THE COMMON LAW OF SOUTH AFRICA • VOL NATHAN AND JOHANNES VOET

Publisher's Note

The book descriptions we ask book-sellers to display prominently warn that this is an historic book with numerous typos, missing text or index and is not illustrated.

We scanned this book using character recognition software that includes an automated spell check. Our software is 99 percent accurate if the book is in good condition. However, we do understand that even one percent can be a very annoying number of typos! And sometimes all or part of a page is missing from our copy of a book. Or the paper may be so discolored from age that you can no longer read the type. Please accept our sincere apologies.

After we re-typeset and design a book, the page numbers change so the old index and table of contents no longer work. Therefore, we usually remove them.

Our books sell so few copies that you would have to pay hundreds of dollars to cover the cost of proof reading and fixing the typos, missing text and index. Therefore, whenever possible, we let our customers download a free copy of the original typo-free scanned book. Simply enter the barcode number from the back cover of the paperback in the Free Book form at www.general-books. net. You may also qualify for a free trial membership in our book club to download up to four books for free. Simply enter the barcode number from the back cover onto the membership form on the same page. The book club entitles you to select from more than a million books at no additional charge. Simply enter the title or subject onto the search form to find the books.

If you have any questions, could you please be so kind as to consult our Frequently Asked Questions page at www. general-books.net/faqs.cfm? You are also welcome to contact us there.
General Books LLC™, Memphis, USA, 2012. ISBN: 9781150018299.

* * * * * * * *

Of South Africa"

A TREATISE BASED ON *VOET'S COMMENTARIES ON THE PANDECTS,* WITH REFERENCES TO THE LEADING ROMAN-DUTCH AUTHORITIES, SOUTH AFRICAN DECISIONS, AND STATUTORY ENACTMENTS IN SOUTH AFRICA. BY MANFRED NATHAN, LL.D., ADVOCATE OF THE SUPREME COURTS OF THE CAPE OF GOOD HOPE AND THE TRANSVAAL; ADVOCATE OF THE HIOH COURT OF THE LATE SOUTH AFRICAN REPUBLIC. *IN TWO VOLUMES.* VOL. I. GRAHAMSTOWN, CAPE COLONY: AFRICAN BOOK COMPANY, LIMITED, Xaw publishers. LONDON: BUTTERWORTH & CO., 12, BELL YARD, TEMPLE BAR. *SOU* PKEFACE.

At the beginning of a new century, when the consolidation of British power in South Africa is no longer a nebulous vision, but actually within grasp, it has been thought desirable to attempt a work which has not hitherto been undertaken—the setting forth of the principles of the Ronian-Dutch Law, which is the common law of all the South African colonies, as well as of Ceylon and British Guiana. The history of South Africa for the past twenty years has made it clear that in constitutional matters a radical change in legislation was not only desirable, but a matter of absolute necessity. In the Transvaal, for instance, such obnoxious measures as the Aliens' Expulsion Law, the Press Law, and the Judge's Testing Bight Law have had to be taken off the statute book without delay. The political laws regulating citizenship and the franchise will have to be altered, and fiscal reform is greatly needed. A policy of pruning and weeding out has also been adopted in the Orange River Colony—will perhaps be adopted even in the Cape

Colony—though to a less extent than in the Transvaal. But the common law of the country, the system under which the great mass of the people daily exercise and enforce their rights, cannot be changed by simple legislation. Nor is there any necessity for such a course.

The Roman-Dutch Law is practically the Roman Law, gradually adapted to the growing needs of a modern community; and the Roman Law is the basis of the jurisprudence of most modern countries, where it has been found to work admirably. During a working experience in South Africa of a century under British rale, the Roman-Dutch system has fulfilled all that could reasonably be expected of it. There is no apparent reason why it should not remain in vogue until the end of time. In matters for which it does not provide (such matters, mainly, as Roman lawyers were never called upon to deal with practically) the English Law is invoked for decision; and hitherto the two systems have not clashed. Modern commercial usages have evoked and evolved a peculiar and special code of rules, known collectively as English commercial law. In connection with such usages it would be manifestly absurd to apply the Roman Law. But for all the personal, everlasting relationships of life the great Roman and Roman-Dutch lawyers made provision; and modern experience has shown how equitable were the rules which they laid down and enforced. The Roman-Dutch Law, as we know it, is definite and clear; but it is to be gathered from a vast number of authorities, which are not always ready to one's hand. It has, therefore, been thought desirable to make a collection, however feeble, of the principles of Roman-Dutch Law, comparing the authorities where they differ, and stating the effect of modern decisions by South African judges, who are the best commentators on Roman-Dutch Law as a practical working system.

In this compilation of law the principles laid down by John Voet in his *Commentaries on the Pandects* have been adopted almost in their entirety. Voet is such a universally-recognised authority, *par excellence* the prince of Dutch jurists, that no apology is needed for this absolute reliance on him. At the same time it has not been forgotten that his great work is a collection of university lectures and expositions. Consequently, all explanatory or argumentative passages have been discarded in making selections from his work. At the same time, obsolete matter, and rales purely local to the Netherlands in then-application, have been omitted. To every statement of law by Voet or other Dutch authorities, a note has been added giving the effect of modern decisions, where such decisions exist, or indicating the alterations effected by legislation in South Africa.

It is hoped that the index to this work will also serve as an index to Voet's *Commentaries*. The references to Voet's work have been given at the end of the sections of this work. The numbers at the end of a section refer to the corresponding section in Voet's *Commentaries*. Thus, " 23,2 § 85 " refers to the eighty-fifth section of the second title of Book XXIII. of Voet's work.

This work does not profess to give every decided case in South Africa. But decisions on every subject have been cited, and reference to those decisions will indicate where other decisions bearing on the same point are to be found.

M. N.

Johannesburg, *April,* 1904.

TABLE OF ABBREVIATIONS.

—»—

A. C. B Appeal Court (Cape) Reports, 1880—188G.

Bach Buchanan's Reports, Cape Supreme Court, 1868—1879.

Bugnet Bugnet's edition of Pothier's *Treatise on Obligation.*

C. B Common Bench Reports (England).

Cens. For The *Censura Forensis* of Van Leeuwen.

C. L. J Cape Law Journal.

CoL Colquhoun's Summary of the Roman Civil Law.

C. T. R Cape Times Reports of the Cape Supreme Court, by J. D. Sheil and others.

E. D. C Eastern Districts' Court (Cape) Reports, by E. J. Buchanan and others.

Exch Exchequer Court Reports (England).

Foord Foord's Reports of the Cape Supreme Court for 1880.

Greg, or Gregorowski.. R. Gregorowski's Reports of the High Court of the Orange Free State.

Grot.or Grotius Hugo Grotius' *Introduction to Dutch Jurisprudence.*

G. V. B Reports of the High Court of Griqualand, by P. M. Laurence and others.

Hertzog Hertzog's Reports of the Transvaal High Court for 1893.

H. L. C House of Lords Cases (England).

Holl. Cons The *Dutch Consultations.*

Inst, or Instit The Institutes of Justinian.

Juta Sir H. Juta's Translation of Van del Linden's *Institutes.*

K. or Kotze Chief Justice Kotze's

Translation of Van Leeuwen's *Commentaries.*

K. B Reports of the Transvaal High Court, 1885—1888, by J. G.

Kotze and S. H. Barber. Kotze's Rep J. G. KotzS's Reports of the Transvaal High Court, 1877—1884.

L. J., Ch. or Ch. D Law Journal (England) Reports, Chancer or Chancery Division.

L. J., C. P. or C. P. D.... Law Journal (England) Reports, Common Pleas or Common

Pleas Division.

L. J., Eq Law Journal (England) Reports, Equity Cases.

L. J., Q. B., or Q. B. 1). Law Journal (England) Reports, Queen's Bench or Queen's

Bench Division.

L. R., Ch. D Law Reports (Kngland), Chancery Division.

I R., P. D Law Reports (England), Probate and Divorce Division.

L. R., Q. B. or Q. B. D... Law Reports (England), Queen's Bench or Queen's Bench

Division.

C.L.—VOL. I. c

M Menzies' Reports of the Cape Supreme Court by the Hod.

J. Buchanan.

Maasdorp A. F. S. Haasdorp's translation of Grotius' *Introduction.*

N. L. R Natal Law Reports.

N. R Natal Reports (1860—1872).

0. F. S. Rep Reports of the High Court, Orange Free State (1880—1881).

Ord Ordinance.

0. R.,S.A.R.orOff. Rep. Official Reports of the High Court of the South African

Republic (1894—1897).

Proc Proclamation.

R. or Ros Roscoe's Reports of the Cape Supreme Court.

R. D. L Van Leeuwen's *Commentaries on Roman-Dutch Law.*

S M. *W.* Searle's Reports of the Cape Supreme Court (1850—1867).

S. A. L. J South African Law Journal.

Sande, *Decit. Frit* Johannes a Sandc's *Decisions Frisicae.*

S. C Reports of the Cape Supreme Court, by Juta, Buchanan and others

(1880—1901).

Schorer *(ad Grot.)* Schorer's notes to Grotius' *Introduction.* 1902 T. H Reports of the Witwatersrand High Court. 1902 T. S Reports of the Transvaal Supreme Court.

T. R Term Reports (England).

V. D. K. or Van der Van der Eeessel's *Select Theses* of the laws of Holland and

Keessel Zeeland.

V. D. L. or Van der L.... Van der Linden's *Institutes of Holland.*

Van L Van Leeuwcn.

Van Zyl C. H. Van Zyl's *Judicial Practice of South Africa.*

Voet Johannes Voet's *Commentarius ad Pandectas.*

Watermeyer E. B. Watermeyer's Cape Supreme Court Reports.

ERRATUM.

On p. 935 (§ 1005) *torpiguns* read *pignus.* THE COMMON LAW OF SOUTH AFRICA.

INTRODUCTION.

I.

The history of the growth of the study of Roman Law, and the spread of that remarkable system of jurisprudence throughout Western Europe, is familiar to all students of law or of mediaeval history. Much has been written, by Von Savigny, Ortolan, and others, of the rise of the Italian universities, and the predominant position assumed in their curriculum by the study of the system of jurisprudence promulgated by the Emperor Justinian. They tell us how the trend of its teaching lay westward, and with what eagerness the Franks adopted the Roman Law. The biographies of the glossatois, and of the jurists who succeeded them, are familiar; and from a perusal of their writings it may be gathered that the Roman Law was mainly introduced into France and Spain by the clergy, whose influence was not limited to the States of the Church, but extended to every place in which ecclesiastical influence was felt. This influence was felt to a slight degree in Germany, but a more powerful impetus to the study of Roman jurisprudence was given by the order of the German kings, who published a collection of Roman Law for

use throughout their realms. This collection was known as the *Breviarium Alarici,* or Roman Law of the Visigoths. It was published in Southern Gaul, but extended its influence to the North. It consisted of a summary of the Roman Law as it existed before the time of the Emperor Justinian. Its influence was felt for a considerable time, but the effect of local customs was such that it was deemed desirable to promulgate the

C.l.—vOl. I. B

Roman Law anew, with all the modifications that had been introduced into that system by the Emperor Justinian. This was done by Charlemagne, or Charles the Great, who made a collection of Capitularies or Imperial Constitutions. They were addressed to all the nations subject to his sway, including the Romans, Franks, Frisians, and Saxons. Thenceforward the Roman Law took firm root in France, and (though to a slight extent necessarily modified by local customs and ordinances) formed the basis of its jurisprudence until the Code Napoleon was promulgated. The Code Napoleon made radical changes, notably in regard to the tenure of property and rights of contract, but the Roman Law still remains to some extent the Common Law of France. It acquired great authority in Germany, and though Prussia in the first instance, and afterwards the German Imperial Government, followed the fashion of code-making set by Napoleon, the Roman Law is still likewise the basis of German jurisprudence in its practical modern application. With regard to the introduction of Roman Law into France and Germany, then, one is on pretty sure ground; but the same certainty does not exist in the case of the Netherlands generally, and of Holland in particular. It is certain that the original body of observances and rules which governed the people of Holland in their conduct, transactions and mutual intercourse, was of customary growth, and Teutonic in its origin. The introduction of Roman Law, although it modified, did not wholly abrogate the Teutonic Customary Law, which survives in several forms in the modern Roman-Dutch

Common Law. The system of marriage in community, and the laws of intestate succession (known as Aasdom's law and Schependom's law) are specimens of Teutonic Customary Law, which survive in modern Roman-Dutch Law, almost wholly unaffected by the influence of Roman Law. The rise of this purely Customary Law of Holland must have been somewhat similar to the growth of the English Common Law, although (except for statutory legislation) the English system has come down to us practically unchanged, and quite uninfluenced by the intrusion of a foreign system, as is the case with Dutch Law, which has been greatly modified and coloured by Roman Law. It seems clear, from the traces of sacerdotal legislation still to be found in most of the collections of Dutch jurisprudence (such as the regulations bearing on divorce, and separation from bed and board), that the monks and priests were to some extent responsible for the introduction of certain portions of the Roman Law into Holland. The law thus imported was not the system generally termed Roman or Civil Law, but was that which jurists distinguish by the name of the Canon Law. It was engrafted upon the Customary Law, and modified it, but not very largely. It remained of effect in Holland until the Reformation, when, in consequence of the great reaction against the influence of the Pope, and Roman Catholicism in general, so much of the Canon Law as was still distinctly traceable was eradicated from the body of Dutch Law. An attempt, which did not succeed, was made by the Emperor Charles V., and his successor Philip II. —mainly through the instrumentality of Cardinal Granvelle—to reintroduce the Canon Law. The spread of the feudal system, and the adoption with it of many Frankish or French, as opposed to German, ideas and customs, brought in their train the introduction of Roman Civil Law. There is no certainty as to dates, but this seems to have taken place in or about the ninth or tenth century of the Christian era. The Feudal Law (we have it on the authority of Van Leeuwen) was specifically made the Common Law of the Netherlands, by proclamations issued at various times by the Emperors Henry, Lothair, Conrad, and Frederick Barbarossa. It did not contain much Roman Law, but the influence it exercised was such that the way was made clear for the wholesale introduction of a new body of law, published or promulgated by decree of the Sovereign. The feudal system had reduced the people to a state of subjection in which they received without protest, and with passive obedience, whatever legislation the Crown deemed necessary to enact. It may be taken for granted — the point cannot be here elucidated— that the Roman Law would never have acquired its preponderating influence in Western Europe, had the feudal system never existed. One of the feudal lords of Holland and the adjoining territories was King William II., the 18th Count of Holland, who "being crowned and confirmed as

King of the Romans by the Princes of the Empire when he was about twenty years of age, resolved that the Dutch should use the Roman Law in the future." When the Canon Law was abrogated, Roman Civil Law—that is, the secular system—entirely supplanted it, and thenceforth the two systems, Teutonic Common Law and Roman Law, became indissolubly blended, and formed the system known as Roman-Dutch Law. The Roman-Dutch Law, then, consisted, in the first place, of customs. Some of these were general, being in force throughout the Netherlands; others were provincial, being confined in their application to one or two of the provinces of Holland and Zeeland; others, again, were local to a town or village, and had no sanction beyond its limits. Where such customary law, general or local, did not apply, the Roman Law, particularly that which was found in the Code, Pandects, Institutes, and Novels of Justinian, was resorted to by the general Court of Pleas in Holland. This was the earliest Dutch Court. Prior to that time the Court was movable, following, in general, the place of residence of the Sovereign, like the old English *Curia Regis.* The Roman Law was not adopted in its entirety, for the introduction of more moder n ideas and usages had rendered many of its provisions unnecessary and unsuited to the times. So much of it, however, as was still applicable was enforced. An insensible amalgamation with local usages took place, so that in time, although the basic law was wholly Roman, the form it had come to assume was very different. As novel circumstances, to which the Roman Law did not apply directly, or could not be made to apply by way of analogy, arose, general or special laws, known as Placaats or Ordinances, were framed and promulgated to meet the needs of the inhabitants of the Netherlands. Such Placaats or Ordinances, when general in their application, were embodied in the Roman-Dutch Law, which, unlike codified systems of law, may be said to resemble a mosaic. We find, then, that the process in the formation of the system now known as Roman-Dutch Law was as follows: Roman Law did not replace Dutch Customary Law, but Roman Law, as a system, was introduced into the Netherlands, and The cases, of course, are not precisely parallel. As to the *Curia Regis,* consult Pollock and Maitland's *History of English Law,* and Carter's *History of English Legal Institutions.* then modified by Customary Law. Of course, in order that such a modification by custom might be of general effect, it had to conform to the usual requirements for giving custom the effect of law— namely, antiquity, certainty, universality, and regularity. If a custom was not as universal as the original law which it modified, or professed to modify, the original law still remained in force in those places where the modifying custom was not in vogue. Thus the general Roman-Dutch Law remained unaltered, unless the custom altering it was as universal as the altered portion of law was in itself. For instance, a custom modifying the application in the town of Amsterdam of the general Dutch Law did not alter that Law; and if the Dutch Law was afterwards imported bodily into another country (such as the Cape of Good Hope), the Amsterdam custom did not affect it. If the modifying custom had, on the other hand,.been of application throughout Holland, the modification would have had effect at the Cape of Good Hope as well, provided such modification existed at the time when the Roman-Dutch Law was introduced at the Cape of Good Hope, or at any time during the Dutch occupation of the Cape of Good Hope. The modification might also take place by means of a general statute. A special statute, like a special custom, would operate only in the place where, and with reference to which, it was promulgated. Lastly, the Roman-Dutch Law was modified by abrogation. A leading authority on modern Roman-Dutch Law summarises the arguments on the question of abrogation of laws by disuse in the following way: "There is a passage in the Digest (of Justinian) which, if taken literally and without qualification, would settle the point. 'The doctrine,' says Julianus, 'has been most properly accepted, that laws are abrogated, not only by the vote of the legislator, but also by the tacit consent of all, through disuse.' It would serve no useful purpose to quote the remarks made by the many commentators upon this passage, and upon analogous passages in the Code. Voet would seem to confine the operation of the doctrine to countries in which a democratic form of government prevails, that is, in which the power of legislation rests with the people as distinguished from i The alternative proviso is, of course, open to controversy.

those in which the power has been delegated to a *princeps*. It is not clear what his view would have been in regard to countries like ours, in which the power is delegated to a representative body elected by qualified electors. He admits, however, that there are instances, and his commentaries are full of such instances, in which well-established laws have been deprived of their obligatory force through not having been acted upon for a long series of years. Van iler Linden says that customs which are founded on good reason and have been properly proved are not only of force where the written law fails, but have

even this force, that they may abrogate the written law. By the written law I presume he means the Roman Law as embodied in the *corpus juris.* In his chapter on 'Punishments' he mentions several which had been abolished through disuse. He mentions several others as being in use in his time which, although not abolished by our (Cape) Legislature, would be as impossible at the present time as if they had been actually abolished." This view has the support of the majority of modern jurists, and does not require discussion. It follows that, unlike systems embodied in a rigid, unchanging code, the Roman-Dutch is a progressive body of law, which has constantly adapted itself to the changing requirements of the times in which it has been applied. It must be remembered, however, that Roman-Dutch Law, though in full vigour at the present day, is no longer capable of alteration. Any alteration, whether by statute, proclamation, or custom, which has been made in the Roman-Dutch Law after its importation from Holland into any other country, is not Roman-Dutch Law, but the law of the country where such alteration takes place. The RomanDutch Law is, and can only be, the Roman Law as it existed in Holland and as it was modified by Dutch customs and ordinances. Thus, the Roman-Dutch Law as applied in the colony of British Guiana is the law as it existed in that colony at the time of its cession in 1814. Any subsequent changes in legislation, whether made by the Crown in Council, by the Governor on the advice of the Executive Council, or by the Court of Policy, though they may change, modify, or repeal provisions of Roman-Dutch Law, do not constitute Roman-Dutch Law, but British Guiana Law. n.

The Roman-Dutch Law, then,'consisted of the body of Roman Law as it existed in Justinian's time, together with the modifications introduced by general Dutch Statutes, Placaats, or Customs. It was not contained in any one enactment, or in any series of enactments, and remained an undigested mass until it was stated in concise form by the ju-

rists of Holland, who made compilations of varying length. The reputation of these compilers, who were at the same time commentators, was so great that in course of time they came to be regarded, not merely as guides, but as authoritative expositors of Roman-Dutch Law, whose *dicta* were as reliable as those of any contributor to the Pandects of Justinian. It is possible that in some cases the reputation acquired was greater than was deserved, but it may safely be said that, on the whole, no body of lawyers so conscientious, so exact, and so much entitled to universal respect has ever existed as the expounders of Dutch jurisprudence who flourished during the period from 1500 to 1800. Their writings are uniformly distinguished by a faithful observance of the spirit and intention of the Roman Law. There is a marked absence of the casuistical hail-splitting in which the German commentators on the Civil Law—Puchta, Baron, Ihering, Mackeldey, Bluntschli, Von Vangerow, and others—have indulged. In brief, this characteristic of the Dutch lawyers may be described as "unimaginativeness." All of them appear to have striven to give a faithful account of the law as it stood, leaving comment and interpretation to those who were more, or very likely less, skilled than they. Under these circumstances, it is no wonder that the law schools of Holland, particularly the Universities of Leyden and Utrecht, acquired a reputation for legal learning, the glamour of which is still fresh in the dawn of the twentieth century. Law students flocked thither from all parts of the world, and Stevenson's record, in *Catriona,* of David Balfour's adventures with a copy of *Heineccius* has the merit of *vraisemblance.* The downfall of Dutch naval power greatly reduced the influence of Holland in European politics, and the Universities suffered somewhat in consequence. But the authority of the great jurists survived the shock of political vicissitude, and bids fair to last as long as the Roman-Dutch Law itself. It would serve no useful purpose to compile a complete bibliography of Roman-Dutch Law. Here one can only give an imperfect list of the chief jurists and their works.

One of the earliest, as well as one of the greatest of these jurists, was Hugo Grotius, whose *Introduction to Dutch Jurisprudence* was the first concise statement of Dutch Law as it stood in his day. His work may be regarded as the foundation stone of the vast and enduring structure reared by the jurists who came after. It was not the earliest work written by a Dutch jurist, but no previous work professed to give an account of contemporary Roman-Dutch Law.

Grotius was preceded by Andreas Gail or Gayll, who, in 1536, published at Amsterdam a work entitled *Practicarum Observationum Libri duo,* a Dutch version of which, entitled *Observantien van de kaysarlijke praktyke,* was published in his lifetime. He died in 1587.

In 1597 Antonius Faber published a work entitled *De erroribus pragmaticorum et interpretum juris.*

Grotius was born in 1583, at Delft. He was educated at Leyden, and entered the diplomatic service of the States General of the Netherlands. In 1608 he married. In 1618 he was sent as ambassador to England. He was charged, together with John of Barneveld and others, with high treason, and was sentenced to imprisonment for life in 1619. In 1621 he escaped from the Castle of Loevestein, and went to Paris, where he became Swedish Ambassador. He died at Rostock in 1645. He wrote numerous works, the most important being *Introduction to Dutch Jurisprudence* (written 1620, published 1631), *Dejuri Belli ac Pads* (written 1623—1624, published 1625), and *History of the Netherlands.*

In 1620 there was published, at Antwerp, a posthumous work on the Roman Law in the Netherlands, entitled *Commentariorum de jure novissimo libri sex,* by Gudelinus.

In 1624 appeared the two earliest collections of Dutch Statutes and Ordinances—*Handvesten en privilegi'en van Amsterdam,* and *Keyserlicke Statuyten, Ordonnantien, Costumen ende Gewoonten.*

In 1633 Jacob Coren wrote *Observantien van Oordeelen van den Hoogen Raedt* (Observations on Decisions of the Supreme Court).

Matthaeus is still regarded as an important authority on RomanDutch Law. He was Professor of Law at the University of Utrecht. He published his famous work on Crimes *(De Criminibus)* in 1644. In 1653 appeared his work on Sale *(De Auctionibus).* Two works by him, *Paroemiae* and *De probationibus,* were published at Leyden in 1667 and 1678 respectively, both being posthumous.

About the same time Johannes a Sande, senator of the Supreme Court of Friesland, wrote a commentary on the title *De regulis juris* of the Pandects. He also published a well-known work on Restraints on Alienation *(De prohibita rerum alienatione),* five books of Decisions of the Court of Friesland (1670), a work on Feudal Customs *(ConsuetudinesFeudales),* and one on Cession of Actions *(De actionum cessione).*

In 1648 a collection of the Dutch Placaats or State Proclamations was published at the Hague. Several subsequent proclamations were published and collected at various dates thereafter. These Placaats are of importance, as most of them were general, and declared or amended the Roman-Dutch Law.

Antonius Merenda, who died in 1655 at the age of 77, wrote twenty-four books of Disputations on the Law *(Controversiarium Juris).*

Bemhard van Zutphen, advocate, published a work at Utrecht in 1642, entitled *Nederlandsche practijk.*

In 1642 a valuable work on Procedure, called *Papegay ofte Formulier Boeck,* was written by Van Alphen, and published at the Hague.

Christian Rodenburg, senator of the Supreme Court at Utrecht, published in 1658 a treatise on Marriage Law *(Tractatus de jure conjugum).*

About the same time Cornelius van Nieustad, better known by his Latinised name of Neostadius, published his collection of Judgments of the High Court *(Vonnissen van den Hoogen Jtiaad).* A Dutch version of this work was published at Rotterdam in 1655, by Adriaan van Nisper, the original having appeared in Latin.

Paul Voet, father of the great John Voet, and son of the famous theologian, Gysbert Voet, was bora at Heusde, in Holland, on June 7th, 1619. He became successively Professor of Logic, Metaphysics, Greek, and Civil Law at the University of Utrecht, where he died in 1677. In 1646 he wrote a work on Duelling *(De duellis Ileitis et Ulicitis).* In 1654 he published a work with the paradoxical title *Harmonia erangelica.* This was followed by a treatise, *De usu juris civilis et canonici in Belgio unite* (1657). In 1661 appeared his most important work, the precursor of modern treatises on Private International Law *(De statutis corumque concursu).* This was followed by *Commentarius ad institutiones iuris* (1668), and other works.

Pieter Bort, in 1649, published his collected works, which include *Hct Hollandts Leen Recht* (Dutch Law of Laud Tenure), *De Domeynen van Hollandt, De Hoogc en Ambachts-Heerlijckheden, Complaincte en d'Arresten,* and *Proceduyren in Criminele Saccken te houden.*

In 1651 appeared an authorised edition of *Decisien en Resolutien van den Hove van Holland* (Decisions and Orders of the High Court of Holland). This kind of work achieved great popularity, and in 1661 the well-known *Hollandsche Consultation* (Dutch Consultations) were published at Rotterdam. In 1676 the lawyers of Utrecht followed suit, and published the *Utrechtsche Consultatien.* These compilations contained the opinions of the foremost lawyers of the day, many of them *ex parte,* but none the less valuable for all that. The collection forms a veritable mine of jurisprudence.

In 1656 Gerard Roseboom published, at Amsterdam, his *Recueil van verscheyde keuren en costumen.*

In 1656 the work on *De Practyke of gebruyk zoo van Civile als Criminele zaken* (Practice in Civil and Criminal Cases) of Joost de Damhouder reached a second edition.

Peter Peckius, in 1659, published, at Dordrecht, a work entitled *Vcrhandclinghe van handt-opleggen ende besetten*. A complete collection of his works *(Opera Omnia)* appeared at Antwerp in 1666.

In 1661 Antonius Perez, or Perezius, Professor of Law at the University of Louvain, published his famous commentary on the Code *(Praelcctiones in duodecim libros Codicis)*. This work contains some very valuable annotations and dissertations, particularly those relating to water-rights.

Gerard van Wassenaar, in 1660, published a work on Judicial Practice at Utrecht *(Practijk Jztdicicel)*. This was followed, in 1661, by a treatise on Notarial Practice *(Practijk Notarieel)*.

At Utrecht, in 1658, appeared Johannes a Someren's *Tractatus de jure novercarum* (Treatise on the Law relating to Second Marriages). In 1676 was published his work on Representation *(Tractatus de representatione)*.

Simon van Leeuwen, whom Chief Justice Kotze, with perhaps pardonable exaggeration, ranks next after Grotius, and before John Voet, as a jurist, was born at Leyden in 1625. He was an advocate, and assistant registrar of the Supreme Court of Holland, Zeeland, and West Friesland. In 1656 he published, at Leyden, his *Paratitla juris novissimi*, a summary of Dutch Law in Latin. In 1662 he published an edition of the *Corpus Juris*, with annotations, founded on the *Corpus Juris Ch ilis* of Dionysius Gothofredus. In 1642 appeared his *Ccnsura Forensis*, and in 1667 came the *Costumcn van Rynland*. His works were of a very practical kind, and consequently obtained a wide circulation among practitioners, who had tested the value of his *Practycke der Notarissen*, which was published in 1656. In 1678 appeared his *Commentaries on Roman-Dutch Law*. Van Leeuwen died in 1682.

In 1664 Brouwer published a treatise, which attained some reputation, entitled *De Jure Connubiorum* (Law of Marriage).

Simon van Groenewegen van der Made was distinguished for his concise, logical annotations to the *Introduction to Dutch Jurisprudence of Grotius,* an edition of which he issued in 1644. In 1664 he published what is still a very valuable work—*De legibus abrogatis et inusitatis in Hollandia* (Abrogated and Obsolete Laws of Holland).

Franciscus Zypaeus, or Van Zype, wrote *Notitia juris Bclgici,* which he published at Antwerp in 1665.

Gerard Noodt, a distinguished lawyer, was born in Gelderland on September 4th, 1647. He was educated mainly at Utrecht, but travelled widely, and received the degree of Doctor of Laws in five universities. In 1774 he published *Probabilium juris Civilis liber primus,* which was afterwards completed. In 1684 he became Professor of Law at Utrecht. He published a Commentary on twenty-seven books of Justinian's Pandects, and valuable treatises on the Aquilian Law and kindred subjects. His inaugural oration at Utrecht was entitled *De causis corruptae jurisprudence.* His Latin style is the purest of any of the Dutch commentators on Roman Law.

In 1669 Peter Vromans published, at Leyden, his *Tractaat de foro competenti.* This work contains some most valuable observations on tbe Law of Domicile.

In 1670 Van den Saude, as above stated, published, at Leeuwarden, *Vijf boeken der gewijsder iaken voor den Hove van Vrieslandt.*

Johan Tjassens, in 1670, published at the Hague a curious and interesting work on Maritime (Naval) Law, entitled *Zeepolitie der Vereenigde-Nederlanden.* At the present day, however, this work possesses only an antiquarian interest.

Ulric Huber published *Digressioncs Justiniancae* in 1670. He also wrote *Hedendaegsc Rechtsgeleertheyt,* which attained a wide circulation, *De Jure Civitatis,* and a posthumous treatise, *Eunomia Romana,* published in 1700. Zacharias Huber issued a collected edition of Ulric Huber's works, and himself wrote *De casibus enucleatis quaestionum forensium ex jure Romano et hodierno,* published in 1712.

Van den Berg issued, at Amsterdam, in 1692, a work called *Nederlands Advysboek.* This, and *Nieuw Nederlands Advysboek,* by the same author, enjoyed great popularity.

In 1692 Abraham a Wesel wrote *Commentarius ad Novellas.* He likewise published treatises on the subject of Community between Spouses, and on Remission of Rent. The lust-mentioned treatise has been much resorted to in the Transvaal Courts since the war.

In 1705 Paul Merula published his *Manier van Procederen,* which continued to be reprinted at various times throughout the eighteenth century.

Antonius Schellinga published his *Nutae ad Pandectas* in 1652. He also wrote *Jurisprudential vetus ante-Justinianea,* and *Dissertationes,* editions of which were issued at Leyden in 1714 and 1717.

Van Dalen, who died at the commencement of the eighteenth century, wrote, in 1634, a work entitled *Recueil van Resolution,* containing an account of the practice of duelling, and the law affecting duelling and military matters in general.

In 1701 Hohius van der Vorm published at Hoorn his *Verhandeling ran het Versterv-regt.*

Georg Bruksulberg, in 1687, published an interesting bibliography of works of commentators on Roman Law, together with an index to the Digest and Code of Justinian, entitled *Memoriale iuridicum novum.*

Abraham de Pape published his *Obserrationes* on Law in 1702.

Johan Schrassert wrote, at Haardewijk, an elaborate work entitled *Consultation, Advysen en Adrertissementen,* which was published in six volumes, at Amsterdam and Utrecht, in 1728.

Arnold Vinnius wrote various essays *(De pactis, jurisdictione, eollationibus, transactionibus et quaestionibus juris selectis)* in 1541, and his celebrated *Commentary on the Institutes* in 1542. This was republished at Leyden by Heineccius in 1747. Heineccius ranks Vinnius as equal in authority to Cujacius, one of the greatest jurists the Western world has seen.

Cornelius van Bynkershoek, who is recognised by most modern lawyers as a sound and reliable authority on Public International Law, whose opinions still carry great weight in the councils of European statesmen, was born in 1673. He became President of the Supreme Court of Holland, Zeeland, and Friesland. His treatises *De Dominio Maris* (1702), *De foro legatorum* (1721), and *Quaestiones Juris Pitblici,* place him, as stated, among the highest authorities. In 1719 appeared a volume of *Opuscula,* which was followed in 1730 by *Opera Minora,* and *Observationum Juris Eomani libri quatuor* in 1733. His great work on International Law, *Quaestionumjuris publici libri duo,* appeared in 1737. A posthumous work, *Quaestionum juris privati libri quatuor,* was published in 1745. Bynkershoek died at the Hague in 1743.

In 1780 Everard Otto published *De jurisprudentia symbolica,* and in 1733 he issued at Utrecht a collection of the writings of the principal modern commentators on Roman Law, French and Spanish, entitled *Thesaurus juris Romani.* This work, probably the bulkiest legal publication in existence, is a marvel of human industry. It is, however, nearly rivalled by the works of Strykius.

Jan Cos in 1733 published various essays on Marriage Law *(Boedelmenging, Huwelijkze voorwaarden, Gemeenschap van winst en verlies).* In 1736 appeared his work *De rei vindicatione,* in 1738 *Over de trouivbeloften en het huwelijk,* and in 1738 *Verhandeling over de Wetten.*

In 1749 Voorda published *Electorum liber singularis quo difficiliora quaedam juris Romani loca explicantur.*

In 1753 Averanius published at Leyden a volume of *Interpretations of Law.*

In 1767 William Schorer, President of the Court of Flanders, and Superintendent of Feuds, published his *Annotations to the Introduction qfGrotius,* which are marked by great ability.

In 1777 Franciscus Kersteman published his *Hollandsch Rechtsgeleerd Woordenboek,* to which he afterwards wrote an *Aanhangsel* (Supplement).

In 1783 Hendrik Johan Arntzenius

published *Institutiones juris Belgici.*

Dionysius Godtfried van der Keessel was born at Deventer in 1738. He was educated in his native town, and at the University of Leyden. He practised as an advocate at the Hague, and then became Professor of Roman Law at the University of Groningen. In 1770 Van der Keessel became Professor of Roman Law at the University of Leyden. In 1800 he published at Leyden his wellknown *Theses Selectae Juris Hollandici et Zeelandici* (Select Theses on the Laws of Holland and Zeeland), a commentary on the *Introduction* of Grotius. He left a valuable work in manuscript, *Novae Praelectiones Institutiomim Autographae sive Commentarius ad Bbckelmanni Compendium* (1771), which is well worthy of translation and publication. Van der Keessel died in 1816. He succeeded Rucker, Professor of Roman Law at Leyden, who was born in 1702, and died in 1778. Rucker published a treatise, *De naturali et civili temporis computatione,* in 1749.

An attempt to discredit the teaching of Roman Civil Law was made in 1772 by Professor van der Marck, of Groningen, who published his *Institutiones Juris Civilis privati, communis, et reipvblicae Groningae Omlandicae proprii.* In this he attempted to substitute for the influence of the Civil Law the authority of the Teutonic Customary Law. The attempt was vigorously opposed, particularly by Van der Keessel, and deservedly failed.

The last of the distinctively Roman-Dutch writers in Holland was Joannes van der Linden. During the time when he practised as an advocate at Amsterdam came the Napoleonic occupation of the Netherlands, and with it the introduction of the Codes, which have ever since governed Holland and Belgium. From this time the Roman-Dutch Law, by a strange paradox, disappears as a system from the jurisprudence of Holland, although the Roman Law is still the basis of the judicial practice in that country. Consequently, Dutch writers after Van der Linden do not elucidate the problems of Roman-Dutch Law to

any extent. And the importation of the Roman-Dutch Law into other countries, and its interpretation there, is not influenced by Dutch legislation after the conquest of Holland by Napoleon. Thus, Roman-Dutch Law is interpreted only by Van der Linden and the writers before him, and to no other authorities can reference on this subject be made. The Roman Law, of course, has been commented upon by numerous other writers; and, where the Roman-Dutch Law fails, and Roman Law has to be applied, those commentators are of authority.

Van der Linden, who was a pupil of Van der Keessel's (to whom the former dedicated one of his works), published his valuable *Verhandeling over de Judicieele Practijcque* at Leyden in 1794. In 1803 he issued a *Verzameling van merkwaardige gewijsden der gerechtshoven in Holland* (Collection of important Decisions of the Courts of Justice of Holland), which he did not complete. In 1806 he published, at Amsterdam, his celebrated *Rechtsgeleerdheid Practicaal en Koopmans Handboek* (Institutes of the Law of Holland), which is still recognised as the best elementary treatise on Roman-Dutch Law.

The writings of Grotius, Van Leeuwen, and the earliest jurists paved the way for the great work accomplished by John Voet. This remarkable man, whom modern authorities, both those who have to administer the law practically as judges, and writers on the theory of the Roman Law, have agreed to place at the head of all Continental expositors of jurisprudence, was the son of the jurist Paul Voet. He was born at Utrecht on October 3rd, 1647. He studied law at the University of his native town, and took his degree of Doctor there. His reputation as a student of law was so great that, at the age of twenty-two, he was appointed Professor of Roman Law at Herborn. In 1670 his treatise on Military Law *(De jure militari)* was published at Utrecht. In 1678 was published an essay, *De familia erciscunda* (on the Division of Inheritances). Both these works were printed in octavo. In 1674 Voet left Herborn, and, after practising as an advocate, became Professor at the University of Utrecht in 1681. He then went to Leyden, and there became Professor of Civil Law. He had now acquired a European reputation, and students flocked from all parts to hear him. His lectures were most luminous expositions of the Roman Law, combined with statements of the Dutch Customary Law, and the extent to which the two systems of law had acted and reacted upon each other. At the same time he summarised and discussed the views of the leading Dutch jurists.

His portrait, painted about this time, which still hangs in the Hall of the Faculty of Law at the University of Leyden, represents him as a small, wizened man, with a face showing great intelligence and kindliness. Notwithstanding his physical defects, his vast intellect triumphed over everything, and he was twice elected *Rector Magnificus* of Leyden (corresponding to the Vice-Chancellor of the English Universities). For thirty years Voet was an ornament of the University. He published his academic and rectorial addresses, which showed that he possessed no ordinary literary talent. His interests were by no means confined to jurisprudence, and he wrote a powerful polemical treatise in support of his grandfather, Gysbert Voet, the theologian. He then set about collecting his lectures, which had consisted of dissertations on the Digest of Justinian, interspersed with references to Dutch Customary Law and the writings of Dutch jurists. The collection, which placed Voet at the head of modern jurisprudence, was published in two folio volumes at the Hague, by Abraham de Hondt, in 1698. It is entitled *Commentarius ad Pandectas* (Commentary on the Pandects or Digest), and has the sub-title *In quo praeter Romani juris principia ac controversial illustriores, jus etiam hodiemum, etpraecipuae foriquaestiones excutiuntur* (wherein, besides the principles of Roman Law, and the more important juristic controversies, contemporary law and, in particular, questions of judicial procedure are discussed). The first volume con-

tains a commentary on twenty-two books of the Digest, and the second volume discusses the remaining twenty-eight books. The work attained an amazing popularity, and the sixth edition was published in 1781. The *Commentary* was dedicated to William III. , "King of Great Britain, France, and Ireland," and Stadtholder of the United Provinces of the Netherlands. There has been a remarkable consensus of opinion among lawyers with regard to the *Commentary*. A French jurist refers to it as *Ce commentaire Va place au premier rang parmi les jurisconsultes.* Eduard van Zurck, whose brother wrote the *Codex Batavus,* addressed a commendatory Latin poem to Voet, in which, after stating that the latter had transcended the glory of his brilliant father (Paul Voet) he proceeded: *Nunc absoluto certa volumine*
Pubes sacratam per Themidis domum
Procedit, et celsum tribunal Tequefori
vaga turba gestit
Dootore mentem, juraque pandere
Quae quinque lustris pervigili manu,
Et voce vivaci recocta Posteritas memorabit omnis.

Judges in countries where the Roman-Dutch Law prevails have echoed this praise of Voet. Sir Henry de Villiers, the Chief Justice C.l.—Vol. i. c of the Colony of the Cape of Good Hope, has, in various judgments delivered by him, referred to Voet's *Commentaries* as "a great work," "our standard authority," and in *Alexander* vs. *Perry* (Buch. 1874, p. 61) he stated that " the opinion of so learned an authority as Voet deserved and was always received in this (Cape Supreme) Court as deserving great weight."

The great characteristic of Voet's *Commentaries* is the logical clearness of the reasoning contained therein, and the author's wealth of illustration. There is scarcely a problem which may arise for consideration that he has not touched upon. Even if a question has not yet been decided in concrete form by any Court, Voet is ready with an answer which exactly meets the circumstances of the case. In discussing the views of an opposing nature advanced

by other jurists he is always temperate, although he does not hesitate to indicate his contempt for mere quibbling arguments. He has a reason for everything, and the reasons which he adduces invariably carry conviction with them. Moreover, his style is so lucid that a child can grasp his propositions. It is, therefore, not remarkable that his work has attained the popularity it deservedly enjoys. The *Commentaries* are valuable, not merely as an exposition of Boman-Dutch Law, but as a discussion of the principles of jurisprudence in general, and of Koman Law in particular. There is probably no work in the whole range of juristic literature to which the proverb "Good wine needs no bush " applies with such fitness as Voet's *Commentaries.*

After an honoured life, Voet died, at the age of sixty-seven, at Leyden, where he lies buried.

IV.

By the labours of Voet and the other Dutch jurists, the principles of Boman-Dutch Law were digested into intelligible form, although, in treating of the subject, Voet and many of his colleagues adopted the somewhat haphazard arrangement of Justinian's Digest. The law became more certain, and its application in judicial matters more regular and satisfactory. Voet was cited as an authority, not merely in the Dutch Courts, but overseas as well. The Dutch East India Company, in founding their settlements in the East Indies and at the Cape of Good Hope, took with them to their Colonies the law of Holland, which thus came to be administered in two hemispheres. The Reformation, and the leading part taken in it by Dutch divines, had attracted many Scotch students to Holland. They, on their return, carried with them the works of Voet, which Scotch lawyers soon came to regard as having great weight in interpreting the principles of Roman Law. "The Civil and Canon Laws," says Erskine, "though they are not perhaps to be deemed proper parts of Scotch written law, have undoubtedly had the greatest influence in Scotland." Voet is still a leading authority in the Scotch Courts.

By the middle of the eighteenth century, Roman-Dutch Law was administered in the Netherlands; at the Cape of Good Hope, at Java, in Borneo, Sumatra, Celebes, Moluccas, Sunda, and part of New Guinea, in the East Indies; at Curacao in the West Indies; and at Guiana, in South America.

In 1795 a British force captured the Cape of Good Hope, which became a British possession until 1802, when it was restored to the Batavian Republic. The Cape of Good Hope was recaptured in 1806, and has ever since remained a British possession. At the time of the first capture, in 1795, the Roman-Dutch Law then in force, including all the general Placaats issued by the Dutch East India Company, was retained. No general legislative change was made at the annexation in 1806. The force and obligation of the Roman-Dutch Law in the Colony of the Cape of Good Hope is thus summarised by De Villiers, C.J., *(Seaville* vs. *Colley,* 9 S. C. 44): "The conclusion at which I have arrived as to the obligatory nature of the body of laws in this Colony, at the date of the British occupation in 1806, may be briefly stated. The presumption is that every one of those laws, if not repealed by the local Legislature, is still in force. This presumption will not, however, prevail in regard to any rule of law which is inconsistent with South African usages. The best proof of such usages is furnished by unoverruled judicial decisions. In the absence of such decisions the Court may take judicial notice of any general custom which is not only well established but reasonable in itself. Any Dutch law which is inconsistent with such well-established and reasonable custom, and has not, although relating to matters of frequent occurrence, been distinctly recognised and acted upon by the Supreme Court, may fairly be held to have been abrogated by disuse. The law of retraction as applied to the sale of debts is inconsistent with the reasonable and well-established custom of persons engaged in commerce in this country, and, until the recent decision in the Eastern Districts' Court *(Deschamps* vs. *Van Onselin,* 8

C. L. J., p. 163), it had not been recognised and acted upon by the superior Courts of this Colony, although numerous cases must have arisen to which it was applicable." From this it is clear that, in South Africa, in accordance with the general rule, local statutes, proclamations, and ordinances are first observed. Where these do not apply, resort is had to judicial decisions, which are founded on the RomanDutch Law, except in regard to procedure and evidence (wherein, by the Cape Evidence Ordinance of 1830, the Natal Law, No. 17, 1859, and the Transvaal Evidence Proclamation, 1902, the practice of the English Courts is followed), and in the Cape Colony in regard to maritime law, shipping law, fire, life, and marine assurance, stoppage *in transitu,* and bills of lading, in which cases the law administered by the High Court of Justice in England for the time being, so far as the same shall not be repugnant to, or in conflict with, any Ordinance, Act of Parliament, or other statute having the force of law in the Cape Colony, has (by the Cape Act, No. 8, 1879, §§ 1, 2) been declared to be the law to be administered by the Cape Supreme Court or other competent Court. Where judicial decisions do not apply, well-established custom indicates the rule to be observed. Failing such unoverruled judicial decisions and well-established custom, the Roman-Dutch Law is applied.

In the Colony of British Guiana, which was acquired by England in 1814, the Dutch Law which prevailed in the Colony at the time of its acquisition by Great Britain is followed, where local ordinances and proclamations having the force of law do not apply.

In the Colony of Natal, which was proclaimed as a British possession in 1840, the Common Law of the Cape of Good Hope, which is the Roman-Dutch Law, was by proclamation made to apply. Consequently, in that Colony local statutes, proclamations, and ordinances are first resorted to, and, in cases for which they do not provide, the Roman-Dutch Law is applied.

In Rhodesia, the ordinances of the

Legislative Council of Southern Rhodesia (which are subject to confirmation by the High Commissioner of South Africa, and to disallowance by the Secretary of State for the Colonies) are first applied. Failing these, certain Cape ordinances and statutes, which were proclaimed as of force in Rhodesia, are resorted to; and when these fail, the Roman-Dutch Law is followed.

In the Orange River Colony, at the date of its conquest and annexation, the local laws were first resorted to. Chapter 9 of the Constitution of the Orange Free State (§ 57) provided that "RomanDutch Law shall be the principal law of this State, in cases where the Volksraad has made no other law applicable to the circumstances." The law dealing with the jurisdiction of the High Court (§ 48) provides, with regard to practice, that "where no regulations as to procedure in civil cases exist, the Roman-Dutch Law must be followed." Despite certain necessary changes in constitutional law of the country, the Roman-Dutch Law remains the Common Law of the Orange River Colony. This is in accordance with the principle stated by Judge Tarring, that " Laws contrary to the fundamental principles of the British Constitution cease at the moment of conquest" *(The Law of the Colonies,* p. 28). It may be here stated that, as a general rule, in the case of civilised nations, the laws prevailing at the time of conquest are continued in force by the conquering nation; whereas, in the case of uncivilised nations, the principle of the British Constitution is that the English Common Law prevails from the date of conquest.

In the Transvaal, the original Constitution of the country (known as the Thirty-Three Articles) enacted that "in all cases for which this law does not provide, the Dutch Law shall be taken as the basis, but in a reasonable manner, and in accordance with the custom of South Africa, and for the benefit and advantage of society" (May 23rd, 1849). An amplifying resolution was passed by the Transvaal Volksraad or Legislature on September 19th, 1852, and provided that "the legal treatise of Van der Linden *(i.e., the Institutes of Holland)* shall remain, in so far as it does not conflict with the Constitution, other laws, and resolutions of the Volksraad, the source of legal authority in this State. If the said work does not deal clearly enough with any subject, or omits to deal with it, the legal treatise of Simon van Leeuwen *(i.e., the Commentaries on Roman-Dutch Law),* and the *Introduction* of Hugo de Groot shall be binding." Thus the writers on Roman-Dutch Law were expressly made authoritative in the Transvaal. Moreover, in the case of *McHattie* vs. *FUmer* (0. R. 1894, pt. 4, p. 9) the Transvaal High Court expressly adopted the decision of the Cape Court in *Seaville* vs. *Colley.* These principles are still acted upon. Thus, in the Transvaal, local laws and resolutions having the force of law are first of all applied, and thereafter the general Roman-Dutch Law. Many of the objectionable enactments on the Transvaal Statute Book have been repealed, but, as indicated in the case of the Orange River Colony, the Roman-Dutch Law remains the Common Law of the Transvaal.

With regard to all British Colonies, it must be noted that all questions of personal *status,* such as citizenship and naturalisation, are governed by the law which regulates the relations between the Sovereign and his subjects. In other words "the *status* of persons domiciled in a Colony is determined by English Law; the rights and liabilities incidental to such *status* by Colonial Law" *(In re Adam,* 1 Moo. P. C. C. 460).

The jurisdiction of the various South African Courts, in which the Roman Dutch Law is mainly applied, may be here briefly stated. The principal Court of Justice in Cape Colony is the Supreme Court of the Colony of the Cape of Good Hope. It is both a Court of original jurisdiction and a Court of Appeal for cases from the Eastern Districts' Court, the High Court of Griqualand West, the Resident Magistrates' Courts of the Cape Colony, and the High Court of Southern Rhodesia. Its original jurisdiction extends over all cases arising within the Cape Colony.

Three Judges are permanently assigned to the Supreme Court, one of whom is the Chief Justice of the Cape Colony. Three Judges of the Supreme Court, one of whom is designated Judge-President, sit in the Court of the Eastern Districts of the Cape Colony, which has original jurisdiction over all cases arising within certain specially proclaimed districts in the eastern portion of Cape Colony, and hears appeals from the Courts of Resident Magistrates within such districts. Three Judges of the Supreme Court, one of whom is designated Judge-President, sit in the High Court of Griqualand West, which has original jurisdiction over all cases arising within the Province of Griqualand West, and the Province of British Bechuanaland, and appellate jurisdiction over cases from the Courts of Resident Magistrates within the said Provinces. The Resident Magistrates' Courts have a limited original jurisdiction in civil and criminal cases, which is defined by statute. The High Court of Southern Rhodesia has original jurisdiction over all cases arising within the Province of Southern Rhodesia. From this Court an appeal lies to the Cape Supreme Court. The Resident Magistrates' Courts in Southern Rhodesia have the same jurisdiction as Resident Magistrates in Cape Colony. In Natal, the Supreme Court of Natal has original jurisdiction over all cases arising within the Colony of Natal, and appellate jurisdiction over cases heard in the Resident Magistrates' Courts of Natal, which have a limited civil and criminal jurisdiction defined by statute. There is also a High Court in Natal for the trial of native cases.

From the decisions of the Cape Supreme Court and the Natal Supreme Court an appeal lies to the King in his Privy Council.

The High Court of the Orange River Colony has original jurisdiction over all cases arising within the Orange River Colony. From this Court an appeal lies to the Transvaal Supreme Court. The Supreme Court of the Transvaal has original jurisdiction over all cases arising within the Transvaal, and the Witwatersrand High Court has similar jurisdiction on the Witwatersrand. The Courts of the Resident Magistrates (formerly called Landdrosts' Courts) have a limited jurisdiction in civil and criminal cases denned by statute. From such Resident Magistrates' Courts an appeal lies to the said High Courts of the Orange River Colony and the Transvaal respectively. From the Supreme Court of the Transvaal an appeal lies to the King in his Privy Council.

PART I. ON LAW IN GENERAL.

I.—Justice And Law. EL.—Law And Custom. III. —Constitutions Of The Head Of The State. IV. —Statutes—Private International Law. PART I.

ON LAW IN GENERAL. CHAPTER I. JUSTICE AND LAW. 1. The Romans were the first authors of a systematised exposition of law. The greatest collection of the principles of Roman law is that contained in the Pandects, the Code, and the Institutes of Justinian (1, 1 § 1). 2. Where there is a dispute between two or more persons, recourse is to be had, firstly, to the written municipal or provincial (statute) law, following the intention and spirit thereof if there is no direct authority in the words themselves; thereafter, recourse must be had to the unwritten laws and established customs of the country, including such maxims of law as have been confined by long usage. If no assistance is derived from the foregoing sources, a solution is to be sought in the Roman Law. There can be no recourse to such parts of Roman Law as have, by universal custom, fallen into total disuse (for example, adoption, slavery, manumission). The rule or maxim, " what is omitted from a statute must be supplied from the Civil Law, and decided according to it," only applies where the Civil Law has formerly been adopted in Holland as to the matter in question, and additions by statute were made to, or deductions made from, the Civil Law in relation to the matter (1, 1 §§ 2, 3). See Van der Keessel (§§ 6, 7, 8, 9—25). 3. Jurisprudence is the knowledge of things divine and human, the science of what is just and unjust, or the art of what is right and what is just (1, 1 §§ 4, 5). 4. Equity is comprehended in the laws generally, and in the definition of written law. What is omitted from the wording of the law must be supplied by interpretation, by the authority of the Judge, by reasoning from the manifest meaning of the law to similar cases whenever the same reason and ground of utility appears to underlie them. Equity is to be observed in the interpretation of laws. Even in interpreting written law equity should be observed. He is said to act *in fraudem legis* who, holding to the words of the law, acts contrary to its meaning and intention (1, 1 § 6).

There is as much of an Equity system in Boman-Dutch Law as under the Chancery system in England.

5. The end of jurisprudence is justice, which is defined as the constant and perpetual desire to render unto each one his due. Constancy and perpetuity are necessary in the nature and perfection of justice. Justice is divided by the civilians into (a) Commutative justice, and Distributive justice. Commutative justice treats of things in *commercio*. Things *in commercio* or *in patrimonii* (see *Colquhoun,* § 922) are those which are capable of individual possession and enjoyment, divided into *res corporales,* or such as are capable of corporeal possession (which migbt be *mobiles* or *immobile»*), and *res incorporales,* or such as are incapable of corporeal enjoyment. In commutative justice what is called the arithmetical proportion is observed, when there is only a comparison of thing with thing, and the equality of the things compared is regarded, not the equality of the persons between whom the transactions stand and the agreements are entered into (i.e., whether nobles or plebeians, magistrates or private persons). Distributive justice is that which treats of rewards and penalties awarded to individuals according to merit or demerit. In this what is known as the geometrical proportion is observed. Grotius *(De Jure Belli ac Pads,* 1, 1, 8) divides justice into *expletrix* and *attributrix.* The former division includes all things and acts, which one is not merely bound to give and fulfil from reasons of equity, but which he, when unwilling, can be compelled to

give or fulfil by competent legal remedies. Under this class are comprehended not merely all things due to us by the law of ownership, and by obligations arising from pacts or from real and quasi contracts, but also those which every one owes to the public, or to private individuals by way of penalty for delicts or crimes. The latter division *(attributrix)* is applied to those things which one may be bound to do according to equity and natural reason. The latter class is more assimilated to rules of morality. Thus, where wine in cask is sold on condition that it shall be removed before the following vintage, if the buyer does not remove it the law gives the seller the power to throw it away or pour it out of the cask. Morality would prescribe a different course of conduct. This case, then, is an example of what is not *justitia attributrix.* In brief, *justitia expletrix* comprises those rules of law or equity which can be legally enforced; *justitia attributrix* such rules of morality as are incapable of legal enforcement (1,1 §§ 7, 8, 9, 10). 6. The less practical definition of *jus,* or law, is that it is a standard or rule of action, or a rule of moral action, obliging us to do what is right. This definition is too wide, as it embraces pure morality. The general tendency of the civil law is in favour of the definition laid down by Justinian, which comprises the following maxims: to live honestly, to hurt no one, to give every one his due *(Inst.* 1, 1, 3). (1, 1 § 11).

The foregoing definition is not so much a definition of law as of the moral principles on which it is based.

7. The law of Nature, as defined by Justinian and Ulpian, is that which Nature has taught to all animals *(Inst.* 2, pr.). It is not right to conclude from this that everything that man does is just, or according to natural law (although man is clothed with reason), in cases where brute beasts act in the same way from instinct. The possession of reason does not justify men in committing incest, adultery, acts of wanton lust, or acts of violence without cause. Some place the foundation of natural law, or the law of Nature, in its agreement or disagreement with logical and social reason. But

this is begging the question. Others, not rightly, seek the beginning of natural law in the social fellowship of man. The only foundation for it is (according to Voet) the beneficence of the Creator, implanting a certain tendency in the minds of his creatures.

This was recognised by man in the beginning, and has always been acted upon by mankind. Thus the Romans include in the category of rules of natural law the following observances, in order: *(a)* Duty to the immortal gods, *(b)* Duty to one's country, (c) Duty to one's parents, *(d)* The law of self-preservation, (e) The conservation of the human race, by the procreation and education of offspring. (/) Duty to society at large, and to the individual members thereof. From this, says Voet, arises the principle that no one should do to another what he would not wish done to himself; that each should give to others what he would desire for himself from others; and that each should apply the same law in his own case which he desires to lay down for others. The law of Nature is firm and immutable. The law of Nature is, nevertheless, subject to exceptions, as in the case of justifiable homicide and slavery (1, 1 §§ 12, 13, 14, 15, 16, and 17).

This is not the place for a metaphysical disquisition on the law of Nature. The subject is fully treated of in Austin's *Jurisprudence,* Lectures 5 and 32. Care must, however, be taken not to accept Austin's theories *in toto,* as much of what he laid down is now discredited.

8. The law of nations is what obtains, and is uniformly observed, among all nations, or at least among such as are more civilised. Primeval law is the law of Nature as originally received among nations. Secondary law of nations is what nations have subsequently laid down for themselves and what human necessities require. There is no law originally introduced as binding on all nations, as nations, or as binding all peoples in public commerce existing among nations; so those nations or individuals who departed from this law were not at first punished. As mankind

advanced in ideas, whatever was by reasoning considered useful and suited for promoting intercourse among men was gradually approved by the use now of this and now of that nation, and so at last of many nations. The nations were not at first bound by any general obligation beyond this. Nations were not looked upon as offending, or breaking the principles of justice, who interdicted commerce with Voet here appears to lay down not so much strict juristic principles, as his conclusions of faith derived from the Sermon on the Mount. other people on their own soil, thereby disapproving and forbidding among their own citizens certain kinds of contracts, which they determine not to allow in their own territories (compare the prohibitions issued by Napoleon against trade with England, and the retaliatory measures adopted, 1806). Laws of embassy and solemn declarations of war are not evolved from the law of Nature, but from the practice and wish of nations. The recognition of ambassadors sent to allied and friendly countries, and the sacred character accorded them, are derived from promises given, and from the principles of the law of Nature which teach that faith once guaranteed, even to a private individual, must be observed. From the constant practice of rules relating to these and kindred matters, such as the mode of conducting war, and the binding effect of treaties, a body of usages sprang up, so regularly and continuously enforced as to amount to a positive law (1, 1 §§ 18, 19).

Voet here distinguishes between the *jus gentium,* the body of legal principles observed among and common to all nations, and the *jus inter gentes* (modern international law), the rules which regulate the intercourse of nations, considered as individuals, with one another.

The definitions of the law of nations, and the right of embassy, are fully treated of in Woolsey's *Introduction to the Study of International Law* (Introductory chapter, caps. 1 and 4), and in Hall's *Treatise on International Law* (4th ed. , pp. 1—42, 87—105, 310—338). Voet had a far more rational conception of the meaning of International Law than

Austin had. 9, The civil law (the municipal law of the State) is that which every nation establishes for itself. From the dictates of the law of Nature, or the rules of the law of nations, it approves particular portions and adopts them as suitable for its own purposes, and to these, at its own convenience, the nation adds others at discretion. In this sense Gaius says that all nations who are governed by law and custom use partly their own law, partly that common to all men. Voet divides the civil law into (a) original civil law, or civil law by origin, and *(b)* civil law by adoption. Civil law by origin is that which is established in a State without any certain or peculiar foundation of natural law, although it is not wanting in a certain See the remarks of Grotius, the father of modern International Law, in his *Prolegomena to De Jure Belli et Pads, passim.* He holds it to be "most certain that there is among nations a common law of Bights which is of force with regard to war." general equity. To this division belong wills and most other solemn deeds, the deduction under the *lex Fcdcidia,* the disposition of the *Senatusconsultum Macedonianum* and the *Senatusconsultum VeUeianum,* and many other laws of Roman origin. Civil law by adoption is what is established among other nations by natural reason, or by logical deduction, and which has been received by our own people as just and right (1,1 § 20).

See Justinian's *Institutes,* 1, 2, 1 and 1, 2, 10: "The law which a people makes for its own government belongs exclusively to that State, and is called the civil law, as being the law of the particular State." "*Jus civile* is the law peculiar to any one nation in particular.... The Romans, however, when they used the term *jus civile* without any distinctive adjective, meant emphatically their own national *jus civile,* which consisted more especially in the interpretations of the *prudentes*" (Colquhoun's *Boman Law,* § 297).

10. In the early times of Roman law, the mere will of the kings stood in place of the law. Afterwards, some formal laws were made by the kings themselves, and

collected by Papirius, being called the *leges regiae* after their authors, and *jus Papirianum* after their collector. The Decemvirs borrowed and adapted various laws from the Greek States, which they embodied in ten tables, to which two were afterwards added. This collection was known as the Law of the Twelve Tables. Then came the actions at law, the *legis actiones,* fixed and solemn forms accommodated by the jurisconsults to the principles briefly set forth in the Twelve Tables. Afterwards came a large number of laws made day by day, *plebiscite, senatusconsulta,* and edicts of the magistrates, both temporary and perpetual. After the Roman Republic had become a monarchy, there came Imperial Constitutions, partly collected privately by Gregorianus and Hermogenianus, and partly published b public authority by Theodosius the younger. Justinian finally caused the rules and principles of Roman Law to be collected and published in the Institutes, Pandects, revised Code, and Novels (1, 2 §§ 1 to 7).

Voet gives a somewhat meagre account of the history of Roman Law, and of the law as it existed after the time of Justinian. A great deal of information on the subject will be found in Ortolan's *History of Roman Law,* translated by Prichard and Nasmith; in the first volume of Colquhoun's *Summary of the Roman Civil Law;* and in the article on Roman Law in the *Encyclopedia Britannica,* by Prof. J. Muirhead.

1L The Jurisconsults at Rome were distinct from the pleaders of causes. They were for the most part specialists, who confined themselves to the study of one particular branch of the law (1, 2 §§ 8, 9).

"*Jurisprudent* was he who combined a competent knowledge of principle and practice, a professor of jurisprudence" *(Colquhoun,* § 294).

CHAPTER II. LAW AND CUSTOM. 12. Papinian has defined law, in a wider sense, as "a general precept, the decision of prudent men, the controlling of wrongs committed either of one's own motion or through ignorance, the engagement binding the whole State." In the sense of "the decision of prudent men," the definition indicates that a law ought not to be passed rashly, nor at the mere will of the legislator, but after mature deliberation as to its justice, fairness and public utility. In the sense that it is "a controlling of wrongs committed either of one's own motion or through ignorance," there is no wrong where the mind is incapable of making a distinction between what is right and what is wrong. Those are not held to commit a crime who are incapable of wrong, either on account of innocence of purpose by reason of their youth, or on account of misfortune by reason of insanity or idiocy. Wrong may, however, be done without *dolus,* or evil intent, so that there is a necessity for its being restrained. Hence damage caused whether through evil intent *(dolus)* or negligence *(culpa),* even of the slightest degree, is counted a wrong. Thus the Roman law permitted actions for wrongs to be brought against those who, without permission, had, through ignorance of law, summoned those to whom reverence was due; or against Judges who gave a wrong decision, through ignorance of law; or against those who, through error of law or fact, had taken away from the possessor certain things as if they belonged to the taker (spoliation). Furthermore, the law must be "an engagement binding the whole State," in so far that the people, in its collective sense, tacitly promises to subject itself to the law (1, 3 §§ 1, 2, 3, 4).

See *Austin,* Lecture 1, *passim,* and the commentators on Austin, such as Holland.

13. Law should be just and reasonable. It should preserve equality in its form, and bind all citizens alike. It should not, unless it be a *privilegium,* or private law, be made for individual persons, but generally. There are certain laws which do not bind the whole people, but only particular classes as a whole. Such are the laws restraining the contracts of women and of minors, like the law which prevented one woman from suing for another, or a minor from borrowing money so as to bind his estate. In this class of laws, binding particular classes

of the population only, the maxim *cessante rations leyis cessat ipsa lex* (where the reason for the law does not apply the law itself does not apply) does not hold good. Perpetuity is another requisite for a law. It should be established with the intention that its obligation shall never cease, unless on account of the changed condition of men or of the times, or the total cessation of the reason for the law (1, 8 §§ 5, 6, 7). 14. The law should be passed by those who have the power of making the law—in a monarchy, by the King; in an aristocracy, by the nobles; in a democracy, by the whole people (1, 3 § 8).

See *Austin,* Lecture 1, *passim,* and his commentators.

15. Promulgation is also a requisite for the validity of a law. Without promulgation the people cannot become sufficiently acquainted with the law, nor can the law then bind people ignorant of it through the fault of the law-giver. As laws do not bind before promulgation, it is likewise true, according to the Novels of Justinian (66, c. 1) and the earlier views of the Courts of Holland, that they do not bind citizens immediately on promulgation, but only two months after promulgation. Voet's view, however, is that they bind upon promulgation. It appears to depend on the mere will of the legislator from what time the promulgation of the law shall date. Thus it is not unusual that shorter or longer times are fixed by our modern law also, according to the different circumstances of the case. If the time be not expressed, it is more correct to think that our laws bind immediately on promulgation (1, 8 § 9).

In England, by 33 Geo. III. c. 13, a statute begins to operate from the time when it receives the royal assent, unless otherwise provided. But, by 48 Geo. III. c. 106, where an Act expires before a Bill continuing it has received the royal assent, the latter Act takes effect from the expiration of the former, unless otherwise provided, and except as to any penalty.

It is now the usual practice to insert in every statute the date when, or after which, it is to be of force and effect.

In *Lyons* vs. *Crosly* (4 S. C. 17) it was said: "As far back as Lord Coke's time it was a recognised principle that as soon as Parliament has concluded anything, the law intends that every person has notice of it, for the Parliament represents the body of the whole realm (4 *Inst.* 26). It is clear that by our *(i.e.* RomanDutch) law promulgation is necessary. By some of Justinian's Novels (66 and 116) definite periods were fixed after the date of the promulgation when the law first became of binding force, but according to Groenewegen *(ad Nov.* 66), who is supported by Voet (1, 3, 9), a statute becomes binding immediately upon its promulgation, unless a different intention can be gathered from the terms of the statute itself. By the 85th section of the Constitution Ordinance of Cape Colony it is enacted that the Governor shall cause every Act of Parliament which he shall have assented to in Her Majesty's name, to be printed in the *Government Gazette* for general information, and that such publication shall be deemed in law to be promulgation of the same." As to the Transvaal, see Proc. No. 8 of 1901, § 2. As to Natal, see Law 3, 1887, § 6.

16. It is clear that an unpromulgated law does not bind. When a law or universal edict has been published almost everywhere throughout a whole country, but the publication has been omitted in some place, town, or village, whether by neglect of the proper officer, or other cause, then such law will bind the inhabitants of those places in which it has been proclaimed, but will by no means bind those of such places where it has been neglected (1, 3 § 10).

This principle is scarcely applicable now. Most laws or statutes, on or before promulgation, are at the present day published in the *Government Gazette* or official organ of the country where they are passed or become law, and publication in such organ is taken to be publication to the whole world. If, however, the Constitution of a State provides another mode of promulgation, then promulgation in such mode is binding.

17. When a law has been passed in accordance with the requisites previously

enumerated, it is binding on all persons of whatever degree, public and private, noble and plebeian. The law does not bind subjects only, but visitors and strangers as well, as long as they remain in the territory where the law is in force. It binds its own subjects only as long as they have their domicile in the place where they are subject to the law in question: for when they change their domicile, and transfer it to another place, they are neither bound by the laws of their former domicile nor by its jurisdiction (1, 3 § 11).

Some modern nations apply the principle of exterritoriality to this extent, that they hold their subjects amenable to the jurisdiction of their native land for acts committed outside its jurisdiction. The questions of the binding effect of foreign laws, and of domicile generally, are briefly discussed by Voet in the second part of the following title. The question of domicile is very fully treated of in Phillimore's *International Law* (vol. 4), Story's *Conflict of Laws,* Dicey s *Conflict of Laws,* Westlake's *Private International Law,* Foote's *Private International Law,* and Burge's *Commentaries.* 18. By a fiction of law, ambassadors, being regarded not as private individuals but as representing the absent Powers by whom they are sent, are looked upon as absentees also, and as residing beyond our territories. Consequently, they are not bound by the civil law of that nation amongst whom they reside for the purposes of their embassy, not more so than any one else who in fact has his domicile beyond such territory. But if they act contrary to duty, and contumeliously trample upon the laws of the land to which they are sent, in an open manner, they may be ordered to leave the country, a complaint being also sent to those whom they represent. The rule is similar with regard to delegates who are away from the town or province in-which they have their domicile, while representing the States or federated provinces in the more general assemblies of the federated provinces, the State council, and similar assemblies. These should, with regard to their daily manner of life, obey the laws of the place where they are residing, but must follow the law of their domicile, or of the place which they have left in the public service, with regard to intestate succession to movable property when they die, to the benefit of inventory, to the appointment of a *curator bonis,* and similar personal matters (1, 8 § 12).

Voet is very guarded in his statement regarding the immunity of ambassadors. Westlake (Pr. *Int. Law,* 3rd ed p. 232) says: "So far as concerns an ambassador or public minister himself, the immunity extends to such an extent that not only is his person privileged from arrest, and his goods or chattels from seizure, but he cannot be sued at all, even for the purpose of obtaining against him a judgment which may be enforced by execution after he has This is, of course, written in reference to the States of Holland, which had, tor most purposes, inter-State relations with each other, more so even than is the rule with the States of the American Union to-day.

ceased to be entitled to the privilege. Nor can he be made a defendant as representing his Sovereign or State, with the view of giving him an opportunity to appear and defend the rights of such Sovereign or State when they may be adjudicated on. Nor, when a foreign Sovereign or State is made a defendant in such a case as last mentioned, can the writ be served on the ambassador or minister as a means of bringing it to the knowledge of such Sovereign or State. " See the same authority further with "regard to the immunity of servants of an ambassador. As to the immunity accorded to those in an ambassador's house, see *Phillimore* (vol. 4, 3rd ed. § 173). 19. Those who are students in a foreign land fall under the general law, that is, they must obey the laws of that place in which they sojourn for the sake of their studies, in the same manner, and so far, as other sojourners are bound while they are in the territory. When particular provision is made with regard to the manners, coercion, and jurisdiction over students, they do not use the same law as the other inhabitants of the place. Such, for instance, is the case with students at the University of Leyden (and, so far as intramural rules of discipline are concerned, in England at Oxford and Cambridge). In successions and the like, students follow the law of their true domicile in regard to movables. In regard to immovable property, the law of the place where the thing is situated is followed (1, 8 § 13). 20. Law either obliges, or commands, or forbids, or punishes, or permits, or persuades, or distributes rewards, or pardons. Laws which counsel or allow (permissive) have, properly speaking, no force of obligation with respect to those whom they counsel or permit, for they leave what they counsel or permit entirely to the discretion of those who come under the law, without imposing a necessity to obey. With regard to other citizens they have a binding force in this way, that those who are not counselled or permitted by the law have no privileges under it (1, 3 § 14). 21. Even according to the Roman Law, though its principles would at first sight appear to militate in a contrary direction, the Princeps, or Head of the State, was not placed above the jurisdiction of *all* laws. Whatever the Roman Princeps had, he derived wholly from the Roman people, as his power was conferred on him wholly by the *lex regia,* which treated of his *imperium.* The Princeps was bound in his conscience by the divine laws, and by the natural laws, and thus by those which are received by the nation as emanating from the dictate of right reason (1, 8 § 15). 22. If anything has been done or agreed upon contrary to the laws, it is *ipso jure* null and void. It is, therefore, not to be observed, even if no declaration of nullity has been specially added to the law. It is otherwise if the laws only permit or counsel a thing, for then they leave it to the discretion of those whom they permit or counsel to follow or neglect what is laid down in the law, or if the law contains a favour for the benefit of a private person only *(privilegium),* for every one may renounce a law introduced for his own benefit alone *(omnis jari pro se introducto renuntiare potest).* What is done contrary to law may hold good, with the consent of those for whom, and in whose favour, the law was introduced. There is nothing to prevent the public law (that is, the law constituted by public authority), when it refers not to public loss but to the affairs of private persons, being abrogated by the agreement of private persons. It is otherwise *(i.e., acts done in derogation of the law are forbidden)* where the public utility is concerned (or where the act would be contrary to public policy), or where those for whose benefit the law has been introduced are forbidden to injure themselves by their consent and act, against their own advantage—as in the case of the alienation of a dotal estate with the consent of the wife, or where minors, prodigals, and the like, contract to their own loss. That which is done contrary to law is not *ipso jure* null and void, where the law is content with a penalty for its breach or infraction. Where there is a taint of fraud in connection with a contract entered into *bond fide,* as in an alienation made for the purpose of changing a Court *(i.e., changing the venue),* the party acting fraudulently or contrary to law is bound to make compensation to the extent of the damage resulting from his act, while the contract itself remains of full force and effect. Since many laws which forbid certain things to be done neither nullify what is done contrary thereto, nor fix a penalty, the maxim originated, that " many things, the performance whereof is prohibited in law, nevertheless hold good when done." Thus the *lex Cincia* formerly prohibited donations above a certain amount, but did not nullify the donation or decree a penalty if a larger donation were given; and though a soldier was forbidden to act as *procurator,* what he did in Court was ratified, if not repudiated by his adversary or by the Judge. Those things especially are not null and void which are done contrary to law, if the law expressly provides for the rescission of the acts; as in the case of an invalid will, alienations in fraud of creditors, things done under duress or fear (Voet's expression is somewhat obscure; but he seems to mean that the act does not become null until its rescission has been obtained before a Court) (1, 3

§ 16). 23. It is clear that laws prescribe a mode for future transactions, and cannot relate back to things that are past (i. e., previous transactions cannot be governed by laws passed subsequently). Those things remain valid which were done in accordance with the old law, and before the new law was made. If a punishment has to be imposed for a crime committed before a new law laid down heavier penalties for the commission of that crime, the punishment must follow what is laid down in the old law, not what is laid down in the new law. It is otherwise where the legislator has treated specially both of things done at the present time and of past transactions. It is objectionable to change those things which were done, compromised, or decided before the new law, either according to the old laws themselves, or according to the interpretation which has always been placed on the laws. Laws which give an interpretation or explanation of previous doubtful laws, that is, which are declaratory of existing law, have naturally a retrospective effect. This is true of such laws as would have no meaning if they did not refer to the past, for where there is a doubt, that signification of the law is to be approved which is free of defects. There is a retrospective effect where an exception, remission, or relaxation is introduced by the new law (1, 3 § 17). 24. Such interpretations of the law as are necessary are made by the law-giver alone, to the extent to which the interpretation is to have the force of law. (This refers to legislative, not judicial, interpretation.) Interpretation of law is a prerogative of the Head of the State, as the authority making the law. Law is also interpreted by the use and custom of the people. If any question arises as to the ambiguity of the law, we must first find what law the State has formerly used in similar cases; for inveterate (i.e., ancient) use fixes the doubtful meaning of a law, and custom is the best interpreter of the law. Special judgments of the Courts cannot alter the law (i.e., the law which is clear and unambiguous); but decisions of a similar nature constantly given have the force of law. In

the interpretation of law, one must not decide concerning the intention of the law, unless one has examined the whole law—for the meaning of the law often becomes clear from what precedes and what follows the part to be interpreted. That interpretation is to be had recourse to, which is free from defect, more suited to accomplishing what is intended, and more in accordance with the will of the Legislature. There should not be a conflicting interpretation, or such as does not carry out the intention of the legislator, so that a thing may happen which is in conflict with the spirit of the law, though not directly forbidden by it. Nor should there be an interpretation which renders the law useless, inapplicable, and of no effect, nor an interpretation which occasions or may occasion loss to one in whose favour it was introduced. Nor should one interpret from particular cases, or a particular law, deducing therefrom a general rule; or from something done in error. One (i.e., the person interpreting the law) should not recede from the proper signification of words; and in doubtful cases, as Ulpian says, one must not depart from the exact words of the edict. That the legislator wished to depart from the proper signification of the words can be gathered from the antecedent or subsequent words of the law, from its preface or conclusion; also from the reason of the law underlying it. In the case of legal fictions, the same rules of interpretation applying to actual cases may be extended to feigned cases. The meaning of a law may be gathered from arguments taken from a contrary meaning, unless a wrong meaning results, or encouragement is given to crime, or unless another law especially forbids such a construction in a particular case (1, 3 §§ 18, 19, 20, 21, 22, and 23). 25. The object of interpretation, made by the Head of the State or by judicial authority, is to discover the probable intention of the legislator with reference to doubtful laws. Dispensation can only be granted by the Head of the State, and is the removal of the obligation of the law on certain persons or things or acts, the force of the law remaining unimpaired in other cases and with reference to other persons. Since dispensation is an abrogation of the law, and it is necessary that every obligation should be relaxed in the same way as it was made, the highest authority in the State is necessary thereto. Not even those who have the highest authority can rightly relax the divine moral law, or the natural law and its obligations. No dispensation should be granted except for a just and urgent cause, and for the sake of public utility (1, 8 § 25). 26. Statutes which derogate from, or take away the effect of, the civil law should be interpreted, not from the civil law, but from the statute or common law of the country (1, 8 § 24). 27. Custom is unwritten law, gradually introduced by the customs of those using it, and having the force of law. In customary law, as in written law (or law specially enacted), justice and reasonableness are desirable. Not only should there be a long lapse of time, but the acts relied on should have been done freely and frequently, and without force or fear. The time for establishing customary law has nothing to do with the period of prescription, for prescription is very different in its nature. A law introduced by prescription does not bind others forthwith, whereas the whole people is bound as soon as a custom is recognised as law. It does not matter in what mode the people declares its will, whether it be judicially or extra-judicially. There need not be express consent to the adoption of a customary law; but the people may consent tacitly. Extra-judicial custom must be proved. Custom will not, though frequent, have the force of law, unless the acts relied on are uniform. If there be a variation in the acts, the custom will not have the force of law (1, 8 §§ 25 to 31).

"Prescription must not be mixed up with the doctrine of custom, for prescription is acquisition by enjoyment for the period required by law, and therefore is law, not custom " *(Colquhoun,* § 339).

28. Notorious customs do not require proof, but, as with every other kind of written law, it is sufficient to allege them in Court.

Among notorious customs are such as are reduced to writing by public authority. He who alleges and relies on a custom must prove it, in case of dispute, as this is a question of fact—whether it be the plaintiff who relies on it for his summons, or the defendant who relies on it for his exception or defence. Voet thinks the better opinion is that a large number of witnesses, not one or two, should prove a custom, since it ought to be known to all. Even a crowd of witnesses does not suffice, when they are witnesses deposing singly to different facts. The simple negation of a fact is not sufficient for the proof of a custom a, 3 §§ 32 to 85).

29. The force of a custom is that, equally with a special law, it binds citizens to its observance. It is interpreted in the same way as law, and by parity of reasoning its principles are extended to similar cases. Those maxims are erroneous which say that "customs are matter of strict law *(stricti juris),* and should not be applied beyond the special cases to which they refer." Not only is a former law abrogated by a subsequent law, but by custom as well, since it makes no difference in what way the people declares its will. So the laws may be removed or changed, not only at the will of the legislator, but by the tacit consent of the community, through disuse. Custom which has come into vogue through error has not the force of law. Custom is introduced by the people, not against law, but without a special law bearing on the subject. It will come to have the force of law if the supreme authority in the State does not either contradict the custom (even if the supreme authority was ignorant of it), or remove it (1, 8 §§ 36, 87). 30. A law is said to be refused *(antiquari,* from *antiquo,* "I hold to the former law," the formula for recording one's vote against the passing of a new law) which was not carried through all its stages, or not passed, being proposed or asked for, and rejected. A law is abrogated which, after having been once carried, has been wholly deprived of force and effect. A law is derogated from when either the first part of the law has fallen into disuse, or when, by a new law, that is forbidden

which was sanctioned by the former law, which is thereby derogated from. A law is surrogated when anything is added to the former law; and obrogated when anything in the former law is changed (1, 3 § 38).

The foregoing distinctions are now of no practical importance, and are only given here to assist those who may meet with the terms when reading the commentators on the Roman Law.

31. Whoever alleges the abrogation of a law once published and received, must prove his allegation. The presumption of law is in favour of the continuing obligation and enduring use of laws, until the contrary be proved. In case of doubt we must presume in favour of the use of a promulgated law, and equally in favour of its first reception and the duration of its reception. A law never received, and never observed, has no force, if a long time has elapsed since its promulgation, and the people has followed a previous law which which is contrary to the law in question. Though a law is not abrogated by disuse alone, it loses its force *ab initio,* or is deprived *ex post facto* of the strength of its obligation, when acts contrary to it are frequently done and not repudiated by the legislator (1, 3 §§ 39, 40, 41, 42).

The principle of English Law is that no custom to the contrary can override a positive and unrepealed statute *(Colquhoun,* § 342).

32. The maxim *cessante ratione legis cessat ipsa lex* (the reason for the law ceasing, the disposition of the law itself ceases), explains itself. The interpretation of a new law which amends a former law should be strict, and ought not to be extended to other cases than are necessary to preserve the meaning and accord with the justice of the new law (1, 3 §§ 43, 44). CHAPTER III. CONSTITUTIONS MADE BY THE HEAD OF THE STATE. 33. After the Roman people had transferred all rule and authority to the Emperor by the *lex regia,* he came to have the same power as the people anciently had. Thenceforward the right of passing laws and depriving laws of effect resided in the Emperor (1, 4, 1 § 1). 34. A constitution of the Emperor was

what the Emperor deemed should have the force of law. The Imperial constitutions were announced in the form of edicts, rescripts, decrees; of interlocution, which was a simple pronunciation of the Imperial wish without any solemn form; of oration, which the officers of the Emperor recited in the Senate when he wished to declare his wish with regard to a decree of the Senate; of mandate, or commissions issued to those who represented him in the provinces, or who were sent on special missions; of subscription or annotation, in which he answered very briefly the letters in which private persons made requests; and pragmatic sanctions, which were full answers to the requests of bodies and colleges concerning their public matters, answers made with the advice of pragmatics or learned men (1, 4, 1 § 2).

The Imperial constitutions were first promulgated by virtue of the authority conferred on the Emperor by the *lex reyia*. Augustus, after having established his power, obtained, by degrees, the transfer of Imperial rights to his own person; always, however, under protest. The succeeding Emperors became more independent of the people, and, consequently, less scrupulous in asserting their power *(Colquhotm, § 313)*.

"The generic name of ' *constitutiouet'* embraces all the acts of the Emperor; but they must be divided into three distinct classes: 1st, the general ordinances spontaneously promulgated by the Emperor *(edicta)*; 2nd, the judgments rendered by him in cases which he decided in his tribunal *(decreta)*; 3rd, the acts addressed by him to various persons, as, for example, to his lieutenants in the provinces; to the inferior magistrates of the cit"; to the praetor, or proconsul, who interrogated him on any doubtful point of law; to private individuals, who petitioned him in any circumstance whatever *(mandate, epistolae, rescripta)"* (Ortolan, § 330).

35. Rescripts were the constitutions more frequently published. They fell into disuse if they were obtained by an express falsehood in the statements of the supplicating petition, by a suppression

of the truth which influenced the Emperor in making the grant, by a partial suppression of the truth, or by a confused and perplexed narration of facts. Suppliants who acted in this manner not merely lost what they obtained, but were subject to punishment for the crime of falsity, or fraud. If there had been fraud in obtaining the principal portion of a petition, the accessory portions were thereby vitiated. Personal rescripts which had no mention of the date or of the consul's name had no effect. Without the addition of the date or the consul's name it was impossible to decide whether the aid of a rescript was obtained or not by a petition lodged in a legal or illegal space of time. And though in Voet's time it was possible to put in a petition even during the pendency of a lawsuit, whenever one wished to obtain the benefit of restitution, yet the ancient law requiring the addition of a day in rescripts was not to be departed from. Rescripts not strengthened with the signature of the Emperor or magistrate were equally wanting in authority. Proof was furnished by production of the original rescript, not by copies thereof. Those rescripts were inefficacious which were contrary to law or injurious to the public treasury *(fiscus)*. Rescripts were invalid which deprived a third party of a right acquired by him. The Emperor could not by rescript weaken a peremptory exception, nor grant delay to a debtor to the prejudice of the creditor, nor impair the force of contracts or obligations lawfully entered into, nor revive a lawsuit that had been settled. For just cause, the Princeps might properly deprive a private person of a right, whether by way of penalty (such as the total or partial confiscation of an estate for crime), or where the public good required it, provided that, 'in the latter case, an equivalent were given which would repay loss of the right or thing taken away. Without the consent of the owner, stones might be cut for public purposes from his quarry, payment being made as laid down by custom or rescript. If the public roads were washed away by the swiftness of a river, or if a chasm were formed in

them, the nearest neighbour was bound, on receiving remuneration, to allow a road through his property. By authority of the State, it might be decreed that the neighbouring houses could be broken down for the purpose of constructing the public workshops or any other public work. By Dutch law, both the buildings of private persons and their lands may be taken for public use by the State magistrates or the prefects, on paying their value to the owner, for the purpose of building walls, widening ditches, making ducts, making or repairing mounds, whether the magistrates or prefects are authorised to do so by a general privilege from the head of the State, or have specially obtained the power to do this in certain cases (1, 4, 1 §§ 3 to 7).

In *Town Council of Cape Town* vs. *Commissioner of Crown Lands and Public Work* (Foord, 21), the Kailway Department of the Cape Colony required a portion of the Cape Town "Parade" for railway purposes. The Governor, in terms of the Cape Act 1 of 1861, gave the Council leave to alienate the ground. The railway department could not come to terms with the Town Council, and appropriated the land in question under the provisions of the Cape Act 19 of 1874, and Act 9 of 1858, leaving the question of compensation to be settled afterwards. The Town Council applied for an interdict to restrain the railway department from thus expropriating the land. It was decided that, even independently of Act 9 of 1858, the Crown may, when authorised by the Legislature to construct roads for the use of the public, take or use any lands, not its own, required for the purpose, upon paying a reasonable compensation to the owner. '' The right to make the roads involves the right to exercise such powers as are absolutely necessary to enable the Crown to make the roads (cf. *Voet,* 1, 4, 7)."

There are numerous English and South African statutes regulating the expropriation of private property by the State, subject to arbitration. See the Cape Act No. 6, 1882, Transvaal Proclamation No. 5, 1902, and Natal

Law 16, 1872.

36. The State does not deprive a private person of his acquired rights when it orders wrongly constructed or badly constructed buildings to be removed, such, for instance, as destroy the symmetry of a street, or obstruct other members of the public, or narrow the streets, or such as menace the safety of public works and buildings (1, 4, 1 § 8).

The power of supervising the erection of buildings in towns is usually delegated to Municipal Corporations, Such powers are conferred on municipalities in Cape Colony under Acts 4o, 1882, and 22, 1893, in the Transvaal by Procs. No. 16, 1901, No. 28, 1901, and No. 7, 1902, and in Natal by Law 19, 1872, and Law 22, 1894.

37. The Princeps does not deprive persons of an acquired right by giving to a private person the right of building in a public place, even to the damage of his neighbours, since one who obtains simple permission to build in a public place is not, when there is a doubt, considered to have obtained permission to act to the disadvantage of his neighbours. For, as a private person can build on his own ground, or concede to another the right of building thereon, even although he may threaten damage to another, by obscuring his light or obstructing his view, provided a servitude has not been granted entitling those who suffer damage to light or a free view, one cannot deny the Princeps the same right in regard to public places, whereby the Princeps or his grantee may build in a public place to the detriment of the neighbours, provided no servitude has been granted to the latter in respect of such public places (1. 4, 1 § 9).

Voet's meaning appears to be this: The Princeps, or Head of the State, may grant the right of building to others, provided they do not infringe some negative servitude previously granted to others, or damago some other person, in which latter case that other person will be entitled to an interdict or damages, according to circumstances. The law will surely not be strained so far as to allow people, under a grant from the Crown, to deface open spaces (such as squares) which have been left open for the enjoyment or recreation of the public!

38. No infringement is made on the acquired rights of a private person, when the Crown interdicts a person from wasting his substance, or from using unnecessary violence (to accomplish certain ends), or from demanding a debt due to him prematurely; for it is to the interest of the State to see that no one misuses what is his own (1, 4, 1 § 10).

The interdiction of prodigals is treated of elsewhere in this work. The Court will also interfere in the case of lunatics and drunken husbands who are dissipating property held in community during marriage.

39. No infringement on private rights will be made by the concession of benefits and privileges (1, 4, 1 § 11).

The spirit of modern legislation and political economy is opposed to the granting of monopolies. Privileges are granted, nowadays, in general, by private legislation, *e.g.,* the obtaining of a private Act of Parliament. The privileges granted under general laws at the present time are such as are in the nature of patent rights, copyrights, and trademarks. It is submitted that privileges granted in general restraint of trade would be illegal.

40. Privileges are divided into—(a) those which are granted to a particular person, and (6) those which are granted in respect of a particular thing. Personal privileges, such as are conceded to a particular person, are extinguished by death, and do not pass to his heirs. Real privileges are such as adhere to the thing, and are transmitted to heirs and other successors. Personal privileges are not only those which are given to one person alone, but those also which by a general law are conceded to a whole class of particular persons; for example, those accorded to minors with regard to the administration of their guardianship, to wives for the recovery of their dowry. Real or causal privileges are not granted to one person or to one class alone, but are granted generally (1, 4, 1 § 12).

41. Personal privileges are transmissible neither by inheritance nor by cession, nor by right of action. Privileges attaching to things or actions are capable of cession. When there is a doubt whether a privilege has been granted to a person (or is personal), or in respect of a thing, one must ascertain whether it has been given as a gratuitous or as an onerous concession. Privileges given without consideration are, in cases of doubt, looked upon aa personal, while onerous privileges are accounted real (i. e., those given for valuable consideration). There should also, in case of doubt, be an inquiry whether a privilege is favourable to public utility and to the rights of third persons, or whether, on the contrary, they are odious in themselves, and prejudicial to the rights of others. In the former case, the presumption is that the privilege is real rather than personal. In the latter case, they should be regarded as personal, so that an odious concession may not extend beyond the person who has obtained it (1, 4, 1 §§ 13, 14). 42. In interpreting privileges, the rules regulating the interpretation of laws and statutes hold good. Where privileges have been obtained on a previous petition, such petition may be referred to for

C.l.—vol. I. E the sake of interpretation. When privileges are special rights *(Jura singularia),* granted in respect of a certain person or thing, or corporation *(universitas hominum),* they should, where strict interpretation is necessary, not be extended beyond the persons or cases for which they were introduced— unless it can be gathered from the facts of the case *(ex circumstantiis evidentibus)* that the grantor intended that the privilege should have effect with regard to persons not specially enumerated. Where such circumstances are wanting, the privilege is not extended (1, 4, 1 §§ 15, 16).

43. If in a privilege anything is derogated from the common law, or from the right of a third party, the strictest interpretation should be applied. This is especially the case when it is clear that the privilege is odious, granted against the public utility and the public laws and asserting or strengthening individual rights. Where privileges primarily

favour only certain persons or causes, they must be construed, in doubtful cases, so as to operate with as little prejudice to general public rights as possible (1, 4, 1 § 17).

In *Stellenbotch Div. Council* vs. *Myburgh* (5 S. C. 8), it was decided that the Council had the right to take gravel from uncultivated quit-rent land within its division for the repair and maintenance of roads beyond the limits of such land. It was said: "I cannot agree to the doctrine that we are bound to adopt such a construction as would involve the least possible interference with private rights. Such a doctrine would perhaps not be out of place where the private rights of one or more persons are interfered with for the private benefit of others, for in such a case it would be quite reasonable to presume that the Legislature desired to limit the interference within the narrowest limits. But where the sole object of the interference is to benefit the public, the same presumption would not necessarily exist The reservation to the Crown of the right of taking materials for the making and repairing of public roads was certainly made for the public benefit, and if the language used is really doubtful the interests of individuals ought, according to Voet (1, 4, 17), to yield to the public good." 44. Privileges should, however, not be so restrictively interpreted as to have no force or no operation against the common law, for then the granting of them would be futile. A later privilege should not be considered to take away one which is previous in time, but should rather be regarded as an augmentation or addition, without destroying completely the validity of the earlier privilege (1, 4, 1 § 18).

45. If privileges do not deprive others of their rights, or only deprive the grantor of certain rights, they should have the widest interpretation (1, 4, 1 § 19). 46. Personal privileges are extinguished by the death of the person to whom they were granted; real privileges are extinguished by the termination of the existence of the thing in respect of which they were granted. If a privilege has been granted to a State, a college, or a corporation, and the grantees have been destroyed or disturbed in their corporate existence by hostile violence or an incursion of robbers, the privilege is not thereby necessarily lost, but it may revive on the restoration of the State or corporation to former rights. But where dissolution takes place by a voluntary process, such as an act of State, or a resolution of the corporation, the privilege thereby ceases (1, 4, 1 § 20). 47. The better juristic view is that which gives the Princeps the power of revocation in the case of those privileges which flow from his mere liberality, and do not originate from a foregoing or a subsequent agreement or obligation. Such revocable privileges, moreover, must have been conceded indefinitely, without any definite period being stipulated, or must be accompanied by a reservation of the right of revocation, alteration or diminution. If, on the other hand, a privilege has been granted by means of a contract, or for valuable consideration, or for something done or to be done, or a present or future gift, or for services rendered, the Princeps cannot lawfully arrogate to himself the right of revocation unless such legal reasons are found as would justify revocation. If privileges for a certain number of years, or in perpetuity, were obtained from the grantor by the suppression of truth or by the suggestion of falsehood (i.e., by fraud), they may unquestionably be revoked or cancelled. The same thing applies in the case of artificers or workmen who abuse the privilege conceded to them, contrary to the intention of the grantor, and in fraud of other subjects of the State; or if, pretending that they have a privilege, they take the law into their own hands, without obtaining the previous sanction of a Court to what afterwards turn out to be wrongful acts. This applies, in the case of a corporation of artificers, to corporate acts: for acts done by individual members of a corporation under colour of the privilege granted to the corporation as a whole should not he held to prejudice the whole body (1, 4, 1 § 21).

The privileges granted to artificers are in modern times regulated, in every State, by patent laws or trade-mark laws, which are privileges granted to the first inventors of articles in the arts or in manufacture, of a beneficiary nature, securing to them the exclusive right in their own discovery for a limited period, but which do not extend (in English and British Colonial law at any rate) to conferring the exclusive right to carry on any trade or manufacturing monopoly. "The conditions are, that they be not contrary to law, hurtful to the State, injurious to trade, or generally inconvenient, and that the patentee be the original inventor; that the manufacture be new in the country where the patent is taken out, or a new improvement at least not in use" *(Col. § 322)*.

The case of corporations generally comes up for consideration in connection with charters granted to trading companies, such as the guilds of the City of London, or the British South Africa Company, or, again, certain English boroughs. Where such chartered or privileged corporations, by a corporate act (such as a resolution binding the corporation in the ordinary way, passed by the required majority of its members), do something contrary to the terms (or even, it is submitted, to the intent not expressly stated) of the original charter, the charter would, in the manner indicated by Voet, be liable to revocation.

48. A privilege is also terminated by renunciation, since *quisque juri acfavori pro se inlroducto recte renunciet* (every one may lawfully renounce a right or benefit introduced for himself). This may be done expressly, or may be inferred from conduct, as in the case where a privilege consists in exemption from performance *(in non faciendo),* and the grantee does an act wholly and directly contrary *(e.g.),* performs the very act which he was exempted from doing). In such a case, however, the act must have taken effect, aud not be merely tentative. Renunciation, however, which is gathered from conduct must be very strictly interpreted—for a renunciation of a privilege is, as it were, a donation, and *nemo in dubio praesumitur donare velle aut suum jactare* (no one, in case of doubt, is presumed to

make a gift or to abandon that which is his own). It follows that where a person, in a particular instance, does that which he could by virtue of a privilege have declined to do, in such a manner as to do a single act deviating from the privilege (though not wholly contrary thereto), he is not, in particular instances afterwards arising, thereby deprived of his privilege (1, 4, 1 § 22). 49. Where privileges have been granted to corporations, no part of them is lost to the corporation by the renunciation of individuals, nor is the privilege destroyed by acts of individuals done contrary thereto—*cum nemo juri alieno renunciare possit* (since no one may renounce or alienate the right of another). The general view of jurists is that whenever privileges contain a " null and void " clause, annulling all acts done to the contrary, such privileges are neither lost by renunciation, nor by any act done contrary thereto (1, 4, 1 § 28).

Voet is not very explicit in the last sentence of the foregoing paragraph. One can scarcely imagine that where a person possessed of a privilege does an illegal act, he is still to have the benefit of the privilege whose terms or spirit he has thus contravened.

50. Where privileges consist in performance (in *faciendo*), and in the exercise of some act, and if, during the whole time which custom or the laws have fixed as the period of prescription, no opportunity for the exercise of a privilege has arisen, the privileged person cannot be met by a plea of prescription. If, on the contrary, the opportunity for exercising the privilege had not been wanting, and the grantee had not availed himself of his privilege from the time when the opportunity for making use of it first arose, onwards through the whole period fixed by law or custom for the period of prescription, he would certainly lose his rights by prescription (1, 4, 1 § 24). 5L Privileges are not extinguished by the death of the Princeps who granted them, but the rights of the Princeps with regard to the granting or revocation of a privilege pass to his heir (1, 4, 1 § 25). 52. Rights under privileges which have been disturbed are vindi-

cated by suits before the Courts, in the nature of possessory remedies (1, 4, 1 § 26). CHAPTER IV. STATUTES PRIVATE INTERNATIONAL LAW. 53. In order to regulate the controversies arising with regard to the authority and force of statutes, laws, and customs, both municipal and territorial, the extent of jurisdiction, and the conflict of laws of different jurisdictions, one must inquire how far a people can extend and protect its own laws, and exclude other laws from recognition within the limits of its jurisdiction; how far comity of nations allows the extension of statutes and decrees beyond the territory of the lawgiver, no law binding him thereto, and how far treaties have been made between States to preserve this comity; and to what extent a citizen or foreigner may recede from the provisions of municipal or provincial law, whether by express agreement or by tacit fact or arrangement presumed from the circumstances of the case (1, 4, 2 § 1).

Consult Phillimore's *International Law*, vol. 4, p. 251.

54. The principal division of statutes is into *(a)* personal, (6) real, (c) mixed. It is generally agreed that personal statutes are those which are principally concerned with the universal or quasiuniversal condition *(status)*, quality, capacity or incapacity of persons— whether no reference at all be made to things or property; or whether things or property be mentioned, though in such a manner that it is clear that the main intention of the person making the statute was to make regulations with regard to a person, and that the consideration of the thing or property was quite subsidiary. Such are statutes determining whether one is a citizen or alien, noble or commoner, outlaw or within the King's peace, able to testate or not; or declaring a person a prodigal, or giving one *venia aetatis;* or regulating the admission to professions and occupations; or generally affecting the condition of persons (1, 4, 2 § 2). 55. Heal statutes, again, are those which are principally concerned with things or property, and dispose of things or property, whether there be mention of a person or not—provided

the main intention of the person making the statute was to make regulations with regard to things or property, and that the consideration of persons, where persons are mentioned, was quite subsidiary. Such are statutes regulating intestate succession to property, though they state the order in which persons shall succeed to each other *ab intestato;* prohibiting or allowing donations between spouses; governing community of property during or after marriage (1, 4, 2 § 8). 56. Mixed statutes are those which treat, principally, neither of persons nor of things, but define the form, manner, order, and solemnities of acts by persons in connection with the transaction of things or in regard to property, whether judicial or extra-judicial (1, 4, 2 § 4). 57. With regard to the force and efficacy of statutes, strict law and natural reason lay down the general rules (from Faulus, in *Dig.* 2, 1) that "beyond the territory you may with impunity disobey the person making the law" *(extra territorium jus dicenti impune non paretur)*, and "an equal has no right to rule his equal, or power of compelling him" *(pari in par em nullum competit imperium, seu cogendi potestas).* It follows that neither real, personal, nor mixed statutes can of themselves have any operation beyond the territory of the person making the statutes, nor have any effect elsewhere, without the consent of the legislator in the place where they are sought to be applied—because statutes cannot have more force than they receive from the legislator making them— whose power is confined to the limits of his territory, to which the force of his statutes is, consequently, confined. Any one is said to be a subject, in respect *(a)* of his goods, when he has any goods situated in any territory, although he has his domicile fixed elsewhere (in modern law this would, in general, refer only to immovable property); *(b)* of his person, when he has his domicile in any place, although the greatest part of his property may be situated elsewhere, or where he is only temporarily residing in the territory (which claims jurisdiction over him by virtue of his temporary residence), or where he is passing through it as a traveller, which likewise renders him temporarily a subject (1, 4, 2 § 5).

The principles enunciated in the foregoing section were applied in the case oi *Blatchford* vs. *Blatchford's Executors* (1 Ros. 7), which will be treated of later on in this work (§ 403). In *Haupt* vs. *Haujit* (14 S. C. 39), where the parties had gone to England with the intention of returning to Cape Colony and residing there, and the marriage took place during their temporary residence in England, it was held that Cape Colony was the matrimonial domicile, and that, in the absence of an antenuptial contract, the marriage (in accordance with Cape Colony law) was in community of goods.

58. There is a general opinion that personal statutes extend beyond the territory of the legislator, so that the capacity or incapacity which attaches to a person in the place of his domicile follows him everywhere. Thus when a person's right or capacity in respect of his civil acts is inquh-ed into, the decision must be left to the Judge of his domicile alone. (This means, that the Judge of the domicile alone has the power of fixing the *status* of a person: it does not mean that the Judge of a place in which the person whose rights are in question finds himself, but wherein he is not domiciled, has no right to decide cases arising with regard to such person, but that in all matters respecting his personal capacity or *status* reference must be had, not to the law of the country in which he is temporarily, but to the law of his domicile). The personal capacity which the Judge or the legislator of the domicile decides to attach to the person in question, follows him everywhere, whether such personal statutes were laid down with reference to a class of men, or to an individual. So one who is a minor or a major according to the law of the domicile is to be considered so all over the world, even in places where greater or lesser age is needed to attain majority. So when one is declared illegitimate by the law of his domicile he is regarded as such everywhere, nor can he by change of residence abandon his ca-

pacity or incapacity, or assume another capacity. Voet, however, holds that, as there is no authority in Roman Law for the foregoing principle, personal statutes cannot extend beyond the territory of the person making the statute any more than real statutes, whether directly, or by inference *personalia non magis quam realia territorium statuentis possunt excedere)*. There is no reason, he says, why a statute, which denies or gives a greater quality to a private person, should extend its force to places where anything different or contrary is laid down by law as to the cppacity or quality of persons. For, where the magistrate of one

State cannot compel the magistrate of another State, the two States being equals, to carry a statute of the former State into effect, he cannot expect the latter, from any reason of law, voluntarily to give effect to such statute. Hence it was that letters requisitorial came into use, by which magistrates of one nation or territory sought the privilege, offering a similar privilege in return, that judgments given by the requestor should be allowed to be executed on goods situate in the territory of the party requested (1, 4, 2 §§ 7, 8).

Voet gives other reasons of a similar nature for the view he takes. The mass of modem opinion, practice, and precedent is opposed to him, and follows the doctrines laid down by the authorities whom Voet condemns merely because the Soman Law is silent on the subject. The general opinion now is that a personal *status* follows the person everywhere. Those who wish to gain a clear idea of the subject, from the theoretical as well as the practical point of view, would do well to consult Story, Burge, Phillimore, Dicey, Foote, Nelson, and—perhaps greatest of all!—Westlake. In Voet's time Private International Law was an unknown science, and—except in regard to a few points—one cannot but be surprised at the clearness of vision and depth of insight he displays with regard to what was, at that time, almost a *terra incognita*. So far as concerns the special point now under discussion, the veiy argument of the au-

thorities who favour the exterritoriality of a personal *status,* which Voet sneers at so bitterly, is looked on as valid nowadays. "It is necessary that the *status* of men should receive its law from one certain place: for how absurd it would be that, in as many places as a person making a journey or sea voyage is detained at, he should change his *status* at each separate place; that at one and the same time he should be here a major, there a minor; that a wife should at the same time be in and out of her husband's power; that in one place a person should be a prodigal, in another a frugal man." This statement is perfectly true so far as regards the proposition that due recognition is given to a man's *status,* as fixed by his domicile, in all countries other than his country of domicile. But the Courts of other countries are perfectly entitled to exercise jurisdiction in other respects.

59. Where a capacity or incapacity is imposed on a subject by the statute of his domicile, with reference to goods situated in the place of his domicile, and not elsewhere, such capacity or incapacity is not lost, wherever such person travels or passes through. So if a person who has been declared a prodigal by Dutch Law (in Holland) goes to Friesland, where he is not regarded as a prodigal, and there makes a contract, after which he returns to Holland, he cannot be summoned in Holland on his contract made in Friesland. There is nothing to prevent the Judge of the domicile laying down a law whereby he forbids any one subject to him by reason of the domicile from doing anything in regard to immovables situate in foreign territory, or even from doing any acts in foreign territory. He may fix a penalty for such acts, which penalty may be enforced on the return of the subject to his domicile, or may be levied on the goods of the subject found within his domicile (1, 4, 2 § 9). 60. The foregoing rules hold also with regard to real and mixed statutes, which provide as to the solemnities attending the execution of acts. In strict law, magistrates are not bound to recognise dispositions of property, or relating to agreements, made in other

places, so far as concerns goods situate within their jurisdiction, when the solemnities observed were those of the place where the business was transacted, neglecting those required by the statutes of the place where the things were situated (1, 4, 2 § 10).

Story has treated this question at great length and with his usual lucidity. Voet's last proposition should, strictly speaking, be limited to immovable property.

61. Voet next discusses the general doctrine that in regard to successions, capacity to testate, contracts and other things, movables are governed, wherever situate, by the law of their owner's domicile, and not by the law of the place in which they are found. The reason for this rule seems to be that movables have no fixed and certain place of situation, are not attached to any certain place, and can easily, on the owner's wishing it, be transported and taken to the domicile, and often seem to be most useful to the owner when they are in his presence, whereby he has an actual physical control over them, and not one merely symbolical. Thus arose the doctrine that an owner is looked upon as wishing his movable goods to be situate, or to be considered as situated, where he had established his home and the principal seat of his business *(ubi fortunarum suarum larcm summamque constituit),* that is, in the place of his domicile. Consequently, if the Judge of the domicile have laid down anything with regard to movables, it applies to movables wherever situate, for no other reason than that they are considered to be in the place of the domicile itself. This view is to be ascribed to comity, which each nation shows to every other, rather than to the rigour of law. What are considered movables at the place of domicile, but immovables where they are situated, are governed, like all immovables, by the law of the place where they really are (1, 4, 2 § 11).

It will not escape notice that, in the passage immediately preceding this, Voet refuses to adopt the general view with regard to personal *status,* because it is not sanctioned by Roman Law; while

now he deliberately disregards the "strict rigour of the civil law," and says that his view on the question of movables is sanctioned by the comity of nations. Fortunately, the view is a correct one. The subject is fully discussed in Westlake's *Private International Law,* 3rd ed. §§ 150, 151, 153.

62. From their real statutes magistrates will not, and cannot, recede. But with regard to movables, which follow the law of the person, the strict rule has been relaxed, and universal practice has sanctioned the rule that movables, where there is a doubt, are governed by the law of the place where their owner has his domicile, wherever they may be situated (1, 4, 2 § 12). 63. In reference to mixed statutes, so far as the solemnities of any acts are concerned, the acts will be valid if the formalities which the law of the place where the act was done has prescribed as necessary have been observed. What is thus done has effect with regard to all movables and immovables, wherever situated, in other territories, whose laws may require very different and more elaborate solemnities. This rule holds good unless it appears that any one, to avoid the more inconvenient and perhaps more expensive solemnities of his own domicile, has, without any necessity, and in fraud of the statute of his domicile, gone to another place for the purpose of executing the act, and immediately returned. In such a case the act is, of course, invalid (1, 4, 2 §§ 18, 14).

Not only where a person goes to another jurisdiction to avoid expense, but where, by reason of relationship or personal incapacity, there exists in his domicile an insuperable obstacle to the celebration or execution of the act, the act will, after performance out of the domicile in a country where such obstacle does not exist, be regarded as invalid within the domicile. So, in *Brook* vs. *Brook* (9 H. L. C. 193), where the parties, domiciled in England, and prohibited from marrying by the law which prevents a man from marrying his deceased wife's sister, went to Denmark, and there celebrated the marriage, it was held invalid in England. See also *West-*

lake, § 2.

64. Voet holds that where a person, doing an act in one place, neglects to follow the solemnities enjoined by the law of that place, but follows either the statutes of his domicile or the law of the place where the thing is situate (which would, in this case, be immovable property), the act is valid (1, 4, 2 § 15). 65. Voet next refers to agreements (which have been previously adverted to) whereby the magistrate of one jurisdiction, on principles of comity, agrees, when asked to do so by " letters requisitorial," to allow execution to be levied on goods within his jurisdiction, in satisfaction of a judgment obtained in another jurisdiction (1, 4, 2 §§ 16, 17).

On this subject the student of modem Private International Law would do well to consult *WestlaJee,* 3rd ed. Chapter V. p. 92.

66. The next question for consideration is the extent to which private persons may, by pacts and agreements, recede from the disposition of statutes. In the case of statutes having for their main object public utility (such as those regulating public morality, or those regulating the forms and solemnities prescribed for acts publicly executed), since the public law cannot be altered by private agreement, and State rights do not fall within the scope of private business, and, moreover, one cannot renounce State rights (seeing that no one can renounce a right which enures in favour of another person), no private person can lawfully contract as to things which concern, not his own private personal estate, but the public utility, and which may result in loss to the public. The case of statutes regulating the private rights of individuals may be looked at from two points of view: *(a)* Statutes which are prohibitory, by which it is forbidden that anything shall take place (such as the law prohibiting donations between spouses; the *lex hoc edictali);* but not statutes which merely state the law from a negative point of view (such as those which declare that community of property shall not be introduced between spouses by marriage, *e.g.,* antenuptial contracts). Where statutes are

prohibitory, whatever is done or contracted against such prohibition is to be considered as of no force, or whatever is directed by last will against such prohibition, with reference to goods situate in the territory of the maker of the statute—whether this be done by those who are domiciled in the territory of the maker of the statute or by those who are domiciled elsewhere, where such prohibitions are not in force, *(b)* Statutes containing no prohibition, but simply declaratory of the rights of private persons. These may be renounced or receded from by agreements (pacts) and dispositions. If, for instance, the statutes define the order of intestate succession, a person who has the power, given him by statute, to testate, may depart from the prescribed order of intestate succession and leave his property in what order he pleases, calling those more remote in preference to those nearer in relationship (1, 4, 2 § 18).

A single example will suffice to make the case of prohibitory statutes clear. A. (husband) and B. (wife), both domiciled in Holland, reside for a time in Russia. There A. makes a gift to B. of a farm situate in Holland. The gift will not pass the property by Dutch law. Again, A., domiciled in Russia, makes a gift to B. of his farm situate in Holland, such a gift being (for the sake of illustration) permissible by Russian law. The gift will be similarly inoperative in Holland. 67. Permissible renunciations or departures from statutes may be made both expressly and tacitly. In case of doubt, there is a presumption that a person contracting with reference to his own property wished to do or establish that which the law of his domicile dictates. Hence arises the maxim, *quisque censetur in dubio se conformare voluisse in contrahendo et adaptasse sui domicilii statutis* (every one, where a doubt arises, is presumed to have desired, in contracting, to conform to and adopt the laws of his domicile). From this it follows that a community of goods, which is of statutory force in the place of domicile of those contracting marriage, extends to all goods, even those situate in places where the statutory community of

goods is unknown. On the other hand, where marriage is entered into in a place where a community of profits only exists by statute, and the parties are there domiciled, no universal community arises from the fact that the spouses possess goods situate in another territory where universal community obtains (1, 4, 2 § 19).

See *Blaichford* vs. *Blatchford'a Executors* (1 Ros. 7).

68. Tacit agreements of the foregoing kind do not, of course, extend to places where prohibitory statutes are in force. Furthermore, a person is not presumed to have intended to recede from his private rights any further than the statutes of his domicile give him power to do so. Where the domiciliary law is absolutely prohibitory, there can, of course, be no presumption of intention to recede from one's rights (1, 4, 2 § 20). 69. There is no presumption that a person intended to conform to the law of his domicile, where he has neither done nor contracted anything with regard to goods situate beyond his domicile, and has wholly abstained from making dispositions allowed him by the law of the place where his things are situate (1, 4, 2 §§ 21, 22).

The question of presumptions may be put briefly thus: A person who makes a contract, where it is doubtful whether he intended to contract with reference to the law of his domicile or the law of the place where he contracts, is presumed to have intended to follow the law of his domicile. Where a person dies in a country where he is not domiciled, and makes no testamentary disposition, he is not presumed to have wished to leave his property in accordance with the rules of succession enjoined by the law of his domicile, but the disposition of his property must be regulated according to the law of the place in which he died. This is a deduction from Voet's statements, but the latter proposition is open to question.

The different cases with respect to domicile, jurisdiction, and conflict of laws generally, must be sought in the chapters relating to the different relationships and contracts wherewith they are concerned. For instance, cases relat-

ing to marriage domicile will be found in the chapter relating to marriage, and the chapter relating to jurisdiction. In the foregoing chapter only the broadest general principles have been adverted to.

PART II. PUBLIC LAW. *A. STATE RIGHTS.* Chap. I.—Citizenship And Public Offices. ,, II.—Public Property And Public Works. ,, III.—Rights Of The Treasury. ,, IV.—Taxation.

,, V.—Military Law. ,, VI.—Embassies. *B. MUNICIPAL EIGHTS.* Chap. I. —Markets. PART n.

PUBLIC LAW. *A. STATE RIGHTS.*

CHAPTER I.

CITIZENSHIP AND PUBLIC OFFICES. 70. The various public offices existing under the Roman Republic and the Roman Empire are treated of by Voet in his first book (titles 9 to 22, inclusive). All these offices are obsolete, and remarks with reference to them have only an antiquarian interest, and do not apply for modern practical purposes, especially in British countries. The law of our time on such subjects may conveniently be found in such works as Sir W. Anson's *Law and Custom of the Constitution,* or Professor A. V. Dicey's work on the Constitution. 71. After discussing the public offices existing at Rome, the mode of attaining them, and the duties appertaining to them, Voet proceeds (in Book 50) to discuss municipal offices. Just as the Treasury, he says, has its rights, so are municipalities governed by special laws, both statutory and customary. After adverting to the distinction between *municipium* and *colonia* in Roman Law (for which see Poste— *Gaius,* p. 818, 3rd ed.—who says that all townships in Italy with the exception of Rome were, by the *lex Julia municipalis,* called *Coloniae* when they had been founded as colonies from Rome, *Municipia* when they traced their existence to some other origin), Voet says that in Roman-Dutch Law *colonia* is a property c.L.—voL. I. F in the country, possessed by a *colonus,* who derives the fruits from it (50, 1 § 1). 72. *Municipes* (subjects) are citizens of a State, participating in public honours and civil duties, and they become such by birth, by manumission and adoption (the two latter modes being obsolete now), and, as regards the State, by naturalisation, or, as regards towns, by occupying property or paying municipal rates. A person may participate in municipal duties and honours by reason of residence, by fixing his domicile in a place, and establishing there the chief seat of all his affairs, whence he does not intend to depart unless specially called away, and being regarded as a traveller when absent from it. He who resides or sojourns for a time in a territory which is not his own city or State, is not bound to perform those duties or undertake those offices which fall to the lot of subjects (50, 1 § 2). 73. Both persons originally born in a place, or subjects, and persons merely inhabiting it for an indefinite period, are subject to the jurisdiction of the magistrates of the place. So, a native and subject of France, while he is in Holland, must obey the laws of Holland; and an inhabitant of Worcester who contravenes, during a visit, the municipal regulations of Wellington, is amenable to the municipal jurisdiction of the latter place. Those who are subjected, by reason of birth or origin in a place, to the laws of that place, against their will, and remain amenable to the laws of their place of origin through life, do not discharge themselves of their liabilities by departure from the place of origin, but may be called upon after migration from the place of origin to another place, to discharge their municipal duties in both places—with the proviso, that they return to their domicile of origin before they are called upon to perform the duties in question. Those who have submitted themselves to a territorial jurisdiction of their own free will, and to the performance of municipal duties, are able to avoid such duties by departing at their own wish—although before departure they were bound to obey the laws. No one can be without a place of origin. Origin is generally to be sought in one place alone. But one can, says Voet, be without a place of domicile, and thus a subject of no place, and, on the contrary, capable of being domiciled in several places at

the same time (50, 1 §§ 3, 4).
The subject of domicile of origin, and the questions whether a man can be without a domicile, and whether he may have more than one domicile, are exhaustively discussed in Phillimore's *International Law,* vol. 4.

74. *Municipium* is derived from *munus* (a public duty or office, or duty generally), and Voet accordingly (after the discussion of certain obsolete matters in the second and third titles) proceeds (in the fourth title) to a discussion of municipal duties. Where a municipal law enacts that only men of a certain class are to occupy certain public positions, this must be taken with the limitation, that they are in other respects fit and qualified to hold such positions.

This is also right, that those who have been allowed to occupy public positions cannot be removed from office before their term

Las expired, unless they are guilty of misconduct. But revocation of a grant of office is permissible where it has been granted on condition that it may be revoked at will of the grantor, provided that such revocation takes place without detriment to the reputation of the holder of the office, where he has not misconducted himself; but this does not apply where he has been appointed for life, or for a fixed term of years. Where (in olden times) an office had been granted to a person for himself and his heirs, this might pass even to female heirs, to such an extent that they might transact the business of the office by substitution (50, 4 §§ 1, 2, 3).

Such a case as that last mentioned can hardl arise under modern systems of government. The question might be raised in the case of such an office as the Hereditary Earl Marshal of England, where the sole heiress might or might not be a peeress in her own right. If an heiress were not created a peeress in her own right, the peerage would become extinct, and it is assumed that the office would likewise cease.

75. Those who have been nominated to positions of honour and public offices may be compelled to fill their duties against their will, in the same modes

as guardians are bound to accept a guardianship, if they have no just ground for excuse—lest otherwise, if every one were permitted to excuse himself from such duties, there would be no one to fill the offices of State. In Dutch Law, " vacating" office denotes the effect of a valid excuse, so that those are said to "vacate" office, who have been excused from performing their duties for just causes approved by law; and they have not the right of " vacation" in whose cases just causes for excuse are wanting

In modern practice, no one can be compelled, against his will, to take up a public duty. But it would appear from the foregoing, and from the remarks of the Roman jurists, that where a person offers to fill a certain position, he may be compelled to perform his duties. A member of the English Parliament who stands for election may not (according to *Anson,* 2nd ed. p. 88, vol. 1) resign after his election; and it is submitted that a person who offers to become Permanent Head of a State Department, and, on appointment, refuses to enter upon the duties of his office, may be compelled to do so, not only on the basis of the doctrine above laid down, but on the liability attaching to an ordinary contract of service. There are many interesting English cases on the subject.

76. Those who are excused by general law from the performance of public duties (except where a special statute, for instance, prescribes a certain age for militaiy service) are persons under the age of majority, other offices which formerly exempted from service being obsolete at the present time (50, 5 § 2).

The principal laws in modern States which regulate the liability of citizens to public service are July Acts (at the Cape, Acts 22 and 23 of 1891; in Natal, Law No. 10, 1871, and amending laws; in the Transvaal, Ordinance No. 10, 1902); and laws relating to military service (in Cape Colony, Act No. 7, 1878; in Natal, Law 19, 1865, and Act 23, 1895; and in the Transvaal, Ordinance 33, 1902).

77. Among those exempted from public duties are, in general, women. In the

case of men, poverty is a ground of excuse (it being, in modern times, a general matter of State policy that insolvents shall not hold a public office) as long as it lasts, ill-health, absence on State duty from the State, and attainment of the age of severity years (50, 5 § 3).

It would seem that under this rule civil servants in Holland could be compelled to retire at the age of seventy. In the Cape Colony (1901) a rule of the Civil Service makes civil servants compellable to retire at sixty. In Natal, by Act No. 26, 1897, it is enacted that "in the case of an officer of the Civil Service over the age of fifty years, whose faculties have become impaired, or whose retirement may be otherwise desirable in the interests of the public service, it shall be lawful for the Governor in Council to require him to retire on a pension." 78. Men who had five children were also excused from the performance of public offices. Several other grounds of excuse, now obsolete, are then mentioned (50, 5 § 4, 5).

79. Besides excuse or exemption from office there is a relief known as immunity, which frees one from performing duties and likewise from rendering tribute. It may relate to persons, or to things, and may be temporary or perpetual. The subject of immunity from taxation is treated of in *Voct* (Book 89, c. 4; see Chapter IV. of this Part). He who alleges immunity from the payment of taxes must bear the burden of proof (50, 6 § 1). 80. Where a person claims exemption by reason of prescription, he cannot rely on the mere fact of prescription. Immunity being an indulgence in the nature of privilege, must receive the strictest interpretation, so that general rights are derogated from as little as possible. If there is no clear evidence of intention on the part of the person granting immunity, immunity from taxation refers only to present taxes, not to future taxes, nor to taxes imposed *de novo,* which were unknown and unthought of at the time immunity was granted. It would be otherwise if an already existing tax was increased, for an accession or addition must follow the principal subject. In that case, the per-

son enjoying immunity is also excused from paying the increased taxation. In like manner an immunity granted in respect of one's property, such as an estate, does not free from the burden such property as is afterwards acquired by the person enjoying the immunity, because the present time is always presumed to be intended, if no other time has been mentioned, or if circumstances do not show a different intention; but the immunity will hold, if fresh property has not been acquired, but the old estate has been increased by alluvion or otherwise (50, 6 § 2). 81. Voet then treats of a distinction, which appears now to be obsolete, between personal and real immunities, and proceeds to discuss immunities granted to persons and their descendants. If an immunity be bequeathed to "my *genus* and his descendants," this will go only to male descendants; if to " my children and their descendants," it will go to female descendants as well as males. This is a distinction founded on the Roman law, for a woman was considered as the beginning and end of her *genus,* and on marriage merged in another *genus;* whereas the designation of children includes not only those in paternal power, but every one, whether male or female, or descended of females (50, 6 § 4). 82. An immunity conceded to a college or corporation benefits not only those who at the time of grant were members thereof, but those who become members by surrogation or co-optation at any time thereafter in the stead of those who vacated office—since colleges or corporations are not held to die or terminate, but continue their existence notwithstanding a change in the composition of the whole body of their members. It would be otherwise, if a grant had been made, not to the college itself or to the body of members as a whole, but to individuals, or to members of the college specially named.

But a grant made to a college or corporation does not benefit everyone associated therewith, but only those who expend labour in connection with the college, and are its workers (50, 6 § 5).

The last sentence has been inserted,

though it would probably be obsolete now. The members of a corporation to whom a grant applies will generally be indicated by the torms of the grant. Voet's reference was probably to the Dutch trading guilds, which were numerous in his day, with which, besides the actual participators in guild concerns, many honorary members were associated. The general doctrine laid down by him is universally recognised in modern low —that a corporation's existence does not terminate with the existence or membership of its constituents, and that, consequently, a grant made to it as a whole is not affected by a change in the constitution of the body of members.

83. A person, of whatever class or dignity, who has a grant of immunity, is not discharged from such burdens as are imposed by an extraordinary necessity of the State. If a person, who has an immunity, of his own free will takes upon himself burdens, whether personal or real, from which he might have excused himself, he is not on that account regarded as having wholly renounced his right of immunity, but may assert his freedom from other burdens (falling within the scope of his grant of immunity) which he has not yet undertaken (50, 6 §§ 6, 7). CHAPTER II. PUBLIC PROPERTY AND PUBLIC WORKS. 84. The next matter for consideration is the duty of those persons who are appointed to the charge of works of the State (public works), the care of landed property of the State (Crown or State lands), the collection of taxes, the sale of State property, and those who look after provisions (such as supplies of wheat) purchased for the use of the State. Their first duty is the giving of sufficient security for their proper administration; and then comes the rendering of an account of acts done during their period of office. Such persons are liable for fraud and negligence (here called *dolus lata* and *levis culpa,* the distinctions between which are briefly adverted to later on, Vol. II.), the latter implying a certain degree of diligence—although there is this diiference between their fraud and negligence, that, if damage has been caused

by their negligence, they are liable for the amount of the damage only *(in simplum)*; but if damage arises from their fraud, those who have caused it are liable for double the amount of damage *(in duplum),* though their heirs are only liable for the single amount of damage *(in simplum),* lest the penalty for the fraud of one who is dead should descend to them. It ought, however, not to be ascribed to their fault or fraud if the Princeps or Head of the State has chanced, in the plenitude of his power, on the ground of necessity, to take and apply public moneys in their charge to the uses of the State (50, 8 § 1). 85. Those persons who are liable to account for their administration are only liable during their own term of office, and not during the term of their successors. Consequently, if, for instance, a fanner of the taxes has, during his term, faithfully rendered account of what he has collected, and his successor sub-lets the collection of revenue to him, the predecessor, and there is a loss or deficiency in the amount collected (not, of course, due to such fraud as would render him criminally liable), the successor, who sub-let the collection of the taxes (or, in the case of a fanner of public lands, who sub-let the land to him) is liable to the State for the loss (50, 8 § 2). The question is by no means so antiquated as would appear. The public revenue is still farmed in a few cases, such as the collection of tolls. It is doubtful whether the doctrine laid down in this section is sound. The question would, in the last resort, simply be that of a subtenant's liability to his landlord (as to which see a later part of this work).

86. If moneys have been received for certain State purposes, they cannot be applied to any other purpose than that for which they were received, except by the authority of the Head of the State or the Legislature——certainly not for the private purposes of the person who receives them; for when a person detains State moneys in his hands, without showing any just ground for retaining them for any considerable length of time, he is liable to pay interest on the same. In case of doubt, receivers of revenue are not considered as entitled to grant delay in payment to debtors of the State. They must show a distinct authority for so doing, and there must be no unreasonable delay (50, 8 § 2). 87. Just as diligence is required in receiving money from debtors of the State, so it is necessary in paying State creditors; and that which is due by the State to creditors may rightly be demanded from administrators of the revenue during their term of administration—for if the term is completed, they can only be called upon if a novation has taken place during the term of their administration and they have given security for the amount of the debt novated (50, 8 § 8). 88. Sureties for revenue administrators are liable, but only *ad rem* (for the subject-matter of the debt), and not for penalties for which their principals may be condemned. Where there are joint-administrators of revenue, and a division of the money received has been made among them, each is nevertheless liable for the whole —because State rights cannot be changed by a private agreement (50, 8 § 4). 89. Voet then treats of decrees of a kind now in disuse, and of the care of public buildings and monuments, which are governed in modern law according to a different system, which prescribes varying regulations for the custody of (a) State property, belonging to the general Government, and *(b)* Municipal property, belonging to the governing body of a particular town (50, 9 § 1 and 50, 10 § 1). 90. To prevent the necessary materials for erecting public works being sold for too great a price, and to prevent the substitution of inferior materials for those of a better class, it has been provided in Holland that the officers in charge of public works and erections, their attendants, bailiffs, constables, and other assistants, shall not sell any timber, stones, or other building materials for use on public works over which they have superintendence, whether by themselves or by their parents, brothers, sisters, children, or any person related to them by affinity, under penalty of deprivation of office, and other penalties at discretion (50, 10 §§ 2, 3). CHAPTER III. RIGHTS OF THE TREASURY. 91. Under the early Roman Emperors there was a distinction between *fiscus* and *aerarium,* the former belonging to the Emperor, the latter to the people. Afterwards the rights of the two departments became intermixed, although a distinction was still preserved between the public moneys or goods (now known as *bona fiscalia,* no matter whether they originated from the *fiscus* or from the *aerarium)* and the private patrimony of the Princeps, inasmuch as by the law of ownership private patrimony was the personal property of the Princeps, while he had only the use or usufruct and administration of fiscal moneys or goods, the property or ownership in which remained vested in the Treasury, as representing the people (49, 14 § 1). 92. Although Modestinus has laid it down that he is not in fault who, in case of doubt, declares against the rights of the Treasury, and it may thence appear that the position of the

Trensury is less favourable than that of a private person—yet, since this does not hold unless there is a question about penalties and fines and the taking of imposts and similar gains, it follows that there is no reason why the Treasury should not have the benefit of various privileges. In many cases, indeed, it has a tacit hypothec (49, 14 § 2).

In *Collector of Customs* vs. *Cape Central Raihvays* (6 S. C. 407) it was said: "Thero is abundant authority in the civil law for the proposition that the State is entitled to the same measure of relief as minors who have suffered lesion.... In the Netherlands this rule of civil law was fully adopted, and, according to Matthaeus *(de Auct.* 1, 16, 29 and 30) and Voet (4, 4, *oo*) was extended to the *fiscus* as the custodian of the public treasury. The latter author enumerates the several rights which the *fiscus* and minors have in common, as for instance that of tacit hypothecation upon the estates of persons administering their respective properties, and in the title *de juri fisci* (49, 14, 2) he repeats the statement that the *fitcus* is entitled to the *restitutio in integrum* in the same manner as minors. There are, of course, many points in which the resemblance fails. For instance, the Crown would not be relieved, like a minor, against prescriptive occupation of land which the Crown has the power of alienating, but in respect of land which it would be illegal for the Crown to alienate there can be no prescription." So, where defendants imported into Cape Colony cement, upon which a duty was leviable, and the Premier of the Colony, as representing the Government, agreed (without being so authorised by law to do) to abandon the duty and allow the cement to be landed free of duty, and the cement was landed and used by defendants, who received a warrant for landing from the proper officer, the defendants, on being sued for the duty by the Collector of Customs, were held liable to pay it. "It is the illegality of the abandonment of duty by the Premier which makes the analogy complete in the present case. If this had been an action to recover money on behalf of minors, the plea that they or their guardian had abandoned their claim would have been bad, when once it was established that, but for such abandonment, they would have been legally entitled to the money." 93. On every contract the Treasury receives interest on account of delay, but does not pay interest, except in so far as it succeeds to the rights of a private person. It acquires pecuniary penalties for wrongs and various contracts entered into against the laws, and also fines for public crimes (crimes against the State, as distinguished from torts). The Treasury *may* sell property acquired by it jointly with another person, even against the will of the co-proprietor. It sometimes retains farmers of the revenue against their will in office beyond their term. If the Treasury sells a property let to a third party, the purchaser is bound to hold to the lease just as if that had been expressly agreed upon. If it sells an inheritance bequeathed to it, the purchaser will have to bear the actions arising out of the inheritance, even against his will. An alienation is regarded as having taken place in fraud of the Treasury, if a person involved in a bond (i.e., binding both person and property) has diminished his patrimony,

and a person alienating in fraud of the Treasury is liable in double damages. Up to the present time the law has prevented usucapion of fiscal property. In fiscal suits the Treasury has a peculiar privilege in suit *(fori):* restitution is granted to the Treasury just as in the case of minors. When Treasury goods have been sold by public auction, and awarded to the highest bidder, a further addition to the price is admissible (this seems to mean that, notwithstanding the goods have been knocked down to the highest bidder, the Treasury may increase the price to be paid for the goods). Thus, A. bids *50l.,* B. 60?., and C. *70l.* The goods are knocked down to C, the highest bidder. Then the Treasury say: "We want 80/." C. refuses to pay this, but A. agrees to the price. A. would seem to be entitled to the goods (49, 14 § 2).

94. An important part of the law relating to the Treasury is the enumeration of the *regalia,* or rights of property appertaining to the State. Among them are moneys paid in the way of fines and penalties, *bona vacantia* (goods having no owner, as to which see the remarks on treasure trove and title by occupancy), and goods belonging to those who suffer confiscation for crime (confiscation for crime is abolished in South Africa). Then there are possessions which in themselves afford sufficient evidence that they belong to the State, such as public roads, navigable rivers and the means and appliances which render them navigable, harbours, coin of the realm, the power of appointing magistrates to further the administration of justice, and certain other modes of acquisition now obsolete.

Then there is the charge for carriage by means of ferry-boats from shore to shore of a river (49, 14 § 8).

In *Uitenhage Divisional Council* vs. *Rted* (Buch. '68, p. 134) this form of rovenue—fees derived from ferryboats—was recognised as one of the stillexisting *reijalia* of the State.

95. More broadly, among *regalia* are included all rights which the Head of the State has in respect to the banks of public streams with regard to taxation and

charges of transport from bank to bank; likewise dock dues for shipping; *census* (a tax levied in Roman days on land, in proportion to area and value, now obsolete, but the principles relating to which might be applicable in regard to similar taxation *(Col.* § 437)), and tribute; mines of precious metal, with regard to which Voet dissents from an expressed opinion that they belong to the State whether they be situate on public or on private property, and holds that only those discovered in public places belong to the State. (In the Transvaal, for instance, this matter has been expressly set at rest by a statement in the Gold Law that "the right of mining and disposal of all precious stones and precious metals belongs to the State" (Law 15, 1898, § 1, and previous statutes on the subject).) If the State does not retain its right to mine, it may claim a certain portion of the product of the mines. Among *regalia* are also included royal palaces, dedicated to the use of rulers of the State, which may not be applied to private purposes (49, 14 § S). CHAPTER IV. THE FARMING OF TAXES, AND TAXATION GENERALLY. 96. *Publicani* are such persons as carry on any transactions on behalf of the Treasury. In a more restricted sense, they are those who collect the taxes on their own account, having them allotted to them (the *publicani)* by the State Treasury or by municipalities in cases where municipalities can collect taxes. But those who farm municipal taxes are not excused from guardianship, as are farmers of the State revenue (89, 4 § 1).

It was the custom at Rome, and frequently in Holland as well, to let out the collection of the revenue derived from taxation to *publicani* or fanners of the revenue. At Rome, "the *publicani* were engaged in collecting the *vectigalia* and *tributa* under their denominations, appropriate to the sources from which they were drawn " *Col.* § 1669).

97. No one can be compelled to undertake the farming of taxes or collection of the revenue; nor can any one, who has completed his term, be compelled to continue the collection of taxes, whether for the same, or a lower

rate. Neither by the civil nor the modern law is a person, who has completed his term of collection, and offers as much for continuing the collection of taxes as does another person who has not yet undertaken the collection, entitled to the privilege of further collection. He can only obtain it by making a higher bid, for no privilege of the kind enures in favour of collectors of the revenue such as applies in the case of lessees (also called *conductores)* of public land, who are preferred on the completion of their lease to new lessees, provided they agree to pay the increased price bid by their rivals *(i.e.,* those who desire to become the new lessees) (39, 4 § 2). 98. Among those who cannot collect taxes are debtors of the State or of the Treasury, unless they supply suitable sureties, who are prepared to satisfy their debts; likewise tutors and curators before they have rendered accounts of their tutorship or curatorship; minors, soldiers, and women (39, 4 § 8). 99. By decree of the States General of Holland, all Government officials are prohibited from farming or collecting the revenue except as servants of the Treasury—that is, they cannot farm on their own account, so as to receive a percentage or share of the taxes (39, 4 § 4). 100. Whoever is prohibited from farming the revenue, is prohibited from doing so by means of other persons, and cannot be a partner or participator in such farming. Nothing, however, prevents succession (of lawful heirs) to a farmer of the revenue who dies before his administration of the tax has ended (89, 4 § 5). 101. The mode of farming and letting out taxes to farm is regulated in modern times by decrees of the Legislature. If two or more persons apply at the same time to have the taxes let out to them, and it does not appear who is prior in time (assuming that their bids are equal), the tax must be given out to be tendered for again. *Publicani* who do not pay the fixed rent for farming the taxes are liable in their persons as well as in property, if it does not appear that the failure in collection of the tax was due to unwonted drought or to some unforeseen cause, and they are liable for

any negligence. And any crime whereby the Treasury is defrauded of the revenue is punishable by penalties at discretion, and such punishment is not capable of prescription like other crimes (39, 4 § 6). 102. Lessees of taxation may ask for a remission of the payment due by them on account of unwonted drought, war, sedition, and epidemic disease. It is also remitted in part, if navigation has been interdicted, or if the import or export of merchandise subject to import or export dues has been stopped. If the conditions agreed upon at the time of entering into a lease of the taxes have not been inserted in the contract the *publicani* may claim the damage sustained by reason of an omission to insert such conditions (89, 4 § 7).

The latter part of this section is somewhat obscure. It means that where no exemption is specified in the contract on the ground of drought, disease, or suspension of trade, a remission of the money due by the *conductor* to the Treasury may nevertheless be claimed. 103. Taxes are imposed by the Head of the State or by the Legislature alone: sometimes by municipalities on special permission given by the Head of the State (regulated at present by the statutes relating to municipal government), in which case the Head of the State lends his authority to such an act of the municipality, precisely as if the tax had been imposed by the Head of the State (see *Town Council of Capetoicn* vs. *Colonial Government,* Buch. '79, p. 174). No other taxation may be imposed which has not the sanction of the Crown and the Legislature (89, 4 §§ 8, 9). In Holland, only the States General have the right to impose or remit taxation for general purposes (89, 4 § 10). 104. In the widest sense, *vectigal* denotes all revenue arising from the sale of goods, from property, from inheritances, quit-rents on lands, and rent of State properties, and, in fine, all fruits and advantages derived from both public and private sources, which go to the Treasury (89, 4 § 11). 105. There is likewise included all public taxation, paid as tribute *(i.e.,* in the form of a general tax levied on the whole population).

Voet gives a list of the taxes payable in his time, which is not repeated here, as the mode and incidence of taxation fluctuate in accordance with the necessities of different States (39, 4 § 12). 106. Personal taxation is that which is imposed in respect of persons, and follows the person, being claimable only by a personal action, or by *parate* execution, the State having a preference over chirograph creditors for such taxes, but no tacit hypothec (see the discussion on tacit hypothecs). Real taxation is that which attaches to a thing, and accompanies it in such a manner that the Treasury has a tacit hypothec for the amount of the tax over the thing, in respect only of the thing on account whereof the tax is owing to the Treasury. According to modern usage, one may easily ascertain what taxes are real or personal. For instance, transfer dues on the sale of land, or taxes on successions, are real, for they adhere to the thing, and burden the possessor of the thing, even if he is not either a subject or an inhabitant, but only a *peregrinus* (traveller or temporary sojourner from foreign parts); and that such transfer dues are real may be furthermore gathered from the fact that this species of taxation only applies to immovables actually situated in the country where the tax is applied, not to property in a foreign country (39, 4 § 18). 107. After detailing various taxes enforced in Holland in his day, and briefly noting the policy of taxation, Voet states that in every case laws imposing taxation must receive a strict interpretation, so that they should not be extended to things similar to those which are liable to taxation—because, as freedom from burdens is favourable, so, on the contrary, liabilities imposed on things are to be regarded as unfavourable, especially as it is in the power of the Treasury clearly to state and declare in respect of what things taxation should be imposed (39, 4 §§ 14 to 18). 108. Extortion under the guise of collecting taxes is punishable. So are all frauds perpetrated in connection with collection of the revenue. Besides the criminal penalty, a collector of taxes is liable in a civil action to refund the money embezzled by him, and upon his death his heirs are liable, but only if there has been joinder in issue *(litis contestatio)* with the deceased before his death, or if any money acquired by the fraud of the deceased has come to his heirs (in which case, it is submitted, they are liable only to the extent of the money received) (39, 4 § 19). 109. After detailing various frauds on the revenue and their punishments, Voet states that where loss is caused to the Treasury by persons who have attained majority, without fraud on their part, they are not liable for loss arising through error, but must pay the tax over again (there is some doubt about this sentence, *publicanos duplicate vectigali contentos esse,* which can also be read as meaning that twice the amount due to the Treasury should be paid: but it seems better to take the first interpretation). Minors who have caused loss, without fraud, are not liable. In the case of majors, there must be a reasonable and probable ground of mistake; and a pretended and artificial cause of error, whereby the Treasury is defrauded, is no ground for excuse. A,great deal is now left to the discretion of the Judge, a strict standard of error being required, and even minors are not easily excused (89, 4 §§ 20 to 26). c.l.—Vol. i. 110. There is no liability for taxation in the case of those who have an immunity from payment. The person claiming immunity must prove it, by showing either that he is protected by a special privilege, or that the articles in respect of which the tax is claimed and refused are exempt from taxation. Since the question whether a privilege has been granted is a question of fact, the burden of proof lies on him who alleges the privilege, just as on a person alleging a custom. This privilege is granted only by the Head of the State, or with his consent by the executive. Where taxes have already been let out for collection, the Head of the State cannot allow any immunity in respect of them, to the detriment of farmers of the revenue (39, 4 § 27). 111. Among those who enjoy immunity from taxation according to the civil law, are the ambassadors *(legati)* of foreign nations, with regard to arti-

cles which they export, but not with regard to things which they import from their native land. Immunity is also enjoyed by the Treasury, and by the Head of the State (39, 4 § 28). It might appear to be mere surplusage to allege that the Treasury, or the Crown, is not liable to pay taxation. But the question might often arise where there are different administrative departments of State, and each conducts the collection of its own rovenue: for instance, where the Post Office claims postage from other departments of State; and more intricate questions might arise where municipalities or divisional councils claim assessment rates or sanitary fees in respect of Crown property situate within their respective jurisdictions. Following on the foregoing *dictum* of Voet, it was held in *Town Council of Cape Town* vs. *Colonial Gorernmeid* (Buch. '79, p. 169) that Crown propert)' situate within the limits of the Cape Town Municipality, occupied by the servants of the Government (although this circumstance was not necessary to the decision) for Government purposes, was not liable to be assessed for municipal rates, even although such property was not specially exempted in the Municipal Act. It was said by De Villiers, C. J., that "according to the law of England the Crown would not be liable to pay rates in respect of property owned or occupied by them, and the question is whether the same law applies to this Colony. A passage was quoted from Voet, in which it is clearly laid down that the *fiscus,* who represents the Crown to all intents andpurposes, is not liable to pay *vectigalia* (taxes). The only question which occurred to me was whether the *vectigalia* could be considered (as being) in the nature of a State tax, or whether the word might also be used in regard to rates imposed by municipalities, but on reference to other passages in Voet, I find that the very same word is used by him in the very same book (see § 103 above), in reference to rates imposed by municipalities." The Court consequently held that the exemption applied to municipal rates as well.

112. If certain property belonging to two persons, one of whom enjoys immunity, while the other is liable, is transferred, or transported anywhere, the tax (whether in the shape of toll, customs dues, or transit dues) is payable in proportion to the share of him who is liable. If, again, goods liable to dues have been mixed in a ship with other goods free from tax, and they cannot be distinguished from each other, the law of Holland provides (or provided in Voet's time) that tax shall be paid on all the goods. It would be otherwise if the goods were separable (39, 4 §§ 29, 80). 113. The imposition of taxation implied, in former times, a right to import or export. Consequently, if one imports or exports goods which the law prohibits from being imported or exported, no tax is levied, but the goods may be confiscated by the State together with the ship bringing them, and a personal punishment besides (39, 4 §§ 31, 32). CHAPTER V. MILITARY LAW. 114. Voet next proceeds to the treatment of the law relating to captives, and postliminy. The science of International Law is of wholly modern growth, and he has very little to say that is of any practical value at the present day. Principles and opinions on the subject must be sought in the pages of modern text-writers, such as Westlake, Woolsey, Hall, Holland, Wheaton, Forsyth, and the Italian School of International Law. This is not the place for a treatise on the subject. Some remarks of Voet, which may be applicable at the present time, may, however, be noted here. In a just war, he says, captured property belongs to the enemy effecting the capture, but when recovered by the original owner have the benefit of the law of postliminy, and revert to such original owner. It does not matter in what way the recovery is effected (49, 15 §§ 1. 2). 115. Grotius holds that booty is only claimable when it is taken within the confines of the enemy's country, but Voet dissents, and considers that booty becomes the captor's property wherever it is captured (49, 15 § 8). 116. Ships containing cargo, captured by the enemy in time of war, and recaptured, ought to return to

their owners by the law of postliminy, on condition that a certain amount, assessed according to circumstances, is repaid to the recaptor (Ordinance of the States General, April 18th, 1677). If goods are captured in a hostile ship, and such goods do not belong to a hostile owner, they shouldbe restored to their owners (in other words, Voet holds that neutral goods in hostile ships go free). In case of doubt there is a presumption that goods found on hostile ships are hostile goods (49, 15 § 5). 117. If a neutral ship, which cannot on that account be captured, is taken by the enemy, and afterwards taken from the enemy by us, it should be restored to the original neutral owner, since the ownership in the ship was not acquired from the neutral owner by a lawful title (49, 15 §§ 6, 7). 118. The next subject of discussion is military law, which is governed at the present day by special statutes, and by that body of modern usages, customs, and opinions known collectively as International Law. For the purposes of this work it is unnecessary to enter into a discussion of such statutes and usages. It is sufficient here to state that the statutes and internal customs of a country regulate such matters as the enlistment and maintenance of armed forces, foreign enlistment, the prerogative of declaring war and making peace, and the effect of war upon the property and contracts of private individuals; whilst International Law regulates the mode in which hostilities are notified to the State on which war is declared and to neutral States, the usages of warfare, and the rights of intercourse between belligerents and neutral powers (49, titles 16, 17, and 18).

In the recent Transvaal case of *Alexander* vs. *Pfau* (1902 T. S. 155), the principle was applied that "it is not in conflict with the principles of International Law for a State to requisition the property of resident aliens, and *a fortiori* that of hostile resident alions, in order to supply the necessities of war." CHAPTER VI.

EMBASSIES. 119. Another branch of International Law to which Voet briefly adverts is that connected with the right of intercourse between nations, by means of ambassadors. The word *legatus* was used in Rome in more than one sense. It denoted *(a)* the governor of a province, accredited and sent by the Republic or the Emperor to rule over the province; *(b)* the coadjutor of a pro-consul; (c) those who were sent by the nation to foreign States, or sent to Rome by such States. It is with this last class that we have to deal. They may not be molested with arrest of their persons, their goods, their attendants or servants; and by the law of nations *(jure gentium)* they are sacred and inviolable on account of the guarantee of public faith given for their security. An ordinance of the States General provides that those who are guilty of defamation (libel or slander) of ambassadors, or who do any injury to their houses, or strike them, or raise a tumult or incite a mob in front of their dwellings, are liable to corporal punishment (which seems to denote any punishment at the discretion of the Judge, not necessarily whipping or torture, but punishment by fine and imprisonment—the special mention of punishment in this place being due to the fact that such offences were not crimes against the private law of the State, but against the law of nations) (50, 7 1). 120. Ambassadors may be appointed not only in person, but during their absence as well, provided they are suitable persons, and are not infamous, deprived of the right to bring actions (which, it is submitted, would include insolvents, who may only sue in certain cases), or debtors of the State. Those who have three children may free themselves from the obligation of embassy (now obsolete, since no one is at present obliged to undertake an embassy). A person may discharge an embassy by means of a representative (provided they have the authority of the State originally sending the ambassador). It is the duty of ambassadors to abstain from taking gifts, unless they wish to render themselves liable to the law relating to bribery. They must not leave their places unless they prove just grounds of necessity (50, 7 §§ 2 to 6). B. *MUNICIPAL RIGHTS.* CHAPTER I. 5IARKETS.

121. Voet has very little to say that is applicable to municipal law at the present day—municipal matters being regulated by modern statutes, and regulations made by the governing authority of the State or the municipality under statutory powers. The Municipal Act of the Cape Colony (Act 45, 1882) is a typical statute of the kind, and the principal headings of the Act may be given here for the purpose of indicating what such statutes are supposed to contain: Application of the Act; Constitution of Municipalities; Municipal Council; Retirement and Vacancies in a Council; Electors and their Qualification; the Making of Voters' Rolls; Election of Councillors; Nomination of Candidates, Polling Places and Polling; Election and Privileges of the Mayor or Chairman; Auditing of Municipal Accounts; Proceedings of the Council; Contracts by and with the Council; Officers of the Municipality and their Duties; the Making and Scope of Bye-laws and Regulations; Property subject to Rates; Making of Valuations; Making of Rates; Recoveiy of Rates; Loans; Powers and Duties of the Council; Municipal Lands. 122. The subject of taxes, State and municipal, as well as the disposal of State property, have been treated of previously to some small extent (see §§ 74, and 84 to 95). The next matter dealt with is public markets. These have their origin either (a) from longcontinued custom, or *(b)* from special proclamation and granting of leave to establish the same. In former times, there was a privilege from arrest in the case of those attending public markets in good faith, which is now obsolctc (50, 11 §§ 1 to 4). 123. A market which has been established by custom can no longer be used if there has been a period of prescription, amounting to thirty years, during which the people have neglected to make sales on the market; but if there has in the meanwhile arisen no occasion to make use of the market, the right to use it is never lost by prescription (50, 11 § 5). This is probably now obsolete, as marketplaces are now generally governed by express municipal regulations. 124. Another subject of municipal and State right

about which there might be some question, is the land tax, known at Rome as *census,* and similar taxation in modern times. It was a tax imposed in respect of citizenship and of ownership of land. Those who had not the use of their land, through earthquake or flood, or other destruction, were relieved from the burden of the tax (50,15 §§ 1, 2).

PART III. THE LAW OF PERSONS. *A. PERSONS IN GENERAL.*

Chap. I.—Status.

„ II.—Public Persons.

III.—Persons (1) Independent, And (2) Undbr Power. *B. DOMESTIC RELATlON-SHIPS.*

Chap. I.— Parent And Child.

„ II.—Minors In General.

„ III.—Guardian And Ward.

„ IV.—Husband And Wife.

PART III.

THE LAW OF PERSONS. *A. PERSONS IN GENERAL.*

CHAPTER I.

STATUS. 125. There are certain distinctions, entailing certain legal consequences, between men and women. In some respects the condition of women is better, in some worse, than that of men.

Their condition is better, in that they have the benefit of the *Senatusconsultum Velleianum* (as to which see §§ 511 to 524). On the other hand, they cannot be magistrates, nor fill public positions and perform duties of citizenship, *i.e.,* political duties (1, 5 § 1).

In *Ex parte Van Pelt and Another* (13 S. C. 476) it was decided that a woman was admissible as translator of the Supreme Court of Cape Colony. It was said: "It may be a question whether the *dictum* of Voet is applicable, without any qualification, to this country at the present time, but, even if it be so applicable, I am satisfied that the office of translator to the Supreme Court is noither public nor political in the sense intended by Voet." 126. Although those still in the womb cannot, since they are unborn, be regarded as men, yet by a fiction of law they are regarded as already born when there is a matter which is of advantage to them. Inheritances as of right (legitimate portions, and inher-

itances designed to descend to one's children, or the children of certain persons or classes of persons) may be transferred to those yet to be born, and still in the womb, as well as to those already born. Their portions by inheritance are reserved for them until they are born. If the question be the benefit not of those in the womb, but of third parties, the fiction that the unborn are considered as already born ceases. But if the unborn child cannot receive a benefit without a benefit accruing at the same time to another, the fiction of law holds good (1, 5 § 5).

"A perfect separation from the body of the mother, and subsequent signs of life, are necessary to constitute birth: hence a child still-born is not considered to have been bom at all: but it is indifferent by what means this separation is effected; consequently, a child cut out of the mother's womb after her death, if it live but for an instant, is held to have been born for all legal purposes, although, as fat as regards the mother, she cannot be said to have brought it forth.... It is not necessary that the child continue to exist for any period" (CW. § 354). The question may be of importance in a case such as this: A. leaves property to B.'s children, if he have any, and their next-of-kin after them; if B. loaves no children, the property is to go to C., a stranger. A child is born to B. in the manner described, and dies immediately thereafter. The property goes, not to C., but to the persons who would have been next-of-kin to B.'s child had it lived.

127. The word *caput,* in Roman Law, signified all the rights that a man can possess, comprehended in the enjoyment of freedom, of citizenship, and the relation he bears to a family. Any loss in such rights was known as *capitis deminutio.* This subject is treated of by Voet in the fifth title of the fourth book. The treatise on the subject contains nothing of practical value at the present day. CHAPTER II. PUBLIC PERSONS. 128. The public offices which existed at Rome died with the Empire, and the remarks with reference to them, with some slight exceptions, are no longer

applicable. In the case only of the *praetors,* who exercised an equitable jurisdiction at Rome, analogies might be drawn upon the occasions on which courts administering Roman-Dutch Law find it necessary to give decrees founded not so much on law as on equity.

"Those decisions which had been established by custom and transmitted from edict to edict, formed a species of magistrate-made law known as the *jus honorarium* or 'honorary law.' It consisted of two principal parts, praetorian law *(jus praetorium)* and aedile law *(jus aedilium),* of which the former is far the more important. This is the origin of that praetorian law which advanced, so to say, in a parallel line with the Roman Civil Law. It did not rest upon any direct legislation; it admitted of modification, and was grounded on the principles of equity and natural justice; it contributed in a great degree to Soman civilisation, and prepared the way for the gradual disappearance of the old legal system" *(Ortolan,* trans, by Cutler, 2nd ed. p. 197).

129. Where there has been an informality in the appointment of a praetor, notary, or magistrate, through his having been incapacitated to hold his office from the beginning, or becoming incapacitated later on, anything done before such magistrate or notary, by those who are ignorant of the incapacity, or in good faith, and not in collusion, is to be regarded as valid (1, 14 § 6).

The above statement of the law as laid down by Voet is put forward with considerable diffidence. Indeed, one might have wished to discard it altogether as obsolete, but for the fact that Mr. Justice James Buchanan, who translated the first book of Voet, did not translate the titles relating to Roman public offices, with the exception of this very section and the succeeding ones, with fhe remark that the sections translated "are of importance." It is submitted, with deference, that even the moderate proposition of Voet in this section, as above formulated, would not hold, in accordance with modern usage. This view has been taken in the High Court of the Transvaal, in a case where Mr. Esser (afterwards Judge Iisser) was appointed to act as Judge on circuit, and went on circuit without having been sworn in with the proper formalities. He sentenced a prisoner who was tried and convicted before him, and, on appeal, the prisoner was discharged, the High Court holding that, as the appointment of Mr. Esser had not been validated by the usual formalities, all sentences passed by him were invalid too. The author, in accordance with this view, and with the maxim *quod ah initio non valet in tractu temporis non cmivahscit,* is constrained to adopt the view that no act or formality executed by a notary, magistrate, or Judge whose appointment is invalid, or who labours under some incapacity, can be valid, and therefore regards the whole section of Voet as obsolete.

130. Acts done by notaries or magistrates subject to a foreign jurisdiction must be authenticated before they can be made use of or applied in our jurisdiction or territory (1, 14 § 7).

Before judgments, decrees, or documents made or drawn up in a foreign State can be available for legal purposes in a country, they must be legalised by the certificate of some State official, representing his State in dealings with other countries, or of sufficient authority to conduct intercourse with other States. The certificate is to the effect that thereby credence is given to the document attached to the certificate, and identifying the person who executed the document. (This is, strictly speaking, a subject within the scope of the Law of Evidence.) See Cape Deeds Office Regulations, §§ 47—50; Natal Govt. Notice of February 19th, 1897; Transvaal Govt. Notice No. 465, 1902; O. R. C. Govt. Notice No. 33, 1902; Rhodesia Deeds Regulations, §§ 48, 49. CHAPTER III. INDEPENDENT PERSONS, AND PERSONS UNDER CONTROl OB' OTHERS. 131. In Roman days, freemen or freedmen were divided into two classes: (a) Those who were under the control of no one; *(b)* those who were subject to the control of the head of a family, the *paterfamilias.* The subjec-

tion to external control lasted only as long as the head of the family lived, and upon bis death the males who were under his power, unless they still had a father or other ancestor living (for a grandfather was a *paterfamilias* as against his grandsons), became independent, or *sui juris.* Every male person then became a *paterfamilias* or *sui juris,* even though he had not attained the age of puberty, and was still under tutelage. Servants or slaves were under the control of their master, forming members of the *familia* of which the *paterfamilias* was the head, and were therefore not *sui juris.* Women by marriage passed into the power of their husbands, and a wife was subject to her husband's control, if he were a *paterfamilias,* or to the control of the person who was the *paterfamilias* of the *familia* of which the husband was a member (1, 6 § 1). 132. Paternal power is the control which male Roman citizens, not females, had over their children—whether legitimate, legitimated, or adoptive. This power existed whether a father was aware he had offspring born to him, or not; and even if, owing to madness, idiocy, or other mental defect, he was unable to exercise the paternal control. Paternal power in ancient Roman days was very extensive. The father had power of life and death over his child. Afterwards the severity of the law regarding children was mitigated, and the paternal power was curtailed in many ways. The paternal power existing at Rome, even in the last days of the Empire, has almost wholly disappeared. Roman-Dutch Law has deprived the

C.l. VOl. i. H father of the right, existing in Roman Law, to sell his child in case of necessity, to have the usufruct of the child's *peculium adventitium* (the *peculium adventitium ordinarium* was whatever the children gained neither from or through the father, but by their own exertions, or from their mother, or other persons), and to make pupillary substitution with those consequences which it used to have according to Roman Law (pupillary substitution is the substitution on the part of the father of an heir to his infant son, who may or

may not have a *peculium,* and may or may not inherit from his father in addition; this power vested in the father or grandfather— direct male agnate ascendant alone—but not in the mother; the father testated for his son, naming an heir for him, and consequently had first to make his own will; *posthumi* could be substituted, being considered as already born in the eye of the law, as the substitution was to their advantage; but the grandfather could not substitute should the children fall under the father's authority on the grandfather's death, hence the father must die before the grandfather). The Roman-Dutch Law retains the requirement of the father's consent to the marriage of his minor children, and, when there is no father, the mother's consent is required, until the children attain their majority. Although in Roman Law, grandsons bom to a son still under paternal power were in the power of their grandfather, in Roman-Dutch Law they are in the power of their father only, and not of their grandfather, and even on the death of their father they do not pass into the grandfather's power. Thus, only the consent of father and mother, not of grandparents, is required for the marriage of minor grandchildren (1, 6 §§ 2, 8).

"The *patria potestas* signifies the power a Roman father had over his children and their descendants by virtue of his paternity, and its foundation was a legal marriage. The Romans distinguished between the *patria potestas* and *dominium* by making the rights of the *filius familias* superior to those of the slavc, thc most important right belonging to the former being the capacity of being *suiis haeres,* or *haeres domesticus,* of the father—capacity, because the father could disinherit him and substitute another person. The *patria potestas* was acquired by marriage and *legitimation* or *adoption.* A son *sub potentate* laboured under no disadvantages with regard to thejiw *publicum;* he could vote in the *comitia tributa,* fill a *magistratus,* or be a tutor; he had the *jus connubii,* but if his marriage were accompanied by the *in manum conventio,* his wife came under the power of his father, not of her husband; and as long as the husband -was *sub patria potentate,* so long were his children under the power of their grandfather: thus a son *sub patria potestate* who marries, is *pater,* but not *paterfamilias*; on the contrary, if a man *sut juris* be married, he is *paterfamilias,* but not necessarily *pater;* conversely, a *filiusfamilias* may be *pater,* if married, and simply *filius* if emancipated."

With regard to property coming to minors by inheritance, the practice is to place such property under the control—in South Africa at least—of the Master of the Supreme Court; and no part of such property may be alienated, burdened, or disposed of without the consent of the Supreme Court. The law on the subject is regulated, in Cape Colony, by Ordinance 105, 1833, 23, 24; in the Orange River Colony, by the Orphan Chamber Law, §§ 34, 35; in the Transvaal, by Proc. No. 28, 1902, §§ 63, 77, 85 and 94; and in Natal, by Act 38, 1899, §§ 42, 44 and 46.

133. In modern law, a man acquires paternal power over his children if they are born within the lawful period fixed after conception, that is, from the beginning of the seventh month to the beginning of the eleventh month—so that the child born in or after the seventh month from marriage is regarded as legitimate; and a child born more than ten months after the absence of the husband or the dissolution of the marriage is regarded as illegitimate. There is, in the opinion of Voet, no absolute test of time, and each case should be left to the discretion of the Judge. Thus he gives a case from Friesland, where, public report being favourable to the woman, and the presumption of modesty being extended to her advantage, a child born twelve months after the alleged intercourse with the husband was held legitimate (1, 6 § 4).

Voet is here considering only the case of children born during marriage, concerning whose legitimacy there is a doubt. Children born before marriage are, of course, legitimated *per subsequens matrimonium.* There is the very

strongest presumption in favour of the legitimacy of children born during marriage, even before the seventh month after marriage, or after marriage, in view of the maxims *pater est quem nuptiae demonstrant* and *si quis praegnantem v. xorem reliquit, non videtur sine liberis decessisse* (although the latter maxim refers mainly to the law of inheritance). Colquhoun (§ 674) has given an extremely interesting and concise summary of the law on the subject, which the author takes leave to reproduce here: "In Scotland, indeed which adopts the Boman Law, legitimation may be performed by subsequent marriage: not so in England, where it is provided that, to be legitimate, the child must be born in wedlock, or within a competent time after the decease of the father... but it is not necessary that he be begotten on a married woman...." In § 677 he says: "Posthumous children were in certain cases considered as *in esse:* thus a will is avoided if posthumous children be born of whom no mention has been made Colquhoun is describing the Roman Law, and it is sufficient for this purposo that the child live but a moment after birth; the child must, however, be born within ton months after the death of the father, for otherwise he cannot be considered legitimate. This being considered the extreme period of gestation, a woman was forbidden to remarry within this time... the Civil Law ordaining that no widow should marry *infra annum luctus."*

Mr. D. Ward, in his little work on *Marriage Laws* (pp. 5, 6), points out that, although a period of mourning was fixed in a proclamation made by Commissary de Mist, this proclamation has not been incorporated with the authorised edition of the Statutes of Cape Colony. He, therefore, holds that there is no provision as to an *annus luctus* in the Cape Colony. In the Transvaal, it was enacted by § 9 of Law No. 3, 1871, that no remarriage could take place, in the case of a widower, within three months of his wife's death, and, in the case of a widow, within 300 days of her husband's death. The provision with regard to widowers was introduced to

prevent remarriages from taking place with unseemly haste—a very necessary provision, as remarriages are both frequent and rapid among the Dutch farming population. In the Orange River Colony, by Law No. 26, 1899, § 13, a widower may not remarry within three months of his wife's death, and a widow may not remarry within 280 days of her husband's death.

134. If a person has had intercourse with a girl before marriage and afterwards lawfully marries her, and does not deny such previous intercourse, the child born immediately after the celebration of the marriage, or even on the very day of marriage, is regarded as legitimate—just as children born before marriage are thereby legitimated (1, 6 § 5).

In *Horak* vs. *Horak* (3 S. 394) a marriage was declared void on account of the previous *siuprum* (unchastity or debauchery) and pregnancy of the wife, where such *sluprum* was unknown to the husband. A child bom six months after the marriage was declared illegitimate, the husband not having cohabited with his wife after knowledge of the *stuprum.* In *Nel* vs. *Nel* (1 M. 274) it had previously been decided that *stuprum* before marriage on the part of the wife, unknown to the intended husband, does not give ground for a dissolution of the marriage. From the judgment in that case it was clear that the Court did not bind themselves as to what they/would have done had the suit been one for a declaration of nullity of marriage. A divorce was sued for. At first sight, this might appear a mere technicality; but there are important differences between the two cases. A decree of nullity produces the same effect as if no marriage had ever taken place, and renders children born of the union illegitimate; a decree of divorce does not make the children illegitimate. The judgment in *Horak's* case makes no reference to *Nel* vs. *Nel,* though the argument of plaintiff's counsel does. The Court deciding *Horak* vs. *Horak* must be presumed to have taken the law to be as above stated. Not only was this section quoted, but also later ones (Forf, 25, 3, 3 and 24, 2, 15).

The first of these passages states that: "If a *foetus* be born during the marriage, one may inquire whether the husband must acknowledge it as his, and ho is not forced to do so if he can prove clearly that it was not conceived from him— as, if he shall find a child one year old, on his return home after nn absence of ten years; or if he is so impotent and infirm as to be incapable of procreation. " The other passage states that one of grounds on which a marriage maybe declared null and void from the beginning, is "marriage with a woman deflowered and pregnant by another man, where the husband has not, upon discovery of the defloworing *(stuprum),* cohabited with his wife, or in any other way condoned the offence." Cohabiting with one's wife after knowledge of her guilt constitutes condonation. See also *Cens. For.* 1, 15, 10; and *Grot.* 1, 12, 3 *(Schorer, §* 50).

135. Following on the maxim *pater est quern nuptiae demonstrant,* it is sufficient, in order to prove that a child is legitimate, to show that it was born from a marriage lawfully solemnised. Where there is a doubt, both the power of procreation, and sexual intercourse between spouses living together, are presumed. Where a husband is impotent, or abstains from intercourse with his wife, a child born in his house is not, where such impotency or abstention is clearly proved, considered as his child (1, 6 § 6).

The mere statement or admission of a woman that a child born during her marriage is illegitimate will not be taken as conclusive in every case. Thus, in *Johnson* vs. *Story* (Natal L. R. 1869, p. 116) an affiliation action in which the declaration relied on the birth of a child in wedlock eight months after marriage, was dismissed with costs. It was held that on grounds of public policy a child born in lawful wedlock cannot be bastardised where it is perfectly consistent with the facts of the case that the husband might be the father.

The case of *Horah* vs. *Horak* was commented upon by Sir *F.* Jeune in *Mots* vs. *Moss* (Prob. Div. Rep. 1897, p. 273). This case decided that, so far as

English Law was concerned, concealment by a woman from her husband at the time of the marriage of the fact that she is then pregnant by another man does not render the marriage null and void. It was said: "The English law of the validity of marriage is clearly defined. There must be the voluntary consent of both parties. There must be compliance with the legal requirements of publication and solemnisation, so far as the law deems it essential. There must not be incapacity in the parties to marry either as respects age or physical capability or as respects relationship by blood or marriage. Failure in these respects, but I believe in no others, renders the marriage void or voidable." 136. The reason why the unsupported confession of the wife that the child is illegitimate should not be taken is to prevent injury to her own reputation, and harm to the child, who must be acknowledged by the husband, and is entitled to inherit his legitimate portion, where children have a right to that, or to succeed *ab intestato* in places where the legitimate portion is not claimable as of right (as in Cape Colony, Act 28, 1874, § 2, and in the Transvaal, Proc. 28, 1902, § 128). Even if the wife, in addition to her own admission, be convicted of adultery, a child bom during marriage will be presumed legitimate. Where the origin of a thing is traceable to either a lawful or an unlawful act, in case of doubt there is a presumption in favour of the lawful act and of morality.

The effect of these rules is that a person alleging illegitimacy in such cases is bound to furnish the requisite proof (1, 6 §§ 7, 8).

In *Abrahams* vs. *Adams* (Buch. 1878, p. 86) it was laid down, following Voet, that the husband is presumed to he the father of all children horn in wedlock, and the strongest proof is necessary to rebut the presumption. The uncorroborated evidence of the wife was held insufficient, where there was possibility of intercourse with the husband, to fix paternity on the defendant, though there was no denial of intercourse by the defendant. Here the mere fact that it was possiblo for the husband to have been

the father was held sufficient to warrant the child's legitimacy, though the wife stated that the defendant was the father and he did not deny this. See also *Richter* vs. *Wagenaar,* 1 M. 262. The obvious reason of the law, apart from the child's interests, is the prevention of collusion between husband and wife. We may now deduce these rules: (a) Where previous *stuprum* is unknown to the husband, and a child is born before the seventh month from marriage, and the husband does not cohabit after knowledge of the *stuprum,* the marriage may be declared null and void, *(b)* Where previous *stuprum* is known to the husband, the marriage will stand, (c) Where a child is conceived during marriage, even if the wife admits adultery, when there is a possibility of access by the husband, and no direct proof is furnished from other sources that another than the husband is the father of the child, the child must be held legitimate. 137. Where a woman remarries within the *annus luctus,* and gives birth to a child at such a time—before ten months from the death of the first husband, or during the seventh mouth from the second marriage—that either husband might have been the father, in case of doubt the second husband will be deemed to be the father—since he must rebut the presumption that the child born in his house is his own, and it is due to his own act that the marriage took place so soon after the first husband's death (1, 6 § 9).

This rule would apply even in places (such as Cape Colony) where the *annus Indus* is not enforced. The question is not whethcr a person is prohibited or not from remarrying within a certain time of the first husband's death, but whether paternity is attributed to one of two persons.

138. Where a child is born to persons betrothed to each other, and the father dies before all the formalities requisite to a valid marriage have been gone through, the child is illegitimate (1, 6, § 10). 139. Where persons have been divorced, and again marry each other, children thereafter conceived and born are to be regarded as legitimate, just as

if the tie had never been broken. Where there has heen a voluntary separation between spouses, without judicial decree, and they again come together, children born thereafter will be legitimate. Where the marriage has been dissolved by decree of the Judge, the ordinary formalities of marriage must be gone through again, to render the fresh union valid. Unless those requisites are observed, the children will be illegitimate (1, 6 § 11).

Voet speaks, in the first place, of a separation without judicial decree, and, secondly, of divorce. He does not say what would happen if there had been a judicial separation. It would seem that the effect and requisites of remarriage would be the same as in the case of a voluntary separation. A judicial separation is no divorce, which is clear enough from the fact that adultery during a judicial separation is ground for a divorce. Consequently, judicial separation has not the effects of a divorce, and if the parties agree to waive the separation and again unite, the marriage will be regarded as resumed, even though it has not been again solemnised with the usual formalities—formalities which would be necessary where the parties had been divorced (see *Mackillican* vs. *Mackillican,* 9 Natal L. R. 193).

139a. Those are reckoned among lawful children who, while having the human form, have not all the parts of the body in perfection, but diminished or deformed in some way. Monsters and prodigies are not to be regarded as children at all (1, 6 §§ 12, 18). 140. Adoption, as a binding contract, no longer holds in RomauDutch Law, as it did in Roman Law. So adopted children have no right to succeed to their adoptive father, nor, when the adoptive father speaks of "children" in a will, are they included in that appellation, unless they are specifically mentioned (1, 7 §§ 1 to 8).

In *Robb* vs. *Mealey's Extcutor Dative* (9 C. T. R. 94) the Chief Justice of Cape Colony said: "The law of this Colony does not recognise adoption as a means of creating the legal relationship of parent and child. Under the Roman Law this relationship was created, but the Dutch Law did not, in this respect, follow the Roman Law. In matters of succession, the adopted child is regarded as a stranger to the adopter, so that an adopted child could not, under the former law of the (Cape) Colony, claim the legitimate portion and cannot, under the still existing law, claim a right of succession *ab intestato* in respect of the adopter's estate." In this case the plaintiff had been adopted by the testator and his wife, and had lived with them for twenty years until the testator's death. The testator made a will, which was written on three leaves, and signed by the testator at the end of the will in the presence of two witnesses who appended their signatures. The second leaf of the will did not bear the signature of tho testator, and the first and second leaves did not bear tho signatures of tho attesting witnesses. According to Cape Law (Ordinance 15, 1845) the will, if an unprivileged will, had to be signed at the foot of one side of every leaf by the testator and two witnesses, in the presence of each other. A privileged will was one whereby a testator disposed of his property entirely among his children, and was in the handwriting of the deceased (holograph) and signed by him alone, as will be seen later on). A privileged will did not require the attestation of witnesses, provided it was holograph, and signed by the testator. Plaintiff claimed that the will in question was privileged, as she was the child of the testator, and even if the will was not duly witnessed, that it was still valid, as privileged wills did not require the attestation of witnesses. After stating the law as above quoted, the Court went on to say, "it would be an unwarrantable extension of the doctrine of privilege to hold that, because the plaintiff was the adopted daughter of the testator, his holograph will, although not duly attested, is valid in so far as it confers benefits on her. " It was thus decided that plaintiff was not entitled to the inheritance. In 1900 a special Act, in the nature of a *privilegium,* known as the Mealey Will Act, was passed by the Cape Colony Parliament, wherein it was declared that the plaintiff in the above case was entitled to the inheritance. See also *Voet,* 28, 1, 15, 16; Van Leeuwen's *RomanDutch Law* (1, 13, 13); *Cans. For.* (23, 2, 21); Bulge on *Colonial Laws* (vol. 4, p. 398); *Grot.* (1, 0, 1); Groenewegen, *de Legibus Abrogatis* (Inst. 1, 11).

140a. Paternal power is dissolved by the natural death of father or son (1, 7 §§ 9, 10). 141. Children may be released from paternal power if they are willing, and if it be not against the will of the parents *(i.e.,* if it be with the consent of the parents). The emancipation from paternal power may be judicial, where the father declares before a Court that he absolves his son from his control, and the Court gives a decree accordingly. Grotius agrees with Voet that there may be a judicial declaration of emancipation. It is doubtful whether a modern Court will give such a decree. Such a decree is to be distinguished from a judgment in which the Court holds, from the circumstances of the case, that a son must be taken as having tacitly emancipated himself from parental control. With regard to tacit emancipation, Voet says it is doubtful whether the wish to emancipate may be deduced from acts and circumstances, such as a son's separate residence from the father with the father's consent, or his carrying on business, conducting his own affairs, or founding a family. He says it is clear that the paternal power is not lost if the father is unaware, or absent, or unwilling to allow his son to do these things. But, if the father agree and consent, whether by express words or conduct, the paternal power is considered as dissolved. Grotius does not draw a distinction between the two courses of conduct on the father's part, though lie hints at it *(Introduction,* 1, 6, 4). Tacit emancipation, he says, takes place, for instance, when a child "is permitted to live and carry on business by himself. When children are released from the paternal power by one or other of these means, they acquire the right to administer their own property, and to appear for themselves in Court" (1, 7 §§ 11, 12, 15).

There are thus three kinds of emancipation from paternal power: (i) Attaining the age of twenty-one.

(6) Judicial emancipation, or the decree of a competent Court declaring the son emancipated. (c) Tacit emancipation, where a son lives apart from the father, or carries on business for himself and at his own risk, and the father by conduct or words agrees to such emancipation. In *Cairncross* vs. *De Vos* (Buch. 1876, p. 5), a minor of about eighteen years-of-age, whose father was dead, who had been living apart from his mother for some time, and carried on the trade of a blacksmith, for his own benefit, was held to have acquired *a. persona standi in judicio,* and to be liable in an action for money lent. See also Van Leeuwen *(R. D. L.* 1,13, 5), and Van derKeessel (107). 142. Paternal power is not lost by insanity. It is not lost, according to the old Dutch Law (no longer in force), by marriage, where such marriage takes place without the consent of the parents. But even now, if the parents set aside the marriage of their child under age, the *patria potestas* continues (1, 7 § 18). During insanity, a father will, of course, lose control over his children. But if he is again restored to his right mind, he will resume control over his children, which he would not have been able to do had his insanity absolutely dissolved, instead of merely suspending, the paternal power.

According to general Boman-Dutch Law, "the father of a minor child who was married without his consent, expressed or implied, was entitled to have such marriage set aside as null and void. The mother's consent was also required, but, in case of a difference of opinion, the father's wish had to prevail. If the father, knowing of the intended marriage, took no steps to stop it, he was deemed to have given a tacit consent to it, and, in the absence of fraud on the part of either or both of the spouses, the publication of banns, which was compulsory, was considered as notice to the father." So in places where (as in the Cape Colony, under the Marriage Order in Council, 1839) publication of banns is required, notice is deemed to have been given to the father on such pub-

lication. This does not, however, hold in the case of marriages by special licence. See *Johnson* vs. *McIntyre* (10 S. C. 318).

143. Where a marriage has been dissolved by death or divorce, the widow or divorced wife who is still under the age of majority does not again come under the parental control of her father or mother, and their consent is not required for her subsequent marriage (1, 7 § 14). *B. DOMESTIC RELATIONSHIPS BE-TWEEN PERSONS.* CHAPTER I. PARENT AND CHILD. 144. The principal object of marriage is the procreation of children. On their birth, they are to be nourished and brought up in accordance with the dictates of natural reason. Since no one is compellable to support the children of other persons, it follows that, when the support of children is in question, they should in the first place be recognised as one's own children. Both those born during the subsistence of a marriage, and those born after divorce or after the death of the father—no other marriage, which might have established another paternity, having followed—are to be recognised as children to be supported (25, 3 §§ 1, 2). 145. As previously explained, the husband cannot be compelled to recognise and support a child in circumstances similar to those of *Horak* vs. *Horak.* See § 184 of this work (25, 8 § 8). 146. It makes a difference whether the obligation to support is due to contract or testamentary devise, or to natural affection alone and the obligation thence arising. If support is due as the result of a contract or testament, the terms of the agreement or testament must be specially referred to. Where support is due by reason of that natural affection which parents owe to children, much is left to the discretion of the Judge as regards the mode of support. Under support due from natural affection and the bond of law thence resulting are included not only food and clothing, in accordance with the means and position of the persons to be supported, but residence (i.e., the shelter of a roof), medicine for the cure of diseases, and instruction in the art of reading and writing, and the first principles of

religion. The general education of children must be left to the discretion of parents; while guardians ought to supply from the patrimony of their wards the means of educating the latter in accordance with the requirements of their station (25, 8 § 4).

There is no legal obligation on parents or guardians to educate children in a particular way, though probably it would be within the competence of a Court,.where parents could afford it or, in the case of guardianship, where minors had enough money to be applied to the purpose, to order the child to receive at least the rudiments of education. The teaching of the Christian religion, or of any religion, is, of course, not now obligator-.

147. The first person bound to support children on account of natural affection, and compellable thereto, is the father—and he is liable whether the children be still in his charge or emancipated (where they have not sufficient means for their own support), and whether they be legitimate or illegitimate. Incestuous children also are to be supported, Bince those should not be punished who have done nothing wrong (25, 8 § 5).

It is not easy to find a word to use as an equivalent for *ex officio pietatis* in Voet's *dictum.* The author has employed the term "natural affection," although one can hardly say that there is natural affection in the case of a man whom the law must be called upon to compel to support his own children!

Voet states later on (25, 3 § 18; § 159 of this work) that the obligation to support children, where there is no contract or testament to that effect, does not bind a person's heirs. This refers to support due to a child from the moment of the death of the person who was previously bound to support the child. Where, however, before the death of the person obliged to support, a certain sum is due to the children in lieu of the support which they should have received, a Court will, under certain circumstances, decree the payment of such sum to the children, whether legitimate or illegitimate, it being essential that the obligation to contribute such money for support should have accrued before the death of the person bound to support. Thus, in *Ex parte Levengeld, In re Tait* (4 S. C. 64), where a woman lived with a man as his wife for many years, and children were born of the cohabitation, who were maintained chiefly through her industry, and the man died intestate in 1877, leaving a sum of 275/., and no one claimed the money, and there was no reason to believe that there were any heirs, the Court, upon the application of the mother to bo declared entitled to the said sum for the past maintenance of the major children during their minority, and for the past and future maintenance of the minor children, granted such an order, the executor who had paid the money into the hands of the Master consenting. It was said: "The present application is not founded upon the seduction of the applicant by the deceased, but upon the general right which children, even if they are illegitimate, have to maintenance from their father." 148. A father will not be released from the obligation to support his children from the fact that he has already assigned a portion of his goods to them, which has been lost through prodigality or misfortune. The same thing holds if a marriage portion or gift in consideration of marriage *(donatio propter nuptias)* has been assigned to a child (25, 3 § 5).

With reference to the decision in *Ex parte Levengeld, In re Tait* (4 S. C. 64), it may be here stated that the decision in that case does not appear to be wholly reconcilable with the case of *Kramer* vs. *Findlaifs Executors* (Buch. 1878, p. 52). In the latter ease, judgment at the suit of the mother was given against the executors for the *maintenance* of an illegitimate child, of which the deceased was the putative father. The deceased, Findlay, supported the child up to the date of his death. The decision was founded on *Voet* (48, 5 § 5); and on the face of the decision, as reported, the judgment was for maintenance due to the child. On reference, however, to *Voet* (48, 5 § 5), it will be seen that the cause on which such action is founded is not maintenance, but compensation, to the woman

for her seduction. It was in accordance with this that the statement was made in *Tait's* case: "The death of the seducer does not, according to *Voet* (48, 5 § 5), put an end to her right of action for the tort committed upon her." The distinction between the two positions should be carefully drawn. A man's executors or heirs are liable for maintenance of his illegitimate children only up to the date of his death; they would not seem to be liable for maintenance for the period after his death, but they will be liable for compensation in the nature of damages to the woman seduced. Among such damages are not only to be reckoned her outlays for the maintenance of the children, but other expenses to which she may have been put in connection with the birth of the children. On any other hypothesis it is difficult to reconcile the *dicta*—not the actual decisions—in the two cases of *Tait* and of *Findlay.*

Having now distinguished between the liability for maintenance and the liability for compensation, one comes to the question whether children of the age of majority may claim support. The statement in *TaWs* case was that the mother could claim for the maintenance of the major children during their minority, and this might cause an inference that the father was not liable after majority. In *Tail's* case that question was not raised. But in *In re Knoop* (10 S. C. 198) it was said: "The obligation to protect a child against want may revive even after such child has reached an age at which he can maintain himself, if he is in distress and unable to work through bad health, and if the parents are possessed of the requisite means." Of course, an age at which a child may maintain himself need not necessarily be the age of majority.

149. If the father is too poor to support the children, and the mother has means, she may be called upon to do so. The mother must also support her children, if it is uncertain who is the father. If a marriage has been dissolved by divorce, not only the guilty party, but the innocent party as well, may be called upon to maintain the children, in proportion

to their means, at the discretion of the Judge (see *Painter* vs. *Painter,* 2 E. D. C. 147) (25, 8 § 6). 150. Voet says that it is a rule of Roman-Dutch Law, derived from Roman Law, that when father and mother are unable to maintain their children the duty of doing so falls on the grandparents. Faber holds that a grandfather in such a case is liable to support the illegitimate child of his legitimate son. If that is the case—and Voet holds that it is so—then is a grandfather likewise liable to maintain the legitimate child of his illegitimate son? (25. 3 § 7). 151. On the other hand, indigent parents must be supported by their children, not only if the parents maintain their ordinary rectitude of conduct, but even if the mother sells her honour for the purpose of getting money (25, 8 § 8). *In re Knoop* (10 S. C. 198) laid down that just as parents are obliged to support their children, "the latter owe a reciprocal duty to their parents. If a father or mother is in distress and unable to work or obtain work, his or her children who have the means can be compelled to contribute towards their parents' support. It would make no difference that the children if able to maintain their parents are minors, for the obligation does not arise out of any implied contract, but out of the sense of dutifulness which every child is presumed to entertain towards his parents." So, where a son had been declared a lunatic by the Supreme Court, and had more than enough to support himself, the Court authorised the payment of 5/. per month out of the lunatic's income to his father, who had been reduced to extreme poverty. 152. Voet further lays down that indigent brothers or sisters are to be supported by their brothers or sisters who have means. Justinian also laid down that natural or illegitimate children are to be supported by the legitimate children of their parents (i.e., by their legitimate brothers or sisters). As to this last rule— not that relating to legitimate children being supported by legitimate brothers and sisters, which still holds good— Voet expresses no opinion; but it is submitted that, in consonance with modern principles of equity, there is no longer any obligation on legitimate children to support their parents' illegitimate children. As marriage is the joining together of husband and wife by a mode of life in which they are inseparable, spouses are obliged to support their indigent husbands or wives respectively (and, indeed, the husband is at all times liable to support his wife). Where a divorce has been decreed on the ground of adultery or malicious desertion, the innocent spouse is not compellable to support the guilty spouse, if the latter be indigent, as the conduct of the latter has broken the bond of marriage. But the guilty husband, after dissolution of the marriage, may be ordered to support the children of the marriage (25, 3 § 8). 153. There is no obligation to support relatives more remote than brothers or sisters. A donee of all the goods of the donor is not compellable to support the donor, if the latter has nothing (25, 3 § 9). 154. Parents-in-law (father-in-law or mother-in-law) who are indigent may compel their sons-in-law to support them, on account of the connection with them derived from marrying their children (25, 3 §§ 10, 11, 12). 155. In order to compel a person who is bound to support one to render maintenance, one must proceed, not by action, but by petition to the Court, which grants an interlocutory order decreeing a certain amount to be paid, in proportion to the necessities of the applicant. Where the person to be supported is a minor, his nearest relations may petition on his behalf. If a person called upon to supply maintenance denies that he is the father, or generally such a person as the law charges with liability to support, no payment of alimony is to be decreed before a summary inquiry has taken place on the matter, and it appears probable that he who denies himself to be the father, son, or other relation bound to support, is in fact such a relation as is liable; or unless it appears that a person has been occupying the position of a son or father (although it may later on be found that in reality he is not the son or the father), in which case such a summary decree that a person is the son or the father shall not prejudice his future

rights (25, 3 § 13). 156. The obligation to support ceases, and the right to compel maintenance likewise, if the children are actively carrying on a trade, from which they are able to support themselves. If, therefore, children are in any way enriched by their labour, such acquisitions may be appropriated by the parents, providing the parents are then supporting them (25, 3 § 14). 157. There is no obligation to support, if the children can maintain themselves sufficiently from what they have already received from father, mether, or other sources. So, even if a stranger has left property to a child, on condition that the income thence arising shall be added to the capital (e.g., for a term of years, or until the child attains majority), the parent who has to support the child may lawfully claim that the income from such gift or inheritance shall be applied to the maintenance of the child (25, 3 § 15). 158. A parent cannot, however, apply the principal sum which a child has received by way of inheritance or gift, whether from his parents or other sources, to the maintenance and education of the child, but must supply the necessary amount from his own daily earnings or patrimony—unless the parent is in so indigent a condition that he cannot support the child from his own resources, in which case he should obtain special leave of the Court (25, 8 §§ 16, 17). 159. The obligation to support others ceases generally, if one is so indigent as to be unable to support oneself; also, if the person claiming support has behaved in so undutiful a manner as to entitle the parent, according to general Roman-Dutch Law, to disinherit him. The question of the transmissibility of the obligation to heirs or executors has already been treated of in §§ 147, 148. The author must not be understood as stating that the obligation is not transmissible, but must be taken merely to have given Voet's statement on the law, and the substance of the decisions in the Cape Supreme Court. Voet here says that this obligation to support does not pass to the heirs, qua heirs, and so, although a son or brother has, of his own free will, or on the mandate of a Judge,

taken upon himself or been declared liable to support his father or brother, as the case may be, yet, on the death of such son or brother, his heir does not succeed to the burden of maintenance (25, 8 § 18). 160. On the death of the person to be supported, or claiming support, the obligation to maintain disappears, even where the obligation arises from contract or inheritance (25, 8 § 19). 161. On a divorce taking place, the question of maintenance of a spouse or of the children of the marriage is left entirely to the discretion of the Judge (25, 8 § 20).

In Simey vs. Simty (1 S. C. 17G) it was said: "When the Court grants a decree for the dissolution of a marriage or for a judicial separation, the custody of the children is in the discretion of the Court, which must look to all the circumstances of the case, and be chiefly guided by the consideration of whatisbest for the children. Prima fade, a guilty parent would not be a proper person to have the custody, but there might be circumstances that would make it desirable that the children, or some of them, should be brought up by him or her." The editor of the report of this case (Sir H. Juta) has a learned note on the decision in Edmeades vs. Edmeades (1 S. C. 173), which may be consulted with advantage. See also Painter vs. Painter (2 E. D. C. 147), and Voet, 25, 3 § 6 (§ 149, above).

162. Voet next considers a legal proceeding at Rome known as ventris inspcctio, which was applied for by a husband who had divorced his wife, and was desirous of establishing the fact that he was the father of a child born shortly after such divorce. The praetor or Judge had the power to nominate three physicians, skilled in obstetrics, to examine the woman, and furnish a report on her condition. Although this was a regular procedure in the early Roman period, regard for female honour caused it to be applied afterwards only when there was no other means of ascertaining what was wanted. If a husband alleged that his divorced wife was pregnant and, after examination, this was found not to be the case, the woman

had an *actio injuriarum* against her husband—provided there was an *animus injuriandi* (intention to injure) on the part of the husband, which was presumed to be absent, if the husband had just grounds for his belief (25, 4 §§ 1, 2).

Colquhoun (§§ 677, 678) says: "It has not yet been determined what shall be considered as the *ultimum tempus pariendi,* this point being left to the decision of a jury on hearing competent witnesses, and judging from the circumstances of the case. Lord Coke lays down nine solar months, or forty weeks, as the extreme time; but this has been so variously decided that no rule can be adopted.... This gives rise to a proceeding at English Common Law, when a widow is suspected to feign herself with child in order to produce a supposititious heir to the estate.... In this case, the heir-presumptive may have a writ *de ventre inspiciendo,* to examine whether she be with child or not, and if she be, to keep her under proper restraint until she be delivered, which is entirely conformable to the practice of the Civil Law." The proceeding mentioned by Voet is then detailed. The procedure under the writ *de ventre inspiciendo* has fallen into disuse: but English Law is so tenacious of old forms and old customs that it would be unsafe to say absolutely that it has become abrogated in this respect. The Roman Law practice has not been followed in Roman-Dutch Courts, within the last century at any rate. Voet, however, does not tell us that the procedure was obsolete in his day; and as the action for an inspection under such circumstances is in all respects similar to other Roman Law proceedings to obtain extraordinary remedies which are still in use, it has been thought desirable to give a summary of Voet's observations on the subject.

As to the time of life when women are presumed to be no longer capable of child-bearing, it may be remarked that there is a singular dearth of RomanDutch authority on the subject, singular, as so much attention was devoted to other matters connected with the birth

and parentage of children. It is a question that may often be of importance in connection with the law of inheritance. Owing to the absence of authority, it was decided in *Re Estate of Meyer* (13 S. C. 2) that there is no fixed rule of law as to the age at which a woman must be conclusively presumed to be past childbearing; but after fifty years of age a Court would require less evidence than before.

163. Au inspection also takes place, if a woman, on the death of her husband, declares that she is pregnant by him (25, 4 §§ 3, 4). 164. When it appears that a woman is pregnant, according to her allegation, the praetor orders her to receive support from her deceased husband's estate, until the child is born. Fraud is, however, to be carefully guarded against (25, 5 § 1; 25, 6 § 1). 165. Voet then proceeds to treat of the subject of concubines, whose *status* is no longer recognised as it was in Roman times. The rights of women who have entered into illicit connections with men fall, in modern practice, under the head of the law of torts, and, in particular, within those branches of it which relate to seduction and affiliation (25, 7 §§ 1 to 17). The rules laid down by him on the subject of legitimation may, however, be briefly summarised. In the time of Justinian there were three modes of legitimation. The first was known as *legitimatio per oblationem curiae,* which is now wholly obsolete. Then there was legitimation by subsequent marriage, which finally gave the right of legitimating all *natural* children born to the parents before marriage. The legitimate grandchildren of a man whose son, the father of such grandchildren, was of illegitimate birth though legitimated by his father's subsequent marriage, are legitimate in all respects as if their father had been originally legitimate, and consequently succeed to the grandfather in the ordinary way. For this species of legitimation it is necessary that the father shall have been unmarried, or a widower

C.L.—VOL. I. I or already divorced— that is, that the woman with whom he formed the illicit connection should not

have committed adultery with him—at the time of conception of the children: for adulterine or incestuous children cannot afterwards be legitimated (25, 7 §§ 4 to 8).

Van Leeuwen *Roman-Dutch Law,* 1, 7, 7, Kotze's ed. vol. 1, p. 51) agrees with Voet that children procreated in adultery or incest cannot be legitimated *per subsequens matrimonium.* Decker, in his note to Van Leeuwen, disagrees with this view, holding that the Head of the State has the power in all cases of granting *legitimatio per rescriptum.* But he forgets that legitimation by rescript is a totally different mode of procedure. Furthermore, this appears contrary to the view expressed by Decker on p. 34 of Kotze's edition (vol. 1), where he says that a Sovereign cannot grant dispensations to the prejudice of his other subjects. It would, therefore, seem best to adhere to the view expressed by such great authorities as Voet and Van Leeuwen.

166. The length of time supervening before the marriage makes no difference with regard to the effect of legitimation: so that a death-bed marriage is even sufficient to legitimate the children previously born, since one is capable of entering into a marriage as long as life lasts—provided the necessary solemnities of marriage have been observed, although there has been no cohabitation after the ceremony (25, 7 §§ 11, 12). 167. The next mode of legitimation is by rescript of the Princeps, when, on the petition of the father, or of the children desiring legitimation, the Head of the State grants a decree of legitimacy. This decree is only given if the father has no other legitimate children in existence—otherwise they would be entitled to succeed *ab intestato* with the other legitimate children, and the Head of the State does not grant privileges to the detriment of other persons. This legitimation is to be sought from the Head of the State to whose jurisdiction the person to be legitimated is subject, not from any other Princeps. The Princeps alone is able to grant a decree of legitimation (25, 7 §§ 18 to 17). CHAPTER II. MINORS AND THEIR RIGHTS. 168. Strict-

ly speaking, the rights and liabilities of minors should be included in that department of law which treats of capacity to contract. For the sake of convenience, however, their rights are treated of in this place. In Roman-Dutch Law, majors were those who had completed the twenty-fifth year of their age. The laws of the various Colonies in South Africa have fixed the age of majority at twenty-one years. Minors are those who have not yet attained full age, whether they be under the power of others or emancipated, and whether they have or have not attained the age of puberty. The last day of minority is regarded as completed at the moment of its inception, when it is to the minor's advantage that this should be so; but when the minor seeks *restitutio in integrum,* the period of minority is reckoned to extend to the close of the last day of minority, *de momento in momentum* (to the very minute) (4, 4 §§ 1, 2). 169. There are certain persons who are regarded as majors, even although they have not completed the necessary number of years. Such are those who have obtained *venia aetatis,* and persons who marry. No special age is now necessary to obtain *venia aetatis,* although those who apply for it should be mature, and have conducted themselves with such rectitude, or given such proofs of ability, that it may appear perfectly safe to entrust to them the management of their own affairs. In making application for *venia aetatis,* the Courts of Holland required the applicant's exact age to be stated (4, 4 § 8). 170. The power of conceding *venia aetatis* resides in the Head of the State alone, since thereby a relaxation of the general law is granted, and a special law with reference to an individual is introduced. It was considered a breach of their authority on the part of magistrates at Rome to grant *renia actatti.* Voet says that the method employed in his day was for the minor to make an application to the States General (the supreme Legislature of Holland), which body often referred the matter to the Judge having jurisdiction over the minor, and acted upon his report. At Utrecht the Courts granted *venia aetatis*

without reference to the supreme governing body; likewise at Mechlin, Antwerp, and Leyden. Voet, however, holds with Groenewegen, that the general Courts of Holland have no power to grant *venia aetatis* (4, 4 § 4).

Groenewegen cites the case of a namesake of his (in his notes to the *Introduction* of Grotius, 1, 10, 3), whose application for *venia aeUitis* the Court of Holland would not entertain, on the ground that none but the Sovereign power could declare a minor of age, since this declaring of age before the legal age does not consist in any legal compulsion, nor in a single command, but in an undefined right of the Sovereign power.

In accordance with this view of Voet and Groenewegen, the Supreme Court of Natal, in in re *Fenton* (Natal L. R. , March 3rd, 1863), refused the application, made with his father's consent, of a minor aged nineteen, for an order to enable him to hold property, make contracts, trade, and sue and be sued without the control of his father. In the case of *Ex parte Stretch* (1 N. L. R. 96) the same Court went farther, and held that not only had the Supreme Court no power to grant a decree of *venia aetatis,* but that such power rested with the Sovereign alone, and could not be exercised by the Governor of the Colony of Natal. Perhaps this was an extreme view to take; but it was at any rate more cautious than the decision of the High Court of the late South African Republic (in 1899), in *Ex parte Daly,* when the applicant, aged nineteen, was granted *venia aetatis,* and admitted to practise as an attorney. The decision in this case was contrary to that in *Ex parte Botha* (10 C. L. J. p. 174). That the Transvaal Government adopted Voet's view is clear from *In re Barrett (Staats Courant* of the South African Republic, February, 1894). In *Ex parte Cachet* (8 C. T. R. p. 9), the Cape Chief Justice said: "In the absence of any clear authority that the Court has power to declare a minor to be a major in law, I am not prepared to exercise such a power in the present instance; that order might have a very far-reaching effect" See also *Ex parte Streicher* (3 S. C. 58) and *Ex*

parte Moolman (1903 T. S. 159).

171. The effect of obtaining *venia aetatis* is that acts done by minors thereafter are in all respects as valid as if done after they had attained the age of majority—so that they cannot obtain *restitutio in integrum,* even if they are proved to have been unskilful in the management of their affairs. There is an exception, however, in respect of immovable property, which cannot be alienated or mortgaged without consent of the Court (4, 4 § 5). 172. In Dutch Law, marriage has this effect, that from the very moment of marriage a minor husband is regarded in all respects as a major, and is discharged from guardianship and paternal power, as if he had actually attained the limit of age prescribed by law — and that not only as regards the administration of his affairs, but as regards absolute freedom of alienation of property as well (4, 4 § 6). 173. Voet holds that, where a minor has been granted *venia aetatit* with regard to the disposition of his property, majority or freedom of disposition does not extend beyond tbe jurisdiction of the Sovereign granting *venia aetatis,* and affects only goods situate within his territory, not goods subject to another jurisdiction (4, 4 §§ 7, 8, 9, 10).

The learned translator of and commentator on Van Leeuwen's *Roman-Dutch Law* (see 1 Kotze, p. 88) states that Voet's doctrine on this point is opposed to the general opinion of Continental jurists. Decker, whose note is also translated, expresses himself very vigorously on the subject, criticising Voet sharply, and holding that a person who has obtained dispensation of years, and, consequently, freedom to administer his property, is everywhere to be regarded as if of full age. In view of the general trend of opinion, Voet's *dictum* on this subject would appear to be incorrect.

174. Where a person has desired, by testament or contract, that anything shall be done, and has made mention of the legal age of majority in connection therewith, in case of doubt the attainment of the actual legal age (twenty-five, or twenty-one years in South Africa) is to be considered as intended,

and one who has obtained *tenia aetatis* is not to be regarded as included (4, 4 § 11). 175. Restitution is granted to minors, where it appears that they have suffered harm by reason of minority and the weakness of youth. The age of persons seeking restitution must be proved, not only by means of witnesses, but by documentary evidence, such as birth certificates. There should be no suspicion of fraud. A deposition by the parents, made at a time when a dispute arose concerning restitution, is not to be admitted. The burden of proving minority lies on him who claims restitution (a major being able to claim restitution for what was done during his minority, provided he has not ratified the same on coming of age),—whether he seeks restitution as plaintiff in a suit brought for that purpose, or, when summoned to fulfil a contract adverse to his interests, he defends himself by stating that he is under age—since in either case the ground of the claim or the exception is the age of the party, and the burden of proving an exception falls no less on the defendant than the burden of proving a claim falls on the plaintiff; and, moreover, in case of doubt, every person making a contract is presumed to have had full capacity to perform the act which is in question: so that the burden of proof rests on one who asserts the contrary (i.e., that the party contracting did not possess the requisite capacity) (4,4 § 12). 176. It is necessary that the minor should be shown to have suffered some loss, either by having lost something which he possessed (as by donating, selling, or by other means); or by having omitted to acquire that which it was possible for him to get (as by repudiating an inheritance or legacy); or, lastly, by subjecting himself to a burden which he might have avoided (as by standing surety for another, or accepting a burdensome inheritance). In case of doubt, such loss must not be presumed, but must be proved by the person alleging it, and consequently by the person who alleges that he was deceived through the weakness of youth. But, where the transaction on which the claim against the minor is founded is

such as to be in its very nature injurious to the minor, such as a suretyship, a donation, or a loan, the burden of proof is on the person making the claim (4, 4 § 18). 177. On proof of such circumstances, restitution is granted to minors on account of judicial as well as of extra-judicial transactions (4, 4 § 14). 178. A minor may have relief on account of a sale of his goods which has not been 'prohibited by law from taking place. This restitution may be sought even where the Judge prohibited the sale from taking place: for, notwithstanding such prohibition, loss might in any case result to the minor. Belief is also given to the minor, in case the thing has been sold for less than it is worth, and damage has resulted therefrom (4, 4 § 15). Loss such as that last mentioned will not in every case amount to *laesio enormis,* as to which see a later part of this work *(Voet,* Book 18, tit 5, § 4 *et leqq.).* 179. If a minor's property has been sold, not by himself, but by another person who sold it as if the property were his own (and not the minor's), whether privately or by public auction, and transfer of such property takes place privately, without the sanction of a

Judge, there is no doubt that the minor need not claim restitution, but may claim restoration of the property by the ordinary remedy of vindicating it against the purchaser, as possessor: because my property cannot be transferred to another without any act on my part, and on the private initiative of another. Voet holds that, even where a public sale takes place, after publication of notices calling upon all persons interested to put in their objections, and a decree is given for the sale, and the ownership of the thing passes to the purchaser—there is no reason why, on proof of damage to a minor on account of the weakness of youth, assistance should not be granted to him, and the possession as well as the ownership of the property be restored to him. In such a case the minor will not have to restore the purchase-price to the purchaser, since the sale did not take place through the fault or for the advantage of the minor, but through the imprudence of the seller,

and for the advantage of the contracting parties. But a choice has been given to the minor by Dutch Law (see Matthaeus *de Auctionibus,* 1, 18, 2, 3), and he may elect whether to claim restoration of his property or to sue the seller or his heirs for the purchase-price obtained from the purchaser (4, 4 § 16).

The foregoing rules on restitution, as well as those that follow, coincide with the views on the subject expressed by Story (in his work on *Contracts),* and have been treated as binding in the Cape Colony (excepting the case of *laesio enormit,* when the Cape Act 8 of 1879 applies). In *Van der Byl* vs. *Solomon* (Buch. 187", p. 25), the Court quoted with approval the following passage from Story on *Contracts* (§ 114): "There is a distinction between those acts and words which are necessary to ratify an executory contract, and those which are sufficient to ratify an executed contract. In the latter class of cases, any explicit acknowledgment of liability will operate as a ratification. But in order to ratify an executory agreement made during infancy, there must be not only an acknowledgment of primary liability, but an express promise, voluntarily and deliberately made by the infant upon arriving at the age of maturity. No act or word, therefore, which does not unequivocally imply a new and primary promise by the infant himself, will be sufficient to create a liability on his executory contract." In other words, an executory contract must be expressly ratified on attaining majority; while an executed contract may be impliedly ratified. In the above case, the father of defendant (a minor) bought at auction a piece of land in the minor's name at a price exceeding its value, but did not pay the price or receive transfer of the land. After attaining his majority, the defendant offered to pay a small sum of money as forfeit instead of completing the purchase. It was decided that there had been no ratification of the contract. See also *Grot.* 3, 1, 26; 3, 43, 10; *Pothier,* § 40.

180. In like manner a minor will be protected against a sale of pledges purporting to be hypothecated by him, made by

creditors. A distinction must be made as to whether the minor has himself entered into a lawful pledge, or a predecessor in title to whom the minor becomes heir, or whether a judicial pledge has arisen from levying execution on his goods in order to follow up a judgment. If the minor has himself constituted the pledge, he is to be protected against sale by the creditor, if such sale will result in harm to him. If the pledge was constituted by a predecessor in title of the minor, a sale made during minority will not entitle a minor to rescission of sale, even if loss appears to have resulted, but he may claim damage from his curators who permitted the sale to take place, or from the pledge-creditor who acted *mala, fide* in connection with the sale—unless there was collusion and fraud between both the creditor making the sale and the purchaser, in which last case the minor will be entitled to rescission of sale (seeing that even majors who suffer loss in this manner are entitled to rescission of sale). If the goods are subject to a judicial pledge or *pignu s praetorium,* and they have been properly sold for the benefit of creditors, and the minor afterwards receives restitution against the sentence or decree by virtue of which the sale took place, he will, indeed, be able to recover the price of the goods thus sold; but the sale will not easily be rescinded by means of restitution, unless it is clear that the minor has sustained excessive or enormous damage *(laesio enormia)* on account thereof. Voet states that the general opinion of Dutch lawyers was that, as the sale of pledges took place with many formalities, such sales should stand, whether the pledge were legally entered into *by* the minor, or by a predecessor in title, and whether for his own or for the predecessor's debt lawfully contracted. The rule as to enormous loss or damage still holds good (4, 4 § 17).

It has been thought best to let the whole of the above passage stand, not discarding the rules of Roman Law on the subject as obsolete. It is submitted that the fact that the sale of pledges took place with formalities—except in the case of sales by judicial decree—would not af-

fect the right of the minor to restitution, especially as the sale of pledges is no longer conducted with the same formalities as were observed in Holland in Voet's time; while the rules of Roman Law appear to be *dictata rectae rationis.* 181. Donations by minors may similarly be rescinded. Although rescission was possible in Roman Law in the case of marriage portions, this does not hold in Dutch Law, as the statutory effect of marriages under Dutch Law is to constitute a community of all property between spouses, unless there be an antenuptial contract (4, 4 §§ 18, 19).

182. Compromise of suits is another matter against which a minor may obtain restitution; likewise division of joint property (4, 4 § 20). 183. If a minor makes payment of that which is legally due by him, on the authority of his guardian, he cannot claim restitution, since he cannot be said to have sustained injury who paid that which he was compellable to pay. If payment were made without his guardian's authority, he may recover such money as still remains in the hands of the payee, but not such as has been spent. It is very doubtful if this distinction would hold at the present day. If a minor pays what is not due by him, it would appear that he can reclaim what has been paid by a *condictio indebiti* in the same manner and subject to the same conditions as bind majors in the same circumstances (4, 4 § 21). 184. If a minor receives payment, by a decree of a Court and through the intervention of his guardian, such payment will operate as a complete discharge of the debtor, and no restitution will be available. If a judicial decree or the guardian's intervention be wanting, payment will not operate as a discharge of the debtor, unless the minor appears to have been enriched (i.e. , to have profited) by the transaction. Where payment has taken place through the intervention of the guardian alone, without judicial decree, the question whether the minor is to have restitution or not will depend on circumstances. By modern law, debtors receive an absolute discharge if they make payment to the guardian of a creditor who is a minor, so

that the Roman Law rules on the subject are practically obsolete (4, 4 §§ 22, 28). 185. Assistance on account of youth is also granted in case of admission to take an inheritance. The distinction between those who are and those who are not *sui heredei* is of no practical importance now. If an inheritance has been adiated by a minor, which turns out to be burdensome to him, he has the right to claim restitution, to this extent, that he may obtain a *separatio bonorum* (4, 4 §§ 28 to 28). 186. Usucapion and prescription admit of restitution on the ground of minority. If a minor has omitted to interrupt the period of usucapion through the weakness of youth, he may claim restitution. In the case of prescription, a minor is not deprived of his remedy if prescription takes place during his minority, according to special statutes laid down in each place on the subject. The general rule is that a minor may obtain relief against prescription (4, 4 §§ 29, 30).

In Cape Colony, prescription against minors is regulated by the Prescription Act, No. 6, 1861, § 6. As to Natal, see Law No. 14, 1861, § o.

187. Besides extra-judicial transactions such as the foregoing, a minor may have restitution in the case of judicial acts, where he suffers loss through insufficiency of proof *(i.e.,* by failing to adduce evidence sufficient to establish his case), or where he has failed to put in his pleadings within the proper time—unless loss occurs to him through contempt or contumacious disobedience of the Court, in which case the minor is not to have restitution (4, 4 § 31).

As a minor has ordinarily a *curator ad litem* in judicial proceedings, restitution of this kind is never likely to be sought. 188. The claim of a minor to restitution or relief against a judicial decree may even be heard, if he considers that he has suffered loss by allowing the time for prosecuting an appeal to go by, or if he desires the granting of relief without appeal, by the same Judge, perchance, as gave the original judgment. Dutch Law does not allow minora to obtain restitution against the sentences of inferior Judges, unless the time for prosecuting an ordinary appeal has gone by, and the power of appealing to a higher Court is then specially granted to them. If there is an invalidity in part of a judgment, the whole sentence must be reversed as invalid. It makes no difference whether the sentence against which restitution is sought is definitive or interlocutory (4, 4 § 82).

The cases in this section are to be distinguished from those mentioned in § 187. That section treats of relief against acts which occur during the course of proceedings in a suit, which relief is sought before judgment is given. If, for instance, a minor has been debarred from pleading, he may claim to have time allowed hiTM to plead. Of course, if judgment has been given against him on default of plea, he may ask to have the case reopened (though, as before stated, this cannot apply where there is a *curator ad litem*). But, when a Court has given judgment against a minor, and he claims restitution on account of the inadmissibility of evidence against him, or some other informality or irregularity whereby he claims to have sustained injury (in that the Court was thereby influenced to give judgment against him), it would seem that the minor has the choice between two remedies: (1) He may petition the Court which gave judgment against him to reopen the case; or (2) he may forthwith go to a higher Court, and ask it to reverse the judgment of the Court below. In the latter case, the judgment is similar in effect to an appeal, but the procedure is by way of petition to secure restitution against the judgment of the Court below.

189. If a widower or widow is in possession of the joint property of the marriage which has been massed (as *boedelhouder),* and has appeared in an action on behalf of himself or herself and the children of the predeceasing spouse, jointly, and a decree has been given in the said cause, the minor children injured by such a decree cannot obtain restitution against the sentence, unless there has been collusion between the parent bringing the suit and the opposing party, or there are grounds which are sufficient to entitle majors to resti-

tution as well (4, 4 § 83). 190. In cases where majors can obtain restitution on account of absence or the operation of a general clause *(clausula generalis)* importing liability, minors may also obtain indemnity as a concession to their youth (4, 4 § 34). 191. Restitution is granted, generally, to a minor against those who have caused injury to him, even against the Treasury when the Treasury has sold the goods of the minor as if they belonged to the Treasury (not on account of a debt due by the minor). If a minor contracts with a *filiusfamilias* (person under paternal power, in modern law a minor), and sustains damage through such contract, Voet says he will have a remedy against the father of such *Jiliusfamilias.* But such remedy would only seem to be available where the father has himself benefited by the contract. If no damage results to either of two minors contracting with each other, restitution will not be granted. As far as third parties are concerned, who obtain possession of things which are disposed of by contract between minors, restitution cannot be claimed against them, unless the third parties acted fraudulently and collusivery in obtaining such possession (4, 4 § 85). 192. Where a minor seeks restitution, all persons who may suffer through such restitution, or to whose interest it will be that such restitution shall not be granted, must be called upon to appear, not only to defend themselves against the claim, but also to ask for restoration to their former position by return of the purchase-price of things bought, or otherwise. If, as previously indicated, another person has unlawfully sold as his own the property of a minor, the minor need not make restoration of the purchase-price. But if creditors have sold a thing by right of pledge, the whole purchaseprice is to be restored, whether we find that the minor has been enriched by the transaction or not. If a minor has himself made sale of his property, on obtaining restitution against such sale he is not liable to restore the purchase-price to the purchaser to an extent greater than he has been enriched by such a transaction. The burden of proving whether, and to what

extent, the minor has been enriched by payment of such purchase-price rests, in Voet's opinion, on the purchaser (4, 4 § 86). 193. When a minor obtains restitution, and renders to his adversary that which is to be rendered to the adversary, he may in turn claim restoration of that whereof he has suffered the loss, such as the thing which he has alienated together with the fruits, or the purchase-price with interest thereon (if he has bought anything that proves burdensome to him, and restores such property on obtaining restitution) (4, 4 § 87). 194. The benefit of youth *(i.e.,* restitution on account of it) is granted not only in respect of things which are wholly real, or wholly personal, but in respect of mixed transactions too. This benefit passes to heirs as well, and so, if a major succeeds to a deceased minor, he is to have a period of four years reckoned from the time of adiation of the inheritance within which to obtain restitution for matters in regard to which the minor, whose heir he is, was or would have been entitled to restitution. If a minor becomes heir to a minor, he is to have a similar period of four years, reckoned from the time when the minor heir becomes a major. If such minor becomes heir to a major who was entitled to such term of four years, and the four years have not expired during such deceased major's lifetime, the minor heir is entitled to avail himself of the right to restitution for the unexpired portion of such term of four years, to be reckoned from the time when such minor heir attains the age of majority (4, 4 § 88).

The position, briefly, is this: A., a minor entitled to restitution, dies without obtaining it. B., his major heir, succeeds to the right of restitution, and has four years in which to avail himself of the right. C, a minor, succeeds to A.; in this case C. has four years after attaining the age of majority. Or C. succeeds to B., three years after B. has succeeded to A. ; in this case C. hasone year after he (C.) attains the age of majority, in which to claim, restitution.

195. The case of sureties of minors is not the same as that of their heirs. Such sureties cannot in general obtain resti-

tution. Grotius agrees with Voet on this point (8, 48, 12), saying that this relief may not be obtained by a surety, who will still remain liable. This circumstance differentiates this kind of relief from others. Voet says the exceptions to this rule are (a) if the minors havebeen injured by fraud on the part of the person opposed to them,, or (6) if sureties have intervened for a minor, not in his capacity as minor, but as sustaining the character of another person. So, if a minor has without a mandate to that effect defended the suit of another person, and given security for satisfaction of the judgment, relief by means of *in integrum restitutio* may be granted not only to him, but to his sureties as well. The same holds good, if a minor heir has given sureties to the creditors of the testator's estate, and afterwards obtains restitution against adiation, for in that case his sureties must obtain the same measure of relief when called upon to make good contracts relating to the inheritance—for that is not a liability on the minor's own contracts, but on the testator's (4, 4 § 89). 196. As regards particular successors of minors, such as legatees or donees, there is no reason why they should be different in this respect from heirs. So, if a minor has left as a legacy, or donated, a thing in respect of which he has rendered himself liable, by pledging it or imposing a servitude upon it, restitution may lawfully be granted to those who have relieved the thing from the bond of pledge or servitude. The same rule does not apply to the case of purchasers from minors of property thus burdened (4, 4 § 40). 197. Restitution is not allowed by virtue of the minor's right to any third parties, besides heirs, sureties, and particular successors. So, when a minor does anything on the mandate of another, from which the person giving the mandate sustains damage, restitution is not even granted to the minor. And if a minor has a thing or cause in common with another, for instance, when minor and major heirs have jointly adiated a burdensome inheritance, or have made sale of a joint property for a lower price than the value, restitution will be grant-

ed to the minors with regard to their share of the inheritance or the thing sold, but not to the majors participating in the same thing, whom the minor's benefit of age will not avail. If, however, the joint purchaser of a property, on the minor receiving restitution as regards his share of the purchase, desires to withdraw wholly from the contract, because it was not his desire to purchase a part of the property but the whole in community, he will be heard (4, 4 §§ 41, 42). 198. Restitution on the ground of minority will be refused if a person is held in interpretation of law to be a major at the time of entering into the contract—when, for instance, he has obtained *venia aetatis,* or is regarded as having attained majority by marrying, or if he has fraudulently represented himself as a major to the person with whom he has contracted, if the other acted *bond fide* and under a genuine mistake; or, finally, if at the time of the contract he was held generally to be a major—not through a foolish mistake or ignorance of law—having acted publicly and fulfilling duties as a major. If a minor acts fraudulently, and represents himself as a major to one who knows that he is in reality a minor, the person so contracting with the minor cannot avail himself of the minor's fraud, as he was aware of the deceit. The proof of knowledge on the part of the person contracting with the minor that the minor pretending to be a major was in reality a minor will be on the minor, since fraud on the part of the other person will not be presumed, unless such person is a blood relation of the minor's, for then the presumption is that he was aware of the minor's age (4, 4 § 43). 199. If a person, having attained majority, ratifies a contract made during minority, he cannot obtain restitution on account of having been a minor at the time he entered into the contract— whether his ratification be express, or deducible from acts and deeds. This holds, for instance, if a minor has been promised a loan of money, and only receives the money after he attains majority. If a transaction be wholly completed during minority, anything done in consequence thereof af-

ter majority does not amount to ratification, as, for instance, where a minor carried on a lawsuit and had judgment given against him during his minority, and after attaining majority satisfies the amount of the judgment (as when a writ of execution is issued against him), he may still obtain restitution. This is so, because things happening as a direct and necessary consequence of a preceding act are regarded as having been transacted at the time of the principal act. If an act done during minority was *ipso jure* null and void, as when a minor's property is alienated without a decree, or when he has contracted without his tutor's or curator's authority, a payment, acceptance, or claim made by him after attaining majority induces a supposition of a tacit ratification —since no one can be compelled by judicial authority to perform an act which is *ipso jure* null and void, whence it follows that fulfilment of such an act after majority necessarily amounts to ratification. If, instead of completing such an act, the minor on attaining majority recommences it *de novo,* his act will be taken to amount to a ratification (4, 4 § 44). 200. A minor cannot obtain restitution against marriage on account of minority alone (4, 4 § 45).

In *Haupt* vs. *Hau.pt* (7 C. T. R. 49; 14 S. C. 39) it was laid down that the marriage of a minor must bo deemed to be valid until annulled by judgment of a competent Court. Minority is not *per se* sufficient ground for annulling a marriage. If either party is entitled to restitution by reason of the fraud of the other, proceedings must be taken within a reasonable time after discovery of the fraud. This *dictum* must be borne in mind in considering the case of *Johimm* vs. *McIntyre* (3 C. T. R. 426; 11 C. L. J. 40; 10 S. C. 318). There the father sought to set aside the marriage, which was solemnised by special licence, without his consent; the special licence had been fraudulently obtained; and the minor child herself objected to the marriage, being a party to the suit to have it set aside. "If the father, knowing of the intended marriage, took no steps to stop it, he was deemed to have given a tacit consent to it, and, in the absence of fraud on the part of either or both of the spouses, the publication of banns, which was compulsory, was considered as notice to the father." See § 142, above.

201. If a minor causes damage under the Aquilian Law (in other words, commits a tort), and this happens through his fraud, he cannot claim restitution. But he will not be liable, if the damage happens through his *culpa levis* or *levissima* (ordinary or slight negligence), without intent to injure (4, 4 § 45). 202. After discussing certain rules of law now obsolete, Voet says that a minor cannot claim restitution for damage which he would have suffered had he been a major—for instance, if the father of a minor or another major person, to whom the minor succeeds, enters into a contract which is burdensome, provided the minor uses the general law: for an heir of whatever age is compellable to make good such a contract of his predecessor. The same thing holds, if accidental damage, due to the act of God, results, for one cannot claim compensation for what happens without the fault of any one (4, 4 §§ 46 to 49). 203. If a person who is a minor, while carrying on a profession, trade or occupation, sustains damage, he cannot claim restitution, since a person cannot profit by his own wrong (4, 4 § 50). This refers to those who enter into agreements in the course of such business, and sustain loss through ignorance of their art or occupation—provided it is clear that the minor so contracting and sustaining damage belongs to the trade in which he is alleged to have been engaged, which is proved from his possession of a shop, office, or other evidence that he carries on business. Here restitution is in conflict with the exercise of a public business. It makes no difference, if to minority is added the fact that one belongs to the female sex, for married women are regarded as acting, not on their own account, but at the instigation of their husbands, and restitution in such a case is granted not so much to the wife as to the husband, who is a major, whether in point of years or by virtue of his mar-

riage (4, 4, §§ 60, 51).

See *Gantz* vs. *Wagenaar* (1 M. 92). In *Gericke* vs. *Keyter* (Buch. 1879, p. 147), where a minor had, with the consent of his tutor dative, gone on a trading trip, and while so trading had exchanged certain oxen for mules, and given a promissory note for the difference in value, his minority was held to constitute no defence to provisional sentenco on the promissory note.

204. If a minor is *ipso jure* freed from liability, he cannot have recourse to restitution—for instance, if landed property of the minor has been sold without a judicial decree; or if he has contracted without consent of his guardian; or if, having a curator, he has contracted a loan without the curator's consent, and has not been benefited thereby (4, 4 § 52). 205. If the minor is not *ipso jure* freed from liability, but has other actions open to him for obtaining an indemnity, he has the choice between bringing such actions and obtaining plenary restitution, where both modes of procedure are available against one and the same person. But where a third person is in question, he must first employ the ordinary mode of procedure. So, where a minor sustains damage on account of a mandate which he has given or accepted, he cannot obtain restitution against a third person so causing damage, unless he cannot be indemnified by a direct or contrary action of mandate. If a minor has given a deposit as security, which was not due, he may proceed against the person to whom he gave such security for the return of the deposit by either a *condictio indtbiti* or a petition for restitution. If a minor has done a thing through the intervention of his tutor or curator, he may obtain restitution, although the action on the guardianship or curatorship against the guardian or curator is still open to him (4, 4 § 58). 206. The remedy of restitution is not to be denied to a minor, who has sustained injury, when his adversary (the person causing the injury) is prepared or offers to adjust the deficiency in the price of the property bought and to make good the difference in value. In such a case the minor may claim a

rescission of the contract, notwithstanding the offer of the other party, and return of the

C.l.—vol. i. K property with its fruits. If, however, the only injury to the minor appears to be that he has sold the property for a lower price, the purchaser's offer to make good the price, together with interest for the period intervening between the sale and the offer, may be entertained (4, 4 § 54).

207. What has thus far been said of minors (with regard to restitution) may be extended to persons declared prodigals, madmen, and others placed under curatorship owing to some defect of body or mind. There is likewise no difference between the law relating to restitution of minors and the law relating to restitution of the

State or the Treasury (4, 4 § 55).

See above, § 92. In the case there quoted, *Collector of Customs* vs. *CajK Central Railways* (6 S. C. 407), it was said, after quoting the maxim *respublica minorum jure uti solet, ideoque anxilinm restitutionis implorare potest,* "if this had been an action to recover money on behalf of minors, the plea that they or their guardian had abandoned their claim would have been bad, when once it was established that, but for such abandonment, they would have been legally entitled to the money." So, in the same way, where a public administrator had abandoned a claim on behalf of the Treasury, the Treasury was, nevertheless, held entitled to recover the amount of the claim.

208. In the case of the Treasury the same reason holds as in the case of minors, that all their affairs are administered by others, and therefore they are unaware of what is done by their administrators, while it is not just that unskilfulness or want of knowledge should harm those who, since they are properly not persons able to act of themselves, cannot administer their own affairs. The same thing,

Voet says, applies to a church, as a corporate body *(ecclesia).* The

Treasury and minors are equal in this respect, that they have a tacit hypothec over the property of their administrators. The rights of the Treasury are superior in this, that it has a tacit hypothec over the property of those who contract with it, and that it has a preference before a minor for tribute and taxes due to it; and, lastly, a sale (apparently by the Treasury itself) of a property to pay taxes due on it may be rescinded, if the property fetches less than the amount of the taxes due, and the debtor or another person offers payment of the full amount of the tax (4, 4 § 55).

The Cape Tacit Hypothec Amendment Act (No. 6, 1861) abolishes the tacit hypothec of the Government on the estates of those entering into contracts with them for the performance of such contracts, with the proviso that no person liable for rent or other periodical payment is to be deemed a contractor. In the Transvaal, by Proc. 28, 1902, § 130, the tacit hypothec of minors on the estates of their guardians or administrators is abolished. By the same section, the tacit hypothecs of the Government for taxes, and on the estates of collectors of revenue, or of contractors with the Government, are also abolished.

209. According to Roman Law, an emancipated son, who was sued in respect of debts contracted while under the paternal control, soon after his emancipation, where he had received nothing, or only a portion of his paternal inheritance not commensurate with the debt, could claim the *beneficium competentiae.* Voet says that this was not the case in Roman-Dutch Law, and Van Leeuwen, Grotius, and Van der Linden are all silent on the subject. Voet says that in Dutch Law a child who was still a minor or under paternal control (i.e. , before his emancipation), could be called upon to fulfil a contract *in solidum,* unless he applied for and obtained the benefit of restitution under the circumstances above detailed in this chapter. The practical effect of the law is that, in addition to the cases in which a minor can claim restitution, he cannot bind himself without the knowledge and assistance of his guardians, except for necessaries, nor can he pass any deed, or appear in law without the immediate assistance of his guardian or a *curator*

ad litem specially appointed for the purpose—except in criminal cases (14, 5 §§ 1—4).

See *Le Roux* vs. *Le lioux and Joel* (Transvaal Official Reports, 1897, p. 100), where an exception was made and sustained on the ground that a minor had been summoned without the assistance of his guardian.

210. The *Senatusconsultum Macedonianum* provided that persons who made money loans to children under paternal power should not institute any action or claim for the recovery of the money against the minors, after the death of the parent in whose power they were. It was passed for the protection of minors who were in the habit of anticipating their right of disposition over prospective property by means of loans, and simply deprived creditors of a subsequent remedy against those to whom they had lent money, as *filiifamilias,* not in the more legitimate commercial transactions of sale or hiring—the object of the law being simply to prevent an anticipation of property. Afterwards the law was extended to all loans, whether of money or other things. To make the law effectual it was sufficient that at the time of the loan the minor should be under power (in *potestate).* Voet mentions the different conditions under which this *Senatusconsultiim* could be applied. In modern law, however, a minor is in the same position with regard to a loan as with regard to any other contract, and the general law relating to restitution sufficiently protects him. The *Senatusconsultum Macedonianum* may be said to be wholly obsolete at the present day. None of the principal Dutch writers mention it as still existing and in force in their day (14, 6 §§ 1—10). 211. Voet next treats of the *peculium* of a child under paternal power. In Roman Law a child might acquire property in various ways, over part of which the father might have the right of disposition *(jus disponendi),* while other things the father could not touch. Such property of the child was known collectively as *peculium* (see § 182, above). It was divided into *(a) peculium militare, (b) peculium quasi cas-*

trense, (c) peculium paganum, (d) peculium profectitium, (e) peculium adventitium ordinarium, (/) peculium adventitium extraordinarium. As modern law places all the property of a minor under the curatorship of his father as natural guardian, or of his tutors testamentary or dative, or curator nominate, the Roman Law does not wholly apply with regard to *peculium.* There are certain modes, however, according to Voet, in which the principles relating to *peculium* apply by way of analogy. There is no doubt, he says, that the Roman Law applies to the acquisition of certain property by minors. His *peculium profectitium* at the present day includes baptismal gifts from sponsors and others (unless an express statement was made to the contrary at the time of making the gift); and of this the parents may have the use. Parents may likewise have the use (not the right of alienation) of things acquired by minor children who are with their parents and supported by their means, as long as the children remain with and are supported by the parents—whether such acquisitions come from the parents or from the labour of the children; and there is no harm in things acquired from the parents reverting to the parents. If, however, a son lives in his father's house, and carries on business separately on his own account, or together with his father, but as a partner, the profit which he acquires by means of such business goes to himself alone, not to the father. Much more will this hold, if the son lives not with the father but separately, or in another country. In the latter case the son, on his side, must support himself, and cannot claim alimony from the father, even if it has been provided in an assignation of the property of one of the predeceasing parents made by the survivor that the survivor so assigning shall have the burden of providing alimony until the children reach majority—since he is considered as providing sufficient support who provides his children with suitable training in arts or workmanship, whereby they are enabled to support themselves honourably in accordance with their condition in life (15, 1

§§ 1—4).

Grotius states that whatever children who are maintained by their parents acquire by way of profit or wages, goes to the parents in full ownership (1, 6, 1). On this Van der Keessel (§ 104) remarks: "That which children acquire in «ither Service i.e., military or civil they should have solely for themselves, by light of *pecuhum cagtrensc,* even after the death of the father; but that which they acquire by their own industry passes, by right of *peculium profectitium,* to the father, and even to a mother by whom they are maintained. In the latter class, however, gifts made to the children by their sponsors cannot properly be included, as decided by the Supreme Court" of Holland. Schorer has the following note on Grotius *Muaadorp,* p. 381): "What children acquire by their own labour and industry is acquired for their parents; nor may the children keep back any of it for themselves, it being reckoned as a set-off against their maintenance, even though the father or mother may have promised to maintain the children till their majority, in consideration of the usufruct of the goods of the predeceased parents" adopting Voet's views as stated in other words in this section, "for in that case he or she is considered as having in addition had in contemplation the profit to be derived from the labour of the children. An exception must, however, be made where a son who is a famous artificer has very largely increased his father's estate, more especially so in the case of a division of an inheritance between a stepfather or stepmother and stepchildren, in which case some moderate siun. .. must be awarded to the son before the division is proceeded with"—such sum to be awarded by a third party, a *louus vir.* Two problems arise in connection with the foregoing opinions: (1) Has the father the absolute *dominium* over his son's property acquired as above? In Roman Law, according to *Colipthnun* (§ 1044), "such *profectitium* belongs altogether to the father—that is to say, he has the legal estate and civil possession thereof; the children have nothing but the corporeal possession and admin-

istration.... If the father emancipate his children without demanding this *peculium,* he is held to have tacitly given it to them; in case of the father's death, however, the children must account for such *peculium profectitium* in the schedule of the estate." This passage would seem to imply that the father must actively, by word or deed, assert his ownership over the *peculium;* otherwise, on the son's emancipation, by majority or other liberation from paternal control, the son could take his *peculium profectitium.* When the father died, however, the son had to bring this *peculium* into collation. Now if the son could thus acquire the administration of the *peculium,* his father could not have had *dominium plenum* (full ownership) over it. Some colour is lent to this view by the fact that Voet never uses the word *dominium in* connection with the father's power over the *peculium profectitium.* It would be interesting to know what was the exact limit of the father's *jus disponendi.* (2) Were baptismal gifts made by sponsors subject to the law governing other *peculium,* consequently vested in the parents'? Voet, in the foregoing passage, says that such gifts were regarded as *peculium profectitium,* except when tho contrary was expressly stated. Van der Keessel quotes the decision of the Supreme Court to the effect that they were not so regarded, without making any distinction. Van Leeuwen *(R. D. L. ,* 1 Kotze, p. 454; 3,16, 7) inclines to Voet's view, stating that "it was held by the Supreme Court that presents given to the children by their godparents *(pil-gaven)* must on a division be first of all awarded to such children, for they are given not to the parents but to the children, and are not derived out of the estate of the parents." However, Van Leeuwen then mentions cases in which the Court of Holland held that " gifts made by godparents to the children belong to the parents of the children, and accordingly may be claimed by creditors." After adverting to the Placaats on the subject of baptismal giftt, he proceeds: "We ought still to understand that presents made by godparents *(pil-gaven),* in so far as they aro not of con-

siderable value, belong not to the parents but to the children, and ought to be received by them in advance before a division, as having been made to them by way of remembrance." Van dor Keessel's note simply refers to Van Leeuwen, and it must be taken that the decision of the Court of which Van der Keessel speaks is that first mentioned byVan Leeuwen, which Van Leeuwen himself says is not general Roman-Dutch Law. One can, therefore, have no hesitation in discarding Van der Keessel's view. Van Leeuwen himself, in the sentence last quoted, is somewhat ambiguous, as he does not indicate where the line is to be drawn in regard to gifts "not of considerable value." Voet's opinion, on tho other hand, is clear and unequivocal, and therefore seems preferable.

212. If a son who lives with his father or mother, and has carried on business, not separately, nor in partnersbip with a parent, but on account of and for the use of the parent, and has by his industry considerably increased the parent's means, he ought to obtain a share of his earnings even after the death of the parent, and equity lays down that before the inheritance is divided a certain amount, to be fixed on the arbitration of a *bonus vir,* shall be awarded to the son in compensation for his labours in thus increasing the paternal or maternal estate (15, 1 § 5).

Van Leeuwen (cmis. *For.* 1, 2, 12, 4) says: "If a son by his labour and industry has greatly increased his father's property, account must be taken of this in dividing the estate left by the father, umpires being appointed who aro to decide how much more the son ought to take on account of this profit." The modern practice in the law of inheritance would not seem to allow of such an adjudication being made.

213. As regards the *peculium adventitium (ordinarium,* whatever the children gain neither from or through the father—*profectitium* being everything received from the father, or which comes to the *Jdiusfamilias* through the father—but by their own exertions, from their mother or other persons; *extraor-*

dinarium, where the property has been gained against the father's wish), Dutch Law, differing in this respect from Roman Law (see § 132, above), provides that a father has not the usufruct of the *peculium adventitium,* unless those who have bequeathed or donated the property to the child have expressly given the usufruct to the father, or the usufruct is necessary for the bringing up of the children (15, 1 § 6).

The distinctions between the various kinds of *peculium* are not very clearly drawn. What is acquired from the parents may be used by them, and the parents have also the use of what is earned by their unemancipated children who are with them and not carrying on business; the same applies, in Voet's view, to gifts from sponsors. Things derived by children from other sources, by way of gift or inheritance, or where they carry on an independent business and earn an income therefrom, belong absolutely to the children, and parents have not even the usufruct, unless this is specially given to them.

214. With respect to every kind of *peculium profectitium* an action lies against the father and the proprietor of the *peculium* irrespective of sex or age, and against any possessor thereof, whether heirs, legatees, or any other into whose hands the *peculium* comes. This action originates when the father has given his son a *peculium profectitium.* If there are several owners, the action lies against them *singuli in solidum.* But if there are several heirs to one man, the action lies against them jointly, in proportion to their shares. The object of this action is to obtain the surrender of whatever the *pectdium* consists in, to be calculated as to value at the time judgment is given (15, 1 §§ 7—10). 215. According to Dutch Law, 'parents are not liable on the contracts of their children where they have not given their authority or consent. Hence, if a son has paid a debt after his father's death, which the son contracted while paternal control still existed, he cannot have any claim for the amount of the debt against his father's other heirs—unless either he contracted on the authority or com-

mand of his father, or his father entered into a contract on his (the son's) behalf (15, 1 § 11). 216. If a *peculium* is extinguished or disappears (by death, emancipation, or alienation), the action *peculio* also vanishes. Equity has, however, given a year within which to bring this action, to be reckoned from the period after the extinction of the *peculium* when the right to vindicate it first accrued—unless the law specially provides that certain actions brought in respect of the *peculium* shall be prescribed before that time (15, 2 §§ 1—4). This action *de peculio* was one brought by creditors for recovery of debts contracted in connection with, the *peculium.* It was given on the contract or quasi-contract of the son, but not on his delicts, unless the father had profited by such delict *(Voet,* 15, 1 § 7), or unless the son had previously been condemned for the delict, and so bound his *peculium* for the amount of damages awarded. It lay even if, at the time of joinder in issue *(litis contestatio),* nothing was found in the *peculium (i.e.,* if the *peculium* amounted to nothing), for the action was personal, although when there was a *peculium* it might be directed *in rem (Voet,* 15, 1 §§ 9, 7).

217. According to Dutch Law, if a *JUiusfamilias,* being a minor under age, dies during his father's lifetime, a claim is to be brought on his contract in an action *de peculio* within one year, not against the father, but against the heirs of the deceased son *in solidnm*—which will include the father, if he is heir to his son (15, 2 § 5). 218. There is also an action known as the action *de in rem verso,* which lies in favour of those who have given a loan to a *JUiusfamilias,* which has been applied to the uses of the father. It lies against the father; and claims whatever has been applied to the father's use, together with interest—either that agreed upon or that which arises from delay in payment *(mora).* It makes no difference whether the father knows or does not know that the money has been applied to his uses, as long as the creditor is in a position to prove that the son concluded the business directly for the benefit of his father, or that

he applied that which he may have received to his father's purposes, and, further, that the money alleged to be so supplied was actually paid over by the creditor. It is not sufficient, if the son purported to receive the money on his father's behalf, but did not apply it to his father's purposes. If only a portion of the loan has been applied to the father's uses, the action will lie for such portion only. If the son originally received the loan neither on his father's behalf nor to be applied to his father's uses, but for his *peculium,* and then, changing his mind, applies it to his father's uses, the action *de in rein verso* will also lie, for the father should not be enriched by the creditor's loss (15, 8 §§ 1—8). 219. It makes a difference whether the loan has been contracted of necessity, for use, or for pleasure. If a loan has been given to be applied to the necessities of the father, the whole amount is recoverable; if it has been given only for his use or advantage, so much only as has been useful or advantageous to the father is recoverable; if the son has contracted a loan to obtain food and clothing, the father's position in life must be looked to, and only so much as is reasonable in accordance with the father's position is claimable. Loans for extravagances of the son, or to the extent to which they are used for extravagant purposes, are not recoverable. If a son makes payments in error to persons whom he supposes to be creditors of his father, and contracts a loan for the purpose, the action *de in rem verso* will lie against the father, unless the son has made these payments on his own behalf, and in respect of his own *pectdium* (15, 8 §§ 4, 5). 220. If a son has contracted a loan for the purpose of procuring clothes, and obtains the clothes, but loses the money before making payment to the tailor, the father will in both cases be bound for a conversion to his own uses, and will, strictly speaking, be liable both to return the loan and pay for the clothes, as both contracts were made for his benefit. But, as it would be wrong to condemn the father *de in rem verso* (as for a conversion to his uses), Voet holds that the condition of the possessor will be the better in law. The same, he says, will hold if the garment as well as the money has been lost or destroyed (15, 8 §§ 6, 7).

Yoet's opinion here seems to be that, if the clothes are made, but not delivered, the maker of them may keep the clothes, while the man who lent the money to the son loses it. The theory of the action *de in rem verso* must be carefully borne in mind. It is for the father's benefit that his son is supplied with clothing, or with a loan to procure clothing. Now, if the father authorises the son to get the loan or the clothing, he will be liable for both debts, as on a contract of agency. But, if the son gets the loan or the clothing without the paternal authority, it will be necessary, in order to hold the father liable by the action *de in rem verso,* to show that the money actually cable to the use of thfr son, and, *per consequentiam,* to the use of his father. If the son got the money and lost it, he never had the use of it, and therefore the father cannot be liable. If the clothes were made but not delivered to the son, he did not have the useof them, and thus the father cannot be held liable. But, with all deference to the great authority of Voet, it must be submitted that, if the clothes were delivered to the son, the father cannot escape liability. The giving of a loan to procure clothes, and the making of clothes, are two contracts entirely independent of each other.

221. The action *quodjussu* is a personal action given to a creditor who has contracted with the son on the authority of the father, whether such authority be general or special; and lies against the father, claiming the amount for which the father gave his authority to the contracting of the debt. If the creditor exceeds this amount, he cannot recover the excess by this action, but must recover it by the action *de peeulio* or a similar process. This action does not lie, if a man has authorised a loan to one who is not in his paternal power, or if the person giving his authority for the loan has revoked it before the loan is made, or if he has only authorised his son to execute the contract (but not to

be liable on it), or if he has stood surety for his son so contracting—because in such a case he is regarded not in his position of father, but as a stranger. The action does not lie if a ward has contracted without his guardian's authority. If a tutor, curator, or any one appointed to administer affairs of State, authorises a loan to the minor or to the State, an action *quod jussu* may be brought against them, if the loan was to their personal advantage. A father is liable on a direct action of mandate, where he has given his son a mandate to contract a loan (15, 4 §§ 1-8). CHAPTER III. GUARDIAN AND WARD. 222. It is a fixed rule of law that the government of children is left to their father, as long as he has them in his power, unemancipated. If, for any reason, the paternal power fails, children who are still unemancipated are placed under guardianship. Guardianship is the right and power to protect one who is unable, on account of his age, to defend himself. Similar in many respects to guardianship is curatorship, which is the right and power of protecting the property of one who on account of his age or weakness of body or mind is unable to protect such property himself. Frequently a person called *actor* or *adjutor tutelae* (joint guardian) is appointed by the Judge or by the Head of the State (Governor), when the guardian is himself prevented from carrying on the business of the guardianship. Such appointment may take place at the desire and risk of the guardian, or he may apply for the Judge's sanction to the appointment, if the minor is absent (26, 1 § 1).

The Cape law of guardianship, in addition to what is laid down in RonianDutch Law, is to be found in the Ordinance No. 105 of 1833. The Ordinance (§ 23) specially enacts that the Dutch Law on the paternal and maternal authority over, and the maintenance and education and custody of, minors in vogue prior to the passing of the Ordinance, is to be retained. At the Cape the assumption of other tutors by testamentary tutors is regulated by Ordinance 105, § 8. As to Natal, see Act No. 19, 1894, § 6. As to the Transvaal,

see Proc. 28, 1902, §§73—113. As to Orange River Colony, see Orphan Chamber Law, §§48—51.

223. Guardianship carried with it a certain public obligation, inasmuch as it might be imposed on persons against their will, provided they had no just ground of excuse (26, 1 § 2). 224. The duties of guardianship are gratuitous, unless the guardian is in poverty, when he may receive a salary or solatium from the person appointing him (26, 1 § 2).

Prom the fact that a guardiau who was in povorty might be paid, the Cape Supreme Court deduced tho supposition that guardians who wero paupers or insolvent had held office without objection in Holland under Roman-Dutch Law; and on this a decision was founded, in *De Villiers* vs. *Stuckeris* (1 M. 377), to the effect that a guardian is not *ipso facto* deprived of office by reason of his insolvency. But see now Ordinance 105, 1833, § 17, and § 282 of this work. See also *Cens. For.* 1, 1, 16, 23.

225. All persons who are able to make testaments may become guardians; likewise all who are not by law prohibited from acting as guardians. Roman-Dutch Law prohibits a person from acting as guardian before attaining the age of majority, and thereby becoming emancipated from paternal power (26, 1 § 8). 226. Debtors or creditors of minors are prohibited from acting as their guardians if the fact of their being debtors or creditors affords a just ground for exemption. This is left to judicial discretion. Those are prohibited whom the father or the mother (after the father's death) in their testaments have forbidden to act as guardians. In modern law, all ecclesiastics and ministers of religion may act as guardians, though they may excuse themselves on the ground that they are ecclesiastics. If a minor pretends to be a major, and so takes upon himself a guardianship, he will be liable on the guardianship just as if he had actually been a major, while fraudulently giving himself out as one (26, 1 § 4).

The Cape Act No. 22, 187G, § 1, enacts that, "If any person shall attest the execution of any will or other testamentary instrument, and such person or the wife or husband of such person shall in and by such will or other testamentary instrument be nominated or appointed guardian thereunder, the appointment of such person or the wife or husband of such person as such guardian shall be null and void." This statute has been adopted, in identical terms, in the Transvaal (Law 7, 1895, § 4). As to Natal, see Law 2, 1868, § 7, whereby the appointment of a witness as guardian stands.

227. If a minor receives *renia aetatis*, or becomes emancipated by marriage, he cannot be compelled, against his will, to accept a guardianship (26, 1 §§ 5, 6). 228. Guardians are appointed to persons, not to things, unless that follows as a natural sequence, so that, in case of doubt, a guardian is considered to have been appointed to a whole patrimony (i.e., to the charge of the minor's property as well as to the control over the minor's actions). It makes no difference whether the ward consents to the guardian's appointment or not —since a guardian may be given to a minor both without bis knowledge and against his will. Nor does it matter whether the ward is legitimate or illegitimate. If a minor is insane, he is to receive a person to control his actions, not as curator to a lunatic, but as guardian over a ward (26, 1 § 7). 229. Guardianship may he threefold: testamentary, legitimate, and dative. There is no natural guardianship in Dutch Law—see *Shepstone* vs. iVeiZ. N. L.R. 1867, p. 9 (26, 1 § 8). 230. Testamentary guardianship is that which is constituted by a father (or paternal grandfather), whereby a guardian is appointed over children still under paternal power, by means of a testament or a codicil confirmed in a testament—provided such testament is the last will of the deceased, and is not revoked, falsified, or invalidated on any ground. It makes no difference whether the father so making a testament was a major or a minor (26, 2 § 1). 231. Tutors or guardians are granted to all minor children under paternal power, whether male or female; and so, if a will makes mention of "sons," without mentioning

the female children, the daughters are regarded as included under the same appointment; but, on the contrary, when "daughters" only are mentioned, sons are not regarded as therein included (since, Voet adds naively, it would be a very bad example, that males should be comprehended in an epithet relating to females). Under the appellation of "sons" or "daughters" are also included posthumous children, but not children already born, of whom the testator was unaware, and whose inclusion he could not have intended. Clearly, if a testator appointed a guardian to "my son," and he had several sons, of whose existence he is aware, the appointment must be taken to refer to all the sons (26, 2 § 2). 232. It makes no difference whether the children, over whom a guardian has been appointed, have been instituted as heirs or disinherited (26, 2 § 8). 233. Testamentary tutors are appointed unconditionally, or from a certain date, or to a certain date, or under certain conditions. Such a day or condition is in Dutch Law considered to have been tacitly included, if spouses have instituted their children as heirs and have left the usufruct of all their property to each other mutually; inasmuch as the tutors appointed under the will (assuming that neither of the surviving spouses is appointed tutor) cannot interfere with the administration of the property while the usufruct lasts, but must allow the usufructuary to administer the property, though they may demand an inventory (26, 2 § 4).

The case above referred to is that where the surviving spouse is *boedelhouder* or administrator of the joint estate, but there is another testamentary guardian. Where the survivor is at the same time *boedelhouder* and tutor, the Cape Ordinance No. 105, 1833, § 18, provides that such survivor may make a sealed inventory, to be transmitted to the Master of the Supreme Court, under conditions set forth in the Ordinance. Where the surviving spouse is not appointed by the will *boedelhouder* or administrator of the joint property, the tutor testamentary may get an inventory (Ord. 105, § 22) from the survivor under conditions reg-

ulated by § 14 of Ordinance No. 104, 1833. As to Transvaal, see Proc. 28, 1902, §§ 89, 14, 16 and 18. As to Natal, see Act 38, 1899, § 10, whereby the Dutch law as to *boedelhouderschap* is retained.

234. A tacit condition is presumed, when a minor or a lunatic is appointed tutor under a will, namely, that the minor shall have become a major, or the lunatic be restored to his right mind, before either undertakes the guardianship. A guardian may be appointed on condition that he is willing, or that he is able, to undertake the guardianship (26, 2 § 4). 235. There is nothing in the old Dutch Law to prevent a paternal grandfather, a mother, a maternal grandfather, or even other blood relations, from appointing a guardian, even if the father has already by testament appointed a guardian over his children. Such guardians may have administration with reference to what is bequeathed to or directed to be done for the children by the will of the person appointing them, so long as their sphere of action, does not conflict with the administration of the guardian appointed by the father. There is no doubt that tutors may be appointed under codicils not confirmed by testament, just as if they had been appointed by testament. Van Leeuwen disposes *(Cens. For.* 1, 1, 16, 4) of this question as follows: "Can a guardian be appointed by codicils where a man dies intestate as having made no will? All authorities say he cannot. Yet in our Roman-Dutch practice nothing is more frequent, because there is little or no difference between a will and a codicil, as to the formalities, force, and effect of the instrument; so much so, that the appointment of an heir is not necessary to the validity of a will, and it is generally admitted that an inheritance may be directly given or taken away by codicils. " From this, says Voet, it follows that it is not necessary in Dutch Law, in order that a tutor appointed by will may assume his guardianship, that the inheritance under the testament shall have been adiated (26, 2 § 5).

At first sight the above opinion of Van Leeuwen, which is adopted by Voet, may seem to conflict with what is laid down in § 230, above, concerning the appointment of guardians by codicils. But there is nothing inconsistent in the two passages.

236. If a tutor testamentary has been properly appointed, there is no need, in general Koman-Dutch Law, for a judicial confirmation of his appointment (26, 3 § 1).

The Cape Ordinance 105, § 2, enacts that no tutor testamentary shall assume or enter upon the administration or management of the estate or property of any minor, except in so far as may be necessary for the preservation and safe custody of the same, until letters of confirmation shall have been granted to him by tho Master of the Supreme Court. As to the Transvaal, see Proc. 28, 1902, § 74; as to Natal, see Act 38, 1899, §§ 25 and 28—32, and 38.

237. If tutors, without receiving letters of confirmation (this must now be taken generally, although in Dutch Law letters of confirmation were only required in certain cases), interfere in any way with the property of the minors, they will be liable, not only in an *actio tutelae* (to account for their guardianship), but in an *actio negotiorum gestorum* to make good all or any loss the minors' property may have sustained (26, 3 § 1).

See Cape Ordinance 105, 1833, §§ 2 and 8; Natal Act 38, 1899, §§ 10, 16, and 25, and Natal Act 19, 1894, § 6; Transvaal Proc. 28, 1902, § 74; O. R. C. Statutes, chap. 54, § 48.

238. Tutors may be confirmed without inquiry, or after inquiry when security is not given, or after inquiry made and security given. There need be no inquiry, where the father appoints a tutor when leaving something to an emancipated son, or to a natural son, or by codicil not confirmed by testament, or by testament which is invalidated or destroyed. In such cases the Judge or the official appointed by the Court (in South Africa the Master of a superior Court) may appoint a tutor dative without inquiring into the appointment of a tutor testamentary specially appointed under such circumstances. In confirming a tutor's appointment, inquiry should be made as

to whether it was always the father's intention that the appointment should stand—for instance, where the father of the minor has quarrelled with the designated guardian, or the guardian is found guilty of crime or immoral conduct, or similar circumstances (26, 8 § 2). 239. Confirmation by inquiry without the giving of security is to be made when the father has appointed a guardian to his natural son, to whom he has left nothing, or where a mother or grandmother has placed a son or grandson under tutelage (26, 8 §§ 3, 4).

The following rules with regard to the confirmation and appointment of tutors testamentary and tutors dative are enacted by the Cape Ordinance 105, 1S33: (re) See note to § 236. (6) Only the father of any minor or mother of any minor whose father is dead may by will or deed appoint a tutor or tutors to care for the person or administer the estate of the minors, (c) Any person bequeathing property to minors or lunatics may appoint curators to administer such property during such minority or lunacy, (d) Letters of confirmation to tutors testamentary are to be granted upon application in writing made to the Master, on production of a valid deed of appointment, (e) Where the Master finds that a person appointed tutor testamentary has not made application for confirmation, he must write to such person asking him if he is willing to act, and if such person consents, letters of confirmation are granted. This abolishes the Roman Law rule that guardians could not refuse to act. (/) No letters of confirmation are to bo granted to persons legally incapacitated or disqualified. *(g)* Curators nominate must similarly be confirmed. (A) The security for the administration of the minor's property, as required by Roman-Dutch Law, must still be given, (i) "Where there are no natural guardians or tutors testamentary, the Master must by edict call on the minor's paternal and maternal relations to attend on a day not less than three nor more than eight weeks from publication of the edict, either at his office or at a magistrate's office, to put in objections, if an-, or to propose a person or per-

sons as tutors dative. The Master shall then appoint a tutor or tutors dative. The persons to be selected are the mother and one or more of the nearest paternal or maternal male relations, above the age of twenty-one, who are willing to act. If any valid objection exists to the appointment of such persons, they shall be passed over, and some other fit person appointed. Such appointment of the Master is subject to review by the Supreme Court, on application by any relations, paternal or maternal, *(j)* Any assumed tutor or curator must receive letters of confirmation. (£) On death, incapacity, or removal from office of any tutor, testamentary, dative, or assumed, similar proceedings to those enacted previously with regard to the appointment of a tutor dative see sub-section (»') shall again be taken. (*l*) Letters of confirmation may be revoked by the Supreme Court or a Circuit Court, if it is shown that the deed appointing the tutor is null; or the Master may revoke the appointment of tutors dative, if a valid deed appointing a tutor testamentary be produced (§§ 1—11).

In Natal, by Act 19, 1894, § 6, the Registrar of Deeds grants letters of administration to tutors testamentary. By Natal Act 38, 1899, §§25 and 21, tutors dative are appointed in the same way as executors dative. As to the Orange River Colony, see the Statute Book, Chap. 54, §§ 48—51.

The Transvaal rules for the appointment and duties of tutors testamentary and tutors dative are contained in Proc. 28, 1902, §§ 73—99. They are, briefly, as follows: (a) Only the father, or the mother where the father is dead or has abandoned the minors, may by will or deed nominate and appoint tutors. But other persons who give or bequeath property may appoint curators to manage such property during the minority or insanity of the legatee or donee. (6) Tutors testamentary cannot act without letters of confirmation from the Master, save for the purpose of preserving the minor's property, (c) The Master grants letters of confirmation to tutors testamentary or to curators nominate, *(d)* Curators nominate and tutors testamentary must give security *ran pupilli sulvam fore,* when ordered to do so by the Supreme Court or a Judge on the application of the Master, (e) Failing tutors testamentary, the Master appoints tutors dative. A notice of meeting of next-of-kin of the minor, paternal and maternal, is published by the Master in the *Gazette.* At the meeting, or upon the report of the Resident Magistrate of the district where the minor resides, the Master appoints a tutor dative. Where there is no property of the minor besides what is in the hands of a curator nominate, or of the Master himself, the Master need not, though he may, call a meeting to appoint a tutor dative. (/) The Master's appointment of a tutor dative is subject to review by the Supreme Court or a Judge, *(y)* A tutor testamentary or curator nominate may assume some other person as tutor of any minor or curator of the estate, under any power committed to such tutor testamentary or curator nominate by will or deed, *(h)* If any tutor, testamentary or assumed, or any curator, nominate or assumed, dies or becomes incapacitated, the Master appoints another tutor or curator in the same way as tutors dative are appointed, (i) The Supreme Court or a Judge may revoke the appointment of a tutor testamentary or curator nominate if the will or deed appointing either is null, or has been revoked. The Master may rovoke the appointment of a tutor dative on production of a valid will appointing a tutor testamentary. (/) The Master may appoint a curator dative to the property of absentees, *(k)* Under the Common Law, the Supreme Court or a Judge may, where necessary, appoint a curator *ad litem,* or a curator *bonis.* (I) Tutors dative or assumed, and curators dative and curators *bonis,* must give security for due administration. (m) All the disqualifications at Common Law for the offices of tutor and curator still apply. (. «) On insolvency, tutors and curators are *ipso facto* removed from office, (o) Executors, tutors, and curators may, for cause shown, be removed or suspended by the Supreme Court or any Judge. *(p)* Tutors and curators must make an inventory of property in their charge.

They have the ordinary duties and liabilities of tutors and curators at Common Law. They cannot alienate immovable property without an order of Court. They must file proper accounts of their administration.

240. Voet then treats of legitimate tutors, those who step into the position of guardians on failure of tutors testamentary. As the invariable modern practice (regulated by statute) is to appoint tutors dative on failure of tutors testamentary, the selection of tutors

C.Ii.—vol. I. L legitimate need not now be discussed. The only legitimate tutors at the present time are the parents, the father having precedence over the mother. The father cannot by testament prohibit the mother from becoming guardian to her children, unless he at the same time indicates in his will another person who shall be guardian of the children. A mere prohibition of the mother's guardianship will not suffice. On the other hand, the Court caunot confirm as guardians those whom the father or mother has prohibited bywill from acting as guardians (except where the mother is prohibited in the circumstances just mentioned) (26, 4 §§ 1—3).

The phrase "natural guardian" is sometimes used in practice in speaking of father and mother. But, strictly speaking, there is no natural guardian known to Roman-Dutch Law. The only guardians are guardians legitimate, testamentary, assumed, and dative.

241. Modern law leaves it almost entirely to the judicial discretion as to who shall be confirmed or rejected as guardians. Where a mother has been appointed guardian by will or by decree of the Court, or becomes such by operation of law, she is not taken to renounce such guardianship by a second marriage or by virtue of a renunciation of the *Senatusconsultum Velleianum.* A person who has been appointed tutor testamentary by the father of minors remains their guardian, if he marries the mother of the minors (26, 4 §§ 4—6). 242. Tutors dative are given to minors who are subject to the jurisdiction of the Court or official appointing the tutors dative, whether they are subject by reason of

having such jurisdiction as their place of origin *(ratione originis),* or by reason of having their domicile in that place *(ratione domicilii),* or by reason of having property there *(ratione rerum ad se pertinentium,* which would also include transactions affecting the minors, as well as the actual possession of property). If there is a competition, with regard to the appointment of guardians, between the judicial officers of the place where the minor is domiciled, and the place whence he originates (his native land), the magistrate or Judge of the place whence the minor derives his origin is entitled to make the appointment of guardian (26, 5 §§ 1, 2).

In *Letterstedt's Curator ad litem* vs. *Letterstedt't Executors* (Buch. 1875, p. 42), where the plaintiff, who had been appointed curator *ad litem* to a minor, "with power to institute any action which he may be advised on behalf of the aaid minor," brought an action for the amendment of certain accounts relative to the testator's estate, and the minor on whose behalf the action was brought was at that time in a foreign country (Sweden), the defendants excepted to the claim on the ground that when the order was made the minor was out of the jurisdiction of the Court. It was decided, on the authority of the foregoing statement of Voet, and of Burge (vol. 3, p. 1005), that the exception was bad, as the jurisdiction of the Court to appoint a curator existed *ratione bonorum* as well as *rati&ue domicilii.*

With regard to the authority of foreign guardians, Dicey *(Conflict of Laws,* rule 130) lays down the rule of English Law that "a guardian appointed under the law of a foreign country has no direct authority as guardian in England; but the Court recognises the existence of a foreign guardianship, and may, in its discretion, give effect to a foreign guardian's authority over his ward." Where two minors, Austrian subjects, were sent to England for education, the Court of Chancery *(Nugent* vs. *Vetzcra,* L. R. 2 Eq. 704) refused to interfere with the discretion of the guardian, appointed by an Austrian

Court of competent jurisdiction, when he wished to remove them from England in order to complete their education in Austria; but, English guardians having been already appointed, the Court refused to discharge the order by which they were appointed, and merely reserved to the foreign guardian the exclusive custody of the children to which he was entitled by order of the foreign Court (Dicey, p. 494). It was said: "With regard to the English guardians of these children, I hold that the Court has power to appoint them, and I continue those that have been appointed.... Out of respect to the authority of the Austrian Courts, by which this gentleman has been appointed, I reserve to him, in the order I am about to make, all such power and control as might have been exercised over these children in their own country if they were there, and had not been sent to England for a temporary purpose." 243. A judicial officer can lawfully appoint as tutors such persons only as are subject to his jurisdiction. It makes no difference, however, whether the tutor is present or absent at the time of his appointment, so long as he is subject to the jurisdiction, and signifies his willingness to be appointed within a reasonable time, according to Roman Law, thirty days (26, 5 § 8).

244. No one may appoint himself as guardian. In modern practice, the administration of estates is often left to Orphan Chambers. At the present day, they have no power of appointing tutors, who are all appointed by the Master of the Supreme Court, unless the father or mother has designated a tutor testamentary (26, 5 §§ 4, 5). 245. On failure of tutors, certain persons may ask for tutors to be appointed to minors, such as their cognate and agnate relations, relations by affinity, the friends of their parents, and those entrusted with their education. Those who desire to bring an action against minors, or to obtain eviction of a thing bought from the minor, must first of all obtain the appointment of a tutor or curator to the minor, by petition to the judicial officer who has the appointment of tutors. In the same way a guardian, on the com-

pletion of his guardianship, when he desires to render an account of his administration, must, at Common Law, failing statutory directions, obtain the appointment, or must counsel the minor to obtain the appointment, of a curator, to supervise the affairs of the minor (26, 6 § 1). 246. On failure of tutors, a mother may obtain the appointment of guardians, whether her children be legitimate or illegitimate. The mother must also obtain the proper confirmation of a tutor not properly appointed by the father or grandfather, where the latter has the power of appointing tutors testamentary. Since guardianship in Dutch Law extends to the age of majority, nothing prevents minors who have reached the age of puberty from applying for the appointment of guardians to themselves (26, 6 §§ 2—4). 247. As soon as guardians have ascertained that they have been lawfully appointed or confirmed, and cannot excuse themselves on any lawful ground, they are bound forthwith to administer the affairs of the minor, and to look after their moral training and education. If they fail in any of these respects, they not only do so at their own risk, being liable to make good all damage suffered through their negligence, but they may in addition be compelled to carry out their administration, forfeiting pledges or securities they have given, or they may even be fined. But all tutors are not liable to administer—for instance, honorary tutors are not compellable: when the father, appointing several tutors testamentary, imposes the liability of administration on one of them alone; or when one of the tutors testamentary, or of those appointed after inquiry, gives security for the indemnification of the minor, and has preference over his co-tutor or co-curator in the administration; in which case the others have the burden of the administration, but no risk attaches to them (26, 7 § 1).

Where the defendant, at the request of the deceased wife of the father of certain minors, "kindly took upon himself," together with such father, who had married a second time after executing a notarial deed of kinderbevnje (bond to se-

cure their portions of inheritance to the children from the estate of the first wife), the guardianship of the minors, and the father became insolvent, owing a large amount to the children of his first marriage, the defendant, as superintending guardian, was sued for the deficiency in the father's estate, of which the father had continually had the administration. It was decided that the defendant, as a mere tutor honorarius, was not liable (Brink vs. Smuts, 3 M. 81). 248. The administration of a guardian is preceded by the giving of security and the preparation of an inventory (26, 7 § 2).

The Cape Ordinance 105, 1833, § 5, enacts " that it shall and may be lawful for the Supreme Court or any Judge thereof, on the application of the Master thereof, or of any relation, or of any person having an interest in the due administration of the estate or property of any minor, in every case in which, prior to the passing of this Ordinance (i.e., under general Roman-Dutch Law), any tutor testamentary might by law have been required to give security rem pupilli sal mm fore, to make an order that letters of confirmation shall not be granted to any such tutor testamentary or curator nominate as aforesaid until he shall have found security to the satisfaction of the said Master to such an amount as in the circumstances of each particular case shall be reasonable, for the due and faithful administration and management of such estate or property. " § 16 of the Ordinance enacts " that every tutor dative and every curator dative who shall be appointed by the Master of the Supreme Court or any Court or Judge to administer the estate or property of any minor or lunatic or insane or absent person shall, before he shall be permitted to enter on the administration of such estate or property," find security to a reasonable amount in accordance with the circumstances of the case to the Master's satisfaction. These enactments practically re-state the Roman-Dutch Law, which still applies with regard to security. See the Natal, Transvaal, and O. R. C. Statutes, previously mentioned. The Rhodesia law is the same as that of Cape Colony.

249. With reference to security, all guardians and curators are bound to promise, on the bond of such security, that they will appear for the minor in actions at law. If they refuse to appear in such actions, they are not only responsible for any damage, but are liable to removal from office. Voet next mentions certain persons, such as tutors testamentary and tutors appointed after inquiry, who were exempted from giving security; but such exemptions may safely be said no longer to apply, with the statutory exceptions previously referred to (26, 7 § 2).

Van Leeuwen (Cent. For. 1, 1, 17, 3) says: "Since all a guardian's property is subject to a legal lien for proper administration, and by reason of the onerous duty he already bears, it is scarcely possible to add to his burden; and, further, since in our day all guardians are invariably appointed or confirmed in their appointment, after due inquiry; the above-mentioned security is not so necessary in our practice, but is manifestly discretionary; the exacting of it being entrusted to the fidelity and prudence of our pupillary magistrates." Voet also (26, 7 § 2) states that it is scarcely required that tutors testamentary should now give security, as minors have a tacit hypothec upon the estates of their guardians (such hypothecation is limited, at the Cape, by Act 5, 1861, § 3; and in the Transvaal, by Proc. 28, 1902, § 130). See also Grotius, 1, 9, 2; Sande, 2, 9, 9, 10 (Decis. Fris.). 250. Nothing may be transacted in connection with a minor's business, nor may his property be touched, until an inventory has been made—unless something has to be done which cannot admit of delay. In such inventory are to be included all things possessed by the minor, together with the burdens attaching to them, both movables, immovables, incorporeal property (such as patents and copyrights), debts and credits, and all deeds belonging to the patrimony. A description of specific things is to be made in such a manner, that a thing of less value cannot be substituted for that inventoried, after the inventory has been filed.

In short, all details have to be given regarding all the property, especially with regard to situation and area of immovable property (26, 7 § 3).

The Cape Law on inventories is to be found in Ordinance No. 105, 1833, §§ 18—22. See above, § 239.

251. Inventories must be made with all the usual formalities necessary and prescribed by law, not at any time after entering on the guardianship, but as speedily as possible, seeing that it ought to precede administration. It must be left to the discretion of the

Judge to decide how soon the inventory should be filed. In Holland tutors, in order that they may make their inventory, may claim an account of the property from the surviving father or mother of the minors, or from the executor of the deceased (26, 7 § 4).

See Grotius, Introduction, 1, 9, §§ 3, 4, 5. Van der Keessel (§§ 135 to 13S) says that on the death of either of the parents, the survivor, and even the step-father or step-mother, as the case may be, should furnish the guardian, at his request, with an accurate inventory of the estate. According to Dutch Common Law, the first-dying parent cannot by will absolve the survivor from preparation of the inventory, which it is the duty of the survivor to furnish. As to the case where the survivor is boedelhouder, see § 233, above.

252. Where a testator absolves a guardian from making a public inventory, this does not discharge from the liability of making a private inventory of all the minor's property (26, 7 § 4).

Van Leeuwen (Cent. For. 1, 1, 17, 1, 2) says: "In practice the rule goes to the length that, even if the testator has expressed his wish that an inventory be not made by the guardian, the Judge may, nevertheless, upon legal grounds, order the guardian to complete an inventory." 253. The penalty for the failure of a tutor to make an inventory is that he is liable for any loss that may result therefrom, and must be dismissed from his guardianship. This will also apply, if an inventory has actually been made, but certain assets or credits have been fraudulently (dolo malo) omitted

from the inventory, or certain debts have been similarly added to the inventory, when such debts were not actually due. If the guardian have any share in such property, thus fraudulently omitted from or included in the inventory, he loses his share in the property, according to Grotius (1,9,4). It will be otherwise, if such omissions from or additions to the inventory are made bond fide, by mistake, which will excuse the tutor. If a tutor has included more in the inventory than can afterwards be found, he will be so far prejudiced, that in case of doubt the property of the minor will be regarded as consisting of what is actually stated in the inventory. It is, however, open to the tutor to show that such additions to the inventory have been made bond fide, and that they do not in reality exist; and, if he has been made to pay, he may obtain restitutio in integrum with regard to such additions (26, 7 § 5).

Van der Keessel (§ 139) says: "A surviving parent who in preparing the inventory fraudulently conceals any property forfeits his share therein. Voet incorrectly denies this, and cites Groenewegen, whose opinion cannot, however, have any weight against a subsequent decision, which is mentioned by Van Leeuwen, or against a law i.e., a local Dutch statute which has since been enacted." The author has carefully gone through the passage of Voet (26, 7, 5) cited by Van der Keessel, but cannot find anything to justify the latter author's view that Voet is incorrect. All that Voet says is that a tutor acting mald fide is liable for damages, and to removal from the guardianship—'' unless one thinks with Mynsingerus (cent, (i, observ. 39, num. o) and others, that he is liable for double the amount of fraudulent omissions; or, with Grotius (Introduction, I, 9, 6, 7), that he must forfeit his share in the thing in question." Voet does not thereby state his disagreement, but leaves one the choice of opinions on the subject. He does not himself state what is to be the exact penalty. Mynsingerus says it is double the value; Grotius, that the penalty is a forfeiture on omission. Grotius clearly refers only to omissions; and, as Voet does not specifically deny this—in fact, appears to approve—it would seem that the law, in such cases, must be taken to be, that the guardian forfeits his share; but, with regard to other fraudulent dealings with the inventory, *Voet's* opinion would seem to be of force and effect, that the tutor is liable for any loss, and to dismissal from the guardianship. The only reference to Groenewegen in the whole of Voet's passage is with regard to the obtaining of *restitutio in integrum,* where the tutor has made payment on account of a *bona fide* error. It is noteworthy that neither Van Leeuwen nor his commentator, Decker, accuses Voet of making any mistake. Indeed, there is nothing in Van Leeuwen's passage *(R. D. L.,* 1, 16, 7) to conflict with Voet. He mentions a case, when the share was forfeited, '' where a widower or surviving possessor had in making out and rendering an account and inventory, *mald fide* concealed some property," and goes on to say, "if such concealment or suppression be made by other guardians they will be punishable for the same, and liable to make good the loss." The last clause is Voet's opinion, in identical terms. Now, the *dictum* of Grotius in (1, 9, 4 of) his *Introduction* clearly refers to the persons (mentioned in 1, 9, 3) who are the surviving parents or stepparents. The law would, therefore, seem to be as follows: *(a)* Surviving parents or step-parents, who fraudulently omit anything from an inventory, forfeit their share in such property as comes under the inventory, *(b)* Surviving parents or step-parents (if they have no share in the property under the inventory), and all other tutors, are liable for all loss arising from any additions to or omissions from the inventory, and at the same time cease to be guardians.

254. A tutor must see that his ward is provided with all the necessaries of life, and that he is instructed in moral training and educated in a manner befitting his position. The tutor should, however, give away or spend nothing but what is absolutely needed to maintain the ward's position. It follows that a tutor cannot remit portion of a debt due to the

minors by their father, unless the other creditors of the father have at the same time made an equivalent reduction of bis debts to them *(Dutch Consultations,* part 2, No. 678). In the same way, the fatber cannot receive a loan out of moneys belonging to the ward from the tutor, unless the father gives the same security as other persons do when furnishing a pledge or a surety *(Dutch Consultations,* part 2, No. 328). In the same way the tutor cannot extend the term of payment of a debtor of the ward (26, 7 § 6). 255. With regard to the property of the minor, the principal duty of the tutor is to preserve it, and secure it against loss or damage. He must see that houses, which the minor has inherited or acquired by any other title, do not become dilapidated, and take care that the value of the minor's property is not diminished by any causes within his control. If the father or any other person, whose heir the minor is, has left any house in a dilapidated state, the tutor must repair the house *(Dutch Consultations,* part 1, No. 297). He must pay debts of the minor on the due date, lest the minor suffer damage on account of delay (ex *mora),* or his goods run the risk of being sold. If a minor has to pay quit-rent, or to discharge the debt incurred subject to a penalty by a person to whom he is heir, or to pay an annual tribute on real property owned by him, the tutor will have to make good out of his own means whatever damage may result to the minor from neglect to pay such quit-rent, debt, or tribute. It makes no difference whether the debt be due by the minor to a stranger or to the tutor himself: since the tutor can not only pay himself, but must do so, lest he afterwards charge interest on the debt for the intervening period—unless the money of the minor has been invested in fixed property, and the tutor has been unable to obtain a judicial decree authorising him to pay himself out of the proceeds of such property. A tutor must fulfil conditions imposed on the minor, where their performance will be followed by gain to the minor, and their omission will be attended with loss to him. Thus, if a donation has been given to a minor under a

suspensive potestative condition, or unconditionally with the addition of a certain *modus* or limitation, non-compliance with which will avoid the gift, the loss accruing to the minor through neglect of the condition attaching to the donation must be borne by the tutor (26, 7 § 7). 256. On the other hand, the tutor must claim payment of everything which is due to the minor, and must himself pay what he owes to the minor. If debtors who are called upon by the tutor to make payment do not give satisfaction, the tutor may sell their securities, if any have been given for the debt, observing the usual rules and formalities in connection with the sale of securities and pledges. If through the tutor's negligence money due to the minor has not been recovered, the tutor may be held personally liable to make payment—unless the minor's money was lent, deposited with, or invested with a person who was, according to competent and general public opinion, in a good financial position *(Dutch Consultations,* part 1, No. 117 and No. 260); or unless the credit of the debtor ceased to be good after the minor's death, or after he attained majority, or after the termination of the guardianship, or when the minor, having attained majority, had signified his approval of the debt contracted with his guardian by the debtor (26, 7 § 8).

"A guardian," says Van Leeuwen *(Cens. For.* 1, 1, 18, 12), "is exonerated from this risk if the ward on attaining majority in person take interest from the debtor on money of his lent by his guardian, and placed out at interest. The ward, by such conduct, recognises the debt, and approves of the conduct of his former guardian, whom he cannot afterwards make responsible." 257. A guardian will not be liable if he has received a debt due by a debtor, whose credit was bad, from a predecessor in the guardianship, unconditionally, and without recognising or approving of the debt, or if he was negligent in the case of debts contracted with the father of the minors *(i.e.,* which debtors incurred with the father's consent), so long as his conduct was free from fraud or gross negligence, which in its effect amounts to fraud (26, 7 § 8).

See the Appendix to the *Dutch Consultations*, vol. 1, p. 33, part 3.

258. Money, plate, documents, and securities of the minor, and whatsoever is not changed by lapse of time, must be deposited in safe custody by the tutor. Grotius (1, 9, 9) says: "All documents and acknowledgments of debt belonging to the wards, either solely or jointly with others, are deposited and kept at the Orphan

Chamber meaning here the official department having the control of minors' estates unless the Orphan Chamber has been excluded by last will." Modern practice leaves more to the guardian's discretion (26, 7 § 9).

The Cape Ordinance 105, 1833, § 25, enacts that all moneys belonging to an estate under guardianship shall be paid to the Master of the Supreme Court, and failure to pay over such moneys makes the tutor dative or curator dative or curator *bonis* liable for interest at the rate of 10 per cent, per annum, and liable to removal from office. Actions may be instituted against tutors or curators to recover the money. By § 26 tutors testamentary or curators nominate are empowered to pay over moneys to the Master. Such moneys are, by § 30, to be deposited in the Guardians' Fund. The Master may, by § 31, make necessary payments out of such fund to the tutors or curators, and (§ 32) may lend money out on mortgage, the bonds to be payable (§ 33) to the Guardians' Fund. See Transvaal Proc. 28, 1902, § 95, and O. R. C. Statutes, chap. 54, § 35.

259. If a tutor (in South Africa, a tutor testamentary, or curator nominate, who has been allowed to retain the ward's money without paying the same to the Master) is able to lend out the minor's money at interest on good security, and neglects to do so, he will be liable, after the lapse of six months from his entrance on the guardianship, to pay interest on such moneys as remain uninvested and can be invested on good security. It will be otherwise if he was unable to find a person to whom to lend the money on good security—unless the

tutor has been able, at the same time, to lend his own money on good security. If the tutor has applied the minor's money to his own uses, he will be liable for interest on the whole of the minor's capital thus employed, nor will any extension of six months as above be given to him He will, however, not be liable to *pay* more in the way of interest than the whole amount of the debt (26, 7 § 9).

In *Mekerk* vs. *Niekerk* (1 M. 454) the Court held the rule of the Dutch Law to be clear, that interest could not be claimed, even from a guardian, to a greater amount than that of the capital on which the judgment was founded.

260. According to modern Roman-Dutch Law, guardians must invest the money of minors in the purchase of estates, or put it out at interest on the security of mortgages or pledges or sureties able to pay. Otherwise they will be liable to pay interest besides returning the capital. Grotius (1, 9, 10) says the guardians must take care "that the money put out at interest is secured by proper mortgages, or good personal securities who are to bind themselves as sureties *singuli in solidum* and co-principal debtors, and they must stipulate further (a privilege peculiar to minors) that the debtor is to pay up the capital when the ward attains majority." Van der Keessel says (§ 158) that "a guardian may legally invest the moneys of the ward in the purchase of profitable estates in the country;" and (§ 154) "in respect of the purchase of annual rents with the money of the ward... these obligations should properly be contracted in the presence of the Orphan Chamber *i.e.,* the Master of the Supreme Court, and should have the same right of preference as the *Schepenkennissen,* which right should be held to subsist even after the ward has attained majority (contrary to the opinion of Voet, who proceeds on the authority of an opinion given before the Law of Holland of September 12th, 1592, was passed)." Van der Keessel then (§ 155) says: "The money of the ward may be safely lent to the Dutch States or to the Public Treasury of Holland.... It does not, however, follow from this that such money can-

not be either invested in the purchase of country farms, or lent out at interest to private parties on good mortgage and personal security. Without this security it cannot properly be lent out either to private citizens or to foreigners, and if lent by the parent or testator, it is not at the risk of the guardian, who is free from gross fault" (26, 7 § 10).

On this important subject the Dutch jurists are all agreed. The only point on which Van der Keessel differs from Voet is the duration of the preference on money wherewith annual rents have been purchased, Voet (20, 2, 14) holding, on the authority of the *Dutch Consultations* (part 4, No. 267) that such preference does not last beyond the age of majority, Van der Keessel that it does. The law, then, empowers a guardian (including a parent who is guardian) to invest the ward's money in (a) Purchase of estates; *(b)* Loans on mortgage, pledge, or with good personal sureties (bound, according to Grotius, as joint principals and *in s(ilidum); (c)* Annual rents, purchased with the Master's authority; *(d)* Loans to the State or the Treasury. If the guardian is not the father, and the father has lent out or invested the money, the guardian will only be liable for gross negligence or fraud. If the guardian or the father (as natural guardian) invests money in any other way than the modes indicated, he will be personally liable to repay the whole amount of the money invested, with interest. So, where a father had subscribed for certain shares in a banking company as guardian on behalf of his minor daughter, and the trust deed of the bank provided that "a person who has subscribed for shares as guardian of a minor is only personally liable to pay any calls or claims which might accrue ou account thereof so long as the person for whom he shall hold the same shall remain under age," a call was made in respect of the shares, and shortly after the call was made the minor daughter became of age. The father sought to have his name removed from the list of contributories, on the ground that his minor daughter had attained her majority; and the liquidators of the bank sought to make the father liable for the calls. The Court held that the father was responsible for the calls *(Cape Commercial Bank* vs. *Porter,* 3 S. C. Co). Here the money had been invested in shares during the girl's minority. The trust-deed limited the father's liability, but it could not abrogate the general law introduced for the protection of minors under guardianship. See also Van Leeuwen *Gens. For.* 1, 17, 9); *Butch Consultations* (part 1, No. 260, and part 2, No. 323). Voet proceeds to say that the term of six months above referred to is no longer strictly observed, but the investment of moneys must depend upon circumstances.

261. If the father of minors has during his lifetime carried on a mercantile business, it is clear that the guardians may continue it at the risk and in the name of the wards, in such a manner that all profit or loss accrues to the latter, if the father has expressly enjoined this. And guardians who continue a mercantile business which was carried on by the father are presumed to continue it not in their own name but in that of the ward. Lastly, guardians are not only able, but ought to continue a business in the name of the ward—provided they carry it on in the same way as it was carried on by the deceased (26, 7 § 11).

See Carpzovius, *Defin. Forens.* 2, 11, 38; *Dutch Consultations,* part 4, No. 394. Van Leeuwen *(Cens. For.* 1, 1, 17, 12) says: "It is laid down as a general rule that, as often as a guardian does anything to which he is in duty bound, as guardian, although he does it in his own name, he is, notwithstanding this, regarded as having acted in the name of his ward.... On this rule the Judges of Leipzig following the Roman Law decided that a written acknowledgment, or a debt, which arose on consideration of money that was a ward's, accrued to the ward—although the guardian had procured the insertion of his own name as creditor in the acknowledgment of debt; and that not only was the guardian presumed to have made such payment out of the ward's estate, but that, in continuing the business of the ward's father, he (the guardian) must be regarded as hav-

ing continued it in the name of the ward. " 262. An important part of a guardian s duty is to appear for a minor in lawsuits, whether the minor be still in his infancy, or absent, or whether he have passed the age of infancy (though not the age of majority) and be present, so far as to institute action on the minor's behalf, or to defend an action brought against the minor: provided the minor has a just ground for taking up an action. And if the minor, having a good cause, has judgment given against him, the tutor may appeal on his behalf from an unjust sentence, unless he prefers to make good the minor's loss from his own means. If the case of the minor appear to be groundless, it is the tutor's duty, so far from bringing an action or making a defence, to recognise good faith of his own accord, and pay what is actually due by the minor without a judicial decree, or generally to abstain from a litigious case *(i.e.,* one which is merely vexatious, and not *bond fide)*— lest otherwise the tutor be compelled to pay out of his own means the costs of an action which he has unnecessarily instituted or defended. In modern law the guardian must obtain leave from the Court to institute or defend an action on the ward's behalf; otherwise, if the ward fails in his suit, the guardian will be liable to pay the costs himself (26, 7 § 12).

So it was said, in *Van der Walt* vs. *Hudson and Moore* (4 S. C. 327): "Under the Roman Law the *iatria jwtestas* was very wide, and the father had the right of bringing actions on behalf of his minor children. Under tho Dutch Law the powers of the father were very much contracted, but this right of bringing actions on behalf of his minor children was retained. It was qualified, however, to this extent, that if he does so and is unsuccessful, he does so at the risk of paying the costs personally. The authorities show that this qualification was introduced for the benefit of the minor." In this case a minor brought an action, and was represented by his father, and the defendant filed a plea in abatement to the action that the father was an undischarged and unrehabilitated insol-

vent, and that the action could not be maintained without leave of the Court, which leave had not been obtained. The plaintiff excepted to the plea, on the ground that it formed no defence to the action. The plaintiff's exception was sustained. After stating the law as above quoted, the Court laid down that the defendant could not take the objection that no leave was obtained from the Court, the regulation as to obtaining leave not having been introduced for his benefit. But the father was insolvent, and, as the law threw on him the risk of paying the costs personally, it was decided that the defendant should have security for his costs before the action was proceeded with. The exception, however, was sustained as above stated. See also *De Villiers* vs. *StuekerU* (1 M. 377); Prince vs. *Berrange* (1 M. 435, 437); Grotius (1, 8, 4); Groenewegen *(ad Cad.* 5, 37, 6); and Van der Linden (1, 5, 5).

263. In his next section Voet discusses the rule which lays down that a tutor has not the right of alienating his ward's property for the sake of gain, and may sell no more than is absolutely required for the preservation of the ward's estate. This subject has been treated of in § 260, above. The ordinary risks of mercantile business, where a trade or commercial transaction is carried on on behalf of the ward, may be undertaken (26, 7 § 18). 264. Whatever guardians are called upon to perform with regard to third parties, they must do in reference to themselves *(i.e.,* they must regard themselves as third parties, with an even greater obligation towards the ward, since they cannot proceed against others without bringing an action, while they ought themselves to pay what is due to the ward without having an action brought against them). They must keep a vigilant eye on the proceedings of their co-tutors or co-curators, for although they cannot exact accounts from such while the administration last, yet they may proceed against them as "suspected" guardians if their co-tutors or co-curators refuse to reveal their transactions in relation to the guardianship. Finally, guardians must display the same diligence in their wards' affairs as

in their own (26, 7 § 14). 265. Although the ending of the period of guardianship terminates the guardian's duties, he ought to bring to a conclusion such transactions as are still in an incomplete or inchoate stage, which have been commenced during the ward's minority, whether they be judicial or extra-judicial: so that one who relinquishes the prosecution of such transactions does so at his own risk, just as if the guardianship had not yet expired, unless accounts of the guardianship have been rendered (26, 7 §§ 15, 16). 266. The authority of a guardian (auctoritas) is a present consent and approval of what is done by the ward, and, though given unconditionally, it may apply to a transaction having a condition attached to it. It must be given by a guardian, being present at the time: so that authority given by letter or through a messenger is of no effect—although the authority will hold, if the guardian is present at the time with the ward, but the other party to the transaction is absent, and communication has to be made with him by letter. There must, furthermore, be an express declaration of authority, whether verbal, by acts, or in writing; and although it makes no difference whether the ward himself indicates his consent to a contract verbally or by conduct, the mere presence of the tutor, combined with silence, is not to be construed as indicating an authority to act. A subsequent ratification, however, by the guardian will operate as a previous mandate to the ward, and give authority to the ward's acts (26, 8 § 1). 267. The authority of a guardian is not required in cases where the ward improves his condition, and does not, in turn, make himself liable to another person. He may, however, be liable without the guardian's authority in case of crime, provided he is doli capax (capable of having a criminal intent). And he will be liable on quasi-contracts, where he has been enriched to the loss of another, in which case such other person may claim from the ward the amount by which the ward has been enriched (26, 8 § 2). 268. The authority of the guardian is necessary in all cases where it is

sought to bind the ward, and where injury to the ward is likely to result from the very nature of the contract. If a contract has been concluded without the guardian's consent, and the person with whom the ward has contracted has bound himself to fulfil the contract, he may be called upon to do so at the choice of the ward, while the ward may himself decline to perform (resile from) his part of the contract. If the ward claims performance from the other party, with whom he has contracted without the guardian's consent, of the contract, and performance of the ward's obligation is a condition precedent to performance by the other party, the ward is bound first of all to fulfil his part of the contract. But in stipulations and other transactions where performance on one side only is necessary (such as donations), or which are otherwise detrimental, the authority of the guardian must be given whenever it is sought to bind the ward. The guardian's authority must also be given in all renunciations of legal privileges made by the ward. In those cases where gain results to the ward, but the ward has certain burdens in return, the guardian's authority must be given: for instance, a ward cannot adiate an inheritance, which brings money to the ward, without the guardian's consent, nor can he accept without such consent a universal fideicommissum to be restored to himself. The same thing applies to acceptance of a legacy, or particular fideicanmi$tum, with burdens attached, so that one must consider whether it will be more advantageous to accept the legacy with the burden or to reject it. Nor can a minor accept a pledge without his guardian's authority, on account of the risk of having an action brought against him for recovery of the pledge by a creditor of the pledgor (26, 8 § 8). 269. Although a minor is not civilly liable on a contract which requires the guardian's authority, he may, nevertheless, be held naturally liable on such a contract (provided the minor at the time of the contract was more than seven years of age). Hence it follows that a surety may validly intervene on behalf of a minor

without the guardian's authority. Furthermore, a promise of a ward made without his guardian's authority may effect a novation of a prior obligation (26, 8 § 4).

Suretyship, being a stipniatio in Roman Law, cannot be entered into by a minor without the guardian's authority (Voet, 46, 1, o), "provided they do not obtain restitution." But the suretyship of a person who intervenes on behalf of a minor, who cannot himself be bound (without the guardian's authority), stands on a different footing. "When the principal contract is absolutely void," says Burge (Law of Suretyship, p. 6), "as the contract of a married woman, by the Law of Holland, the obligation of the surety is void. But if the person undertaking as surety knows that the contract of the principal debtor is void, on account of his incapacity, he must be considered as incurring a principal and not merely a collateral obligation. He undertakes to secure payment to the creditor, notwithstanding the minority or coverture of the debtor might protect him from payment. Again, although no action can be sustained against the principal, yet the surety may be liable. Thus the surety for the performance of an obligation called natural, as distinguished from a civil obligation, will be bound, although no action could be maintained against the principal; of this description is the contract of a minor, made without the authority of his guardian, a demand which, although it could not have been sued for, yet, having once been paid, cannot be recovered back." 270. If, however, a ward makes payment of what he has promised without the guardian's consent, he may sue for return of the money paid by a condictio indebiti, just as if there was no natural obligation. But if a person who has attained his majority ratines a contract entered into by him during minority without the guardian's consent, lie will become civilly liable (26, 8 § 4).

In Nel vs. Divine, Hall & Co. (8 S. C. 18) the foregoing rules were approved of by the Cape Supreme Court. It was said: "There is no question in this case, as there was in Cairncrots vs. De Vos

(Buch. 1876, p. 6; see § 141, above), and in *Gericke* vs. *Keyter* (Buch 1879, p. 147; see § 203, above), whether the defendant, at the time of the purchase, was emancipated or not, nor does the question of ratification after majority arise. The simple question is whether to an action brought against a person of full age for goods purchased during his minority without his parents' or tutors' consent and without proof that it was for his benefit that the articles were bought, the plea of minority affords a valid defence. If the contention be correct that an unemancipated minor, having a parent or tutor alive, labours under an absolute incapacity to enter into any contract, without such parents' or tutors' consent, it is clear that even with proof that the contract was for the minor's benefit, it could not be enforced against him. That no such incapacity, however, exists, is evident when it is borne in mind that a person who contracts with a minor is bound to abide by his part of the contract if the minor insists on it *(Voet,* 26, 8, 3), and that the minor himself becomes bound if after attaining majority he ratifies the contract *(Voet,* 26, 8, 4)." In this case an action was brought against the defendant, after her marriage, for the price of goods, purchased during her minority without the guardian's consent. The burden of proving that the purchase was for the minor's benefit was held to lie on the plaintiff. It was decided, on proof that the goods were bought for the defendant's sister, that the purchase was not for the minor's benefit.

271. In the next place there are cases where the guardian's consent is, indeed, necessary, but where even that is not sufficient— as in the alienation of immovable property of the ward; and payments to be made by the ward, unless annual rents or payments of interest are due (26, 8 § 5).

It is with some hesitation that payments are here included in the prohibition stated by Voet. The compiler of this work would prefer to havo left it out: for certain payments the guardian is authorised, and indeed bound, to make—for instance, such as are necessary for the

minor's support, or to carry on his business. In fact, the minor may validly pay for necessaries without the guardian's consent. This *dictum* of Voet's is, unfortunately, exceedingly obscure, and he throws no further light on the subject. CL.—VOl. I. H 272. Again, in certain cases the tutor's authority is absolutely null and void: lor L. stance, where the tutor acts for the ward directly and as principal *in rem siiam,* as, if an action arises between guardian and ward, or if the tutor makes a stipulation (such as suretyship) with the ward, or enters into any other contract with him—so that, in those cases, the ward is not bound on his guardian's authority, where the guardian has paternal authority, and on that account acquires the things agreed upon for himself, and not for the ward. So, if the ward has been instituted heir, and is asked to restore the inheritance to the tutor, he does not validly make such restoration on the tutor's authority; and still less will a delegation (a transfer of debt, where one debtor is released by substituting another, who is willing, in his stead: *Grotius,* 8, 44, 2) made to the ward by the guardian, or to the guardian by the ward, hold good.

There is, however, no doubt that, on the authority of a co-tutor, a tutor may validly bind a minor to himself, and even carry on a suit against the minor (26, 8 § 6).

Grotius (1, 9, 4) says, without qualification, that "if guardians themselves have any dispute with their wards, one or more other guardians are appointed for the management of the matter." It is clear that the law is as above stated by Voet. As we have seen, in other legal proceedings guardians, failing the consent of the Court, are personally liable for cost (above, § 262). Such legal proceedings must be instituted in the name of the guardian: *Letterstedt's Curator* vs. *Letteretedfa Executor* (Buch. 1874, p. 45).

273. Where a father and his son are co-tutors, the one cannot give his authority to the other to contract with a minor under guardianship (26, 8 § 6). 274. If several persons are guardians of one ward, the authority of all is not required, but

that of one will suffice—unless a testator, when appointing testamentary guardians, has expressly provided that one shall not be able to act without the consent or assistance of the other; or unless the other tutors forbid the performance of that for which one tutor has given his authority. It makes no difference whether the tutor giving his authority is the actual administrator of the guardianship or only a tutor *honorarius,* since, in ordinary circumstances, the authority of a tutor *honorarius* is sufficient. If a guardianship has been distributed or divided in respect of different localities, so that the administration of affairs in one province has been entrusted to two or three guardians, and the administration of affairs in another province to two other guardians, only the consent of those appointed for one province is required for transactions relating to the guardianship within that province (26, 8 § 7). 275. According to modern law (differing from the Roman Law) a guardian may be compelled, even if he be unwilling, to authorise an act of the minor, when a decree of the Court has been obtained for the purpose (26, 8 §§ 8, 9, 10). 276. If a tutor or curator has contracted with regard to a thing relating to a ward, either in the ward's name or in his own name, an equitable action *(utilis actio)* will lie, in certain cases, in favour of the ward on such a contract. So, if a tutor has purchased an estate with the ward's money, or has given the ward's money as a loan to a third person, the minor will have an equitable action to vindicate (obtain possession of) the estate, or a *condictio certi* (claim for a specified amount) to recover the money lent, whether the transaction has been entered into by the guardian in his own name or in that of the ward (26, 9 § 1).

The strict rule of Roman Law was that no one could recover on the contract of another. In order to remedy this, certain persons were by a fiction allowed to bring a fictitious action *(utilis actio), as* in the cases above-mentioned. The *actiones directae* proceeded from the civil law; the *utiles actiones* were invented to supply a remedy. See Savigny, *System ties heutigen Romischen ReekU,* vol. 1, § 15, p. 56; vol. 5, § 215, p. 72.

277. On the other hand, if a guardian receives a money loan and converts it to the uses of the ward, an action will lie against the ward for recovery of the money. So also will an action of hiring lie in favour of a lessee against a ward if the guardian has let the ward's property. If a tutor is co-heir with his ward to a *fideicommissum,* and gives security for the whole of the *fideicommissum,* the tutor will, on the ward's attainment of majority, have an equitable action against the ward for recovery of the share due by the ward on the *fideicommissum.* The execution, too, of a judgment given against a guardian who appears for his ward in a case must be directed against the property of the ward as an equitable proceeding, unless the guardian has in addition bound himself and proceeded on his own behalf— which, however, will not be presumed in case of doubt, or unless the guardian has raised a bad exception or plea against a *bond fide* plaintiff, in which case the minor must pay the amount of the judgment as really due, while the guardian may be compelled to pay the unnecessary costs of his bad exception or plea— though this would seem very doubtful at the present day (26, 9 § 2).

Van Leeuwen *(Cms. For.* 1,1,1", 13) says: "If a judgment be given against the guardian as guardian, he cannot be compelled to allow it to be executed upon his own property, even if he was under an obligation for the minor in his own name; provided the judgment did not pass against him in his own name. " 278. Although, while the guardianship endures, actions may be brought against the minor under the circumstances before mentioned, and also against the guardian while he continues in his office, yet, when the guardianship is terminated, all actions *ipso jure* pass against *(i.e.,* may be brought against) the ward alone which formerly lay against the guardian—so that, on laying down his guardianship, the guardian can no longer be called upon for debts of the ward, unless he has transferred the obligation to himself, or given his per-

sonal security in the matter. But if, during the administration the guardian has bound himself by his fraud *(dolus),* the obligation arising out of such fraud will remain after the guardianship is terminated, and an action on that ground will lie against the guardian himself—for fraud ought to harm its author alone, and that which has been done by the fraud of guardians should not be transferred to the ward after he has attained majority. Again, if the guardian has contracted in the ward's name at a time when it was certain that the ward was no longer solvent, it is clear that the guardian will, on account of his fraud, be liable *in subsidium (i.e.,* recourse must be had to him in the second place, after excussion of the ward) to the person with whom he thus contracted, for the amount which cannot be realised from the ward's estate (26, 9 § 8).

In the case last mentioned, could not the guardian be sued in a direct action for a wilful misrepresentation, and be made liable for all the damage suffered? 279. On the question whether the ward may himself be made liable for his guardian's fraud, one must consider whether the fraud relates to the guardian's own affairs *(i.e.,* whether the guardian was acting on his own account and in his own name *in rem suam),* or to the affairs of the ward. In the former case, the ward will not be liable; in the latter case, the ward will be liable to the extent to which he has been enriched by the guardian's fraud. If, however, nothing has been acquired by the ward through the guardian's fraud, he will not be liable, if the guardian is insolvent; if the guardian is solvent, the ward will be liable, having his recourse against the guardian's property—provided, however, that the ward, when summoned, may always be discharged from liability in such a case, if the ward makes cession to the plaintiff of the action for indemnity which he has against the guardian. Voet says the effect of the rule laid down by Javolenus still holds good, under the foregoing circumstances, namely, that "neither in interdicts, nor in other cases, shall the fraud of the guardian hurt the ward, whether the guardian be

solvent or not" (26, 9 § 4).

See *Grotius,* 3, 1, 30, and *Van der Keesse l* (§ 133).

280. In case of doubt, the guardian who transacts business in connection with the ward's affairs, is presumed, even if this is not expressly stated, to have contracted in the name of the ward, especially when the person with whom he contracted was aware of his capacity. It will be otherwise, if the guardian contracts with regard to things which concern him and the ward equally— for instance, if he has lent money or purchased an estate, when he holds both his own money and that of the ward, and does not express his capacity as a guardian: for then he is regarded as having transacted his own business rather than that of the ward (26, 9 §§ 5, 6).

Van Leeuwen (CW *For.* 1, 1, 17, 12) says: "Although, according to general law, one who contracts or acquires anything is presumed to have contracted and acquired in his own name and not in that of another, yet the rule is otherwise in the case of a guardian, who, on making a purchase with his ward's money, though in his (the guardian's) own name, is nevertheless presumed to have bought for the benefit of the ward, and consequently to have acquired the property for him: wherefore the ward becomes owner of the thing, and has a real action to recover it." 281. An action existed in Roman Law, known as that for the removal of a suspected guardian *(suspecti tutoris).* It was much stricter in Roman times than at present, but Voet holds that such an action for the removal from office of a guardian will still lie under Roman-Dutch Law, as the other actions against guardians, for the rendering of accounts of administration and repayment of losses under certain circumstances, can be brought only on the termination of the guardianship. The action for removal from guardianship no longer entails infamy or corporal punishment, as it did in Roman times (26, 10 §§ 1, 8).

282. The action lies against one who does not act conscientiously or according to his duty in the administration of a guardianship. The circumstances which

give cause for such removal lie mainly within the discretion of the Judge. Among those given by Montanus *(de tutelis,* c. 86, 1) are enmity of the guardian to the ward or the ward's father; any immoral conduct on the part of the guardian subsequent to his appointment; prodigality and licentiousness of the guardian; fraudulently causing a ward to abstain from an inheritance; fraudulently involving the guardian's financial affairs with those of the ward; fraudulently selling the property of the ward without a judicial decree; refusal of a guardian to act conjointly with a co-guardian; failure to perform the general duties of guardianship after appointment; generally, character so bad as no longer to entitle a guardian to remain in office (which does not include insolvency, for the guardian may counteract the circumstance that he is in poverty by providing sufficient security—though in South Africa insolvency deprives a tutor of office). The kind of guardianship makes no difference, whether it be testamentary or dative. The action for removal of a guardian is no longer criminal or quasi-criminal, seeing that it is not followed, on removal, by corporal punishment of the guardian. It must be brought during the guardianship, not at its termination. At the present day all who have the power to appoint, have the power to remove guardians (26, 10 §§ 1—12).

The exception above mentioned, with regard to insolvent guardians, does not apply in Cape Colony. Ordinance 105, 1833, § 17, provides that tutors, testamentary or dative, and curators, nominate or dative, whose estates shall be sequestrated as insolvent, shall *ipso facto* be removed from office. By § 23 of the same Ordinance it is provided that the general Roman-Dutch Law as to actions competent to minors shall be retained. The same disability holds in the Transvaal (Proc. 28, 1902, § 87), nor, in that Colony, may an absentee act as guardian (§§ 75 and 26). In Natal, by Act 19, 1894, § 6, letters of administration shall not be granted to any person who shall at the time be by law disqualified or incapacitated to hold office.

283. The effect of a charge being made against a guardian, on which an action for his removal from office is founded, is that while the case is pending the administration is taken away from the guardian. This is now only done if there are grave doubts as to the *band fide* conduct of the guardian (26, 10 § 7). As to this action, see Van Leeuwen *(Cens. For.* 1, 1, 17, 14, 15, 16). Van der Keessel (§ 162) says: "When guardians, whether testamentary or dative, are suspected, the superior magistrates, and in some places even the pupillary magistrates, may, after hearing the relatives of the ward, remove them... but in most cases without injury to the guardians' reputation." 284. The action for removal of a guardian under the foregoing conditions may be brought by any relative of the ward, whether male or female, or by any friend interested in the ward's welfare (26, 10 § 4). 285. According to the strict rule of Roman Law, a guardian could not refuse to accept a guardianship, or to perform the duties thereto appertaining. But, in modern practice, a guardian is entitled to ask permission to be excused from the guardianship. While his application is pending, the guardianship may be entrusted to a temporary curator, but the risk of and responsibility for such temporary curatorship will attach to the guardian making application for excuse from duty (27, 1 §§ 1—5).

Grotius (1, 7, 14) says: "Guardians, whether testamentary or dative, are at liberty to apply to the Court to be excused on the ground of inability or inconvenience, which application will be liberally considered, but no one can claim exemption as of right. Whoever is aggrieved by the decision of the Court may appeal to a higher tribunal; but in the meantime one or more other guardians are appointed in his stead, and that at his costs and charges if he should ultimately be decided to have been in the wrong." Van der Keessel (§ 124) says: "A guardian desirous of excusing himself should, within fourteen days (to be computed from the day on which he became aware of his appointment), or within such other time as may

be fixed by law, submit his excuse to the Orphan Chamber, or, upon appeal, to the ordinary Judge, supported by good reasons, which, however, are to be left to the decision of the Judge. The executors of a testament under which they are appointed guardians need not allege any such excuse." The statement of Grotius, that no one can claim exemption as of right, simply means that sufficient reasons must be alleged by the person appointed guardian. The Cape Law (Ord. 105, § 3) imposes on the Master the duty of writing to the person appointed tutor testamentary, to ask if he is willing to act. Therefore, at the Cape, tutors testamentary need not apply to be excused before undertaking the guardianship. If the guardianship has once been undertaken the guardian must thereafter apply to be excused in accordance with the general Roman-Dutch Law, for § 9 of the Ordinance refers only to proceedings to be taken on the death, incapacity, or removal from office of a guardian by decree of a competent Court; and even if the words "removal from office by decree of any competent Court" applied to the voluntary removal of a guardian at his own request, the procedure under the general law would have to be followed (except as regards tutors testamentary, as above stated). See Transvaal Proc. 28, 1902, §§ 73—75.

286. The guardian must cause the ward to be educated in accordance with the desire of his father. If the father wishes a certain person to instruct his child, and that person refuses to do so, the guardian must see that the child is educated as nearly as possible in consonance with the father's wishes. If the father professes one form of religious belief, and the guardian another, the child should be brought up in the belief of the father (27, 2 § 1).

On the subject of religious education the English cases (the *dicta* in which appear to coincide with the civil law) may with advantage be consulted. In *Agar-Ellis* va *Lascelles* (10 Ch. D. 49), where a Protestant father had, on marriage, promised his Roman Catholic wife that the children of the marriage should be brought up as Roman Catholics, and soon after the birth of the first child the father determined to bring up the children as Protestants (to which determination he adhered), and the mother, unknown to the father, had so indoctrinated the minor girls with Roman Catholic views that ultimately they refused to go with their father to a Protestant place of worship, the father claimed to have the children made wards of Court. It was decided that he had not forfeited his right to have the children brought up according to his own religious views, and that the Court would aid him in enforcing his right, leaving it to the father to do what he considered to be best for the temporal and spiritual welfare of the children. A stronger case was required to cause the Court to interfere with a father than with a testamentary guardian. In *Ha wksworth* vs. *Hawksworth* (6 Ch. 539), the father, a Roman Catholic, was dead. He left no instructions as to the faith in which the children were to bo educated. His widow, a Protestant, brought up the children as Protestants for eight years. On a suit being instituted with regard to the administration of the father's estate, the Court gavo orders that the children should be educated in the Roman Catholic faith. See also *In re Montagu* (28 Ch. D. 82); *In re Newbery* (1 Ch. 263); *Skinner* vs. *Orde* (4 P. C. 60); *Andrews* vs. *Salt* (S Ch. 622); *In re Clarke* (21 Ch. D. 817); *In re Scanlan* (40 Ch. D. 200).

287. Means of support or alimony in accordance with his station must be furnished to the ward, following the directions imposed on the guardian by the testament. If there are no testamentary directions, the guardian, if means are wanted for the ward's support and education, must apply to the Court for directions, or for permission to use a part of the ward's patrimony or the income thence arising for the support of the ward (27, 2 § 2).

The Cape Ordinance 105, 1833, § 21, enacts that no curator, nominate or dative, shall have any power or authority as to the maintenance, education, or custody of the person of any minor or lunatic or insane person, except in so far as the same may have been committed to him by the decree or order of any competent Court or Judge. § 23 enacts that the general law touching and concerning the maintenance and education of minor children, either by their parents or others, shall be retained, with the foregoing exception under § 21 (which is really a re-enactment of the Common Law). *In re Fehrzeu* (3 M. 74) decided that the Court were authorised and required to interpose their authority (according to Roman-Dutch Law, apart from statute), where a tutor applied for an advance out of a capital sum, being the minor's inheritance, the interest of which was insufficient, the minor having the intention of proceeding to Europe for his education. See also *Prince* vs. *Berrange,* (1 M. 435).

288. If the minor's capital should, by some means or other, be diminished, the sum applied for his maintenance or education should be reduced in proportion. If a Judge, being unaware of the amount of the minor's patrimony, makes an order for an amount to be applied which is beyond the minor's means, the guardian, being aware of the minor's monetary position, should reduce the amount for the minor's maintenance (27, 2 §§ 8, 4). 289. Guardianship is terminated by death; or by the arrival of a day or the fulfilment of a condition which is expressly or tacitly fixed for the termination of the guardianship; or by the ward's attainment of majority. The termination of the period of guardianship does not at once put an end to the guardian's liability, but the guardian's property is subject to a tacit hypothec in favour of the ward for everything done by the guardian during his term; and the liability of a guardian lasts until he has rendered accounts of his administration, and satisfaction has been made of all claims against the guardian to the ward or his heirs (27, 8 § 1).

This tacit hypothec at Common Law has, as we have seen, been abolished by statute in Cape Colony and in the Transvaal.

290. In order to obtain the rendering of accounts by the guardian, an action lies in favour of the ward, known as the direct action on the guardianship *(actio tutelae directa),* just as an action *(actio tutelae contraria)* lies in favour of the guardian to indemnify him for losses sustained during the term of guardianship. These actions are brought on the termination of the guardianship. The actions of guardianship are general, and include accounts and liability for all transactions during guardianship. The bringing of the action depends on the termination of the guardian's tenure of office, not on the ward's emancipation. Thus, if the guardian dies, or is banished, or removes, or is excused, or otherwise superseded, the new guardian, or the ward himself on the authority of the new guardian, may claim the rendering of an account from the former guardian or his heirs (27, 3 § 2).

The Cape Ordinance 105, 1833, § 23, provides for the retention of the general law as to the actions competent to minors against their tutors or curators, or competent to their tutors or curators against minors. § 38 requires tutors testamentary or dative or curators to lodge accounts with the Master, before February 15th in every year, of the administration of the estate or property under his guardianship up to December 31st of the year preceding, unless in the will or deed appointing a testamentary guardian or curator nominate it has been directed that such guardian or curator need not lodge an account. The survivor of two spouses whom the will appoints administrator of the joint estate and tutor of the minor children is also exempted from lodging an account. See Transvaal Proc. 28, 1902, § 97.

291. The guardian, if he has agreed to do so when he undertook the guardianship, may be compelled to file yearly accounts of his administration, by action brought for that purpose (27, 8 § 8).

The Cape Ordinance 105, 1833, § 38, provides that the guardian, on failure to render annual accounts, shall forfeit any fees due to him for the guardianship for the period for which he ought to have rendered accounts. This does not take away the guardian's liability to have an order made against him that he shall render accounts, on action brought for that purpose. So, in the Transvaal, by Proc. 28, 1902, § 98, the Master may summon a tutor to show cause why any account has not been lodged. See also §§ 55, 56, and 57 of the same Proclamation.

292. If accounts are rendered during the guardianship, the first account (as in the case of yearly accounts) must be based on the inventory of the minor's property. In the later accounts, all the transactions connected with the estate must be detailed and accounted for (27, 3 § 8).

Van der Keessel (§ 157) says that the annual accounts which guardians are by statute required to render to the Orphan Chamber or Master should not be confounded with those accounts which ought to be rendered to the ward himself, at the termination of the guardianship. This would seem to mean that, if the guardian has agreed to deliver annual accounts to the ward, these accounts must be delivered to the ward apart from the annual accounts to be delivered to the Master of the Court. Van Leeuwen *Vent. For.* 1,1,18, 2) says: "In the proper rendering of accounts it obtains in general practice that when the first accounts are rendered the formally drawn inventory is looked into to find whether all payments and receipts, and each item of the ward's income are stated in the accounts, and tally with the inventory—for the inventory is the basis of all the accounts. When this has been done, an appraisement must be made of the value of the rents and goods of the ward; then an examination of the expenses which the guardian claims to deduct, to see whether they were lawfully incurred and are in keeping with the ward's means. But when second and further accounts are rendered, the last accounts previously rendered are inspected *(i.e.,* compared with that now rendered)." 293. The direct action *(actio tutelae directa)* lies in favour of the ward and his heirs. In modern practice it is also competent to the husband of a girl who has been placed under the control of guardians or curators, to bring such an action; since marriage dissolves guardianship or curatorship of the person, the wife passing by marriage into a new and perpetual curatorship (except where she is under trusteeship with regard to certain property, specially constituted under the terms of an antenuptial contract). This action also lies in favour of the creditors of a ward, if he has made cession of his property in bankruptcy (27, 8 § 4).

294. The action *(directa)* must be brought against the guardian or his heirs, and against other successors to his property. Thus it may even be brought against the Treasury, if he has made *cessio bonorum* of his property (abolished in South Africa, and replaced by sequestration under the insolvency laws). It may also be brought against a successor in the guardianship of a tutor deceased or removed from office: inasmuch as it was the duty of the substituted tutor to demand an account and delivery of the ward's property from his predecessor or his heir; and if the successor does not do so, the ward suffers damage, and therefore has his recourse against the successor. Where a guardian has been married in community of property, since a woman is in such a case liable on the contracts and quasi-contracts of her husband, even if she is ignorant thereof, and even if made against her will, his widow will be liable in such an action. And where a woman, who is guardian of the children of the first marriage, marries a second time, without having previously rendered accounts of the guardianship, her second husband will be liable in the direct action (27, 8 § 5). 295. Even if a guardian has handed over the administration of the guardianship to some one else, such as the mother, grandfather, or relative of the pupil, on condition that such temporary administrator shall indemnify the guardian for whatever happens during the administration, the guardian will be liable, having his personal right of recourse, if he thinks fit, against the temporary administrator. The guardian is not freed from liability by transferring his duties during his term of guardianship (27, 3 § 6). 296. The general object of this direct action on the guardianship is to secure and obtain for the ward whatever property of the ward is to be found with the guardian, and all profits or gains that are earned, or damages which may arise from the fact that the guardian has not done that which, in accordance with his duty, he should have done. Since particulars concerning these things cannot be arrived at, unless the means and property of the ward have first of all been collated, together with an inventory, the first requirement is that the guardian should render accounts of his administration: such accounts should be examined and debated, to guard against omissions, mistakes, or falsifications (27, 8 § 7). 297. The guardian must then restore the property as inventoried, and pay over what has been acquired in addition to what has been included in the inventory, together with interest, if he has made delay in rendering accounts or restoring what belongs to the minor according to the inventory, or over and above the inventory; and whether damage result from the act of the guardian or of his co-guardian; especially if he has converted the moneys of the ward to his own uses. If it is not due to the fault of the guardian or his co-guardian that the accounts have not been rendered in time, or if he has placed the property of the minor under consignation (a judicial deposit, by placing the property or thing due in charge of the Court, which, according to Decker, had this effect, that the debtor was thereby completely absolved, and interest consequently ceased to run), the guardian is not liable to make payment of interest (27,3 § 8). See also *Dutch Consultations,* part 3, vol. 1, No. 87, 88.

298. Proof must be furnished of what is actually in the guardian's possession. The guardian is not discharged from liability to deliver up the ward's property in his hands, by the fact that he has been absolved from rendering accounts by the testament appointing him. Guardians are also liable in general for any loss resulting through their fraud, gross negligence, and ordinary negligence in administration, although no benefit results therefrom to the guardian personally, while so conducting the administration (27, 3 §§ 9—12).

Van Leeuwen *Cens. For.* 1, 1, 18, 10)

says: ""*When* guardianship is at an end the consequences of his fraud or negligence must be made good by the guardian in the accounts of his administration; and he is liable for the consequences not only of gross but even of slight negligence." 299. There are even cases where the guardian is liable for the very least degree of negligence—for instance, where he is generally most diligent in the transaction of his own affairs, since he is not free from fraud who applies less care in the transactions of others that have been entrusted to him, than in his own affairs (27, 3 §§ 12, 13). 300. The following acts of a guardian will be looked upon in the light of fraud or negligence: not giving an exact account of property in his charge, or suppressing details concerning such property; not selling those things of the ward which are of a. perishable nature, or deteriorate with time; lending out money of the ward, when the borrower afterwards becomes insolvent or unable to pay; not taking steps to secure the appointment of a curator, where the ward needs a curator (27, 3 § 14).

Voet then states that the guardian will not be free from blame, where he has followed the advice of the father or mother or blood relations of the ward. He quotes Chassaneus *ad consuetudines Burgundiae,* rub. 6 § 6) and Van Leeuwen *Cais. For.* 1, 1,18,10). The latter disagrees with Voet, stating that the guardian need not account for what has been done upon the advice of the ward's relatives, since fraud is presumed to be absent from all acts of a guardian who contracts in the presence of the ward's relatives. That may be so, but the question is here not so much one of fraud, as of gross negligence. Even if the presumption of negligence in this case did not exist, according to Voet, the ward could still claim to be indemnified if he proves fraud or negligence on the part of the guardian in connection with things done on the advice of the ward's relatives. In other words, fraud or negligence not being presumed, the ward may still obtain damages on proof of fraud or negligence, where the relatives of the ward advised the acts causing

damage. This liability extends so far, says Voet, that the guardian is not discharged even if the father has directed the guardianship to be carried on with the advice of the mother of the wards. See Menochius, *de praaumptionibus* (3, 128, 2). See also *Dutch Consultations* (5, 67, 2).
301. No fraud or blame is to be presumed from the fact that at the terminatiou of the guardianship the guardian is rich, who was poor at the commencement thereof. There is, however, such a presumption in the case of administrators of the public funds (27, 8 § 15).

See Perezius on the Code (*arbitrium tutelae,* 12; *de jure fisci,* 21), Uenochius *(de praesumptionibiw,* 6, 28, 2), Mascardus *(de probationibus,* 1399, 9).
302. The action to compel the rendering of accounts may be brought at any time within thirty years from the termination of the guardianship. If accounts have once been rendered and approved of in solemn form, the guardian cannot be compelled again to render accounts of his administration—unless there is a question of an error in the calculation. If it is shown that there has been fraud or negligent omission of items from the account previously rendered, a new account may be claimed (27, 3 § 16).

See *Dutch Consultations* (3, 1, 87, 88; 2, 44).
303. Accounts must be rendered in the place where the administration was carried on. If a ward has several guardians, eacli must render accounts of his special guardianship work. Tutors dative must render accounts to the judicial officer by whom they have been appointed. A testamentary guardian must render accounts in the domicile where the guardianship has been administered (27, 8 §§ 17, 18).

See Van Leeuwen *(Cens. For.* 2, 1, 14, 10).
304. If the guardian has during the guardianship converted or made sale of the property of the ward, fraudulently, with or without intending appropriation thereof to his own uses, an action will on the termination thereof lie against the guardian (but not against his heirs, as it is penal), in favour of the ward

and his heirs or successors, for recovery, as a penalty, of double the value of the thing sold in such manner. But, although damages resulting from such fraudulent sale may also be claimed in this action, double the amount of damages will not be awarded. A claim on the Aquilian Law (i.e., in tort), and one for theft (embezzlement) may also be joined in this action, provided there was the intention to appropriate to the guardian's own uses *(animus furandi).* If one claim, where there are several distinct claims in such an action, fails, the other claims are not extinguished, but judgment may be given in the plaintiff's favour on them (27, 3 § 19). 305. A similar equitable action is given to persons under curatorship against curators. This action, if the curatorship is limited to a certain time, as a term of years, can only be brought after the termination of the curatorship; if the term of curatorship is unlimited, the action may be brought at any time—seeing that it is uncertain when a lunatic will return to sanity, or a prodigal become fit to be trusted with managing his own affairs. If a minor has had a curator *ad litem* or another curator for doing a particular thing appointed, the action against such curator may be brought at any time, as it is uncertain when such curatorship will end (27, 3 § 20). 306. The guardian has, on his side, an action against the ward, known as the contrary action of guardianship (*actio tutelae contraria).* It lies in favour of the guardian and his heir, on the termination of the guardianship, against the ward and his successors, even if the ward has not previously brought a direct action on the guardianship; and even if the guardian has been removed from his office as a *tutor suspectus,* owing to wrongful administration of the ward's affairs, or his having been summoned in an action of theft, or arising out of a wrongful sale of the ward's property. There is nothing to prevent a tutor being *suspectus,* and at the same time having the right to recover what is over and above the necessary amount spent on the administration of the ward's affairs. The object of this action is to indemnify the guardian, and secure for him before everything the expenses or disbursements he has been put to in connection with the ward or his patrimony, together with interest at the customary rate (even after the termination of the guardianship, until the ward restores the money spent by the guardian), unless the guardian has money of the ward on interest, out of which he may repay himself. It makes no difference whether the guardian has made the disbursements during the guardianship, or on the termination of his duties, or even before the guardian began his duties, provided the payment of disbursements took place sooner or later in connection with such transactions as were concerned with the undertaking or carrying on of the guardianship administration, or provided such disbursements were made by one acting as a pro-tutor before the administration of the guardianship ended. If the transactions with which such disbursements were connected took place after the guardianship had terminated, and therefore were unconnected with the guardianship administration, an action on the transaction of another person's affairs *(contraria negotiorum gestorum actio)* will rather lie (as to which see later, vol. 2). If anything was due to the guardian by the ward or the ward's father before the gunrdianship ended, such as a loan, the former action *(tutelae contraria)* must be relied on (27, 4 § § 1—8). 307. The fact that the ward has derived no benefit from the expenses incurred on his behalf will be no bar to the guardian's bringing this action. It will be sufficient if, according to the general estimation of men, gain was hoped for from such a transaction, and the guardian has had adverse results in connection with what he undertook in good faith and to the best of his ability. A guardian cannot, however, recover the expenses of a lawsuit undertaken on the ward's behalf without the consent of the Court. The guardian (provided he has obtained the consent of the Court) will not be prevented from recovering that which he has paid on behalf of the ward upon a judicial decree, although he could not have been

compelled himself to pay the amount against his will—since it is enough for the ward to have been liable naturally and civilly, and thus effectually bound. If the guardian has disbursed more than the means of the ward, derived from his patrimony, were sufficient for, he can only recover the same if such disbursement resulted in profit to the ward, or if it were made after obtaining a judicial decree authorising the disbursement. If the guardian has made unnecessary expenditure in connection with the transaction of the ward's affairs, such as he would not have made on his own account, he cannot recover the same by this contrary action (27, 4 §§ 4, 5). Voet instances as such unnecessary expenditure the furnishing of a horse and escort for the ward, where in the same circumstances the guardian would go on foot, excessive expense in connection with lawsuits, or in connection with the funeral of the ward's father. 308. If the guardian has paid anything on the ward's behalf which is not due by the ward *(solutio indebiti),* as this has no relation to the ward's affairs, and cannot be ratified *by* the ward, the guardian cannot recover the same from the ward by the contrary action (27, 4 § 6). 309. Damage attaching to the guardian in connection with payments made on the ward's behalf must also be considered in relation to this contrary action. If the ward is liable in an action for division of a joint property *(communi dividundo),* when he lias caused damage to the property owned jointly with another, the guardian will be able to recover such damage, paid on the ward's behalf, from the ward. And if the guardian has suffered damage, not from the ward, but from another, in connection with his guardianship duties (for instance, if he has been robbed during a journey undertaken on the ward's behalf, and has also been attacked and wounded, having to pay for medical attendance in consequence, or if he has lost his belongings in a shipwreck when voyaging for the ward), he will be able to recover the same from the ward by the *actio contraria* (27, 4 § 7). Voet says the case of the guardian is

the same as that of a mandatory. In a previous passage (17, 1,13), referred to later on in this work (vol. 2, "Agency "), he states that according to strict Roman Law a mandatory could only recover such expenses as arose directly from the performance of the mandate. Those arising from accident or chance were to be borne by the mandatory. This was altered by Dutch Law, under which an equitable action was introduced, given to the mandatory for the recovery of losses sustained by him by accident, or tort of third parties, while transacting the business of the mandator. Yoet says a similar action was introduced for the benefit of partners and guardians. 310. That which a guardian is able to recover by means of the contrary action of guardianship, he may also set off in accordance with the rules relating to compensation or set-off, that is to say, if there is a debt of the like quantity and of the same kind. If such requirements are wanting, the Judge cannot decree a set-off. Only after such set-off has been decided upon and rejected can the guardian recover by the contrary action such amounts due to him as were held incapable of being set off against each other—unless the Judge has decided that the amount so claimed to be set off by c.L.—Vol. I. N the guardian were claimed in bad faith, for then they are not recoverable by the contrary action (27, 4 § 8).

As to the requirements for set-off (which are discussed later in this work, vol. 2), see *Brett* vs. *Soliman* (4 S. C. 9). 311. In this contrary action the guardian may claim not only that his disbursements shall be paid to him, but that the actions against his co-tutors shall be ceded to him, if he has suffered loss through the negligence of all, and not through his own negligence (much less through his own fraud). Equitable actions, however, may be brought against co-tutors without cession (27, 4 § 9). 312. Even if the guardian has bound his own property in pledge to the creditors of the ward, or has rendered himself liable (in *proprid persona*) to such creditors, by making a contract for the pupil's benefit in his own name, by undertaking a suretyship, or giving a mandate, under similar conditions, he may lawfully claim in this action that the ward shall release the guardian's property from pledge, and the guardian himself from his obligation on the ward's behalf (27, 4 § 10).

Yoet has a long dissertation on the merits of this question, which may with advantage be consulted by those who are curious with regard to the subject.

313. Although the office of guardianship is in its origin gratuitous, a guardian is enabled to claim remuneration where he is poor, or has had great trouble in transacting guardianship affairs, not by means of a contrary action on the guardianship, but in a special action. The salary of a guardian may be fixed by testament, or by the magistrate or judicial officer appointing him (27, 4 §§ 11, 12).

Van Leeuwen *(Cent. For.* 1, 1, 18, 20) says: "A guardian cannot demand a salary, for he performs a gratuitous labour. Yet in practice the matter is discretionary." The Cape Ordinance 105, 1833, § 39, enacts that tutors testamentary or dative, and curators nominate or dative, shall in respect of the administration and management of any estate be entitled to claim, receive, or retain out of the assets of such estate a reasonable compensation for their care and diligence in the said administration, to be assessed and taxed by the Master of the Supreme Court, subject to the review of the Supreme Court on the petition of any such tutor or curator or of any person having an interest in the said estate. A similar provision is made in Transvaal Proc. 28, 1902, § 58. See also the Transvaal Master's notice of June 4th, 1902.

314. An equitable action, similar in all respects to the contrary action in favour of guardians (and known as *contraria actio utilis curaXumis causa),* lies in favour of curators (27, 4 § 18). 315. Tutors or curators are either true or false. Persons are said to be false tutors when, not being in reality tutors, they administer the affairs of minors as if they were their guardians, whence they are said to act as tutors *(pro tutore gerere).* This

may happen if they believe themselves, in good faith, to have been appointed guardians, or if they know perfectly well that they are not guardians and yet pretend to be such. Among those who act in this manner are such persons as were tutors, but have ceased to be such, and still continue to transact the business of the wards who were under their control; or such as, having been validly appointed by will, carry on the business of the guardianship while unaware of their appointment— since, in order to be liable in an action on the guardianship, it is necessary that one should know that he is a guardian. From such protutorial transactions (carried on as if the person doing them were in reality a guardian) an action on the *protutela,* direct and contrary, arises. The direct action is a personal one, on good faith *(bonae ./Wei),* hi favour of the ward and his heirs, against the person acting as guardian *gerew pro tutore)* and his heirs. It claims an account of the administration, and payment of all profits, or compensation for all loss arising out of such administration, requiring the same good faith and diligence as are necessary in the case of a real guardian. A person so summoned is liable not only for things actually done, but for things omitted to be done as well. If a person has believed himself to be guardian, but afterwards becomes aware that he is not in reality a legal guardian, and desires to abstain from interference in the ward's affairs, he must inform the nearest relatives of the ward, in order that they may obtain the appointment of a guardian (27, 5 §§ 1, 2).

In *Hoffman's Creditors* vs. *Wolmarans* (1M. 534) it was decided, on the authority of what has been said above, that a person who had acted and described himself as guardian (protutor) was liable as such to the minors, who claimed a preference by virtue of their tacit hypothec on the guardian's estate. Act No. 5 of 1861 (Cape), § 8, sub-section 3, provides for the abolition of the tacit hypothec of minors upon the estates of their protutors, and upon the estates of agents or others (not being their guardians) intermeddling with the prop-

erty or affairs of such minors, and upon the estates of tutors who have been assumed, substituted, or surrogated, or who have been appointed by order of Court, in security for the debts due and owing by such persons in such capacity to such minors. The hypothecation on tutors' estates is limited to three years (§ 3). The tacit hypothec in question has similarly been abolished in the Transvaal.

316. A contrary action is given to protutors or persons acting similarly against wards, for the recovery of an indemnity for disbursements, similar to the contrary action given to guardians. The alienation, however, of things belonging to wards, by protutors, will not be valid where alienations made by guardians under similar circumstances are valid. The action of protutorship may be brought during as well as after the administration. A protutor who brings an action on behalf of a ward may be repelled at the commencement of the suit by an exception *(exceptio tutoris illegitimi)* that he is an illegal tutor, and consequently in the position of an unauthorised agent, and may therefore be prevented from proceeding further in the suit—an exception which cannot be raised against a guardian (27, 5 § 3).

See also Van Leeuwen *(Cens. For.* 1, 1, 17, 17).

317. A person who, on the authority of a true guardian, contracts with the ward, remains, as we have seen, validly bound, and cannot be relieved against his contract by any ordinary or special remedy; but one who contracts with a minor on the authority of a false guardian (or protutor), believing such false guardian to be a true guardian, may obtain plenary restitution *(in integrum restitutio)* on the ground of his just error, lest one deceived by the pretended authority of a false tutor should suffer loss—unless the Judge gives a decree ratifying what has been done by the protutor (in which case the contract receives validity from the authority of the Judge, not from that of the protutor). No restitution will, however, be given to a person contracting with a protutor who knew that such protutor or person

acting as guardian was not in reality a guardian, or knew that the person acting as guardian could not interpose his authority, because he was a lunatic—unless the ward contracted with a knowledge of all the circumstances, or upon judicial authority. If a person contracts with a ward on the authority of two persons, one of whom is in reality a guardian, while the other is a pretended guardian, no restitution will be given to the person so contracting. It makes no difference whether the person who gave his authority to the ward knew that he was not a guardian, or, on the contrary, believed himself in good faith to be a guardian. A person acting in good faith as guardian, and interposing his authority as such, is liable to the ward only in an ordinary action of protutorship, while there is no remedy open to those who have, on such authority, knowingly or unwittingly contracted with the ward. But one who knows that he is not a guardian, and wrongfully, with a fraudulent intent, interposes his authority, is liable in an action for all damages (in *factum)* thence arising, to the person who contracted on such authority with the ward. One who has, in bad faith, induced another person to hold himself out as guardian, is similarly liable for all damages that may thence ensue. This action, being penal, lies in favour of the plaintiff's heirs, but not against the defendant's heirs. It is prescribed after one year. Where several people jointly cause damage in this manner, the action lies against them severally for the whole amount of damage *(singuli in solidum),* but on payment by one the others are discharged. If the first defendant, on being summoned, cannot pay the whole amount, the remainder may be recovered against those who have been participators with him in causing damage (27, 6 §§ 1, 2). 318. As above stated (§ 249) guardians are frequently compelled to give security *rem pupilli salvam fore* (that the property of the ward shall be safe), in order that the wards may satisfy their claims upon the guardian from the property of his sureties. Sureties and their heirs may be called upon by the wards and their heirs

in an action on the stipulation of suretyship *(actio exstipulatu stricti juris),* on account of what has been wrongfully or neglectfully done by the guardians during their term of administration, to make good that for which guardians may be condemned in a direct action of guardianship *(actio tutelae directa),* or should have been condemned, so that the sureties may even be called upon to pay interest due by the guardians on account of delay, no matter in what manner they have intervened on behalf of the guardians. On the other hand, sureties have the same right of recourse as the guardians against the wards. But if, after the term of guardianship has expired, the guardians have transacted some business of their former wards, not being compelled to do so in virtue of their guardianship duty, such business not being connected with their administration, their sureties will not be liable, on the ground of their suretyship, to make good such transactions to the wards. Those are also looked upon as sureties who, being present, are nominated by guardians as sureties, and do not contradict such nomination, but, knowing of it, allow themselves to be referred to in '. public documents as sureties. Although, as a general rule, sureties have the benefit of division, yet, if several sureties intervene on behalf of one guardian, they are liable each for the whole amount *(singuli in solidum),* and the exception of the benefit of division cannot be raised. If there are several guardians, who have the benefit of division amongst themselves (concerning which see later, vol. 2. of this work), and different sureties have bound themselves for each guardian, each surety will have the benefit of division in right of the guardian for whom he has bound himself, lest otherwise the position of the surety shall seem to be less favourable than that of the principal debtor (27, 7 § 1).
The rules of the Cape Ordinance 105, 1833, on the subject of suretyship to tutors are very simple. § 5 enacts that the Master or any person interested in the due administration of the minor's estate, where by Roman-Dutch Law any tutor

testamentary might have been required to give security *rem pupilli aalvam fore,* may apply to the Supreme Court or any Judge for an order that letters of confirmation shall not be granted to a tutor testamentary or curator nominate until he shall find security, to the Master's satisfaction, to a reasonable amount, for the due administration of the estate. § 16 makes it obligatory on tutors dative and curators dative to find security for the administration of the estate or property in their charge, to the Master's satisfaction, before entering upon such administration. § 41 requires the Master to keep a register of all sureties for tutors testamentary or dative, or curators nominate or dative, and of all sureties for other debtors to minors. In case of insolvency of sureties for tutors or curators, the Master shall require the tutor or curator whose surety has become insolvent to give further security, to a reasonable amount, for the estate or property under guardianship. Certain regulations are also laid down as to publications in the Cape *Government Gazette.* The Transvaal provisions as to security are contained in Proc. 28, 1902, §5 "7 and 85. As to Natal, see Act 38, 1899, §§ 28—33, and § 25. As to O. R. C., see Statutes, chap. 54, § 33.
319. If one surety, being called upon for payment, discharges the whole amount of the debt, he may have recourse, when the action is ceded to him, not only against his co-sureties, but against the coguardians of the guardian for whom he has stood surety as well—. just as the guardian would himself have had; and this recourse is only for a wrongful act on the part of the other guardians short of fraud, there being no recourse against the other guardians for a fraudulent act on the part of all the guardians, or for loss suffered through the fault, fraudulent or not, of the guardian for whom the surety has bound himself-It will be otherwise, if the surety claims cession of action against his co-sureties; for this he lawfully claims, the ward being entitled to call upon him to make good not only the negligence of the guardian for whom he stood surety, but his own fraud or gross negligence as well (27, 7

§ 2).

Voet has put the latter part of the foregoing passage somewhat obscurely. It would seem to mean—in default of any judicial interpretation—that the surety has recourse for the acts of the guardian who is his principal not only against his co-sureties, but against his principal's co-guardians as well, unless the loss results from *(a)* the sole negligence of his principal, (6) the fraud of his principal. The surety will (it is submitted) have no recourse against his co-sureties where the loss occurs through (a) his fraud, *(b)* his gross negligence.

320. In Roman Law persons who nominated guardians were liable for their acts; this is not the case in Roman-Dutch Law, unless there has been fraud in connection with such nomination (27, 7 § 3).

In case of fraud on the part of persons nominating guardians, it would seem that such persons, when called upon to make good loss arising from such false and fraudulent nomination, must be made defendants in a general action on tort. They fill no official position, such as that of a guardian, or even a pro-tutor, and therefore the *actio tutelae* or *protutelae* will not apply.

321. As regards the liability of the heirs of guardians, the rule of modern Dutch Law is that, as heirs succeed to all the goods of the deceased, a person who has been injured through the fraud of a deceased guardian, whether it arises out of a contract or not, has an action for indemnity against the heirs of the deceased for the whole amount *(in solidum)* of the loss, even if no gain has thence resulted to the heir, or even if the inheritance (i.e., the estate) of the deceased is insolvent, so long as it has been adiated without an inventory: since it is better that damage arising from the fraud of the deceased should be borne by him who acquires gain by right of the deceased, or at least hopes for it, by adiating an inheritance as if it were in a flourishing financial condition (27, 7 § § 4—6).

See *Dutch Consultations* (part 3, vol. 1, No. 165); Van Leeuwen *(Cent. For.* 1, 3, 1, 2); Paid Voet on the *Institutes* (on obligations arising from delict, No. 3).

322. Voet then proceeds to the consideration of actions against magistrates. The rules laid down by him can scarcely be said to be applicable at present, as he expressly excepts *magistrate majores,* and considers only the liability of *magistratus municipales.* In South African practice, all the work with reference to the appointment of guardians, and the care of funds belonging to wards, is in the hands of Masters of the Superior Courts, who discharge the functions which were in Holland—and at the Cape of Good Hope, before the establishment of the office of Master—entrusted to Orphan Chambers (27, 8 § 1). At the Cape, Ordinance No. 103 of 1833 provides for the abolition of the Orphan Chamber within the Colony, and for the performance thenceforth (from July 5th, 1833) of the duties discharged before that time by the Orphan Chamber by the Master for the time being of the Cape Supreme Court. The subject of actions against the Master is provided for in Ordinance 103, § 10, and in Ordinance 105, § 43. As to the Transvaal, see Proc. 28, 1902, §§ 56 and 118. As to Orange River Colony, see Statutes, chap. 54, §§ 9 and 53. As to Natal, see Act 38, 1899, §§ 61 and 62.

323. Upon a consideration of the passages in Voet's *Commentaries* bearing on the subject, and of Van Leeuwen's remarks *(Cens. For.* 1, 1, 17, 4), it would not appear safe to lay down unreservedly that actions against magistrates lie in favour of wards. Vau Leeuwen says: "The decision of this doubt is a difficult and intricate matter." Both writers hold that the action can only be brought where there is fraud or gross negligence (though Van Leeuwen would seem to go further, and to hold that slight negligence also creates a liability) on the part of the magistrate. It would (it is submitted) be safe to say that wards have an action where there has been fraud, collusion, or gross negligence (in connection with the funds in his charge) on the part of the Master (27, 8 §§ 2—5).

Grotius, in the *Dutch Consultations* (vol. 5, No. 133; *De Bruyn,* p. 466), lays down that where no proper security has been given by guardians, the Orphan Masters are liable in default.

324. With reference to the order in which guardians and others previously mentioned in this chapter are to be called upon for payment, the following rules must be observed: If there is only one guardian, he must first of all be summoned, next his sureties, and next the magistrates (if they can be held liable for anything). If several guardians have been appointed, one must find out whether one of them alone has administered the guardianship, or several. If one alone, he must be excused before the others who did not administer, and next to him his heirs and sureties, if he has furnished any, the other guardians who did not administer having the right to avail themselves of the benefit of order or excussion, if they are called upon first of all, no matter whether one took upon himself the administration by private agreement, last will of a testator, or judicial authority (see Van Leeuwen, *Cens. For. 1,* 1, 18, 15, 16, 17). The same rule holds, if one of several guardians has of his own accord conducted the administration alone, the other guardians failing to administer, although they were aware of their appointment—so far as things which he has done of his own accord are concerned, and also matters connected with such doings; but with reference to things omitted or neglected by him, who has of his own accord done certain things, the risk and responsibility attaches to all the guardians alike; and one person, who has done certain things, cannot be excused first in respect of what he has left undone or omitted. But those are also considered to have administered a guardianship, who have given an express mandate to another guardian to conduct the guardianship; or who have accepted from a co-guardian as sufficient security *rem pupilli salvam fore* offered by him, and have allowed him to administer the whole of the guardianship; or who have ceded the administration to their co-guardians (27, 8 § 6).

In order to bind a co-tutor who has not

actively administered the guardianship, so as to render him liable to excussion, either along with the active administrator, or immediately after such active administrator and before the nominal guardians, there must be some conduct on the part of the co-tutor which is capable of being construed as an interference, in some way or another, with the guardianship. He must not be merely passive, silently acquiescing in the acts of the administering guardian. There must be some positive act, such as those instanced above; otherwise the co-tutor whom it is sought to make liable will have the benefit, not the burden, of excussion.

325. If all the tutors have had the administration, it must be seen, whether they have administered guardianship affairs jointly or severally. If they have done a thing jointly and collectively, they may be summoned at the choice of the ward to make payment each for all *(singuli in solidum),* having the benefit of division, if the remainder who were not summoned are solvent at a time when, the guardianship having ended, they could be called upon for payment —it being otherwise if, afterwards, on account of the ward's delay, some of them had ceased to be solvent (27, 8 § 6).

In other words, A., B., and C. are guardians. On the expiry of the guardianship, A. is called upon to pay 300/. C. is insolvent. A. pays 300/., and can then claim 100/. from B. If hoth B. and C. are solvent, A. may either claim 100/. from each, or may claim 200/. from B., leaving it to B. to proceed against U. for the remaining 100/.

326. If the guardians have conducted the administration separately, either as regards portions of the ward's property, or different places where the property is situate, one must again determine whether the division of administration has been made by private authority, or by authority or decree of the Judge or the testator. If the administration has been divided by private arrangement amongst the guardians, the ward may proceed against one of them in precisely the same manner as if the administration

had been conducted jointly. In such a case, the guardians cannot claim the benefit of order or excussion. If the division of the administration has been made at the will of the testator or of a Judge, each guardian is held liable for the portion which he has separately administered, not for the portion administered by his co-guardian—unless he were negligent in claiming the removal of a suspected co-guardian, if it came within his province to claim such removal (27, 8 § 6).

The rules contained in the three foregoing sections (§§ 324, 325, 326) were acted upon by the Cape Supreme Court in *Niekerk* vs. *Kiekerh* (1 M. 452). There certain children claimed from the defendant, one of their grandmother's executors, and one of the guardians of the said children while minors, their shares of the inheritance coming from thoir said grandmother. They sought to moke defendant liable as having administered the estate along with the other executors and guardians. Defendant admitted his appointment as executor and guardian, but denied that he had administered the estate in such capacities, and claimed that the plaintiffs should first of all have recourse against the administering executors and guardians. The Court adopted the rules laid down by Voet (see § 324); held, that the least act of administration respecting the estate of a minor renders the person who commits it an administering tutor, and deprives him of the benefit of claiming a previous excussion of the other administering tutor or tutors; and decided, that by making himself a party to and signing the liquidation account of the estate, the defendant must bo deemed to have been an administering tutor. It was furthor held that, if the late administering guardian or any of the other two guardians were insolvent at the time when, by reason of their coming of age, the plaintiffs were entitled to have brought their *actio tutelae* against those guardians, the defendant could now be called upon to pay every deficiency which had been occasioned by the maladministration of the estate, reserving to him his right of relief, *pro raid,* against

his co-guardians who were solvent; but that, if any of the co-guardians who were solvent at the time of the expiry of the guardianship, consequent on the majority of the plaintiffs, had since become insolvent, the amount of their share of the deficiency must be deducted from the amount of the claim of the plaintiffs, and the loss which had thus been occasioned by the delay of the plaintiffs must fall on them, and not on the defendant, who, by the delay of the plaintiffs, had been prevented from operating his relief from the co-guardians who were solvent at the expiry of the guardianship, but had since become insolvent The Court gave judgment for the plaintiffs, as claimed. See also *In re Liesching* (2 M. 329), and *llrink* vs. *Smuts* (3 M. 81).

327. There are cases where a co-tutor cannot even be held liable secondarily *(in subsidium)*—for instance, if a guardian, being possessed of means, suddenly becomes insolvent, when no blame can be imputed to the co-guardian; or if the co-guardian, who bad to be called upon first of all, was able to pay at the time when action was instituted against him, and on account of delay ceased to be solvent (27,8 § 7).

§ 41 of Ordinance 105, 1833, as we have seen, regulates the proceedings in case of insolvency of guardians in the Cape Colony. Similar proceedings are taken in the other South African Colonies.

328. Guardians are prohibited, in general, from alienating without judicial decree the immovable property of their wards, or such movable property as is capable of preservation and does not perish or deteriorate in value by effluxion of time, such as gold, silver, garments, gems, and other movables of value, like heirlooms and plate. The right to alienate a ward's movables without a judicial decree refers to such things as cannot be preserved by keeping, such as fruits and natural products, superfluous animals, worn-out clothes, and similar things which the guardian should alienate, unless he wants to cause loss to the ward. The alienation of such things may take place by private sale out of hand

(27, 9 § 1).

See *Grotius* (1, 8, 6; *Maasdorp,* p. 26). Van der Keessel (§ 130) adopts the same rule, and lays down that guardians are incapable of alienating, not only immovable property, but public, State, or foreign securities as well. Before application to sell immovables is granted by the Court, Van der Keessel (§ 131) says the advice of the Orphan Chamber or Master should be taken, the decree being given by the Court appointing the guardian, or to whose jurisdiction the guardian is subject (§ 132). The Cape Ordinance 105 of 1833, § 24, provides that no tutor testamentary or dative, and no curator nominate or dative, and no curator *bonis* shall sell, alienate, or mortgage any immovable property belonging to any minor, or forming part of any estate under the guardianship of such tutor or curator, unless the Supreme Court or any Judge thereof shall by any order made by such Court or Judge have authorised such sale, alienation, or mortgage, or unless the person by whom any such tutor testamentary or curator nominate shall have been appointed shall have directed such sale, alienation, or mortgage to be made. As to the Transvaal, see Proc. 28, 1902, § 94. As to Natal, see Act 38, 1899, §§ 42 and 60.

329. Amongst the immovable property of the ward which the guardian cannot alienate without judicial decree or direction of the testator, are to be reckoned such incorporeal things or rights as are included in the category of immovables. The right of emphyteusis or superficies (as to which see a later part of this work, vol. 1.), cannot be alienated without decree, nor certain servitudes attached to the soil, such as mining rights. Nor, generally, may usufruct or other servitudes, personal or real, be alienated without decree. The same applies to annual rents, compositions on land, or payments in fee. Nor may actions relating to such real property or real rights he ceded or alienated without decree, or generally, any obligation in favour of the ward, by the mere authority of the guardian (27, 9 § 2).

See Perezius on the *Code (tit. qyando*

decreto Opus nan est, No. 1).

330. Alienation includes any act of the guardian whereby the real rights *(jus in re)* of the ward are lessened or diminished, or whereby the ward is prevented from availing himself in any way of his rights. Thus alienation includes not only sale or exchange, but the suffering of usucapion, the ceding of real rights in payment of a debt, the handing over of an estate bequeathed to a ward as fiduciary heir, gifts of real rights or of property or marriage gifts (27, 9 § 3).

In *Wolff* vs. *Solomon's Trustee* (12 S. C. 42; 5 C. T. R. 72), the father of the plaintiff, a minor daughter, purchased a farm in the Transvaal for the plaintiff, and had the same transferred into her name. Two years later the father became insolvent. Two years after that the trustee of the insolvent estate obtained from the father the title-deeds of the farm, together with a power of attorney, signed by the daughter (who was still a minor), authorising the transfer of the Transvaal farm, the insolvent having admitted that he had paid the price of the farm in fraud of his creditors. No steps were taken by the trustee to set aside the transfer to the minor, or to recover the purchase-price (as an equivalent for the farm) from the minor assisted by a curator *ad litem.* The daughter afterwards married, while still a minor, and did not become aware of the delivery of the title-deeds until her husband discovered this fact two years after the marriage. Nine years after this discovery the plaintiff brought an action against the trustee to recover the title-deeds, and to have the power of attorney declared null and void. It was said by De Villiers, C.J.: "It is perfectly clear that neither the delivery of the title-deeds nor the execution of the power could in any way prejudice the plaintiff during her minority. Even if the power had been carried into execution, by transfer of the farm *coram lege loci,* such transfer would have been null and void without the consent of a competent Court. On this point all the authorities are agreed." As there was no sufficient proof of fraud on the plaintiffs part, or of ratification after majority, she was

held entitled to succeed.

331. Among obligations, which are prohibited equally with the alienation of the property or real rights of minors, are included not only the giving of pledges, by which the detention or natural possession passes to a creditor, but also the giving of a mortgage, by which the thing is bound for a debt, the bare detention or natural possession of the thing remaining with the ward. This is true to such an extent that, if a ward, with the sanction of his guardian, acquires a property on condition (entered into without leave of the Court) that the estate shall remain bound to the seller in right of pledge, such pledge shall be of no effect It will be otherwise, if the question be one of a tacit or legal, not a conventional, mortgage or hypothec: for the property of wards is liable to legal or tacit hypothecs just as the property of any other person. Thus if a ward purchases a property from the Treasury, the Treasury will have a binding tacit hypothec over the same, as the property of one who contracts with the Treasury. In one case only can a mortgage be validly constituted over a minor's property by a guardian, without judicial decree—namely, where a minor has lent money to another minor who purchases an estate, on condition that the estate shall remain under mortgage in favour of the lender until the loan is repaid (27, 9 § 4).

In the Cape Colony, by Act 5, 1861, § 8, sub-section 2, the tacit hypothec of the Government on the estates of persons contracting with it is abolished. This hypothec was abolished in the Transvaal by Proc. 28, 1902.

332. As above stated, the decree authorising a sale must be made by the Judge of the Court under whose jurisdiction the guardian or the ward's property is. This judicial decree will only be given, if there is a just ground for alienating the ward's property. One cause of alienation for which a decree may be given is payment of the ward's debts, care being taken that only so much is alienated as will realise sufficient to cover the debts. Another cause is the contracting of marriage by the ward, where money is nec-

essary for the ceremony and for household expenses; or if the ward cannot be supported, or fed, clothed, and educated in accordance with his position, unless an alienation be made (27, 9 §§ 5—8). 333. If a judicial decree authorising alienation has not been given in regard to things that are not to be alienated without judicial decree, everything that takes place in connection with such alienation is *ipso jure* null and void. The same thing holds good, if it is afterwards shown that the decree has been obtained from the Judge by fraud; or if a decree has been given that the ward's property shall be mortgaged, and the guardian makes sale of the property. If the Judge decrees that the property shall be mortgaged or alienated (sold), the guardian may choose either of the two modes of disposing of the property (27, 9 § 9). 334. From this certain actions arise, both against the guardian alienating or binding, the ward's property in a unlawful manner, and against those in whose favour the guardian has made such unlawful alienation or obligation, or in whose favour the guardian has unlawfully remitted debts or other rights competent to the ward. Against the guardian the ward may bring the *actio tutelae* in respect of such transactions taking place without judicial decree. A debtor of the ward, in whose favour an unauthorised remission of the debt has been made, will be liable in the original action to enforce payment of the debt, just as if no remission had been made. If the possession of property alienated without authority has passed to another person, the ward and his heirs will have a vindicatory action to recover such possession, together with all the fruits, if the person who holds the property is a possessor *(mala fide)* in bad faith. But if a person from whom the property is recovered be a possessor in good faith *(bond fide),* only the fruits which exist at the time of joinder in issue *(litis contestatio)* need be delivered. The possessor may defend himself by an exception of bad faith *(doli moli),* if the ward who vindicates the property has received the price paid for the same by the possessor, either wholly or in part (or if the price

has been wholly or partially applied to the ward's uses), and the possessor may detain such property until he has received a refund of the amount paid to the ward or applied to the ward's uses. If the possessor, without raising an exception of bad faith, has restored the property wrongfully alienated, he may nevertheless, by a *condictio sine cansd,* recover from the ward the amount received by the ward or applied to the ward's uses. The burden of proving whether any amount and what amount has been received by the ward or applied to the ward's uses lies not on the ward, but on the purchaser (27, 9 § 10). 335. If there is a doubt, it is presumed, in favour of minors, that an alienation of the ward's property has not been validly made, and the purchaser must show that he has not neglected any formalities requisite to the purchase of the property. If he fails in such proof, the property must be restored to the ward claiming the same. So long as a decree of the Court has been obtained, it makes no difference, in modern Dutch Law, whether the decree was given before or after the sale (27, 9 § 11).

The practice of the Deeds Registry offices throughout South Africa makes, or ought to make, it absolutely impossible for such alienations to take place without the previous sanction of the Court.

336. There are certain cases, in which alienation may take place of necessity without a decree of the Court: for instance, where a ward holds a property in common with another person, and the joint owner claims a division of the property; if a property has been mortgaged by the father of the ward or any other person to whom the ward is heir, and the creditor wishes to enforce his rights by sale of what has been mortgaged to him; if, on account of failure to pay annual tributes, such as quit-rent, the property is sold by the Treasury; if the Court has given authority to mortgage the ward's property in order to satisfy a judgment. Voet adduces other instances. It is, however, submitted that the nature of them all is such as to make alienation inoperative without judicial decree. Thus, with regard to the division

of property held in common, it is submitted that at the Cape (and the law on this subject is the same in the Transvaal, Orange River Colony, Natal, and Rhodesia) there can, in terms of § 24 of Ordinance 105, 1838—which forbids sale, alienation, or mortgage of any immovable property " forming part of any estate under the guardianship of the tutor or curator "—be no division of a joint property, and thus no alienation even of that portion which does not belong to the ward, without judicial decree. In the second case mentioned in this section, again, the creditor must of necessity obtain a judicial decree declaring the mortgaged property executable before he can sell the same (27, 9 § 12). 337. A ward may alienate without judicial decree, on the ground of necessity, where he has, with his guardian's authority, purchased an estate from a third person with the suspensive condition attached to the sale, or a condition for re-sale, for in such cases, if the conditions are unfulfilled, the property *ipso jure* reverts to the seller, the dominion over the estate sold having passed, not absolutely but conditional!y. In such case, the position is the same as if no sale had taken place. If a testator, whether the father or another person to whom the ward is heir, has laid down in his will or codicil that a certain estate coming from him shall be alienated, the obtaining of a decree authorising such sale will be superfluous, since it was the will of the testator that the property should be alienated, and the guardian is therefore required to alienate in the manner prescribed by the testator (even if, says Voet, the will should afterwards be invalidated—although this seems a very bold statement). If the testator has not enjoyed the sale by his testament, but merely gave out or stated during his lifetime that the property was for sale, alienation cannot take place after his death without a judicial decree (27, 9 § 12).

Even where there is a condition on the sale of land for re-sale, or reversion to the seller upon non-payment, the South African practice favours a judgment of Court to justify such re-sale or reversion.

338. If a guardian takes upon himself the suit of a minor who is summoned in an action, he may, where such a course is necessary, give security on the minor's behalf to abide the result of the action without judicial decree. In like manner he may sell, without judicial decree, a thing pledged to his ward for a debt (since landed property mortgaged cannot be sold without a decree). The same thing holds, if the father, or other person to whom a ward is heir, has pledged or mortgaged a thing or estate for a debt, or if the ward has given a similar pledge or mortgage (after obtaining judicial authority), and the tutor afterwards obtains a loan at the same or a lower rate of interest than that charged on the pledge or mortgage, and with the money so lent discharges such pledge or mortgage. Where the money has been borrowed at a higher rate of interest than was charged on the mortgage, and the mortgage is discharged, such loan will not be valid, unless there is a judicial decree. The sale of immovable property, which a minor has made without judicial decree and without his guardian's authority, will be valid, where the minor has conducted and represented himself as a major, and so deceived the purchaser (27, 9 § 18).

The terms of § 24 of the Cape Ordinance 105, 1833, are so imperative that one might be justified in holding that even where a minor represents himself to be a major, a sale of landed property cannot take place without a decree of the Court. There is no decision of any Court on the subject, and it would be safer to hold with Voet that in case of fraud the minor is bound by the sale, especially as, if this were not so, the onus of proving that the minor was of full age would be on the person who contracted with him.

339. Any alienations, which were null and void at the beginning, may be thereafter ratified, if the minor has attained the age of majority. Such ratification may take place even against the will of the adverse party, and may be express or tacit. A tacit ratification will be inferred if the ward, having attained majority, institutes an action of guardianship *(actio tutelae)* against the guardian (or a similar action against a curator), to recover the value or price of what was unlawfully sold (i.e., without judicial decree) during his minority. Such a ratification is entire, and cannot extend to one part of a transaction, while another part is neglected. If there has been ratification, the transaction may nevertheless be rescinded, if the former ward can show that there has been *laesio enormis* (though in Cape Colony, in terms of Act 8, 1879, § 8, relief on the c. i.—Vol. i. o ground of *laesio enormis* is no longer obtainable). Ratification, according to Voet, is also implied where, since majority, the following terms have elapsed without an action brought by the former ward to set aside the transaction: (1) In the case of alienations with a burdensome title *(ex oneroso tibulo),* five years; (2) in the case of alienations with a lucrative title *(ex lucrativo titulo),* ten years where the parties are present, twenty years where the parties are in different jurisdictions (27, 9 § 14).

The first case of prescription mentioned by Voet refers to alienations where the title is given for valuable consideration *(onerosum)* to the party acquiring from the ward; the second case refers to alienations without valuable consideration to the ward who alienates. It will be seen that the principle of law, that everything is to be construed in favour of minors, is followed in this matter as well, the term of prescription being much longer where the minor is in a less favourable position.

340. If a decree for an alienation has been made without hearing relatives or persons interested in the alienation of the ward's property, such relatives or interested persons may, before the sale, apply to the Court for such an order as may be deemed fit under the circumstances (27, 9 § 15).

See Grotius (1, 8, 6; *Maasdorp,* p. 26). Schorer (note 37) agrees with Voet that the relatives may obtain an interdict restraining the alienation. See also *Dutch Consultations* (part 1, No. 153).

341. Voet says that what has been laid down with regard to the alienation of minors' property applies to the property of churches, asylums founded for the benefit of orphans, and similar institutions, the persons having the administration of such property being quasitutors or curators (27,9 § 17. § 16 has been considered above, § 178). 342. Although there are many rules of law which apply to tutors and curators indiscriminately, there is this difference, that a tutor is generally regarded as appointed to the person, and a curator to the property, of the ward—although, in modern usage, guardians have jurisdiction over both persons and property. A guardian may be appointed to a minor even against the minor's will; but not a curator in Roman Law, except a curator *ad litem,* or a curator specially appointed to obtain an account of a guardian's administration. In modern law, however, there is no distinction (27, 10 §§ 1, 2). 343. Curators *ad litem* are not appointed so much by the Judge of the minor's domicile, as by the Judge of the Court before which the action, in which it is sought to make the minor a party, is brought. A curator *ad litem* cannot be compelled to give security *rem pupilli salv am fore* (27, 10 § 2).

See Van Zyl's *Theory of the Judicial Practice* (chap. 2, p. 17, ed. 1893; 2nd ed. p. 20, and the authorities there collected) on the appointment of a curator *ad litem.* 344. Curators are appointed to insane persons, and those who have not the proper control of their mental functions, since they cannot give their consent or apply their will to anything, have no mind of their own, and are not capable of committing wrong, so that they are, by a fiction of law, treated as persons who are absent, asleep, or dead. According to Roman-Dutch Law (although this is otherwise in South African practice), a judicial or magisterial decree is not necessary to declare a person of unsound mind.

Everything done by a lunatic before the appointment of a curator, during lunacy, is *ipso jure* null and void; and, on the contrary, what is done by a lunatic during a lucid interval, or after his reason is finally restored to him, will hold good. A judicial decree is necessary for the appointment of a curator to a lunatic, in order that such a curator may interfere without risk in the administration of the lunatic's affairs (27, 10 § 3).

Curators to lunatics or prodigals are in all respects analogous to curators of the property of minors, and the subject is, therefore, treated of in this place. In the Cape Colony, the rights and duties of curators to lunatics are regulated by Act No. 1, 1897. § 34 of the Act provides for the appointment by the Court of curators over the property of persons declared lunatic. § 13 of the Act appoints the Attorney-General, Solicitor-General, and Crown Prosecutor of Griqualand West ex-officio curators ad litem of persons detained under the Act by magisterial or judicial order. By § 34, the ex-officio curator ad litem may apply for the appointment of a curator of the property, where no curator has been appointed, and the estimated value of the corpus of the lunatic's property does not exceed 500/., or the income therefrom 50/. per annum. Where the lunatic is capable of managing himself, but not his property, a curator may be appointed to the property, not to the person (§ 35). The Court (§ 36) may dissolve a partnership where one partner has been declared a lunatic by the Court. A copy of the order appointing a curator over a lunatic must (§ 37) be lodged with the Master of the Supreme Court. The Master grants (§ 38) a certificate of appointment to such curator, who must file an inventory, just as in the case of the estate of a deceased person (§ 39). Curators ore entitled to the same remuneration (§ 40) as executors. If a lunatic dies intestate, or if he dies testate and there is no executor, or none willing to act, the curator of the lunatic (i.e., curator bonis) shall continue to administer the estate, and distribute the assets as if he had been appointed executor dative (§41). The Court may (§ 42) grant authority to the curator to (1) sell the lunatic's property; (2) exchange or make partition of such property; (3) carry on or discontinue the lunatic's business; (4) grant leases of the lunatic's property; (o) perform an-contract relating to such property entered into, before

the lunacy, by the lunatic; (6) exercise any power or consent to such exercise where it is for the lunatic's benefit; (7) raise money on mortgage of the lunatic's property to pay his debts, or expenses of past, present, or future maintenance; (8) apply money for maintenance or benefit of the lunatic; (9) make such reports to the Court or the Master as the Court may deem fit. The terms of the Cape Act are practically identical with those of the Transvaal Proc. No. 36, 1902. As to Natal, see Law No. 1, 1868.

345. A curator, where a lunatic has lucid intervals, has the administration of the lunatic's property only during actual insanity. It is left to the discretion of the Judge to decide whether things done by a lunatic, who sometimes has lucid intervals, were done during a period of insanity or not. If there is no trace of insanity in what has been done, but everything seems to have taken place in accordance with custom and ordinary care, the burden of proving that the act was done during insanity should be on the person contesting the validity of the act. If, on the other hand, there are any signs of insanity, or if the alleged lunatic did not transact everything necessary to the business in hand, signifying merely his assent to what was proposed by a simple affirmation or response, the presumption will be that such an act was done during lunacy (27, 10 § 4). 346. It is the duty of a curator, while insanity lasts, to defend and protect the lunatic by his (the curator's) discretion and labour, and to look after his property, in the same way as guardians are bound to do in relation to their wards (27, 10 § 5). 347. It is still customary in modern law to interdict from the administration of their property, and to appoint curators over, such persons as place no limit to their expenditure, on the petition of their parents or other near relations. After such interdict has been granted, persons declared prodigals cannot alienate any goods or bind themselves, without the authority of the curator—so that not even a surety intervening on behalf of persons declared prodigals is validly bound (unless the transaction be entered

into by the curator). just as if he had stood surety to a lunatic. There is, however, this difference between the acts of a lunatic and those of a prodigal, that the contracts of a lunatic are ipso jure null and void, in what manner soever they have been entered into, even before a curator has been appointed to the lunatic as such (in other words, the acts of a lunatic during insanity, even before a curator's appointment, are void); while the acts of a prodigal, who squanders his substance, before a curator has been appointed and a judicial interdict given, are valid. If a prodigal has been placed under curatorship, he cannot again have the control of his affairs, even if his conduct improves, unless he first of all obtains the sanction of the Judge, and a decree restoring to him the right to administer his own affairs. According to Voet, a judicial decree restraining a prodigal from control of his own affairs is not sufficient of itself. The decree must be made known by publication. In this he is followed by Grotius (1, 11, 4), and Van Leeuwen Cent. For. 1, 1, 16, 28). Van der Keessel (§ 165), and Van der Linden (1, 5, 8; Juta, p. 42) are silent on the subject. Van Leeuwen says: "Curators are appointed to spendthrifts, upon cause shown, not by the pupillary magistrate the Master, but by the Court of Holland or the ordinary Judge; and the appointment is publicly proclaimed, and also the interdict, in order that all may have notice." Van Leeuwen (1, 1, 16, 28) and Van der Keessel (§ 166) concur with Voet in holding that a prodigal must be discharged from curatorship by judicial decree. In the same manner as a minor, a prodigal may, by contracting, improve his condition, where he contracts without his curator's assent. A prodigal may adiate an inheritance with his curator's authority. The fact that a person has been declared a prodigal does not absolve him from liability for crime or tort. A testamentary appointment by a father of curators to his major children who are insane or prodigals will not be valid. The Court may appoint not only parents as curators to their children, but children also as curators to their parents. Voet holds that a wife may be appointed curator to her husband (27, 10 §§ 6—10).

In holding that a wife may be curator to her husband, Voet draws no distinction between person and property. Van der Keessel arbitrarily states (§ 168) that the Dutch Law does not allow of a married woman being appointed curator over her husband if insane or prodigal. Grotius (1, 11, 7) draws a distinction, stating that "the wife, being a minor, cannot be appointed guardian to her husband in case he should be afflicted by lunacy or prodigality, though she may sometimes be allowed the management of the property." Schorer (note 47) contents himself with quoting Voet, whom he interprets to lay down that the wife may have the curatorship of her husband's goods and her own. This view was followed by the Cape Supreme Court (*In re De Jager*, Buch. 1876, p. 228), which laid down that a wife cannot be appointed curator of the person of her lunatic husband, though she may be allowed the management of the property.

The power of the Court to appoint curators over the property of prodigals is undoubted (*In re Chism*, 9 S. C. 61). At the Cape, a drunken father has been placed under curatorship on the petition of his daughter (*In re Miller*, 9 S. C. 414). Where the Court was unable to declare a respondent of unsound mind, yet, as some restraint over the administration of his property was necessary, and as the defendant himself consented to the order, a curator *bonis* was appointed (*The Master* vs. *Lehmann*, 4 E. D. C. 308) to administer his estate and (in accordance with § 25 of the Cape Ordinance 105, 1833) pay over the proceeds to the Master. See also *In re Filmer* (Buch. 1875, p. 2); *In re Printloo* (9 E. D. C. 181); *In re De Jager* (16 S. C. 222); and *Combrinck* vs. *Combrinck and Another* (Buch. 1877, p. 72).

348. As to the validity of a decree, appointing a curator over the prodigal, beyond the jurisdiction of the Judge making the order, Voet holds that, as there has been no publication of the decree beyond the jurisdiction, a person who contracts in good faith with the prodigal

beyond the jurisdiction will have a just ground of action against the prodigal, on the score of *justus error*, in the same manner as if there had been no interdict (27, 10 §§ 11, 12). 349. Curators may also be appointed to persons who suffer from such bodily defects as render them unable to have the sole control of their affairs, wherefore they require the assistance of others to some extent in their transactions, such as deaf and dumb persons, and those who suffer from a perpetual disease (such as leprosy).

The curator in such a case is only required to give his assistance or authority in transactions to such an extent as the person suffering from such bodily defect is incapable, on account of his infirmity, from completing the transaction by himself—in the same way as curators to lunatics who have lucid intervals act as curators only while such lunatics are insane (27, 10 § 13).

Where curators (since dead) had been appointed to a deaf and dumb person, and there was a sum of money belonging to him in the hands of the Master, and he applied for an order (1) declaring him capable of managing his own affairs, (2) releasing his property from curatorship, and (3) authorising the Master to pay to applicant the sum in the Master's hands, the Court held that there had not been sufficient cause shown for releasing applicant entirely from curatorship, and appointed a curator, who would, however, "only exercise such powers as are required to supplement the applicant's physical defects" (*In re Rens*, Foord, 92; see also *In re Hens*, 3 M. 100). Such curators are not appointed over the persons of deaf and dumb people. See *Grot.* 1, 11, 2; *Van der Kernel*, § 164; Yinnius on the *Institutes*, 1, 2, 3, 4; *Digest*, 29, 2, o, and *In re Rensburgh* (3 M. 99).

350. Curatorship ends, in the case of lunatics, with their restoration to sanity; in the case of prodigals, with their reformation, and the certainty that they may be once more trusted to manage their concerns properly. In their case, it appears that a judicial discharge from curatorship is necessary. In the case of minors, guardianship ends with attainment

of the age of majority, or marriage, or obtaining *venia aetatis* (27, 10 §§ 14—16).

See *In re Kemp* (3 M. 101), where the Court, on motion, released a person who had been declared to be of unsound mind from curatorship on the ground of his recovery.

CHAPTER IV. Husband And Wife.

(1) Promise Of Marriage.

351. Simple consent of parties is sufficient to constitute a binding agreement to marry, and this may be signified in person or, when the parties are away from each other, by letter or messenger. All persons who may validly contract marriage may enter into a promise to marry. Minors may promise to marry, and so may widows within the *annus luctu8*, although the former cannot marry without the consent of parents or guardians, nor the latter during the year of mourning (28, 1 §§ 1, 2).

A minor making a promise to marry without the consent of parents cannot be sued for breach of promise of marriage (*Gray* vs. *Rynhoud*, 1 M. 150). But a minor may sue, duly assisted, for damages for breach of promise of marriage. 352. There is nothing to prevent prodigals from making a promise to marry, since marriage has more relation to the persons than to the property of the contracting parties. This is the rule of the civil law. But Voet prefers to hold that, as marriage is followed by a statutory community of property, prodigals who have been interdicted cannot make a valid promise of marriage. This would, therefore, seem to be the modern law (28, 1 § 3). 353. Fraud or intimidation (duress, *metus*) are sufficient grounds to avoid a contract to marry. If the fraud is discovered, or the intimidation ceases, and a fresh promise of marriage, free from fraud or duress, is made, this will bind the parties (28, 1 § 4). 354. If the persons who enter into a contract to marry are under guardianship, the authority of the guardian is necessary, according to Roman Law. But this is not the case in Dutch Law, according to Voet (28, 1 § 5). This consent refers more to the actual marriage than to the promise to marry; though, as above stated, a minor is not liable in damages for breach of promise.

Voet (in 23, 2 § 16) says that the law of Holland does not require the consent of guardians to the marriage of minors, and quotes an edict of the Government of Holland, dated 1580 (art. 3). Van Leeuwen also *(R. D. L.,* 1, 14, 9; *Kotze,* 1, 106) says: "The consent of guardians to the marriage of their wards is not necessary." Van der Linden (1, 3, 6; *Juta,* p. 20) says that if the parents of the parties who wish to marry each other are alive, their assent or consent must be previously obtained. But with regard to guardians, he holds that at Common (Dutch) Law their consent is not necessary. Van der Keessel (§ 77) says: '' Under the term 'parents,' without whose consent the proclamation of espousals (».e., of banns) is not permitted to minors, are not included grandfathers and grandmothers, uncles, or guardians. " The Cape Marriage Order in Council of 1838, S§ 10, 17, requires, however, the consent of guardians. There is no difference between the consent to a marriage and the consent to a promise to marry, and, therefore, the consent required is the same for both. In the Transvaal, by Law 3, 1871, §§ 4 and 16, the consent of parents or guardians, failing which, that of the magistrate, is required. As to Natal, see Law 7, 1889, § 4. As to Orange River Colony, see Law 26,1899, § 19. The Rhodesia law is the same as that of the Cape.

355. A condition, a *modus,* or a day may be incorporated in a promise to many. The condition must be in accordance with public policy, and not immoral. It must be a possible condition, and must be fulfilled before the obligation to marry can arise, unless the contracting parties have foregone the condition, either expressly, or tacitly by having carnal intercourse with each other. The condition must be of a kind, the fulfilment of or omission to perform which depends on the will of the parties who have promised to many (28, 1 § 6).

See Van Leeuwen *(Cent. For.* 1,1,11,5); *Dutch Consultations* (part 5, No. 106, p. 358); Vinnius on the *Institutes* (on paternal power, 1, 9, 1, 5, ed. 1709, p. 44).

356. Mere intercourse, though it will avoid such a condition as that just mentioned, will not constitute marriage, according to Dutch Law (28, 1 § 6). From this it follows that, if the condition attached to the promise of marriage depends upon the will of a third person, the act of the parties who are to marry cannot affect the fulfilment of the condition by such third person. Thus Van Leeuwen *(Cens. For.* 1, 1, 11, 6) holds that if the promise be made subject to the father's consent, and intercourse takes place between the parties before such consent is obtained, such consent on the part of the father will still be required to confirm the promise of maniage (28, 1 §§ 6, 7). 357. In Dutch Law, adopting the Roman Law (to which the Canon Law is contrary), an impossible condition attached to a promise of marriage vitiates the contract—unless the condition is attached by way of negation, as a promise to marry " if you shall not touch the sky with your finger. " In such a case the contract is regarded as unconditional, and it is clear that an obligation thereon immediately arises (28, 1 § 8).

In other words, where the performance of the contract of marriage depends upon the performance of a thing which is impossible, the whole contract is avoided. Where a condition is attached to the contract that the marriage shall take place if an impossible thing does not happen, such a condition is treated as *von scripta,* and the promise to marry is binding.

358. Where an impossible condition, or one which infringes good morals, public utility, truth and honour is attached to the promise, the law will regard such a promise as entered into with no serious intention to marry, and the agreement will therefore be treated as null and void. But, where a serious and binding agreement to marry was originally entered into, the subsequent addition of an immoral condition (although immoral conditions generally vitiate contracts) will not discharge the contract to marry. So, if a youth promises marriage to a girl whom he has seduced, on condition that she shall procure abortion by

means of poison, the promise will stand, the desire to avoid public disgrace being the motive for the procuration of abortion, and the seduction constituting a sufficient consideration for the promise to marry. The same rule will hold, if the man promises marriage on condition that the girl will permit of previous intercourse. It makes no difference whether such conditions are fulfilled or not. In either case, the girl may sue for breach of promise of marriage (28, 1 §§ 8, 9). 359. If the da) has been fixed for the marriage, no suit on the promise of marriage can be brought until such day has elapsed. If consent is required to a promise to marry, failure to obtain such consent avoids the promise of marriage. If the statutes of any place prescribe any form for a binding promise of marriage, noncompliance with such statutes renders the marriage null and void (28, 1 §§ 10, 11). 360. The opinion of Van Leeuwen *(Cens. For.* 1, 1, 11, 10), and Grotius (1, 5, 16), apparently followed by Van der Keessel (§ 86), is opposed to the view of Voet, who holds that an oath is sufficient to establish a promise of marriage. The other commentators consider that if the mere oath of the plaintiff stands against that of the defendant, there should be absolution from the instance in favour of the defendant, and the mere fact that the plaintiff has been seduced by the defendant will not of itself raise a presumption that there has been a promise of marriage. It would seem, according to moder n practice, that the latter part of the rule would hold good, and that seduction by itself raises no presumption of a promise to marry. The question whether or not there has been a promise is an ordinary question of fact, which must be left to the discretion of the Judges. Consequently, Voet's view would seem to be quite in accordance with modern usage (28, 1 § 11).

There seems to be considerable doubt as to the question whether the oath of a man should be taken to have preference over the unsupported oath of a woman in cases of seduction and breach of promise of marriage. In *Gleeson* vs. *Durrheim* (Buch. 1868, p. 244; followed in *Van der Berg* vs. *Elsbeth,* 3 8. C. 36) the rule of Dutch Law was deliberately adopted by the Cape Supreme Court, that if there was no evidence *aliunde* to lead the Court to doubt the man's oath, his oath was entitled to preference. But in a case of incest tried on circuit at Swellendam, Cape Colony, on April 10th, 1900, where counsel for the defence relied on the foregoing rule, the learned Judge who presided, in summing-up the case to the jury, said this rule was a survival from ancient times, when women were regarded as inferior to men, but that at the present day women were in all respects on terms of social and intellectual equality with men, and the rule might therefore be regarded as non-existent. No doubt this is the correct view to take. But, in the face of the decisions of the Cape Supreme Court, and in the absence of statutory provision on the subject, was not the learned Judge—apart from the facts of the particular case before him—bound to lay down the rule of law as stated in *Gleeson* vs. *Durrheim 1* 361. From promise of marriage arises the expectation of marriage (apet *matrimonii),* and an obligation to marry. In Dutch Law, a person who fails to perform a promise of marriage may be ordered to make specific performance, by marrying the other party.

On failure to perform the marriage, the party ordered to do so may be sentenced to imprisonment (28, 1 § 12).

This rule (as to which see also Van Leeuwen, *Cena. For.* 1, 1, 11, 26) was acted upon by the Cape Supreme Court in *Jooste* vs. *Grobbelaar* (1 M. 149; June 12th, 1832), when the defendant, who had seduced the plaintiff, was ordered to marry her within a month. The Cape Marriage Order in Council of 1838 abolished this procedure (§ 19), making it impossible for a Court thereafter to give a decree enforcing specific performance of a promise of marriage. This legislation has been imitated in the Transvaal (Marriage Ordinance No. 3, 1871, 517). § 20 of the Cape Ordinance provides for an action for damages for breach of promise of marriage, but such provision was unnecessary, as the ac-

tion exists at Dutch Common Law. In Natal (Marriage Order in Council, § 19), Orange River Colony (Law 26, 1899, § 20), and Rhodesia the law is the same as in Cape Colony.

362. Either of the parties may break (recede from) the promise of marriage where he or she discovers that the other party has been guilty—without the connivance of the person receding from the contract—of immorality *(stuprum),* and intercourse with others; or, according to Voet, on account of prodigality; or where there is a difference of religious belief (provided this was unknown to the party breaking the contract, at the time the promise was made); or on account of impotence (inability to beget children); or the taking of monastic vows, or insanity. Again, if a man promises to marry a girl, and continues to live in the same place *(i.e.,* does not go to another country in the interval) for two years, and fails to marry her, the girl may marry another person without being liable in an action. One party may repudiate espousals, where, before the engagement, the other had been guilty of fornication, of which the person to whom the fornicator was engaged was ignorant—provided there is sufficient proof of unchastity, such as birth of children, or abortion; mere suspicions or vague rumours not being sufficient ground for repudiation of the engagement (28, 1 § 13).

In English Law, as in Roman-Dutch Law, promise of marriage by a lunatic would appear to be void: for in English Law the marriage itself of a lunatic is void *(Hancock* vs. *Peaty,* L. R. 1 P. & D. 335, 341; 36 L. J. Mat. 57), if such marriage takes place during insanity.

363. Where a man who has promised marriage procures the seduction or debauchery of the girl to whom he is engaged by another person, he cannot be excused from his promise. In the same way, if a girl has been compelled to have connection with another, as in case of rape, the man cannot avoid his promise to marry. If a person promises marriage to a widow, believing her to be a virgin, he cannot break his promise when he discovers that she is a widow.

On the other hand, in addition to the cases mentioned above, the following grounds are sufficient to avoid a promise to marry: leprosy or venereal disease in either party,, conviction of crime, insolvency, fraudulent promise of marriage gifts, and similar grounds, in the discretion of the Court (28, 1 §§ 14, 15).

See Van Leeuwen *(Cent. For.* 1, 1, 11, 27—33).

364. Voet holds with Van Leeuwen *(Cent. For.* 1, 1, 11, 13 that betrothals between minors are not absolutely binding unless and until the party making the promise (and whom it is sought to bind) attains the age of majority. Minors have the same right of restitution against this as against other contracts (23, 1 §§ 16, 17). 365. On breach of the promise to marry, an action lies in favour of the injured party, to recover not only whatever presents havebeen given in earnest of the promise, but whatever amount the party sued has been enriched in by the agreement to marry. In. addition to this, the injured party may claim what gains he or she expected to obtain on account of the expectation of marriage—in other words, prospective damages for loss of position, wealth, or other advantages. According to Grotius (3, 2, 19; *Maaadorp,* p. 207) a donation made in contemplation of marriage must be returned in case the marriage does not take place (28, 1 §§ 18, 19).

In *Mocke* vs. *Fourie* (3 C. T. R. 315) it was said by De Villiers, C.J.: "I cannot find that our law makes any distinction between the case of a man suing for damages for breach of promise of marriage and a woman suing for breach of promise of marriage. In either case damages are recoverable, if there has been a deliberate breach of the promise to marry and consequent damages sustained by the party." So, where the plaintiff, a man, threatened legal proceedings,, and the defendant (the woman) then gave a promissory note in full settlement of all claims which the plaintiff might have against her, arising out of breach of the contract to marry, the plaintiff was held entitled *(Van*

Stailen vs. *Kocks,* 4 E. *D.* C. 24) to judgment on the promissory note. In other words, breach of promise by the woman was held a sufficient consideration for the note.

366. According to Van Leeuwen *(Cens. For.* 1, 1, 13, 12), where a person is betrothed to more than one individual, the earlier engagement is a bar to the later one. Voet does not agree with this. And at the present day one engagement is no bar to another. The party can make his choice, and marry one girl to whom he is. engaged, running the risk of being sued by the other girl or girls, for breach of promise (28, 1 §§ 20, 21). 367. Donations are not forbidden between engaged persons, nor is adultery, committed with one of the parties to the engagement, the contrary being the case where the parties are married. There is no period of mourning for an engaged person who is dead, nor is a widow prevented from entering into a promise of marriage during the period of mourning *(annus luctus).* Engagement does not make the children of the parties legitimate, nor create affinity between the relatives of the parties, nor does it create statutory community of property or the right to claim such community (28, 1 § 22).

The curious reader may consult an amusing chapter on the subject of espousals in Van Zyl's *Theory of the Judicial Practice* (ed. 1893, pp. 378—402; 2nd ed. pp. 394—417).

(2) The Contract Of Marriage. 368. Polygamy is forbidden in Roman Law, which is followed in this respect by Dutch Law. A second marriage contracted during the subsistence of the first is void (28,2 § 1).

Van der Keessel (§ 64) says that if a second marriage has been contracted during the subsistence of the first marriage in good faith on the part of both spouses, it is so far valid that the children born of the second marriage are legitimate under the Canon Law (which, he says, has been adopted in this respect by the Court of Holland, and by the States General). The same author (§ 65) goes farther, and says that even if the second spouse alone has acted in good

faith, being deceived by the bigamist, a child born of such a union is likewise to be regarded as legitimate. With all deference to the authority of Van der Keessel and the Court of Holland, it is submitted that the children in such a case are illegitimate. In the first place, as we have seen, the second marriage is absolutely void. The only persons whom the law recognises as legitimate are those born from a valid marriage— i.e., a marriage not void—or born out of wedlock but legitimated by a subsequent marriage. Secondly, the rule prohibiting dual marriages has been introduced, not so much to punish individuals, as to provide against polygamy on grounds of public policy. However innocently the parties may have acted, public policy cannot be infringed in favour of one or two parties who have acted in good faith.

The punishment for bigamy, in Cape Law, is discretionary. The Transvaal Marriage Oidinance, No. 3, 1871, § 10, enacts that bigamy shall be punished with three years' hard labour (an enactment described by Justice E. J. P. Jorissen as "barbarous "),' and further provides that on conviction of a person for bigamy the second marriage shall be declared null and void—which is Notwithstanding Judge Jorissen's *dictum,* however, it is clear that the punishment of three years' imprisonment fixed by the Transvaal statute must be regarded as a maximum.

unnecessary, as the second marriage is void at common law. In *Hatch* vs. *Hatch* (9 S. C. 1) the defendant, who had been deserted by her husband, and believed that she was a widow, married the plaintiff. It was subsequently discovered that the first husband was alive. The second marriage was declared void, and the custody of a child born during the subsistence of the second marriage was given to the mother. 369. In Ronian Law, consent and cohabitation, or one or other of them, were held sufficient to constitute a valid marriage. This is not the case in modern law. But cohabitation will be taken as evidence of a marriage subsisting between the parties (28, 2 § 2).

In *Hoffman* vs. *Hoffman* (1 M. 281), where a witness saw the parties go into church together to get married, had visited them when they lived together as man and wife, and had heard the man call the woman his wife, the Court decided that there was sufficient *prima facie* evidence of the marriage. See also *Kemball* vs. *Kemball* (1 M. 281), *Schlechting* vs. *Schlechting* (Buch. 1875, p. 26), *Potter* vs. *Potter* (7 E. D. C. 148), *Matomela* vs. *Matomela* (2 E. D. C. 12), *Tradesmen's Benefit Society* vs. *Du Preez* (o S. 0. 269), and *Bronn* vs. *Bronn's Executors* (3 S. 313).

370. According to Dutch Law, marriages can only be contracted lawfully after publication of banns on three Sundays or market-days, in the place of domicile of the bridegroom and bride, or, if the domicile is but newly acquired, in the former place of domicile. The marriage will then proceed, unless some person comes forward and alleges some just cause or impediment sufficient to prevent the marriage. If there has been no due publication of banns, the marriage is *ipso jure* null and void. Even Jews are required to submit to three publications of banns, and it is not sufficient that they should have entered into a marriage in accordance with Jewish Law (23, 2 § 8).

See Van Leeuwen *Cens. For.* 1, 1, 14, 7). The publication of banns at the Cape is regulated by the Ordinance of 1838, §§ 2—6, and notice of marriage before a magistrate is regulated at the Cape by Schedule A. to Act 16, 1860. The law as to banns in the Transvaal is regulated by §§ 1 and 7 of Law 3, 1871. As to Natal, see the Marriage Order in Council, §§ 2—6. As to Orange Biver Colony, see Law 26,1899, § 3. Special licences are regulated at the Cape by § 11, Ordinance of 1838, and § 5, Act 16, 1860; in the Transvaal, by §§ 3, 4 of Law 3, 1871, § 2 of the same law regulating marriages before Landdrosts or Magistrates. Special licences in Natal are regulated by Law 7, 1889, and in Orange River Colony by Law 26, 1899, §§ 8 and 9. Jewish and Mohammedan marriages are regulated at the Cape by Act 16, 1860, § 4, which provides for the appointment of special marriage officers, and in Natal by Law 19, 1881, § 1.

371. "It is a universally accepted principle that the question whether a valid marriage was contracted must be decided according to the law of the place where it was celebrated. Voet, whilst admitting the general principle, claims the right for every State to refuse recognition of marriages entered into by its own subjects in other countries with the view of avoiding the publicity required by the law of their own country " (De Villiers, C.J., in *Ngquobela* vs. *Sihele*, 10 S. C. 852). Voet's opinion seems to have been based upon the terms of the Dutch Echt Reglement (Marriage Edict), which applied specially to marriages in Holland, and he does not, in the portion of his *Comvientaries* now under consideration, lay down any general rule on the subject (28, 2 § 4).

The right of a State to refuse recognition of marriages entered into in other countries in evasion of its own laws was discussed at length in the leading English case of *Brook* vs. *Brook* (4 Jur. N. S. 317; see also *Ruding* vs. *Smith*, 2 Hag. 384; *Lindo* vs: *Beluario*, 1 Hag. 216; *Goldtmid* vs. *Bromer*, 1 Hag. 324), which was referred to in *Broun* vs. *Bronn's Executors* (3 S. 329).

372. Mere companionship and cohabitation of a man with a woman do not constitute any absolute presumption of marriage. There must be further proof of the marriage (28, 2 § 5).

See § 369, above.

373. Consent of the contracting parties is essential to constitute a valid marriage. If such consent is wanting, or given under circumstances from which one may infer loss of reason, undue influence, or fraud, the marriage is *ipso jure* null and void—for instance, if one of the contracting parties be a lunatic, or has been deprived of his or her reason through drunkenness, or if there is a mistake in the identity of one of the parties, or in an essential quality of one of the parties (though not in an accidental quality, such as appearance, wealth, rank, and similar qualities). The case of fraud, according to Voet, can hardly arise, as it is necessary, in a modern marriage ceremony, for both parties clearly to express their consent. But surely consent may in some cases be obtained by fraud! (28, 2 § 6). 374. Besides the consent of the parties to the marriage, the law requires the consent of certain persons under whose control they may be. In the first place, the consent of the father is necessary to the marriage of his minor children. The consent of the father may be express or implied. It is implied if the father knows that the marriage of his minor child is about to take place and does not forbid it. Since a marriage without paternal consent, where such consent is necessary, is void, the children of such a marriage — unless it be ratified subsequently by the consent of the parents or by the party who married during minority recognising the marriage after attainment of the age of majority—will be regarded as illegitimate. Failing the consent of the father, that of the mother, as surviving legitimate guardian, is required for the marriage of children under the age of majority. Where there is a difference of opinion between the father and the mother, preference is to be given to the wish of the father, by virtue, firstly, of his judicial standing, and secondly, of the marital control he has over his wife. Where a surviving parent enters into a second marriage, his or her consent is still necessary to the marriage of minor children of the first marriage. The consent of parents is not required for the marriage of major children, or of emancipated children. The consent of persons who have been declared prodigals is not necessary for the marriage of their minor children though this does not dispense with such consent of others as may be necessary. The consent of grandparents is not required. No consent is necessary to the second marriage of widows or widowers who are still minors. Where publication of banns is made in an underhand way, and the parents come to know of such publication, and do not object to the marriage, their consent will be implied in the same manner as if such publication had originally been open and free from fraud. The same rule holds if the parties acted in good faith, but publication without the parents' consent is allowed to take place through the negligence of those public officers who have to make the publications (28, 2 §§ 7—10, and 12—18).

The Cape Marriage Order in Council of 1838, § 17, provides that where the parent) or guardians of minors are insane, absent from the Colony, incapable in law or in fact of consenting, or unreasonably and improperly induced to withhold consent to a proper marriage, or dead, any person desirous of marriage may apply to the Chief Justice of the Cape Colony for his consent to the marriage. § 14 of the Order prevents marriage officers from solemnising marriages (except in case of a widow or widower) after the same shall have been forbidden. § 10 provides that

C.L.—VOL. L P *bond fide* marriages of minors by marriage officers do not entail any penalty on such marriage officers. The solemnities of marriage in the Transvaal are regulated by Law 3,1871, §§ 12—17. As to the consent of guardians to the marriage of minors in Roman-Dutch Law and Cape Law, see above, § 354. In Natal, the consent of guardians is necessary for the valid marriage of a minor. So, where there had been a marriage without compliance with this rule, the Natal High Court refused to authorise the marriage, intimating that the guardian could give his consent (*In re McDuling and Brown*, 6 N. L. R. 88). In the same case it was decided that the marriage, even after banns, of a minor, one of whose guardians objected, though the other consented to the marriage, would be void under the Natal Marriage Ordinance. In *Lee* vs. *Donlon* (5 N. L. R. p. 270), the Natal Supreme Court laid down that the marriage of a woman under twenty years of age is, in Roman-Dutch Law, invalid, or may be invalidated, if it be without the consent of the father, or, if not, of the mother, if surviving, unless it has been authorised by judicial authority. The marriage of a person who has attained full age cannot, however, be assailed without his or her consent, unless some interest is liable to be affected. As to Orange River Colony, see Law 26, 1899, §§ 9,13 and 19. In *Johnson* vs. *McIntyre* (3 C. T. R. 426; 11 C. L. J. 40; 10 S. C. 318), the defendant, in collusion with the mother of a girl, who was a minor aged fourteen, obtained from a magistrate a special licence to marry her. The licence was granted without production of the father's consent, defendant having made a false representation that the girl was the daughter of a deceased man. The marriage was then solemnised by a clergyman upon production of the licence. Some weeks after, the father became aware of the marriage, and immediately applied for and obtained an interdict restraining the husband from having access to the girl, pending an action (now brought) to set aside the marriage. It was decided that no presumption of notice to the father existed, as this was a marriage by special licence. The marriage was therefore set aside as null and void. The Second Schedule to the Cape Act 9, 1882, provided for the following declaration to a magistrate by a person applying for a special licence: "I have no knowledge of any just impediment or lawful objection by reason of any kindred, relationship, or alliance of any former marriage, or the want of consent of parents or guardians, or any other lawful cause whatever." It was said by De Villiers, C.J.: "A special licence dispenses with previous notice to the public, and the magistrate in granting it has to rely upon the declarations made by the intended husband and wife under Act 9 of 1882. If one of them be a minor the licence cannot be granted without the written consent of the parents or guardians, as the case might be, or of the Chief Justice of the Colony. If through the fraud of one or both of the persons intending to marry the magistrate is led to believe that the requisite consent has been given, and to issue a licence accordingly, the common law right of the father to have such a clandestine marriage set aside remains, in my opinion, intact. The fact that the mother was a party to such a fraud would not affect the father's right, for, as I have already observed, in case of

a difference of opinion, his wish must prevail." 375. The penalty for contracting a marriage with a minor, without the consent of the father or mother, or the guardian or guardians where the consent of guardians is nec essary, is laid down by the Placaat or Edict of Charles V., of October 4th, 1540, § 17, a section as celebrated in Roman-Dutch Law as are the fourth and seventeenth sections of the English Statute of Frauds. This section enacts that persons marrying minors without such consent first had and obtained shall derive no benefit from the property of the minor whether present or in expectancy, and whether obtained by way of gift, dowry, inheritance, legacy, or otherwise. In other words, there is to be no community of property between spouses so married, and, if they marry by antenuptial contract, no gift from the minor spouse shall benefit the major spouse. Even where such marriage of minors is subsequently ratified by consent of the parents or guardians, the penalty laid down in § 17 of the Edict of 1540 still applies. The penalty holds as against the spouse misleading the minor, not against the minor spouse who has been misled. So the spouse who was a minor at the time of the marriage, and induced to enter into the marriage through the undue influence of the other spouse, may succeed to the property of such other spouse and may receive gifts, or benefit from the statutory community of property to this extent, that such benefit shall not entail any corresponding disadvantage upon the party receiving such benefit. The penalty only applies where, at the time of the marriage, the parents or guardians had a just ground for opposing the marriage. Where judicial consent has been obtained, the penalty will not be enforced. The question as to what is or is not just ground for refusing consent is a matter of judicial discretion. If marriages have already been clandestinely contracted, and the magistrate thereafter becomes aware of the grounds of opposition, he may declare that the grounds of opposition are invalid, and ratify the marriage; but (as the marriage was itself clandestine) the penalty under the Pla-

caat of Charles V. will still apply. Where parents object to the marriage of their minor children, Voet inclines to the view that they should state their reasons against the marriage. In South Africa, it is submitted, according to the tenour of the various marriage ordinances, such statement of reasons is not required. The statutes require the consent of the parents, without any further stipulation; and the onus of proving that such consent is wrongfully withheld would seem to lie upon the person who attempts to have the marriage celebrated (28, 2 §§ 11, 19-22).

A translation has been issued in Cape Colony of this title of Voet's. The translator renders into English the latter portion of § 21 in such a manner as to make Voet's statement of the law far from clear, as follows: "If, in cases of clandestine marriages afterwards lawfully contracted, the magistrate, shortly after giving his consent, became aware of the reasons of opposition, he may pronounce that the marriage ceremony was not entered upon with the requisite consent, and order the marriage to be ratified; and in this case the penalties apply as ordered by the Edict of Charles V. " On the penalty under the Placaat of Charles V., see *Mostert* vs. *The Master* (Buch. 1878, 83), *Mosiert* vs. *Mostert's Trustees* (4 S. C. 35), and *Ruperti* vs. *Ruperti's Trustees* (4 S. C. 22). See also *Greeff* vs. *Verreaux* (1 M. 155), and, as to the validity of a minor's marriage without consent, *Gray* vs. *Ryuhoud* (1 M. 150). On the question of consent of the Chief Justice of Cape Colony, see *In re Wishart* (7 E. D. C. 8).

376. Where it has been decided that the opposition of parents to the marriage of a minor child is groundless or frivolous, the parents cannot retain possession of such minor child's property, but it passes into the power of the husband, where the marriage takes place in community of property (28, 2 § 28). 377. The law does not prohibit marriage between guardians and their wards; but it is submitted that, in Cape Colony and Natal at least, when the wards are still under age, judicial consent to the marriage must first of all be obtained (28, 2 §§

24—26).

In the Transvaal and Orange River Colony, in the absence of parents or guardians, the magistrate must give his consent.

378. According to Voet's interpretation of the Dutch Law, marriages between Christians and Jews or Mohammedans are forbidden. Van Leeuwen *(Cens. For.* 1, 1, 18, 8) dissents from this view, holding that such marriages are not forbidden. Yet Van Leeuwen immediately goes on to say that "marriage between followers of different religions or creeds must be celebrated before the local magistrates." He thus admits that marriages under such circumstances before ministers of religion would not be valid. Voet's strict interpretation of the Dutch statutes appears perfectly sound (23, 2 § 26).

Difference of creed or religious belief is at the present day no bar to marriage, and a marriage between persons of different creeds, if valid in other respects, is not invalidated by the circumstance that it has been performed by a minister or priest professing one of such creeds.

379. Marriages, says Voet, are not allowed in cases of rape, unless the ravisher has obtained a pardon from the Crown, or the woman who has been ravished freely consents to marry the man.

Marriage cannot take place between an adulterer and the woman with whom he has committed adultery. The Canon Law in this matter differed from the Roman Law, but the matter was settled by two edicts of the States General of Holland, the Echt Reglement of March 18th, 1656, § 88, and the Placaat or Decree of July 18th, 1674 (28, 2 § 27).

In *Daniel* vs. *Daniel* (3 S. C. 231) the plaintiff had been divorced from her husband on the ground of adultery with the defendant, with whom she subsequently went through a form of marriage. Afterwards plaintiff brought an action against defendant to have the marriage with him declared null and void, relying upon her own adultery while she was married to her former husband as a ground for setting aside the marriage. It was said by De Villiers,

C.J.: "For myself, I cannot come to the conclusion that Courts of law exist for any such purpose. If people act in the way the plaintiff has acted, they must take the rL-k upon themselves. If an innocent party had applied to the Court for a declaration that the marriage was null and void, it would have been a serious matter for consideration. But I cannot bring myself to think that this Court should give any assistance to the plaintiff." The application for an order annulling the marriage was accordingly refused. It is submitted that, this case notwithstanding, if the rule with regard to the marriage of persons who have committed adultery still applies, it is unnecessary for either spouse to obtain an order declaring the marriage null and void; and such spouse may then marry again without incurring the penalties of bigamy. This view is by no means in conflict with the decision in *Daniel* vs. *Daniel.* See also Groonowegen on the *Cade, (ad,* 1, 27, on the *lex Julia de adult, mere),* and *Dutch Consultations* (part 3, vol. 1, §§ 52, 53, 54, and vol. 2, §§ 71, 72).

380. The States General of Holland, in the Echt Reglement of March 18th, 1656, § 49, forbade the marriage of lepers, which had not been prohibited in Roman Law. Insane persons can marry during a lucid interval—that is, where they are sane for the time being, and not kept under restraint as insane (23, 3 § 28). 381. Marriage is forbidden between persons who are too closely related by consanguinity or affinity. Consanguinity is relationship by blood arising from the fact that persons have a common ancestor.

Affinity is connection by marriage subsisting between one spouse and the blood relations of the other spouse. The lines of consanguinity are direct or collateral. In the direct line are ascendants and descendants only, *in infinitum.* In the collateral line are persons not directly descended from each other (or who stand to each other in the position of ascendants and descendants), but who trace their origin to a common ancestor. In order to tell by how many degrees of relationship persons are separated from

each other, the rule of the Roman Law is that there are as many degrees as there are generations, or persons counted, not including the stem or person from whom the enumeration proceeds. A father is related to his son in the first degree, a grandfather to his grandson in the second degree. In the collateral line the descent is first traced back to the nearest common ancestor. Thus, two brothers are related to each other in the second degree. First cousins, the sons of two brothers, are related to each other in the fourth degree. A paternal uncle and his brother's son are related to each other in the third degree. By marriage, one acquires the relationship (by what are known in the civil law as quasi-degrees) of one's spouse to such spouse's blood-relations. Thus a father-in-law, mother-in-law, become parents through marriage to the son-in-law or daughter-in-law (28, 8 § 29).

382. The Roman-Dutch Law, like the Divine (biblical) Law and the Roman Law, forbids marriages between ascendants and descendants in *infinitum.* This applies not only to direct descendants, but to persons related by marriage in the ascending or descending line. Thus a father cannot marry his daughter, a great-grandfather his great-granddaughter, a father-in-law his daughter-in-law, a stepfather a step-daughter, nor a stepmother a step-son; nor can a grandfather marry the widow of a deceased grandson, who is called a granddaughter-in-law. The foregoing cases are only given as examples, but the rule applies to all persons similarly related. The Roman-Dutch Law forbids marriages in the collateral line as well. Thus, an uncle cannot marry his niece, or his grand-niece, or greatgrand-niece, nor an aunt her nephew, or grand-nephew, or great-grand-nephew. The same applies to persons similarly related by marriage. So, a widower may not marry the daughter of his brother-in-law or of his sister-in-law. This does not so much follow from the rule that a man cannot marry his deceased wife's sister, who is a relation by marriage (and therefore stands, by virtue of the fiction of law mentioned in § 881, in the place of one's own sister),

but because the child of a brother and a sister-in-law or a sister and a brother-in-law is a relation by blood. This prohibition does not extend, in Roman-Dutch Law, to persons who have merely been adopted into a family, and are not otherwise related. The prohibition in the collateral line extends to relationships in the fourth degree, but excludes that degree (although the Canon Law included it). Thus marriages between first cousins, being the children of brothers or sisters, and so related in the fourth degree, are permitted by Roman-Dutch Law. Voet appears to adopt the view that according to the Dutch Law (though not according to Roman Law) marriages between persons related in the ascending or descending line in the second species of affinity—derived through a second marriage—are not prohibited. Thus a man can marry the widow (being the second wife) of his son-in-law, or a woman can marry the widower (being the second husband) of her daughter-inlaw, the child of the ascendant marrying being in either case the predeceased husband or wife of the wife or husband respectively whom the ascendant marries. In simpler language, A. can marry B., the second wife of C., who was first married to D., A.'s daughter; or F. can marry G., the second husband of H., who was first married to K., F.'s son. The death of one of two persons married to each other does not put an end to the affinity between the survivor and the relations of the predeceased spouse. Although no affinity arises between a person who has had illicit intercourse with another and the blood relations of the latter, yet, according to Voet, it would seem that marriage between the person deflowering a woman and her blood relations is not allowed. He lays it down as a fixed rule that the blood relationship arising out of the fact that a person has promiscuous intercourse with another constitutes a bar to marriage just as much as the relationship arising out of a lawful marriage would do. Thus, a man cannot marry his illegitimate daughter; nor can a woman marry the son of the man with whom she has had illicit intercourse.

Marriages are not forbidden which are contracted between the blood relations of one spouse and the blood relations of another spouse, so long as the parties proposing to marry are not blood relations of each other. In other words, A.'s son B. by A.'s first marriage with C. can marry D., the daughter of E. (A.'s second wife) by E.'s first marriage with F., there being no blood relationship between C. and D. (28, 2 §§ 80—86, and 89).

The prohibited degrees were defined in Holland by the Political Ordinance of 1580. § 5 prohibited marriage between ascendants and descendants, blood relations, *ad infinitum.* § 6 forbade marriage between brothers and sisters, whether of full or half blood. § 7 forbade marriage between uncles and their nieces, or aunts and their nephews, *ad infinitum,* continuing the same relationship onwards. § 8 forbade marriages in affinity (relationship by marriage) within the same degrees as in consanguinity (relationship by blood). §§ 8 and 9 prohibited marriage between a man and his step-mother, or the widow of any of his ascendants, or his daughter-in-law, or the widow of any of his descendants, or his mother-in-law, or any of his deceased wife's ascendants, or his step-daughter, or any of his deceased wife's descendants; in the same manner marriage was prohibited between a woman and her step-father, or the widower of any of her ascendants, or her son-in-law, or the widower of any of her descendants, or her father-in-law, or any of her deceased husband's ascendants, or her step-son, or any of her deceased husband's descendants—in all cases *ad infinitum.* § 10 prohibited marriage between a man and his brothel's widow or his deceased wife's sister, and between a woman and her deceased husband's brother or her sister's widower. This refers both to the full and the half blood. §11 prohibited marriage between a man and the widow of his brother's or sister's son or other descendant, or his deceased wife's brother's or sister's daughter or other descendant, and between a woman and the widower of her brother's or sister's daughter or other

descendant, or her deceased husband's brother's or sister's son or other descendant. See also Van Leeuwen *(l!. D. L.,* 1 *KotzS,* pp. 110—116, 1, 14, §§ 12—14; *Cutis. For.* 1, 1, 13, §§ 13—24), Grotius, 1, 5, §§ 5—13; Colquhoun, §§ 617—636. The English law prohibits the following marriages by reason of consanguinity or affinity: 1. Grandmother. 2. Grandfather's wife. 3. Wife's grandmother. 4. Father's sister, 5. Mother's sister. 6. Father's brother's wife. 7. Mother's brother's wife. 8. Wife's father's sister. 9. Wife's mother's sister. 10. Mother. 11. Step-mother. 12. Wife's mother. 13. Daughter. 14. Wife's daughter. 15. Son's wife. 16. Sister. 17. Wife's sister. 18. Brother's wife. 19. Son's daughter. 20. Daughter's daughter. 21. Son's son's wife. 22. Daughter's son's wife. 23. Wife's son's daughter. 24. Wife's daughter's daughter. 25. Brother's daughter. 26. Sister's daughter. 27. Brother's son's wife. 28, Sister's son's wife. 29. Wife's brother's daughter. 30. Wifo's sister's daughter. The corresponding degrees in the case of a woman marrying are prohibited in English law. In the Transvaal, Law No. 3, 1871, marriage is prohibited to the following extent (§ 4): (a) Between all persons in the ascending and descending lines *in infinitum,* and between collaterals in the third degree, that is, between uncle and niece, or aunt and nephew, whether related by blood or by marriage; *(b)* between "own" cousins, that is, both of whose parents on one side are brothers and sisters of the parents on the other side. This means that where A., brother of B., marries C., and B. marries D., C.'s brother, E., the child of A. and C., cannot marry F., the child of B. and D.

The Cape Act 40 of 1892 enacts (§ 2) that it shall be lawful for any widower to marry the sister of his deceased wife, provided such sister is not the widow of a deceased brother of such widower, or to niarry any female related to him in any more remote degree of affinity than the sister of his deceased wife, save and except any ancestor of or descendant from such deceased wife. § 3 enacts that any marriage contracted between persons both of whom should bo alive at the date of passing of the Act which would be void, or voidable, by reason of any law (meaning thereby the general Roman-Dutch Law) by this Act repealed, should be deemed to be as valid as if duly solemnised before the taking effect of the Act; provided such marriugo shall not have been dissolved or declared invalid by the decree of any competent Court (only Judges of the Supreme Court having jurisdiction to decree a dissolution of marriage). § 4 enacts that nothing in the Act contained shall be deemed to legalise or render valid the marriage of a man with the sister of a wife from whom ho has been divorced. With regard to marriage between persons related through illicit intercourse, reference may be made to the case of *R.* vs. *Areiids* (8 S. C. 176), in which it was decided that carnal intercourse by a father with his illegitimate daughter constitutes the crime of incest. In such a case there must, of course, bo clear proof that the blood relationship exists. See also *Digist* (23, 5, 6, 8) and Carpzovius *(def. for.* 4, 23, 10); and *R.* vs. *K.* (Bucb. 1875, p. 98). In the Orange River Colony, by Law 26, 1899, § 13, it is generally enacted that marriages are unlawful between persons who are related to each other in the prohibited degrees of consanguinity. Those prohibited degrees have to be sought in the general Dutch Law.

In *Mills* vs. *Acting Resident Magistrate of the Cape* (11 C. T. R. p. 438; 19 5. A. L. J. 61), it was decided that a nophew may marry his aunt, provided that the relation between them be that of affinity only. The Court came to the conclusion, on a review of the authorities, that the balance of opinion among Boman-Dutch jurists is in favour of the prohibition extending to such marriages. But it was decided, on a consideration of the Cape Act No. 40, 1892, § 2 (which makes it lawful for any widower to marry the sister of his deceased wife, provided such sister be not the widow of a deceased brother to such widower, or to marry any female related to him in any more remote degree of affinity, save and except any ancestor

of, or descendant from, such deceased wife), that " if, as the Act stands, it removes the restriction against intermarriage between a widower and his niece by affinity only, she being a femalo related to him in a more remote degree than his sister-in-law, on principle it should be held that it also permits the marriage of a widow with her nephew, to whom she is related by affinity only. " 383. Voet then considers the question whether a dispensation from the foregoing prohibitions can be granted by the Supreme Power in the State. There is no doubt, he says, that this can be done in the case of marriages which are only prohibited by the Roman Law, not those prohibited by Divine Law *(i.e.,* the prohibitions contained in the Book of Leviticus). Great care must be exercised in the granting of such dispensations (28, 2 §§ 87, 38).

See Grotius (1, 5, 13 *Maasdorp*, p. 15, and Groenewegen's note, No. 17). 384. The Cape Marriage Order in Council enacts (§ 9) that marriage shall take place within three months of the publication of banns; and, if such period elapses, the publication becomes void, the law requiring a fresh publication before the parties can be married by banns. Declarations must be made by the parties before the marriage officer (§§ 7, 15). Marriages must be solemnised with open doors (§ 21) between the hours of eight in the forenoon and four in the afternoon, in the presence of two or more credible witnesses besides the minister or marriage officer who shall solemnise the same. Immediately after the ceremony an entry thereof shall be made in a marriage register book to be kept for such purpose by the minister or marriage officer. A duplicate original register is to be kept, which must be transmitted within one month from the date thereof by the minister or marriage officer to the Colonial Secretary of the Colony, who is to file and preserve the same. Searches may be made in such duplicate original register, and copies taken (§§ 22, 28). The remuneration of marriage officers—other than magistrates (who, by § 7 of Act 16, 1860, are not entitled to any fee,

gratuity, or reward for acts done under the marriage laws)—is to be fixed by the Governor (§ 24). Marriages by special licence are regulated at the Cape by Act 16, 1860, § 5, by Schedule A. to the same Act, and by Act 9, 1882. Persons desirous of marrying before a magistrate must give fourteen days' notice in writing to the magistrate of their intention to marry. If the parties live in two different districts, such notice must be given to the magistrate of each district. The magistrate must keep a marriage notice book, which shall be open to inspection without fee. Such notice shall be affixed in some conspicuous place, and shall be read aloud at the next sitting in Court of the said magistrate, and twice thereafter in Court, provided that three clear days shall elapse between each reading, and provided that the three readings shall take place within twenty-one days next after the receipt of notice of intention to marry. Objections to intended marriages must be made in writing, addressed to the magistrate. Marriages by magistrates may, after notice, be solemnised between nine and twelve in the forenoon, with open doors, in the presence of two or more credible witnesses besides the magistrate.

The parties shall make a declaration, and the register shall be signed and attested as in the case of marriages before ministers or marriage officers appointed by the Governor in terms of Act 16,1860. All objections to such marriages shall be referred by the magistrate to the Resident Magistrate's Court of the district for decision. (Schedule A. , Act 16, 1860, §§ 1—28). Act 9, 1882, § 8, provides that resident magistrates may issue special licences, which shall be void (§ 4) if no marriage is solemnised in pursuance thereof within three months. Certain declarations are required (§ 5, and in the case of widows or widowers, see § 6), and minors must produce the written consent of parents or guardians before obtaining a special licence. Questions may be put by the magistrate (§ 8) and a penalty of imprisonment, with or without hard labour, for a term not exceeding five years, is imposed on persons who wilfully make false declarations or statements, or forge or fraudulently alter any consent in writing to the marriage of minors, or similarly alter any licence to marry (§ 9). Similar provisions are contained in the marriage ordinances of the Transvaal, Orange River Colony, and Natal (see Transvaal Ord. 3, 1871, §§ 3, 4; Natal Law 7, 1889; O. R. C. Law 26, 1899, §§ 8, 9).

(8) Consequences Of Marriage. i. *Capacity to Contract; and Community.* 385. The first consequence, in Roman-Dutch Law, of a valid marriage is that the wife assumes the dignity or *status* of her husband, which she retains during widowhood (i.e., until she marries again, when she takes the *status* of the second husband). The wife also follows the forum of the husband, and likewise his home or domicile. The paternal control over a woman ceases with her marriage, which emancipates her from paternal control by placing her under the curatorship of her husband. The husband becomes the curator of his wife even if he be still under the age of majority, for he is emancipated by marriage. The wife has no judicial standing of her own, and her husband must sue and be sued for her (28, 2 §§ 40,41).

As to the *status* of the wife, see Colquhoun (§ 602). Tho fact that the domicile of the wife is that of the husband entails as a necessary consequence the rule that a wife must be sued in the same Court or forum as her husband A wife may, however, under certain circumstances acquire or establish a forum for the purpose of suing her husband for divorce. "The matrimonial domicile is that in which, at the time of the marriage, the consorts expect and intend to live together. It will therefore bo in general the domicile of the husband at the time of the marriage, though perhaps, if it were agreed between the parties that the husband should adopt another domicile immediately after the celebration, and he adopted it accordingly, such agreed domicile might be considered the matrimonial domicile" (Westlake, *Pr. Int. Law,* 3rd ed. p. 36). As to divorce, see *Westlake* (3rd ed. pp. 74—

88). In *Adams* vs. *Adams* (2 S. C. 24) it was said by De Villiers, C.J.: "The ordinar-maxim is *ubi uxor ibi damus,* that is, the supposition is that if a man leaves his wife behind he does not intend to change his domicile." In this case, leave was applied for in 1882 to sue the husband by edictal citiition for a divorce, where he had left his wife in 1878, and had gone to the Transvaal, where he was living in adulter-. Leave was granted, the Court saying: "It does not follow that he has changed his domicile from the sole fact that he has remained away for some time." See *Cunningham* vs. *Cunningham* (Buch. 1875, p. 99), *Bell* vs. *Kennedy* (L. R. 1 H. L. Scotch Cases, 307), *Mason* vs. *Mason* (4 E. D. C. 330), *IVJiipp* vs. *Whipp* (12 S. C. 174), and *Peters* vs. *Peters* (9 C. T. R. 289). In *Peeves* vs. *Peeves* (1 M. 249, following *Voet,* 5, 1, 95, 101; 23, 2, 40; and the *Code,* 10, 39, 9) it was laid down that the *forum domicilii* of the husband is, by the law of Cape Colony (i.e., Roman-Dutch Law), deemed *Om forum domicilii* of the wife, whether she be at the time actually resident within the territory of the said *forum* or not, and this for the trial of all questions, not only arising between the wife and third parties, but between the wife and the husband, and respecting the rights and obligations and duties of both parties, which result from their relation as husband and wife. See also *Bestandig* vs. *Bestandig* (1 M. 280), *Hawkes* vs. *Hawkes* (2 S. C. 109), and *Ex jiarte Atkinson* (Off. Rep. Transvaal, 189.5, p. 289).

The South African Courts have always held themselves bound by the decision of the Judicial Committee of the Privy Council in *Le Mesurier* vs. *Le Misurier* (1895, A. C. p. 517), where it was held that jurisdiction to pronounce a decree of divorce *d vinculo* depends on the domicile. So, in *Ex parte Kaiser* (1902 T. II., p. 165), it was held that a wife cannot establish for herself a domicile in tho Transvaal, apart from that of her husband, so as to enable her to sue her husband for divorce, the marriage having been celebrated in Cape Colony, and tho husband never having resided in the Transvaal. See also *Brunsclncik* vs.

Brunschwik (1902 T. H. p. 2-,S), *Walker* vs. *Walker* (6 C. T. R. 388; 13 S. C. R 363; 14 C. L. J. 51), *Lea* vs. *Lea* (19 S. A. L. J. 391), *In re Bright* (19 S. A. L. J. 3S1), *Ex parte Rosenwax* (11 C. T. R. 10), *Thomas* vs. *Thomas* (23 N. L. B. 38; 19 S. A. L. J. 388), *Moreland* vs. *Moreland* (19 S. A. L. J. 288), *Frirdmau* vs. *Friedman* (19 S. A. L. J. 390; 23 N. L. R. 25), *Gilbert* vs. *Gilbirt* (22 N. L. R 201; 19 S. A. L. J. 74), *Schoeman* vs. *Schoeman* (3 C. L. J. 262), *Wolter* vs. *Wolter* (11 E. D. C. 89; 14 C. L. J. 137), and *Murphy* vs. *Murphy* (1902 T. S., p. 179).

As to tho judicial standing of the wife, see Grotius (1, 5, 22), Schorer *(ad Grot,* § 21), Van der Keessel (§ 95),'Van Leeuwen *P. D. L.* 1, 6, 7; 1 *Kutze,* p. 41; *Cens. For.* 1, 1, 7 §§ 6, 7). In *Prince* vs. *Anderson* (1 M. 176), a widow hud re-married out of community of property, and was summoned, without her second husband's name being mentioned in the summons, to confess judgment on a bond executed before the second marriage. It was objected on behalf of the husband, that, as the wife was under his legal guardianship, she could not appear in Court without his consent. The objection was sustained. And so, in *Landjiberg* vs. *Marchand* (1 M. 200), it was decided that where a woman married out of community is sued the summons must be served also on the husband'. See also *Schuster* vs. *Bnfe* (9 C. L. J. 123), *Clark* vs. *Johnson* (4 C. T. R. 42S; 11 S. C. 414), and *Binjes* vs. *Verxigman* (Buch. 1879, p. 229). In *Klette* vs. *l'fitzi* (6 E. D. C. 134) a husband, married in community, was sued for a slander uttered by his wife. The wife's name was not mentioned in the summons. It was decided that either the wife must be sued, assisted by her husband, or, if the husband were sued, he must be sued in the capacity of husband in community to the wife said to have uttered the slander. See also *Flurian* vs. *Colonial Government* (3 C. T. It. 139; 10 C. L.J. 222). Where the marriage is in community, each spouse is liable for half the debts of the other spouse. In order to make a person so married liable on a summons, it must bo shown that the liability arises *(a)* out of the fact that the husband is married to his wife in community, or *(b)* on the part of the husband, out of the fact that his wife is subject to his marital power. Where the marriage is not in community, the necessity for mentioning the husband in the summons arises from the requirement of law that he must stand by and assist his wife in judicial proceedings. The law deprives a married woman of judicial standing by herself during marriage, and she acquires no separate judicial standing from the circumstance that the parties entered into an antenuptial contract excluding community of profit and loss, and the marital power.

386. According to Dutch Law, a wife cannot bind herself or her husband by a contract entered into without his authority, and neither the husband nor the wife can be sued on such a contract during the marriage or after its dissolution, the contract being *ipso jure* void. The ratification subsequently given by the husband is equivalent to a previous authority. If the husband is present when the wife enters into a contract, remains silent, and does not forbid his wife to enter into the contract, the law presumes the husband's consent to the contract from his silence. There is considerable doubt as to whether a contract entered into by the wife, without the husband's ratification or consent, express or implied, revives upon dissolution of the marriage. Voet says that if the marriage has been dissolved by death, the widow may in such a case claim the fulfilment of the contract, for during the marriage she was in the same position as a minor who is under guardianship, and enters into a contract, without the guardian's or curator's authority, which produces mutual obligations: the minor being able to bind others to himself, but not being bound to them in turn (unless he has received profit out of the transaction). Van Leeuwen *(K. D. L.* 1, 6, 7; 1 *Kotze,* p. 48; see also his *R. D. L.* 2, 7, 8), on the other hand, says: "Whatever transaction or agreement a woman has entered into without the consent of her husband becomes *ipso jure* void; and

such acts do not revive upon a dissolution of the marriage." Voet goes on to say that husband and wife are bound by a contract entered into by a wife without the husband's consent, whenever they have been enriched thereby. If one is to adopt the strict analogy of the law of guardian and ward, it must be laid down that such contracts of the wife become null and void, unless the wife is enriched by them, when she (and her husband, in virtue of marriage in community) will be liable; although, even where she has not been enriched, the wife may, according to Voet (but not Van Leeuwen), upon dissolution of the marriage, claim fulfilment of the contract, in her own right. In other words, the guardianship of the husband during marriage makes his consent necessary; if his consent is not given, the wife is not bound, unless she was enriched by the contract; but after marriage the guardianship ceases, and the wife then has an equitable action in her own right to claim upon the contract. Van Leeuwen appears to have overlooked the fact that upon dissolution of marriage the wife is emancipated from the husband's guardianship; and it is therefore submitted that Voet's exposition of the law is correct. The wife may lawfully contract without her husband's consent, where she stipulates for or obtains something by means of an unilateral contract which is for her sole benefit, since in such a case she lawfully acquires gain for her husband, on the analogy of a ward acquiring gain for himself; provided that the debt arising from such an obligation is to be paid to the husband alone, not to the wife without the knowledge of the husband. From this it would seem that where a debtor has bound himself on such a contract, and secretly paid the debt to the wife, the husband may again claim payment from the debtor, if the husband received no benefit from the payment to his wife. Another exception to the rule that a wife cannot contract without her husband's consent is the case of a woman who is a public trader with the sanction or authority, or without the prohibition, of her husband, provided the contract has

relation to the particular trade or business of the wife. In such a case the wife makes both herself and her husband liable. In such a trade contract the wife creates a liability whether she binds herself as principal or as surety, or by representation, or if she pledges the stock-in-trade of her business or even immovable property, provided local laws or statutes do not prohibit the mortgage of such property for the wife's business. It does not matter, in the case of a public trader, whether the wife is a minor or a major. If a woman who is a public trader contracts or makes a promise with reference to matters which are beyond the scope of her trade, she will not bind herself or her husband, unless there has been consent, express or implied, or ratification on the part of the husband. Where a woman has been a public trader, and her husband prohibits her from trading any further, she will not after that create a liability on her contracts in respect of her trade, provided parties contracting with the wife are aware of the husband's prohibition, having the prohibition brought to their notice by publication or by some other means. The previous sanction of the husband to the wife's trade will only bind after a prohibition, if the prohibition has been made at a time when the state of the wife's affairs had changed for the worse, or she had become insolvent, or if the wife claims the right of disposing of her separate property by will in such a manner that the property of the husband is not rendered liable. The contracts of the wife with regard to the management of household affairs, such as purchases of necessaries, bind herself and her husband, for the husband is presumed to have relinquished the management of household affairs to his wife—unless the husband obtains an order of Court interdicting his wife from the management of household affairs. The question as to what constitute necessaries in a household contract must be left to judicial discretion to decide (28, 2 §§ 42—46).

The conflict of opinion between Van Leeuwen and Voet on the question whether a wife is liable, on a contract entered into without authorisation of the husband before marriage, after dissolution of the marriage, may be reconciled by laving down that it is optional for the wife after dissolution of the marriage to take up the contract or not.

As to the agency of a wife for her husband, see *Selby* vs. *Freimond* (5 S. C. 266). In that case the wife was sued. Her husband had carried on a business, the licence for which was in his name. The goods were supplied for the purposes of this business. The husband left for the Transvaal, and the wife continued the business (that of an hotel-keeper) in the husband's name for some months. At the same time she earned on business in her own name as a grocer. The goods in question were siipplied after the husband's departure. The wife was summoned in her own name (apparently on the ground that she was a public trader), without the assistance of her husband. She excepted on the ground that her husband should have been joined in the summons. The Court decided that there was nothing to show that the woman carried on the hotel business for her own benefit. The licence was in the husband's name, and whatever profits his wife earned wero earned for him. The defendant was therefore only the agent of her husband. Consequently, the defendant's exception was sustained. See also *Brown* vs. *Dyer and Dyer* (3 E. D. C. 267; 1 C. L. J. 43), *Smith* vs. *Muff*, (11 S. C. 20), *Janicm* vs. *WaUon* (G N. L. R. 234; 2 C. L. J. 349). In *Von Plaster's Creditors* vs. *Jones, Rudd & Co.* (2 E. D. C. 122), a wife gave to a creditor two promissory notes as a consideration for or inducement to the creditor to forbear opposing the rehabilitation of her husband, an insolvent, who managed a business carried on in the name of his wife, to whom he was married out of community of property. The insolvent was present at the transaction (the giving of the notes), and took part in its negotiation, though, as he alleged, only as agent for his wife. The creditor received the notes upon the said consideration, withdrew his opposition, and the insolvent received his dischargo. It was said by Shippard, J.: "I hold that,

according to the rules of the Roman-Dutch Law, the act of the wife in this instance, notwithstanding the fact of her nominally carrying on a separate trade, must be deemed and taken to be the act of her husband, on the ground so clearly stated by Voet (23, 2, 44)—namely, that where, as in this case, the transaction is beyond the scopo of the wife's separate business, the husband's preseuce and his assent, express or implied, are requisite to render his wife's contract binding against either or both. Where, as here, the husband is not merely a consenting party, but personally negotiates the whole transaction to the point of actual signature, it is clear that if the promissory notes were valid at all (as but for the statutes they might have been), they would have bound the husband no less than the wife; and therefore the giving of these promissory notes must, in my opinion, be deemed and taken to have been in law the act of the insolvent himself." See also *Poclding-ton* vs. *Cowey and San* (6 N. L. R. 118).

As to the liability of a woman who is a public trader, see Van Leeuwen (*R. D. L.* 1, 6, 8; *Kotzt* 1, p. 43; *Cens. Fur.* 1, 1, 7, 7; *R. D. L.* 2, 7, 8); Van der Linden (1, 3, 7; *Jain*, p. 23); Grotius (1, 5, 23; *Opinions*, de Bruyn, p. 31); *McIntyre* vs. *G«odi.ion* (Buch. 1877, p. 83); *Jligy* vs. *Witt* (7 E. D. C. 183); *Oai* vs. *Lumsden* (3 S. C. 152); *Smith* vs. *Muff* (11 S. C. 20); *Drury k Co.* vs. *Daly* (13 N. L. R. 257); and *Janion* vs. *WaUon* (N. S. C. 1885; C. L. J. vol. 2, p. 349).

As to the liability for household necessaries, see *Grassman* vs. *Hoffman* (3 S. C. 282), which decided that where a wife had purchased necessaries for herself and her children during her husband's desertion, and had obtained a divorce, she was liable, after that, for half the price of tho necessaries supplied. In *Miism* vs. *Bernstein* (14 S. C. 504) it was held that the engagement of a midwife by a woman about to be confined, without any notification to the midwife that the husband would not be responsible for her fees, constituted a necessary contract for household purposes on which the husband was liable. See also Van Leeuwen (*R. D. L.* 1, 6, 8, and 2, 7,

8; and *Cent, For.* 1, 1, 7, 8). See *Schultz* vs. *Preller* (O. R., S. A. R '95, p. 208). 387. Where a husband is unavoidably absent, the wife has, in Roman-Dutch Law, under a general mandate, without restriction, the power to transact business and to contract on behalf of her husband. There need, in such a case, be no prior mandate, but a subsequent ratification is sufficient. Voet states that there is one case where the contract of a wife, entered into without the previous or subsequent knowledge of her husband, will be held binding— namely, where the wife makes terms in order to free her husband from captivity or imprisonment, provided such terms are freely made and are not unreasonable (28, 2 § 47).

The Courts in South Africa have frequently granted authority to a wife to contract in the absence of the husband. In *Ex parte Fourie* (8 S. C. 115) a woman, married in community, had been deserted by her husband for four years. The husband took all the joint property of the marriage away with him. The wife heard nothing from her husband of his doings or whereabouts. He then became entitled to an inheritance, which was in the hands of the Master of the Supreme Court. A rule *nisi* was granted, calling upon the husband to show cause why one-half of the inheritance should not be paid to the wife, and one-half to the children for their maintenance; and on the return-day the rule was made absolute, the husband not appearing. See also *In re Hartmann* (5 C. T. R. 484; 13 C. L. J. 45), *In re Henry* (5 S. 308), *In re Julias* (2 S. C. 103), *Clinton* vs. *Clinton* (6 E. D. C. 104), *Ex parte Mewes* (4 C. T. R. 131), *Ex parte Wtsterdijk* (Off. Rep. 8. A. R. 1894, p. 48), *Sissing's Executor* vs. *Registrar of Deeds* (2 C. L. J. 99), *In re Ate Williams* (6 C. T. R. 148), and *Re Bouwer* (1902 T. H. 103).

388. Mere insanity on the part of the husband, without a special authorisation to the wife by a competent Court, does not enable a wife to contract as though she were an unmarried woman. Insanity does not put an end to marriage or the marital power. The wife of a lunatic

cannot against her will be compelled to contract with the assistance of her husband's curator. The wife must permit such contracts to be entered into by her lunatic husband's curator as are advantageous for her husband and for their joint property. Voet suggests that, failing this mode of procedure, the wife may apply to have herself appointed curator of her husband's property,

C.L.—VOL. I. Q either alone or together with the husband's nearest blood relations (28, 2 § 48).

See *Vuyk* Vb. *Vuyh* (S. A. R. 2 Kotze, p. 19); *In* re *De Jager* (Buck 1876, p. 228).

389. As a wife cannot, in general, enter into a contract without her husband's authority, so she cannot, in like manner, break or avoid an obligation once validly contracted. So the act of a wife will be void if, without the knowledge and implied consent of her husband, she enters into an agreement not to claim something due to her *(pactum de non petendo)*, or releases a debtor by way of gift from the debt without any consideration *(acceptilatio)*. As stated above (§ 886), payment by a debtor to the wife without the husband's knowledge, or against the husband's wish, does not release the debtor from liability, except to the extent by which the husband has actually received benefit from such payment (28, 2 §§ 49, 50). 390. Upon the dissolution of the marriage, a wife or her heirs may sue upon contracts entered into during the marriage by the husband, and having reference to her own property, or the joint property of the marriage. After the marriage has been dissolved, the wife and her heirs may be sued for half the liability arising from contracts entered into by the husband during the subsistence of the marriage in community. It makes no difference whether the debt incurred were necessary or not, so long as the husband is not publicly interdicted from managing his own affairs. When the wife is unwilling any longer to be bound by the extravagant liabilities of her husband, she may petition the Court for a decree dividing the property *(boedelscheiding)*; and, upon such division and the

publication thereof, the husband cannot bind the joint property or his wife's property. For a debt contracted during the subsistence of the marriage the husband or his heirs can alone be sued to the whole extent thereof *(in solidum)*; while the wife can be sued for the half thereof only: but the husband, upon payment of the whole amount of the debt, may have recourse against his wife or her heirs for the half thereof. If, during his lifetime, judgment is given against the husband, and he points out the dowry of his wife as property for seizure under a writ of execution, and dies thereafter, the wife may claim that only so much of her dowry property shall be seized as will satisfy half of the judgment; and she may stop such execution by tendering half of the judgment debt to the creditor. But the husband may, by virtue of his marital power, during the subsistence of the marriage pledge or mortgage certain property of his wife, and such property will be executable by virtue of such pledge or mortgage (28, 2 §§ 51, 52). sMiel vs. *De Wet* (5 E. D. C. 58) decided that although a surviving spouse may be liable for debts contracted by her deceased husband to whom she was married in community, the declaration, when she is sued on such debts, must show that the amount was not recoverable from the joint estate of the marriage. This decision was approved in *Faure* vs. *Tulbagh Divisional Council* (8 S. C. 72). See also *Brink* vs. *Louw* (1 M. 210), *Grassman* vs. *Hoffman* (3 S. C. 282), Grotius (1, 5, 22; *Maasdorp*, p. 18; *De Bruyn*, p. 31); Van der Keessel (§ 93); Van der Linden (1, 3, 7); Van Leeuwen *(R. D. L.* 4, 23, 6; 2 *Kotzi*, 186—187; *Cent. For.* 1, 1, 12, 20, 21). 391. In case of a marriage in community, the wife is liable to account for profits and losses arising out of a guardianship undertaken by the husband, in the *actio tutelae*. The wife is liable for half the amount on a suretyship entered into by her husband. The wife becomes liable in such a case by virtue, not of the community, but of the husband's marital power (28, 2 § 58). Van Leeuwen *(Cens. For.* 1, 1, 12, 21) agrees with Voet that a wife married in

community of profits and loss is liable to the creditor for half the amount of a suretyship entered into by her husband: but he holds that the wife may thereafter have recourse against her husband and his heirs for the amount so paid by her, where the suretyship was entered into without the wife's knowledge and consent. With this Voet disagrees, holding that the wife has no recourso against the husband for half the suretyship debt so paid by her. Voet says that since the wife married in community is liable for half the husband's torts, *a fortiori* she will be liable, without recourse, on a suretyship.

In *Brink* vs. *Louw* (1 M. 210) a husband, married in community, entered into a suretyship on which he became liable. He then became insolvent. His widow was held liable for half the amount of the suretyship debt. See *Van der Keessd* (§ 93).

392. Donations, though excessive and immoderate, made by the husband to third parties, will hold good against the wife, unless there has been clear fraud on the part of the husband. There must be no intention on the part of the husband directly to prejudice the wife. There is a presumption of fraud on the part of the husband where he makes a donation to his children by a former marriage, or to blood relations at a time when his wife is ill, or at the point of death; and in such a case the wife or her heirs are entitled to restitution. On the dissolution of the marriage the wife may first of all deduct from the estate the amount which was unreasonably applied by the husband to donations or other uses in prejudice of the wife's interests. If there is not enough left in the estate after payment of debts to satisfy the wife's claim in this respect, she or her heirs may bring an action *(actio Pauliana)* to revoke the donation to the extent to which she was defrauded out of her property (28, 2 § 54).

See *Linde* vs. *Beyers* (not decided, 1 S. C. 411).

393. The torts of a husband, which give rise to a civil action, will bind his wife, where the spouses are married in community. But the wife will not be liable

for her husband's crime, and accordingly a money fine for a crime of the husband is not leviable on his wife (28, 2 §§ 55—57). 394. By virtue of his marital power a husband married in community may alienate all the property of the joint estate, movable and immovable, without his wife's consent; but he cannot do this where the marriage has taken place on an antenuptial contract, excluding the marital power, or specially prohibiting alienations. Where the husband misconducts himself the wife may obtain an interdict preventing the husband from alienating the property of the marriage, whether it be a marriage in community or upon antenuptial contract. Any alienation made after such interdict will be null and void, and the wife will have an action to recover property so alienated (vindication), unless adverse possession during the term of prescription (to be reckoned from the dissolution of the marriage) has deprived her of the right to recover. The prohibition of alienation must be express, in order to render the alienation null and void, and entitle the wife to recover (23, 2 § 58; 23, 5 §§ 1—8).

As to the right of a husband to alienate, see Grotius (1, 5, 21, 22, 24, 25); Van der Keessel (§§ 92, 9", 98, 99, 231); Van Leeuwen (*R. D.L.I,* 6, 7, 4, 24, 4, 7; 1 *Kotzi,* 43; 2 *Kotze,* 196—200; *Cens. For.* 1, 1, 12, 5, 6); Van der Linden (1, 3, 3, 4, 7). The latter says that if the husband clearly abuses his marital power, and is likely to reduce his wife to poverty, the law affords the wife the means of restraining him within bounds. The South African Courts hare frequently restrained husbands from alienating property pending suits to dissolve marriage. See *Sture* vs. *Sture* (1 R. 51); *Hay ward* vs. *Hayward* (6 E. D. C. 192); and *Unujulwa* vs. *Umgulwa* (7 E. D. C. 73). As to restraint in case of marriage by antenuptial contract, see *Steytler* vs. *Dekkers* (2 R. 116). See also *Van der Merwe* vs. *Van der Merwe* (5 C. L. J. 301).

395. Voet states that in questions of jurisdiction the law of the marriage domicile must be followed in considering what is the extent of the marital control

over the movable property, and what a wife under marital control can do with regard to the movable property. With regard to immovable property the law of the place where the property is situate must be looked at *(lex loci rei sitae).* The same rules which apply to the estates of minors in foreign jurisdictions apply to the estates of women who are under the marital power of their husbands (28, 2 §§ 59, 60, 61). See "*Westlake (Pr. Int. Law,* 3rd ed. §§ 34, 35, 36, 167).

396. Although guardians cannot contract with their wards (unless there are co-guardians, and the contract is entered into with the authority of the co-guardians), there is nothing to prevent husbands from contracting with their wives, provided tbey do not infringe the rule which prevents spouses from making a donation to each other. If a woman enters into a contract with her husband's authority she cannot claim restitution against it if the contract results disastrously for her. The husband, as guardian by marriage of his wife, is not compellable to render an account of his marital administration to his wife or her heirs, nor is he compellable to indemnify her if her property has been diminished by his negligence. Voet here adopts the opinion of Neostadius, that the estate of a wife may be wholly dissipated by value of the husband's marital power, unless the antenuptial contract shall have stipulated otherwise. This must be taken with the proviso (see § 892) that the husband has not fraudulently donated the wife's property. In Dutch Law a wife has no tacit hypothec on the estate of her husband for the restitution of the dowry or property brought by her into the marriage (28, 2 §§ 62, 63).

In *Ziedeman* vs. *Ziedeman* (1 M. 238) it was laid down that all contracts which spouses may lawfully and effectually enter into with each other before marriage may lawfully and effectually be entered into by them during the subsistence of the marriage, in so far as they are personally concerned, provided such contract does not constitute, directly or indirectly, a gift, or deed of gift, from

one spouse to the other. See *Steyn* vs. *Steyn's Trustee* (Buch. 1873, p. 109); *Gibbon* vs. *Gibbon* (2 E. D. C. 293); *Albertus* vs. *Atbertut' Executors* (3 S. 202); *Hall* vs. *HalVs Trustee and Another* (3 S. C. 3); *Brown* vs. *Brown* (Transvaal Off. Rep. 1897, p. 386).

397. Where no special stipulation to the contrary is made by a contract entered into before a marriage (the nature of which antenuptial contract will be discussed later on), marriage, in EonianDutch Law, produces *ipso facto* a legal or "statutory" community of property and of profits and loss between the spouses. Into this community come all possessions of the spouses, present and future, real and personal, transfer of either movable or immovable property from one spouse to the other not being necessary. It does not matter if one of the spouses at the time of the marriage possesses nothing, for a universal partnership between the spouses results in any case. In the community are included all inheritances, legacies, and donations (28, 2 §§ 64—70).

In *Nortje* vs. *Nortj'e* (6 S. C. 9) it was said: "By virtue of the community of property, the defendant (in a suit for divorce on the ground of adultery, where there had been an order for a separation of the property, but no decree of forfeiture of the benefits resulting from the marriage) was entitled at the date of the decree to one-half of the plaintiff's future as well as present estate." So, where parties, married in community in 1862, were divorced in 1882, without a decree declaring that the husband, by reason of adultery, had forfeited the benefits coming to him from the marriage, and an inheritance came to the wife in 1886, the husband wns held entitled to one-half of the inheritance. In *Tessefaar's Trustees* vs. *Blankenberg's Executors* (Buch. 1877, p. 54) it was held that a bequest to the wife, described as "her free and own property without any deduction," went into the common estate of tho marriage.

398. Fideicommissary property does not come into the community where husband or wife is fiduciary heir, and the property passes to some fideicommissary heir on the arrival of a certain day

or the fulfilment of a certain condition. All that may be claimed to belong to the community by virtue of such & *fideicommissum* is what is due as the Trebellianic portion, or as the legitimate portion. The same rule applies where property is left to a spouse on condition that such property shall revert to whence it came if the spouse die without children, and the spouse thereafter dies childless. The same thing applies to donations where the donor or person making the gift has stipulated that the property shall not pass into the community; in such a case the spouse to whom the donation is made retains the sole ownership of the property donated (28, 2 §§ 71—77).

Under the *Senatusconsultum Trebellianum*, a direct heir who accepted an inheritance burdened with a trust or *fideicommissum* was entitled to deduct a fourth share, in which case he became liable for his share of the debts, but not for the legacies; and, if he paid more than his share of debts, he was entitled to demand the sum paid in excess from the fideicommissary heir. In RomanDutch Law, children had to be instituted heirs to at least one-third of what they would have got out of the estate *ab intestato,* both profit and loss being taken into account. If there were more than four children, they were to be instituted heirs to at least one-half of the testator's estate. In the Cape Colony, Act 26, 1873, § 1, enacts that "in no case shall any heir of any one dying be entitled to deduct out of the estate of the person so dying any portion under or by virtue of the laws known respectively as the Falcidian and Trebellian Laws, which, but for such laws respectively, such heir would not be entitled to claim or deduct." As to the Transvaal, see Proc. 28, 1902, § 126. The Capo Act 23, 1874, § 2, provides that " no legitimate portion shall be claimable of right by any one out of the estate of any person who shall die after the taking effect of this Act." As to the Transvaal, see Proc. 28, 1902, § 128. As to donations which do not go into the community, see *Van Vuuren* vs. *Van Vuuren* (5 S. C. 418); *Bosman* vs. *Richter* (2 S. 78); *Blignaut's Trustee* vs. *Celliers*

(Buch. 1868, p. 206); *De Ville* vs. *Theunissen* (Buch. 1878, p. 171); *Van der ByVs Trustees* vs. *Michau's Executors* (2 S. C. 430).

399. Gifts made by the husband to the wife before marriage during betrothal *(arrha)* do not come into community. Such are jewellery and sums of money. Where the marital power is not excluded, mone, which has been received in return for property which did not fall into the community, is regarded as belonging to the community (28, 2 §§ 78, 79).

See *Hall* vs. *HalVs Trustee and Another* (3 S. C. 3); *Union Bank* vs. *Spence* (4 8. C. 339); and *Thorpe's Executors* vs. *Thorpe's Tutors* (4 S. C. 488).

400. Another consequence of community in marriage is that all debts of the spouses are shared in common, not only those contracted during the marriage, but those contracted before the marriage as well. Accordingly the property of one spouse can be seized in execution for the debt of the other spouse premaritally contracted. If the creditors of one of the spouses, where the debt was contracted before marriage, have taken no action on the debt during the subsistence of the marriage, they cannot sue the other spouse after the marriage has been dissolved by death or judicial decree, having recourse after the dissolution of the marriage against the spouse only who contracted the debt. During the subsistence of the marriage, of course, either spouse may be sued. The spouse who contracted the debt, and is sued upon dissolution of the marriage, may recover from the other spouse, or from the estate of such other spouse, half the amount paid to creditors. With regard to debts contracted during the marriage, the wife (if the debt has been contracted by the husband, debts contracted by the wife, except in regard to necessaries or to a public trade carried on by her, being void) is liable to the creditors, upon dissolution of the marriage, for one-half the amount of the debt. The husband will, after the dissolution, be liable for the whole amount of the debt (28, 2 § 80).

Briefly, the position is this: A wife

married in community is liable to creditors (A) during marriage, for (1) all debts contracted before marriage; (2) all debts subsequently contracted, but not for fines for criminal offences; (B) after marriage, for (1) half of the debts contracted during marriage, but not for fines, nor for debts contracted before marriage (though, according to Voet, the husband who pays the whole of such debts has recourse against the wife or her heirs for half the amount so paid by him). See *Reis* vs. *Gilloway's Executors* (1 M. 186). As to the general law regarding the liability of spouses for each other's debts, see Grotius (1, 5, 22, 23, 24); Van der Keessel (§§ 222—225); Van Leeuwen *(R. D. L.* 4, 23, 6; 5, 3, 13; 2 *Kotze,* pp. 186 and 371); and Van der Linden (1, 3, 7).

401. Where a parent marries a second time in community, the second spouse is liable to the children by the first marriage of his or her wife or husband for alimony and support of such children. The amount required for this purpose is a charge upon the joint estate, and must be deducted prior to a division of such estate (28, 2 §§ 81, 82). 401a. The funeral expenses in connection with the interment of a deceased spouse do not form a charge upon the community, but must be borne by the heirs of the deceased. There can be no doubt about this, for such expenses only arise after death, which dissolves the community (28, 2 § 83).

See *Tiffin* vs. *Harsant* (Buch. 1876, p. 50).

402. All profits and loss arising out of community are shared by the parties to the community, provided the cause of such profit or loss resulted from the community, even if the amount payable accrued or became due after the termination of the community. Tims, if A. , who is married to B. in community, brings a suit on a cause of action arising out of such community, and B. dies after joinder in issue *(litis contestatio),* and A. then marries C. in community, after which judgment is given in the suit in favour of A., half of the amount due under such judgment will go to A., and half to the heirs of his first wife B. If

property has been left to G. (who is married in community to H.) in trust for X. , with the proviso that the property shall only pass to X. on the performance of a certain condition, and this condition is not performed, wherefore the property vests, after G.'s marriage is dissolved, in G., half of such property will go to G. and half to H. or her heirs, since acquirements of property under a conditional trust, where the condition fails, are retrospective in their effect, and relate back to the time when the property was acquired. The same rule applies to debts arising from a cause existing prior to the marriage, as, for instance, where a judgment is given against one of the parties on such a debt after the marriage has been dissolved (28, 2 § 84).

The only condition necessary to create the community of profit and loss is that the cause of profit or loss shall have arisen before or during the subsistence of the marriage. Where, during a marriage in community, the husband entered into a suretyship for which he became liable, and afterwards surrendered his estate, his surviving spouse was held liable (in *Brink* vs. *Louw*, 1 M. 210) for half the amount of the suretyship. See *Pappe* vs. *Home* (1 M. 212); *Union Bank Liquidators* vs. *Kiver* (8 S. C. 146).

403. Voet mentions the opinion of Argentraeus *(ad consuetudines Britan.* § 218, gloss. 6, Nos. 83—85), Peckius *(de testamentis conjug.* bk. 4, c. 28, § 5), and Matthaeus *(Paroemia,* 2 § 60), who held the view that with regard to the movable property of the spouses one must follow the law of the domicile, while with regard to real or immovable property the law of the place where the property is situated must be regarded *(lex domicilii* governing movables, *lex loci rei sitae* governing immovables). Voet's own opinion is that both movable and immovable property are governed by the law of the husband's domicile, which the wife follows. In support of this view he cites Molineus (§ 53), Burgundus (on the *Constitutions of Flanders,* p. 1, § 15), Choppinus *(de moribiis Farisiensibus,* 2, 1, 4), Charondas (bk. 2, § 64), Goris (1, 6, 4),

Someren *(de jure novercarum,* c. 12, § 2), Rodenburg *(de jure conjugum,* preliminary title, 2, 5, 14, 15), and others. Where a Hollander married a young lady of Friesland (where community of property did not prevail) at Amsterdam, without an antenuptial contract, and the wife had real property situate in Friesland, Grotius *(Dutch Consultations,* 4, 22) was of opinion that the husband could sell the property of the wife and invest the proceeds as he thought fit without restraint by the former guardians of the wife. Community existing between spouses in one country does not *ipso facto* bring into community property situate in another country (the first country being the marriage domicile) when community does not exist in the second country, but each spouse acquires a personal right with reference to property so situated in a country where community does not exist. Persons who marry are regarded in law as having tacitly agreed, on marriage, according to the usages, customs, and laws in force with regard to their persons and property in the place where the contract was made. In the first place reference must be made to any specific agreement between the spouses, and, failing this, to local customs or statutes referring to marriage property. In case of doubt, marriage is presumed to have been contracted in the husband's domicile. If a tacit agreement is then held to have taken place, this will have, in the absence of proof to the contrary, the same force as an express agreement; and for this reason Voet takes the tacit contract of marriage to extend to property, real or personal, wherever situate. If it clearly appears from the circumstances of the case that the husband intended to relinquish his own domicile, and adopted his wife's domicile (which must, of course, be done *animo et facto),* the law of the husband's new domicile must be adopted with reference to questions concerning community. If at the beginning of the marriage universal community, according to the law of the husband's domicile, was introduced between the spouses, or, on the other hand, was excluded, and then, after a

lapse of time, the spouses change their mind and transfer their domicile to another place (for instance, if they go from Holland to Friesland, where only community of profits, and not of property, or of loss, prevails), the removal by itself cannot alter the community of property once introduced between the spouses, but in the new domicile the community previously introduced will remain, and what is excluded from the community in the old domicile will be excluded from the community in the new domicile, removal effecting no change with regard to contracts made before marriage. Where there is a doubt which constitutes a husband's domicile at the time of marriage, the place where he chiefly resides, and where most of his property is situate, should be regarded as his domicile—the rule generally followed being *ubi uxor ibi domus* (where the wife is the domicile will be found). In doubtful cases there is a presumption in favour of the existence of community, where the law of the husband's domicile introduces community in marriage (28, 2 §§ 85—91).

See *In re liobb* (3 S. 279). The case of *Bhitch/ord* vs. *Blatchford's Executors* (1 E. 3; IE. D. C. 365) decided that the law of the domicile of marriage will prevail to regulate the rights of the spouses in regard to property acquired in the Colony by persons married elsewhere, who subsequently removed to the Colony *animo remanendi.* The same case decided that community of gains or profit subsequent to the marriage was not introduced by change of domicile to the Colony, where at the domicile of marriage no community existed between the spouses. So, where the parties married in England, where no community of property exists, and thereafter came to Cape Colony, where the husband acquired considerable property, which he bequeathed, with the exception of a small annuity to the wife, to an illegitimate son in England, and the wife claimed that under the Cape Law she was entitled to half the marriage property, the Court held that she was not so entitled. In *Chi well* vs. *Carlyon* (7 C. T. R. 83; 14 C. L. J. 131; 14 S.

C. 67), the following rules were laid down by the Cape Supreme Court: *(a)* Assuming that two spouses were domiciled in Cape Colony at the time of their marriage there, and remained so domiciled during their joint lives, immovable property in England purchased by the husband during the subsistence of the marriage would fall within the community of property created by the marriage; *(b)* assuming that the spouses were so domiciled at the time of their marriage, but subsequently changed their domicile to an English domicile before the purchase of the immovable property, but during their joint lives, such change of domicile would not have any effect upon their respective rights in regard to the said property. See *Black* vs. *Black's Executors* (3 S. C. 200); *In re Estate of Barnes* (1 E. D. C. 5); *Aschen's Executrix* vs. *Blythe* (4 S. C. 130); Story *(Conflict of Laius,* §§ 183—186); Phillimore *(International Law,* vol. 4, § 445); Burge (pt. 1, c. 7, § 8); Savigny *(Private International Law,* § 24); and Westlake *(Pr. Int. Law,* 3rd ed. pp. 65—74).

404. The principal differences between the community of property resulting from marriage and a universal partnership are that a universal partner, unlike a husband, cannot bind the partnership property for amounts spent on luxury or gambling; while one partner is liable to the other for fraud or negligence, and a husband is not accountable to his wife in similar circumstances. Again, in a partnership profit and loss are shared in geometrical proportion, while in community profit and loss are shared in arithmetical proportion— which means that husband and wife in community divide profit and loss equally, while partners divide profit and loss in proportion to their share in the partnership (23, 2 § 92).

See *Van der Keessel* (§ 706). It must be noted that there is no rule forbidding leonine partnerships between spouses. One spouse may bring nothing into community, yet both will share profits and loss equally. Both Voet and Van der Keessel state that a universal partner, by the civil law, cannot alienate more than his own share of the common property. But this is not so in modem practice.

405. The consequences of marriage, whereby community of property is introduced, come into operation immediately upon solemnisation of the marriage, even though no cohabitation *(concubitus)* subsequently takes place. Not cohabitation but consent constitutes a valid marriage (28, 2 §§ 93—97). 406. If a husband is absent from home, and it is uncertain whether he is alive or not, his wife is not at liberty to remarry. There is no presumption of death from absence, however prolonged. It was ordained by the States General of Holland, in a decree dated March 18th, 1656 (vol. 2, Placaats of Holland, § 90, p. 2446) that if the husband had been absent for five years, and no information had been received or was obtainable about him or his whereabouts, the wife might obtain a judicial decree authorising her to marry again (23, 2 § 99).

Van Leeuwen *(Cois. For.* 1, 1, 15, 12) states the Roman Law to be that a wife who has heard nothing during four years about her absent husband can marry again, under certain conditions. The period was extended by Novel 22 (c. 14) to ten years. Such absence was required to be intentional and malicious. In case of absence on account of military or other necessary duty, the wife could not many again, unless she had absolute proof of her husband's death. If the husband is not proved to be dead, but merely absent, the wife cannot marry again unless she first of all obtains a decree of divorce on the ground of malicious desertion. The Placaat of 1656, quoted by Voet, would not seem to apply in the Cape Colony, where it has been laid down that there is no presumption in Roman-Dutch Law that a person who has not been heard of for seven years is dead; although the Court would be justified in holding that in the Cape Colony absence for seven years would be sufficient to justify the Supreme Court in ordering a distribution of the estate of the absent person upon due security *(la re Booysen,* Foord, 187). So, where a woman had been abandoned by her hus-

band, of whom no tidings had been received for twenty years, and she was desirous of remarrying, and applied to the Court for an order authorising her to enter into a fresh marriage, the application was refused. By Dutch Daw a person, whether husband or wife, is not punishable as for bigamy if he or she reasonably and in good faith believed that his or her spouse was dead at the time of the second marriage. Such belief is neither unreasonable nor entertained in bad faith if the spouse has been absent for seven years or more and, notwithstanding proper inquiry, has not been heard of or from during that period. See *Dormehl* vs. *Morison's Executors* (7 S. C. 152); *In re Miller* (Buch. 1874, p. 28); *In re Nelson* (Buch. 1876, p. 130); and *Van der Ketssel* (§ 64).

407. Before entering upon a second marriage, the survivor of two spouses married in community must pass a bond securing the portions of inheritance of the minor children of the first marriage who are heirs to the predeceased spouse. The tacit hypothec of children on the estate of their surviving parent, in virtue of his guardianship, is lost by the passing of a deed securing their inheritance *(kinderbewijs).* In Roman-Dutch Law the penalty for failure to pass a deed of *kinderbewijs* was forfeiture by the surviving parent of his or her inheritance from the predeceased spouse (28, 2 §§ 100, 101).

At the Cape it is enacted, by Act 12,1856 (§§ 1, 2), that no second marriage of a widow or widower, having minor children by the first marriage, shall be allowed to take place unless the magistrate or minister solemnising such marriage shall first of all receive from the Registrar of Deeds a certificate showing that a deed of *kinderbewijs* has been passed by the widow or widower, and that the portions of the minor heirs of the first marriage have been secured. The penalty for remarrying before the shares due to the minor children of the surviving spouse have been ascertained and secured or paid is forfeiture by the survivor of one-fourth of his or her share in the joint estate for the benefit of the minor children (Act 12, 1856).

The rule that tacit hypothecs are lost by the passing of a deed of *kinderbewijs* was exemplified in *Naude ve. Naude's Trustee* (Buch. 1869, p. 166). There the *kinderbeivijs* contained only the general clause, and no special hypothecation. It was decided that the bond was to be postponed in the ranking of creditors to a general mortgage clause contained in a prior special conventional mortgage 408. A parent who marries in community for a second time, and takes the portion inherited by a child from the predeceased spouse upon the death of such child under intestate succession *(ab intestato)* is bound to share such portion equally with the children of the survivor and the predeceased spouse. It is different if the child so inheriting from the predeceased spouse bequeaths his or her portion to the surviving spouse, who need then make no division with the children of the first marriage; and there need be no division if the deceased child so bequeathing property to the surviving parent has acquired the same from any other source. A surviving parent who succeeds, jointly with his or her children, *ab intestato (by* intestacy) to his legitimate portion of the inheritance of a deceased child who acquired such inheritance from the predeceased parent, is entitled not to the ownership of such legitimate portion, but only to the usufruct thereof. The foregoing rules were introduced as penalties for a second marriage, and the latter rule with regard to the usufruct holds good so long as the children of the first marriage for whose benefit the rule was introduced are living. The Roman Law provided that a surviving spouse cannot by his or her own disposition confer a special benefit on any of the children of the first marriage in particular, with regard to property coming from the predeceased spouse, but such property must, if descending *ab intestato,* be shared equally between the children without distinction, and if the property descends by testament, the dispositions of the first-dying spouse must hold good, for a mutual will is the will of the first-dying spouse. Where a surviving spouse remarries more than once, the children of

each marriage take only the property coming from their own parents, and have no interest in the property of a marriage between one of their parents who has in such manner remarried and his or her spouse in a previous marriage. The children of the first marriage are entitled to their shares, unless they have been specifically disinherited. They do not transmit their right to descendants, and can only claim the ownership of the property where they have been instituted heirs jointly with the surviving spouse, if they outlive the surviving spouse. If all the children of the first marriage die in the lifetime of the surviving parent who has remarried, the survivor has full power to alienate property accruing to him or her either directly from the first spouse or from a child or children of the first marriage *ab intestato;* and, likewise, alienations of such property made by the survivor during the lifetime of the children of the former marriage, who have since died, will become ratified (28, 2 §§ 102—109).

Voet does not clearly lay down which of the rules summarised in this section were or were not obsolete in Holland, and the subsequent portions of the title cast no light on the subject. It would seem from Van der Keessel (§§ 313—320) that the Trebellian Law *(Senatus-conaultum Trebellianwn),* on which the foregoing rules are founded, was in full force in Holland in his day. He even goes so far as to state specifically that the procedure enjoined by Justinian *(Inst.* 2, 23, 12; *Cole,* 6, 42, 32), whereby the heir was put to his oath as to the trust which he had or had not received, had been adopted in Dutch Law. See Van der Linden (1,9, 8), Van Leeuwen *(II. D. I.* 3, 11, 1—11; 1 *Kotzi,* pp. 413—418); and Grotiua (2, 20, 6—14). The rules would seem to be obsolete in the Cape Colony, where Act 26, 1873, § 1, provides that " In no case shall any heir of any one dying after the taking effect of this Act be entitled to deduct out of the estate of the person so dying any portion under or by virtue of the law known as the Trebellian Law, which, but for such law, such heir would not be

entitled to claim or deduct." The Trebellian Law is also repealed in the Transvaal. This does not affect the general rules relating to *fideicommissa* or trusts, which Voet treats of in Book 36.

409. The next penalty provided in the case of second marriages is that a survivor cannot give by deed *inter vivos* or bequeath by testament to his or her second spouse more than the sum given or bequeathed to that one of the children of the first marriage to whom the least portion has been left; and, if more than such smallest portion is given or bequeathed to such second spouse, the gift or bequest is void to the extent of such excess, and the excess must be divided equally among the children of the first marriage alone. If there are not only children, but grandchildren of the predeceased spouse as well, such grandchildren succeed by right of representation to the share of the excess due to their parent (who is the child of the marriage between the survivorand the predeceased spouse). This law (which is found in the *Code,* 5, 9) is known, from the first words of the introduction, as the *Lex hdc edietali* (28, 20 § 11).

Colquhoun says (§ 582): "The parties to a second marriage can give no more to one another than the portion of a child of the first marriage; and if their portions be unequal, then the same as the child who has the least. All excess over this is equally divided among the children of the first marriage: this applies to gifts, legacies, or heritages under *quocunque nomine.* Whatever one receives by operation of law is not to be included in such sum." The *lex hdc edictali Codicis de secundis nuptiu* was introduced by the Emperors Leo and Anthemius. Neostadius (on *Antenuptial Agreements,* 4) states that the law was first introduced in the Netherlands in or about 1529. See also Van Leeuwen *(li. I). L.* 4, 23, 5; 2 *Kotzt,* 185).

410. If only grandchildren of the predeceased spouse survive, the amount which has been given or bequeathed to the survivor's second spouse in excess will go to such grandchildren not *per capita* but *per stirpes.* Thus if there are five grandchildren, two being children

of one son, and three children of the other son of the predeceased spouse, the first two grandchildren will each take one-fourth of the excess, and the next set of (three) grandchildren will each take one-sixth of the excess. The same rules apply not only to second marriages, but to all subsequent marriages. Voet mentions an opinion of Sande (Law relating to Step-parents) to the effect that if a survivor has left less to a child of the first marriage than his legitimate portion, such legitimate portion must first be made up to its full value from the excess, for the balance of the excess is distributed among all the children of the first marriage; but Voet dissents from this view (28, 2 § 111).

The foregoing rules of the *lex hdc edictali*, as well as those following, were repealed by the Cape Act 26, 1873, § 2, which provides that " from and after the taking effect of this Act the sixth law of the ninth title of the fifth book of the Codes *(sic)* of Justinian, commencing with the words 'Hac Edictali,' and commonly called or known as the Law or Lex Hac Edictali, shall be and the same is hereby repealed." This law was repealed in the Transvaal by Proc. 28, 1902, § 127. Van der Keessel states (§§ 222, 232) that community of property subsists in the case of a second marriage notwithstanding the *lex hdc edictali* (even where such community has been introduced by antenuptial contract). In such a case, either spouse will become liable for debts contracted before marriage; and, where the *lex hac edictali* is still in force, a second spouse will in consequence be liable to the children of the first marriage (the survivor of which marriage such second spouse has married) for their legitimate portions and for the excess paid, given, or bequeathed to such second spouse.

411. The children of a first marriage are not deprived of this benefit by the fact that they have adiated the inheritance left them by will of their surviving parent who married a second time (28, 2 § 112).

See *Blignaut's Trustee* vs. *Celliers' Executor* (Buch. 1868, p. 206); and *Salmon* vs. *Duncombe and Others* (5 N. L.

R. 103, and 7 N. L. R. 182), and *Barrett* vs. *Meyer's Executes* (6 N. L. R. 169).

412. When a husband has contravened the *lex hdc edictali* by making an excessive gift *inter vivos* to his second wife (or, *vice versa,* the wife makes a similar gift to a second husband), which gift is made irrevocably, the benefit of the penalty given by the law in favour of the children of the first marriage becomes vested in them, so that they cannot even be deprived of such benefit by an agreement between the husband and his second wife (or between the wife and her second husband, as the case may be) cancelling the donation. "But it does not necessarily follow," says De Villiers, C. J. (in *Lucas* vs. *Hoole* (Buch. 1879, p. 145), "that the rights of the children to the penalty would vest where the gift to the second wife is made not by way of *donatio inter vivos,* but by way of bequest or inheritance. In the latter case it would remain uncertain until the husband's death whether his second wife would receive any benefit at all; in the former case the gift would take effect immediately, and it could be easily ascertained, by comparing the gift with the husband's means, whether or not the gift was excessive and contravened the law." If a father who has made a gift to his second wife dies insolvent, the said gift being in contravention of this law, the excess will go to the children of the first marriage, and not to the creditors of the deceased, unless the gift was clearly made in fraud of the creditors. A second wife cannot deprive her husband's children by a former marriage of the benefit of the *lex hdc edictali* by renouncing a legacy which exceeds the amount which the law allows to be given to her, the law conferring the excess on the children of the first marriage immediately upon the death of their father. The law will also not be defeated by the fact that the father has made the gift or bequest to his second wife with a substitution (failing the second wife) in favour of a stranger or of the second wife's children. A gift exceeding a child's portion, made by a step-mother, who has children by a prior marriage, to her step-child or step-children, will be void to

the extent of the excess, but only if it clearly appears that the *lex hdc edictali* was contravened by the very fact of making such step-child the recipient of the gift. The penalty in such a case will, of course, enure in favour of the step-mother's own child or children (28, 2 §§ 113—117).

See Van Leeuwen *(Cens. For.* 1, 1, 12, 13; 1, 3, 4, 50), *Dutch Consultations.* (1, 90, 3; 3, 1, 44); Johannes a Someren (3, 1, 1).

C.L.—VOL. I. R 413. The *lex hac edictali* does not prevent a surviving spouse who remarries from leaving more property to the children of his or her second marriage than to the children of his or her first marriage.

The children of the first marriage must be satisfied if they receive the legitimate portions due to them from the estate of their parent (28, 2 §§ 118, 119).

See Van Leeuwen (1, 3, 4, 50, *Cent. For.),* Saude *(Decisiones Frisicae,* 2, 3, 6), *Dutch Consultations* (1, 90, 3; 3, 1, 44), and Johannes a Someren (3,1, 1; 9, 2, 3).

414. Prohibited gifts under the *lex hac edictali* include "morning" gifts (jewellery and similar presents in consideration of marriage), dowry, and the like. The usufruct of property is likewise included, unless it be shown that the usufruct does not amount in value to a child's portion. The same rule applies to household furniture left or given to the second spouse (28, 2 §§ 120, 121).

The question whether community arises or not in the case of a second marriage, notwithstanding the *lex hac edictali,* has been discussed above (§ 410). Voet is of the same opinion (23, 2 § 122) as Van der Keessel. He then proceeds to consider the effect of antenuptial contracts on property, with reference to the *lex hac edictali,* but as the decision in each particular case depends on the interpretation of the special contract, the subject need not be further gone into here. Profits arising from the community introduced by the second marriage, and money or property earned through the industry and labour of the parties to the second marriage, are not to be reckoned as included in the children's portions of the first marriage (23, 2 §§ 123, 124).

415. Spouses of survivors of a first marriage will not be able to retain more than the child's portion due to them under the *lex Me edictali,* by showing that the children of the first marriage have already received more than their shares of inheritance from their predeceased parent. If a second spouse has by antenuptial contract stipulated to receive from his or her wife or husband a child's portion of the inheritance coming from such wife or husband, and the portions paid out to the children have been increased, the child's portion for which such spouse has so stipulated by antenuptial contract should be similarly increased. If a wife promises her second husband a dowry of all her goods, having already paid or provided for payment of a sufficient portion to the children of her first marriage, and thereafter reduces her dowry in order to increase the portions of the children of the first marriage, her second spouse can recover the amount of such reduction of the dowry promised to him from the children of the first marriage, by the *actio Pauliana* (which is a real action, enabling him to recover the property of which he has been deprived from the children of the first marriage), or he may on his wife's death deduct the amount so owing to him from his wife's estate. A person who marries a second time, and promises a child's portion to the second wife or husband in consideration of the second marriage, cannot burden such child's portion with a trust or *fideicommissum.* The child's portion is in all cases to be calculated by a computation of the mass or whole amount of the patrimony or possessions of the spouse marrying a second time, without any previous deduction of the legitimate portion of the children of the previous marriage—which would appear to mean such share of the legitimate portion due to the children of the first marriage from the side of the surviving spouse who remarries, not from the side of the predeceased spouse. The computation must date, not from the second marriage, nor from the making of the donation or testament, but from the death of the spouse according to the value of whose estate the children's portions are reckoned, since donations between spouses are only confirmed by death, while death alone gives effect to testaments. If all the children of the first marriage die during the second marriage, the surviving spouse of the first marriage may lawfully institute his or her spouse in the second marriage as heir to the whole patrimony. If the surviving spouse of a first marriage has left less to one of the children by such marriage than will amount to a legitimate portion, or has passed over or disinherited such child, the second spouse to whom the same has been given or bequeathed may, nevertheless, claim the legitimate portion due to him or her (28, 2 §§ 125—130).

416. If a person leaves one child by a former marriage, and disinherits the same, leaving all the property to the second spouse, such disposition will hold, if the child has been lawfully disinherited. If the child has been disinherited unjustly, he may claim a child's portion from each marriage, that is, two-thirds of the inheritance; and if more children than one have been disinherited, they will all be entitled, under similar circumstances, to their portions. From this view of Voet's Van der Keessel (§ 288) dissents, holding that a disinherited son is in such circumstances entitled to one-half of the inheritance (28, 2 §§ 181, 182).

Apart from the abolition of the *lex hdc edietali* in Cape Colony and the Transvaal, as well as Natal, this rule no longer applies there, since legitimate portions are no longer claimable as of right (Cape Act 23, 1874, § 2; Transvaal Proc.28, 1902,§128; and Natal Law 7, 1885, §§2, Sand 4), and parents may (§ 3) disinherit children, parents, or other relatives or descendants without assigning any roason for doing so. Voct's next section deals with the disherison of children, apart from the loss of tho legitimate portion, for good reasons, such as prodigality and drunkenness. He says it would be against the *lex hdc eilictnli* to institute the children of such disinherited children in their stead. Schorer dissents from this view (§ 101, *ad Grotius,* 2, 12, 6), holding that the same reasoning applies as in the case of a child who has been deprived of his legitimate portion. Schorer appears to be correct (23, 2 § 133).

417. Where there are only grandchildren of a predeceased spouse, their children's portions will be calculated *per stirpes,* not *per capita* (23, 2 § 134). See also § 410, above.

418. When a question arises as to the amount that has been paid to a second spouse in excess of the lowest child's portion, the burden of proof lies on the children of the first marriage who claim the excess, or their descendants (28, 2 §§ 135, 136).

Voet further (23, 2 § 136) considers the offect of a change of domicile as affecting the operation of the *lex hdc edietali.* Ho practically holds that the general rules, that movables follow the law of the domicile of the owner, and real property follows the law of the place where it is situate, apply. A solution of such problems must be sought in modern works on Private International Law.

419. Another penalty of a second marriage is loss by the mother (not the father) of the guardianship over and right to educate the children. This penalty no longer applies in South Africa, where the various statutes and ordinances relating to guardianship clearly recognise the right of both parents, even if a second marriage has been entered into, to act as guardians of the minor children of the first marriage. The other penalties still apply in general RomanDutch Law (not where they have been repealed specially by statute, or abrogated by disuse) even if the children of the first marriage consent, approve, or do not object to the second marriage (23, 2 §§ 137—139). (8) Consequences Of Marriage. ii. *Dowry; and Antenuptial Contracts.*

420. The signification of dowry in Roman Law is different from the meaning which it bears in Roman-Dutch Law, for in the latter system marriage introduces a statutory community, unless a special dotal agreement has been entered into beforehand. "Dos" or dowry consists of the property which is given

by a wife, or by some other person on behalf of the wife, to the husband, for the purpose of sustaining the burdens of the marriage. If the marriage does not take place, the giving of dowry is null and void. If it takes place, the giving of the dowry is irrevocable, if the contract relating to it is entered into by the person who gives it with the intent that it shall always remain with the husband. "Under the Dutch Law, the term *dos* acquired a wide signification, and included, in the absence of proof to the contrary, all the property given to the husband for administration by the wife, but she acquired no tacit hypothecation in respect of such property, unless it was specifically secured against alienation by antenuptial contract excluding community of goods." Property included in the dowry or *dos* might be corporeal or incorporeal, personal or real, debts, inheritances (whether direct or fideicommissary), usufructs or interest. A guardian may agree on behalf of his female ward that all her property shall form her dowry, provided he considers that this will be advantageous to the ward. If the guardian or curator in good faith represents the amount of the dowry to be greater than it actually is, he will not be liable to the husband; but if he makes a misrepresentation as to the amount in bad faith *(dolo malo)*, he will be answerable to the husband for the difference between the amount represented and the actual amount. Not only property presently owned, but future property as well, is included in the dowry. But in case of doubt only things owned at the time the dowry is transferred will be considered as belonging to it. A dowry may be constituted either before or during the marriage; and a dowry fixed before the marriage may be increased during the marriage. If a dowry is promised by a woman, without mention of any specific articles or any fixed sum of money, it is presumed that she has given all her property as dowry. If pa)'ment of the dowry is delayed, interest on the amount will begin to run from the date of marriage, according to some authorities, or from the date when action is brought by the husband to ob-

tain the dowry or its value (Abraham a Wesel, *de connubiali societate,* 2, 1, 41; Van Leeuwen, *Cens. For.* 1, 4, 4, 15; *Dutch Consultations,* 2, 210, p. 425). Parents or other relatives or friends of the wife are not, in modern law, liable for a dowry, or the amount thereof, unless they have made a promise to pay the same, in consideration of which promise the marriage takes place, or unless they have become sureties on behalf of the wife for the amount of the dowry. Roman-Dutch Law imposes no necessity on either parent to contribute a dowry on his or her daughter's marriage. Where a marriage has taken place in community, the dowry or its value must be brought into collation, for the purpose of ascertaining the sum total of the estate owned in community and dividing the same. If a child has property of her own, and her father promises a dowry, he is presumed in Dutch Law to have promised payment of the same, in his capacity as guardian, out of his daughter's property, not of his own resources. The distinctions between various kinds of *dos* or dowry *(aestimata* and *inaestimata; numerata* and *cauta; profectitia* and *adventitia),* known to Roman Law, no longer exist in Roman-Dutch Law. The effect of giving a dowry is that the husband acquires the fruits or income thereof, and has the right of dominion over it. He has consequently an action to vindicate the same, if others have acquired possession of it, or if his wife or others have alienated it (28, 8 §§ 1—20).

Dowry is a private contract between the spouses. Dower in English Law is precisely the opposite of dowry in Roman Law, with which we are now concerned. In England, the word dower or *dos* (as used by Bracton and other English lawyers) denotes what tho husband gives the wife. The Roman jurists used "dowry" to signify the portion brought by the wife to the husband. In Roman-Dutch Law, the husband has no action, during the marriage, against the wife for recovery of the dowry *(Van iier Keessel,* § 256); but he can bring such an action during the marriage to obtain the dowry, or its amount, against the father of the

wife or any other person who has promised a dowry. Upon dissolution of the marriage, the husband may claim, as against the wife or her heirs, that the amount of the dowry which has not yet been paid shall be collated or brought into computation in a division of the marriage property. The giving of a dowry entitles the wife to a tacit hypothec upon the estate of her husband, where she has stipulated for such hypothec either expressly, or tacitly by desiring, in an antenuptial contract, that her own property should be reserved to her *(Van der Keessel,* § 263). This tacit hypothec will be preferent not only as against subsequent mortgage creditors of the husband, but as against those also who are prior in date *(Nederl. Adv.* 3, 90; Van L., *R. D. L.* 4, 13, 14; 2 *Kotze,* 99). This last statement is made on tho authority of Van der Xeessel (§ 263), who refers to Van Leeuwen. But it is quite clear that Van der Keessel misread Van Leeuwen. It is, therefore, submitted that this preference of the wife has priority only over the rights of subsequent creditors. The wife will have no preference at all where, by antenuptial contract, she reserves to herself " free control over her property, as fully and effectually as if no marriage had taken place." In such a case, no question of *dos* or of tacit hypothecation can arise. So, where the wife lends her husband money to assist him in his business or otherwise contracts with him, having been married under an antenuptial contract such as the foregoing, she can claim no greater rights upon his insolvency than any other creditor with whom she has dealt *(Rupert? s Trustee* vs. *Rupert i,* 4 S. C. 22). "Having by antenuptial contract freed herself from the disabilities which would otherwise attach to her married state, she cannot claim the benefit of a privilege which was introduced by reason of those disabilities." See also *Mostert* vs. *Mostert's Trustee* (4 S. C. 35). It is thus clear that the wife's hypothec is lost where the husband is deprived of his marital power and control over the wife's property; but it remains if the parties are married in community or by antenuptial contract, where the husband retains the marital power, when the amount of the dowry and the existence of an agreement—which, it is submitted, need not be in writing—are clearly proved. Voet states that the agreement constituting the dowry may be entered into before or during the marriage; and he draws no distinction between Roman Law and Dutch Law in this respect. Now Dutch Law absolutely prohibits donations between spouses during marriage. There is no modern case on the subject; but it is submitted that at the present day dowry cannot be constituted during marriage. The agreement for dowry would, then, seem to be wholly antenuptial. There is no necessity for transfer of landed property which passes from one spouse to another as dowry (*Van der Keessel,* § 202). An antenuptial contract between spouses may stipulate for tho payment of dowry by the bride's father, or by a stranger—who may promise it either absolutely or upon his death *(Van der K. , § 244)*. A reservation may be attached to the giving of such dowry, making it returnable either to the donor or any other person, or to the side whence it came. When it is returnable to the donor, he may himself reclaim the dowry, of which the husband will have only the usufruct *(Van der K., § 245)*. Tho case of *Steyn* vs. *Steyn* (Buch. 874, p-16), which was decided in the Cape Colony before the passing of the Cape Antenuptial Contracts Act (No. 21, 1875), laid down, as a proposition of general Roman-Dutch Law, that an antenuptial contract cannot secure to the wife, in The expressions "marital power" and "exclusion of the marital power" are frequently used in a very loose sense. Practically speaking, no contract is ever effectual to exclude the marital power completely.

competition with creditors, any of the husband's property not at the time of the marriage vested in trustees, to be administered by them without any right of interference on the part of the husband. This would seem to refer only to the husband's property settled on the wife. But where the wife's dowry is specially stipulated for in the contract, and the husband retains the marital power, it dues not seem necessary that the dowry should be vested in trustees to enable the wife to reclaim it. The tacit hypothecation of the wife on the estate of her husband for the amount of her dowry is prescribed by the lapse of a third of a century (*Vvet,* 23, 4 § 52). 421. Another form of gift between spouses known to the Roman

Law was the *donatio propter nuptias.* This was a gift, intended to be devoted to the marriage expenses, made by the husband to the wife in contemplation of marriage (as distinguished from *dos)*. The term no longer has the special meaning attaching to it in Roman

Law, and now means a marriage settlement. Such a settlement, if made by antenuptial contract, will remain unimpeachable by creditors if the contract is valid, with the exceptions provided for in special statutes, such as the Cape Antenuptial Contracts Act,

No. 21, 1875 (28, 3 §§ 21, 22).

See also O. R. C. Law 7, 1892, and Law 23, 1899. As to Transvaal, see Law 13, 1895, § 39.

422. A gift made in contemplation of marriage, under an antenuptial contract, which provides that a surviving spouse shall receive, by way of gift or donation, a certain sum out of the estate of the deceased, is known in Dutch Law as *douarie (Van dcr Linden,* 1, 3, 4). Kotze, C.J., in his edition of Van Leeuwen *(R. D. L.* vol. 2, p. 100), defines *douarie* as a marriage gift promised as a provision for widowhood. This seems a more reasonable definition than that of Van der Linden, which is too wide: for it can hardly happon in modern times, and with the prevalence of modern ideas, that a wife should promise money or property, to be given on her death, as a support for her husband while he is a widower. It is true that Kotze, C. J., makes no express distinction of sex. But tho distinction is of no great importance, since the generic term "marriage settlement" is applied to all gifts in contemplation of marriage, whether under antenuptial contract or otherwise, so long as they can bo clearly and validly distinguished from the prop-

erty of the donor. Van Leeuwen holds *(R. D. L.* 4, 13, 14; see also Decker's important note on the subject, in 2 *Kotze,* 100—102) that a wife has no preference with regard to her *douarie,* but is postponed to all other creditors. Jewellery and other personal presents given by the husbajid to the wife before or at the time of the wedding, belong to tho wife alone (Van L., *R. D. L.* 4, 24, 13). As to dowries in native marriages, see *Hamite* vs. *Mzalunza* (7 E. D. C. 149), *Afalga-t* 78. *Gakava* (6 E. D. C. 225); *Sengane* vs. *Gondele* (1 E. D. C. 195), *Nanto* vs. *Malgaa* (5 S. C. 108).

423. All contracts having reference to the property of the spouses, and to their marital rights, must, according to Dutch Law, be entered into before the marriage takes place (28, 4 § 1).

See Grotius (2, 12, 5; *Maatdorp,* p. 81); Schorer (§ 100, *ad Grot.);* Van der Keessel (§ 231); and Van Leeuwen (B. *D. L.* 4, 24, 1; 2 *Kotze,* 194). Where parties have all along intended to enter into an antenuptial contract, but have in good faith omitted to do so, or where no contract has been entered into or registered through circumstances beyond their own control, the South African Courts will permit a contract to be entered into and registered after the marriage has taken place, saving, however, to creditors such rights as they acquired between the date of the marriage and the date of registration of the contract. So, where an antenuptial contract was not signed by the notary before whom it had been executed, and the notary died shortly after, and the marriage took place, the Court ordered a contract to be registered after the marriage, saving creditors' right *(In re Moolman,* 1 S. C. 25). In *Ex parte Peacock* (Transv. Oft Rep. 1897, p. 287), a similar order was made where the parties had not signed a contract before marriage. See also *Ex parte Minnaar* (Transv. Off. P,ep. 1897, p. 163); *Ex parte Purchase* (3 S. C. 84); *Re Moore and Siaayman i* C. T. R. 4); *Twentyman* vs. *Hewitt* (1 M. 156); *Schoombie* vs. *Schoombie't Tnutees* (5 8. C. 189); *Dale* vs. *Registrar of Deeds* (5 G. W. R 184); *Ilutcheon* vs. *Kaffrarian Registrar of Deeds* (3 E. D. C. 229);

and *In re Pu ters* (9 C. T. R. 468).

424. Voet holds that an antenuptial contract need not be in writing, and in support of his view cites Neostadius (on *Antenuptial Agreements,* §§ 18, 19); and *Dutch Consultations* (8, 1, 149, 164). Van Leeuwen *(Cens. For.* 1, 1, 12, 9) takes the same view of the matter. Voet, a little further on, proceeds to state that antenuptial contracts containing gifts amounting in value to above 500 *aurei* (fixed in modern practice at 500Z.), require to be in writing, although even then they need not be notarial. It is the same, Voet says, with antenuptial contracts which provide for the future devolution of property by inheritance. Van der Linden (1, 3, 8; *Juta,* p. 15) says distinctly that the contract must be in writing, and must be contained in a notarial instrument, although, in general Dutch Law, no legal registration thereof is required (23, 4 §§ 2—4).

Van der Linden's view was followed by the Cape Supreme Court, which decided that an underhand antenuptial contract signed by the spouses and attested by witnesses could not avail as against the wife's creditors, who claimed payment of a debt contracted by the wife before marriage (*Wright* vs. *Barry and Another,* 1 S. 6; 1 M. 175). Van der Keessel (§ 229; see also *SteytUr* vs. *Dekkers,* 1 R. I11) holds with Voet that antenuptial contracts need not be in writing. Van der Linden's is the more modern opinion, and, supported as it is by the opinion of the Cape Supreme Court (given in 1850), would appear to be correct as to general Dutch Law. In the Cape Colony all doubt on the subject was removed by the passing of Act 21, 1875, § 1 whereof repeals the sixth section of the Placaat of the Emperor Charles V., relating to antenuptial contracts, and bearing date October 4th, 1540 (which postpones the claims of wives under marriage settlements until the claims of the creditors of the husband are satisfied). § 2 of Act 21, 1875, then goes on to enact: "No antenuptial contract executed after the taking effect of this Act shall be valid or effectual as against any creditor or creditors of either of the spouses unless the same shall

be registered in the Deeds Registry Office of this Colony, in conformity with established law and custom, and unless a duplicate original or notarial copy of such contract shall, at the time of the registration of the original, be deposited in the Deeds Registry aforesaid, there to remain for general information, and such duplicate or copy may be inspected by any person who shall, by payment of the fee for the time being payable for a search in the Debt *(sic,* probably 'Deeds') Registry, be entitled to inspect the register of antenuptial contracts, and no separate or further fee shall be demandable, and no such antenuptial contract as aforesaid shall be registered until such duplicate or notarial copy as aforesaid shall have been deposited." Voet himself (23, 4 § 50) says that publicity is required; but this only means that a notarial contract is necessary; and the necessity for such notarial contract is limited by Voet, as stated above, to gifts of 500/. and upwards, of landed property, and of property to go by way of inheritance. As to the view of the matter token by Natal Courts, see *Fuller! Trustees* vs. *Fuller* (4 N. L. R. 37), and *Doran* vs. *Doran* (13 N. L. R. 29). In the Orange River Colony antenuptial contracts must be notarial and registered (Law 7, 1892).

425. No particular form of words is necessary in an antenuptial contract in order to exclude the marital power. It is sufficient if the intention of the parties is unmistakably conveyed (28, 4 §§ 5, 6).

See the remarks of Bell, J., in *Steytler* vs. *Dekkers* (2 R. 98); and *Marshall* vs. *Murshall* (5 S. 145). Per Cloete, J., in the latter case: "It is quite clear that the law is well fixed that when spouses marry without community, the husband retains, by virtue of his marital authority, the right of administering all the separate property of the wife." So, where the wife reserved to herself the free administration of her separate property, the marital power was held to have been excluded. Where a wife reserves to herself free administration, and vests her separate property in trustees, she may afterwards recall the trust, and resume

possession of and administration over her separate property. But, as previously indicated, the marital power remains for most practical purposes, even where a contract purports to exclude it. Thus, except in matrimonial suits, no woman (perhaps not even a public trader) may sue without the assistance of her husband.

426. No subsequent private contract can derogate from an antenuptial contract once publicly entered into, whether the contract be merely notarial or registered in the public registry (28, 4 § 7).

The remarks of Voet on this subject are extremely amusing, but better fitted for a place in a romance than in technical lectures on the law of marriage.

427. Among clandestine agreements (which, therefore, cannot detract from the force of an antenuptial contract) are those which refer not only to the formal stipulations in the contract itself, but to the expunging of or addition to items in the inventory of goods attached to the antenuptial contract (23, 4 § 8). 428. If the parties, when entering into an antenuptial contract, refer to a document to be drawn up afterwards, which is to contain a specification or valuation of property forming the subject of settlement, such document must be executed with precisely the same formalities as the prior antenuptial contract (28, 4 § 9).

It would seem that such a document cannot be anything more than a specification, or valuation of the property conveyed by the previous contract. If it purports to transfer any property from one spouse to another (assuming it to be executed during the marriage), or to give one of the spouses additional rights, it will be invalid as infringing the law which prohibits donations between spouses. If executed before marriage, the same formalities must take place as with the original contract. There will then be two antenuptial contracts, the later being the supplement of the contract which is prior in time. If the contract, properly executed, is merely an explanation of the prior agreement, or such a modification of the prior contract as will convey no additional right or rights on either party, it would appear to be valid. But see *Van der Linden* (1. 3, 6).

429. Antenuptial contracts may be entered into either by the spouses themselves, or by their parents, where certain settlements or arrangements with regard to dowry are stipulated for. Strangers or relatives who wish to exercise liberality towards the spouses may become parties to an antenuptial contact, even against the will of the girl to whom a dowry is to be given for the purpose of contribution towards the marital estate; and such other parties may stipulate for a return of the property settled on dissolution of the marriage. If a stranger has once unconditionally agreed to make a certain settlement, he cannot thereafter impose a condition providing for the return of the property to him. If a person once acquires a right of action for recovery of property under a marriage settlement, such right of action cannot be taken away from him by last will and testament of either spouse; unless the person having such right of action becomes heir to the spouse making the testament; or unless the wife who contributes dowry by antenuptial contract has vested her rights in an agent or trustee, to whom she gives a mandate to stipulate for return of the dowry —for in this case the heirs of the wife have an action of mandate against the trustee for recovery of what he obtained on the stipulation (for entering into which he had the wife's mandate); or unless the wife has allowed a stranger to stipulate for the property as a donation, and afterwards burdens it with *fideicommmum*. Parents, guardians, or strangers cannot stipulate in an antenuptial contract to the prejudice of either spouse, where such spouse *(e.g.,* a minor) is unaware of the terms of the contract, and their consent, express or implied, has not been obtained. If such contract be prejudicial, and its terms unknown to a spouse, such spouse will not suffer, and the statutory community of property will result from such a marriage (28, 4 §§ 10—18). 430. Any agreement which has reference to a dissolution of a marriage is opposed both to law and public morality; and so is any antenuptial contract which pur-

ports to convey, during marriage, a gift from one spouse to the other (23, 4 §§ 14—16).

In *Braude* vs. *Braude* (9 C. T. R. 666; 17 C. L. J. 64), all the Judges were of opinion that a contract providing for a future voluntary separation was not binding. But it was laid down by De Villiers, C.J., that a contract providing for the disposition of property in case of a judicial separation was not contrary to the policy of the law. See also *Croker* vs. *Croker* (6 C. T. R. 20; 13 C. L. J. 137). Several English cases have been decided having reference to this subject, and the law in England may be said to be somewhat intricate. It is thus generally stated by Sir William Anson, in his work on *Contracts* (5th ed. p. 197): "Agreements providing for separation of husband and wife are valid if made in prospect of an immediate separation. But if such agreements provide for a possible separation in the future they are illegal, whether made before or after marriage, because they give inducements to parties not to perform ' duties in the fulfilment of which society has an interest.'" The judgments in *MMregor* vs. *McGregor* (21 Q. B. D. 424), *Wilson* vs. *Wilson* (1 H. L. C. 538), *Besantxs. Wood* (12 Ch. D. 605), and *Curtwright* vs. *Cariwright* (3 De G. M. & G. 982) should be consulted; see also Brett's *Commentaries cm English Law* (2nd ed. p. 577).

431. An agreement that the wife's dowry or *dos* should remain with the heirs of the husband, in whatever way the marriage is dissolved, or that the wife should not have her dowry returned to her, deprives the wife entirely of her dowry. An agreement whereby it is provided that a husband shall make good fraud alone, which may be perpetrated in connection with the *dos,* is null and void, as contrary to public policy (although Groenewegen holds that this is not the case in modern Dutch Law). There can be no subsequent extension of time given, as in the case of other debts, by the wife to the husband for return of the dowry, when once the antenuptial contract has provided for its return on the dissolution of the mar-

riage. The modern law rejects the fine distinctions of the Roman Law with regard to modification or deterioration in the value or condition of property, originally given as dowry, upon its return. Agreements which provide with regard to profits arising from dotal property will be valid if they are to take effect only after the wife's death. In Dutch Law nothing prevents a condition being attached to a contract, whereby a portion of the dowry goes to the heirs of the husband, while the remainder is restored to the surviving wife alone (28, 4 §§ 17, 18). 432. In Dutch Law all antenuptial contracts which are in accordance with natural reason and justice, with good morals, and which conform to custom or statute, are valid. Agreements in such contracts may be general or special, and may have reference to the laws or customs of various places, and to the effects produced by a change of domicile; provided that the laws of the future domicile, with reference to which the parties contract, do not forbid anything contained in the contract upon which the parties intend to act in such domicile (28, 4 § 19). 433. An agreement whereby it is provided that the husband shall be in the power of his wife is especially illegal. So also is an agreement illegal which provides that the husband shall not appear in judicial matters for his wife, but that she shall alone appear in suits; or which provides that the husband shall never change his domicile (28, 4 § 20).

See *Prince* vs. *Anderson and Others* (1 M. 176).

434. Among unlawful agreements, which can never become lawful, are those which give the spouses the right to do those things which are plainly contrary to statutory prohibitions (in other words, which contravene statutory dispositions), such as clauses permitting the spouses to make donations to each other which are prohibited by law. The law prohibiting such agreements has been introduced, not for the benefit of the parties, but upon grounds of public policy. Consequently, the spouses cannot, by contract, exclude the operation of the law. The same rule applies to

agreements which deprive one spouse of a privilege or enjoyment which is imposed on the married state by law or by custom—not privileges introduced for the benefit of a particular spouse, for such privileges may be renounced. So, an agreement which deprives one spouse of the right to dispose of his or her property by will or testament is invalid (28, 4 § 20).

Where husband and wife were married by antenuptial contract, under which it was agreed that they should be entitled to benefit each other by donation, and that certain shares settled by the husband on the wife (which were vested in the wife's trustee appointed under the contract) should not be realised and transferred by the trustee without the wife's consent in writing, the husband, after marriage, exchanged a piece of land for his wife's shares. The wife's written consent to such exchange was never given to the trustee. The land was sold by the wife's agent (not her trustee), who retained the proceeds of such sale, which were claimed by the trustee of the husband's insolvent estate. The wife brought an action against her agent and her husband's trustee to recover the purchase-price of the property. It was decided that, as the spouses could not make a donation to each other, and as the trustee under the antenuptial contract could not transfer the shares without the wife's written consent, there was a total failure of consideration for the transfer by the husband to the wife of the land. The proceeds thereof were, therefore, held to belong to the husband's insolvent estate *(Hall* vs. *Hall's Trustee and Mitchell,* 3 S. C. 3; 1 C. L. J. 94).

435. On the other hand, an agreement whereby the husband is deprived of the power, granted him by statute or common law, of alienating the wife's property, is valid, since it tends not so much to diminish the marital power as to secure more firmly the retention by the wife of her dotal property (28, 4 § 20).

See Grotius (1, 5, 24; see *Maasdorp,* p. 19), and Van der Keessol (§ 97).

436. An agreement for the increase of a dowry—provided it does not consti-

tute a donation between spouses—or for a donation *propter nuptias*—provided it be given before marriage—is legal. If an agreement has been made before marriage for the payment or transfer of some thing or some property, and a condition (to be subsequently fulfilled) or a future date is attached to such agreement, the agreement will be binding, in case of a dissolution of marriage by death, if a time certain has been established for the fulfilment of the condition or the expiry of the period agreed upon. If the agreement be based on a condition or expiry of a period which is uncertain, the agreement will not bind. If there is a difference between the laws of various jurisdictions in regard to antenuptial agreements and the performance of conditions attached to them, the law of the husband's domicile should be followed (23, 4 §§ 21—25).

In the interpretation of contracts, the law of the place where the contract was entered into is generally followed—*lex loci contractus.* But where the parties contract with reference to a particular domicile, the rules laid down in *Black* vs. *Black's Executors* (3 S. C. 200), *Chiwell* vs. *Carlyon* (7 C. T. R. 83), and similar cases must be noted.

437. Where there is no statutory community of property on marriage, such community of all property may be introduced between spouses by antenuptial contract. Or the contract may exclude such community in whole or in part. An agreement providing for universal community will hold good so long as there are no children of the first marriage, for such an agreement will contravene the *lex hdc edictali* (except in countries, such as Cape Colony, where the *lex hdc edictali* has been repealed). An antenuptial contract may provide that the universal community introduced between the spouses may be regulated, not according to the laws of the husband's domicile, to which the wife has by marriage transferred herself, but according to the laws of the wife's domicile, or according to the laws of any other domicile chosen by the spouses (23, 4 §§ 26, 27).

Such an agreement as that last men-

tioned by Voet would not seem to hold good, according to the principles of modern private international law, unless the parties remove to the domicile by whose law they intend their property to be governed. Keeping in mind the principle *locus regit actum,* one must remember, in the first place, that immovable property is governed by the law of the place where it is situate *(lex loci rei sitae),* while the policy of the law is opposed to a husband contracting in such a manner, by following the law of his wife's domicile, as to evade his responsibilities to creditors in his own domicile. On the other hand, due weight must be given to the fact that an antenuptial contract providing for such change of domiciliary law has been made notarially and publicly registered, applying the maxim *caveat emptor.* 438. Just as antenuptial contracts with regard to community of property hold good, so will similar contracts having reference to community of acquisitions or gains during marriage be validated.

If an antenuptial contract provides for the exclusion of the statutory community of property which follows on marriage, but makes no mention of profits or gains, a community of acquisitions or gains between the spouses is considered to have been tacitly agreed upon.

But where, on the contrary, an express agreement has been made providing for community of profit and loss between the spouses, and no mention is made of community of property, the law regards such community of property as tacitly excluded. Nor does the law forbid an agreement which provides that the community of profit and loss shall commence from a certain date or run to a certain date, or subject to a condition (28, 4 § 28).

Van Leeuwen *(Cens. For.* 1, 1, 12, 10) says: ""When community of goods has been excluded, community of gain and loss arising during the marriage is notwithstanding considered to have taken place by operation of law.... If community of goods be excluded, community in gains accruing or losses resulting is only held to be excluded if that be expressly stated." See Schorer *(ad*

Grotius, § 24); Grotius (2, 12, 9); Van der Keessel (§§ 247—249); and Bynkershoek *(Decisions on Private. Law,* II. c. 1); also *Schultz* vs. *Prellsr* (Transv. Off. Rep. 1895, p. 208); and *Blatchford* vs. *Blatchford's Erecutors* (1 R. 8).

439. If a community of profits has been introduced between spouses by statute or antenuptial contract, it makes no difference in what place the things which make the profits have been acquired during the marriage. So even immovable property which, by the law of the place where it is situated, accrues to the husband, becomes the joint property of the spouses, if it is in the nature of a profit or gain. In such a case, if community of profits has been provided for by contract or statute, both the dominion over and possession of property acquired as profits will be joint and common, even if the husband has acquired the property by a contract or transaction entered into, not in the names of himself and his wife, but in his own name alone (28, 4 §§ 29, 30). 440. Where it is not possible to ascertain from which side certain property has come, and the surviving spouse does not satisfactorily prove that such property has come from himself or herself, or the heirs of the deceased spouse do not satisfactorily prove that such property came from the deceased spouse, the law will, in such case of doubt, presume that such property belongs to profits or acquisitions obtained during marriage, and the property will belong to the spouses jointly. Among things which come into community of profits is reckoned whatever has been obtained by the industry and labour of the spouses from some business, work, manufacture, exercise of a profession, from exercise of public dignity or office, or other means; or whatever one spouse acquires through title by occupancy, as belonging to no one, such as captured wild beasts, abandoned property found on the sea-shore, and treasure trove; likewise whatever has been acquired by fraud, theft, or other crime, so long as the spouse committing the crime is not compelled to make restitution of the property wrongfully acquired by him or her. Community of profits likewise includes natural fruits, profits acquired by industry—natural fruits being the vegetation naturally produced by the soil or the natural product of animals, industrial fruits those acquired by tillage, vintage, and similar farming operations; rents; interest on property or on money lent—whether due on things belonging to either spouse at the time of marriage, or on things subsequently acquired. If a usufruct has been left to one spouse, the fruits will, during the marriage, go into community of profits; and after the marriage the spouse to whom the usufruct has been left may claim only the fruits accruing from the date of dissolution of the marriage. Into the community of profits come all things, whether movable or immovable, which have been purchased during the marriage in the joint name of the spouses. If the husband has purchased immovable property for himself alone, and has obtained transfer into his own name, he is considered in law to have done so by virtue of his marital power, and to have desired, where there is community of profits, that such property

C.l.—Vol. i. s should be regarded as acquired for himself and his wife. It makes no difference whether he has acquired the dominion, during marriage, revocably or irrevocably. Garments which have been acquired during the marriage are, in case of doubt, regarded as belonging to the community of profits. If a thing has been purchased with money which was brought into collation for the purpose of contributing to the expenses of the marriage, on the antenuptial condition that such money should on the dissolution of the marriage revert to the spouse who contributed it, the thing so purchased will belong to the community of profits, but the contributing spouse may on the termination of the marriage reclaim the money so brought into collation, while the thing purchased with such money will be divided equally between the spouses—even if it has been agreed upon by antenuptial contract that dowry money (i.e., money brought into colla-tion by either spouse) shall be spent in the purchase of landed property. It will be otherwise if the husband, when making the purchase, expressly states that he does so for the wife's benefit with the wife's money, that he spends the money in furtherance of the wife's business interests, and that he regards the property purchased as standing in place of the money originally contributed by the wife. The same principles apply with regard to purchase-money, where the husband sells his own property or that of his wife, and with such purchase-money buys another property. It makes no difference whether the husband obtains property from another person by sale or exchange, so long as what is given in return for the property obtained, even if it be not money, belongs to the wife. Nor does it matter whether the husband obtains possession of specific property in the manner above indicated, or of a universality of property *(universitas rerun),* as by the purchase from the heir of a deceased person of the inheritance of such heir. Where inheritances accruing subsequently to the marriage are excluded from community of profits, and the husband, being co-heir to a certain person deceased, purchases the shares of those who are joint heirs with him (whether by testament or intestacy), such shares will be regarded as having come to him, not by inheritance, but by purchase. Anything which has been acquired, or the right to which has vested in a spouse, prior to the marriage, does not fall into the community of profits. Thus, if one of the spouses has bought a property before the marriage takes place, and transfer thereof is only made after marriage, the property will belong to the spouse who purchased it alone, even if the purchase price has been paid out of the joint moneys of the spouses—because transfer is only a secondary step *(sequela,* sequel) following on the contract of sale, and the purchaser, from the moment the sale is concluded, has a personal action to obtain transfer, it being only reasonable that the effect of the contract should benefit the person who entered into it. It makes no difference whatever terms have been annexed to the payment of the purchase price of such a sale. The same rule holds good if the property of a third party has been assigned by judicial decree to, or declared executable in favour of a spouse, who sued to obtain such property before marriage. If, during the subsistence of the marriage, the husband sues for a certain property or thing belonging to himself or his wife, it will, upon recovery by judicial process, belong to the spouse in whose name the dominion has been asserted and recovered. If a property has been captured during time of war, before or during the marriage, by enemies, and returns by the law of postliminy *(jus postliminii)* while the marriage still subsists, it will be regarded as belonging to the spouse to whom it belonged previous to its capture. The same rule applies to such movable property as is capable of reversion by the law of postliminy; but it will not apply if such movable property has been purchased from the captor by the spouse who lost it. If a spouse before marriage sells property, movable or immovable, unconditionally, without stipulating for resale, such property, if again purchased by the same spouse after marriage, will be regarded as belonging to the community of profits, and will therefore belong to the spouses jointly. If a stipulation has been made for resale, and the spouse originally selling avails himself or herself, during the marriage, of the right to repurchase, the property will go to such spouse, and not into the community of profits, where the original sale was made before marriage (28, 4 §§ 31—41).

44L Voet, after discussing the matter at length, lays down that inheritances, legacies, or donations coming from a stranger to one of the spouses pass into the community of profits; but inheritances, legacies, or donations from parents or blood relations of a spouse do not go into the community of profits (28, 4 §§ 42, 43).

Voet states that he had previously been of opinion with Sande *(decisiones Frisicae,* 2, 5, 5), Fontanella (on *Antenuptial Agreements,* 11, 7), Maevius (on the *Law of Liibeck,* 2, 2, 12, 59),

and Coren *(Opinions,* 18 § 23), that all such inheritances, legacies, and donations did not come into the community of profits. He gives reasons for his subsequent change of view, resulting in the distinction drawn above. See also Van Leeuwen *(Cens. For.* 1, 4, 23, 23). This distinction, Voet adds in the next section (23, 4 § 44), only holds so long as the nature of the thing given or bequeathed is not repugnant and opposed to community. He goes on (23, 4 § 45) to state that this distinction only holds where it is not certain that the stranger making the bequest, legacy, or donation wishes the same to go to a particular spouse. If the stranger expressly states that he wishes the property to go to the community, effect must be given to such wish or intention. If parents or blood relations direct that property bequeathed or donated by them shall go to the community, their intention must similarly be carried into effect.

442. If it is agreed upon in the antenuptial contract that property contributed to the support of the marriage shall return to the side whence it came, and no mention is made of property afterwards acquired by inheritance, such inheritances, legacies, and donations as come during the subsistence of the marriage to one of the spouses —with the exceptions mentioned above (§§ 440, 441)— will be divided equally between them, where statutory community of all property is shown to exist—for *expressio unius est exclusio alterius.* If an unconditional agreement has been made that during the marriage profit and loss accruing to the spouses shall be in common, and inheritances have not been specifically added to the agreement for community of gains, there will be a presumption of a tacit agreement against community with respect to such inheritances (28, 4 § 46).

See Grotius (2, 12, 9—14); Van der Keessel (§§ 247—25"); and Van Leeuwen *(Cens. For.* 1, 1, 12, 19).

443. Interest on debts or moneys or bonds due to one of the spouses before the day of marriage is not reckoned among the profits of the marriage, but increases the dowry or portion of the

spouse to whom such debts, moneys, or bonds belong. Nor do augmentations of separate property of either spouse come into the community of gains, whether they be external, as alluvion, or other accessions to soil (like buildings), or internal, such as an increase in the value of property (28, 4 § 47). 444. The same principles apply to community of loss as to community of profit; and if it has been agreed upon by antenuptial contract that profits acquired by the spouses shall be in common, no mention being made of losses, loss will nevertheless be shared equally among the spouses. As we have seen, this distribution differs from the liability in partnerships, in which losses are divided in proportion to the shares of the partners (28, 4 § 48).

See *Grotius* (2, 12, 9), and *Van der Keessel* (§ 247).

445. Just as augmentations of separate property are not shared, so diminutions in the value of such property, or other damage or loss occurring to the same, are borne by the spouse holding such property alone (28, 4 § 49).

Grotius (2, 12, 15) states that the spouses may claim compensation for property excluded from the community—in other words, may demand a division of the loss with the other spouse—where such separate property has been destroyed or injured, or where expense has been incurred in or about such property. Van der Keessel (§ 247) dissents from Grotius, stating that an accidental or casual loss occurring to the property of either of the parties is not common to both, but attaches to the owner of such property; "as rightly held by many authors since the time of Grotius," among whom he cites Voet and Coren (No. 18). The same rule applies to necessary expenses of an extraordinary nature. But useful expenses should be refunded to the extent to which the property has been thereby improved. The reason for this appears to be that during marriage the spouse to whom such separate or dotal property does not belong has the benefit of the improvements. Therefore, only improvements during the marriage will be taken into consideration (see *Voet,* 25, 1 § 4). Van der Keessel quotes

Voet (25, 1 § 5) to show that luxurious expenses *(i.e.,* costs of ornamentation, which improve a property, but do not increase its products) are to be shared by the spouses; but Voet distinctly states that such expenses are borne by the spouse alone who owns the property.

446. During marriage spouses married without community of property, but with community of profit and loss, are liable for debts contracted after marriage by their husbands or wives respectively. But they are not in similar circumstances liable for debts contracted before marriage. If it has been simply provided in an antenuptial contract that the property shall revert to the side whence it came, and that there shall be a community of profit and loss, one spouse, if otherwise liable to excussion for debts of the other contracted before marriage, will not be rendered the less liable by such a contract. It is sufficient, in order to avoid liability to such excussion, to provide generally by antenuptial contract that the husband shall not have any right, during marriage, of alienating property brought by his wife, or subsequently to be acquired by her; in which case the wife will have a vindicatory action for return of property alienated in contravention of the contract. The wife *may* also escape liability by means of a special stipulation in the antenuptial contract, that the property of the wife may not be pledged or excussed for debts of the husband contracted before the marriage.

Such an agreement, according to general Dutch Law (see Placaat of

States General, July 80th, 1624, § 4, vol. 1, p. 877), had to be in writing; and, since the time of Van der Linden, as we have seen, must be notarial. It is not necessary that an inventory of property, brought into the marriage by the spouses, should be attached to the antenuptial contract, in order that the contract may have effect against creditors; and it is sufficient if the spouse, who claims that his or her property is not liable for debts of the other spouse, proves that he or she has sole dominion and ownership over such property (28, 4 § 50).

So, where no schedule of goods belonging to the wife is appended to the antenuptial contract, it will be sufficient if proof that such property belongs to the wife is furnished from other sources *(aliunde).* As to publicity of antenuptial contracts, see *Wright* vs. *Barry* (1 S. 6), *In re Smith* (1 M. 167), and § 424, above.

447. The effect of a contract, whereby it is agreed that a wife's property shall be separate, that she shall not be liable on her husband's contracts during marriage, and that she shall not share in any profit or loss accruing to the husband during marriage, is, that the wife will not be liable to creditors on the dissolution of the marriage, and will have a preference for the recovery of her separate property (dowry or *dos*) upon the estate of her husband, before other creditors, whether hypothecary or otherwise, with whom the husband contracted debts during marriage; but her preference will not take precedence over conventional or legal hypothecations acquired by creditors over the husband's estate before the date of the marriage. But if any creditors have lent money to procure necessaries or provided such necessaries, during the marriage, the wife will have no preference over such creditors for necessaries, since she is liable even after dissolution of the marriage for half of the amount of necessaries, despite the antenuptial contract—having recourse for the amount so paid by her against her husband's heirs (23, 4 §§ 51, 52).

As to the wife's hypothec, see *Mostert's Trustees* vs. *Mostert* (4 S. C. 35), and § 420, above. As to liability for necessaries, see *Grossman* vs. *Huffman* (3 S. C. 282), and § 386, above. On the wife's preference, see further Van Leeuwen *(Cms. For.* 1, 1, 12, 3).

448. It is lawful for the spouses to enter into an antenuptial contract, whereby the wife may elect whether she is to share in the profits or losses arising out of the marriage, while the marriage lasts, or, having renounced such share in profit and loss, to claim the restoration of her property upon dissolution of the marriage. If she makes the latter choice,

she will have her ordinary preference for dowry on the husband's estate. If, on the other hand, the wife chooses to share profit and loss, the husband, if called upon after dissolution of the marriage to make payment to creditors for debts contracted during the marriage, may have recourse against his wife or her heirs for her share of the debt (28, 4 § 53).

See Van Leeuwen *(Cent. For.* 1, 1, 12, 11).

449. The right of the wife to elect, under the antenuptial contract specially entered into for that purpose, is transmissible to her direct heirs (children and descendants through them), when a question with regard to the wife's liability arises between the creditors and such heirs; but if a question arises between the husband or his heirs and the wife's heirs, the right of option will benefit all the wife's heirs, however remote (28, 4 § 54). 450. If the parties enter into an antenuptial contract which gives the wife such a right of election, and thereafter establish themselves in another domicile by the laws of which no contract between the spouses can avail to defeat the rights of creditors who became such during the marriage, and the spouses then again establish their domicile where they lived previously (and where the wife had the right of election), the wife may again avail herself of such an agreement as against creditors with whom they contracted whilst they were domiciled in the place where the contract conveying the right of election was valid (28, 4 § 55).

In simpler words, A. and his wife are domiciled in Holland, where such a contract is valid. They remove to a domicile where such a contract will not hold. Then they return to Holland. The contract will revive, and will avail against creditors who became such before the departure from or after the return to Holland.

451. In Dutch Law, a wife who has stipulated by antenuptial contract that her dowry shall be secured to her, or who has reserved to herself the right of election previously mentioned, and consequently receives a preference over other

creditors, has the right of intervening on behalf of her husband, and of subjecting herself of her own free will to the burden of some debt or other during the subsistence of the marriage (23, 4 § 56). 452. An agreement, whereby the wife stipulates that she shall in any case have her dowry secured to her, and shall, moreover, receive half of any profits acquired during the marriage, does not give the wife any right of preference over the property of her husband before other creditors, and furthermore postpones the claim, which lies in favour of herself and her heirs as against her husband and his heirs, until such other creditors have been satisfied (28, 4 § 57).

See Groenewcgen's note to Grotius (2, 12, 9; *Maaidorp,* p. 81); and Van Leeuwen *(Cens. For.* 1, 1, 12, 11).

453. The wife's claims are similarly postponed to those of other creditors if she stipulates for the return of her dowry, while the husband agrees to maintain, keep in repair, and improve the dotal property, and the husband or his heirs thereafter makes or make no claim against the wife for the expenses so incurred by the husband (28, 4 § 57). 454. Agreements in antenuptial contracts which provide for future succession to property of the spouses are valid. Such agreements may provide for succession by surviving spouses or by third parties. An agreement that on death of spouses the property shall return to the side whence it came is valid. So are agreements providing that the heirs of a predeceased spouse shall be satisfied by payment by the survivor of a certain amount or of certain property; that after the survivor's death the relatives of both spouses shall share equally in what is left of their property; that only children of a first marriage shall succeed, and that children of the second marriage shall receive only a certain amount out of their paternal inheritance; that things (whether movable or immovable) situate in the domicile of the spouses shall be governed according to the law of the domicile, while property situate elsewhere shall devolve according to the law of the place where such property is

situate (23, 4 § 57). 455. The effect of an antenuptial contract is that it gives rise to an action to compel fulfilment of what is therein and thereby provided or stipulated, provided marriage has followed upon such a contract, which, according to Dutch Law, need not be consummated.

There can be no alteration of an antenuptial contract by deed *inter vivos* (after marriage), whether such deed be private or publicly registered. For every change of the kind implies a donation betwccn spouses *inter vivos,* as, for instance, where the statutory community between the parties is amended or altered by such a deed. Such changes are wholly opposed to Roman-Dutch Law (23, 4 §§ 58, 59).

In *Albertus* vs. *Albertnt' Executors* (3 S. 212) it was said by Watermeyer, J.: "Whatever contracts could be made between a man and his wife voluntarily, in case of living separately, a contract by which community is changed into a severance of goods is not one of those contracts. Voet clearly lays down likewise, first, that there can be nothing in the nature of a donation, and then as clearly as words can lay it down, that the change of community into separation would be a donation." The whole of this judgment is valuable, and should be carefully studied. See also *Braude* vs. *Braude* (9 C. T. R. 666); *Booysen* vs. *Booysen* (1 M. 242); *Grotius* (1, 5, 20—26); and *Van der Keeise!* « 231).

456. In order to make a testamentary disposition by virtue of an antenuptial contract invalid, it is not sufficient that there should be a simple revocation of all othcr bequests than those contained in the will then being made, but the testamentary disposition under the antenuptial contract must be specially revoked in the same manner as the antenuptial contract required to be made (23, 4 § 60). 457. If it has been agreed upon by antenuptial contract that the property shall revert to the side whence it came, the spouses have the right of designating a particular person to whom the property is to go. According to Dutch Law, a wife cannot leave to her husband property which was given as

dowry by the wife's parent on condition that the wife should only have the right of disposing of property acquired during the subsistence of the marriage, but not of the dotal property (28, 5 § 61).

See Van Leeuwen *(Cms. For.* 1, 1, 12, 17).

458. If spouses have brought their property into the marital estate, and it has been agreed by antenuptial contract that one spouse shall succeed to the estate of the other in whole or part, one spouse cannot without the knowledge or without the consent of the other dispose of property in prejudice of the rights of such other spouse. If the consent of the other spouse has been obtained to a change in the testamentary disposition under the antenuptial contract, the surviving spouse may elect whether to take under the antenuptial contract or under the change of disposition, provided the consent of the predeceased spouse be clearly proved (28, 5 § 62).

See *Scorey* vs. *Scorey's Executors* (1 M. 235).

459. If spouses have by antenuptial agreement designated as liens not each other mutually, but other persons, in general terms (such as, that the property shall return to the side whence it came), the spouses are not thereby prevented from disposing of their property in another manner, and from instituting other persons as heirs. The same rule applies if particular persons have been designated as heirs. An agreement, whereby children of a second marriage succeed to a greater portion of the property of the twice-married spouse than the children of the first marriage, or *vice versa,* may be changed by will of the survivor. If it has been agreed upon before marriage that upon the death of the survivor the children of both of two marriages shall succeed in equal shares to all the property, the order of succession may not only be changed by either spouse with the consent of the other, while the spouses are alive, but the last survivor will have the free right of disposition of his or her share of the joint property, and can therefore substitute other heirs to his or her share in the place of those originally agreed upon (28, 5 § 68).

Voet dissents from Grotius (2, 15, 9), who holds that when the first dying of two spouses has bequeathed the survivor any benefit, and has directed how the property of the joint estate is to go after the survivor's death, the survivor cannot, after enjoying the benefit, dispose of his or her share by last will in a manner contrary to the will of the first-dying. Van der Keessel (§ 283) expresses a modified view, which is in agreement with the qualification expressed by Voet in a later portion of the same section (23, 5 § 63), that the survivor cannot make a separate disposition, where both spouses have by onamon consent made a disposition of the common estate or of the share of the survivor. See also Schorer *(ad Grotius, §* 114). The views of the Dutch jurists on the subject were examined and reconciled or explained, and the law finally settled, in *Mostert* vs. *South African Association* (Buch. 1872, p. 33; and Buch. 1874, p. 40).

460. If spouses make a contract providing for future succession, they do not thereby revoke previous testaments made under the autenuptial contract, providing for succession by the survivor or other persons than those mentioned in the antenuptial contract, if they agree unconditionally that the property shall revert to the side whence it came. But if particular persons have been designated as heirs in the later will, to whom the succession *ab intestato* would not go in any case, or not in the way defined by the testament, the prior testament must be considered as revoked (28, 4 §§ 64, 65). 461. If spouses by antenuptial contract regulate the succession, not to their own property, but to that of their children who succeed them (for instance, where they lay down that the brothers of their first-dying children shall succeed to the portions of such first-dying children, or that if the last surviving of their children die without issue the property shall revert to the side whence it came), no *fideicommissum* or trust is thereby created; and the children have the full right of disposing of their property, so coming to them from their parents, by deed *inter vivos* or by last will. If the

property is left to the children in express terms indicating that such property is subject to a *fideicommissum* in favour of some other person or persons, the children may not dispose by will of any other portion of their paternal or maternal inheritance than that which constitutes their legitimate or Trebellianic portion (28, 4 § 66).

See Grotius (2, 29, 3). Schorer (§ 198) contents himself with referring to Voot, who considers the cases where the children exercise their right of disposition; while Grotius holds with Voet that if the children do not exercise their right to dispose, that is, if they die intestate, the succession is regulated by the antenuptial contract of the parents.

462. Where third parties share in the making of an antenuptial contract (such as parents or relatives who contribute to the dotal property of the wife), they are bound, according to Dutch Law, by such a contract, and accordingly cannot make such a disposition of the dotal property as will affect the succession of the property as it has been fixed by the spouses in the antenuptial contract (28, 4 § 67). 463. Where succession to property has been fixed by antenuptial contract, and such succession has not been burdened with *fideicommissum,* no subsequent testamentary disposition may be made which will have the effect of burdening such property with *fideicommissum,* if the succession in general has been unconditionally bequeathed without reference to the claim of one heir conjointly with others (a *concursiis,* as Voet terms it), or if a certain thing or a certain amount has been bequeathed. If the spouses have agreed that the survivor shall succeed jointly with the children or other relatives, nothing prevents the portion of the survivor so inheriting from being burdened with *fideicommissum,* provided the portions of the others who succeed with such spouse are likewise burdened with *fideicommissum* (28, 4 § 68). 464. When a question arises as to the law which ought to be followed in respect to a change of succession under an antenuptial contract, the law of the place of domicile of the spouses must regulate the disposition of

movables, while immovable property will be regulated according to the law of the place where it is situate (23, 4 § 69). 465. If the spouses omit to provide for any contingency in an antenuptial contract, such omissions must be looked upon as express, and what is provided for in one case cannot be extended by implication to another case with regard to which no provision is made. So, if provision be made for a thing in case of divorce, the same provision will not apply if the marriage be dissolved by death. Therefore, if the parties neglect to dispose of certain of their property by antenuptial contract, such property will follow the law of community (28, 4 § 70). 466. Where there is a doubt as to the meaning of parties in au antenuptial contract, the law permits an inquiry into the intentions of the spouses, although the same are not express, but to be inferred by conjectures from the circumstances of the case, and ordinary presumptions of law. So, if it has been expressly agreed that there shall be community between the spouses of acquisitions or gains, one will rightly conclude that the parties desired to exclude the statutory community of all property. Again, if the parties have agreed to exclude the statutory community in favour of their cognates or strangers who are their heirs, they will be presumed to have done so in favour of their own children as well. In case of doubt, where one thing is provided for, its opposite will also be held to have been provided for; and thus, if the parties provide that there shall be community of profits or exclusion of such community, they are presumed to have provided that there shall be community of loss or exclusion of such community. Again, if it is provided that the husband shall have all the profits acquired during the marriage, it follows that he shall also be liable for all the debts contracted during marriage (28, 4 § 71).

See Van Leeuwen *(Cent. For.* 1, 1, 12, 18).

467. Where a contract is obscure, and the intention of the parties cannot be inferred from surrounding circumstances, the customary form of antenuptial con-

tract should be applied in order to interpret the contract under consideration (28, 4 § 72).

In other words, reference should be made to the form of antenuptial contract in common use to elucidate or explain a contract which cannot be otherwise interpreted or given effect to.

468. If parents give a dowry to their daughter on condition that if she dies during marriage the dotal property shall revert to them, they are, in case of doubt, considered to have intended that the property shall revert if the daughter die without issue; and, in such case of doubt, the dotal property will go to the children of such daughter—the main reason for this being that, in Dutch Law, a daughter is, upon marriage, emancipated from the parental power (23, 4 § 78). 469. Antenuptial contracts should, in general, receive such an interpretation as will make it appear that the statutory community of property has been departed from as little as possible, and any form of liberality in such contracts should receive a restrictive interpretation. So, if it has been agreed that all movable property shall remain in possession of the surviving spouse, this will not, in the absence of express terms to that effect, include rights of action, which are not regarded as movables, but fall within the category of incorporeal property (28, 4 § 74). 470. The Cape Antenuptial Contracts Act (No. 21, 1875) provides that antenuptial contracts, whereby one spouse settles on the other spouse, or the children of the marriage, or their descendants, any property, movable or immovable, shall not be valid as against creditors of the insolvent estate of either spouse, where such spouse becomes insolvent within two years from the time of execution of the contract, where the debt or demand of the creditor existed at the date of registration of the contract, provided it is shown that the same was made by the insolvent with intent to defraud or delay the creditors in obtaining payment of his or her debts (§ 8). This enactment has also been made in the Transvaal, under the Insolvency Law of 1895; and in the Orange River Colony by Law 28,

1899, § 1. Where one spouse settles an annuity on the other, or makes a settlement of other property payable at death or any other time, no payment, transfer, or other act necessary to carry out such covenant or agreement shall be valid against creditors of the insolvent estate of one or other spouse, where the debt existed at the date of such payment, transfer, or other act, if it be proved that such payment, transfer, or other act was made with intent to defeat or delay creditors of the insolvent spouse, at a time when the liabilities of such insolvent spouse, fairly calculated, exceeded his or her assets, fairly valued—provided that no such payment, transfer, or other act shall be impeached by creditort after five years from the making thereof, and that this enactment shall not impair or affect the operation of any special conventional hypothecation granted by either spouse at the time of entering into such covenant or agreement in order to secure the same (§ 4). In the Orange River Colony the period of impeachment is three years

Law 28, 1899, § 2). Where contracts have been registered, the payment by either spouse of premiums on policies of life assurance, settled under such contracts, cannot be impeached by creditors of an insolvent spouse as being undue preferences (Cape Act, § 6).

In *Leigh's Trustee* vs. *Leigh* (1 S. C. 7o), a husband, by antenuptial contract, settled a sum of money on his wife, which was to become hers if she survived him; but if she did not, the money was to revert to and form part of his estate. It was agreed that the wife should have a preferent claim for the money, payable on the husband's death or insolvency. It was found that the husband was insolvent at the date of the marriage. The wife claimed as a concurrent creditor of her husband. It was decided that the claim of the wife could not be sustained, but that it might be admitted as a contingent claim, payable if she survived her husband. Her claim was, therefore, postponed to the claims of her husband's other creditors. See also *Hurley* vs. *Patier* 1 S. C. 154).

(4) Donations Between Spouses. 471.

As we have seen, donations between spouses are absolutely prohibited; but if an unconditional donation has actually been made by one spouse to another, the natural possession passes in fact—though not in law—to the donee, to such an extent that the donee has the rights of a *bond fide* possessor to this extent, that he or she may, on ejectment from an estate given to the donee, recover possession by means of the interdict *unde vi.* But the legal possession does not vest in the spouse who is the donee of such property, whence it follows that the donee cannot acquire ownership of the property by usucapion. From this point of view the donee is a *mald fide* possessor, is said to hold in the place of the possessor *(pro possessore),* and has no valid title to the property, although the donee may enjoy the produce of the property *(fructus industriales)* gained through the donee's industry (24, 1 §§ 1, 2). 472. It thus follows that the spouse who is the donee has not the dominion over the property or thing donated. The donor, his heirs, successors, or assigns may accordingly vindicate or recover possession of the property donated, even if it has been transferred to other persons. The person vindicating such property must refund to the donee the amount of money spent on the improvement or maintenance of such property, over and above the value of the produce of the property which the donee has had the use of *(fructus percepti).* The donee has, however, the option of paying the value of the property donated, on security against eviction being given her. Alienation by the donee to other persons does not become valid until the donation is confirmed by the death of the donor, which event makes the gift retrospectively valid. If the things donated have been consumed (such as perishable produce), the donor or his assign has an action *(condictio)* to recover the value by which the recipient of the things was enriched up to the time of joinder in issue *(litis contestatio).* A similar action lies if the recipient—whether donee or donee's transferee—has fraudulently made away with the property donated. A spouse is considered to be enriched, and therefore to stand in the position of a donee, when such spouse has been released from payment of a debt due to the other spouse; or if the spouse's property, which was subject to a servitude in favour of the other spouse, has been released from the burden of such servitude. The donee is not liable to return the produce *(j)-uctus industriales)* raised by the donee's labour on the farm donated to him or her. The donee is not regarded as enriched where he or she purchases property with a sum of money donated, and the value of the property thus purchased is greater than the amount of money donated; and in such a case the donee is liable to return only the sum of money originally donated. On the other hand, the donor, where the value of the property purchased is less than the sum originally donated, may claim only the property, for which he will have a vindicatory action, even if the donee becomes insolvent (24, 1 § 3). In *Van der Bi/Vs Assignees* vs. *Van der Byl and Others* (5 S. C. 176), it was said by De Villiers, C.J.: "If there is one doctrine more firmly settled in our law than any other it is that, until the death of the donor, gifts between husband and wife, with certain exceptions, are of no force or effect whatsoever as against the donor or his creditors. 'Let it be known,' says Ulpian *(Dig.* 24, 1, 3 § 10). 'that a donation between husband and wife is so strictly forbidden that the transaction is *ipso jure* of no effect. Accordingly, if it be a corporeal thing which has been given, even delivery thereof is of no avail. And if one has entered into a covenant with the other, or made an entry to the credit of the other, it is of no effect.' And Celsius says *(Dig.* 24, 1, 48), ' Whatever a husband has given to his wife after marriage remains the property of the husband, and may be recovered by him by means of a *vindicatio,* and it would make no difference that large legacies have been left to him by his wife.' The rule, no doubt, lost much of its stringency after the *senatusconsultum* of Antoninus to the effect that all gifts invalid during tho marriage should become valid on the death

of the donor, unless revoked during life or by will, but still, whilst the marriage subsists, the invalidity remains. Voet adopts the opinion of Ulpian, and maintains that the ownership of a thing given by way of gift by one spouse to the other remains in the donor." The case of *Hall* vs. *Halts Trustee and Another* (3 S. C. 3; above, § 434) might at first sight present a difficulty, as the transaction (the giving of a piece of ground by the husband to the wife) purported to be not a donation but an exchange, the consideration being certain shares vested in the wife's trustee. But the trustee's consent to the wife's parting with the shares, which was necessary under the antenuptial contract, was never obtained; and the wife, therefore, made no proper alienation of the shares to her husband. The transfer of the land was thus made without a valid consideration, and was consequently regarded as a donation. The property was therefore reclaimable by the husband's creditors. See also *In re Williams* (6 N. L. E. 200); *Spence* vs. *Union Bank* (4 S. C. 341).

473. As we have seen (§ 472), donations are confirmed between spouses if the donor dies leaving the donation unrevoked. If the spouses die at the same time, so that it is impossible to determine who died first, the donation is likewise validated. A donation exceeding 500 *aurei* must be registered, or ratified in a last will, and if it is neither registered nor bequeathed by will it will be valid only up to 500 *aurei*. A donation of upwards of 500 *aurei* has, in case of registration, a retrospective validity from the time when the donation was made; but, in case of confirmation by will, it has validity or effect only from the date of confirmation (24, 1 § 4).

Colquhoun (§ 1825) estimates the value of the *solidus* or *aureus* of Justinian's age at eleven shillings and sixpence in English currency, and regards twenty-five aurei as equivalent to fourteen pounds and sixpence sterling *(14I. 0s. fid.)* in English money. Therefore, five hundred *aurei* are equivalent to 280*l*. 10s. (two hundred and eighty pounds ten shillings sterling). He differs from Thibaut, who holds that 25 (twenty-

five) *aurei* are equivalent to about *5l*. (five pounds sterling) of English money. Kotze, C.J., in his edition of Van Leeuwen *(R. D. L.* 4, 30, 4, 5; 2 iT. 'pp. 238, 239), uses the word "ducat" as equivalent to *aureus,* although he does not state what value this " ducat" bears in English currency. Van Leeuwen himself states that 72 gold aurei went to a pound apothecaries' weight, and computes the value of an *aureus* at six guilders of Dutch money (in Van Leeuwen's time). At the Cape the *aureus* is considered equivalent to one pound sterling (*Thorpe's Executor* vs. *Thorpe's Tutor, i* S. C. 488). In *Barrett* vs. *CNieVs Executor* (Kotze's Transvaal Rep. for 1877—1881, p. 104),

C.L.—VOL. I. T the Transvaal High Court adopted the rule of Roman Law, that donations above 500 *aurei* must be *publicly* registered, and if they are not registered, they are only valid up to 500 *aurei*. In that case the *aureus* was regarded as equivalent to *11*. 474. Once a donation is confirmed, the donee acquires a vested right in the thing donated, no matter whether the thing donated has actually been transferred or not. If then, a donation has been promised, no delivery of the property or thing donated taking place, and such promise is confirmed by death (there having been no revocation of the donation), the donee may sue the donor's heirs, executors, or assigns to obtain possession of the property or thing donated (24, 1 § 5).

475. If the donor dies insolvent, the donee cannot claim so as to prejudice the rights of creditors who were such at the time of the insolvent's death. The donee cannot claim where the donor has revoked the gift; although the claim will be allowed to this extent, that the burden of proof will be on the heir of the person making the donation, who must show that the donation was actually revoked. There will be a presumption of revocation where a marriage has been dissolved by judicial decree, and no subsequent reconciliation between the spouses takes place. Where the donor makes a voluntary alienation of the thing or property donated, revocation

will be presumed. But a pledge of the thing or property donated establishes no presumption of revocation (24, 1 § 6). 476. If the donee dies before the donor, the donation is void (24, 1 § 7). 477. Not only are direct donations forbidden, but those also which are indirect and in fraud of the law prohibiting donations. This may happen, either where the donor enters into some transaction with the other spouse which will have the effect of conveying a donation, or where the donor exercises the prohibited generosity through the intervention of other persons. The law does not prohibit business transactions between spouses which are entered into in good faith, such as purchase and sale, mandate or agency, partnership, *mutuum* (an agreement whereby one person lends to another some property of his, capable of being measured, counted or weighed, which is to become the receiver's property on condition that the receiver shall afterwards return the same quantity and quality of the same article), *commodatum* (an agreement whereby one person lends a particular thing to another, which the receiver is to use rent-free and afterwards return), deposit, pledge, or unauthorised agency. But such transactions must not infringe the rule prohibiting donations between spouses, and where fraud (i.e., evasion of this rule) is proved, the transaction between the spouses will be of no effect. But where there was no fraudulent intent on the part of the spouses, and the transaction results in a donation, the transaction, if that part of it which constitutes the donation is separable from the remainder of the transaction, will be considered valid except in so far as it constitutes a donation. So, if one spouse in good faith sells something to the other for a certain price, but makes an agreement not to claim the purchase-money, the sale will hold good, and the seller may be compelled to complete the sale, but the agreement to remit the price will be invalid, just as if the spouses, after completing the contract of sale, had entered into a fresh agreement to constitute a donation. Again, if one or more things are sold by one spouse to the other, at

the same time, for a lump sum, which is lower than the real value of what is sold, the sale will hold good, but the dominion of what is sold will only be acquired by the purchasing spouse in proportion to the price paid, and therefore the dominion will be shared between the spouses (24, 1 § 8).

It is submitted that the last rule mentioned above will at the present time only hold good where the spouses clearly contravene the rule prohibiting donations. There is no reason why one party should not sell a thing to another at a lower price than it is worth, so long as the consideration is not so ridiculously low as to make it perfectly clear that the transaction was not quite *bona fide*. The rule is well summarised by De Villiers, C.J.: "Although onerous contracts, that is, contracts for which there is consideration on both sides, will hold good between husband and wife, arrangements between them which in fact constitute an evasion of the law will not be supported, to the extent, at all events, to which the law is evaded" *(Hall* vs. *Halv't Trustee,* 3 S. C. 3). It has been held, in Natal, that the law invalidating gifts between husband and wife is not to be rigidly enforced. Gifts tending as much to the comfort and convenience of the husband and children as that of the wife are not within the spirit of the prohibition. The prohibition does not extend to the occupation of the donor's house free of rent, nor to the allowance of alimony or a moderate income, nor to the gift of ornaments not beyond the husband's station in life; nor if the donor is not made poorer by the gift; nor if the gift is made in good faith, and io as to revert, after the donor's death, to the children of both spouses; nor if the gift be of money for the repair of a house injured by fire, even though the donor is impoverished and the donee enriched thereby *(Williams's Trustee* vs. *Williams,* 7 N. R., N. S. 93). See also above, § 396.

478. A donation which merely amounts to an exchange between spouses is valid. A donation made in contemplation of death or divorce is valid, if it is to take effect upon death or divorce, for

such a transaction contemplates a time when the parties are no longer spouses (24, 1 §§ 9, 10). 479. The rule regarding donations is not to be strictly construed as to trifling articles of property. So no account will be taken of ordinary presents of jewellery, trinkets, articles of clothing, amusement or use, such as is customary between spouses of the station in life to which donor and donee belong. A donation will also be valid if the donor is not made poorer, or the donee richer, thereby. So, the donee is not enriched where the gift is made to the donee as a temporary holder of the gift, as where a husband in good faith makes a donation to his wife, on the understanding that upon her death the thing or property given shall go to their child or children. So, the donee is not enriched where a husband gives money to his wife to purchase gifts for relations. The burden of proof as to the application of moneys given to a spouse will be on the donee (24, 1 §§ 11, 12).

See *Williams's Trustee vs. Williams* (7 N. R., N. S. 93; §477, above); and *Scorey* vs. *Scorey's Executors* (1 M. 235).

480. The donor is not impoverished where money is given, and the donee purchases property with such money, and the value of such property, then or afterwards, is greater than the amount of money originally made over as a donation; and only the amount of money originally given can be reclaimed by the donor. Nor is the donor impoverished if he or she remits a pledge, provided the original debt continues to subsist; or if he or she pays a debt or hands over a property subject to a *fideicommissum,* due on a particular day, before such day arrives. But a spouse cannot restore the *dos* or dowry before such restoration is due. Where a spouse repudiates or fails to take a fideicommissary property or inheritance, which hy reason of such repudiation or failure to take becomes the property of such spouse's husband or wife, there is no contravention of the rule against donations, since the spouse who repudiates or fails to take has never acquired ownership. For instance, a farm is left to A., and failing

him, to his wife B. The husband repudiates the inheritance. The farm will validly pass to B., for, as A. never acquired the farm, he makes no donation of it to his wife. But the husband may not give up to the wife a legacy or inheritance which has already vested in his favour, for he has then acquired the title, and a subsequent transference to the wife will amount to a donation (24, 1 § 18). 481. The law permits a husband, as we have seen, to give a donation to his wife for the purpose of restoring or repairing a house that has been burnt down, but not for the purpose of building a new one (24, 1 § 14). 482. A donation between betrothed persons is not prohibited. Betrothal, in Dutch Law, ends with marriage (whether civil or religious); and after the performance of the ceremony, even if there has been no cohabitation, the parties are regarded as married. A donation made by one spouse to the other before marriage, which is to have force and effect only after marriage, should be considered invalid. A donation made after an actual judicial divorce, where the spouses have not remarried each other, is valid. If the parties have only been separated from bed and board *(a mensu et thoro),* and the bond of marriage still holds in other respects, a donation between the spouses is invalid. A donation between putative spouses, who are not husband and wife in law, will hold good; as, where a marriage of a minor is declared null and void for want of consent (as in *Johnson* vs. *Mclntyre,* 10 S. C. 818), a donation by the husband, being a major, to his putative wife, the minor, will stand (24, 1 § 15). 483. In Dutch Law, differing in this respect from Roman Law, the property found in a wife's possession is presumed to be hers until the contrary is proved, and the burden of proving a donation lies on the person who asserts that the wife has acquired the property by way of donation from her husband; and the presumption is strengthened by the fact that the wife is a public trader (24, 1 § 16). 484. Where the husband has been deprived of the marital power, and his wife makes a donation to her husband's son under paternal power, the

wife cannot on the son's death recover the property donated to him, although the father is heir to the son (24, 1 §§ 17—19). Grotius (3, 2, 8) states that parents cannot make valid donations to their children who are still in their power; but Van der Keessel (§ 485) states that this rule originated from the *patria potestas* of the Romans, and there is nothing in Dutch Law to affect the validity of a donation by a father to his son under power.

(5) Judicial Separation And Divorce. 485. Among the Romans, divorce, that is, the annulling of the bond or obligation of marriage, could be effected by consent of the spouses, or by the mere will of the husband. But, according to modern Roman-Dutch Law, divorce, or dissolution of marriage, can be effected only by judicial decree. Besides a judical decree of divorce, there are other judicial modes of procedure which suspend or abrogate the force and effect of the marriage tie. Such are decree of judicial separation, which separates the spouses as to cohabitation and joint ownership of property (or cohabitation alone), without dissolving the marriage; and decree of nullity of marriage, which declares that no marriage subsisted between the parties from the beginning (24, 2 §§ 1—4). 486. In modern Dutch Law, the only grounds for granting a divorce, that is, dissolving the bonds of matrimony, are adultery of either spouse, and malicious desertion. The two grounds need not exist together. There will be no ground for divorce by reason of adultery where the wife has been ravished or violated without her consent (not against her will, for she may be ravished when asleep, or by fraudulent means, and then her will plays no part whatever in the transaction); or where, after the adultery was committed, a reconciliation took place, equivalent to condonation by the innocent spouse. Such a reconciliation may be proved by the express consent of the innocent spouse, or by acts and deeds, such as cohabitation after knowledge of the adultery. Husbands who are aware of the adultery of their wives, and con-

tinue to live with them for purposes of gain, cannot obtain a divorce (24, 2 § 5).

In *Htathershaw* vs. *Heatherthaw* (1 E. 186) a husband, after living in adultery, sued for a restitution of conjugal rights against his wife, who had deserted him. It was decided that the Court could decree restitution. See also *Wylde* vs. *Wylde* (1 M. 271), *Anhauser* vs. *Anhauser* (7 G. W. R. 115; 12 C. L. J. 57), *Henning* vs. *Henning* (11 C. L. J. 55), and *Nel* vs. *Nel* (1 M. 276). As to condonation, see *McLeodys. McLeod* (N. H. C, May 21st, 1863).

487. Where both the spouses are proved to have been guilty of adultery, the Court will not decree a divorce, unless after the adultery of one of the parties condonation by the other spouse took place, and the condoning spouse thereafter committed adultery.

Adultery previously committed but condoned cannot be set up as a defence, where such condoned adultery was committed by one party, and the same party sues for a divorce (24, 2 § 6).

So, in *Wiezel* vs. *Wiezel* (Buch. 1877, p. 92), a decree of divorce was refused, where it was proved that the plaintiff as well as the defendant had been guilty of adultery. See *Pienaar* vs. *Pienaar* (14 C. L. J. 290), *Wilson* vs. *Wilson* (1 C. T. R. 145; 8 C. L. J. 175), and *Hosier* vs. *Hosier* (13 S. C. 377).

488. It is no defence, on the part of the wife, in a suit for divorce on the ground of adultery, to allege that she has been driven from her husband's house by his cruelty, and that she has been compelled to commit adultery because she was reduced to destitution, or that her husband's abstinence from sexual intercourse drove her to have sexual intercourse elsewhere. If the husband persists in wilful abstinence from sexual intercourse, his wife may seek a decree for restitution of conjugal rights, just as if he had actually deserted her (24, 2 § 7).

In *Hosier* vs. *Hosier* (13 S. C. 377) it was laid down that in an action for divorce on the ground of the defendant's adultery, it is no valid defence that the plaintiff had, by reason of his or her refusal to cohabit with the defendant, conduced to the defendant's adultery; and it makes no difference whether such adultery was committed by the wife or by the husband. See also *Richter* vs. *Wagenaar* (1 M. 264), *Barker* vs. *Barker* (1 M. 265), *Biccard* vs. *Biccard and Fryer* (9 S. C. 473), *Nanto* vs. *Malgass* (5 S. C. 108), *Goodison* vs. *Ooodison* (Buch. 1874, p. 143), and *Van Niekerk* vs. *Van Niekerk* (14 S. C. 178).

489. The allegations as to adultery must be clearly proved before the Court will grant a decree of divorce (24, 2 § 8).

As to evidence sufficient for a decree of divorce, see *Wood* vs. *Wood* (Morcom's Natal Rcp. 1870, p. 43), where a divorce was granted, the evidence pointing clearly to adultery, though actual cohabitation was not proved; *Thompson* vs. *Thompson* (9 N. R. 106); *Clark* vs. *Clark* (8 N. R. 182; holding that evidence of condonation cannot be given unless it has been pleaded by the defendant); and *Wilson* vs. *Wilson* (9 N. R. 100). In *Chester* vs. *Chester and Grahams* (Hertzog's Transv. Rep. 1893, p. 181) it was said: "In order to establish adultery the commission thereof must be made to appear from circumstances from which a man of common sense, acting cautiously, will be led to the conclusion that the act has really been committed. The fact that the Judge does not consider himself justified in declaring that adultery *has not* been committed, does not entitle bim to conclude that adultery *has* been committed." 490. When the parties have been divorced, they can marry again; but the guilty party cannot, as we have seen, lawfully marry the party with whom he or she has committed adultery (24, 2 § 8).

491. As to divorce on the ground of malicious desertion, the procedure is as follows: a formal suit is instituted in respect of the desertion; the fact of malicious desertion is established by evidence; and the deserting spouse is repeatedly summoned, by order of the Court, and publication if necessary, to return to the spouse who has been deserted. If the deserter then contumaciously refuses to return to and cohabit with his or her spouse, the bonds of marriage are dissolved by public judi-

cial decree in the same way as if the suit had been instituted on the ground of adultery. The usual practice is to grant a decree or rule *nisi,* returnable on a particular date, calling upon the deserter to return to the deserted spouse; and if, on the return-day, the deserter has not returned, the decree of divorce is confirmed or made absolute. In any case, the decree should not be given unless it appears that all hope of reconciliation is at an end. Where divorce is decreed on the ground of malicious desertion, a decree may be given declaring that the guilty spouse has forfeited all profits or benefits obtained from the property of the deserted spouse, whether the same arise by virtue of an antenuptial contract or from the statutory community of property, and the guilty spouse is, after such a decree, liable to restore all antenuptial gifts, or gifts during marriage, as well as one-half of the debts incurred during the marriage (24, 2 § 9).

In *Gibbon* vs. *Gibbon* (2 E. D. C. 284), Shippard, J., said: "With regard to the question whether by any rule of the Roman-Dutch Law judgment in a suit for restitution of conjugal rights be a condition precedent to obtaining a decree of divorce *a vinculo matrimonii* on the ground of malicious desertion, it will be observed that, according to the authority of Brouwer (de *Jure Connubiorum,* 2, 18, 12), malicious desertion is regarded as affording even weightier ground than adultery for granting divorce by the law of Holland." After quoting Voet, the learned Judge proceeded: "Voet's words appear to indicate that he contemplates a suit for restitution of conjugal rights as a condition precedent to proceeding for divorce on the ground of malicious desertion; though as the passage is concise to the verge of obscurity, it becomes necessary to ascertain its true construction as far as possible from other authorities." The Judge quoted Van Leeuwen (*Cens. For.* 1, 1, 15, 12, 13, 15), and Matthaeus (de *Criminibnt,* 48, 3, 11), who says: "If any one desert his wife with malicious intent never to return to her, the deserted wife is to be empowered to marry again forthwith *(statim),* that is, without wait-

ing for the death of the husband who has deserted." Shippard, J., proceeded: "The explanation of the word *statim* here given precludes any inferences as to the mere question of practice," and, after quoting Van Leeuwen *(R. D. L.* 1, 15, 4), went on to say: "The practice hitherto prevailing in this Colony, whereby a suit for restitution of conjugal rights always necessarily precedes an action for divorce on the ground of malicious desertion, is based on the practice uniformly observed in Holland down to the cession of this (Cape) Colony; and though I should be inclined to hold, even apart from this, that the practice hitherto invariably prevailing in the Courts of this Colony should be deemed to have hardened into a rule of local law, such as could scarcely be changed without legislative interference, I am not bound to rest my conclusion on such ground; but am, as I consider, entitled to affirm, that by the rules of the Roman-Dutch Law judgment in a suit for restitution of conjugal rights must be obtained as a necessary preliminary to a decree of divorce *d vinculo matrimonii* on the ground of malicious desertion. This being-so, it seems to me to follow that a decree of restitution of conjugal rights so obtained may fairly and openly be treated as a legal fiction, devised with a view to ulterior proceedings for divorce.... The theory of the Roman-Dutch Law appears to have been that divorce should never be granted while there remained a hope of reconciliation. In casos of alleged malicious desertion the Courts required proof that no such hope remained, and therefore would not dissolve a marriage on such ground till after proof of contumacious disobedience of a decree of restitution of conjugal rights.... I hold that under the pleading rules now in force here, as adapted from those framed under the Judicature Act in England, a deed of separation cannot be relied upon as an answer in bar of *a* suit for restitution of conjugal rights, unless specifically alloged in the plea and duly proved." See also the judgment of Buchanan, J., in *Gibbon* vs. *Gibbon;* and the cases of *Alcock* vs. *Alcock* (1 M. 251), *Botha* vs. *Botha* (1 M.

259), *Hodges* vs. *Hodges* (Buch. 1868, p. 297), *Ziedeman* vs. *Ziedeman* (1 M. 238), *Booi/sen* vs. *Booysea* (1 M. 242), *Richter* vs. *Wagenaar* (1 M. 264), *Barker* vs. *Barker* (1 M. 265), *Goodison* vs. *Goodison* (Buch. 1874, p. 143), *Wylde* vs. *Wylde* (1 M. 269), *Weyers* vs. *Stop/orth* (1 M. 273), *Cunningham* vs. *Cunningham* (Buch. 1875, p. 99), *Govgh* vs. *Gough* (1 M. 257), *Reeves* vs. *Reeves* (1 M. 244). In *Mostert* vs. *Mostert* (2 S. 128) it was held that desertion for two days was sufficient to found a decree of divorce, so long as the desertion was wilful.

492. Where a deserted spouse marries again without having previously obtained a divorce, the deserter may obtain a divorce against the spouse so re-marrying. Where a spouse has been absent for a long time, and then returns, repentant, the deserted spouse ought to receive back the repentant spouse, and cannot obtain a divorce on the ground of malicious desertion. Where the husband has committed a crime, and becomes a fugitive, leaving his domicile through fear of a criminal prosecution, his wife may obtain a divorce on the ground of desertion. But where the removal of the husband is necessary and unavoidable, and not caused through fear of arrest for crime, the wife must follow the husband to his new domicile, and if the wife refuses to follow the husband when called upon to do so, the husband, and not the wife, may obtain a decree of divorce on the ground of malicious desertion (24, 2 §§ 10—13).

See *Reeves* vs. *Reevee* (1 M. 244).

493. Where spouses have once been divorced, and are thereafter reconciled, they cannot again become united to each other as man and wife unless they again go through the ceremony of marriage; and mere private consent will not suffice to re-establish a marriage once dissolved. If the parties are once more properly married, in accordance with the laws of the land, the antenuptial contract and other agreements or rights with regard to property revive in the same manner as if the marriage had never been dissolved—unless a division of the property has been made after the di-

vorce. In such a case, the rights under the antenuptial contract will have become affected, and a new arrangement must be entered into. But where the parties are married in full community, no fresh contract need be made (24, 2 § 14). 494. Marriages may be pronounced or declared by the Court to be null and void for causes which existed or arose prior to the marriage. Such decrees may be given on the petition of either spouse, or, in certain cases, even against the will of both spouses. A decree may be made against the will of both spouses where they stand within the prohibited degrees of relationship, whether they are aware or ignorant of the fact; or where minors have contracted a marriage without the consent of their parent or parents whose consent is necessary, where such parent or parents objects or object to the marriage. Marriage may be declared null and void on the petition of either spouse, where there has been an incapacity on the part of the other spouse to procreate (impotence), which is a fundamental incapacity—that is, not such as suddenly arises as the result of a disease or operation, but an original and wholly irremediable incapacity—and (according to Voet) has lasted for three years. But if the incapacity to procreate is not latent, but externally visible, or apparent on the surface, there is no necessity to wait three years, and a decree of nullity may be given at once. A marriage may, as we have seen (§ 184, above), be declared null and void on account of previous *stuprum* or debauchery of the wife unknown to the husband. Marriages cannot be declared null and void where the impotence or incapacity to procreate arises subsequent to the marriage; or where the spouse against whom the decree of nullity is sought catches a contagious disease, or becomes insane—for a spouse cannot take advantage of the purely accidental misfortunes of the other spouse (24, 2 §§ 15, 16).

See *Horak* vs. *Horak* (3 S. 396), *Ne!* vs. *Nel* (1 M. 274), *Van den Berg* vs. *Van den Berg* (1 M. 241), and *Johnson* vs. *McIntyre* (10 S. C. 318). As to decree of nullity for impotence, see *X.* vs. *X.*

(12 C. L. J. 292), and *Ngwende* vs. *Ngwende* (8 B. D. C. 68; 11 0. L. J. 45). As to *stuprum*, see *Seyelecho* vs. *Seyelecho* (14 C. L. J. 298). As to disease, see *Garton* vs. *Garton* (9 C. T. R. 683).

495. Judicial separation, or separation from bed and board (a *mensd et thoro*) is granted by the Court on the ground of the excessive cruelty and severity of one spouse towards the other, or lasting quarrels, disputes, and disagreements, or threats by one spouse to the other, accompanied with imminent danger to the life or person of the threatened spouse. The marriage is not dissolved by such a decree, and the parties are unable to enter into a fresh marriage with other persons. Separation from bed and board will also be decreed judicially on the ground of continued insanity, where the lunatic has been violent (24, 2 § 16). Drunkenness is a ground for judicial separation *(Poggenpoel* vs. *Poggenpoel,* 8 C. T. R. 36; 15 S. C. 37). See also *Hassmjagtr* vs. *Hassenjager* (6 E. D. C. 101), *Powrie* vs. *Powrie* (7 C. T. R. 191), *Van Niekerk* vs. *Van Niekerk* (7 C. T. R. 176; 14 S. C. 178), and *Van den Berg* vs. *Van den Berg* (1 M. 241).

496. Where a separation of marital property has been effected after a judicial decree of separation, the statutory or contractual community of property and of profit and loss still remains, and profits or losses are not separately acquired or sustained unless the husband has been judicially interdicted from dealing with all property, or at any rate that portion of it which goes to the wife as the consequence of the division. If no such order has been given, the wife's property is, after division, still liable for her husband's debts, and the husband's marital power continues unless it has been excluded by antenuptial contract. Of course, where all community of profit and loss and of property was excluded by antenuptial contract, the wife will be no more liable after marriage than she was before. If the wife deserts the husband, he is not obliged to provide for her maintenance; but where the behaviour of the husband occasions a decree of separation, the husband will be ordered to contribute to his wife's

support after the separation (24, 2 §§ 17, 18). 497. Where the spouses live apart by voluntary agreement, whether verbal or written, and no judicial decree has been made, the marriage still exists, and all its consequences on the property of the spouses remain—unless a special agreement has been entered into between them, though this is effectual only as against the spouses, and not as against creditors (24, 2 §§ 19, 20). See *Albertiu* vs. *Albertiu' Executors* (3 S. 211), *Grauman* vs. *Hoffman* (3 S. C. 282), *Booysen* vs. *Booysen* (1 M. 242), *Botha* vs. *Botha* (1 M. 261), and De Bruyn *Opiniont of Grotius*, pp. 45, 40, 153, and 276—279).

498. The dotal property of the wife, where such a course has been agreed upon, may be restored to her during the marriage; and in this case she will have no right to alienate the same, but has the bare detention of the property, with the right of administering it, and enjoying the fruits thereof. Upon the dissolution of a marriage, the wife might sue for restitution of her dotal property (by an action known as the *actio ex stipulatu,* which was a *bond fide* and privileged action). The dowry contributed by a stranger *(dos adventitia)* may be reclaimed by him, either on the wife's death during marriage, or during her lifetime upon dissolution of the marriage where it was agreed upon, when such dowry was contributed on condition that it should on the dissolution of the marriage be returned to him with or without the wife's consent. Such third party may not only have this right to reclaim the dowry, but he may cede the same to another person. If no agreement for restitution of the dotal property was entered into between the spouses and the party contributing it, the wife alone may sue for its restoration. This right on the part of the wife to reclaim her dowry is transmissible to her heirs. Where the dowry has been contributed by the wife's father *(dos profectitia)*, he may, if he has expressly stipulated for its return on dissolution of the marriage, reclaim the same without his daughter's consent; and this action is transmissible to the father's heirs. If the father stipu-

lates for return of the dowry, not when the dotal property is transferred to the husband, but at any time thereafter, provided that when he so stipulates the marriage has not yet taken place, the father may, on dissolution of the marriage, recover the dotal property. But he will lose his right of action where he stipulates for return of the dowry after the marriage has taken place. Voet next distinguishes between the right to reclaim on the part of a daughter who is emancipated *(sui juris),* and one who is under paternal power; but, as, according to modern Dutch Law, all persons are emancipated by marriage, only the rules laid down with regard to emancipated daughters *(sui juris)* apply at the present day. If an emancipated daughter dies during marriage *(in matrimonio),* and her father has entered into no express agreement for the return of the dowry to him, the dowry must be restored, not to the father, but to the daughter's heirs, even if the father has contributed the dowry. If a bride's grandfather contributes a dowry, he has an action for its recovery on the same conditions as the bride's father would have had it; and this action in favour of the bride's paternal grandfather is transmissible to the bride's father, as heir to her paternal grandfather, provided the grandfather gave the dowry on his son's behalf. Where he does not give it on his son's behalf, it will be looked upon as coming from a stranger, and will be reclaimable on the same conditions as dowry coming from a stranger *(dos adventitia)* would be. On dissolution of a marriage by death, the widow may claim not only her separate property, but that property also which it was agreed upon, under the antenuptial contract, should remain in her possession on the husband's death. The dowry can only be reclaimed by the wife or her heirs if it was actually paid over or transferred to the husband; otherwise the claimant or claimants may be defeated by an exception *(exceptio non numeratae dotis).* But the claim will hold good where it is due to the neglect, fault, or default of the husband that the payment or transfer of the dowry has

not been made: as where debts due to the wife have been assigned to the husband by way of dowry, and he has failed or neglected to proceed against the debtors (24, 3 §§ 1—10). 499. In Roman-Dutch Law, restitution of the dowry must be made immediately on the dissolution of the marriage. The husband or his heirs will, however, be entitled to a respite of six weeks, or a reasonable time for the framing of an inventory where it is necessary to frame an inventory in order to determine the amount of the dowry and its accessions (24, 8 § 11). 500. All the accessions to the dowry must be restored, such as alluvion to land, and property acquired by the husband through the medium of the dotal property, such as plantations of trees on dotal property which have not been cut down, standing crops not gathered.

Fruits and produce, however, which have been gathered and used by the husband need not be restored. Trees which have been cut down need not be restored. In other words, as regards produce, whether natural or acquired through industry, the dotal property must be restored in the same condition in which it stood at the moment when the dissolution of the marriage took place (24, 3 § 12).

See Van Leeuwen *(Cens. For.* 1, 1, 15, 20), who holds, contrary to Voet, that no account is taken of fruits or produce as they stand at the time of dissolution of the marriage.

501. Maintenance provided for the benefit of the spouses during the marriage by the wife's parents cannot be reclaimed with the dowry, as long as such parents did not, before the marriage, bind themselves to contribute such maintenance. The same rule holds with regard to small gifts or presents during the marriage (24, 8 § 18). 502. Where the husband is entitled, by law or custom, to sell any of the dotal property during marriage, and does so, the wife or her heirs may claim the price realised by the sale, if such sale were *bond fide.* But where the sale took place with the intention of defrauding the wife, she or her heirs will not suffer by such fraud,

but may recover the full value (24, 8 § 14). 503. In addition to the dowry, upon dissolution of marriage the wife is entitled to one-half of all the profits acquired during marriage, unless community of profit and loss has been excluded by antenuptial contract. If special property has been acquired in this manner, the spouses will have the right to bid for the same, and the property, if both bid, will go to the highest bidder; otherwise the property must be sold by public auction. If there has been a deficiency in the payment to the husband of dotal property as compared with the amount of dotal property promised in the antenuptial agreement, the wife's share in the profits on dissolution will be proportionately reduced (24, 8 § 16). 504. Not only does the action for restoration of the dowry lie against the husband, but it may be brought against sureties for restoration of the dowry as well. This action must be brought in the place where the husband has his domicile (forum domicilii), even if the dotal contract has been concluded or the marriage solemnised in another place—for, on marriage, the wife assumes the husband's domicile. The value of money given as dowry is to be computed according to the standard prevailing, not in the husband's domicile, but in the place where it was given or paid (24, 8 §§ 17, 18). 505. Among the grounds on which the right to claim restitution of the dowry may be forfeited Voet mentions misconduct on the part of the wife, on account of which the husband obtains a divorce. It is submitted, that if there is to be any restitution whatsoever of dotal property, it must proceed upon the supposition that it belongs to the wife, and not to the husband. Dotal property is not to be looked upon as a benefit arising out of the marriage, except in so far as, daring marriage, the husband has the usufruct of the same; and therefore a decree of forfeiture of benefits, following on divorce, given as against the guilty spouse, should not deprive the wife of her dotal property, provided the parties are married out of community. Even ordinary benefits, apart from dotal property, are not lost

by a guilty spouse if there has been no special decree of forfeiture of benefits (see Nortje vs. Nortje, 6 S. C. 9). The right to reclaim is also lost if the agreement gives the dotal property in whole or in part to the surviving spouse, and the husband is the survivor. Where the husband or the children of the marriage become insolvent, the dotal property is not claimable from theui. Where the dotal property perishes without fraud or gross negligence on the part of the husband, its value cannot be reclaimed. If the husband, on the dissolution of the marriage, offers to restore the dotal property, and the wife refuses to accept it, the husband is only liable for fraud occurring after the time when the offer was made. The husband is liable for deterioration in the value of the property where he has neglected to make some necessary outlay upon it. He must use the same diligence in connection with the dotal property as he employs about his own affairs. He is not liable for accidental loss, not traceable to his negligence. The wife's claim with regard to dotal property is to be postponed to those of all her husband's creditors who became such during the existence of the marriage. If nothing of the husband's property is left, that is, if it has been exhausted by the claims of creditors, the wife will receive nothing. The wife, if the claims of creditors have been satisfied, may claim that her dotal property shall next thereafter be restored out of the balance which remains in the husband's estate, where she has stipulated, in the antenuptial contract, for the restoration of her dowry. But where the parties are married in community, the balance remaining after satisfaction of debts will be equally divided between the surviving spouse and the heirs of the deceased or insolvent husband; and in such a case of community no claim on account of fraud or negligence in connection with the dotal property will arise, for in community all losses are shared equally. If there has only been community of profits between the spouses, the dotal property must be restored to the wife in its entirety, and the husband must be compensated for

all improvements made in connection with the dotal property by him; and in this case the husband will not be liable for fraud or negligence, since profit and loss are shared by the spouses. Where the dotal property itself is lost, and there is community of profit and loss, the wife must by herself bear such loss (24, 3 §§ 19—21). 506. On dissolution of the marriage by death, the survivor may claim such profits as are due to him or her by virtue of the community or the antenuptial contract. In case of divorce, the guilty spouse cannot claim such profits as arise from the douarie (see § 422, above). Where a particular thing or property is promised as douarie, only such thing or property need be paid over at death, no matter whether it has been improved or lessened in value in the interval. The surviving spouse (that is, the widow) has no legal mortgage or tacit hypothec over the property of the deceased for the douarie promised her in the antenuptial contract, but her claim may only be satisfied after the husband's creditors have been paid. Where a specific thing or property has been fixed upon as douarie before the marriage, and the spouses afterwards leave to each other the usufruct of all the property left at death, the survivor may nevertheless claim payment of the property left as douarie, and will have the full ownership of this, whilst enjoying only the usufruct of the remainder of the marriage property. But where the douarie consists in payment of an annual income or allowance, it will be absorbed in a bequest of the usufruct of all marriage property (24, 8 §§ 22—26).

The distinction between dos, dowry, or dotal property, and douarie should always be borne in mind. The wife's dowry is the property originally brought by her into the marriage. Douarie is a gift promised by a spouse, to take effect on his or her death, as a provision for the survivor during widowhood: in other words, a settlement to take effect at the death of the settlor. It follows that the wife hat the ownership of the dowry, though not the full and free administration and jus disponendi during the marriage; and her hypothec arises by virtue of her right of ownership. But *douarie* does not vest in the wife until her husband's death; it is a contingent right, and therefore postponed to the claims of creditors and heirs or legatees who have hypothecary rights. See *Steyn* vs. *Steyn's Trustee* (Buch. 1874, p. 16).

507. Where parties are married in community, the community of property may be continued between the survivor and the heirs of the deceased spouse. It does not extend beyond the children of the marriage, unless the law of a country, where such continued

C.L.—VOL. I. *V* community mnny arise, specially provides for its extension to other heirs (24, 3 §§ 28, 29).

This community, according to Van der Keessel (§ 266, 267), takes place between the survivor and the heirs of the deceased either *ipso jure* (and, in such case, either for the benefit of, or as a penalty against, the survivor), or at the desire of the parties to the marriage (declared either by testament or by agreement). Van der Keessel also states that there is nothing to prevent a continuation of the community, not only of property, but of profit and loss as well. Voet, however states (24, 3 § 30) that the community with the children does not take place if it is likely to cause loss to them, since it originated primarily for their benefit. But he goes on to say that if, between the death of the first-dying spouse and the time when the minors demand payment of their portions of inheritance, the estate has first increased, and thereafter decreased, in value, diminishing finally to an amount less than it was valued at when the community began (*i.e.,* on the death of the first-dying spouse), the children or heirs cannot avail themselves of the community in part only, but must elect whether to renounce such community in its entirety and demand their portions of inheritance, or to partake of the community and sustain their proportionate share of loss. Where the heirs of the first-dying spouse have agreed or consented to or acquiesced in the continuation of the community, they cannot object to the assets of the common estate being bound by debts incurred by the sur-

vivor. But where the survivor alienates any of the joint property with the intention of defrauding the heirs of the first-dying spouse, the heirs will have an action *(utilu actio Pauliana in rem)* to recover the property thus fraudulently alienated (24, 3 § 31). Voet does not anywhere state that this community may be continued by direction of the spouses; but Van der Keessel (§ 267) says: "Community may also be continued or introduced by the mutual testament of the spouses who have instituted each other heir, as regards the property which is to be divided after the death of the survivor amongst the heirs of both spouses; and under such community (unless otherwise provided for) donations, legacies, and inheritances subsequently devolving on the survivor should also be reckoned." Where a husband gave his wife, who survived him, the life usufruct of certain property, which was vested in trustees, with the direction that they should from and after her decease "divide the said moneys, stocks, funds, and securities, and the annual income thenceforth" due for the same and accruing should be divided "equally between my children, if more than one, and if only one then to such only child who shall be living at the death of my said wife, and the issue of any of them who may have departed this life, such issue to take equally between themselves, if more than one, the share such parent would have taken if living," and an account was filed only three years after the testator's death (which showed a deficiency in the estate, but did not detail the full interest in a certain business), and no further account was ever filed, it was said by De Villiers, C.J.: "To such an extent were the rights of children recognised by the customs of various parts of the Netherlands, that, in the absence of a proper account, or of a due compliance with the will of the deceased parent, the children were entitled, under circumstances similar to the present, to claim a share in all acquisitions made by the surviving spouse, even though not derived by way of profit from the joint estate itself" *(Atmore* vs. *Chaddock,* 13 S. C. 205). In

Uloete vs. *Clocte's Trustees* (5 S. C. 59) husband and wife, married in community, made a mutual will appointing the survivor and the children of the marriage heirs of the first-dying, of all property left at the death of the firstdying spouse. It was provided that the wife, if she became the survivor, should continue a certain brewery for the benefit of herself and children. Eventually the whole estate was to go to the children. The wife survived, and the joint estate was handed over to her by the executors. She continued the brewery business, and incurred debts. The creditors then sequestrated the joint estate of the spouses. The wife then claimed, on behalf of the minor children of the marriage, that they should be awarded a preference on the insolvent estate for their portions of inheritance. There had been no separation of the minors' portions of inheritance from the estate as held by the mother. It was decided that the children were bound by the continuation of the community directed by the will, and were consequently not entitled to any preferential claim.

508. Decisions as to whether the survivor's second spouse, where there is a continued community between the survivor and the heirs of the survivor's first spouse, is or is not entitled to share in such community, must be left to the equitable discretion of the Court (24, 3 § 32). 509. The continuation of the community ceases or is prevented— where the continuation does not result from testamentary direction— if the surviving spouse makes an inventory and delivers the same to the tutor of the minors, or to the major heirs. By Dutch Common Law such an inventory had to be drawn up within a year and a day from the dissolution of the marriage; and after the lapse of that period, the continued community is presumed to have lasted from the date of dissolution of the marriage (24, 3 § 33). 510. In all questions concerning the continued community, the law of the place where the parties were domiciled when the marriage was dissolved by death must be observed. There can be no change in the application of the law by reason of

the removal of the survivor to another domicile immediately on the dissolution of the marriage, according to Voet; although this statement would seem to admit of some doubt (24, 3 §§ 34—36). (6) Special Privileges. 511. On account of the weakness of their sex, a special privilege was accorded in the Roman Law to women, by the *Senatusconsultum Velleianum*, which forbade women to bind themselves as sureties on behalf of other persons. This benefit, which has been adopted in general Roman-Dutch Law, was originally introduced in A.d. 18. Kotze, C.J., in his edition of Van Leeuwen *(R. D. L.,* vol. 2, p. 38) gives the date of the passing of this important enactment as A.d. 46; but on reference to Colquhoun (§ 1618) it clearly appears that only a re-enactment of the law was made in A.d. 46. The law was framed during the consulship of Marcus Silanus and Velleius Tutor (being named after the latter), in A.c.c. 771 (a. d. 18). It first appears as a statement of the law in A.d. 46 (reign of Claudius), although Ulpian informs us that it was first promulgated in the reign of Augustus. Afterwards, another benefit was introduced in favour of married women, the date of which is uncertain. It is found in Justinian's *Code* (4, 29, 22), and is known, from the opening words of the law, as the *Authentica si qua Mulier.* In *Oak* vs. *Lumsden* (3 S. C. 144), it was said by De Villiers, C.J.: "Afterthe Senate had passed the *Senatusconsultum Velleianum* considerable divergence arose among lawyers as to its operation. Doubts at first arose as to whether the suretyship of a woman was not absolutely void, but it was finally decided that, although prohibited by law, a woman could only take the benefit of the *Senatusconsultum* by pleading it." As to this latter point, it may be remarked in passing that the High Court of Griqualand West, in *Mahadi* vs. *De Kock* (1 G. W. R. 343) decided that the benefit of the *Sejiatusconsultim Velleianum* could be claimed although it had not been raised by the pleadings. De Villiers, C.J., in the case of *Oak* vs. *Lumsden,* went on to say: "I have never found any satisfactory ex-

planation of the passing of the new law known as the *Authentica si qua Mulier,* whereby married women are specially protected against their contracts or suretyships for their husbands, seeing that they were already protected under the general terms of the *Senatusconsultmn.* The explanation I would venture to give, in default of any better, is that the Emperor Justinian wished—to use an English Law phrase—to make the suretyship of a wife for her husband not only voidable, but absolutely void." This latter enactment provided that if a wife gave her husband her consent to an instrument of debt, or bound in writing her property or person, whether for a public or private debt, the obligation of the wife should be invalid, unless it clearly appeared that the debt had been incurred for the special benefit of the wife herself. In *McAlister* vs. *Raio d Co.* (6 N. L. R., N. S. 10), it was held that the *Senatusconsultum Velleianum* and the *Authentica* n *qua Mulier* apply to all obligations of women, including promissory notes, signed by them as sureties; and that public female traders, though not entitled to the benefit of the *Senatusconsultum Velleianum,* are entitled to that of the *Authentica si qua Mulier.* There is no doubt that these rules form part of Dutch Law. In *Whitnall* vs. *Ooldschmidt* (8 E. D. C. 814) it was said by Shippard, J.: "The strict rule of the Roman Law, forbidding a woman to become surety for the debt of any other person, has been adopted by the Law of Holland to its fullest extent;" and in *Oak* vs. *Lumsden* (8 S. C. 144) it was said by De Villiers, C.J.: "It will be necessary for me briefly to state what I have always understood to be the law of this (Cape) Colony relating to contracts of suretyship entered into by women. It is clear that women, whether married or not, suffer under no incapacity to bind themselves by contract, provided they comply with the proper legal forms.... But on account of the real or supposed frailty of women, the law confers upon them certain privileges which it is competent for them to plead in bar of actions brought upon certain classes of contracts. Amongst these contracts is

that of suretyship, which is not binding upon a woman who avails herself of the benefits of the *Senatusconsultum Velleianum"* (16,1 § 1). 512. According to Voet, the above rights in favour of a woman arise not *ipso jure,* but through the putting forward of an exception. This is in accordance with the statement of De Villiers, C.J., but not with the view expressed by the Griqualand Court in *Mahadi* vs. *De Kock* (16, 1 § 1). 513. The benefit of the *Senatusconsultum Velleianum* is available not only to a woman, but to her heirs and sureties as well (whether they became sureties with or without the woman's mandate). This arises from the fact that the benefit is not merely personal, but real as well *(in rem).* A person who, in pursuance of a mandate from a woman, stands surety for a third party, may also plead this benefit, provided he did so in good faith, and was unaware that the creditor was acting contrary to the *Senatusconsultum Velleianum* (16, 1 § 2). 514. The benefit may be pleaded as against a creditor suing on the suretyship of a woman, if he was aware of the woman's intervention, and likewise against such creditor's heir. If a woman first sold her own property unconditionally, and thereafter laid out the money obtained from such sale on her husband's behalf, there will be no suretyship, and the woman will lose the benefit of the *Senatusconsultum Velleianum.* But if she sells her property on condition that the price shall go to pay her husband's debts, or even those of a stranger, such a sale will be regarded as contrary to the *Senatusconsultum Velleianum,* and the woman will not be liable. Even where the creditor is ignorant, the woman, if she acts in good faith, will not be liable; but where the creditor is ignorant, and the woman acts fraudulently, she will not have the benefit of the *Senatusconsultum Velleianum* (16, 1 § 3). See *Oak* vs. *Lumsden* (3 S. C. 154). 515. The exception whereby a woman, or other persons entitled to the benefit, desires to escape liability may be raised not only before or after joinder in issue *(litis contestatio),* but even after judgment, to prevent execution on the property of the person entitled to the benefit. If the exception has been pleaded, or even if it is pleadable though not actually pleaded, an action against principal debtors or sureties which has become extinguished by reason of the woman's intervention revives in favour of the creditor, or where a woman makes a contract in the place of one who would otherwise have contracted (i.e., if the woman had not done so)—as, for instance, where a woman contracts a loan on behalf of one who was to have received the money for his own use. The money is here received, in either case, for the benefit of one and the same person; and, when the woman receives it on behalf of that person, and afterwards avails herself of the benefit of the *Senatusconsultum Velleianum*, the creditor still has an action against the person for whose benefit the loan was received. The original obligation revives subject to all its former limitations: so, where the woman has stood surety for one who was liable to an action limited by a certain term of prescription *(temporalis actio)*, the term of prescription is not extended when the woman's obligation ceases, but expires at the time when it would ordinarily have expired had the woman not intervened. Such actions do not, on the discharge of the woman from liability, revive *ipso jure* in the creditor's favour, but the creditor must obtain plenary restitution *(restitutio in integrum)*. In the case of a *temporalis actio* (action subject to prescription) the time of prescription begins to run anew from the date when the creditor has obtained *restitutio in integrum*. Such plenary restitution in the creditor's favour is not barred by the fact that the date to which or the condition under which the woman stood surety is still pending or unfulfilled; and the creditor is entitled to restitution even if the day has not yet arrived or the condition is still unfulfilled. Nor is restitution barred by the fact that the creditor had freed the original debtor by means of acceptilation *(acceptilatio,* a voluntary release by the creditor by way of donation), where such acceptilation or release was given in contemplation of the woman's sure-

tyship, the obligation being transferred from the principal debtor to the woman—since the release of the principal debtor by the creditor was conditional on payment or discharge of the debt by the woman. Again, restitution is not barred by the fact that the creditor becomes heir to the woman who has stood surety, since he does not succeed in respect of her obligation under the suretyship, the debt being still due to him in his position as creditor, not as heir to the woman; and, *vice versa,* restitution is not impeded by the fact that the woman becomes heir to the principal debtor (16, 1 §§ 4, 5). 516. There will be no restitution in the creditor's favour where the woman has bound herself as surety for an invalid or ineffectual obligation. For instance, there can be no restitution where a woman is surety for a minor who contracts without his guardian's authority. As we have seen, minors contracting without their guardian's authority are *naturally* liable to this extent, that their sureties are bound; but here the woman surety is protected by the *Senatusconsultum Velleianum,* and the minor is not personally liable. If the creditor has another ordinary remedy available, restitution will not be granted to him as of course—where, for instance, the principal debtor has given a pledge or mortgage for his debt, and a woman has, in addition, stood surety for the debt (16, 1 § 6). 517. If a woman stands surety jointly with a man, the latter is alone liable for the whole amount to the creditor, since the man knew, or ought to have known, that the woman was not bound— unless the woman has, as to her own share of the debt, entered into the obligation for her own benefit. The man will not be liable for more than his share where it has been specially agreed that the man and the woman shall each be liable for his or her share only (16, 1 § 7).

Where a mother indorsed a promissory note as surety only, her son indorsing it as an additional surety before the note was taken by the payees and the indorsee, who was the plaintiff in an action against the mother, it was said, by

Shippard, J.: "To such a case must be applied the rule stated by Voet, namely, that when a man and woman jointly sign as sureties, and the woman has not renounced the benefit of the *Senatuscoutultum Velleianum,* the creditor may have his remedy against the male surety, but has none against the female, and has got himself to thank for it, as he was bound to know the law" *Auret* vs. *Hind,* 4 E. D. C. 295).

518. The intervention of a woman generally takes place in three ways, namely, by transferring to herself another person's obligation,, by sharing it, or by binding herself on behalf of another person who contracts a debt. She may intervene by substituting herself in the place of another debtor, by giving a joint promise, by novating a debt, by standing surety, by giving a pledge, by giving a mandate, by appointing a representative with authority to contract debts, by taking up an action on behalf of a defendant, by submitting to judgment, or by contracting for a person who would otherwise have contracted on his own behalf. In all such cases a woman has the benefit of the *Senatusconsultum Velleianum.* Where a woman promises to give indemnity for a debt, and no principal debtor has appeared in the transaction, and no creditor, for whom and to whom respectively she is liable, there is no intervention by her, and she will not have the benefit of the *Senatusconsultum Velleianum* (16, 1 § 8). 519. The benefit of the exception under the *Scnatusconsultmn Velleianum* is lost in certain cases. It is lost where a woman renounces it. A great controversy on the question as to the mode in which a renunciation, in order to be effectual, must be made, has arisen in South African Courts, and among South African lawyers. Into the merits of such controversies it is not the object of this work to enter. It will be necessary, however, briefly to indicate the scope of the dispute. The great point of doubt is whether a renunciation of the *Senatusconsultum Velleianum,* in order to be effectual, should be notarial or not. In *Whitnal l* vs. *Goldschmidt* (8 E. D. C. 314) it was laid down by Shippard, J.:

" The better opinion seems to be, that the Law of Holland, like that of Friesland, followed closely in the lines of the Roman Law on this point, and that, according to the Law of Holland, the renunciation by a woman of the benefit of the *Senatttscmisultum Velleianum,* in order to be effectual, must be made either judicially on oath, or extra-judicially by a public or notarial instrument duly attested, without which, by Dutch as by Roman Law, the engagement itself was null and void; and it is scarcely necessary to add that these rules applied with far greater force to the case of a married woman attempting to become surety for her husband, and, with that object, to renounce the benefit of the *Authentica si qica Mulier."* The learned Judge criticised the views of Voet and Groenewegen *(De Legibus Abrogatis, Code,* 4, 29, 23), who "appear to hold, contrary to Roman Law, that a woman can validly renounce the *beneficium Senatusconsulti Velleiani* by a private, as well as by a public, instrument. But, as remarked by the translator of Van der Keessel's *Theses Selectae* (note to § 496), Voet, for this opinion, cites only Groenewegen, who relies solely on the old French jurist Bugnyon.... I have carefully examined the treatise of Bugnyon, in order, if possible, to verify the citation of Groenewegen, and find it incorrect." After discussing the various authorities, the learned Judge laid down the rule as above stated, adding that the views of Voet and Groenewegen are " not merely opposed, but entirely refuted, by the concurrent testimony of the vast majority of the most eminent jurists of Holland." In *Oak* vs. *Jjumsden* (3 S. C. 144), De Villiers, C.J., took an opposite view, saying: " In my opinion, a notarial instrument is not essential to the validity of the renunciation, whether the woman renouncing be married or not. In the case of a woman who carries on a public trade no express renunciation is required if she undertakes a suretyship for the benefit of her business. And whether the woman be a trader or not, if she became a surety for another on a good consideration, or led the creditor to believe that she had received such consid-

eration, she would not be entitled to the privilege. If, therefore, a woman married out of community makes a promissory note in favour of her husband, as for value received, she cannot, if she has in reality received no value, plead her privilege in an action brought against her by a *bond fide* holder for value, without notice that the note was an accommodation one." Commenting on this, Kotze, C.J., in his edition of Van Leeuwen *(R. D. L.* vol. 2, p. 620) says: "It appears that the learned Chief Justice attaches great importance to the words *for value received* occurring in promissory notes, and holds that if a woman signs a note in this form she is virtually guilty of fraud in having misled the creditor by an assertion that she has received value for the obligation contracted by her. That a woman cannot plead her privilege where she has been guilty of fraud is plain; but ought the mere formal words *for value received,* occurring in every promissory note, to be considered as a practice of fraud by the woman, where she has in reality received no value?" In *Oak* vs. *Lumsden* (8 S. C. 144), De Villiers, C.J., discussed the observations of Shippard, J. , and proved, to his own satisfaction, that a notarial renunciation of the benefit was not essential; concluding by stating: "Even Van der Keessel, whom Mr. Justice.Shippard also cites (§ 496), says: 'It is a rule founded on reason, and confirmed by the authority of many authors, that in order to render effectual the renunciation of the *Senatusconsultum Velleianum* which is permitted by our customs, it ought to be made by a public instrument, without which the engagement itself is void, unless, perhaps, a different rule can be proved to have been adopted in Holland by custom.' We have the testimony of Groenewegen and Voet—than whom no more competent witnesses could be found—that such a different rule had in fact been adopted in Holland; and in the face of that testimony I feel myself bound to hold that a woman, whether married or single, cannot take the benefit of the privileges already mentioned, if she has knowingty and deliberately

renounced her right to plead them, even if she has not done so by a public instrument, provided only the renunciation be clearly proved." Kotze, C.J., in his note to Van Leeuwen, holds with Shippard, J., that the renunciation must be effected by a public judicial or notarial instrument, and states that, even it be proved that in the province of Holland a notarial or judicial renunciation was not necessary— which he doubts—yet this was not a rule of general Roman-Dutch Law (16, 1 § 9).

The following authorities should be referred to for elucidating this knotty point: The learned note in the appendix to Kotze's Van Leeuwen *(R. D. L.* voL 2, pp. 599—621); *McAlister* vs. *Raw & Co.* (6 N. L. R, N. S. 10); *Mackellar* vs. *Bond* (4 N. L. R, N. S. 109; 6 N. L. R, N. S. 178, 196); *Natal Bank* vs. *Bond* (53 L. J. P. C. 97, 98); *Code* (4, 29, 23 § 2); Van der Keessel (§ 496); Van Leeuwen *(R. D. L.* 4, 4, 2; 2 *Kotzi,* 38); Van Leeuwen *(Cens. For.* 1, 4, 17, 4); Sonde *(Decis. Fris.* 3, 11 §§ 3— 5); Gail *(Observ.* 2, 77); Christinaeus *(Decisiones,* 3, 36 §§ 5, 10); Vinnius *(Select Questions,* 1,48); Perezius *(On the Code,* 4, 29 § 23); *Alport's Executors* vs. *Alport* (9 C. T. R. 326); Grotius (3, 3, 19); Brunnemannus (On *the Pandects,* 16, 1, 8); Brunnemannus *(On the Code,* 4, 29, 23 § 4); Zoezius *(On the Pandects,* 16,1 §§ 15, 17, 18); Zypaeus *(Belgian Law,* 4; *On the Sc.* § 4); Noodt *(On the Pandects,* 16, 1; *Opera Omnia,* vol. 2, p. 356); Huberus *(Praelectiones Juris Civilis, Pandects,* 16,1 §§ 15— 20); Averanius *(Interpretationes Juru,* 2 c. 5); Leyser *(On the Pandects,* § 171); Neostadius *(Antenuptial Contracts,* f$ 18, 19). See also the judgment of Bristow, J., in *Stride* vs. *Wepener,* Witwatersrand High Court, September 16th, 1903.

520. An attempt has been made, in *Marico Board of Executors* vs. *Auret* (14 S.C. 458), to reconcile the conflicting opinions on the mode in which a renunciation of the benefit should be effected, by holding that the very highest degree of proof is necessary, not only to establish the renunciation of the benefit, but also to show that a woman was

aware of the effect of such a renunciation. In *Oak* vs. *Lumsden* (3 S. C. 144), the Court had said: "It is important that her renunciation should be effected by means of a notarial instrument, for by this means proof that she deliberately renounced rights which she knew she possessed would be dispensed with;" while holding that a notarial act was necessary to validate the renunciation. In *Marico Board of Executors* vs. *Auret* the Court went a step further. It was said by De Villiers, C.J.: "Among the modes enumerated by Voet, in which a woman may interpose her credit and become entitled to the benefit of the *Senatusconsultum,* is that of giving a pledge for the debt of another, and it has not been contended that the defendant would have been bound by the pledging of the life policy for her husband's debt without a formal renunciation of the benefits. In the document signed by her she purported to renounce both benefits, and if she knew at the time what her rights were, and, notwithstanding such knowledge, deliberately renounced them, she would have no defence to the present action. The document was executed before a landdrost and not before a notary, but it has been stated that under Transvaal Law a landdrost (magistrate) may, in the absence of a notary, perform notarial functions. But I take it that under Transvaal Law also it is the duty of the notary or of the landdrost, as the case may be, to explain to a woman about to become surety for her husband and renounce the benefits of the *Senatuscomultum Velleianum* and of the *Authentica si qua Mulier,* what her rights are and what benefits she is about to renounce. The presumption would always be that this duty has been duly performed, but in the present case the landdrost himself admitted that he was satisfied with asking the defendant whether she knew what she was signing" (16, 1 §§ 8, 9).
In *Stafford* vs. *Fass «fc Co.* (8 N. L. R., N. S. 10) it was said by Connor, J.: "The law throws a certain amount of protection over married women. In order that the renunciation of *benefida* by a married woman who becomes surety for her husband may be effective, it is neces-

sary that the benefits renounced should be explained to her. Where tho bond of a married woman, given as surety for her husband, purports to contain the necessary renunciations and has been registered, that does not protect a third person taking over the bond. If the power of attorney given by a married woman, authorising a mortgage under renunciation of the necessary *benefida,* has in fact been executed without explanation of the protection renounced, the surety is not bound. When, however, the money advanced, for which a married woman is suroty, comes into her own hands, then she is bound, as the bond is a surety bond in name only." The rule that the effect of renunciation must be explained to the woman has practically been adopted by the Privy Council, the highest authority on Roman-Dutch Law in the British Empire, in *Natal Bank* vs. *Bond* (53 L. J. P. C. 97, 98; 4 N. L. R., N. S. 109). In that case defendant, a married woman, gavo hor husband a general power of attorney in the usual form. The husband, by virtue of this authority, executed a special power of attorney to a notary to pass a mortgage bond binding the wife personally as surety, and authorising the notary (the sub-attorney) to renounce, as ho did, the benefit of the *Authentica ei qua Mulier.* It was decided (affirming the judgment of the Supreme Court of Natal) that the general power given by the wife did not, in the absence of express words, authorise the husband to empower the notary to renounce the benefits in question. See also the remarks of Cadiz, J., in *Boin* vs. *Lavaure* (8 N. L. R., N. S. 75).

521. If a woman intervenes on behalf ofher husband, and effectually renounces the benefit of the *Senatusconsultum Velleianum,* she is not thereby taken to have renounced the benefit of the *Authentica si qua Mulier* as well. Both benefits must be expressly renounced. As we have seen, both benefits are to be renounced in the same manner (16, 1 § 10).
See *Oak* vs. *Lumsden* (3 S. C. 155), *Whitnall* vs. *Goldschmidt* (3 E. D. C. 314), and *Smutt, Louw & Co.* vs. *Coetser* (Buch. 1876, p. 55). In the Cape

Colony it is enacted by Act 19, 1893 (Bills of Exchange Act, § 20, sub-section 1), that " to the validity of a bill, accepted or indorsed by a woman, the renunciation of the benefits of the *Senatusconsultum Velleianum* and *Authentica si qua Mulier* shall not be requisite. " A similar change in the law has been effected in the Transvaal, by Proc. 11, 1902, § 20.

522. A woman has not the benefit of these exceptions where she makes a donation to another person, or makes payment on behalf of a debtor (not as surety), or delegates (assigns) her own debtor to another person's creditor without herself intervening in the transaction, or restores a pledge which she holds as a creditor. Where a woman, under pretence of intervening as surety (and getting the benefit of the *Senatusconsultum Velleianum),* really makes a sale to accreditor, she cannot avail herself of the benefit. Nor can she have the benefit, where she intervened fraudulently and with intent to deceive; or if, after the lapse of two years, she renews a former intervention on behalf of a third party or stranger, but not on her husband's behalf; or if the debtor has already paid to the woman the amount for which she stood surety, on the understanding that she should herself make payment of the debt to the creditor; or if the debtor pays the woman, who promises that the creditor will regard such payment as a discharge, and the creditor does not thereafter ratify the payment. Nor can she avail herself of the benefits where she receives a reward, of whatever amount, for her intervention; or if she stands security for a dowry; or for another person to a creditor who is a minor (not for a debtor who is a minor, in which case, as we have seen, she is absolved), and cannot obtain payment of the debt from the person (principal debtor) for whom the woman stands surety; or if she incurs the debt on her own behalf, even if she is a joint-debtor, if the transaction is for her own benefit; or if she stands security for her indigent husband, in order to obtain maintenance and support or sustenance for themselves and family (16, 1

§ 11).

See Grotius (3, 3, 15—17); Schorer (ad *Grotius,* § 297); Van der Keesset (§ 495); *Dutch Consultations* (2, 317). In *Bevern's Trustee* vs. *Kretzschmar* (11 S. C. 18) it was held that a woman who promises to pay the amount of a debt owing by another loses the protection of the *Senatiuconsultum Velleumum* if she has good consideration for the promise. See also *Le Roex* vs. *BrinVt Executors* (4 S. C. 74); *Maekie, Dunn & Co.* vs. *McMaster* (9 S. C. 212).

523. A woman who is a public trader loses the benefits, where she stands security for another in respect of those things which appertain to the particular business in which she is engaged, but not with regard to other matters (16, 1 § 11).

In *McAUster* vs. *Raw A Co.* (6 N. L. R., N. S. 10) it was said by Connor, C.J. : "There is, no doubt, authority for saying that, in Holland, a woman trading publicly could not claim the benefit of the *Senatusconsultum Velleianum,* but could insist on that of the *Authentica si qua Mulier* (Groenewegen *ad Code,* 4, 29, *pr.*). For this proposition Neostadius is cited *(Antenuptial Contract),* §5 18, 19)." In *Oakxs. Lumsden* (3 S. C. 144) De Villiers, C.J., said: "I am of opinion that, even without such a renunciation, a woman carrying on a public trade, who becomes surety for another, is debarred from pleading the privilege either of the *Senatusconsultum* or of the *Authentica,* provided only the contract was made in the course of her trade." The remarks of the same high authority, immediately following, may with advantage be referred to. In *Whitnall* vs. *Goldschmidt* (3 R D. C. 314) Shippard, J., quoted Groenewegen and Neostadius to show that a married woman who publicly kept a shop or carried on trade on her own account had the benefit of the *Authentica si qua Mulier,* though not of the *Senatusconsultum Velleianum.* In this matter Kotz6, C.J., in his note to Van Leeuwen (iJ. *D. L.* vol. 2, p. 621), adopts Voet's statement without comment, holding that a woman who is a public trader cannot set up either the *Senatusconsultum Velleianum* or the

Authentica si qua Mulier. Here again the authorities are in conflict, De Villiers, C.J., and Kotz6, C.J., being ranged against Connor, C.J., and Shippard, J. The question is therefore not finally settled; but Voet's view, it is submitted, appears the most logical one to take, for, if certain principles govern the renunciation of these benefits, the same principles should govern their applicability or non-applicability.

524. If a woman, being aware of her benefits under the *Senatusconsultum Velleianum* and the *Authentica si qua Mulier,* pays what is due by her under a suretyship, she cannot reclaim the money so paid on the ground that she did not renounce the benefits. If she was ignorant of her rights, however, she can claim repayment, where there has been no renunciation (16, 1 § 12).

See *Zeederberg* vs. *Union Bank* (3 S. C. 294); and *Whittaker* vs. *Stewart* (Cape Supreme Court, November 1st, 1900), and *South African Loan Co.* vs. *Sath* (6N. L. R. 18). It is submitted, with great respect, that the explanation given by De Villiers, C.J., in *Oak* vs. *Lumsden* (see above, § 511), is not wholly satisfactory—namely, that Justinian, by introducing the *Authentica si qua Mviier,* wished to make the suretyship of a married woman " not only voidable, but absolutely void." If such a suretyship became altogether void, what necessity would there be for a married woman to renounce the benefit of the *Authentica si qua Mulier f* The maxim *Quisquis juri pro se introducto potest renunciare* applies, and can only apply, to contracts which a party is free to renounce or adopt as he or she pleases. But where the law absolutely prohibits a person from contracting in certain circumstances, by making the contract absolutely null and void, there can be no contract in fraud of such a rule. It follows that suretyship of a married woman was not void under Justinian. Perhaps an explanation may be found in the fact that a married woman was under the *patria potestas* of her husband (being reduced, by marriage, to the position of a minor, even if she was previously emancipated), and that the Roman

lawyers desired to prevent the estates of wives becoming liable for colourable contracts, entered into by women whose husbands exercised an undue influence over them. This is, of course, put forward as a mere tentative explanation.

The case of *Whittaker* vs. *Stnvart,* referred to above, is reported in 10 C. T. R., at page 587. See also *Watson and Co.* vs. *De Wit* (11 C. T. E. 90.) PAKT IV.

THE LAW OF THINGS OK PROPERTY.

A. *THINGS IN GENERAL.*

Chap. I.—The Nature Of Things; And Rights Over Things.

„ II.—Possession And Ownership Of Property. B. *PARTICULAR RIGHTS IN THINGS.*

Chap. I.—Servitudes. IX—Quit-rent Tenure. PART IV.

THE LAW OF THINGS OR PROPERTY.

A. *THINGS IN GENERAL.*

CHAPTER I.

THE NATURE OF THINGS J AND RIGHTS OVER THINGS.

525. The division of things in Roman Law (under the *jus gentium*) which has been practically adopted in Dutch Law, classifies them as (1) things common to all, or *res communes;* (2) public things, *res publicae;* (8) things belonging to corporate bodies created by the State—in other words, things belonging to a whole city, or to a body erected or constituted by charter—*res universitatis;* (4) things belonging to no particular person, but capable of appropriation by a particular person, *res nullius;* and (5) things belonging to individuals, *res singulorum.* A wider division is (1) things belonging to no one in particular, *res nullius;* and (2) things belonging to a special person or body of persons, *res alicujus.* Things subject to the law of man *(humani juris)* and at the same time belonging to no one may, according to the *jus gentium,* be common to all men. Things subject to divine law *(divinum jus)* are *res sacrae* and *res religioscu* (the former, according to the old Roman Law, being dedicated to the celestial, and the latter to the infernal gods, both classes being by law inalienable), and *res sanctae* (things which, without being sacred, were protected against the

injuries of men by having a severe penalty attached to the violation of their security). Things belonging to some one in particular are either public property or the property of individuals. The former are at the disposal of the public or of the State; the latter are subject to the discretion and control of private persons (1, 8 § 1). 526. *Res communes* are such things as, by the *jus gentium,* belong to no one in particular. The Roman Law acknowledges four classes of this division of things, the air, running water, the sea and its coasts, and wild animals as long as they are in a state of freedom. In another sense, *res nullius* included wild animals, implying those things which were by their nature, indeed, capable of individual possession, but which remained unappropriated. They comprised not only wild animals *(ferae naturae),* but bees and gems or precious stones, treasure trove, and pearls in the sea (oysters being fish, and the sea common property). As to *res communes,* Voet says that every one can build on the sea-shore, and not only the building but that part of the shore on which the erection is made becomes the property of the builder. The public use, however, must not be interfered with, nor the rights of private owners in the neighbourhood. In order to build on the shore, it is not necessary to obtain a grant from the Crown, so long as no attempt is made to injure the rights (such as right of way) of the public generally, or of private persons in particular. No one may be prevented by interdict from building or doing anything on a public place, such as the sea-shore or waste land, unless it appears that damage or harm is thereby occasioned to the public or to a private person. Where a person obtains the authority of the Crown to build, he must make good damage arising from faulty construction to those who suffer thereby; but where a person builds of his own accord, without sanction from the Crown, he is liable not only for damage caused by defective construction, but also for that occasioned by defect in the soil or subsoil (1, 8 §§ 2—4). 527. Public things belong by right of dominion to the whole public,

or people of the State. They are distinguished from *res communes,* inasmuch as they have already been taken in possession on behalf of the public, whereas *res communes* are subjects of property still to be occupied, belonging, as it were, to no one. Among public things are included perennial streams and harbours; and as the use of them is common to all, just as of public roads and shores and banks of rivers, so every one is at liberty to sail upon and fish in such perennial streams and harbours, or to draw or lead water from them, provided the water is not there for the general public use, and that the river is not navigable, or of such a nature that another river becomes navigable with its assistance (1, 8 §§ 5—8).
' Public things are properly suck as every one may use—such as rivers, their banks, harbours, and highways; but such things as belong to the whole nation (the *use* of which is, however, not common to every individual) belong *in patrimonio populi (i.e., reipublicae):* and perhaps the clearest distinction is between *use* and *usufruct,* for though *ager publicus* be not actually enjoyed by the nation at large, yet the rents thereof, flowing into the public exchequer, become the common national property."..." The coast of the sea is free to all mankind, but, as in the case of rivers, the *imperium publicum* over it and harbours belongs to the Roman people. The same is the case with public roads."... *"Fundi publici* resembled the present Crown lands, and the revenues proceeding from them flowed into the *aerarium" (Colquhoun,* §§ 924, 925). As to public roads, see *Dobie* vs. *Schickerling* (2 S. 94). Grotius (2, 35, 9; *Maasdorp,* p. 151) says: "High roads *(viae publicae)* are roads common to all, which may be used by every one, the profits thereof going to the Crown." 528. Persons who own estates bordering on a public stream, and are consequently proprietors of the banks thereof, may build or erect in the stream or upon the bank whatever may be necessary to protect their property against the violence or destructiveness of the stream, and they will become the owners of the

works or buildings erected in this manner and with this object—provided they do not in any way injure the upper or lower proprietors whose estates border on their own, or any one having property in the neighbourhood. Nor can they, in so doing, obstruct the public use of the stream, by impeding navigation, or diverting the flow of the water. Where a river is public, and navigable, a proprietor who owns land on both banks cannot erect a bridge across the stream so as to connect his estates on either side of the river. Persons who do not own estates bordering on the stream cannot build anything in the stream or on its banks, since such erections would belong to the owner of the land on the banks of the stream (following the maxim, *quicquid inaedificatur solo, solo cedit),* in the same way as that portion of the river-bed which is no longer covered by water belongs to the owner of the adjacent land. Since the sea-shore and navigable rivers belong to the domains of the Crown, the public, apart from navigation and processes necessary to navigation, cannot make use of the same, unless the Crown has given express leave, or sanction has been obtained from persons to whom the Crown has entrusted the care of the sea-shore or of navigable rivers. Otherwise persons cannot fish, build, or perform other operations on shores or in and about navigable rivers appropriated by the Crown (1, 8 § 9).

In *Anderson and Murison* vs. *Colonial Government* (8 S. C. 293), the applicants had purchased a wrecked steamer which lay on the sea-shore of Dassen Island, the property of the Crown. The Government agreed to allow the removal of the wreck on certain conditions, which applicants refused to comply with. The Government then refused permission to the crew of a vessel belonging to applicants to collect the cargo of the wrecked steamer, and warned the said vessel off the shore of the island. Applicants then claimed an interdict restraining the Government from obstructing the removal of wreckage and stores from the wrecked steamer. The Cape Supreme Court refused the interdict, holding that no ground had been shown for preventing the Government from asserting their ordinary rights as landowners. It was said by De Villiers, C.J.: "Upon the cession of this Colony to the English Crown the laws of the country (Roman-Dutch) were retained. Under those laws the public had the right to the free use of the sea-shore, that is, to the land between high and low water marks, and it is no more in the power of the Government than it is that of any private individual to deprive the public of that right. No doubt the Government are, in one sense, the custodians of the sea-shore, but they are such only on behalf of the public. They may, as Voet points out, grant permission to individuals to build upon the sea-shore, and without such permission no one is at liberty so to build; but that permission is subject to the condition that the rights of the public shall not be interfered with. Any structure between high and low water marks, which materially interferes with the general use of the shore, whether constructed with or without consent of the Government, would be a nuisance which this Court would be justified in restraining. *A fortiori* would the Court restrain any direct interference with the rights of any of the public to recover, or temporarily deposit, shipwrecked goods on the shore. It is a very different matter, however, to ask the Court to interfere with, the right of Government to ward off trespassers from Crown laud." 529. Things belonging to a corporate body *(res universitatu),* whether such body be public or private, cannot at the same time be owned or disposed of by individuals, unless such disposal is made by virtue of a proper mandate from the corporate body (1, 8 § 10).

530. Things are, again, divided into corporeal and incorporeal. Corporeal things are such as are tangible, or capable of actual physical possession. Incorporeal things are such as are not tangible, in other words, which are incapable of physical possession: and they consist in rights, "of which exercise is the proof." Corporeal things are movable (such as furniture or ships), or im-

movable (such as landed property). A thing which is originally movable may be regarded as immovable where it is regarded as part of, and as an accession to, immovable property. Thus fruits, originally movable, are looked upon as immovable where they are ungathered and still hang to the tree *(fructus pendentes),* if the tree is itself looked upon as immovable property. Trees which adhere to the soil, being portions of an estate, are regarded as immovable property. If they fall down, however, or are uprooted, or cut down, they no longer adhere to the soil, and are classified as movable property; and they are not dependent upon the real rights of the house or estate where or upon which they grew; and, on a sale of the estate, they do not, when detached from the soil, go to the purchaser, unless this has been specially agreed upon. If articles, such as beams, or columns, or pieces of marble, which are originally movable, are joined or attached to buildings for perpetual, not temporary use, they form part of the buildings, and are looked upon as immovable property (1, 8 §§ 11—14).

In *Ferguson* vs. *Favill* (1 E. D. C. 219) it was said by Shippard, J.: "The rules of our law with regard to timber are well defined. Trees uncut are reckoned as part of immovable or real property; and though the *emphyteuta,* or tenant at perpetual quit-rent, under his original title, and irrespective of statutory rights, could not cut trees without replanting, or, in other words, could not commit waste (*Voet,* 6, 3, 46), yet as against third parties or trespassers the *emphyteuta,* having *fundum vectigalem,* could maintain the *actio arborum furtim caesarum Voet,* 47, 7, 2), though a usufructuary could not. In this respect there is a strong analogy between the *emphyteuta* of the civil law and the copyholder of English Law, though the right of the copyholder became greater in this respect, namely, that by virtue of his possessory interest he could maintain trespass, even against the lord, for cutting down trees when not justified by the custom." 531. Money intended for the purchase of immovable property, and

set aside for that purpose, cannot be looked upon as immovable; for a mere intention cannot alter the nature of anything. Similarly, the price obtained from the sale of immovable property will not be looked upon as immovable (1, 8 §§ 15—17).

532. Incorporeal things include such rights as inheritances, servitudes, debts, actions, patent rights, and copyright. Inheritances consist of both movable and immovable property, and the law regards them from the point of view of separate things found therein, movables being regulated by the law relating to movables, immovables by the law of immovable property. Praedial servitudes are classed as immovable property, since they are the rights and qualities of immovables, accessions to estates, following the nature of the estate to which they are attached, or diminutions of the right of ownership of real property—inasmuch as the right of ownership of the servient tenement is diminished by the rights of the owner of the dominant tenement. Usufructs over movable property are reckoned as rights to movables; over immovable property they are looked upon as real rights. Actions, again, are divided into actions *in rem* and actions *in personam,* that is, real and personal. Actions *in personam* are classed as movables, whether they relate to movables or immovables, for they follow the person, so long as they are not attached to a *jus in re;* nor does it matter whether such actions *in personam* are instituted to establish dominion over immovables or movables, or to enforce a sale or a purchase, or a lease, or any similar contract. Actions *in rem,* or real actions, again, are to be considered as immovables if they refer to immovable property, and as movables if they are instituted to recover a movable (1, 8 §§ 18—21).

As to praedial servitudes, considered as real rights, see *Hiddingh* vs. *Topps* (4 S. 107); *Judd* vs. *Fourie* (2 E. D. C. 41).

533. Rents which are already due are to be reckoned as movables. Leases which endure for a term of years, rights of toll, rights of way, rights of gathering or collecting redeemable or irredeemable

rents, rent from lands held on tenure of *emphyteusis* (quit-rent), rights of hunting or fishing, mineral rights, are reckoned as immovables (1, 8 §§ 22, 28).

A distinction is here drawn between money due or payable for rent, and the right to leases for a term of years. The former are classed as movables, the latter as immovables. So, where the law requires the registration of a pledge or mortgage of real rights, a pledge of a lease *in longum tempus*—in the case under consideration, for ninety-nine years—in order to be valid as against parties other than the pledgor or pledgee, must be registered in the Deeds Registry or other office for registering real rights *(Collins* vs. *Hugo and Another,* Hertzog, p. 203). It was said by Kotze, C.J.: "A lease of fixed or real property, for the term of ninety-nine years, must be looked upon a *separata bonorum species,* and classed under the category of immovable rather than movable property. Such a lease gives rise to real rights over fixed property, and must be looked upon as fixed property." See also Mackeldey *(Lehrbuch,* §§ 299, 302); *Utrecht Consultations* (No. 75, p. 338); Groenewegen (on the *Code,* 4, 65); Van Leeuwen *(Cens. For.* 1, 4, 22, 5; *R. D. L.* 4, 21, 9; *2 Kotzi,* 177); Van der Keessel (§ 673); and *Maynard* vs. *Usher* (2 M. 178). In *Brooks* vs. *Corner Estate Co.* (Off. R. Transvaal, 1897, p. 421) it was also held that a lease of a piece of ground for a term of ninety-nine years constitutes a real right over that piece of ground. Where a third party was unaware of the existence of a servitude, and the deed of transfer made no mention thereof, he was held entitled to rely on the Transvaal law (No. 3, 1886) which enacted that no servitude should hold good against third parties if not properly indicated in the deed of transfer.

534, Annual rents may be either real or personal. They are personal where no immovable property is charged with the payment of rents; real, when immovable property is specially charged and made liable for the rent, in such a manner that a change of the possessors or occupiers of such property does not alter the liability in respect of the land. Purely real rights or obligations imposed on land are to be regarded as real property. Mixed rents, where both the person of the debtor and immovable property are bound, are looked upon in Dutch Law as movables. Where a debt is secured by an hypothecation of real property, whether the same bears interest or not, such hypothecation is to be classed as a movable; since the principal obligation is not attached to the real property, but arises from a loan of money, or the balance of a purchase-price, which are classified as movables. The mode of securing such hypothecs, however, since they are a charge on real property, is similar to that prevailing in respect to the real property itself: they must be registered *coram lege loci,* and the necessary dues must be paid. The same principles apply to rents due by corporations or *universitates.* In Dutch Law incorporeal things *(res incorporates)* are classed under the head of movables or of immovables only when such classification follows by necessary implication from the form of words used in making a disposition of incorporeal things. Otherwise, incorporeal things or rights are treated as a class wholly separate and apart from things real or personal (1, 8 §§ 24—29). 535. As we have seen, movable property is said to be in, and governed by the law of, the place where the owner of such property has his domicile. Immovables are governed by the law of the place where they are situate. Personal actions, according to Voet, are to be regarded as movables, and will therefore follow the law of the domicile of the creditor who is entitled to sue on them (1, 8 § 80).

Considerable discussion, into the merits of which it is impossible to enter here, has arisen on the question of the law which is to regulate rights of action, where there is a conflict of law on the subject. The subject is treated of in Westlake's *Private International Law* (3rd ed. §§ 311, 312, 321, 322), and Story's *Conflict of Laws.* In *MacCartie* vs. *Bromwich* (Transv. Off. Rep. 1897, p. 403) the Transvaal High Court, where it appeared, *ex facie* of a judgment grant-ed in default by a foreign Court, that the defendant, at the time of the judgment, was not within the jurisdiction of the Court, decided that the pltintiff in an action on such foreign judgment could not succeed unless he proved that the defendant, though absent, was nevertheless domiciled within the jurisdiction of the foreign Court at the time when the judgment was given. See also *Acvtt, Blaine & Co.* vs. *Colonial Marine Insurance Co.* (1 S. C. 402), and *Smuts & 0,.*vs. *Holman* (Transv. Off. Rep. 1897, p. 280)i CHAPTER II.

Possession And Ownership Of Property.

(1) Modes Of Obtaining Possession And Ownership.

536. According to the civil law, dominion over things is acquired by (a) universal, or *(b)* particular title. Universal titles include inheritances; particular titles include usucapion, donation, legacies, and special or particular *fideicommissa.* Dominion, according to the *jus gentium,* is acquired by occupation, accession, and tradition or transfer (41, 1 § 1). 537. Occupation is the legal apprehension or taking of corporeal things, which are common *(rei communes)* by the *jus gentium,* with the intention to acquire the ownership thereof; and by this such tilings as belong to no one in particular *(res nullius)* go to the first occupier, by natural reason. And although capture of property belonging to the enemy, during warfare, is capture of things belonging to some one in particular *(res alicujus),* yet, since the law and custom of war allow the seizure by a belligerent of things belonging to his enemy, such things are reckoned as *res nullius,* and pass as booty into the dominion of the enemy capturing them (41, 1 § 2). 538. Occupation takes place as regards either portions of things or particular things. We may occupy portions of air, of the sea, or the sea-shore. Particular things are occupied by hunting, fishing, fowling, provided they are *res nullius* (belonging to no one in particular). Domestic animals, such as fowls, geese, sheep, and other gregarious animals used by man in domestic work, cannot pass' to one through title

by occupancy, even if they stray, or have flown away, or have been taken away by wild beasts and left alive— since they are in the dominion of individuals, and remain the property of their owners wherever found, nor can they pass out of such dominion without the act of the owner. Therefore, domestic animals must be restored to the owner, and any one who knowingly retains them with the intention of appropriating them is considered to be guilty of theft. The same rule applies to wild creatures that have been domesticated, such as peacocks, doves, or bees, even if they fly away, so long as they have not desisted from their habit of returning to the house or estate of the person who acquired them by occupancy. As to ostriches, see *Le Roex* vs. *Smit* (5 S. 827). It makes no difference whether one captures wild animals or birds in a public or private place, on a property of one's own or belonging to others, or whether the owner of the property knows and consents to their capture or not, or even if he objects to it. This is so, notwithstanding the fact that one cannot hunt or fowl on the land of others against the will of the owner, and that the owner of land, who forbids such hunting, has an action for damages against the party intruding on his property. In spite of this, the animals captured pass to the captor. It makes no difference that the hunter has been enriched through his own wrongful act, for the act of trespass is to be distinguished from the act of acquiring title by occupancy. It is not legal to hunt in another person's preserves, or to fish in another person's fish-ponds. There is nothing to prevent hunting in such forests or woods of others as are not game preserves, or fishing in stagnant waters belonging to others. Game in preserves and fish in fish-ponds or reserved streams are not *res nullius;* while fish in stagnant waters and animals wandering in unpreserved forests have their natural liberty, and are in the possession of no one. Every one is allowed to fish in public streams, and in the open sea. According to Roman Law, if a person hts fished in the arm of a public stream for a term of years, alone, and

without disturbance of his rights, he may, if he possesses the adjoining ground, prohibit others from fishing there, and may, on sale of the ground, insert a condition that the purchaser shall not fish there in infringement of his rights. If his fishing has been interrupted, he cannot complain of interference with his rights. Voet quotes Grotius *(Dutch Consultations,* part 8, vol. 2, No. 178; *De Bruyn,* pp. 180—185) to show that the inhabitants of a country, who have been in possession of a sea-coast for ten years for the purpose of fishing along such coast, may prevent strangers from fishing there. According to Roman Law, nations which occupy or annex unowned or uninhabited islands may prohibit others from fishing off the coasts of the same. With regard to fishing in public streams, it has been laid down that fishing with the net is only allowed to those who own or occupy the neighbouring ground, or have a licence from the Crown or the adjacent occupier; while fishing with hook and line is free, although persons are answerable for trespass on the ground of others. Where persons are prohibited by statute from killing or hunting certain animals, they do not, by killing or captm-ing the same, acquire any title to them, and if such killing or capture is prohibited, one cannot destroy such wild animals even if they trespass and commit damage on one's own ground, but one must be content with driving such animals off or away from one's property (41, 1 §§ 3—7). Voet states the rule of Roman Law to be that wild animals which have been domesticated or tamed by art coase to belong to one if they lose or desist from the habit of returning to the property of the tamer. In modern Dutch Law, he says (quoting Van L., *Cens. For.* 1, 2, 3, 7, and Groenewegen, *Institutes, "* On the Divisions of Things," § 15), this is not the case, even if they go out of one's custody and abandon the intention of returning. As to fishing in the private waters of another, see *Breda and Others* vs. *Midler and Others* (1M. 425), in which damages were awarded for fishing in a lake situate within the boundary

of the private property of the plaintiffs. See also Grotius (2,1, 18, 51, 52, 54; 2, 4, 2— 32) and Van Leeuwen *(Cms. For.* 1, 2, 3, 6—12). The right to hunt game is regulated in Cape Colony by Acts 36,1886, and 38,1891; and fishing is regulated by Acts 29, 1890, and 15,1893. As to whales, see *Langley* vs. *Miller* (3 M. 584), where it was held that a whale mortally wounded so as to render it unable to keep the sea, and so mastered as to make it impossible for it to escape from the person who has mortally wounded it, is the property of that person, and one who assists in such a case to capture is not entitled to a share of the whole. See *Le Roux* vs. *Smit* (5 S. 327) and Transvaal Law 5, 1880, and Ord. 29, 1902.

539. In modern usage, real property captured from the enemy during war goes to the State to which the captors belong. The ownership of movables captured during war depends on circumstances. If the capture is made by an army, or a body of troops, the property is looked upon as booty, and distributed according to prevailing usages. Where soldiers are allowed to capture on their own account, the property will, if taken in accordance with prevailing customs, not contrary to the laws and usages of war, belong to the private captors (41, 1 § 8). 540. Another mode of acquiring title by occupancy is by *inventio,* or discovery, which may be of things movable or immovable— either such as never were in the possession of any person, or such as have been lost or abandoned by their owners. It is not sufficient that one should know where such property is, or should see it, but it is necessary that he should remove it or seize it—since dominion begins from the moment when one acquires natural possession *(dominium rerum a naturali possessione coepit).* Of two finders, who see a thing at the same time, the first occupant, says Van Leeuwen *(Cent. For.* 1, 2, 8, 19), will be preferred. Things which have been lost must be restored to the owners, and, where the owner is not known, they should be deposited in the custody of public officials, such as the police, or publication of their find-

ing should be made. Goods thrown overboard or jettisoned for the purpose of lightening a ship during a storm do not thereby become derelict, but still belong to the former owner, since they were not thrown overboard by reason of a desire to get rid of them, but in order to escape'perils of the sea. Any one seizing such goods on the sea, or when driven on shore, with the intention of retaining them, is, if aware that the goods were jettisoned, guilty of theft (41, 1 § 9).

Voet does not state specifically that the finder must know that the goods were jettisoned; nor is this stated in the *Digest* or *Code (Code,* 6, 2; *Pandeds,* 47, 2, 43 § 11). Colquhoun says: "A distinction is drawn as to the *animus;* thus, if a person cast things overboard to preserve them, they are not abandoned, but if he knew they would perish they are so. On the other hand, if the finder save them with a view of reserving them for the rightful owner, he commits Do theft; it is, however, otherwise, if he have the *animus* of appropriation." Surely, if the intention of the person abandoning the goods makes a difference, the finder must at least know that the goods have been abandoned before he becomes guilty of theft or of wrongful conversion! Of course, any one may be indicted for stealing property the owner whereof is unknown (see *Queen* vs. *Judelman,* 10 S. C. 12). But there would appear to be very exceptional circumstances to provide for where goods have been thrown overboard in a tempest *navis levandae causa.* After speaking of the question of theft, Voet states that no one can acquire title to goods so found by usucapion *pro derelicto,* who falsely holds that he has acquired the property as derelict or abandoned. Here, then, the finder's knowledge is an important element; and so, it is submitted, it would be in a case of theft.

541. In order to acquire title by *inventio* or discovery, the property must be *res nullius.* Such are islands which are uninhabited: gems and precious stones found on the sea-shore, or in the sea itself, shells, and sea sand, unless the Crown prohibits their removal from the shore. Things which have been abandoned by their owners, with the intent never to reclaim them or again to make use of them, go to the finder—for they cease to belong to the owner immediately on abandonment, and at once become *res nullius,* as being held by no one in particular. With regard to real property, the Roman Law provided that lands or fields which were deserted and abandoned by their owners were derelict, and any one could enter on them of his own authority, and, after the lapse of two years, acquire both ownership and possession thereof; but if, before the period of two years had elapsed, the former owner desired to resume the possession and use of the lands, the occupant had to surrender the same, retaining his right to compensation for outlays and improvements. In Roman-Dutch Law, however, one cannot enter upon such land and acquire dominion thereof, except in accordance with the rules of law relating to usucapion (41, 1 § 10). See *Orotiiu* (2, 32, 3; 2, 7, 9); and *Van Leeuwen* (1, 2, 3, 17).

542. Treasure acquired by title by occupancy, generally known as treasure trove, is an ancient deposit of money, which has been concealed during such a long time that the proprietor of it is not known, and cannot be discovered. That is not considered as treasure trove, and does not go to the finder *(occupanti),* which has been placed for the sake of greed, or through fear, or for safekeeping in the ground or in a wall, and has been discovered by another person, while the owner is still alive and remembers (or keeps in mind) the deposit of such money—even if the former owner of the treasure has forgotten the exact spot where the money is buried, or if he has sold the ground where the treasure lies buried and has forgotten to remove it. If a person finds treasure in the ground of another, even if the ground belong to the Crown, half the treasure goes to the finder, and half to the owner of the ground. If treasure trove is found on quit-rent land, half of it goes to the *emphyteuta,* and not to the Crown as *dominus directus* of the quit-rent land. If treasure is found on a property which has been sold, but not transferred, half thereof goes, not to the purchaser of the ground, but to the seller, for he does not lose the dominion over the ground until transfer is made. Voet goes on to say that, as the risks and benefits of a thing sold attached to the purchaser as soon as there is mutual consent to the sale, even before delivery, equity gives the purchaser the right to the treasure found on land sold but not yet transferred. His view would then seem to be that the Roman-Dutch Law, varying the strict rule of Roman Law, gives half of the treasure found on the property to the purchaser of the land. The civil law further provides that if a man employs a labourer to seek for a hidden treasure, the treasure, when found, accrues wholly to the employer, since he had some information or suspicion of its presence, and the presence of the workman employed by him was not a mere accident; but if the workman, being employed for another purpose, casually finds a treasure, he has a claim on it to the extent of one-half (41, 1 §§11, 12). See also *Van der Keessel* (§ 198).

The English Law differs from Soman Law, in providing that treasure trove *(thesaurus inventus),* whether money, coin, gold, silver, plate, or bullion, hidden in the earth or other private place, belongs to the Crown, if the owner thereof is unknown; but if the person who hid the treasure be known, or is afterwards discovered, the owner, and not the Crown, is entitled to the treasure. Hiding is, in English Law, distinguished from abandonment. The treasure must be *vetus depositio pecuniae.* If a man scatters his treasure in the sea, or upon the earth, it belongs, by right of occupancy, to the first finder.

543. Minerals, metals, and precious stones (not being hidden treasure) belong, according to the civil law, to the owner of the ground. If property is sold, the right to such minerals, metals, or precious stones passes to the purchaser; and a usufructuary was entitled to mine for such minerals, metals, or stones on the property over which he held the usufruct. An ordinance of the States General, dated October 13th, 1629

(§§ 24—26, Dutch Placaat Book, vol. 2, p. 1239), provided that all metals, minerals, or precious stones found in the possessions of the Dutch East India Company should belong to the said company (41, 1 § 13).

The Transvaal Gold Law, No. 15 of 1898 (§ 1), provides that the right of mining and disposing of all precious stones and precious metal belongs to the State. In the Cape Colony, the right of mining for minerals or precious stones is vested, in the case of Crown lands, in the Crown; and, in the case of private property, in the owner of such property, unless there is a special reservation with regard to minerals or precious stones in favour of the Crown. See the Cape Acts 9, 1877; 19, 1883; 44, 1887; 12, 1889.

544. Accession *(accessio)* is a mode of acquiring dominion, whereby a thing becomes the property of a person by reason of its acceding or becoming attached to a thing, which is called the principal thing. The accessory object becomes the property of the owner of the principal thing. Accessions may be natural, artificial or industrial, and mixed. Natural accessions are such as are added to the original substance *by* the operation of Nature, without premeditated human design. Artificial or industrial accessions accrue through the presence of a premeditated human design. Mixed accessions are produced through the combination of Nature and premeditated human design (41, 1 § 14).

545. Natural accessions include the offspring or young of animals—since everything born of one's female animal belongs to the owner of such female animal, not to the owner of the male which is the other parent, if the male has a separate owner: unless one's animal, being the mother, is possessed in good faith by another, or unless such other person has the usufruct of the animal. Another species of accession is alluvion *(alluvio)*, which is a latent increment or increase (i.e., one so gradual as to be scarcely visible), whereby an addition is made to one's ground in so slow a manner that it is impossible to ascertain how much has been added at any particular moment. Alluvion takes

place in the case of estates which have no boundaries on the side where the alluvion takes place, and are contiguous, on that side, to a stream or river. It does not take place where estates have fixed boundaries on all sides, or are bounded by a lake or swamp. Hence those who obtain or purchase ground right up to the banks of a river have the right to alluvion, as if the boundary had been undefined. Hence, too, those who purchase or obtain estates bounded, towards the sea, in Holland, by defined dykes, have not the right to alluvion. Alluvion is distinguished from appulsion *(appulsio)*, or avulsion *(avulsio)*, whereby earth is torn away from an estate by the force of a stream or river, C.L.—VOL. L Y and carried to another estate situate along the banks of such stream or river. It differs from avulsion, inasmuch as the increase in the ground to which the earth or soil has been carried by the stream it clearly visible in the case of avulsion. The ground so carried does not immediately belong by right of alluvion to the owner of the estate whither the ground has been carried, but only after the ground has become firmly attached to such estate, when it becomes the property of the owner of such estate, together with any trees or vegetation which it may have carried along with it. An evidence of such attachment is that such trees strike their roots in the soil of the estate to which they have been carried. After the trees have so struck root, neither they nor their value can be recovered by the former proprietor, since it is due to his own negligence that he has not vindicated his right of ownership before such accession or attachment. Islands, likewise, to a certain extent, may be the subjects of accession. If they arise in the sea, they are *res nuUius,* and belong to the first occupier. According to Roman-Dutch Law, the consent of the Crown is required for the occupation (followed by ownership) of such an island by a subject. Voet states that, with regard to islands in streams or rivers, a distinction must be made, according as the island floats, or is attached rigidly to the bed of a river. If the island floats, that is,

if it be a collection of trees and undergrowth to which a certain amount of soil is attached, and does not adhere rigidly to the bed, but moves about freely in the current, it is public, and follows the ownership of the stream. If it is attached to the bed of a river, and is adjacent to the boundariet of a certain estate, being nearer to that estate than to any other property bordering on the river, it does not belong to the owner of such estate, if the estate has specified boundaries on all sides, but to the first occupier. If such island is adjacent to property which has no fixed boundary on the side contiguous to the river banks, it belongs, if it rises in the middle of the stream, to the persons who own estates on either bank of the stream, contiguous to such banks, in proportion to the extent of such estates. If it is nearer to one such estate (having no defined boundary on the riverside) than to the estate on the opposite bank, it belongs, by right of accession, to the owner of the former estate. And whatever adheres subsequently to such island by alluvion belongs to the owner of such island, even if such alluvion brings the island nearer to the estate on the opposite bank. If the island is formed near a usufructuary estate, it belongs to the person who has the ownership and dominion of such estate, and not to the usufructuary. Voet seems to take the view that alluvion benefits the owners of adjacent estates with undefined boundaries, but that, contrary to Roman Law, islands which rise in a stream belong to the Crown, being considered as *regalia.*

Grotius *Introduction,* 2, 10, 14—26; *Maasdorp,* pp. 74, 75) expresses no decided opinion on the matter. Later on (in the same section, 17) Voet shows that there was no very decided and uniform rule on the subject. Van Leeuwen *(Cens. For.* 1, 2, 4, 12) says: "In this matter we think a distinction should be taken between islands in a river which have arisen apart and separate from the lands on its banks, and which are certainly subject to the same rules of law as rivers themselves; and, inasmuch as public rivers are assigned to the ownership of the Sovereign and classed among royal properties, it follows also that the increment which results from them accrues to the Sovereign or the Treasury, or those who are in the enjoyment of a right ceded to them by the Sovereign.

But (in accordance with the *Institutes, de rerum divisione*, 2, 1, 20—22) no law even now prohibits the acquisition for ourselves or our property of other alluvial deposits or accessions to adjacent lands." In view of the uncertainty of the Dutch authorities, it would appear safer to hold that the rules of Roman Law on the subject are still in force (41, 1 §§ 15—17).

Colquhoun (§§ 981—983) lays down the following rules of Roman Law. The word alluvion implies a gradual increment. It differs from *avulsio,* which is a violent separation of a piece of ground by the force of a river, and its annexation to the property of another and neighbouring estate. If an island rise in a public river, and become fixed in the middle of the river, it belongs in common to those who possess the land nearest to the bank on each side of the stream, according to the breadth and length of each frontage. If the whole island is nearer to one estate than to another, that estate claims the whole. Similar rules are laid down in English Law by Bracton. Islands rising in a river belong to him to whom the piscary of the river appertains. If a river between two lordships gain imperceptibly on the one, the owner loses his ground. With respect to an island rising in the sea, the civil law gives it to the first occupant, the English Law to the King. Increments on the sea-shore, if insensible, go, by English Law, to the owner of the soil, following the principle *de minimi non curat lex;* if they are sudden and considerable, they go to the Crown. In the same way, if the sea encroach upon private land, such land accrues to the Crown, for the shore between high and low water mark belongs to the Crown.

546. If a river leaves its bed, and flows in a new course or channel, which channel is upon the land of another, the old channel is divided between the contiguous properties in the same manner as an island rising in a public river, if such properties were not bounded by any fixed limits on the side adjacent to the former channel. The new bed and channel occupied by the river becomes as public as the river which flows along them. If the river leaves this second channel, and returns to its former bed, or follows a new channel, the second channel will be governed, as to accession, by the same rules as the former channel was when deserted. Voet, however, states that in Roman-Dutch Law the deserted bed of a public stream belongs to the Crown, in the same manner as an island which arises in a public stream becomes public and goes to the Crown. Inundation, in Dutch Law, does not deprive the owner of the inundated soil of his rights, unless the owner deserts and abandons the ground. If the ground remains under water for ten years, and during that time the former proprietor exercises no act of ownership (such as fishing in the waters covering his land), the land will be regarded as abandoned, and will go to the Crown (41, 1 §§ 18—20).

See G-rotius *(Introd.* 2, 9, 6, 7; *Maasdorp,* p. 72).

547. Artificial or industrial accessions are such as arise by the industry of man. The Roman Law divisions of this classification are *specificatio, pictura, confusio, adjunctio, commixtio, i/iaedificatio,* and *scriptura.* Specification takes place when a person produces from his own materials and the materials of another a new species or thing. If, for instance, a man mixes his honey with another man's wine, or makes a garment of his own cloth combined with that of another, a new species is produced by way of specification, which belongs to the maker, whether the article can be disintegrated into its former materials or not. Although both owners stand in the same position, as far as the materials are concerned, with regard to the thing which is the result of a combination of materials the maker or manufacturer stands in a better position. If a thing has been made wholly from the materials of another person than the maker, it will belong to the owner of the materials, if it was made at his desire, and on his account; but where a thing is made without the consent of the owner of the materials, it will belong to the maker or manufacturer, if the new thing or *species* cannot be disintegrated or reduced to its original materials; but where it can be disintegrated or reduced to its original materials, the new thing or *species* belongs to the owner of the materials. It makes no difference whether the maker knew or did not know that the materials of which he composed a thing belonged to another. If he acted in good faith *(bond fide),* an action will lie against him for the value of the materials *(actio in factum ex lege Aquilid);* but if he acted in bad faith *(maid fide),* an action will lie both for the value of the materials and for damages *(actio furti et condictio furtiva)* for the wrongful conversion; and in the latter case the owner may even have a real action *(rei vindicatio)* to reclaim his materials. If a man embroiders the silk or purple of another into his garment, the silk or purple goes to the maker of the garment by right of accession; and the owner of the silk, where there has been fraud on the part of the maker, will have an action for damages as for wrongful conversion, but not a real vindicatory action, since it is impossible to recover a thing that has been extinguished (so far as its separate existence is concerned) by a real action. An action may, however, be brought for the value of the silk or purple, not only against the maker who has acted in good faith, but against one who has acted in bad faith as well. There can also be a mode of acquiring title through accession, when there is confusion. This is the mixture of things that can be poured together in a fluid state, whether they are of the same or of different natures, such as wine with wine, wine with honey, or different metals, such as gold and silver. If this mixture or confusion *(confusio)* is made with the consent of the owners of the materials, or by accident, the mixture is common property, when the materials are not separable from each other. If the materials are separable, each remains

proprietor of his own materials. If the materials have been intermingled through the act of one proprietor alone, the mixture, if the materials are of the same nature, such as claret with claret, or lead with lead, will belong to the owners of the materials in proportion to their holdings in the materials before the mixture. If the materials are of different kinds, each remains owner of his own materials, if they are separable after mixture. If the materials are of different kinds, but not separable, the mixture will go to the maker of the new thing or substance. Where metals are easily separated from each other by skilled labourers, such as gold from copper, each remains owner of his materials. Building *(inaedificatio)* is another species of industrial accession. If a person has built with his own materials on the ground of another, or on his own ground with another man's materials, that which has been built adheres or accedes to the soil *(inaedificata solo cedit)*, no matter whether the thing so built touches the ground, or another building or wall. If the ground belongs to no one in particular *(res nullins)*, it will become the property of the person who has erected the building. Where a person builds on his own ground with the materials of another, knowing that such materials belong to another, an action *(de tigno injuncto* or *juncto)* will lie against him. Under the term *tignum* are comprised all the materials from which such erection has been made. The action lies for the value of the materials taken, and damages; and the person who knowingly and in bad faith takes the materials of another can, of course, be prosecuted criminally. The owner of the materials cannot claim the materials themselves in a real action, so long as they remain attached to the building, lest the building should suffer on that account. The action will lie against a person who has taken the materials, whether he has done so in good faith or in bad faith. If the materials become separated from the building to which they were joined, and are distinguishable, they can be recovered by a real action (41, 1 §§ 21—24, and 47, 8 §§ 1, 2). 548. In the same

way as buildings, things that have been planted *(implantata)* and sown *(sata)* accede to the soil. They fall under the category of mixed accessions, for industry is required to bring forth the powers of Nature. They are accessory to the ground, which is the principal thing. If a tree has been planted on the confines of an estate, in such a manner that its roots strike into the adjoining property, it will be the common property of the owners of the adjoining estates. If it is planted on the boandary of two estates, and takes root in one estate nlone, it will belong wholly to the owner of such estate. Whoever has sown the grain belonging to another person in his own ground, is liable to the owner of the grain in an action for the value of the grain. And whoever sows with his grain in another man's ground may recover the value of his grain (which, says Voet, can be done by means of an *exceptio doli,* a sort of claim in reconvention: which would seem to indicate that such a claim can only be raised where an action, such as ejectment or trespass, is brought against the person sowing on another man's ground), whether he has acted in good faith or in bad faith (41, 1 § 25).

On the right to crops, see *Bellingham* vs. *Blommetje* (Buch. 1874, p. 38), and *Albtrtyn* vs. *Van der Westhuysen and Others* (5 S. C. 385).

549. Voet assimilates *scriptura,* or writing, to *implantatio,* or planting, though, strictly speaking, it is a purely artificial mode of accession. All writing, albeit in letters of gold, whether the subject is a poem, history, or oration, follows the ownership, according to Roman Law, of the paper or parchment on which it is written. But a person who has in good faith obtained possession of the paper or parchment, may repel the owner of the paper or parchment who seeks to obtain possession thereof, by a plea of fraud *(doli exceptio),* and may retain the substance on which he has written; and, if he loses possession of the paper or parchment, he may recover the same by action. But Roman-Dutch Law provides, simply, that one who has written on the paper of another may re-

tain the same, upon offering to the owner thereof other paper, which is clean, and equally good. With regard to paintings, the modern rule is that the picture belongs to the painter, and not to the owner of the material on which it is painted; unless a man paints on the wall, ceiling, or floor of another man's house (41, 1 § 26).

See *Nelson and Meurant* vs. *Quin & Co.* (Buch. 1874, 48). For remarks of English Judges on the right to retain one's letters or other writings, see *Boosey* vs. *Jeffreys* (4 H. L. C. 396); *Percival* vs. *Phipps* (2 Yes. & B. 19); *Gee* vs. *Pritchard* (2 Swanst. 402); *Labouchere* vs. *Hess* (14 *Times* L. R. 75); and, as to copyright in reports of speeches, *Walter* vs. *Lane* (L. E. Ch. D. 1899, part 2, p. 749). 550. Among mixed accessions the law classes fruits. Fruits are natural, such as are produced without the care or culture of man; or artificial, such as are produced hy human skill; and there is a third class, by a fiction of law called fruits, known to the Roman lawyers as *fructus civiles,* which includes profit in the shape of rent or interest. Natural fruits, or natural fruits artificially produced, are again divided into (a) ungathered fruits, *fructus pendentes,* fruits which still adhere or are attached to the soil, and *(b)* gathered fruits, *fructus exstantes,* which have been separated by reaping, or other mode of gathering from the soil to which they were attached. Fruits may accrue either to the owner of the soil, to a usufructuary, a lessee, a creditor having a pledge by virtue whereof the fruits arising from the property pledged are to go in payment of interest on the pledge, or to a possessor in good faith or bad faith. The owner of a property, when he has gathered the fruits growing thereon, at once acquires title by ownership to the fruits, *ipso jure.* But a *mald fide* possessor of another man's property does not acquire the fruits for himself, but is liable to restore them together with the property to the real owner who claims them, whether such fruits be natural, industrial, or "civil." If a *mala fide* possessor has collected the interest on money belonging to another, the interest is not to be paid over to the real owner of the money, unless he takes upon himself the risk attaching to the principal sum. A *mala fide* possessor of another man's money is liable for the interest due on such money, if he could have obtained such interest, even though the owner of the money was not about to obtain such interest, or, on the contrary, where the owner of the money was about to acquire the interest, although the *mala fide* possessor was himself unable to collect it. In other words, where a person is wrongfully possessed of moneys or securities belonging to another, on which interest is due by a third party, the presumption is that the wrongful possessor has received interest, and he must account for the same. With regard to a *bond fide* possessor, it is laid down that he is only liable for such fruits as are in existence at the time of joinder of issue *(litis contestatio),* or such as are gathered thereafter, or even for such as are still to be gathered, where it is the fault of the *bond fide* possessor that they have not been gathered (41, 1 §§ 28, 29).

Where a husband and wife, married in community, made a mutual will, by which, in case of re-marriage of the survivor, the children of the marriage were to receive one-half of the whole of the joint estate, and there was one child of the marriage, the husband, who survived, married again. He awarded to the child one-fourth of the whole joint estate, which would have been the portion due to the child but for the mutual will. Afterwards, the child discovered that she was entitled to one-half of the joint estate of her parents, and brought an action against her father's executors to recover the one-fourth part still due to her, and for interest. It was decided that she was entitled to her one-fourth part, and to interest from the date of summons only. The Court held that the father had been a *bond fide* possessor of the property in the interval subsequent to his wife's death, and that he was consequently not liable for interest obtained or acquired, and consumed, *before litis contestatio (Cleeuweek* vs. *Beryh,* 2 M. 396). Voet's rule was adopted, that a

bond fide possessor is not liable for interest before *litis contestatio,* even if he has been enriched thereby.

551. Where an action is brought to recover an inheritance, the fruits which have been consumed by a *bond fide* possessor before *litis contestatio* must be restored to the extent to which he has been enriched thereby. In cases of vindication of property (ret *vindicatio),* and similar modes of judicial proceeding, one includes in the category of fruits consumed by the *bond fide* possessor not only those which he has himself had the use of, or which have otherwise ceased to exist, but also such as have been sold, exchanged, or given away by him—even if he still has the value of such fruits; and in such cases the value cannot be recovered from him. The position of a usufructuary is the same as that of the owner, and the usufructuary can only claim against a *bond fide* possessor what the full owner can claim— seeing that fruits, when gathered, at once belong by operation of law to the usufructuary or the owner, as the case may be. Although fruits are acquired by the *bond fide* possessor as soon as they have been separated from the soil, or gathered in other ways, yet it does net follow that they are not to be restored to the owner, who claims his property, together with such property, if they still exist at the time of *litis contestatio.* Here the dominion of the *bond fide* possessor, so far as the fruits are concerned, is revocable, and the purchaser in good faith of fruits from another man's property is considered in law " to make them his own, for the time being, by gathering them," until the real owner claims such fruits as are still in existence, together with the thing or property from which such fruits were gathered or obtained (41, 1 § 29).

In *White* vs. *Adams* (14 S. C. 159) it was successfully argued that even in the case of a usufruct, "one cannot follow *fructus consumptos* against *bona fidt* possessors, and Voet is a direct authority for stating that sale makes *fructus consumptos,* which cannot be followed up. The words 'the purchaser in good faith' *(quippe quos emptor,* etc.) apply only to

a sale of *res aliena."* The Judge President (whose judgment was reversed) quoted Voet for the proposition, "That the acquisition of dominion by a *bona fide* purchaser in such cases, though absolute at the time, is not irrevocable, and that it is still open to the owner to vindicate from him *fructus adhuc exstantes,* together with the property itself. " It was argued by counsel for appellant that Judge President Laurence, in his reasons for judgment, said that the claimholder had a sort of usufructuary right to the claim, and he based his opinion on Van Leeuwen (1 *KotzS,* p. 24; 2, 9, 4): but that passage was based on the yearly growing of things, which, counsel argued, could not be said of diamonds. The Supreme Court (De Villiers, C.J., Buchanan and Maasdorp, JJ.) thereupon held, where the plaintiff, being the holder of a claim in an alluvial digging, had temporarily left it, and another digger took out a licence for the claim and found a valuable diamond in it, but thereafter the inspector of claims decided that the plaintiff was entitled to the claim upon payment of the licence on renewal, and the plaintiff then brought an action against the digger who found the diamond (joining as defendant a person who bought it without knowledge of the trespass), to recover the diamond or its value, that the ownership of the diamond was not vested in the plaintiff. He was therefore held not to be entitled to recover the diamond from a *bona fide* purchaser.

552. It makes no difference, with reference to the question whether a *bond fide* possessor has been enriched by fruits that have been consumed, whether such fruits are natural or industrial. Natural fruits, however, can only be acquired if the *bona fide* possessor has a just title *(justus tituhts).* If he has no just title he is only enriched by the value of such fruits as are the product of his industry; but " natural" fruits he is not enriched by, having to account for their value. If he has a just title to the property, the fact that the *bond fide* possessor has no special usufruct of the thing from which the fruits are derived makes no difference, and the *bond fide* possessor is, neverthe-

less, entitled to both natural and industrial fruits. If a possessor has for some time held the property *bona fide,* and at other times has held the same property *mald fide,* he is entitled to the fruits during the period when he has had *bond fide* possession. If at any time he becomes aware of a defect in his title, and ceases to be a *bond fide* possessor, he no longer has a right to acquire possession of the fruit, even by taking them *(capio)* through a long period of time—seeing that in usucapion the beginning of the occupancy alone is looked at, and there *bond fides* must be present. If a deceased person has possessed property *mald fide,* and his heir thereafter holds the property *bond fide,* the heir is liable to restore the fruits gathered by the deceased, because they never belonged to the deceased; but the heir is not bound to restore the fruits which he has himself gathered and consumed (41, 1 §§ 80—38).

See Grotius (2, 6, 3), and Van Leeuwen *(Cen. For.* 1, 2, 6, 3, 4).

553. Tradition or transfer is the next mode whereby property is acquired. It is the giving or transference of possession from one person to another *(de manu in manum).* It may be actual (real) or fictitious. Real or actual transfer takes place when a corporeal tiling, movable or immovable, is transferred from hand to hand, or by induction into possession. Fictitious transfer is that by which transfer of a thing is assumed or feigned to have taken place, which does not take place in actual fact. This fictitious or constructive transfer, again, is divided into three species: *(a)* transfer *brevi manu* (with the " short hand "); *(b)* symbolical delivery; and *(c)* transfer *longa manu* (with the "long hand"). Transfer with the short hand *(brevi manu)* is that by which a thing which has been previously transferred for another cause, is feigned to have been again transferred for a new cause, and thus another or twofold transfer is avoided. Symbolical delivery is that which takes place by means of a symbol or external sign, which intervenes instead of actual transfer: by this means, transfer of the keys of a granary, in front of the granary,

constitutes a transfer of the goods or produce therein contained. Transfer with the long hand *(longae manus)* is' said to take place when the thing to be acquired by transfer is placed in sight of the transferee, which is allied to placing one in actual custody of the thing (41, 1 § 84).

The case of *(yCallaghan's Atsignees* vs. *Cavanagh* (2 S. C. 122) is a good example of transfer *brevi manu.* There a restaurant keeper put a servant of his in charge of a certain business as manager. The servant then lent his employer money, on condition that he (the servant) should retain the fixtures and furniture in the restaurant managed by such servant as a pledge. The assignees of the employer claimed the furniture from the servant, but it was decided that the pledge to the servant was valid, for "if a servant has goods of his master in his possession, and by a subsequent contract, either by pledge or sale, the property is intended to be passed to the servant, there need not be an actual fresh delivery." In *Heydenrych* vs. *Saber and Others* (17 C. L. J. 68; 10 C. T. R. 129) it was said by De Villiers, C.J.: "No doubt, a mere symbol is not sufficient to effect delivery; the goods must be subjected to the power of the person to whom delivery is intended to be made. That would be effectively done by giving him the key at the warehouse itself. A pledgee who is at the warehouse and has the key in his hand is in a position to exercise immediate power over the contents of the warehouse. The key is in one sense symbolical, but it *is* more than that, for it is the means by which the pledgee is enabled to have access to and retain control of the goods. The fact that the plaintiff did not obtain an assignment of the lease (of the store in which the goods were placed) does not affect the validity of the delivery." In this place Voet does not treat of delivery by *eonstitutum 2,ossessorium,* which will be discussed later on in this work. Symbolical delivery may be ordinary (as in the case of handing over keys), or may consist in cession of a right of action, or may consist in the handing over of title-deeds. In the latter case it

must be noted that, in Dutch Law, transfer *coram lege loci,* is required in the case of immovable property. Delivery *longat maniis* takes place by means of physical transfer, up to a certain point. "It is delivery *de manu,* but not in manual" (De Brayn's *Grotius,* p. 494). For cases on delivery generally, see *Terrington* vs. *Simpson* (2 M. 110. *Goosen's Trustees* vs. *Goosen* (3 E. D. C. 386), and *Haupt's Trustees* vs. *Haupt & Co.* (1S. 296); as to constructive delivery, see *Mills and Sous* vs. *Trustees of Benjamin Brothers* (Buch. 1ST6, p. 115), *Reus* vs. *Barn's Trustee* (2 M. 89), *Ortun* vs. *Reynolds* (3 G. W. B, 219, and 2 A. C. R. 102), *Stewart's Executor* vs. *De Morgan* (2 E. D. C. 205), *Smuts* vs. *Stack and Others* (1 M. 297), *Morkel* vs. *Holm* (2 S. C. 57), *Laing* vs. *Zastron's Executrix* (1 M. 229), *Chapman* vs. *Braham's Trustee* (2 G. W. R. 423), *Coaton* vs. *Alexander* (Buch. 1879, p. 19), *In re Russouw* (1 M. 479), *Hare* vs. *Heath's Trustee* (3 M. 32), and *Guest* vs. *LeRoex's Trustee* (5 S. C. 119). In *Frit* vs. *British United Diamond Mining Co.* (7 S. C. 17), a contract of sale was entered into, whereby the plaintiff was to receive two engines from defendants. The engines were on defendants' property. The question in the case was whether, notwithstanding the fact that the engines remained upon the defendants' premises, there had been such a legal delivery of the engines to the plaintiff as to vest the property in him. It was not stipulated that the sale should be on credit. The plaintiff obtained possession of some fittings forming part of the engines, but the most bulky portions remained upon the defendants' premises. The High Court of Griqualand West (Laurence, J., and Cole, J.; Solomon, J. , dissenting) held that there had been no such delivery of the goods to plaintiff as to vest the property in him. The Supreme Court (De Villiers, C.J., Smith, J., and Buchanan, J.) affirmed this decision. De Villiers, C.J., said: "It is not pretended that it ever entered into the mind of either the plaintiff or of the defendant company's manager that the fittings (which were removed) should be taken as symbols of the engines.

Whether the fittings were removed for safe preservation, as urged by the defendants, or in pursuance of the contract, as urged by the plaintiff, they were not removed for the purpose of symbolising that species of delivery which the law requires in order to effect a transfer of the property." Laurence, J., said: "In order to establish a completed sale according to our (Dutch) Law there must not only be a delivery, either actual or symbolical, but there must be an intention on the part of the vendor to transfer the ownership, and the purchase price must be paid or secured or credit given. " 554. The dominion in a thing does not pass by transfer, unless the person making the transfer is owner of the thing which is the subject of transfer, or unless he transfers with the owner's consent —for instance, if he is a procurator or attorney having a special mandate to transfer, or if he is a general agent with unrestricted powers. There must be the intention to transfer the ownership, and likewise the power to make an alienation of the property: consequently, a minor or a prodigal will make an invalid transfer where the authority of the guardian or curator, as the case may be, has not been given for the transfer. Things which cannot form the subject of private contracts (res extra commercium) can also not be transferred. In order to pass the dominion in a thing, there should be a just cause for the transfer. With transfer must go acceptance, to be made by the person to whom the transfer is intended to be made—so that there may be a common intention on the part of both contracting parties, and a joint act of their will in transferring the ownership. It is also required, in the case of a sale, that the price of the article sold shall be paid to the seller who makes transfer, tir that credit shall be given for the price (41, 1 § 35).

As to the requisites for transfer of ownership, see *Naude's Executors* vs. *ZiervogeVt Executrix* (3 M. 354), and *Beuhes* vs. *Steyn* (Buch. 1874, p. 18), in which the foregoing rules were adopted. In *Greenthields* vs. *Chisholm* (3 S. C. 220) it was said by De Villiers, C.J. : "By English Law the sale of a specific chattel transfers the property to the vendor without delivery. When the agreement for sale is of a thing not specified, as of an article to be manufactured, or of a certain quantity of goods in general, without a specific identification of them, the contract is an executory agreement and the property does not pass. The appropriation of specific goods to the contract which by our law is the test whether the risk passes to the purchaser is, under the English law, the test whether the property passes. By our law the property does not pass to the purchaser until he has performed his part of the contract by accepting delivery, and where the sale is for cash, by paying for the goods or by receiving credit—except where tho purchaser becomes insolvent, in which case, under the (Cape) Insolvent Ordinance, § 105, the vendor loses his *dominium* unless within ten days (in the Transvaal, twenty-one days) of the delivery he had reclaimed the possession of the property by notice in writing. The mere delivery is not enough; there must be an acceptance by the purchaser, 'in order that thus,' to use the language of Voet, 'the minds of both contracting parties may concur and consent to the transfer of the property.' Their intention must, of course, be gathered from their acts; and where a purchaser, through his carrier, has obtained delivery, there is *prima facie* proof of acceptance, but it is not conclusive. If the rest of the evidence clearly shows, as it does in this case, that the purchaser did not accept the goods or intend to accept them, the bare fact of delivery to his carrier is not sufficient to pass the property to him." See *Darnelt* vs. *Cooper* (1 E. D. C. 174).

555. According to Roman Law, if the person making a gift or transfer, and the person receiving the same, are not in agreement as to the cause for the transfer, but agree as to the thing itself which is the subject of transfer, the transfer, if in other respects valid, will hold good. If, for instance, the transferor believes that he is bound to make the transfer, in accordance with the terms of the will, and the transferee receives the property on the assumption that it comes to him by virtue of a stipulation, the transfer will, nevertheless, hold good. If a person pays money to another by way of gift, and that other receives the money by way of loan, the property nevertheless passes. But, where no other act follows in such a case, whereby one party may be made to follow the intention of the other party, the person making the gift of the money may lawfully recall the gift, where such gift has not yet been accepted. But if the recipient of the money has already used the money (believing that it was lent to him) the donor cannot reclaim it, because it was the intention of the donor that the money itself should become the property of the recipient (41, 1 § 36). 556. Where, on the contrary, a person has transferred money by way of loan, and the recipient has taken it by way of gift, the transferor may recover the property. According to Ulpian, if a person by mistake transfers his own property under the belief that it belongs to another, or transfers the property of another under the belief that it belongs to himself, the alienation is null and void. So, if my agent, or the guardian of the minor, makes transfer of his property as if it belonged, respectively, to me or to the minor, the dominion is not thereby lost, since no one loses his property by mistake (nemo *errans rem suam amittit).* Where a person purchases in good faith a thing which belongs to his agent, and thereafter gives a mandate to the agent to sell the same thing to another, and the agent sells the thing while unaware that it is his own property, he will be liable to make transfer to the purchaser; and, if the agent has already made transfer to the purchaser, he cannot recover possession of the thing (41, 1 § 37).

Voet distinguishes between the two cases last-mentioned. Where a man sells his own property under the impression that it is that of his principal, the agent is not regarded as having contracted or sold, but as having transferred on the bare mandate of another—for he has neither bound himself to transfer the thing, nor had he the intention of divesting himself of the ownership. He acts here in the mistaken belief that the thing belongs to another, and the whole transaction is, therefore, based on error. In order to bind himself in such a case, he must know to whom the property belongs, and must have the intention to divest himself of the property. But in the other case, the element of mistake is absent. The agent sells the thing, and his knowledge, mistaken or correct, as to the ownership, plays no part in the transaction. The distinction is very delicate, and is an admirable instance of the hair-splitting in which the jurist Marcellus (on whose authority Voet makes the distinction) indulged. The following is a literal translation of the passage: "The contrary rule has been laid down by Marcellus, where I purchase in good faith and take possession of the slave of Titius, receiving him from a third party, and Titius sells him on my mandate, being unaware that the slave belongs to him. In this case Titius, although he made sale in his capacity of agent, is liable to the purchaser; and, if he has transferred that which is the subject of sale, he cannot revindicate it. There is no conflict between these rules. In the first case (where an agent sells his own property under the mistaken impression that it belongs to his principal) the agent is not regarded as having contracted or sold, but only as having transferred his own property on the mandate of another, as if it belonged to another; and thus, as he never bound himself by his own act to make transfer of the thing to the person to whom he had transferred the thing, on the mandate of another, although it was his own (the Latin words are *tanquam mam,* which may mean either 'although his own 'or 'as if his own'), that nude and mistaken act of transfer could not deprive the transferor of his ownership, seeing that he had never bound himself to transfer the ownership, and never had the intention of transferring the dominion. In the case, again, which Marcellus mentions, the owner sold his own property on the mandate of another, as if it belonged to that other, and transferred the thing when sold; and so he made himself originally liable on his own agreement evidently the contract of agency to the pur-

chaser to make transfer, no less than if he had sold the property of another as if it were his own, so that he could himself, in the case of such a sale, also be called upon by the buyer to make transfer in a direct action of purchase *(actio emti)*—while against the person giving the mandate only an equitable action *(utilii ex onto actio)* would lie. It follows, that if he of his own free will transfers a thing sold by him, he only completes a contract, to the fulfilment whereof he had bound himself; and, by fulfilling it, he makes the person receiving the thing owner *(dominui)* thereof—since in any case it was primarily incumbent on the seller to transfer the thing, and the person doing this, if he were the owner in actual fact, also makes the purchaser owner." 557. In Dutch Law, the mere hadning over of movables is sufficient to transfer the dominion in them, whether this transfer is actual, constructive, or symbolical. Immovable property can only be transferred, to have legal effect, by solemn act in accordance with the law of the place where the transfer is made *(coram lege loci)* and the property is situate; and, upon such transfer, the dues on the transfer must be paid to the Treasury. In the case of such a solemn transfer, acceptance on the part of the transferee is not necessary; and nothing prevents a transfer in favour of an absentee by the owner, or by an agent having a special mandate for the purpose. Nor is revocation of a transfer made in favour of an absentee permissible, seeing that the right of ownership or of possession, once transferred, cannot be revoked in case of repentance on the part of the transferor (41, 1 § 38).

In *Harris* vs. *Buissinne's Trustee* (2 M. 105) it was laid down that: "By the law of Holland, the *dominium or jus in re* of immovable property can only be conveyed by transfer made *coram lege loci,* and this species of transfer is as essential to divest the seller of, and invest the buyer with, the *dominium or jus in re* of immovable property as actual tradition is to convey the *dominium* of movables, and the delivery of the actual possession of immovable prop-

erty has no force or legal effect whatever in transferring its *dominium.* This rule of the law of Holland was not a mere fiscal regulation. It was with the rest of the law of Holland introduced into this (Cape) Colony on its first settlement, and has been acted on invariably ever since, except that, by certain Colonial laws, the Registrar of Deeds has been substituted for the magistrates before whom in Holland transfers were by law required to be made." This is the law all over South Africa. The Cape Ordinance 14 of 1844 provides for the registration of transfer deeds by the Registrar of Deeds. Act 12 of 1858 prescribes the qualifications necessary to enable persons to become conveyancers, for the purpose of transferring land. The transfer duty payable in Cape Law is the sum of two pounds per cent, upon the purchase price or value of any freehold, quit-rent or other leasehold property sold or otherwise alienated. This is payable to the Government by (a) the purchaser of any such property; (6) every person becoming entitled to any such property, by way of exchange, donation, legacy, testamentary or other inheritance, or in any other way than by means of purchase and sale; (c) every person into whose name any such property registered in the Deeds Registry in the name of any other person shall be registered or transferred. Transfer duty must be paid within six months of the date of the sale, exchange, or donation, failing which interest thereon at the rate of 12 per cent, becomes payable. Where property has been bought and sold the purchaser and seller must make solemn declarations in accordance with the forms laid down in the Cape Act No. 5 of 1884 (Schedule 2). Transfer duty generally is regulated at the Cape by Act No. 5, 1884. § 24 of this Act provides that in case of sale by public auction the auctioneer shall ascertain from the highest bidder for whom he purchases, and if such bidder professes to purchase for some other person, the auctioneer, if he approves of the purchaser so disclosed, shall take down the name of the purchaser, whether the bidder himself, or some one for whom he purchases; and there shall be no sale until such, name shall have been taken down. By § 25, if the highest bidder at an auction refuses to disclose his principal when called upon by the auctioneer to do so, the auctioneer shall consider such bidder as being himself the principal purchaser, and the bidder will be held liable as principal; or the auctioneer may, at bis election, treat the sale as null and void. By § 26, if a bidder discloses a principal who afterwards refuses to ratify the sale, and the bidder is unable to produce sufficient authority for the purchase from his pretended principal, the bidder will be personally liable for transfer duty. By § 30 "every private sale or sale made otherwise than by auction, in regard to which the purchaser shall not profess to purchase for himself, in his individual capacity, shall be wholly null and void, unless, at the time of the making and completion thereof, the name of the principal for whom the purchase is made shall be disclosed, and inserted in the note or memorandum in writing, if any, which may be made in regard to such sale." The general lawas to transfer and declarations of purchaser and seller is the same throughout South Africa, with the exception that in the other Colonies the amount of transfer duty on land varies, being 2 per cent, in Natal, and 1J per cent, in the Transvaal. The Dutch Law is derived from the Edict of Charles V., of May 10th, 1529 (Dutch Placaats, vol. 1, p. 373), the Edict of the States General on the fortieth part, § 13 (vol. 1, p. 1957, Dutch Placaats), and the Political Ordinance of 1580 (§§ 37, 38). See also Grotius (2, 5, 13; *Maatdorp,* p. 62), Van der Keessel (§ 202); Schorer (*ad Grot.* § 76); and Van Leeuwen (Cena. *For.* 1, 2, 7, 6). As to the Transvaal, see Proclamation No. 8, 1902, which contains similar provisions to those embodied in the Cape Acts. As to Natal, see Law 5, 1860; Law 19, 1883; Law 19, 1884; and Law 6,1890. As to Orange Biver Colony, see Statute Book, chap. 67.

558. There can be no solemn legal transfer of immovable property in any other place than that in which the property is situate (41,1 § 89).

See *Harris* vs. *Buimnne's Trustee* (2 M. 105), and *Wilson's Trustees. Martell* (2 S. 255).

559. The judicial officer who is charged with the duty of making transfer cannot refuse to give his authority to the transfer, if both seller and purchaser agree to such transfer. If, however, there is no just cause or lawful ground *(Justa causa)* for the transfer of the thing, the officer or Registrar of Deeds may lawfully refuse his authority for the transfer. And, if the contract, on which the solemn transfer is made, is fraudulent or pretended, no transference of dominion is considered to have taken place (41, 1 § 40).

The rules of the Cape Deeds Begistry Office require production to the Registrar of Deeds, before he can give transfer, of the grant or transfer deed C.L.— VOL. I. Z by which the transferor holds the property. The same rules are in force in Natal, the Transvaal, Orange River Colony, and Rhodesia.

560. There are certain modes of alienation, which take effect without any solemn transfer in accordance with the law of the place *(coram lege loci),* and which may be made by mere writing (without registration)—for instance, if the thing passes by way or title of legacy, inheritance, dowry, legal or statutory community of property, or action for division of a joint family inheritance where some special portion of the property is awarded to an individual member of the family. In the consideration of the question, whether a religious body or church may transfer immovable property without solemn transfer in accordance with the law of the place *(coram lege loci),* there is no reason why such cases should be distinguished from those of ordinary persons wishing to transfer their property (41, 1 § 41).

Where a partner in a firm had purchased certain fixed property, and transfer was passed and registration effected in his own name, but the purchase was made with funds belonging to the partnership, it was decided, upon sequestration of both the partnership estate and the private estate of this partner, that the property must be administered as this part-

ner's separate property. The land was, therefore, held to have vested in the partner, and not in the partnership estate, although it was purchased with partnership funds *(Anstruther* vs. *ChippinCs Trustees,* 3 S. 91). The community of property above referred to relates only to community in marriage, and does not refer to ordinary cases of partnership. Voet states (17, 2 § 5) that what a partner acquires beyond the ordinary scope of the partnership he retains as his own property. In support of the contention that the property " vested in the partnership, a case decided by the High Court of Holland (see *Coren,* Obs. 25, No. 49) was cited. There a sharebroker was instructed by his principal to purchase shares in the Dutch East India Company. He purchased them, and with the principal's consent had them registered in his own name. On the broker's insolvency, the Court decided that, notwithstanding the registration in his name, the shares were to be considered the property of the principal. It was said, by Cloete, J.: "It appears to me that, in that case, as reported, the question of registration never was the subject of direct discussion, nor was a doubt ever thrown on the necessity of registration. The whole case there hinged (as it strikes me) on the question in how far property purchased by a broker for his employer could be held to be vested in the former."... "It is clear that by the law of this (Cape) Colony, where a public debt registry has been established to represent all the rights and titles to immovable property, the transfer or title itself is then the only document to which we ought to look."... "It is admitted that the only cases in which our Courts still trace a title to immovable property are those of *fideicommitsum* or entails, or devises under testamentary questions. In these such property may yet be declared to belong to the legatee, devisee, or fideicommissary heirs, without specific title appearing on the deeds registry." See also *South African Loan, Mortgage, and Mercantile Agency* vs. *Cape of Good Hope Bank* (6 S. C. 163), in which it was said that " an agreement between the individual owners of two separate claims to work these claims in partnership would not, by itself, be sufficient to show that they intended each partner to become co-owner of both claims." 561. With the exception of the cases above-mentioned (see § 560), if a person transfers immovable property for a just cause, without solemn form in accordance with the law of the place *(coram lege loci),* he does not by such transfer prejudice his creditors in any way, and they may claim such property equally with the debtor's other goods to satisfy a judgment or claim in insolvency. But such sale will prejudice the seller himself, so that he cannot recover from the purchaser the property thus simply transferred, and his claim may be repelled by an exception *(exceptio rei venditae et traditae);* nor can the seller disturb the purchaser in his possession or in the exercise of his rights of ownership, and if the purchase is dispossessed or disturbed the Court will award him the undisturbed possession. Where possession is transferred in accordance with the local law *(coram lege loci),* there must be no secret or feigned alienation in fraud of creditors. Such a sale will be null and void so far as third parties are concerned, although it will hold as between the seller and the purchaser (41, 1 § 42).

By deed certain title-deeds of a house were pledged. The deed provided that it should be lawful for the pledgees to receive the interest, dividends, rents, and profits, if any, accruing on the bonds and title-deeds mentioned in the schedule to the deed. Afterwards, a deed of assignment, to which the pledgees were parties, was made, whereby the debtor's estate was conveyed to trustees in trust for creditors. It was decided that the original deed of pledge had, nevertheless, the effect of creating an assignment of the rents of the house in favour of the pledgees *(Phillips and King* vs. *Norton's Trustees,* 2 M. 369). See also *Harris* vs. *Buissinne's Trustees* (2 M. 105), and *Wilson's Trustees* vs. *Martell* (2 S. 255).

562. Possession is defined as the detention of a corporeal thing, with the intention of holding it for oneself. It is the de-

tention of a thing certain—whether it be of a thing in common between two possessors held indivisibly (when a thing has been transferred by way of sale or legacy to two persons jointly), or of an undefined share in a defined thing. There can clearly be no possession of an uncertain thing (41, 2 § 1). 563. Possession, in the special meaning with reference to which it is now considered, differs from ownership in certain respects. When an heir achates an inheritance, all the rights in respect thereto, and so all the dominion over the things which are the subject of inheritance, pass to him; but the possession does not pass, unless there is actual natural detention of the things inherited. Dominion may be acquired for one without his knowledge, or even against his wish; but possession must be acquired with the knowledge of the possessor, unless the person who acquires the thing on his behalf makes an express stipulation that the thing shall go to the possessor now in question. Dominion is a matter of law, while possession is a question of fact only (41, 2 § 2). 564. Possession is divided into *(a)* natural, or actual, and *(b)* civil, or juridical. Natural possession is that which exists in actual fact, where a person has corporeal possession of a thing, or holds the thing physically and with the intention to remain the possessor. Such a person may be either the owner *(dominus)* of the thing possessed, or a *bond fide* or *mald fide* possessor. Juridical possession is a legal form of possession, where one has the intention of possessing, and is feigned to possess by right of law, while he has not actual physical possession of the thing. In this way the owner *(dominus)* of a thing, the *bond fide* or *mald fide* possessor, and even a thief, may possess by means of the physical detention of a lessee, borrower, or depositary, or they may even regard themselves as possessing a thing without any physical detention through or by means of any other person. Another distinction is drawn in Roman Law between juridical and natural possession. According to this, juridical possession is that whereby one possesses with the intention or capacity of the owner *(dominus),* in which

way true owners *(domini)* and *bond fide* possessors are said to hold; and natural possession is that mode whereby one holds a thing with the intention of having it for oneself, but not in the capacity of owner *(dominus)*—such as *mala fide* possessors, persons holding by force or secretly *(vi vel clam),* and thieves or robbers. In this way, too, a usufructuary, a creditor holding a pledge, or person holding *jmcario* a thing of which possession has been obtained *precario,* a lessee, or borrower, are said to have natural possession —inasmuch as they severally hold, not with the intention of being owners *(domini),* but with the intention of acquiring for themselves some temporary benefit from possession of the thing (41, 2 § 8).

Savigny *On Possession,* book 1, § 7; *Perry's Translation,* p. 39) lays down the following rules: "Originally, *possessio* denotes mere detention, that is, a nonjuridical physical relation; and it is unnecessary to subjoin any qualification to the term to show that a mere physical relation is intended, so long as no other notion is opposed to it, which makes a qualification necessary. But such detention under certain conditions acquires a legal character, as, through Usucapion, it gives rise to property: it is then called *possessio civilis,* and it now becomes necessary to distinguish every other species of Detention from it in terms; such detention is called *naturalis possessio,* that is, that sort of *possessio* simply which has not become a juridical relation like the *civilis.* But detention becomes a juridical relation in another way also, namely, because Interdicts are founded upon it; it is then termed *possessio* simply, and this is the meaning of the word when it is used without epithet, but nevertheless in a technical sense. All other detention in opposition to Interdict-possession is again called *naturalis possessio,* that is, the physical relation in contradistinction to the last mentioned juridical one, just in the same way as that term is used to express the like antithesis with reference to *civilis possessio."* Savigny then proceeds to give a lengthy exposition of the differences between the two kinds of possession, which is well worthy of reference.

565. Another division of possession is into *(a)* lawful *(justa),* and (6) unlawful *(injusta).* A person is said to have lawful possession when he possesses justly, in the capacity of owner *(dominus),* or without the capacity of owner, but by virtue of legal or judicial authority. In this way persons who hold a pledge are said to have lawful possession (41, 2 § 4). 566. Two persons cannot have corporeal or natural physical possession, *singuli in solidum,* of the same thing at the same time. But they may have possession of the same thing at the same time in different modes, where one of them has the physical detention, and the other has the intention *(animus possidendi)* to possess. Where a farmer goes to town to market, and during his absence another takes wrongful possession of his farm, the farmer has the *animus possidendi,* or intention to possess, while the newcomer has physical possession. Nothing prevents two separate persons from having the *animus possidendi,* or intention to possess, without having actual physical possession. This intention or *animus* may be lawful in the case of the one, unlawful in the case of the other; or both may have an unlawful intention to possess; or both may have a lawful intention to possess. Thus, in the case instanced, the fanner, the rightful owner, may have gone to market, and the usurper may leave the farm with the intention of returning. Here the intention of the farmer is lawful, that of the usurper unlawful, although neither has physical possession. Again, the usurper may have left the farm, intending to return, and during his absence another person may take wrongful possession and leave, intending to return. Here both wrongful possessors have an unlawful *animus possidendi,* without physical detention. Again, during the absence of the lawful owner, a wrongful possessor of the farm may sell the farm to a purchaser in good faith, who may be away from the farm. In this case, both the original owner and the *bond fide* purchaser have a lawful *animus possidendi,* without actual physical detention (42,

2 § 5). 567. All persons may acquire possession, who can have the intention to possess. Corporations may acquire property not by themselves, but through their servants or administrators. Lunatics or minors cannot acquire possession, but their curators or guardians may do so on their behalf, provided they have the intention to acquire for the lunatic or minor, and not for themselves. A minor may himself acquire possession, with his guardian's authority (42,2 §§ 6,7). 568. One may lawfully acquire possession by means of an agent, even without one's knowledge. This possession without one's knowledge may be acquired where at the beginning the principal was unaware that the agent had already acquired those things which were to be acquired under the mandate to the agent. The period of usucapion does not run in favour of persons ignorant that possession has been acquired on their behalf, where the agent has acquired the property of another person. If the agent, to whom possession is given, declares that he wishes to take possession on his own behalf, he acquires, not for his principal, but for himself. But if he only had this intention to hold for himself in his mind, without expressing it, he will acquire possession for his principal, and not on his own behalf. Thus, it was said in *Stewart's Executor* vs. *Be Morgan* (2 E. D. C. 220): "It is abundantly clear that we may retain possession by virtue of our intention through the corporeal detention of another *(Dig.* 41, 2, 3,10). So, instead of acquiring possession in one's own person, we may obtain it through a representative, such as an agent or trustee, the representative acquiring the holding of the property not with the intention of possessing it himself, but for the person for whom he acts and who has the *animus possidendi.* The *constitutum possessorium* is thus a mode of acquisition by substitution through the declaration of the juridical possessor that for the future he will hold in the name of a third person that which he has hitherto held in his own name... . A person who already had the lawful possession of a thing may effect delivery to himself as agent for another

merely by virtue of his own intention, express or implied, to hold the thing in future as agent for another. This intention must, however, be proved not not merely to have existed before the agent obtained the lawful possession, but after he has obtained it; and such intention will not be presumed, but must be proved affirmatively by the person who asserts that a constructive delivery has taken place" (42, 2 § 8). 569. Possession is acquired by tradition (transfer), real or constructive, by occupation, or by accession. It is not necessary that every part of the subject of possession should be physically held, but if one portion of an estate is taken in actual physical possession the whole estate is considered as possessed, provided there is the intention to possess the whole. If there is no such intention, the former possessor retains all such portions of the property as have not been taken in actual physical possession by the new possessor (42, 2 § 9). 570. Possession is not acquired by mere operation of law *(ipso jure),* not even by an heir. Actual possession is not acquired by physical detention alone, or by intention alone, but by both together, although there may be constructive possession *brevi manu,* or by symbolical delivery, or taking by having the thing in one's sight, and declaring one's intention to hold the same. If the subject matter is incorporeal, such as a usufruct, or servitude (whether personal or real), or a right of action, there is no actual possession, but quasi-possession (42, 2 §§'10, 11). 571. Possession is retained by both intention and physical detention; or even by mere intention, so that an absentee owner continues his possession as long as he has the intention to retain it, unless, having become aware that another has acquired wrongful possession, the true owner does not dispute such adverse possession. As we have seen, possession may be retained by intention where there is physical detention by another, such as a lessee, agent, or usufructuary; and such possession is not lost by the death of the persons who have such temporary physical detention (42, 2 § 12). 572. A possessor, while he retains possession, cannot change the ground on which he retains possession *(causa possessionis)*, so far as his own possession is concerned. That is to say, while he has physical detention and the intention to possess, and no external change in the cause *(causa)* of his possession takes place, he cannot resolve to hold on another ground than that on which he has thus far had possession. In other words, assuming that a man has unlawful possession, and no external act has taken place whereby such unlawful possession has become lawful, he cannot, by a mere declaration of intention or will, change his possession from unlawful into lawful detention. This rule holds not only with regard to natural possession, but in the case of civil possession as well. But it does not prevent one from abandoning one's possession on the original ground *(causa)*, and again acquiring possession of the same thing on another ground *(causa)*, by the intervention of some new fact, act, or circumstance, whether actual or constructive. Thus, a depositary may steal the thing or money deposited with him, and apply the same to his own purposes: and, as soon as he forms the intention to steal and appropriate, he ceases to hold the subject-matter as depositary, and continues to hold it as stolen property. An excellent example of this mode of changing the *causa possessionis* is afforded by the case of *O'Callaghan's Assignees* vs. *Cavanagh* (2 S. C. 122), where the manager ceased to hold his employer's furniture as servant, but continued his possession of it as pledgee. Here the *causa possessionis* was changed, the act which sufficed to change it being the constituting of a pledge. The possession was uninterrupted, and no new delivery was necessary, the bare intention to hold thenceforth as pledgee (following upon the contract of pledge) being sufficient. In *Stewart's Executor* vs. *De Morgan* (2 E. D. C. 218) it was said, by Shippard, J.: "Von Savigny, in treating of the *constitutum possessonum*, which in reality, though not in name, was necessarily familiar to Roman lawyers, says that a simple commission without juridical ? judicial au-

thority is sufficient to establish the acquisition of possession through the acts of another; that whoever is in a condition generally to acquire possession for another by his own acts is not the less competent to do so because up to that moment he, the agent, may have had juridical possession of the subject; that in such a case the application of the rule must be differently expressed, inasmuch as the act of prehension, having already taken place, need not be repeated, and the whole transaction may be looked upon as the converse of a *brevi manu traditio;* for, as in that mode of delivery he, who previously had detention without the possession, by mere *animus possidendi* acquires the possession without any new act, so in like manner, in the case of a *constitutum possessonum*, by a mere act of the will possession is converted into detention, and the right of possession itself is immediately transferred to another person— as appears from the following passage of the *Digest:* 'What I possess in my own name I am capable of holding in the name of another; for I do not change the *causa possessionis* for myself, but I cease to possess and make another person possessor through my instrumentality; nor is it the same thing to possess (for oneself) and to possess *(i.e.,* hold) in the name of another. For (in the latter case) the (true) possessor is the person in whose name the thing is held. The agent lends his aid to the possession of another.' In this passage the words ' for I do not change the *causa possessionis* for myself refer to the well-known rule of the Roman Law,'*nemo sibi causam possessionis mutare potest'* —a rule applicable to *possessio naturalis* as well as *chilis.* From what Maicellus says, it is clear that this rule does not apply where the possessor having got rid of his possession wishes to obtain possession of the same thing anew from another *causa"* (42, 2 §§ 18, 14).

See Savigny on *Possession* (book 1, § 7, rule 3; *Perry,* p. 49), and *Haupts Trustees* vs. *Haupt & Co.* (1 S. 296).

573. Besides *constitutum possessorium*, Voet mentions another kind of "*constitutum"* known to the Roman Law.

"Constituere implies an agreement that something shall take place on a certain day or time; hence *pecuniam constituere* is to agree npon a day upon which money owed by the principal, or him for whom he is bound, shall be paid; in the first case it is termed *constitutum debiti propiii*, in the latter *constitutum debiti alieni*. This contract was, of course, of no effect except supported by a stipulation " *(Colqufonm,* § 2076). If a person " constituted " the debt of another by mistake, under the impression that it was his own, this *constitutum* had no effect. All persons could make a *constitutum* who were capable of contracting. The Roman Law gave an action for enforcing this stipulation, known as *actio de constitute pecuniu.* There is, in modern law, no such procedure, and this contract is only mentioned here for the sake of distinguishing it from the *constitutum possessorium.* Voet says this second form *of constitutum,* as distinguished from *constitutum possessorium*, has the effect of suretyship; and the *constitutum debiti,* therefore, would seem to be indistinguishable from suretyship. Even as to the existence of the *constitutum possessorium* in Dutch Law, Voet speaks very doubtfully; and his doubts would seem to be shared by the Judges of the Cape Supreme Court, in *Orson* vs. *Reynolds* (2 A. C. R. 102). It was said by De Villiers, C.J.: "The plaintiff's counsel relies entirely upon the doctrine of the *constitutum possessorium* in support of the appeal. That doctrine has often afforded a refuge to counsel when every other argument has failed, but I am not aware of any case in the Supreme Court in which it has been found applicable. A case has been cited in which the doctrine is said to have been applied by the Eastern Districts' Court, that of *Stewart's Executor* vs. *De Morgan* (2 E. D. C. 205). On reference to the judgments, however, I find that the Judge President alone based his decision upon the *constitutum possessorium*, Mr. Justice Shippard speaking doubtfully upon the point, and Mr. Justice Buchanan not referring to it at all.... In the case of *Mills and Sons* vs. *Trustees of Benjamin*

(Buch. 1876, p. 120), the principles of the *constitutum possessorium were* discussed in the Supreme Court, but the decision was not based upon it.. . No principle is more clearly established than that a *constitutum* is not to be presumed unless its existence necessarily follows from the other circumstances of the case." The Judge President (Barry) appeared to have altered his view after his decision in *Stewart's Executor* vs. *De Morgan,* for in *Orson* vs. *Reynolds* he said: "If the doctrine of *constitutum possessorium* has *any place* in our law, the facts of the present case do not render it applicable." At the same time, none of the Judges have gone so far as to say that *constitutum possessorium* no longer exists in modern Dutch Law. In *Payn* vs. *Yates* (9 S. C. 497) it was said by De Villiers, C.J.: "It is not necessary for Payn to resort to the doctrine of *constitutum possessorium* for the purpose of sustaining his *jus in re.* That doctrine applies where a person who is already a legal possessor undertakes to become the possessor for some one else" (13, 5 §§ 1-14). (2.) Usucapion And Other Modes Op Acquisition. 574. Usucapion was the acquisition of ownership by use. In other words, it was a method of obtaining ownership by continuing possession of the subject of usucapion during a period of time prescribed by the law. This subject is treated of in this place in accordance with what has been laid down by Savigny, although a great many writers treat usucapion, along with servitudes and donations, as one of the species of possession. In reality, the scope of usucapion was much broader, for even servitudes may, under certain circumstances, be acquired by a sort of usucapion. Von Savigny's definition of possession is, perhaps, in some respects, too narrow. He states (book 1, § 2, *On Possession)* that "Throughout the whole Boman Law, there are only two rights which can be ascribed to bare naked Possession independent of all property—namely, Usucapion and Interdicts." This definition has been often criticised; and it is probably incorrect, for the reason that usucapion was a mode of original acquisition of posses-

sion, whereas interdict is a mode whereby possession or ownership, once acquired, is protected or vindicated. Strictly speaking, interdicts would then fall under the law relating to civil procedure. As was stated by Shippard, J., in *Stewart't Executor* vs. *De Morgan* (2 E. D. C. 217), Von Savigny is not quite correct. "Von Vangerow, after mature consideration of Von Savigny's opinions, has enunciated certain propositions which appear to be now generally accepted as sound.... Von Vangerow indicates the true place of possession by distinguishing between the *interdicta retinendae* and *recuperandae possessionis,* the latter, or the *interdictum unde vi,* being really based on an *obligatio ex delicto,* while the former, or *interdicta uti possidetis* and *utrubi,* constitute a primary right universally recognised, or *jus in rem,* having its place in the Code regulating *dominium* along with real actions, or *vindicatio."* But neither Von Savigny nor his critics have made any attempt to place usucapion among the special modes of possession. Modes like use or usufruct confer only a limited possession. But usucapion, once perfected, secured full possession in the same way as title by occupancy, accession, or transfer. A knowledge of this mode of general possession must, therefore, be preliminary to an investigation of the special forms or modifications of possession. It is true that Colquhoun (§§ 1109—1117) makes usucapion a particular mode of acquiring possession; but his classification generally is far from scientific. In the present work, all modes of acquiring possession generally will first be treated of; while special modifications of possession or ownership will be discussed separately. At the present stage, however, the acquisition of title by contract and title by inheritance will not be discussed (41, 3 § 1). Mi Poste (in his excellent commentary on the *Institutes* of Gains, 2, §§ 15—17. third edition, p. 163) says: "We have hitherto spoken of tradition as a title whereby property was acquired. Tradition, however, was only an element, usually the final element, of the complex mode of acquisition jto which it

gives its name. To be capable of passing property, tradition must be accompanied by another element, usually an antecedent element, some contract or other source of obligation, or some evidence of intention to aliene. The same was true of usucapion. Besides possession for a certain term it was requisite that possession should have had an innocent inception or belief of the possessor that he had a right to take possession *(bona /ides).* The second condition of acquisition was indicated by the preposition *pro* governing a noun or participle; the *bona fide* possessor was said to possess *pro emptore, pro donato, pro legato, pro derelicto.* The oondition itself was called the *causa,* or *justa causa,* or *titulus,* of the usucapion; and we may now notice the exact relation of the word Title as used in this commentary to the *Titulus* of the classical jurists. Title, as used by Austin and as used in this commentary, denotes the totality of the complex conditions to which the law annexes any right, *in rem* or *in personam: titulus* as used by the classical jurists is only one portion of the mode of acquisition called Usucapion." This extract suffices to show that usucapion was as general a mode of acquisition of ownership or possession as any other. See *De Bruyn* (p. 483).

575. All persons capable of acquiring ownership could acquire by usucapion. A ward above the age of infancy might have usucapion without his guardian's authority. A lunatic might acquire by usucapion, where the term of usucapion commenced before his insanity (41, 8 § 8). 576 The requisites for usucapion were a just title *(justus titulus),* good faith *(bona fides),* a thing capable of usucapion *(res non vitiosa),* continued possession, a time fixed by law, and absence of mistake in law—which could never be of advantage to the possessor in case of usucapion. Just title *(justus titulus)* is a convenient ground for transfer of ownership, such as purchase or gift—in such a manner that, on the same grounds as the dominion passes on transfer by the true owner, usucapion results where on the same grounds transfer is made by one who is not the

owner. This means that usucapion may take place where the property is passed by one who is not the owner, under the same circumstances as ordinary transfer of ownership would result where title is given by the true owner. In the case of a sale, of course, there is this exception, that ownership is not acquired by the purchaser unless he pays the price, or receives credit for the price; while usucapion *pro emtore* takes place even if the purchase-price has not been paid. This mode of usucapion is discussed later on in this chapter (see § 584). The title must be a true, and not a false one. A false cause does not give rise to usucapion; and so there is no usucapion *pro legato* or *pro dote,* if there has been no legacy or giving of dowry. This, however, does not hold with regard to the acquisition of servitudes by prescription, where *bona fides* (good faith) together with a reputed title *(cum tituli opinione)* is enough, and it is not necessary for the person claiming a servitude by prescription to show how he came by his title. An error in good faith on a matter of fact, as distinguished from error in law, does not prevent usucapion. The necessity for a true title is such, that the burden of proof thereof lies on the possessor. There will be no presumption with regard to the actuality of the title from long-continued possession. If there is a true title, but one which has become null and void by operation of law *(ipso jure),* a distinction is drawn where such nullity arises from mistake in law and mistake in fact. If it arises from mistake in law, as where one imagines that a ward may sell his property without his guardian's authority, or that a donation between spouses is permissible, there can be no usucapion. If it arises from a reasonable mistake in fact, equity— not strict law—permits usucapion: for instance, if a person purchases a thing from a ward without the guardian's authority, believing the ward to be of age, or from a madman, believing him to be sane, or from an interdicted prodigal, when unaware of the interdict. If one title is feigned, while another actually exists—for instance, if a person gives out that he has sold, when he has in reali-

ty made a donation—usucapion will result in accordance with the true mode in which title has been acquired, following the maxim *plus valet quod agitur, quam quod simulate concipitur* (that which is actually done is of greater force than that which is pretended). If a thing is pretended, and neither that nor anything else has been done, there will be no usucapion. If there is a true title, but the possessor is not aware of its existence, there will (according to Sabinus) be usucapion in favour of even the ignorant party (following the maxim *potius substantia sen veritas rei quam opinio spectatiir).* This is different from the case where a person is unaware that possession of a thing has been acquired by his servant or agent. In the latter case, there will be no usucapion—the distinction being that in the first case the possessor is aware that he has possession, but does not know that the title is just; while in the latter case he is not even aware that he has possession (41, 8 §§ 4, 5). 577. *Bona fides* (good faith), the next requisite for usucapion, is a conscientious belief that the property belongs to one, founded on the supposition that the person from whom one acquires possession was the rightful owner *(dominus)* of the thing, and had the power to alienate the same. A person is not regarded as a *bond fide* possessor, who is in doubt as to whether the person from whom he acquired the property was or was not the rightful owner, and had or had not the power to alienate. This *bond fide* belief must exist from the very beginning, and *mala fides* supervening (provided the occupation began in good faith) before the completion of the term of usucapion will not interrupt the usucapion. In this respect usucapion differs from acquisition of ownership by the gathering of fruits *(fructuum acquisitio),* since a *bond fide* possessor only acquires fruits for so long a period as his belief is *bond fide,* and he has no right to the fruits from the moment when he has ascertained that the property from which the fruits are derived belongs to another. The beginning of the period of usucapion is the time of transfer. So, if a con-

tract is entered into for the transfer of the property, and the actual transfer only takes place some time thereafter, the fact that at the date of the contract the transferee believes that the property belongs to another will make no difference, provided that at the date of the transfer he believes that what has been paid or handed over to him has lawfully become his property. In the case of a sale there must be good faith both at the time of the contract and at the time of delivery; and there will be no usucapion *pro emtore* (in the capacity of purchaser), if at the time of purchase the purchaser knew that the property belonged to another than the seller. In the case of a corporation, where occupation begins in bad faith *(mala fide),* and the members of the corporation who have held *mold fide* die or terminate their membership of the corporation, and are replaced by members who continue the occupation of the property in good faith *(bond fide),* their occupation in good faith will not purge or absolve the original occupation in bad faith, and usucapion will accordingly not take place. In case of doubt, there will be a presumption in favour of the *bond fide* possessor, and the burden of proof will be on the person who asserts that the possessor holds in bad faith *(mald fide).* There are certain cases in which usucapion, or prescription *longi temporis* (through a long period of years), takes place, even where the person availing himself of usucapion has knowledge that the thing belongs to another. Thus a discharge from a rural servitude may be obtained in this way: for instance, if A. has a right of way over the property of B., who ejects A. from the way by force, A., if for the period of prescription he ceases to exercise his right, will lose it. Again, if a person has a usufruct, and is ejected by the owner of the usufructuary property, and ceases during the period of prescription to gather the fruits, he will lose his right to them. In the former case the owner of the servient tenement will acquire the right of way, and in the latter the *dominus* (full owner) of the usufructuary property will acquire the usufruct, by usucapion (41, 8

§§ 6—10). 578. The next requirement was that the thing should be capable of usucapion. Servitude and similar incorporeal rights may be the subject of usucapion. Where a building has been joined to another erection, the former must be separately occupied for the period of usucapion *(tignum junctum)*, and the mere fact that the erection!to which it is attached is acquired by usucapion will not give a title to the building so attached, unless that building has been separately acquired by usucapion. In the case of collections of things, such as flocks or herds of sheep or cattle, there will be no usucapion of the flock or herd collectively, but each member of the flock or herd must be separately acquired by usucapion. Things which are incapable of usucapion are: divine or religious things; a dotal estate, if usucapion thereof did not begin before the estate was given at dowry; property burdened with *fideicommissum,* if the same is sold by the burdened person while the condition of the *fideicommissum* is still unfulfilled; adventitious property *(bona adventitia)* of children alienated by their parents, unless the children have neglected, after attainment of majority, to institute proceedings for so long a time that continued possession prevents their claim to the property; property common to all men *(res communes)* by the law of nations; and property of the Treasury or the Crown. This does not apply to unowned property *(bona vacantia),* not yet appropriated by the Treasury: such property is capable of usucapion by prescription of forty years, and after the lapse of that time such property cannot be appropriated by the Treasury, or claimed by the Treasury as unowned property. The appropriation by the Treasury must be made within the period of forty years, to be computed from the day on which it became clear (or was established) that there was no heir or administrator *(possessor bonorum)* of the property. In such a case, there is no need for good faith *(bona fides),* nor just title *(justus titulus),* whether separately or conjointly; and it is sufficient if there has been possession for forty years with the intention of retaining the prop-

erty for oneself. The necessity for prescription during forty years, where good faith and a just title (or one or other of them) are absent, does not prevent one from acquiring ownership by usucapion in the ordinary term of prescription of *bona vacantia* of one year for movables or two years for real property, provided good faith and a just title are present (41, 8 §§ 11—12).

As to usucapion of fideicommissary property, see *De Jager* vs. *Scheepers and Others* (Foord, 123). As to acquisition of Crown property, see *Blanckenberg* vs. *Colonial Government* (11 S. C. 90), and *Jones* vs. *Town Council of Cape Town* (13 S. C. 43). In the latter caso it was laid down that a right to property acquired by prescription affords a cause of action as well as a ground of defence. Voet states, on the authority of Van Leeuwen *(Cens. For.* 1, 2, 10, 10, 11), that prescription of Crown property is, in Dutch Law, the same as that of private property. He does not here use the term usucapion, and it is difficult to ascertain whether he intends in this place to draw a distinction between usucapion and ordinary prescription, or to use prescription as synonymous with usucapion. But from a perusal of Van Leeuwen it seems clear that there is one term of prescription in all cases, whether of usucapion or otherwise—namely, a third of a century. The distinctions of Roman Law between movable and immovable, Crown and private property, have been abolished. In connection with the acquisition of real property by prescription, the *dictum* of the Cape Supreme Court ill *Jones* vs. *Town Council of Cape Town* (13 S. C. 52) should be carefully borne in mind: "Where land has been acquired by prescription, the registered owner may be compelled to do what is in his power in order to confer on the occupier title in accordance with the laws of the Colony." The Supreme Court would seem to have given a free interpretation of the term "a third of a century" required for prescription; for in *Blanckenberg* vs. *Colonial Government* thirty years was taken, both in the pleadings and the judgment, to be the term. See al-

so *Municipality of Frenchhoek* vs. *Hugo* (2 S. C. 248), and *Barnard* vs. *Colonial Government* (4 S. C. 419).

579. The subject of prescription generally forms a portion of the law of civil procedure, and is dealt with under that head. But as prescription is a mode of acquiring possession, it may be stated here that in a latter portion of his commentaries Voet again mentions a third of a century as the period of prescription. The period in Roman Law was thirty years *(longissimi temporis* c.L.—VOL. I. A A *praescriptio, quae jure Romano annis triginta implebatur),* and thit probably led tbe Cape Supreme Court to adopt thirty years as being nearest in round numbers to a third of a century. The former requirement of Dutch Law that there should be undisturbed possession and *bona fides,* is, according to Voet, done away with, and mere occupation for the necessary period will suffice. But one must not allow the period of prescription to be interrupted by disturbance on the part of the true owner, nor recognise him by any conduct or act as the true owner. Interruption will take place where an action is commenced against the possessor, or where he acknowledges his obligation to the real owner, or, in the case of a servitude, permits him to do something in exercise of hit right of servitude (44, 8 §§ 8, 9).

At the present day, prescription occupies the place of usucapion.

580. There is authority in Roman Law for holding that the property of minors, during minority, is incapable of usucapion; and a regulation was made that the prescription of thirty years could not run as against minors. This simply meant that the term of prescription would commence from the attainment of majority. The Roman Law also forbids usucapion of stolen property, unless the stolen property returns to the rightful owner with his knowledge. Van Leeuwen does not refer to the usucapion of stolen property. Usucapion will be still more difficult in the case of property stolen from a minor, for in such a case there is a two-fold objection, that the property is stolen, and that it belongs to a minor.

The same double objection applies to property stolen from a lunatic (41, 8 §§ 13—15).

As bearing on the usucapion of stolen property, it may here be noted that in the Cape Colony criminal prosecutions for theft are barred after the lapse of twenty years. There are similar enactments in the other Colonies and territories of South Africa.

581. The next requisite for usucapion was uninterrupted possession. It must have been lawfully acquired in the first instance, and must have been continuous during the whole of the term requisite for usucapion. There are some cases of actual interruption where the possession is, by legal fiction, regarded as continuous. This happens where a property passes from a deceased person to his heir, from a seller to a purchaser, and in the case of similar universal or particular successors. In the case of possession passing from a seller to a purchaser there must be good faith on both sides, and there must be no defect in the possession. The usucapion of several particular successors in turn will hold good, so long as no one intervenes who possesses in bad faith. If there are five persons, who purchase a thing from each other in succession, and the third purchaser obtains the thing in bad faith (mold fide), and sells it to the fourth purchaser, who takes it in good faith, the fifth purchaser (assuming that he takes in good faith) will only have the benefit of possession by the fourth purchaser, and cannot count the possession of the first and second purchasers (predecessors of the third, who held mald fide) towards the period of usucapion. The good faith of a seller will not avail a purchaser who takes in bad faith. Where, however, a testator has commenced usucapion of a thing in good faith, his heir, even if he act in bad faith, will continue the usucapion, for an heir succeeds to all the rights of the deceased. This will not be the case where the deceased had not yet commenced usucapion of the thing which the heir thereafter acquires from him. Usurpation is opposed to uninterrupted possession: it denotes an interruption of possession and usucapion. By means of usurpation the action in favour of the true owner (dominus) is perpetuated. It may take place either if no opposition is offered by the possessor, or against the will of the possessor. Interruption of the first kind is that which takes place when one abandons a thing, or transfers it to another with the intention of losing the possession: an instance of the latter case is, where one who has begun usucapion of a thing belonging to another, transfers it to the true owner by way of sale, pledge, lease, or similar title. This does not take place where, instead of pledging, one mortgages or hypothecates the thing to the true owner, for, in case of mortgage or hypothecation, one does not part with the possession. Interruption of natural possession takes place against the will of the possessor, where one is forcibly ejected from the possession of immovable property, or if one is deprived of movable property by theft. In such a case, the fact that one afterwards recovers possession of the property by judicial decree will make no difference to the interruption. In a civil (as opposed to a natural) sense interruption of possession and usucapion takes place upon joinder in issue (litis contatatio).

According to Dutch Law (differing in this respect from Roman

Law) a simple summons to appear before a Court is sufficient to interrupt prescription. This view was adopted by the Cape Supreme Court in Van Schalkwijk vs. Hugo and Another (Foord, p. 92), where it was said: "So long as the adverse occupiers remained in actual possession, the course of their incompleted term of prescription could only be interrupted by means of a judicial interpellation in the same way as a creditor can only prevent the term of prescription from running against him by means of a judicial interpellation against the debtor." There will be no interruption of civil possession by a mere extra-judicial interpellation. Judicial interruption of prescription is of advantage only to the person who has taken such legal steps as are sufficient to interrupt prescription, and will not benefit others; following the maxim res inter alios acta alteri nec prodest nec nocet. On the other hand, such interruption will be to the disadvantage only of the person (or his heir) who was a party to such legal proceedings. So, if a debtor has acquired prescriptive possession of a thing which is taken in execution, and the true owner intervenes in the execution, and proves his ownership (in an interpleader suit), and the ownership is adjudged in his favour, the prescription in favour of the debtor is not thereby considered as interrupted—since the interpleader suit took place, not between the debtor and the true owner, but between the true owner, as claimant of the thing taken in execution, and the creditors (41, 8 §§ 16—20).

See Cape Act 6, 1861, § 7; Natal Law 14, 1861, § 6. Both statutes expressly retain the Roman-Dutch Law as to judicial interpellation. 582. With reference to the term of prescription, where the law makes a difference according as a person is present or absent, it is In Hartley vs. Urn kanganyeH (10 N. L. R. 49) it was held that issue of a summons which iB not served isInot a judicial interpellation, and does not interrupt prescription.

laid down that prescription as between persons who are present takes place where they have their domicile in the same territory; while those are regarded as absent who have their domicile in another territory (41, 8 § 21). 583. There were certain special modes of usucapion. One of these is called usucapion by way of payment (pro soluto), which takes place where a person receives that which is the subject of usucapion in good faith as payment of a debt, provided both creditor and debtor believed that the debt was due, and that what was paid belonged to the debtor. If the debt was not due there will be no usucapion, for the debtor will be able to recover what he has paid by the condictio indebiti (41, 3 § 22). 584. Another species of usucapion was usucapion by way of purchase (pro emtore), where a person purchased a thing from one who was not the true owner, or stood (like a ne-

gotiorum gestor, or unauthorised agent) in the place of a purchaser. In this case there must be good faith both at the time of sale and at the time of delivery, and the sale must be unconditional—for as a conditional sale, completed by delivery, does not transfer the ownership to the transferee where the seller is the true owner, so the seller, where he is not the true owner, does not transfer the right to usucapion. It is not necessary that the price shall have been paid, provided the ownership otherwise passes. If a person buys a particular thing, and another thing is delivered to him by mistake, there is no usucapion by way of purchase, because that which has not been sold cannot be the subject of usucapion *pro emtore* (41, 4 §§ 1, 2). 585. The next species was usucapion in the capacity of heir *(pro herede).* Usucapion is continued by virtue of the title of a deceased person, where the deceased had acquired the thing in good faith and by a just title. If the heir knows that the thing belongs to another, he will not acquire it by usucapion; even where he holds the thing by way of loan, lease, pledge, or deposit (having thus acquired it by a lawful title)—since no length of possession will confer on him the property by usucapion, where he is aware that another person is the owner. If a person, who is not the true heir, possesses the property of the deceased in the *bond fide* belief, founded on a reasonable error of fact (not of law) that he is the true heir, or next-of-kin to the deceased, or otherwise entitled to retain the property, he is entitled to usucapion *pro herede,* in respect of such things as were not the property of the deceased—provided he does not know that the things did not belong to the deceased (41, 5 §§ 1, 2). 586. The next species was usucapion by way of gift or donation *(pro donato),* which took place where one received as a gift something from a person who was not the true owner. The gift may be fictitious, for instance, when the transaction is described as a sale, but in reality constitutes a gift. There will, however, be no usucapion, where the transaction is described as a gift, but does not in reality constitute a gift—unless there is a

reasonable mistake of fact, which leads the recipient to believe that the transaction constitutes a gift. If there is a defect in the title to the thing on the part of the donor, such as theft or forcible possession, there will be no usucapion; and there will be no usucapion if the parties are prohibited from making a gift to each other, such as husband and wife. If a thing belonging to another has been given by way of donation *mortis causa,* the donee in good faith may have usucapion against the true owner, but the donor may reclaim the thing so acquired by usucapion from the donee, during the donor's lifetime (41, 6 §§ 1, 2).

Voet states that where a husband makes a gift to his wife of property not his own, but belonging to some one else, without the consent of the true owner, the wife may acquire title by usucapion. It is submitted that the prohibition of donations between spouses is so universal that a husband cannot give his wife another man's property; otherwise the door would be opened to unlimited fraud.

587. Usucapion of abandoned property *(pro derelicto)* was that which took place when a thing had been abandoned by the true owner, in which case it went to the first occupier as if it were *res nullius.* If a person "occupies" a thing abandoned by one who was not the true owner, in the belief that it was abandoned by the true owner, he can acquire the thing by title *pro derelicto,* although he does not know who abandoned it. But if he is aware that it has been abandoned b one who was not the true owner, he cannot have usucapion, since he acts in bad faith. Nor will there be usucapion if one believes that the thing was abandoned, when it was only lost (41, 7 § 1). 588. Another form of usucapion was that which took place by way of legacy *(pro legato).* If a thing belonging to a testator is bequeathed as a legacy, the ownership thereof passes to the legatee by mere operation of law immediately on the testator's death. This form of usucapion takes place when a thing belonging to a third party is bequeathed and delivered to the legatee, who receives the same in good faith, believing

that it belonged to the testator, provided there is no other defect in the title to the thing, such as theft. If a thing belonging to the testator is bequeathed and handed over to the legatee by virtue of a will which is defective, or which, being properly made, is invalidated by a subsequent will or codicil, the legatee may nevertheless acquire title by usucapion *pro legato*—provided the legatee acquired the thing in consequence of a reasonable mistake, not of law, but of fact, believing the will, by virtue of which he has acquired the thing, to be of full force and effect (41, 8 §§ 1, 2). 589. Another species was usucapion by way of dowry *(pro dote),* by which a husband acquired property belonging to another, or held jointly with another, which had been given by way of dowry as if it belonged to the wife. It is necessary that the marriage shall have taken place (41, 9 §§ 1, 2). 590. Usucapion in the belief that the subject thereof is one's own property *(pro suo)* was that which took place when one had obtained the property, in good faith, in any one of the foregoing modes. There are certain other modes treated of by the Roman jurists *(pro transacto, pro jurato, pro judicato, pro adjudicato, pro noxae dedito, pro cesso, pro inanumisso,* and *pro fideicommisso*—which last is similar to usucapion *pro legato),* which have reference to the special procedure of Roman Law, and need not be taken into consideration for practical purposes of modern Dutch Law (41, 10 § 1). (8) Loss Of Possession And Ownership Generally. 591. Possession is lost both by intention and physical act, not by a physical act alone. Thus, a minor docs not lose possession without his guardian's authority, although he ceases to have physical detention of the thing. This refers to legal possession. Actual possession may be lost in various modes, such as theft or captivity of the possessor (41, 2 § 15).

Voet scarcely touches this subject from a general point of view; although there is obviously much difficulty in the distinction between actual physical possession and legal or fictitious possession, such as is not physical, but resides merely in the intention of the person who looks upon himself as the lawful possessor. If, for instance, a person is imprisoned for a term of years, and is at the same time possessed of property, under what circumstances will he lose the legal possession which undoubtedly resides in him, but which he is incapable of exercising during his imprisonment, bearing in mind the fact that he has no actual physical detention? Again, what is the juristic position of an owner of property who, from circumstances beyond his control, is kept away from his country, where he has the *animus possidendi*, but is never able to do anything in exercise of his rights? Von Savigny expresses a view diametrically opposed to that of Voet. In his treatise on *Possession* (book 3, § 31; *Perry,* p. 246) he says: "To enable the Possession to continue, there must be a corporeal relation and *animus.* If either one or the other, or both together, cease, the Possession is lost." This view is supported by Mr. T. E. Holland, who holds that one may acquire possession—apart from market overt—by usucapion of stolen property. The owner of stolen property has the *animus possidendi,* but not the physical ownership. According to the view of most of the jurists who contributed to the *Digest* of Justinian, the thief and holders from him did not acquire possession; but according to the view quoted above, mere loss of physical detention was sufficient to divest one of the possession. It is clear that Savigny refers to physical possession. Voet does not state that he refers to legal possession, as contradistinguished from physical possession. But if Voet refers to legal possession, there is no conflict of opinion between him and Von Savigny. It may be as well to summarise here the views of Von Savigny on loss of possession. The physical relation to the thing possessed, which enables us to deal with it, need not, as in the acquisition of possession, be a present immediate power, but it is sufficient if the relation of immediate dominion over the thing can be reproduced at will, and the possession is only lost when the power to deal with it at will is altogether gone.

The possession of a movable is lost, when another person makes himself master of it, either secretly or by force. Whether the other party actually acquires the possession is altogether immaterial; the physical power of disposing of the subject is withdrawn from us, although no one else may have the right of possession. Our power maybe excluded without the interference of any other party. In the case of immovables, possession is lost whenever the power of dealing with the subject ceases. It is continued so long as this power lasts, except that the notion of this power must be somewhat differently expressed in degree as to continuance, than as to acquisition. The possession of land is lost by every act which disables the previous possessor from dealing with it. It does not matter whether the person who offers the obstruction intends to possess for himself, or merely to put an end to the other's possession. Possession is lost by mere *animus,* whenever the possessor at any moment *intends* to give it up; for, at that moment, the reproduction of the original intention is rendered impossible by the contrary determination of the will, and it is upon this impossibility, as upon the physical impossibility, that the loss of possession arises. As in this case the loss of possession is not founded on a mere negation of will, but on a new act opposed to the former (the *animus possidendi),* it is clear that whoever is incapable of exercising a will cannot lose in this way, any more than he could acquire, possession (§§ 32—34).

(4) Possessory Remedies. 592. The possessor or owner of property is entitled, in RomanDutch Law, upon deprivation of possession, to certain real remedies for recovery of the property of which he has been deprived. Personal actions in Roman Law were known as condictions, while real actions were known as vindications; and the distinction must be carefully borne in mind. Vindication, generally speaking, is the legal assertion of one's right in a thing. In a general sense, dominion or ownership embraces every right in or to a thing; and in this sense dominion may be regarded as ex-

isting in respect even of such incorporeal rights as servitudes. In a stricter sense dominion or ownership is the right by which we own a thing (not merely a certain right of disposal over a thing). In the sense it is either complete, where one is both owner of the thing and possessed of the usufruct thereof, or incomplete, where one has the bare ownership, while another person has the usufruct. Dominion or ownership entitles one to a vindicatory action, which may be denned as a real action whereby we claim that a thing belonging to us, but in the possession of some one else, shall be restored to us. It is a special action *in rem.* A direct vindicatory action lies in favour of those who have acquired ownership of a thing by the law of nations or by municipal law. So a husband will have this action in respect to dotal property, during the marriage, while the wife can only bring such an action upon dissolution of the marriage. Even if the owner of the property is deprived of the usufruct thereof, or has alienated the usufruct, he may bring the vindicatory action. The dominion, whether permanent or temporary, entitles one to the vindicatory action; so fideicommissary property, which only vests Possibly the position may be different where the parties are married by antenuptial contract excluding the marital power. temporarily in a fiduciary heir, will entitle him to a vindicatory action. A person may have such an action even if he had not the possession of the property before the action—for instance, where an heir adiates an inheritance, and so acquires the ownership of the inherited property, without having the possession thereof (6, 1 §§ 1—8).

See Van Leeuwen *(R. D. L.* 4,1, 1; 2 *Kotzi,* 2; and 2, 7, 4; 1 *Katze,* 190) and Colquhoun (§§ 20, 31).

593. In order to sue in this action, the plaintiff must, at the time of the action, have a right of ownership actually vested in him. On the other hand, judgment may be given against the defendant, even if he only acquires possession of the property during the course of the suit. The main question in such a suit is the proof of the plaintiff's title; and he

may recover if he proves his title and shows that the defendant withholds possession from him, or prevents hia obtaining possession: and, for this purpose, mere physical detention by the defendant at any time is sufficient. But if the plaintiff had the dominion at the time of joinder in issue *(litis contestatio),* and lost such dominion before judgment, the defendant cannot be compelled to restore the property to him (6, 1 § 4). 594. One is not deprived of the right of vindication where a third party unlawfully alienates one's property. So a person who has given an express power to an agent to sell a thing for a certain price, say a thousand pounds sterling, may vindicate the property if the agent sells the thing for a lower price than that fixed by his constituent. In the same way, if one authorises an agent to sell for a fixed price, and to give delivery only on payment, and the agent delivers before payment, one may reclaim the thing sold by this action. If a fiduciary heir sells a property before the condition of the *fideicommissum* is fulfilled, the fideicommissary heir, if the condition is afterwards fulfilled, may vindicate the fideicommissary property. If the property was to go to the fideicommissary only on fulfilment of a condition, and he does not fulfil the condition, the fiduciary heir, the property having absolutely vested in him, may part with it if he pleases; but before the time or the opportunity These rules, of course, do not apply to cases where the agent is held out as having full authority. for the fulfilment of the condition arrives, the fiduciary may not alienate. The owner of property alienated by a usufructuary may vindicate the same; and a joint owner, where another joint owner alienates the whole of the property jointly owned, without authority to do so, has the same remedy. In the same way a person may vindicate his stolen property. Stolen property may be recovered, not only from the thief and his heirs, but from any *bond fide* or *mold fide* possessor whatever; nor is there any liability on the part of the true owner to refund the purchase-price of stolen property to a *bond fide* possessor (6, 1 §§ 5—8).

Voet proceeds to give exceptions to the rule that stolen property is recoverable from any possessor. The first exception, he says, is with regard to goods which have been pledged to public pawnbrokers; in this case the true owner cannot recover the goods, unless he first tenders the sum advanced on the goods at the time of pledge to the pawnbroker. There has been no actual decision on this point in South African Courts. Voet does not state that the rule was absolute in Holland. He says that it is usual or general *(quae fere est).* Van der Keessel (§ 184) makes no qualification in this respect He gives three exceptions to the general rule, and states the one now under consideration as follows: There is an exception "in respect of goods, even though stolen, which have been given in pledge to public pawnbrokers." He does not even prefix the term " usually," or "generally." The exception was quoted in *Retief vs. Hamerslach* (2 Kotze's Transvaal Rep. p. 177), but no comment was made on the subject. Other authorities bearing on the point are Van den Berg *(Nederl. Advytboek,* 1, § 223, p. 494); P. Voet (rfe *mobil. et immob. natura,* c. 9, § 8, p. 204); Grotius (2, 3, 6; *Alaasdorji,* p. 53); and Matthaeus *(de Auctionibus,* 1,11, 70). It will be noticed that Grotius makes the qualification with regard to pawnbrokers "unless they knew, or had reasonable grounds for suspecting, that the property belonged to others, and unless they had failed to expose the same to public view for a certain number of days." Grotius treats the case of pawnbrokers and "old-clothes men " on the same footing. Van der Keessel (§ 184), on the othei hand, makes a distinction. Another exception to the general rule, according to him, exists "at some places, in respect of goods sold by 'old-clothes' merchants, after having been publicly exposed for eight days (which is not, however, the general law of Holland, since the purport of the law of March 17th, 1563, and of similar other laws is different). " Van der Eeessel, in the same section, mentions another exception "in respect of gold or silver sold to a goldsmith for a just price, and by him openly ex-

posed." It is conceived, however, that the case of goldsmiths would be in the same position as that of "old-clothes " men, and this view is taken by Barry, J. (3 E. D. C. 105). The enactments relating to both are to be found in a Placaat of the States General, dated March 17th, 1663; and it must be taken that both enactments had the same extent of application. Now, Van der Eeessel states that the exception with regard to "old-clothes" men only existed at some places; and Kotze, C.J., in i?etf«/vs. *Hamerslach,* stated that this exception was only of local application. Van Leeuwen (i?. *D. L.* 2, 7, 4; 1 *KotzS,* 192) makes the eight days' exposure in front of the tradesman's door apply both to " old-clothes" men and goldsmiths; and consequently it seems fairly conclusive that the same conditions applied to either, and that the exceptions with regard to both were of purely local application in Holland, being no longer in force in South Africa. The next exception stated by Voet is one with regard to which some considerable diversity of opinion has arisen in South African Courts. He says that stolen property, which has been sold at markets constituted by public authority *(publicis nundinis,* market overt, public markets), cannot be reclaimed, unless the rightful owner tenders the price paid for the same, provided the purchaser has not recovered the price from the soller. It was decided by the Eastern Districts Court (Barry, J. , Shippard, J., and Buchanan, J.), in *Van der Merwe* vs. *Webb* (3 E. D. C. 97) that the doctrine of market overt, as prevailing in Holland, did not form part of the law of Cape Colony; and, consequently, that the true owner of stolen property sold on the public market at Grahamstown could recover the same as against a purchaser in good faith, without tendering restitution of the price paid by such purchaser. This view of the law was subsequently approved by De Villiers, C.J., in *Woodhead, Plant & Co.* vs. *Gunn* (11 S. C. 4). On the other hand, it was laid down in the Transvaal High Court, by Kotze, C.J., that a purchaser in good faith of stolen property at a public market is entitled to retain such property against the true owner, until the latter repays him the purchase-price *(Retief* vs. *ffamerslach,* 2 Kotze's Bep. p. 171). In *Van der Merwe* vs. *Webb* it was simply said by Barry, J., that: "Unless it be clearly proved that the general law of Holland has imported the exception in favour of public markets there meaning throughout Holland, and moreover that that law has been imported into this Colony, I cannot act upon this exception, and restore to the defendant the price he has paid. The passage to which I referred counsel in Kotze's *Van Leeuwen* (vol. 1, p. 122), and which is a translation of Decker's notes not found in Van Leeuwen's *Commentaries* themselves, is merely a summary of the passage from Matthaeus before quoted, while his reference to Matthaeus *De Auctionibtu* (book 1, 11, 70) only further refers to local customs which I cannot concede are applicable here.... Acting, therefore, upon the civil law maxim so often referred to, as our Common Law, I think that this Court should, like the American Courts, refuse to give effect to privileges of markets where they have not been specially imported into our local law." The maxim in question is *Id quod nostrum est sine facto nostro ad alium transferri non potest* (that which is ours cannot be transferred to another without some act on our part). "From this maxim," said Barry, J., "the owner cannot be deprived of his right of property by the wrongful act of any one who has taken it without title, or who, having it in bis possession for another purpose, sells it." In the same case it was said by Shippard, J.: "It may fairly be argued that as all markets are strictly local, and can only be lawfully held at the stated time in the particular place specified in the grant, the peculiar customs or privileges belonging to markets in one country or district can no more be transferred to another than can the particular grant under which the fair or market is held. This being so, Van der Keessel'srule that the common or general law of Holland cannot be made up or proved out of the particular laws of particular cities or parts of Holland, § 14 applies, and the mere concurrence of

a number of particular laws of particular cities or parts of Holland cannot be regarded as constituting part of the common or general law of

Holland, which on this subject should still be taken to be identical in principle with the Soman Law.... The right to retain property *bond fide* bought, unless the price were returned, applied equally to purchases in every market, great or small, throughout Holland. It does not follow that this last rule has been imported into this Cape Colony. Local ordinances, statutes, or customs can have no force beyond the territory wherein they prevail.... I incline as at present advised to the opinion that what I have ventured to call, for convenience, the Dutch law of market overt, does not form part of the Common Law of this Colony, and consequently that in this case the rule of the Roman Law applies. " Buchanan, J., took the same view. All the Judges in the case admitted that Toet, Grotius, Van Leeuwen, Zypaeus, Matthaeus, and Groenewegen were of opinion that the doctrine of market overt was of general, if not universal application in Holland, but they based their decision on the ground that this doctrine was not shown to be part of South African Law. The case seems to have been decided mainly upon broad grounds of policy. Kotze, C.J., in *Retief* vs. *Hamerslach,* appears to have proceeded on strict legal grounds. He makes the following acute remark: "Grotius, in his *Introduction* (2, 3, 5) says the owner may exercise his right of recovering his property, even from a *bond fide* possessor, without returning the possessor the money he paid for it. Upon which Groenewegen has the following note—that by a charter of Maria of Burgundy, the inhabitants of Holland, Zeeland, and Friesland ' may, with the assistance of the local authority, take possession of their property, which has been stolen or taken away from them, whenever they may find or come upon the same.' If, now, the general rule of the civil law, that an owner may follow up his property at all times, was of such general application in Holland, as asserted by the learned Judges in *Van*

der Merwe vs. *Webb,* what necessity was there for this charter of the Lady Maria of Burgundy?" The author of an article in *The Cape Law Journal* (vol. 5, 1888, p. 70), who criticises the judgments in the foregoing cases, does not attempt—though he dissents from the decision in *Retief* vs. *Hamerslach*—to answer this question: which, indeed, appears unanswerable. It is satisfactory to note that there is agreement on one point in connection with this matter. Kotze, C.J., decided that whatever might be the law as to sale of stolen property in market overt, sales at public auction were not on the same footing as sales in market overt, and property sold by public auction under such circumstances is recoverable by the true owner; and De Villiers, C.J., approved of this view in *Woodhead, Plant & Co.* vs. *Ounn* (11 S. C. 11).

Voet gives another exception, in the case of the recovery of stolen money. According to Roman Law, if money was stolen and paid over by the thief to a creditor, and the creditor mixed such money with his own money, so that the stolen money became indistinguishable, the owner of the stolen money could not recover it from the creditor (presuming that the latter acted in good faith), and had only a remedy against the thief. According to Voet, no such distinction is made in Soman-Dutch Law. It is sufficient if a person received the money in good faith *(bond fide)* from the thief, and it does not matter whether the stolen money is distinguishable or indistinguishable. The true owner of the money cannot recover from the *bond fide* possessor. The mixture or giving in payment of money is regarded as equivalent to spending the same. In *Woodhead, Plant & Co.* vs. *Gunn* (which contains a concise discussion of the subject) it was said: "At the present day every one is agreed that the currency of money is quite incompatible with the right of any one to follow stolen money into the hands of others who have honestly received it for value, whether it has been mixed up with other money or not." Of course, if it is proved that the receiver knew the money to have been stolen, the true owner can recover the same from him (*York* vs. *Van der Lingen,* 1 Ros. 337); and the receiver is also criminally liable. In *Woodhead, Plant b Co.* vs. *Gunn* the Cape Supreme Court extended the doctrine to the case of negotiable instruments which have been placed in such a state that the maker can be sued thereon by any *bond fide* holder, the same being treated in commercial usage as cash. So, where a person stole a Bank of England note for *5I.,* and purchased articles to the value of five shillings from a merchant, to whom he gave the note, receiving in change 47. 15., and the true owner of the note brought an action against the merchant to recover the note, it was decided that he could not succeed. Voet was not cited as a direct authority on the point, but he states clearly (6, 1 § 12) that in one part of the Netherlands, at least—Zeeland—it was enacted by the States General of the province that the owners of written obligations or securities (a sort of debentureshare), made payable to bearer (in the vernacular, *toonder dezes),* cannot vindicate such securities if sold or pledged by others than the true owner, unless upon redemption of the pledge or payment of the price. But, though he states that the custom was prevalent to a considerable extent, Voet considers that the general rule of Roman Law has not been absolutely departed from, and quotes Van Leeuwen *(Cens. For.* 1, 4, 7, 15—17) to show that in Holland such securities could he recovered. It was admitted in *Woodhead, Plant & Co.* vs. *Gunn* that there was a want of unanimity of opinion in the Netherlands on the subject, though De Villiers, C.J., quoted Van der Keessel (§ 525), who states that "When a note or chirograph negotiable instrument has been made payable to the holder, any one who holds it may sue thereon; not only in those places where this is allowed by custom, as in South Holland, Dordrecht, and Amsterdam, but elsewhere also; it being clearly allowed by the reason of our law: excepting, however, where the holder has obtained the instrument from the legal possessor by fraud, and the latter has given timely

notice thereof to the debtor, or the debtor himself can prove *mala fides* on the part of the holder. If the holder himself is in possession of the instrument *bond fide* and by a just title, but the party from whom he derives his title had obtained it by theft, he is still entitled to payment.... If the instrument is made payable to Titius or *the lawful holder,* the holder ought to prove his own right, and if he be a lawful holder, the right of all the prior holders." In any case, whatever might be the Dutch Law on the subject, it was decided in *Woodhead, Plant & Co.* vs. *Gwin* that no doubt existed in the Cape Colony at the present time; and the decision with regard to the *ol.* note was given as above stated. On the authority of Van der Keessel, this may be taken to be the general Roman-Dutch Law on the subject; and Bynkershoek *(Quaestiones Juris Privati,* 2 § 11) agrees with him. The Cape Act 19 of 1893 (Bills of Exchange Act), § 27, enacts that "a holder in due course is a holder who has taken a bill, complete and regular on the face of it, under the following conditions, namely—(o) That he became the holder of it before it was overdue, and without notice that it had been previously dishonoured, if such was the fact; *(b)* That he took the bill in good faith and for value, and that at the time the bill was negotiated to him he had no notice of any defect in the title of the person who negotiated it," and the Act proceeds:

"In particular, the title of a person who negotiates a bill is defective within the meaning of this Act when he obtained the bill, or the acceptance thereof, byfraud or other unlawful means, or for an illegal consideration, or when he negotiates it in breach of faith, or under such circumstances as amount to fraud. A holder whether for value or not who derives his title to a bill through a holder in due course, and who is not himself a party to any fraud or illegality affecting it, has all the rights of that holder in due course as regards the acceptor and all parties to the bill prior to that holder." § 28 of the same Act enacts that " Every holder of a bill is *primd fade* deemed to be a holder in due course; but

if in an action on a bill it is admitted or proved that the acceptance, issue, or subsequent negotiation of the bill is affected with fraud or illegality, the burden of proof is shifted unless and until the holder proves that, subsequent to the alleged fraud or illegality, value has in good faith been given for the bill." The same statutory provisions are contained in Transvaal Proc. No. 11, 1902, 5§ 27 and 28. In *Liquidators of Cape of Good Hope Building Society* vs. *Bank of Africa* (10 C. T. R. p. 597) it was stated that the 27th section of the Cape Act above quoted, so far as it relates to the immunity of *bond fide* holders of stolen negotiable instruments from any claim by the person really entitled to the instrument, was merely a re-enactment of the Roman-Dutch Law on the subject. It was consequently held that where the manager of the plaintiff society, which had an account with the bank, had indorsed cheques made payable to the society (as he was empowered to do), and fraudulently placed them to the credit of his own private account with the same bank, appropriating the proceeds, the bank, which took the cheques in good faith and in due course, was not liable to the society for the amount of the cheques. De Villiers, C.J., in his judgment, stated that the decision in *Woodhead, Plant Jc Co.* vs. *Gunn* was in accordance with the leading English cases, as well as with Roman-Dutch Law. The following English cases (which may with advantage be consulted) were referred to in the judgment: *Raphael* vs. *Bank of England* (17 C. B. 161 —an action upon a bank-note which had been stolen, where the jury found that the plaintiffs had given full value for the note, that they had taken it *bond fide,* that they had no knowledge at the time they took the note that it had been stolen, but had the means of knowledge if they had taken proper care, and the Court held that the plaintiffs, on the finding of the jury, were entitled to judgment in their favour); *Jones* vs. *Gordon* (2 A. C. 616); *Lord Sheffield's Case* (13 A. C. 333); *Joint-Stock Bank* vs. *Simmons* (A. C. 1892, p. 201); *Thomson* vs. *Clydesdale Bank* (A. C.

1893, p. 282); *Hanuaus Lake View Ceutral* vs. *Armstrong* (16 Law Times Eep. 236); *Bryant* vs. *Quebec Bank* (A. C. 1893, p. 179); and *Bessel* vs. *Fox Brothers* (53 L. T. p. 193). To sum up, the exceptions in modern Dutch Law to the general rule that stolen property is recoverable are—(1) in respect of money; (2) in respect of negotiable instruments placed in such a state that the maker can be sued thereon by any *bond fide* holder, and which are by commercial usage treated as cash—but not, it is submitted, in respect of such shares in companies as require some other formality, besides indorsement in blank and delivery, to make them negotiable; as to which see two instructive Transvaal cases, *Warre, Smith and Another* vs. *Phillips* (Hertzog's Rep. 1893, p. 63), and *Afrikanische Bergwerks and Handels Gesellschaft* vs. *Oppenheimer* (Transv. Off. Rep. 1897, p. 432; following *Afrikanische Bergwerks Co.* vs. *French Bank,* Transv. Oft Rep. 1897, p. 471); (3) according to *Retiefva. Hamerslach,* but not according to *Woodhead, Plant Ic Co.* vs. *Gunn,* and *Van der Merwe* vs. *Webb,* in respect of things sold in public market, or market overt.

595. Property taken in war, and sold by the captor, cannot be vindicated by the true owner, for according to International Law the captor acquires full ownership of what he takes in war; and he only loses such ownership on recapture of the property by his enemy (6,1 § 9).

596. Although the true owner can reclaim his stolen property, he cannot claim the price paid for such property, or owing for the same. But the true owner will have a personal action of recovery *(ad exhibendum)* for the price of things stolen and alienated, not only against the thief and his heirs, but against persons who have received the property *mald fide* and with a knowledge that it was stolen, and who have sold or consumed such property. Although, as we have seen, purchasers who acquire property in good faith are liable to return the stolen property to the true owner if it is still in their possession, they are not liable for the price thereof if thereafter they sell the stolen

property in good faith. If a person's money is stolen, and property is bought with such money, the true owner of the stolen money cannot by the vindicatory action claim that the property so bought shall be delivered to him; and he has only a personal action to recover the stolen money, which will lie against the thief, his heirs, or against the person who has, *mald fide* and with a knowledge that the money was stolen, sold his property to the thief for such stolen money. Voet argues strongly in favour of the view that where a depositary, borrower, lessee, creditor, or person holding *precario* holds movable property of another, and sells the same to a *bond fide* purchaser, the same cannot be reclaimed; and in support of his view he goes upon principles of equity, and cites the *Laws of Liibeck* (book 3, tit. 2, § 1), Carpzovius *(Legal Definitions,* part 2, § 26, def. 5, on the Saxon Law), and the *Laws of Antwerp* (tit. 58, § 5): but he does not state that this is general Roman-Dutch Law, and, in the absence of any other enactment of a general nature, it must be taken that in such cases the true owner may claim his property (6, 1 §§ 10—12).

In *Liquidators of Cape of Good Hope Bank* vs. *Be Beers Consolidated Mines and Dunkelsbuhler* (11 S. C. 441), an agent, acting beyond the scope of bis authority, improperly applied certain money of his principal towards the purchase of a concession for himself. He was held liable to account to his principal for all the profits made by him out of the concession, seeing that it was obtained with the principal's money. The agent sold the concession to third parties, who took the same in good faith and for valuable consideration. It was decided that the ownership of the concession had not become vested in the principal, and that the principal could not vindicate the same from such third parties. See also *Castleman* vs. *Strides Executor* (4 S. C. 28).

597. Movable property sold by judicial sale cannot be vindicated by the true owner, where such sale is the ordinary public execution sale for the benefit of creditors, even if the true owner was

ignorant of the sale. Even immovable property, sold by judicial decree, after the customary legal notice, where the true owner does not make timely intervention and oppose the sale, cannot be recovered by vindication. This, therefore, constitutes another exception to the rule as to the recoverability of property wrongfully acquired (6, 1 § 18).

This view was adopted by the Cape Supreme Court in *Lange and Others* vs. *Liesching and Others* (Foord, 55). So (followingalso *Matthaeus,* 1, 11, 33) where property belonging to an insolvent, who held the same as fiduciary heir, was sold by his trustee by public auction, after due notice, it was decided that the fideicommissary heirs, who were of full age and aware of the sale, and did not protest against such sale, could not recover the land from the purchaser, who had bought in ignorance of the *fideicommissum.* From the *dictum* of De Villiers, C.J., to the effect that a public sale of an insolvent's property by his trustee is a sale authorised *ex decreto judicis* (by judicial decree), it follows that in such a case it would have made no difference whether the purchaser knew of the *fideicommissum* or not.

598. Where a person sells a thing, and gives credit for the price, and the ownership thus passes to the purchaser, the seller cannot vindicate what he has sold, and has merely a personal action to recover the price. By delivery he deprives himself of the ownership. If, however, the purchaser obtains the goods on credit, and immediately thereafter surrenders his estate as insolvent, there is no doubt that the seller may vindicate and recover possession of the goods: for in such a cause the sale was occasioned by the fraudulent act of the purchaser, and the sale was itself *ipso jure* null and void, the delivery ensuing without any *justus titulus* in favour of the purchaser. And if, in case of such a fraudulent sale, the fraudulent purchaser has made an underhand or private sale of the thing C.L.—VOL. I. B B bought by him to a third party, the true owner can recover the thing from such third party, without tendering a refund of the purchase-price (6, 1 § 14).

The Cape Ordinance 6, 1843 (Insolvent Ordinance), § 105, enacts that there is no reclamation by vendors Of property sold to an insolvent but not paid for, where no credit was given, and there was an actual agreement or tacit understanding that the price should be paid forthwith in cash, unless either—(o) the vendor reclaims the property in writing within three (altered to ten by Act 38, 1884, § 11) days of delivery of the property and then proceeds, without unnecessary delay, to enforce redelivery of the property by judicial process; or (6) the sale may be rescinded and the property reclaimed on the ground of fraud. See *Harcomhe and Rylands* vs. *Lxlehohn's Trustee* (4 S. C. 225); *Truter* vs. *Joubert't Trustee* (9 C. T. R. 387; 16 C. L. J. 186); *Hare* vs. *KotzS* (2 M. 94); *Quires Trustees* vs. *Assignees of Liddle & Co.* (3 S. C. 322); *Finningly's Trustees* vs. *Breda, Halkett & Co.* (3 S. C. 401); *Drown* vs. *Dyer and Dyer* (3 E. D. C. 267); and *Commissioner for Sequestrator* vs. *Vos* (1 M. 286). In the Transvaal the period of reclamation is twenty-one days (Law 13. 1895, § 42). In Natal, Orange River Colony, and Rhodesia the period is the same as in Cape Colony, under Ordinance 6, 1843.

599. Voet holds that in the case of goods obtained on the fraudulent undertaking that the sale is for cash, and sold on a public market, the same rule applies as in the case of stolen goods sold at market overt, and that the true owner cannot recover the same. But if it be the rule of South African Law (as laid down in *Van der Merwe* vs. *Webb,* 3 E. D. C. 97) that stolen property is recoverable when sold on a public market, the same rule will apply to goods fraudulently bought on the pretence that payment shall be in cash, subject to statutory limitations such as those laid down in § 105 of the Cape Insolvent Ordinance (6, 1 § 14).

600. Voet states that an heir, since he is by a legal fiction regarded as being the same person *(persona)* with the individual whom he succeeds, and is liable for an act of the deceased to the extent to which he is heir, cannot vindicate property of his own sold by the deceased to a purchaser in good faith, to the extent to which he is the heir of such deceased person. In other words, he can only reclaim so much of the value of the alienated property as is in excess of his inherited share. On the one hand, it is difficult to see why the heir should claim at all, as the sale was in good faith, so far as the purchaser is concerned. On the other hand, if the purchaser's liability be admitted, on account of the fraud of the deceased, it is difficult to see why such liability should be limited to the excess above the heir's share. The answer is, of course, that the heir sustains the personality of the deceased *(heres personam defuncti sustinet);* but the rule, from a modern point of view, seems somewhat inequitable. It must, however, be borne in mind that of two innocent persons the one who is the actual possessor has the strongest position *(conditio possidentis).* Despite sentimental objections, therefore, the rule as laid down by Voet must be regarded as still prevailing. He extends it to the case of a ward, who cannot recover from a *bond fide* purchaser property of the ward alienated, without an order of Court, by the deceased person whom the ward succeeds as heir (6, 1 §§ 15,16). 601. A person who, without the true owner's consent, alienates property, cannot vindicate the same if he afterwards succeeds as heir to the true owner, or in any other way acquires the ownership thereof. If a fiduciary heir alienates the property subject to *fideicommissum,* while the condition of the *fideicommissum* is yet unfulfilled, and thereafter, when the condition is fulfilled, becomes liable to fulfil the terms of the *fideicommissum,* and is called upon to do so by the fideicommissary heir, he cannot recover by vindication the property so alienated by him; but the fideicommissary heir (except in the case of a judicial sale of which he has notice, where he does not protest) may recover the property from the purchaser or possessor by vindication, while retaining his right of recourse against the fiduciary heir. If, however, a person has wrongfully alienated property whereof he had not the full ownership, but merely the administration, he may recover

the possession of such property by vindication, unless he brings such vindicatory action for his own advantage, and not for the advantage of the person on whose behalf he administers. So, a guardian, in his capacity as guardian, may recover for the ward property which the guardian has wrongfully alienated (6, 1 §§ 17—19). 602. Those who have never attained the full ownership of a thing have no right to vindicate the same, whether the ownership is to be acquired for themselves or in a representive capacity. Thus persons who have bought and paid for property, which has not been legally transferred to them, cannot vindicate the same; nor have persons the right of vindication to whom a thing has been promised in any other way, but not delivered. Such persons have only a personal action for transfer; and if the property has been alienated, or has passed into the possession of a third party, they can only claim the purchase-price and damages, or damages where the case i& not one of sale. So, if a thing has been sold at different times to two different persons, not the person who first entered into the contract of sale, but the person to whom, on cash payment or on giving credit, the thing was first transferred, will have the vindicatory action—no matter whether the delivery to the purchaser having the right of vindication was actual (even if the documents of title were not handed over to the purchaser) or symbolical (which may take place by handing over documents of title, signature of documents, or *constitution possessorium*— even if there has not been actual physical delivery). If symbolical delivery has first been made to one person, and thereafter actual delivery to another person, the first transferee, on the symbolical delivery, will have the right to vindication. If, however, the property is sold to one person (who receives neither actual nor symbolical delivery), and thereafter another person, knowing of the first sale, buys the property and obtains possession thereof, the first purchaser will have no vindicatory action, because he has not become owner by either actual or constructive delivery; but, according to the opinion of certain jurists (although Voet does not state that this is a general rule of Dutch Law—which it may be taken to be, from an equitable point of view), a personal action will lie against the second purchaser, if his conduct is fraudulent or in bad faith (6, 1 § 20).

Where a person sold an estate to 'another, who paid the purchase-price, and the seller did not give transfer of the property to the purchaser, but surrendered his estate as insolvent, it was decided that the purchaser could not claim as against the trustee of the insolvent estate that the property should be delivered to him, and that the purchaser had only a personal action (ranking as a concurrent claim with the claims of other creditors against the insolvent estate) for the recovery of the purchase-price paid by him. See §§ 553 and 557, above. As to a prior symbolical delivery conferring a better title to vindication than a subsequent actual delivery, see *Clarke* vs. *BradfiM* (6 E. D. C. 23S). See also *Harris* vs. *Buissinne's Trustee* (2 M. 107).

603. An exception to the rule that property purchased with stolen money cannot be vindicated exists in the case of minors, who may vindicate the property purchased with money stolen from them by their guardians. Those persons who have bought or received cession from the true owner of a vindicatory action *in rem* have an equitable vindicatory action against the possessor of the property. Persons who make a donation *mortis causa,* and wish to revoke the gift, or donors *inter vivos,* where the terms of the gift are not fulfilled, have a vindicatory action for the recovery of the gift (6, 1 § 21).

As to cession of a right *in rem,* see *Van Aardt* vs. *Hartley's Trustees* (2 M. 49), In that case a vendor who had not the *dominium* of a farm, but a *jus ad rem,* a right to claim conveyance or transfer, sold the farm, or, in law, his right to the farm, and thereafter surrendered his estate as insolvent without having obtained transfer *coram lege loci.* The *jus ad rem* had been sold and actually delivered before sequestration, and, accordingly, the Court ordered the trustee in

insolvency to give transfer in favour of the purchaser from the insolvent. In a headnote to this case the learned reporter states: "The case of *Harris* vs. *Buissinne's Trustee* (2 M. 105) is distinguished from this case by the fact that there the vendor who had become insolvent had *the jus in re* at the date of the sequestration." 604. The vindicatory action, as we have seen, can be brought against any *bond fide* or *mald fide* possessor (with the exceptions before-mentioned); so that persons who come into possession of property at any time, whether before joinder in issue *(litis contestatio)* or during the pendency of the suit, may be condemned to make restoration of the property. The action lies also against the heirs of the possessor, to the extent of their possession. They are to be sued, not in their capacity as heirs, but as possessors. The remedy will also lie against those who have made themselves parties to the action, unless the plaintiff knows that they had no possession. It will also he against those who have fraudulently ceased to possess, and, if they are dead, their heirs can be sued, being held liable (in an action *in factum)* to the extent to which they have been enriched by such possession; but if action had been commenced before the death of the person who fraudulently ceased to possess, his heirs will be liable to the full extent to which he was liable. Persons who temporarily hold the property, such as lessees, borrowers, depositaries, and the like, may also be sued; though they will be discharged from liability if they indicate the person in whose name they hold the property. No persons are liable to a vindicatory action, who have purchased the property of another from the Crown or the Treasury; and the plaintiif in a vindicatory action against the Treasury must bring his suit within four years (6, 1 §§ 22, 23).

See *Philip Brothers* vs. *Wetzlar* (Buch. 1878, p. 79).

605. It is incumbent on the plaintiff in a vindicatory action to give the full description of what he claims. If, however, he can give no complete description, but is able to furnish sufficient evidence of

ownership from other sources, he may succeed in his action. It is essential, in any case, that the ownership shall be proved. If proof of ownership is not given, the plaintiff cannot succeed. Ownership is proved, by showing that the plaintiff is the lawful possessor of the property, and by proving the cause or title by virtue whereof the dominion passed to him. This may be done by witnesses, documentary evidence, or such other proof as is admissible in a Court of law. In case of the assertion of a claim to immovable property, since such property can only be transferred in solemn form, according to the law of the land *coram lege loci),* if the plaintiff has no other means of establishing his title, it will be sufficient if he proves that transfer was passed to him. Once the plaintiff has proved ownership, he need not show that such ownership is still vested in him, for this will be presumed (6, 1 § 24).

Where a plaintiff claimed certain diamonds from the Chief of the Detective Department at Kimberley, and it was found that the diamonds, though they had been in plaintiff's possession, were not his property, and that sufficient *prima facie* evidence that they were stolen property had been produced by the defence to throw upon the plaintiff the burden of rebutting it and showing that his possession was lawful, the Cape Supreme Court (affirming a judgment of the High Court of Griqualand West), in the absence of such rebutting evidence, gave absolution from the instance in favour of the defendant. It was not proved that the plaintiff knew that the diamonds were stolen. The contention was raised that his bare possession would entitle him to succeed against the defendant unless such possession had been acquired by theft. But it was said by De Villiers, C.J.: "The doctrine that bare physical possession is a good title against a wrong-doer would only apply in the so-called possessory suits, and not in actions for the vindication of an article. Nor would the doctrine apply even in possessory suits unless the wrong-doing amounts to what is termed spoliation. If the defendant, having lawfully acquired physical possession of the article, detains it *bona fide* in the assertion of a legal right, the bare previous possession of the plaintiff would not be enough; but there must have been actual retention of the thing with the object of keeping it for oneself" *(Kemp* vs. *Roper N.O., 2 A. C. R. 141).* For a converse case, see *Robinson* vs. *Roper N.O.* (2 A. C. R. 89).

606. Incorporeal rights cannot be claimed in this vindicatory action. A person may claim part of a thing or property, where he is a part-owner; but he must claim a denned or fixed part, unless he has justification for not knowing exactly what part belongs to him, in which case he may vindicate an uncertain part. This will take place where a legatee sues for the *corpus* of a legacy, and it is uncertain what amount will be deducted by the heir on account of the Falcidian portion (where such portion is claimable); or where things belonging to several proprietors have become so intermixed that they can no longer be distinguished and separated from each other, or even if the mixture is such that separation is difficult. If one's property has to some extent perished, one may vindicate what remains of it. So one may vindicate the site and rubbish (ruins) of a house that has been destroyed. Things which are incapable of individual possession and enjoyment *(commerciis hominum exemtae res,* or *res extra commercium)* cannot lawfully be vindicated. Things which are joined to other things in such a way that, either on account of their natural situation or by disposition of law, they cannot easily be separated, cannot be vindicated (6, 1 §§ 25—29). 607. Property vindicated and recovered by this action must be restored with all its fruits, and in the same condition as it would have been in had it been restored when legal proceedings were first taken. It must be delivered at the place where it is situate, and where the action is brought. If movable property has been fraudulently transferred to another place by the defendant, it must be restored at the place where action is brought at his expense; but if there is no fraud on his part, the plaintiff must bear

the expense of bringing back such movable property. Restitution must be made immediately after judgment, unless the goods are in another place, when the Judge will decree delivery within a reasonable time. If, after judgment, the defendant refuses to give up possession, he may be compelled to do so by force; and he cannot refuse to give possession on the ground that he has a right of pledge or *superficies* (surface enjoyment) or usufruct over the property. If the defendant has not the means of making restitution, and he has fraudulently ceased to possess the property claimed, he is liable for the value of the property, on satisfactory proof of such value being given by the plaintiff, and he cannot claim from the plaintiff any cession of action in respect of such property. If a person ceases to possess through his negligence *(culpa),* not fraud *(dolus),* he is only liable to the plaintiff for the intrinsic (actual) value of the property, and not for the value put upon it by the plaintiff. It makes no difference whether, in such a case, the defendant is a *mala fide* possessor who through negligence has lost possession before joinder in issue *(litis contestatio),* or a *bond fide* possessor who loses possession after joinder in issue; for joinder in issue places a *bond fide* possessor in the same legal position, in this respect, as a *mala fide* possessor was in before joinder in issue. In this case, on restoration, tbe plaintiff must give the defendant cession of action against his predecessors in title, from whom he (the defendant) derived possession, or against the persons to whom the possession has since come. If, however, the property or thing has perished, or the defendant has ceased to possess the same, without either fraud or negligence on his part, but through pure accident (whether inevitable accident or act of God), the defendant, whether *bond fide ormolu fide* possessor, will not be liable. A person, however, who has stolen the thing will in any case be liable. In case of loss by accident, the value of all fruits and other benefits derived from the thing or property up to the date of loss by accident will have to be restored to the plaintiff;

but if the loss resulted through fraud or negligence, the value of fruits or other advantages which would have been acquired, had the thing or property not been destroyed, up to the date of judgment, will have to be paid to the plaintiff (6, 1 §§ 30—35). *Seerf/ervs. Barnato Brothers* (Transvaal High Court, August 29th, 1898) and *Philip Brothers* vs. *Wetzlar* (Buch. 1878, p. 79).

608. If the possessor has incurred any expenses in connection with the thing to be restored, he will have, according to Voet, no action for repayment of such disbursements, but he will have a right of retention until repayment. Nor will he have this right of retention in respect of any disbursements whatsoever made by him. In the case of luxurious expenses (expenses incurred in connection with beautifying a property, or increasing the pleasure thereof), the possessor may remove what has been put up for such purposes, provided this can be done without injury to the property, and retain what has been so removed for himself; but he cannot effect such removal, if the owner is prepared to pay the amount such improvements, if removed, would be worth to the possessor. A possessor, whether *bond fide* or *mala fide,* may also deduct necessary expenses; but a thief cannot claim compensation for necessary disbursements. A *bona fide* possessor may recover useful disbursements to the full extent to which the value of the property has been actually enhanced thereby, although the amount expended may have been greater than the value of the improvement as it stands at the time when compensation is claimed. But if the expense was beyond what was necessary, the *bond fide* possessor may either remove the buildings or erections constituting the improvement (if he can do so without injury to the property), or he may recover from the owner the amount the materials used in improvement would be worth after removal. If, on the contrary, the useful expenditure incurred is less than the actual value of the improvements, the *bona fide* possessor can only recover his actual expenditure. In

other words, his claim is for indemnity, not for probable or possible profits; so that in any case he recovers exactly what he spent. A *maid fide* possessor, on the other hand, has, as a general rule, only the right of removing useful improvements, provided he does so without detriment to the property. After demand he cannot remove the materials, and he can then only claim the amount expended by him for necessary improvements. If the rightful owner knows of the erections made by a *mala fide* possessor, and makes no protest, the *mald fide* possessor may recover, according to Roman Law, not only the necessary, but also the useful expenditure on the property. If the owner is ignorant of the improvements made by the *mald fide* possessor, the latter cannot recover compensation, except, according to Dutch Law, such expenditure as was necessary to protect and preserve the property, and such as comes under the heading of "useful expenses." The *bond fide* possessor is not bound to compensate or set off the fruits or income derived from the improvements against the value of such improvements themselves. But the possessor, whether *bond fide* or *mald fide,* must set off the fruits or income derived from the property itself against the expenses incurred, not only in connection with the acquisition of such fruits or income, but in connection with the property generally (6, 1 §§ 36—39).

The law of Cape Colony (embodying the principles of Roman-Dutch Law) on the subject has been enunciated as follows in *De Beers Consolidated Mines* vs. *London and South African Exploration Co.* (3 C. T. R. 438; 11 C. L. J. 41; 10 S. C. 359)—" (1) A *bona fide* possessor retains his ownership in materials affixed by him to the land until he has parted with the possession. Even after the owner has appeared to demand possession, such *bond fide* possessor may retain possession until he is compensated for his improvements to the extent of the enhanced value of the land, and, failing payment of such compensation, he may remove the materials if he can do so without serious damage to the

land, or he may surrender occupation and recover the compensation by action. (2) A *mald fide* possessor who has affixed materials to the land and, before demand made by the owner, has disannexed and removed them, is not deemed to have parted with his ownership in the materials. After demand, he no longer has. the right to retain the land or remove the materials from the land, nor is he entitled to compensation except for such expenditure as he may have necessarily incurred for the protection or preservation of the land. If, however, the rightful owner has stood by and allowed the erection to proceed without any notice of his own claim, he will not be permitted to avail himself of his fraud, and the possessor, although he may not have believed himself to be the owner, will have the same rights to retention and compensation as the *bona fide* possessor. (3) In the absence of special agreement a lessee annexing materials, not being growing trees, to the soil is presumed to do so for the sake of temporary and not perpetual use, and, as between himself and the owner of the land, does, not, during his tenancy, lose his ownership in the materials. He may, before the expiration of his term, disannex the materials and remove them from the land, subject to the rights of the landlord to demand security against any serious damage to the land, and to interdict any depreciation of his tacit hypothecation for unpaid rent. At the expiration of the lease, however, the owner of the land becomes the owner of all materials then remaining annexed, and even of materials which, having been annexed without his consent, have been disannexed but not removed by the lessee. The lessee has no right of retention after the expiration of his term, but may by action recover the value of the materials annexed by him with the landlord's consent, and the land becomes subject to a legal hypothec for such compensation when duly assessed. Improvements necessary for the protection or preservation of the land may not be removed even during the tenancy, but on the other hand they must be compensated for." The tenant of premises

on a monthly tenancy placed a fence round the premises with the consent of the landlord, and afterwards, upon receiving notice to quit, the tenant claimed from the landlord, as compensation, the value of the fencing material, giving notice at the same time that she would remove the materials before her tenancy expired. The landlord transferred the land before the expiration of the tenancy. It was held, that as the landlord was the person who had let the land to her, with whose consent the improvements had been made, to whose land the materials had been annexed, and who, during the subsistence of the lease, had prohibited the removal of the materials, he was the person from whom the tenant was entitled to recover the value of the materials, and not the present proprietor *(Gibson* vs. *Froet,* 13 S. C. 169). See also *Colonial Government* vs. *Stephan Brothers* (10 C. T. B. 626; 17 C. L. J. 67), *Barnard* vs. *Colonial Government* (5 S. C. 122), *Albertyn and Another* vs. *Van der Westhuysen and Another* (5 S. C. 385), and *Bellingham* vs. *Blommetje* (Buch. 1874, p. 38). In the decision of the case first cited in this note, the Court, while approving of certain views of Voet, preferred to follow Van der Keessel (§ 214), a much later authority, who "places the *maid fide* possessor on the same footing as a lessee who has made improvements without the consent of the lessor." See also *De Vries* vs. *Alexander* (Foord, 43); Huber *(Praelectiones,* 19, 2, 7); Placaat of States General of September 26th, 1658; Burge *(Commentaries,* vol. 2, p. 15); and *Lyons Trustees* vs. *Exploration Co.* (6 G. W. R. 216).

609. The vindicatory action lies in favour of a person who is the full and true owner of a thing or property. In order to protect a person who acquires a thing or property in good faith, but who has not, by usucapion or other mode of perfecting title, acquired the full ownership, an action (known as the *actio Publiciana)* was introduced, which is still in force. The underlying principle of this action is that the right of possession (a fictitious kind of ownership) shall be founded on legal and just

grounds. In this way a person may sue who has acquired property from some person who is not the true owner, provided the transferee acts in good faith and has acquired under a lawful title *(justus titulus)*. In the same way as the true owner may sue in the vindicatory action, the person having this right of possession may sue for its recovery if he loses it without his consent or act. The true owner of property cannot sue in this action, but must rely on the vindicatory action, unless he alleges that he has not sufficient proof of his full ownership, in which case he relies on *bond fide* possession and *justus titulus*. Where the plaintiff sues by virtue of a title which he has acquired through purchase, he need not prove that he has paid for the thing or property. It makes no difference whether at the time of joinder in issue *(litis contestatio)* the plaintiff is a *bond fide* or *mald fide* possessor, provided that the original acquisition was in good faith. Where a person obtained possession in good faith, and his heir afterwards has the possession, and retains it *mald fide,* the heir can nevertheless bring this action. Where a person purchases property from a lunatic whom he regarded as sane at the time of the purchase, he will be allowed this action on equitable grounds (6, 2 §§ 1-5). 610. This action lies against any possessor, whether *bond fide* or *mald fide,* who holds by an inferior title to that of the plaintiff, or who has relinquished his possession by fraudulent means, or has joined in the action as if he were in possession. If, however, a possessor holds the subject of the action by a title which is not inferior, but equal to, that of the plaintiff, the plaintiff will not succeed in recovering possession, in accordance with the maxim *in pari causa melior est conditio possidentis*. This will apply where a *bond fide* purchaser loses possession and brings an action against another person who, after such loss of possession, also purchased *bond fide*. The positions, however, of the plaintiff and the possessor will not be equal or on a par, where the defendant (the present possessor) holds by a lucrative title *(ex titulo lucrativo,* one by which an object

is acquired gratuitously, as by testament or gift), and the plaintiff holds by an onerous title *(ex titulo oneroso,* in virtue of a consideration, such as sale or exchange); and in this case the plaintiff will be in the better position. This action does not lie against the true owner *(dominus),* for his title is stronger than that of any other person (6, 2 §§ 6—8). 611. In this action one may sue for both things corporeal and incorporeal rights, such as real and personal servitudes—provided the incorporeal rights are such as are capable of being acquired by usucapion or prescription (such as rights of surface, *superficies,* and rights acquired under quit-rent, *emphyteusis)*. This action will, consequently, not lie to recover possession of stolen goods; or property of which the law or a last will forbids alienation (and which cannot, on that account, be capable of usucapion); or property, of which there has been neither actual nor symbolical delivery, even if it is such that the property passes, by a legal fiction, without any actual form of delivery (as in the case of property bequeathed to a legatee, and not yet handed over to him or otherwise legally taken in possession). It will be sufficient to entitle one to bring this action if one has had possession for only a moment. The same rules apply with regard to fruits or income, and expenditure or disbursements on the property possessed, as are in force with regard to the vindicatory action (6, 2 §§ 9—11). 612. There are certain other actions to obtain possession or ownership, or to define possession or ownership, which may be conveniently treated of in this place. They are the action for declaration of boundaries *actio finium regundorum),* the action for division of an inheritance *(actio familiae erciscundae),* the action for division of property held jointly in undivided shares *(actio communi dividundo),* and the action for production of property sued for in a vindicatory action or *actio Publiciana (actio ad exhibendum).* 613. "Whenever the boundaries of properties belonging to different owners have become confused in such a way that it is uncertain which is the true boundary of each property,

whether this happens accidentally or through the act of one or other of the owners or of a third party, the action for regulation or declaration of boundaries will lie. Since this action is one for declaration of rights, each party to it appears in a two-fold capacity, as plaintiff and as defendant. Consequently, if a person is empowered as an agent to institute such an action, he is also regarded in law as having power to defend the same. Though regarded in Boman Law as a mixed action, being partly real, partly personal, this action is more in the nature of a vindicatory, and therefore real, action than anything else. It lies in respect of landed properties which are contiguous to one another, or only separated by a private stream. But it does not He if the properties, in respect of which complaint is made that the boundaries are uncertain, are divided from each other by a public road or a public stream—for in such a case no confusion of boundaries is to be apprehended, seeing that the properties are not contiguous, but the public road or public stream which runs between is contiguous to either. So, too, the action will not lie in respect of buildings, seeing that here there can be no disturbance of boundaries, as the buildings are separated by their own wall or a partywall. The action will, however, lie in respect of gardens which are attached to buildings or urban properties, if the boundaries of such gardens have become indeterminate (10, 1 §§ 1—5). 614. The action lies in favour of contiguous proprietors or occupiers of land against those who occupy the property contiguous to that of the plaintiff, whether such contiguous occupiers are full owners, usufructuaries, creditors holding the land in pledge, quitrent holders, or other *bond fide* possessors—since all these have a real right, and it is of importance to their rights that the boundaries shall be defined. But the action cannot be instituted by a *maU fide* possessor; nor by a joint owner of property held in undivided shares, against his co-proprietor, where the boundaries of the plaintiff's private property are confused with the boundaries of the property held in common, unless the joint ownership of such common property shall first have been put an end to, and the shares of the partners determined (10, 1 § 6).

See *Heatlie* vs. *Colonial Government* (5 8. C. 353); *Whitehead* vs. *Shearer') Executrix* (7 C. T. R. 479), *Van Zyl* vs. *Burger* (9 C. T. R. 644), *Huyo* vs. *Russouw and Others* (8 C. T. R. 187), *Swanepoel* vs. *Swanepoel* (9 C. T. R. 584), *Reid* vs. *Surveyor-General* (7 C. T. R. 26), *Barrinyton's Executors* vs. *Colonial Government* 6 C. T. R. 505), and *Barrington* vs. *Colonial Government* (4 S. C. 408).

615. The plaintiff in such an action claims that the Court shall regulate the boundaries which are uncertain, or concerning which there is dispute, and determine what shall be the boundaries of each property. The action may arise out of any circumstances occasioning a confusion of boundaries—whether a party to the suit has built beyond what are regarded as the limits of his property, or planted trees in a similar manner, or removed beacons or terminal stones; or whether such beacons or terminal stones have become indistinguishable through decay or antiquity; or whether trees marking the boundary have been destroyed, or the beacons and boundaries have been obliterated by floods. If the old boundaries cannot conveniently be restored or determined, the Court will fix new boundaries; and, where there has been uncertainty, the Court has the power of removing this uncertainty, and settling disputes, by giving a decree that the boundaries shall run in another direction, or with certain variations; and the Court may even, in order conveniently to fix a boundary, award a portion of land belonging to one party in the suit to the other party, adjudging a reasonable sum of money as compensation. The Court may, in such an action, assign boundaries not to individuals only, but also to several joint-owners holding indivisibly, seeing that the boundaries are assigned, not in respect of the persons, but of the estate in dispute (10, 1 § 7).

In *Hirsch* vs. *GUI* (10 S. C. 156) it was laid down that it is perfectly legiti-mate to refer to the diagram attached to a transfer deed, when the Court wishes to ascertain what the boundary was intended to be. "The case of *Barrington* vs. *Colonial Government* (4 S. C. 408) did not decide, as has sometimes been supposed, that the diagram can be of no service in fixing the boundaries of land. If the diagram is inconsistent with the terms of the grant or with the beacons as pointed out at the original measurement, then the diagram must yield to the evidence afforded by the body of the grant or by such original beacons. But where no such inconsistency exists the diagram affords the most valuable evidence of what was intended to be transferred, and more especially in the case of surveys made since complete accuracy has been insisted upon in the Deeds Office." See also *Van Wyk and Benkes* vs. *Bester* (5 C. L. J. 309), *Clnyton N. 0.* vs. *Metropolitan and Suburban Railway Co.* (10 S. C. 291), *Richards* vs. *Nash and Another* (1 S. C. 312), and *Colonial Orphan Chamber* vs. *Marnitz* (9 S. C. 47).

616. The plaintiff in an action for regulation of boundaries may also claim payment of damages, reparation of injuries sustained through the fraud or negligence, gross or ordinary, of the defendant, and repayment of benefits derived from the possession of the property occupied by defendant which the Court adjudges to belong to the plaintiff (10, 1 § 8). 617. Proof of boundaries may be given by means of public registers relating to land tax, and ancient muniments or documents of title to land; of witnesses who not only state matters within their own knowledge, but state what others relating the circumstances to them had heard and seen in connection with the land in dispute during a long period of time, or what has been handed down by tradition. Where there is a conflict between ancient records and the evidence of witnesses, greater reliance must be attached to the former. Proof may be given as to the boundaries pointed out at the time of sale of one of the properties in dispute by a person who was the owner of both properties in dispute. The Court may also personally inspect the property. The Court may also take into consideration presumptions of law having relation to the matter in dispute (10, 1 § 9). 618. As a general rule, the Court will take as the boundaries those indicated at the last sale of the property of which it is desired to fix the boundaries—the presumption being that such boundaries are still observed and acknowledged, unless they have been altered in the interim by mutual agreement between the contiguous owners. While the action is pending, neither of the owners may interfere with the boundaries (10, 1 § 10).

In *Mostert and De Beer* vs. *Smit* (5 S. 169), certain lots, into which a farm htd been divided after survey, wero sold at auction. The purchasers made no inspection of the ground, but bought according to a plan shown at the auction. The surveyor marked on the plan, in error, a certain line, which purported to be the boundary between the lots held by the parties to the suit; and it appeared that this line was not the boundary intended by the seller. It was not possible, by the adoption of either the line originally intended or that erroneously drawn, to make the superficial area of the lots correspond with the areas indicated in the deed of transfer. The Court held that the purchasers were bound by the plan upon which the sale took place, and that the boundaries laid down in such plan must be taken as binding.

619. This action is prescribed after the lapse of thirty years from the time when uncertainty as to the boundaries first arose. The term of prescription does not run from the date of transfer, but only from the date when the mistake was discovered. Thus, in *Saayman* vs. *Le Grange* (Buch. 1879, p. 10), a transfer deed which, by mistake of the transferor, varied from the terms of the deed of sale of the land, was ordered to be rectified at the suit of the transferee more than forty years after transfer, upon clear proof that the occupation had always been in terms of the deed of sale and not of the transfer deed, and that the mistake had only been discovered within the period of prescription (10, 1 § 11).

A learned translator of this title of Voet states that the time of prescription dates from the time when the dispute first arose. But it seems desirable to substitute "uncertainty" for "dispute," since a defendant may submit to the judgment of the Court without actually disputing the boundaries; and a person may even come to Court and ask for rectification of a transfer without seeking to hold any other person liable. Perhaps the best definition of the commencement of the period of prescription is the time when uncertainty as to the boundaries first arose to the knowledge of the parties concerned.

620. Voet states that no certain rule can be laid down as to the extent of the spaces between buildings. This depends partly on the municipal regulations of the town in which the buildings are, and partly on judicial discretion (10, 1 § 12).

See *London and South African Exploration Co.* vs. *Rouliot* (1 C. T. R. 4; S S. 0. 74).

621. Where a testator has left certain property, which goes to several heirs, and has not indicated how much each heir is to take, the Court decrees a division of the inheritance, in an action brought for that purpose *(actio familiae erciscundae)*. It is open to the coheirs to make a division by mutual arrangement, without going to Court for the purpose. If the action is brought, deduction must in the first place be made of all property in the estate which does not form part of the inheritance to be divided, such as property belonging to a surviving spouse, or property belonging to a third party whereof the deceased had the usufruct or use, or fideicommissary property which was to go to third parties upon his death. In the same way, co-heirs cannot claim a division of damages which the wife and children of the deceased have obtained or may obtain on account of his death through the wrongful act of some person. In the same way, deduction must be made of that which, by virtue of some special law or prerogative of primogeniture, is due to one of the co-heirs alone. Deduction is also made of all prelegacies, which go solely to those whom the testator has indicated as prelegatees. If some of the co-heirs have, in error, permitted division of a thing prelegated to them alone among all the co-heirs, they can obtain plenary restitution *(restitutio in integrum)* against such a division, and a refund of that which is due to them alone and which was erroneously divided among all the co-heirs (10, 2 §§ 1—9). 622. This action lies in favour of those who furnish satisfactory proof that they are co-heirs. If the plaintiff is not in actual possession of the property of which division is claimed, and the defendant denies that the plaintiff is a co-heir, he ought first of all to bring an action for recovery of the inheritance *(hereditatis petitio)*, otherwise his claim may be defeated by a dilatory exception. It makes no difference whether the heirs are testamentary or *ab intestato*, C.L.—VOL. I. C C direct or fideicommissary. An equitable action may be instituted between a purchaser who has bought the share of one of the heirs and the seller's co-heirs. Where there is no denial of the fact that the plaintiff is a co-heir, it does not matter whether the plaintiff, or any of the parties to the suit, are in actual possession of the inheritance, since the matter to be decided is not possession, but ownership. The action may be instituted not against all the co-heirs, but against some of them only; though the Court, where it appears that the interests of the other co-heirs will be affected by the decision, will order them to be joined as parties to the suit. Where co-heirs are absent, the parties instituting the suit may apply for the appointment of curators to represent such absent parties. If one of the co-heirs is dead, his heirs may bring the action which was competent to him against his co-heirs. All such heirs of the deceased co-heir must take action together, or appoint one attorney in the suit to represent them all, for the action cannot be split up. Persons who cannot bring this action are co-heirs conditionally instituted, seeing that they cannot adiate the inheritance until they fulfil the condition of their institution. Those co-heirs who have been unconditionally instituted may, however, bring this action before the fulfilment of the condition by the co-heirs conditionally instituted, saving the rights of the conditionally instituted heirs when they shall fulfil the condition attached to their institution. This action cannot be instituted by wards, lunatics, or prodigals, nor by their guardians or curators; but if it can be clearly shown that the persons under guardianship or curatorship will suffer in their interests if the ownership of the inheritance in undivided shares is continued, leave will be given to the guardians or curators to summon the major co-heirs in an action for division. The Court will also, upon cause shown, order a division of the inheritance, where all the co-heirs are minors. Minors or lunatics may, through their guardians or curators, be made defendants in an action to divide an inheritance (10, 2 §§ 9—16).

623. The costs of such a division will, as a general rule, be ordered to come out of the estate in which the division is made. The Court will not order a division to be made until it is certain that the person owning the estate of which division is claimed is dead. But if a person has been absent for a considerable period, during which nothing has been heard of him, after diligent inquiry, the Court will, in its discretion, allow the heirs, whether testamentary or *ab intestato*, to take possession of the estate, and to divide it in proportion to their shares or claims, on their giving security for the restoration of the property in case the absent person should return (10, 2 §§ 17, 18).

Thus, where a Husband and wife had been married in community of property in 1832, and no will had subsequently been made by either spouse, and the husband sailed for New Zealand in 1864, leaving in Cape Colony his wife and family, with whom he communicated regularly until 1867, when he wrote that he was going to join the war against the Maories, and he was not afterwards heard of, the Court appointed his eldest son to administer the joint estate, to pay over one-half thereof to the wife and to distribute the other half as if the husband had died intestate *(Ex parte Storey,*

3 E. D. C. 150). See also *In re Lavin,* 3 E. D. C. 435), *In re Booysen* (Foord, 187), *Ex parte Westerdyk* (Off. Eep. S. A. R. 1894, p. 48), and *In re Hendrika Julius* (2 8. C. 103). Van der Keessel (§ 163) says: "In case of award's continued absence for a period of sixteen, eighteen, or twenty years, or even a shorter period, his property should, after diligent inquiry has been made in this respect, be delivered over to the next heirs under personal or real security. Where the period has not been defined by law (as in South Africa), it should be left, as well as the matter itself, to the determination of the Judge." See Grotius (1, 10, 5), and Groenewegen *(De Legions Abrogatis, Code* 8, tit. 51).

624. If it is found impracticable to make an equal division, or if it appears that loss will result from such division, particular things may be awarded to certain persons on condition that they shall pay over the excess in value above their own shares to the other co-heirs. The best course to be adopted, according to Voet, is not to award the property to an heir who has the largest share, but to put it up to auction among the heirs, awarding it to the highest bidder, who then pays so much of the purchase-price as is over and above his own share to his co-heirs. If the heirs do not bid, or do not bid sufficient, a stranger may be allowed to come in and buy (10, 2 §§ 19-22).

See *Hoets* vs. *De Smidt* (2 S. 4).

625. Not only one estate or thing, but everything held in common by co-heirs may be made the subject of this action *familiae erciscundae.*

Personal claims—with the exception as to an action for damages for causing the death of the deceased, above-mentioned—fruits derived from an estate or estates, accessions to the property, may all be included in this action. Debts and rights of action are not included, as they are divided among the co-heirs *ipso jure,* so that each heir owes or claims in respect of them in proportion to his share in the inheritance. So, if the estate has been divided, and an heir cannot pay in respect of his proportionate share, the other heirs are not liable for his share. The Court may, in a division

of such claims among the heirs, annex whatever conditions may be just and equitable. A testator may, in his will, whereby he bequeaths property to co-heirs, annex a condition that the property shall not be divided for a certain term, or except on the fulfilment of certain requirements. He may also prohibit any alienation of such property *in perpetuum* (10, 2 §§ 28—29, 82).

626. Once a division of the property has been made by this action, all further actions of the kind are absolutely stayed, unless the division—as we have seen—was made between some of the co-heirs only, and the remaining co-heirs thereafter claim a division. The action for recovery of an inheritance *(hereditatis petitio)* differs from the action *familiae erciscundae* in this respect, that it can be brought against the same co-heirs more than once—provided the claimant is a different person—for the action *familiae erciscundae* is universal in its effect, while the *hereditatis petitio* only settles the rights of a particular claimant. The action *familiae ercvscundae* will also not lie if the testator has instituted one heir in respect of particular property, and another heir without mention of particular property; for the former is regarded as a legatee, and is thus not regarded as having any property in common with the other heir. The same thing happens if one is instituted heir of property in the testator's domicile, and the other heir of property without the domicile; or one is made heir of movables, and the other heir of real property. Where a mistake has been made in awarding a division on a *bond fide* ground of error, the Court will, on cause shown, amend or alter such division. Where a wrong division has taken place by reason of the fraud of one of the heirs, the Court will similarly alter its award. The co-heirs may, even after the Court has given judgment, mutually agree to depart from the terms of the award. Where a division has been agreed upon by common consent, and thereafter the parties continue to hold as if no such division has been made or agreed on, it will be presumed, after the term of prescription has elapsed, that

the division has been tacitly abandoned. Voet does not mention the term of prescription; but it must be taken to be thirty years, as in other actions of this kind (10, 2 §§ 30, 81, 38—48).

627. The next action to obtain ownership or possession is that for division of property held jointly in undivided shares *(actio communi dividundo).* By this action persons who hold a property in such manner ask for a division, and for a performance of such personal obligations as may be due to them in respect of the shares which they hold. It lies in favour of those who jointly hold undivided property, whether there is a partnership between them in respect of such property or not; and whether all, or none, or only one of them is in possession. It does not matter under what titles they respectively hold; whether they are direct owners, or only equitable (such, for instance, as are in occupation of public property farmed out to them); whether they have full ownership, or only surface rights *(superficies);* or whether they are creditors having a right of pledge which has been exercised by their being placed in possession of the property pledged. But other hypothecary creditors, such as mortgagees, cannot claim a division; although, if two persons take a pledge at the same time, an equitable action will lie between them for the division of such pledge. This action does not lie in favour of persons who have a joint praedial servitude in respect of a property which they jointly hold in undivided shares, so far as the division of such servitude is concerned. But an equitable action may be brought to divide the exercise of such servitude, for the purpose of apportioning between the holders of the servitude the extent and times of user. The view of the law in such a case is that it is not a single servitude which is divided, but two or more servitudes existing in respect of the same property, distinguished from each other by their mode of use. This action, likewise, does not lie in favour of partners against a person who has already parted with his share in the property jointly owned; but it will lie in their favour against the person to

whom the outgoing joint-holder has alienated his share. But if the outgoing joint-holder had already incurred a liability in favour of the other joint-holders before alienating his share, whereby he had to perform some personal act, though he will not be liable in the direct action for division, he will be liable in the equitable action. Nor does this action for division lie in favour of persons who hold the property by force, secretly, or on sufferance *(vi clam autprecario)*; nor to depositaries or thieves (10,8 §§ 1, 2). 628. Only things which have been acquired by a lawful title can form the subject of this action; and things acquired on an unlawful or immoral consideration cannot be thus divided. If the Court cannot conveniently make a division, apportionment or allotment must take place in the same way as in the case of an action for division of a joint inheritance *(actio familiae erciscundae)*. In making such division or apportionment the Court will take the course which is most conducive to the interest or wishes of all the parties. "A thing," says Van der Keessel (§ 775), "which does not allow of being divided, such as a house—after it has been offered for competition amongst the part-owners—passes to him who owns the larger share, at the price which the other part-owner has offered for it, unless he prefers to relinquish it for the same price to the smaller shareholder. If the shares of the part-owners are equal, the thing simply passes to him who offers most." If one of the owners in undivided shares has a farm adjoining the common property, the more equitable course is to assign that portion of the common property which adjoins the farm to the owner of such farm, and the other parts to the other owners whose farms do not adjoin. Where one of the joint-owners has, by his fraud, gross negligence, or ordinary negligence, caused loss to the common property, or has prevented the other joint-owners from taking measures for the preservation of the common property, he may be made liable in this action of division for damages as well. So, too, if one of the owners has taken all the produce of the common property,

he may be called upon to pay over to his co-owners their portions; and if necessary, or useful, expense has been incurred in connection with the joint property, such a joint-owner will be liable to make good his portion of expense (see *European Diamond Co.* vs. *Royal Diamond Mining Co.,* 2 A. C. R. 140). But expenditure for luxurious purposes cannot be recovered from him. If a person spends money on property jointly owned by him and others, he will have recourse against such others for their shares, even if at the time he incurred such expense he did not know who such joint-owners were. But if he thought the property belonged to himself alone, he cannot recover the expense by either the direct or the equitable action *communi dividundo;* although he will have a right of retention of the joint property until he obtains a refund of the expenses over and above his share (10, 8 §§ 8, 4). As to claim for partition, see *Dickson* vs. *Stagg* (3 S. C. 115).

629. Where the joint-owners have agreed that for a certain period the joint-ownership shall continue, this action cannot be instituted during such period. But if there was a general agreement that the community should be perpetual, this action may nevertheless be instituted. An agreement, however, for a perpetual community will prevent this action for division being instituted, where the thing or property held in common is of such a nature, that a division would be useless to the joint-owners (in other words, that they could make no use of the parts when divided), and that the property could not be awarded to one or other of the joint-owners without involving great expense to the remaining joint-owners: for instance, where there is a common lobby or yard between two houses (10, 3 § 5). 630. This action may be instituted more than once between the same parties, since it is not so universal in its nature as an action for division of an inheritance, and nothing prevents one from recovering that which has not yet been divided. The action is not barred by the fact that the joint-owners have continued to hold the property in undivided shares for over thirty

years. But it is prescribed if each owner has held a separate portion of the property for more than thirty years (10, 8 § 6).

Voet mentions some trivial cases, which are scarcely worthy of notice for practical purposes. Thus, he says, the action does not lie in respect of a tree growing on the boundary of two properties, or a large mass of stone or rock lying partly on one farm, partly on another.

631. No alteration in the form of the common property (such as a building) can be made by one owner if the other objects. In such a case, the person who objects is in a superior legal position, and he can compel the person making the alteration to restore the property to its former condition. But if one of the joint-owners has knowingly permitted (but not authorised) a stranger, not having a share in the property, to make an alteration, such joint-owner is liable to pay damages for such alteration, but is not compellable to restore the property to its former condition (10, 3 § 7).

See Van der Keessel (§ 777), who agrees with this, but adds that a part-owner, who has the smaller share in a house, may, without the other part-owner's consent, cause the same to be repaired; a view which is in accordance with equity, repairs coming under the head of necessary expenses.

632. There is no doubt that one joint-owner of property held in undivided shares may, against the will of the other joint-owner, dispose of his interest in the property, by sale, donation, or otherwise, to a third party. But such transfer of rights cannot be made after the action for division of the property has once commenced, where the other joint-proprietors object. Voet expresses a doubt as to whether this last rule (as to transfer after commencement of action) has not been abrogated by the *Code* (4, 38, 14); but there is no Roman-Dutch decision on the subject (10, 3 § 7). Van der Keessel (§ 772) does not seem to hold that the rule as laid down by Voet is of universal application. Of course, where there is agreement among all the joint-owners, a division may be

made in whatever way meets with the wishes of those interested. In *Registrar of Deeds* vs. *DeKock* (Off. Bep., Transvaal. 1897, p. 108), it was held that three joint-owners of two forms may divide such farms among one another in equal shares, as they please, without payment of transfer duty. As to modifications or dispositions relating to common property by one joint-owner without the consent of the other joint-owners, see *Oosthuysen* vs. *Du Plessis and Another* (5 S. C. 71), *Van Wyk* vs. *Van Wyk* (2 E. D. C. 403), and *Strydom* vs. *Tiran* (Buch. 1873, p. 84).

633. If a joint-owner sells the portions of the other joint-owners without their consent, he does not prejudice them in any way; unless the property jointly owned consists of merchandise, bought with the object of being resold, for in such a case one joint-owner may sell the whole of the merchandise. If several of the joint-owners agree to the sale of their shares in common property—other than merchandise—while some object, and the property is sold, only the shares of those who consent go to the purchaser (10, 8 § 7). 634. If there is a disagreement between joint-owners of houses or lands as to the letting of such property, in so far as some wish to let the property, and others object to letting it, and the use of such property cannot conveniently be divided among the joint-owners, the entire property should be let—that is, the wish of those joint-owners desirous of letting it should prevail. If one of the co-owners wishes to have the entire use of the property, on payment of the same rent as the stranger offers, the co-owner will have the preferent right to the lease (13, 8 §§ 8, 9). 635. As a general rule (according to Van der Keessel, § 776) one joint-owner cannot compel another to make public sale, by auction, of property held in common by them— with the exception of ships, which may be sold by a majority of the owners, by public aale. This rule follows as a corollary to what has been laid down above (§ 688); for if a joint-owner cannot be injured by a sale without his consent, he cannot be compelled to make such sale. 636. A co-owner of landed prop-

erty is not entitled, without the consent of his co-proprietors, to appropriate part of the soil for the purpose of making bricks, whether such bricks are to be used on the place or not *(Oosthuysen* vs. *Muller,* Buch. 1877, p. 129). 637. Where land has been transferred by one and the same deed to two or more persons, one co-owner has no implied or tacit authority to pledge the transfer deed as security for the charges of a commission agent in attempting to raise a loan on mortgage of the land at the request of such owner without the consent of his co-owners *(Jewell and Rutter* vs. *Hazell and Steer,* 14 S. C. 16). 638. Since there cannot be a vindicatory action without certainty as to the property or thing to be vindicated, a plaintiff, where the thing or property claimed is hidden or detained by a third party, or is joined to some other thing or property (in such a way that a separation can be legally demanded), may have recourse to an action for production of the property which is the subject of the vindicatory or possessory suit, this subsidiary action being known as the *actio ad exhihendum.* It is a personal action, and only movables can be the subject thereof. It lies in favour of those who have an interest (not necessarily of a pecuniary nature) in the movables which form the subject-matter of the action, provided such interest arises from a lawful, just, and reasonable cause, and from a real right in or to the movables *(jus in re).* It makes no difference if the plaintiff afterwards proceeds, not in a vindicatory action, but in a personal action. It lies in favour, not only of those who assert a right of ownership, but of those who claim a right of possession, or who claim a right of pledge, or a right of usufruct; or if those who proceed civilly for recovery of property which has been stolen *(actio furti),* or who proceed by way of interdict. By this action, too, the production of fruit which has fallen into another man's ground may be claimed. This action is prescribed after the lapse of thirty years (10, 4 §§ 1, 2). 639. The plaintiff in this action must give a complete description of the thing sued for: and he must show that it is of impor-

tance to him that the article should be produced, both at the time of joinder in issue *(litis contestatio),* and when judgment is given, in the other action. If the production of the thing is of importance to several persons, each of them may institute an action for production. Any possessor or detainer of the movables in question may be sued; likewise those upon whose ground the movables have been placed by such agencies as inundation or tempest. The movables must either be in the possession of the defendant at the time when the action is brought, or must have been fraudulently disposed of by the defendant (10, 4 § 3). 640. The things which form the subject of this action must be produced together with all fruits and accessions, and in the same condition as they were in when notice of action was first given. Where it is impossible to produce the thing with fruits, or in the same condition, the Court may award damages to the plaintiff. If the thing cannot at once be produced, the Court may order security to be given for its production (10, 4 §§ 3—6). 641. Another mode of procedure to enforce one's proprietary or possessory rights is by interdict. An interdict may be applied for with the object of either acquiring or retaining, or recovering possession. In some respects the Roman and Roman-Dutch mode of procedure by interdict corresponds to the English remedy of injunction, but in the majority of cases interdicts discharge a function to which injunctions can lay no claim—not merely affording relief, partial or total, against the wrongful or tortious acts of another, but conserving and protecting to the fullest extent one's rights of property. Mr. J. J. Casie Chitty (in his excellent translation of *Voet on Vindications and Interdicts)* says: "It is in the law of property and of real actions that ' the superiority both of the Roman and Roman-Dutch Law over the English in point of simplicity and completeness, as well as in freedom from anything approaching to technicality or refinement,' referred to by Mr. Charles Lorenz in his preface to his translation of Van der Keessel, is more distinctly seen." We find, in the first place, that the vindicatory action *rei vindicatio)* is parallel to the English actions of ejectment, detinue, and trover; while the *actio Publiciana in rem* corresponds to trespass, and ejectment as a possessory action. But the Roman and Roman-Dutch Law was very effective, as we shall see, in its interdict procedure. In Roman Law, an interdict was a provisional or conditional command issued by the Praetor on an *ex parte* statement by an applicant—similar to the English injunction in Chancery, or mandamus in the Courts of Common Law. It was open to the defendant or respondent to show cause against such a command, in which case the Praetor remitted the hearing to a magistrate *(judex)* to try the issue of fact. (See Austin's *Jurisprudence,* pp. 508, 609). Justinian somewhat modified the early form of procedure, and interdicts were framed as *formulae,* whereby the Praetor ordered or forbade something to be done. In Roman-Dutch Law, when the matter in dispute was ownership, possession, or quasi-possession, resort was had to vindicatory, possessory, and interdict actions. By an extension of the procedure relating to interdicts, they came to embrace matters which were not within their scope in strict Roman Law. They then came to be issued in cases where irreparable injury or damage would ensue but for the granting of an interdict, or where there would be danger in the delay which would necessarily take place if a regular suit were instituted. With interdicts in their relation to the law of torts we are not now concerned. 642. An interdict may be regularly sought in Roman-Dutch Law by action. It is sufficient for the plaintiff to set forth the facts of the case, and to pray for an order of Court operating as an interdict. The common mode of procedure in an action to obtain an interdict (generally of a perpetual nature), or in a possessory action, is to proceed by way of motion for an interlocutory order, which order, when granted, operates as a provisional interdict restraining the respondent (defendant in the action) from doing certain things until the principal action shall have been decided one way or

another. The claim for a perpetual interdict, in a possessory action, or action for declaration of rights, is in itself a principal suit, and once such a claim has been decided the matter is *res judicata* between the parties. The principal Roman interdicts in possessory cases were *uti possidetit, utrubi,* and *unde vi;* and actions analogous to these still survive in Roman-Dutch Law. Another possessory interdict, in suits of inheritance, was the interdict *quorum bonorum.* There were certain others, to which brief reference will be made hereafter. They were the interdicts *quod legatorum; ne vis fiat ei qui in possessionem viissus erit; dc tabulis exhibendis; ne quid in loco sacro fiat; ne quid in loco publico vel itinere fiat; de loco publico fruendo; de via et itinere publico reficiendo; ne quid in flumine publico ripdve ejus Jiat quo pejus navigetur; ne quid in fiumine publico fiat quo aliter aqua Huat atque uti priore aestate fiuxit; ut in fiumine publico navigare liceat; de ripu muniendd; de vi et vi armatd (unde vi); de superficiebus; de itinere actuque private; de aqua quotidiand et aestixd; de rivis; de fonte; de cloacis; quod vi aut clam; de precario; de arboribus caedendis; de glande legendd; de homine libero exhibendo; de uiigrando;* and *interdiction Salvianum.* Some of these belong to the law of servitudes, such as those relating to rights of way and water-rights, and will be treated of in connection with the law of servitudes. The interdict *de homine libero exhibendo* corresponds to the English procedure under the Habeas Corpus Act, and, properly speaking, forms part of the law of persons; but it will be treated of in connection with the law of procedure (48, 1 §§ 1—8). 643. In possessory interdicts not only the principal thing, but the fruits or income derived therefrom come into consideration. The granting of an interdict relating to a thing prevents the person interdicted from disposing of such fruits as shall have accrued after the date of granting of the interdict, but it does not operate with regard to fruits acquired before the date of the interdict. Neostadius (from whom Voet does not express dissent) is an authority for saying that

where the defendant is a wrongful possessor the interdict will operate as to fruits acquired since the date of wrongful possession (48, 1 § 4). 644. The action to obtain possession and the claim for an interdict entitling one to retain possession (or restraining the respondent from interfering with the possession) may be conjoined in one action. And the claim for an interdict may be instituted while the action to obtain possession, or to confirm one's possession, is pending. Mere enjoyment of possession will not prevent one from obtaining a possessory interdict, for one's possession may be disturbed. The fact that an action has been brought to obtain possession does not operate as *res judicata* (or bar) in an action to obtain a possessory interdict. But if one has failed in an action to obtain possession (such as a vindicatory suit), and thereafter institutes a claim for an interdict, the burden of proof of ownership or right of possession lies upon him, and not upon the person against whom the interdict is sought. There is an exception to the general rule in the case of the interdict *uti possidetis,* which cannot be conjoined with an action claiming possession or ownership, such as the vindicatory action. It is obvious that the two claims are inconsistent: in the suit for an interdict *uti possidetis* one asks for the confirmation of the possession which one has had up to the time of claim; whereas, in the vindicatory action, one seeks possession of that which one has hitherto not had in possession, though entitled to it. But one is not prevented from instituting a vindicatory action in the first place, and then abandoning it, and thereafter resorting to a possessory interdict *(retinendae possessionis).* Interdicts are commonly known in Dutch Law as mandates or "mandaments." The Courts will generally grant such interdict only where it appears that the rights of the applicant are being interfered with, or where another person has exceeded his rights which have been declared to belong to him by virtue of some action, or where there will be danger in case of delay (such, for instance, as would arise from bringing a regular action), or where irreparable loss or damage threatens, or where the law provides no other remedy by action. As a general rule, penal mandates of a prohibitory nature, where the respondent is condemned to specific performance, are only granted where there is danger in delay, or when it is a question of spoliation, and such interdicts are only made to operate for a limited period. In other cases where penal mandates are granted, they are generally granted unconditionally, or so as to take effect for a certain time. No one is to be deprived by means of a penal mandate of possession which he has had for a year and a day, without force, secrecy, or tenure on sufferance (non *vi, clam, vel precario*). Where the interdict is granted in connection with a possessory action, and such action is not decided at the same time as the interdict is granted, the plaintiff usually obtains an operation of the interdict until judgment is given in the principal suit (48, 1 §§ 5—9).

In *Boh* vs. *Transvaal Gold, Exploration and Land Co.* (2 Kotze, Transv. Bep. p. 75), where, from the petition in support of an application for an interdict, it appeared that no act had been committed by the respondent interfering with the alleged rights of the petitioner, nor that any well grounded apprehension existed that such act would be committed, the Court refused to grant the application. In *Ex parte Francken* (2 Kotze, Rep. p. 53), where application was made for an interdict restraining the respondent from alienating or mortgaging his property (under the Transvaal Law 1, 1874, § 55), pending an action to be brought against him by the applicant, it was held that as the petition did not set forth that the alleged debtor was by his acts jeopardising the creditor's interests, the interdict must be refused. Where, upon an application to make absolute a rule *nisi* operating as a provisional interdict, it appeared from the affidavits of the parties that a right of property was in dispute between the parties, and that this right could not be satisfactorily determined on affidavit, the Court refused the application, leaving the applicants to their remedy by action *(Barrett Brothers*

vs. *Rauteribach,* 2 Kotze, Rep. 64). 645, "The interdict *quorum bonorum,* according to Savigny, was the remedy whereby a successor, whether civil or praetorian, and, if praetorian, whether *contra tabulas* or *secundum tabulas* or *ab intestate,* having already, in response to his demand *(agnitio)* of the succession, obtained from the Praetor the formal grant *(datio)* of *bonorum possessio,* maintained his title thereto before the tribunals if he met with opposition; just as *hereditatis petitio* was the remedy whereby the civil successor could have maintained a corresponding claim to the *heredita*" (Poste's *Gaius,* 3rd ed. p. 601). According to Voet, this interdict is still in force in Roman-Dutch Law. It lies in favour of those who have been placed, in the ordinary course, in possession of an inheritance, or who have been declared entitled to an inheritance in a suit brought for that purpose; and is transmissible in favour of heirs or successors. It lies against those who have possession *pro herede* or *pro possessore* (see *Voet,* 41, 5 §§ 1, 2; above, § 585), when their possession is disputed, or when they have fraudulently made away with or disposed of the subject of inheritance—provided no other has acquired title to the inheritance by usucapion. The interdict will not lie against those who assert that they are the full owners of the property in question, if they can prove the plea of ownership—which may be raised in defence to this claim for an interdict. It will not lie against those who have been appointed heirs by will, where the will is clearly free from defect. It will not lie against debtors to the estate (of the deceased), and in this respect differs from an *hereditatis petitio.* The claim to an inheritance *(hereditatis petitio)* will lie in respect of incorporeal things or rights, whereas the interdict *quorum bonorum* has reference only to corporeal things. The interdict is applicable whether the estate devolves by testament or *ab intestato.* If the heirs *ab intestato* have possession of an inheritance, and are confirmed in it by public authority (such as the authority of the Master of the Supreme Court in South African

Colonies), the heir who has been instituted by a testament having no visible defect visible defect, *visibile vitium,* Voet defines as the omission of the date of execution, or the omission of the legal number of witnesses; but not forgery, or destruction, or other informality in a testament, or denial of the testator's power to make a will may obtain possession by means of the interdict *quorum bonorum* from the legitimate heirs *(heredes legitimi),* since mere succession by intestacy is not sufficient to repel the claim of a person who has been designated heir by will. Persons who have been instituted heirs by testament may claim to be admitted to share the inheritance with the heirs ai *intestato* who are in possession. If one person has been instituted heir in a testament, while another is named as heir by substitution, and both claim possession of the inheritance, the instituted heir will succeed, and, if the substituted heir has taken possession of the inheritance, the instituted heir may by this remedy compel him to relinquish possession, and deliver up the inheritance to the instituted heir. Of course, if the instituted heir is dead, the substituted heir may take possession. A fideicommissary heir may avail himself of this interdict, where the inheritance is to be restored to him *verbis* in the express terms of the will) by the fiduciary heir. A person who has been made heir, not unconditionally, but subject to a certain condition, may claim possession by this interdict while the condition is pending, so as to give him the administration of the inheritance in the meanwhile, but he must furnish due security. Where two persons simultaneously claim an inheritance, and neither claimant is in possession, the Court will place neither in possession, but will cause the estate to be administered, until the suit has been decided and the inheritance awarded to one or the other of the parties to the suit (48, 2 §§ 1—9). 646. Another mandatory remedy relating to the estates of deceased persons is the interdict *quod legatorum.* It was given to the heir (who in this capacity corresponded to the executor or administrator of the present day), in respect of legacies or fideicommissary inheritances, where legatees or fideicommissary heirs took possession of the thing bequeathed as a legacy or *fideicommissum* without the consent of the heir (as executor, administrator, or fiduciary holder). The remedy appears fully applicable at the present day. It makes no difference whether the legatee has taken possession of his own accord, or by authority of a public official, such as the Master of a Supreme Court. It lies against those also who have acquired possession of the subject of the legacy, from the legatee, by a universal or particular title—whether bankruptcy, inheritance, sale or gift. Grotius (2, 28, 18; *Maasdorp*, p. 115) says that "the legatee has a real right to the thing bequeathed, if it belonged to the testator; but the legatee may not take possession of it on his own authority, but must demand it from the heir, unless the right to take possession is allowed him by the will." The interdict *quod legatorum* is not available against donees *mortis causa*, since they have obtained the thing at the wish of the deceased donor, and the possession (whence also the full ownership, although it is revocable) has been transferred to them in the lifetime of the donee. If there is a doubt as to whether one possesses the subject of a legacy as heir *(pro herede)*, as possessor (pro *possessore)*, or as legatee *(pro legato)*, recourse may be had either to this interdict or to the claim of inheritance *(hereditatis petitio)*. In this claim for interdict may be included both corporeal and incorporeal property, such as usufructs and servitudes, which the legateé has taken possession of without the heir's or administrator's consent; or even with the heir's consent, but before adiation of the inheritance or recognition of the heir's right to the inheritance. If the legatee cannot restore the thing, he may be condemned to pay the value thereof. If several heirs are burthened with the payment of a legacy, and one of them wishes payment to be made to the legatee, while the others object, this interdict will only be available in favour of those heirs who object. If the legatee has taken possession of a vacant inheritance without fraud, he does not lose his ultimate right to the legacy; but where he takes the thing which is the subject of the legacy by force or fraud, he can never again recover it from the heir—in other words, his right to the legacy lapses. The heir's right to this interdict cannot be enforced, where he is unable to claim the Falcidian portion *(quarta Falcidia)*. Consequently, the interdict is no longer available in Cape Colony, where the heir's right to the Falcidian portion has been abolished by Act No. 26, 1873 (§ 1). This interdict is likewise not available, if the heir, at the time of the interdict, is unwilling to give security for the ultimate payment of the legacies. The heir may also elect whether to proceed in this action for an interdict, or to sue the legatee in a direct claim for the Falcidian portion (48, 8 §§ 1—*1)*.

It may here be noticed that though this interdict *quod legatorum* is available against legatees, they cannot in turn, as particular successors, avail themselves C.L.—VOL. I. DD of the interdict *quorum bonorum*. As to the interdict *quod Itgatorum* generally, see Schorer (§ 164; Maasdorp's *Grotiut*, p. 475). The Falcidian portion has also been abolished in Natal, the Transvaal, and Rhodesia.

647. Another remedy relating to inheritances is the interdict *ne vis fiat ei qui in possessionem missus erit* (against forcible interference with the rights of a person who has obtained possession). It is not only available in respect of an inheritance generally, or of a legacy, but applies to the case of any creditor who has obtained execution by order of the Court, and is prevented from some cause or other from obtaining possession either in his own name or that of another person. It embraces in its scope not only the actual thing claimed, but all loss arising from the detention thereof as veil. It lies in favour of the claimant's heirs, but not against the heirs of the person from whom the thing is claimed, except for so much of the property as has come into possession of such heirs; and it is no longer available after the lapse of one year. It is not in the nature of a penal interdict, and has none of the consequences of a penal interdict. It does not apply to the case of forcible taking by a minor who is *doli incapax* (legally incapable of committing crime); or of a lunatic; or where a major takes *bond fide* possession of the thing or property, in the belief that it belongs to him, or that it is bound to him (by way of pledge), or that it does not belong to the execution debtor. But if there has been gross negligence on the part of such a major, he will be liable to this interdict, notwithstanding his *bond fide* possession. A person may avail himself of this interdict if he has had possession of the property by virtue of his writ of execution, and some one has thereafter disturbed him in his possession—whence it follows that this remedy is both prohibitory and restoratory (43, 4 §§ 1—4). 648. Another interdict was that for the production of testamentary writings, such as wills and codicils, *de tabulis exhibendis*. This has scarcely any practical effect at the present day, as the local ordinances or statutes of most countries governed by Roman-Dutch Law (such as the Cape Ordinance No. 104, 1838, and the Natal, Transvaal, Orange River Colony and Rhodesia statutes) provide effectually for the production to and deposit with the Masters of the various Supreme Courts of such documents by the persons in whose custody they are. This interdict is an "exhibitory " remedy given in favour of those who allege on oath that they have reason to believe that they are interested in a will or codicil, such as heirs, direct or substituted, and successors *ab intestato*. It is not available to legatees and fideicommisBary heirs. It lies against those who detain or are in possession of the will or codicil, and is in the nature of a prayer that the will or codicil shall be produced, immediately if it is at hand, or after a reasonable time (fixed by the Court) if the document is in some other place. If there is an action pending at the time with regard to the will, this interdict will not lie; but the party who has the will may, of course, be called upon to produce the document for reference in such action, in case he refuses inspection there-

of (43, 5 §§ 1-5). 649. The principal interdicts relating to possession in general are, as we have seen, *unde vi, uti possidetis,* and *utrubi.* In the later times of the Roman Law, *utrubi* was assimilated to *uti possidetis.* The essential difference between them and *unde vi* was that the latter interdict was enforced where there had been wrongful deprivation of possession, and it was sought to recover such possession, whereas, in the case of *uti possidetis* and *utrubi,* there was generally a disturbance of possession, without actual deprivation of possession, and it was sought to secure the possessor in his rights, and to prevent future infringement of them by interdict. The mode of procedure was slightly modified in'Roman-Dutch Law, in accordance with the modification in general interdict procedure, but the principle on which the interdicts are based remains the same. The interdict *unde vi* only applied (and its Dutch equivalent still applies) to immovables, not only to the landed property itself, but to all rights connected therewith, and also to incorporeal rights such as usufruct and use of immovable property, of such a nature as, being attached to immovables, are themselves to be regarded as immovables. The interdict *unde vi* also applies to praedial servitudes. A different remedy applies in the case of forcible deprivation of or ejectment from movables such as a ship or a vehicle—in which case recourse must be had to the action of theft *(actio furti),* of forcible deprivation of goods *(actio vi bonorum raptorum),* or of production and discovery *(actio ad exhibendum).* If there are movables situate on a farm or in a house, whence one is expelled, the interdict will also lie in respect of such movables, since they are regarded as accessory to the immovable property—no matter whether they belong to the person expelled, or have only been let to him, or pledged to him, or are things over which he has the right of use or usufruct. It is, therefore, in the discretion of the person expelled whether he will apply for the operation of this interdict in respect of both the immovable property and the movables situate there-

on, or in respect of the immovable property alone. If the immovable property has been restored, the interdict may nevertheless be made to operate in respect of movables removed by the respondent from the land, in case such movables have not been restored with the land. The interdict is open not only to the person expelled by force, but to his heir as well. It makes no difference whether at the time of ejectment the complainant had natural possession (physical and legal detention), or only legal possession (consisting in intention alone), or legal possession conjoined with detention by means or agency of another who has such detention in the name of the legal possessor. If two brothers are co-heirs, and one of them possesses and administers the inheritance with the consent of his brother, and thereafter, without his brother's knowledge, or against his will, makes over the inheritance to a third party, the brother who has been deprived without his knowledge or against his will may claim restoration of his half share of the inheritance from such third party. The full owner of a house or farm which has been leased to another may avail himself of this interdict when the tenant has been forcibly deprived of his possession. If a person leaves his farm or his house, without leaving any one in charge, and is prevented or prohibited from having ingress, or from returning to his property, or is forcibly detained while on his way back so as to prevent his returning to his house or farm, he may avail himself of this interdict. An hypothecary creditor who has been deprived of his possession of the land mortgaged to him may have the benefit of this interdict, but not the debtor who executed the hypothecation in his favour—since the person who gives the property in pledge is regarded as having possession only for purposes of usucapion; whereas the creditor is deemed to have possession for all other legal purposes. In this case there must be an actual pledge (accompanied by delivery) of the land to the creditor; for if the debtor, as mortgagor, still has actual possession of the land, there is no reason why he

should not avail himself of this interdict. Persons who hold the land by virtue of a judicial pledge or hypothec *(pignus praetorium)* cannot avail themselves of this interdict, since they never had possession in a legal sense, but only the custody for a limited purpose. Where a husband has given an estate to his wife, and she has been forcibly deprived of possession, she may avail herself of this interdict, for although gifts between spouses, made during marriage, are null and void, yet such gifts are sufficient to constitute a transfer of natural possession. Tenants or agents, who occupy houses or properties belonging to landlords or principals, have not the right to avail themselves of this interdict except when the true owner *(dominus)* of the house or property is absent, or unable to sue for recovery of possession, or where the agent is empowered to sue for such recovery. It does not matter whether, at the time of ejectment, the person ejected held the property by a lawful or unlawful title, as the interdict is given even to those who hold by force, secretly, or on sufferance *(vi clam aut precario),* and is available against either a third party or against the true owner *(dominus)* himself if he has taken forcible possession of the property. So, if one ejects a rightful owner from his property, and the latter lies by, and for some time takes no steps, and thereafter ejects the wrongful possessor by force, the wrongful possessor may avail himself of the interdict *unde vi,* on the strength of the maxim *spoliatus ante omnia restituendut est.* At the same time, Voet quotes the authority of Hugo Grotius *(Dutch Consultations,* 5 § 157), Menochius *(Recovery oj Possession,* 1 § 118), Peckius *(Dejure sistendi,* 17 § 2), and Wassenaar *(Judicial Practice,* 14 §§ 6, 7), for holding that if such a wrongful possessor applies for an interdict, and has no other colour or title to possession than his own unlawful entry, the *dominus* will succeed on raising the defence of ownership. This latter view is more in consonance with modern jurisprudence. Where a person has been ejected, but continues his possession through his agent or tenant, he cannot avail himself of the interdict *unde vi.* Those, also, cannot employ this remedy who never had possession, whether physically or in intention, but, being anxious to obtain possession, are prevented from fulfilling their object. Voet then lays down a rule which it seems somewhat difficult to reconcile with the modern notion of duress—namely, that if there is no forcible dispossession, but one is constrained by threats or fear to part with one's possession, he cannot avail himself of this interdict to recover possession. In the criminal law, a person is guilty of robbery where he uses no actual physical violence, but by dint of threats or the employment of such other means as induce physical fear compels his victim to part with his property. There seems to be no reason why this doctrine should not apply, in the civil law, to the case of deprivation of one's immovable property. Voet bases his *dictum* on the ground that a person cannot be said to have been ejected by force, who gives his consent to the occupation of the property by another; but at the present day it can hardly be held that such a consent is free and voluntary. The interdict *unde vi* is available against those who have made a forcible ejectment, no matter whether they made ejectment and entered into occupation at the same time, or only made ejectment, without entering into occupation, allowing another to take the vacant possession. The ejectors may be held liable, whether the ejectment has taken place through their own act, or that of their agents or servants, either on their mandate, or with their subsequent ratification. If, however, an agent, falsely alleging that some one else is his principal, makes the ejectment, the agent alone will be liable. It makes no difference whether the person causing the ejectment has a real right *(jus in re),* or not, or whether he still is in possession of the property from which the ejectment was made or not; or whether he has ceased to possess through fraud, negligence, or accident (since, as in a case of theft, he is always regarded as being in fault—*in mora*). The interdict *unde vi* is not available against the heirs

of the ejector, unless they are in possession of the property from which the eject ment took place, or unless they have fraudulently made away with the property. This interdict will lie against the Crown *(Dutch Consultations,* 5 § 8). It does not lie against persons who have in good faith acquired possession from the ejectors by particular title, such as sale or gift. The effect of this interdict, when granted, is that the respondent must yield up possession of the real property together with the movables situate thereon, and also the fruits arising from such property from the date of ejectment, interest, and all damage resulting from the wrongful dispossession. All this must be claimed within a year, and after the expiration of the year one can only claim such property as has actually come into the possession of the ejector (43, 16 §§ 1—7). 650. The interdict *uti possidetis* is one brought to ensure retention of possession, and to guard against its loss, and, at the same time, to prohibit others from forcible interference with such possession. It has also reference to immovable property, and to those incorporeal rights which are classed as immovable property, such as usufruct, use, and praedial servitudes. This interdict lies in favour of one who has possession or quasi-possession at the time of joinder in issue *(litis contestatio),* so long as the possession is not *vi clam vel precario (Sengane* vs. *Gondele,* 1 E. D. C. 201). So long as the possession is not *vi clam vel precario,* it makes no difference whether the claimant holds by a lawful or unlawful title. The claimant may, however, have this interdict if he possesses *vi clam vel precario* from a third party. He has, in order to obtain this interdict, to prove possession on his part, and disturbance on the part of his adversary. There is possession on his part, whether he holds personally, or through another (such as an agent, tenant, or servant) —although the agent, tenant, or servant cannot have recourse to this interdict, unless specially empowered to do so. Execution creditors cannot have the benefit of this interdict. Creditors to whom a pledge has been delivered may

avail themselves of this interdict in respect of such pledge. The heir of a person who has been disturbed in his possession cannot avail himself of this interdict, since the heir is not in actual possession. In like manner, this interdict *wit possidetis* does not lie in favour of one who has already lost possession: since this is an interdict for retaining, not recovering possession. This interdict lies against those who contend that they also have possession, and under that pretext disturb the applicant in his possession, whether by employing force against him, or preventing the possessor from using the land which he possesses at his own discretion, as by sowing, ploughing, building, repairing, or doing anything else to show his exercise of the right of free and undisturbed possession. The interdict lies against them, whether they make the disturbance personally, or through their agents or servants on their mandate, or by subsequent ratification of the acts of agents or servants. The disturbance must take place not only in words (such as threats), but by acts and deeds. If a person is merely threatened with disturbance, he must, if he can prove damage, have recourse to an action of injury *(actio injuriarum),* and cannot avail himself of the interdict *uti possidetis.* If the disturbance takes place on the part of one who does not claim possession, Voet thinks recourse should be had rather to the *actio injuriarum* than to the interdict *uti possidetis;* but, as the interdict *uti possidetis* is designed rather to insure one's safe possession than to decide the adverse claim of an aggressor, there seems to be no reason why, in the case of an aggressor or disturber who does not claim possession, a claim for damages should not be conjoined with a prayer for an interdict restraining the aggressor from any future disturbance of the possessor in his rights. Such an interdict will not be the interdict *uti possidetis,* which has reference only to disputes about the right of possession. Furthermore, the dispute must be about the same thing. If one party possesses the ground, and the other surface-rights and buildings, the interdict *uti possidetis* cannot apply; since the parties do not claim the same right of possession. The object of this interdict is to prevent future disturbance by the persons who have hitherto caused disturbance. The party causing disturbance may also be called upon to provide security against future disturbance, to the extent of the complainant's interest in the land. If a possessor)' suit is pending, the plaintiff who applies for the interdict must, ou his side, provide security, with suitable sureties, for the restoration of the property, without deterioration in value while the suit is pending, in case judgment should go against him; and if the plaintiff does not furnish such security, the property may be handed over to the defendant, provided he gives similar security 48, 17 §§ 1-5). 651. In the same way as the interdict *uti possidetis* applied to immovable property, the interdict *utrubi* applied to movables. The claimant in the interdict *utrubi* must not possess, as against his adversary, *vi clam vel precario;* and in other respects the procedure was the same as in the case of the interdict *uti possidetis* (48, 81). 652. The principle of the foregoing interdicts was retained in Dutch Law, although their form was altered to suit changed conditions, and they were known under different names—other times, other manners. The possessory interdicts in Dutch Law are fully detailed by Van der Linden *(Judicial Practice,* vol. 1, book 2, chaps. 20, 21, 22; 2nd ed. 1829, pp. 298—814). According to him, they were divided as follows: 1. *Ad acquirendam possessionem* (to obtain possession), known in the Dutch Courts as *mandament van immissie* (mandate of placing in possession); 2. *Ad retinendam possessionem* (to retain possession), known in the Dutch Courts as *mandament van maintenue* (mandate of maintenance in possession); and 3. *Ad recuperandam possessionem* (to recover possession), known in the Dutch Courts as *mandament van complainte* (mandate of complaint), and *mandament van spolie* (mandate of spoliation). Of these, the *mandament van complainte* and *mandament van spolie* answer most nearly to

the interdict *undevi;* the *mandament van maintenue* to the interdict *uti possidetis;* the *mandament van immissie* to the interdict *unde vi,* so far as that interdict applies to co-heirs. The writ or *mandament van immissie,* according to Van der Linden, was and is almost solely applicable where one heir ousts another, who has equal rights, out of the possession of the inherited estate. The conclusion of the prayer of the petition for this interdict should be in this form: "That the applicant shall be placed in (or inducted into) possession of the property. " The writ or *mandament van maintenue* asks for an order confirming one in possession, and concludes with the prayer: "That the applicant shall be maintained, supported, and strengthened in his possession" —*dot hij zal warden gemainteneert, gestyft, en gesterkt in de possessie.* The petition for a mandate of maintenance must contain a concise account of the applicant's possession, and of the disturbance by the other party. A rule *nisi* is then granted, which is confirmed or discharged on the return-day. In order to obtain the confirmation of this interdict the applicant must not have obtained possession ri *clam vel precario.* The *mandament van complainte* is granted where one loses possession, and (it is submitted) it is not possible to show clearly that the applicant has been deprived of possession. The petition praying for this mandate must show—(o) that the complainant has possession by himself, or through his predecessors, or by means of members of his family or his tenants; *(b)* that such possession is peaceable, lawful, and just; (c) that it has lasted for more than a year and a day; (d) that the disturbance has taken place within the year. A learned translator of Van der Linden's *Institutes* seems to take the view that the disturbance or loss of possession must have taken place within the year during which the possession must have lasted. But what if the possession has lasted for several years? Perhaps it would be better to construe Van der Linden as meaning that the application for an interdict must be instituted within a year from the time when

the cause of complaint first arose—in other words, fixing a year as the period of prescription of this interdict. This will correspond with what has been said above (§ 649; *Voet,* 48, 16 § 6) as to the prescription of the interdict *unde ri.* The mandate of complaint prays for maintenance of possession, and the prevention of future disturbance. The next interdict, *mandament van spolie* (writ of spoliation) corresponds most nearly to the interdict *unde vi* in its strict sense. The petition must set forth—*(a)* that the petitioner has had the free and undisturbed possession of the thing or property in question; and (6) that there has been forcible removal and deprivation of such property by the respondent. The petition need not set forth the title of the applicant, as the mandate proceeds on the maxim *spoliatus ante omnia restituendus est* (the person despoiled must receive restitution at all costs). The mandate is available in respect of both movable and immovable property, and so combines the interdicts *unde vi* and *utrvbi.* The prayer is for the setting aside of the forcible dispossession, and for the reinstatement of everything in the same condition in which it was at the time when the forcible dispossession took place, with interest, damages, and costs (48, 17 §§ 6, 7).

The procedure by way of *mandament van spolie* (writ of spoliation) is quite common in South African Courts. In *Haupt's Executors* vs. *De Villiers* (3 M. 341), A. sold a wagon to B., on condition that B. should immediately grant A. a promissory note for the price, payable at three months from delivery. B. obtained possession of the wagon, and failed to give A. the note. B. thereafter died. A. then proceeded to B.'s farm, and forcibly retook possession of the wagon. The executors of B.'s estate then claimed a writ of spoliation, which was granted, and made absolute in their favour with costs. In *Swanepoel* vs. *Van der Hoeven* (Buch. 1878, p. 4), applicants hired from respondent a flock of sheep under a five years' lease. While the lease was still running, the respondent, actuated thereto by reports as to the solvency of the lessors, removed the sheep, during the temporary absence of applicants from home, and without their consent. On an *ex parte* application, the Court granted a rule *nisi* (to operate as an interim interdict restraining respondent from leasing the sheep to others) calling on respondent to show cause why-he should not restore the sheep. See also *Crause* vs. *Ryersbach* (2 Kotze, Transv. Rep. 1881—1884, p. 50); *Solomon* vs. *Woolf(I* C. T. R. 224); *Benson* vs. *Van Wyk and Another* (2 C. T. R. 309); *Connell* vs. *Factor and Lax* (6 C. T. R. 100); *Jersipc* vs. *Hart* (7 E. D. C. 85); *Klipplaats Wool Co.* vs. *Leach* (7 E. D. C. 206); *Ncotame* vs. *N'cume* (10 S. C. 207); and Van Zyl's *Judicial Practice* (2nd ed. pp. 343—345; 1893 ed. pp. 329—331). As to possessory interdict procedure generally, see *Kelly* vs. *Kirkwood and Another* (3 S. 5); *Fletcher* vs. *Cape Town Municipality* (10 S. C. 134); *Bultfontein Mining Board* vs. *Armstrong and Another* (8 S. C. 236); *Skippen and Another* vs. *Cape Town Municipality* (6 S. C. 64); *Lippert* vs. *Aries* (1 S. C. 187); *In re Walton and ZieUman* (3 N. L. R., N. S. 23); *Taylor and Williamson* vs. *Oiven* (9 N. L. R., N. S. 70); *St. PauVs Churchwardens* vs. *Johnson and Another* (11 N. L. R., N. S. 60; conflicting, to some extent, with *In re Walton and Zietsman); Hunt and Leuchars* vs. *Anderson* (2 N. L. R., N. S. 64); *Bennett* vs. *Ferguson & Co.* (5 N. L. R., N. S. 198); *Mason* vs. *Lawes* (6 N. L. R., N. S. 8); *Net & Co.* vs. *Oestreich* (6 N. L. R., N. S. 165); *Oriental Commercial Bank* vs. *Snell* (Morcom's Natal R. 1871, p. 97); *Hamilton* vs. *Emanuel* (Morcom's Natal R. 1867, p. 299); *Standard Bank* vs. *Oakes* (1 N. L. R., N. S. 260); *In re Koch* (Morcom's Natal R. 1869, p. 164); *BoshoffvB. Niekerk* (Finnemore's Rep., March 19th, 1861), *John* vs. *Trimble and Others* (1902 T. H. 19), *Goundry* vs. *Jeffery* (1902 T. H. 35), *Burmester* vs. *McColl* (1 T. H. 42), and *Driefontein Mines* vs. *Schlochauer* (1902 T. S. 33).

653. There are certain proprietary interdicts which arise out of the rights which one possesses as a member of the community generally of a State or town.

One of these is the interdict *ne quid in loco publico vel itinere fiat* (against anything done, or to be done, in a public place or public road). Public places are all such as are dedicated to some public use, and at the same time are of benefit to private individuals—for example, public squares, buildings, lands, roads, and walks. Public lands denote such properties as commonages, or parks open to the public; but not Crown lands, because they form the private property of the State, and the general public have no right of interference with or use of such lands. This prohibitory interdict is available where a person does something in a public place whereby another suffers damage, or some detriment or loss is caused to the public. The interdict may be claimed by the person who suffers damage, and by any member of the general public, and has the effect, when granted, of preventing the doing of the thing complained of in a public place. For instance, a person may be prevented from building on land adjoining public property in such a way as to obstruct the public right of way, or to shut off the light from adjoining buildings. But if the interference is of such a nature that no detriment or damage to public property is done, and only a private person suffers, this particular interdict will not lie, and recourse must be had to another interdict, or to an action for damages *(actio injuriarum)*. Where an erection has already been made, this interdict, since it is merely prohibitory, cannot avail; and the erection will have to be removed by State or municipal authority. A similar interdict lies with regard to public roads in the country—town or urban roads being under the municipal authorities—to prevent anything being done on such roads to injure and interfere with their use. This is of a prohibitory nature. An interdict of a restitutory nature is that whereby one seeks the removal of any erection or obstruction on a rural public road. There is also a prohibitory interdict, preventing one from employing force against a person using a rural public road. When a person has received the temporary grant and enjoyment of public property (such

as a lease of public baths, buildings, lakes, or pools), interference with such grantee or lessee is prevented by the interdict *de loco publico fruendo* (for the enjoyment of public places). If, however, the grantees have exceeded the rights which were granted to them, they cannot complain of the employment of force against them. According to Matthaeus *(de auctionibus,* 2, 5, 5), grantees of public land, when disturbed, may call in the public force to protect them. It has been held *(Gifford* vs. *Hare,* 14 S. C. 255) that prescription will not avail as a defence against the abatement of a nuisance proved to cause injuries noxious to life or property (43, §§8, 9). These interdicts are partly connected with the law of torts, where they are classed under the head of nuisance. But it has been thought desirable to treat of them in this place, as they refer to the possession and enjoyment of property, public and private. As to the granting of such interdicts, see *Dell* vs. *Town Council of Cape Town* (Buch. 1879, p. 2), and *Malan* vs. *Cape Toum and Wellington Railway Co.* (4 S. 82).

654. It is the duty of the magistrates or officials entrusted with the care of buildings and streets in towns to see that nothing is done in public places, or in connection with such buildings or streets, whereby the buildings, streets, or their use suffer damage (43, 10).

The Cape Municipal Act, No. 45 of 1882 (§§ 156, 157) regulates municipal duties in regard to public property; and § 109 of the Act defines the powers of municipal councils in regard to byelows. The Cape Divisional Councils Act, No. 40 of 1889, regulates the powers of divisional councils with regard to the construction and maintenance of country roads (§§ 141—143), the taking of materials from land (§§ 143—148), the erection of gates across roads (§§ 152— 154); the erection of tolls and toll-bars (§§ 162—169); and the construction and maintenance of bridges (§§ 170—192). See Natal Law 19, 1872, §§ 52—95, and Act 22, 1894, §§ 2—52. As to Transvaal, see Proc. No. 16, 1901, Proc. No. 39, 1902, and Proc. No. 28, 1901.

655. If a person, or body of persons, duly empowered or legally obliged to repair a public road or place, is engaged on the construction or repair thereof, and is forcibly obstructed in such repair, the Court will grant the interdict *de vid et itinere publico reficiendo* (on the repair of public roads) against the obstructor, and the obstructor will be liable for any damage caused by him. But if a person makes unauthorised repair of a public road, he may be forcibly interfered with, and will be liable for damage resulting to neighbouring proprietors. If a person ploughs or makes an excavation in a public road, he is only compellable to repair the road (43, 11). 656. Another interdict, *ut in flumine publico navigare liceat* (that a person shall be allowed the free navigation of a public stream), prevented interference by force with persons sailing on a public stream or lake, or loading or unloading goods on the shores thereof. This interdict has no reference to private streams, or their banks. It is extended, by analogy, to the sea and the shores thereof— that is, so much of the sea as is within the territorial jurisdiction (48, 14).

Voet treats (in titles 12 and 13) of rights relating to public streams; but his remarks relate to water-rights, and so are best treated of in connection with servitudes.

657. If a person, in order to protect the banks of a public stream against the force of the water, does something which causes a nuisance or obstruction in the stream or on its banks, he may be interdicted from causing forcible damage, and compelled to give security against loss to neighbouring proprietors. The neighbours cannot demand such security after the obstruction has been erected, but must proceed by an action for damages in tort (43, 15).

See *Beaufort West Municipality* vs. *Wernich* (2 S. C. 36); and Van Leeuwen (*Cms. For.* 1, 2, 4, 14).

658. Certain other interdicts in connection with rights of property are those which have relation to forcible, secret, or precarious tenure *(vi clam vel precario)*. The interdict *quod vi aut clam* is given as a protection against those who

injure the property of others, by forcibly or secretly making an erection, causing an obstruction, or making an alteration on or in the property of another, or by making a forcible or secret removal of a building or erection from such property. This sort of disturbance may take place in connection with a public or private building, or any work or erection on public or private land. This interdict *quod vi* (arising from the use of force) must not be confounded with the interdict *unde vi,* which, as we have seen, relates to the forcible deprivation of one's possession. A person is held to act secretly *(clam),* who has not given notice of any erection or alteration on property to another, to whom it was his duty to give notice. If a person gives notice, and does not proceed with the work for a long time, it is his duty again to give notice before proceeding with the work. A person is regarded in law as acting forcibly *(vi),* who has received notice not to proceed with a certain work or erection, and nevertheless proceeds with it, or who actually employs force in the construction of a building, even if he has not received notice. It is sufficient, in the latter case, if force was employed at the beginning, although the use of force did not continue thereafter. A person also acts forcibly who, knowing that he was to be prohibited, forcibly makes an erection or removal to prevent the prohibition being made before such erection or removal is made, or prevents the person about to make the prohibition from having access to the property in question: but the interdict will not lie if these things are done by a third party, without the encouragement, approval, or authority of the person to be prohibited. This interdict relates to erections or obstructions in connection with real property, and does not have reference to movables, unless such movables are regarded as accessory to the soil. It lies in favour of one to whose prejudice something has been done forcibly (ft) or secretly *(clam),* whether he has possession of the property or not, whether he is the true owner *(dominus),* or is otherwise interested in having the erection or obstruc-

tion prohibited (for instance, if he be a usufructuary). It lies against him who acts forcibly or secretly, or who authorised such acts, or who permitted such acts to be done on his own property or that of another when it was his duty to have prohibited or opposed them, and he was able to do so. It makes no difference that the person making such erection or causing such obstruction was not aware to whom the property, on which the erection or obstruction was made, belonged, provided he knew that the property belonged to another, and not to himself. The interdict does not lie against the heirs of the person doing the prohibited acts, except to the extent to which they have been enriched by the act. It will not lie against third parties who come into possession of the property. Where the wrongdoer is in possession, this interdict compels him to restore the property to the condition in which it was before the acts complained of took place, and to pay any damage caused. If the wrongdoer is not in possession, he may be condemned to pay, not only the actual damage caused, but also the amount which it would cost to restore the property to its former condition. If a person is in possession, and the wrong is done to the property without his consent, he is not liable, except that he must allow the removal of the obstruction or building objected to by those who have a right to remove the same. This interdict is prescribed after the lapse of a year, reckoned from the time when the erection or obstruction was completed, or when work was last done on such erection or obstruction. The interdict is not available if the complainant consented to the construction of the building or obstruction; or if there is a lawful ground for doing the work on the part of the defendant, such as ploughing on or cultivating land; or if a building were pulled down to prevent destruction by fire. A person may have this interdict against him if he forcibly or secretly demolishes or removes a building or obstruction forcibly or secretly erected by another: for it is the function of the Court to order the removal of buildings forcibly or secretly erected (48, 24 §§ 1—8). 659. Precarious tenure *(precarium)* is a grant of occupation to one person by another, on condition that such tenure shall last during the pleasure of the grantor. A person may hold by such tenure, not only if he receives an express grant, but where, without any indication of consent on the part of the owner, he possesses without any objection by the owner. The occupation, in the latter case, may be disallowed by the true owner of the property whenever he wishes. The grantee has the use of the property during the time he is allowed to remain in possession thereof, and has possession to such an extent that he may have recourse to the interdict *uti possidetis* against all persons but the grantor or the person who allows him to remain on the property. He is, as we have seen, unable to acquire usucapion of the property. This mode of tenure *(preeario)* gives rise to an interdict *de preeario* (concerning precarious tenure), which is of a restitutory nature, and is perpetual, as it cannot be barred by prescription lasting even for a time immemorial. By this interdict the claimant seeks restoration of the property which the grantee has held on sufferance, with the produce and income from the time of delay in restoration *(a tempore morac),* or from the return-day of the interdict, and damages arising from delay in restoration. This interdict lies in favour of the person who gave the grant, or his heirs, since it is of a vindicatory and real nature.

It makes no difference whether the complainant (applicant) himself made the grant of the property, or his agent; and whether he is himself the owner of the property, or made a grant of it when it belonged to another. The interdict lies against the person who holds by precarious tenure, or against his heir. The holder on sufferance is liable whether he is in actual possession, or whether he has wrongfully caused the property to pass out of his possession; but his heir is only liable to the extent to which he has received possession of the property held on sufferance. A person who has received a grant on sufferance, but does not take possession of the proper-

ty, and does not fraudulently cease to have possession thereof, is not liable to the interdict *de precario*—since this interdict only applies to cases of fraud or gross negligence. The heir of a precarious grantee must, as we have seen, deliver up so much of the property as is in his possession; and so must a minor, who takes possession by this mode of tenure, even without his guardian's authority. This interdict will not lie, if the grantee has given security for the restoration of the property. Precarious tenure is not extinguished by the death of the grantor (48, 25; 48, 26 §§ 1-5).

See *Hart* vs. *Hart* (1902 1 T. H. 247), and an interesting *excursus* on the subject in Hunter's *Soman Law* (3rd ed. pp. 411—412, and 380—382).

660. Another proprietary interdict relates to the cutting down of trees *(de arboribus caedendis).* "If trees," says Voet, "overhang an urban property, and it is due to the fault of the owner of the trees that they are not cut down, the neighbour (whose property the trees overhang), whether owner or usufructuary, who is damaged by such overhanging trees, may obtain from the Court an interdict empowering him to cut down the trees, and to remove the branches, if the owner of the branches is unwilling to remove them; and the interdict will prevent forcible hindrance to the person making the removal. If there are several owners of the urban property, who are injured by the trees overhanging, each of them may have an interdict. Although, in the Roman Law, the Praetor permitted one to cut down not only the overhanging branches, but the whole tree,

C.L.—VOL. I. EE according to Dutch Common Law not the whole tree, whose branches overhang, but only so much of it as actually overhangs the adjoining property, may be cut down." In *De Villiers* vs. *O'Sullivan and Another* (2 S. C. 251), it was remarked that Voet "does not state whether, in his opinion, the Dutch Law preserved intact the distinction between urban and rural tenements, and in other respects followed the law as laid down in the *Digest.* Groenewegen, in his comments upon

this title of the *Digest,* says: 'If a tree overhangs the land *(/undo)* or house *(aedibiis)* of another, it is not allowed by our customary law or that of the French to take out the tree by the roots, but to remove altogether that part which so overhangs.' He, at all events, makes no distinction between urban and rural tenements." The Court then cited the opinions of Grotius *(Introduction,* 2, 84, 21; *Maasdorp,* p. 149), and Van Leeuwen *(RomanDutch Law,* 2, 21, 20; 1 *Kotze,* p. 299); and came to the conclusion that under the later customary law of Holland the owner of land could lop branches overhanging his land without previous notice to the owner of the tree, but could not keep the branches so lopped down for himself, unless the owner of the trees refuses to take them. This rule applies to both urban and rural tenements (48, 27 § 1).

661. There is another interdict which, so far as can be ascertained, has never been granted in South African Courts. It is that known as the interdict *de glande legenda* (concerning acorns to be gathered). Where acorns or fruit generally dropped from trees, growing in one property, on to the property of a neighbour, the owner of the tree was owner of the fruit, and had the right of gathering the fruit within three days. This interdict prevented the owner of the ground on which the fruit had fallen from obstructing or interfering with the owner of the tree in his attempt to gather the fruit. Voet states that at certain places (which he does not specify) a different rule prevailed, and that the fruit belonged to the owner of the property on which the fruit fell. But where no such exception has been received in use, the rule of the Roman Law, that the fruit belongs to the owner of the tree, must be taken to have been retained in Roman-Dutch Law (48, 28 § 1). 662. The foregoing interdicts are in many respects similar to the English injunction—which may, of course, be perpetual or temporary. Injunctions, like interdicts, may be obtained by action, in which the injunction is not only granted, but damages may also be claimed and awarded. *B. PARTICULAR RIGHTS IN THINGS.* CHAPTER I.

Servitudes. (1) Servitudes In General. 663. Servitudes in general, says Voet, may be denned as rights constituted in favour of one person, having reference to property belonging to another person, whereby a property brings profit to another than the true owner, a thing at variance with the usual rights of ownership *(dominium)*. It is thus defined by Colquhoun: "A servitude or service is a real right attaching to the property of another, whereby the owner must suffer something in respect of this property which he otherwise, in right of his ownership therein, would not have been obliged to suffer, or forbear some act, which he otherwise would have had the right to have performed in virtue of his character of owner, for the benefit of some other person or thing. This is more explicatory than, though not so concise as, the definition of the Pandects" (§ 984). The definition of the Pandects is—*Servitus est jus quo res alterius rei vel personae servit* (servitude is the right whereby a thing or person has service done to it or him by a thing belonging to another person). Colquhoun's definition is, at the same time, more accurate than that of Voet. The right of servitude is a real right, inasmuch as there is no good service when there is only a *jus ad rem* or personal claim *jus in personam)*, by which a person must suffer something to be done to his property, or omit to do something. Where, for instance, a lessor, by virtue of the agreement of lease, is bound to allow the lessee to occupy the premises leased, the lessee has no servitude, because, as against the lessor, the lessee has no real right, but merely a personal claim. In other words, the granting or obtaining of a servitude gives the person entitled to it a real right in respect of the property subject to the servitude. But though the right to obtain the servitude, or to use it and enjoy it, is a real right, there is a certain distinction between the various modes in which servitudes are used. By virtue of this distinction servitudes are known as personal servitudes, and real servitudes. The right to the servitude is a real right, because the servitude must always be exercised in

reference to a particular thing *(res)*, whether natural products (fruits), or an estate. But the servitude itself is personal, when it is constituted in favour of a particular person, without reference to any real property owned by that person, and so confers a purely personal right of enjoyment; and the servitude itself is real, when it is constituted in favour of a property *(praedium)*, and has no especial reference to the individuality of the person who owns the right of servitude. A real servitude must always attach to a landed estate, whether such estate be urban or rural. Both personal and real servitudes must exist in respect of a thing or property from which the enjoyment of the servitude is derived. This property, tenement, or *praedium,* is known as the servient property or tenement *(res serviens, praedium serviens).* There must be a servient property in every servitude. Furthermore, in the case of real servitudes, there must be a dominant property or tenement *(res daminans, praedium dominans),* in favour of which the real servitude is constituted and enjoyed. This distinguishes the real servitude from the personal servitude. In the case of the latter there is no dominant tenement, for the right of enjoyment is constituted in favour of a particular person. Servitudes are spoken of as praedial, when they are constituted over one estate, whether rural or urban, in favour of another estate, rural or urban *(praedium urbanum* or *praedium rusticum)*. The principal personal servitudes are—*(a)* usufruct *(ususfructus), (b)* use *(usus),* and *(c)* habitation *(habitatio)*. These will be dealt with in the first place (7, 1 § 1).
(2) Personal Servitudes. 664. Usufruct *(ususfructus)* is the right to consume what the property of another produces, without damage to the substance of the property from which the produce is derived. Full ownership *(dominium)* is divisible into bare ownership *(nuda proprietor)* and usufruct, for when we conjoin the two we have full ownership. Thus, where a principal debtor binds himself to deliver a certain estate, he may give a surety who binds himself to transfer the usufruct of the estate. In

the same way, a testator may bequeath an estate, and thereafter revoke the bequest so far as the usufruct of the estate is concerned, leaving to the legatee the bare ownership, or, on the contrary, he may revoke the bequest as to the bare ownership, leaving to the legatee the usufruct alone (7,1 §§ 2, 8). 665. A usufruct may be conditional or unconditional, and may be made to take effect from a certain day, or to a certain day. Until the condition is fulfilled, or the day from which the usufruct is to take effect arrives, the fruits and profits derived from the property go to the person who has the proprietary rights. If A. bequeaths the usufruct of his house to his wife, for five years after A.'s death, with the provision that after the lapse of that period the usufruct is to go to B. , and A.'s wife dies two years after A. , the usufruct for the next three years goes, not to B., but to the proprietor of the house. If it is clearly the testator's wish that the usufruct, on his wife's death, should immediately go to B., the proprietor of the house will have no claim to the usufruct. If a testator leaves his farm, without the usufruct thereof, as an unconditional legacy to D., and leaves the usufruct conditionally to E., and the condition of the usufruct is not fulfilled, the usufruct, while the condition is unfulfilled, will go, not to the testator's heir, but to D., as the proprietor of the farm. Usufruct may be acquired by mere operation of law: where, for instance, a widow contracts a second marriage, and her minor children are heirs to the property left by their deceased father, the minors will be the owners of such property, but their mother, even after the second marriage, will have the usufruct; in the same way, a father will have the usufruct of his son's *peculium adventitium*. Usufruct is also acquired by prescription; by judicial decree (where a Court decides an action for division of a joint inheritance, and awards the ownership to one party and the usufruct to another—which may also happen in an action to divide a common property), by special agreement, or by last will and testament. According to Roman Law, if a testator leaves a property to A., and the usufruct thereof to B., the usufruct is shared by A. and B. ; but the Dutch Law is otherwise, and the ownership belongs to A., and the usufruct absolutely to B. Where a house, specially designated, the identity of which, as to size and boundaries, is certain, has been left to a person by will, for the purpose of being inhabited or made use of by the legatee, or where an estate has been similarly bequeathed for the support of a legatee, it will be presumed, in case of doubt, that not a usufruct, but the full ownership, has been bequeathed. Where a usufruct has been bequeathed, whether of a particular thing or of a whole inheritance, and it is directed that on the death of the legatee the thing or inheritance shall be restored to a third party, there will be a presumption, in case of doubt, that the ownership with the burden of *fideicommissum* (bequest of property to one person in trust for another), and not the bare usufruct, has been bequeathed— for the legatee, on his death, loses the usufruct by mere operation of law, and therefore more than the bare usufruct must be regarded as bequeathed to him (see *Hiddingh* vs. *Roubaix,* Buch. 1878, p. 42; Van Leeuwen, *Cens. For.* 1, 8,8,8,9; Grotius, *Introduction,* 2,20,14). If a testator bequeaths to his wife, or any other person, the usufruct of a thing, and adds a prohibition against alienation of the thing, or bequeaths the usufruct of a house on condition that the house shall not be enlarged, or that no servitude shall be granted in respect to it, the full ownership, and not the bare usufruct, is considered as having been bequeathed—for a prohibition of alienation only affects the absolute owner (the usufructuary being debarred from alienating by the Common Law), and only the full owner can impose a servitude on property, so that a prohibition to impose a servitude would be worthless if the testator did not intend the legatee to have the ownership *De Geest's Executor* vs. *De Geest's Executor,* 4 S. C. 97). If a usufruct is bequeathed with the power of alienation, unconditionally, the full ownership, with the burden of *fideicommissum,* is considered to

have been left; but if the usufruct has been bequeathed with the power of alienation only in case of absolute necessity or want, the bare usufruct is considered to have been left, and ownership is considered as arising only in case of such absolute necessity or want. There cannot be a bare right of usufruct, and the power of alienation (arising out of ownership), co-existing at the same time. Where a testator appoints A. as legatee of the usufruct of all his property, and institutes B. as heir after A.'s death, B. cannot, during A.'s lifetime, disturb A. in the enjoyment of the usufruct, although B. is heir to the property. In this respect the Dutch Law differs from the Roman Law, according to which the legacy of the usufruct of all the property to A. was void, the heir (B.) being required to adiate the inheritance immediately on the testator's death, and not on the expiry of A's term of usufruct (7, 1 §§ 4—12). 666. Where a bare usufruct has been left, the ownership of the estate which is the subject of usufruct at once vests in the testator's successors *ab intestato* or (where he made a will) in his testamentary heirs, and if such successors die during the existence of the usufruct they transmit their ownership and eventual right to become full owners (i.e., the right to have the bare ownership combined with the usufruct) to their heirs. On the other hand, if a testator leaves to a person the ownership of property, burdened with a *fideicomtnisitim* (trust) in favour of another, the restitution to be made after the fiduciary legatee's death, the fideicommissary heir who dies during the lifetime of the fiduciary heir does not transmit his chance of obtaining the fideicommissary property to his heirs, and the fideicommissary property is only restored to such fideicommissary heirs as are alive at the death of the fiduciary heir. If no persons, to whom, according to the testator's direction, restitution of the fideicommissary property was to be made at the death of the fiduciary heir, are alive at the time the fiduciary heir dies, the fiduciary heir becomes full owner of the fiduciary property, and accordingly his rights as own-

er are acquired by his heirs; and the fiduciary heir, during his lifetime, after the death of the last of the fideicommissary heirs, may alienate or dispose of the fideicommissary property in any way whatsoever. Where husband and wife had, by mutual will, appointed all their children heirs, and bequeathed, after the death of the survivor, their immovable property to their sons, it was held that the surviving testator was a usufructuary, and that upon the death of the first-dying of the testators, each of the sons acquired a vested interest in the immovable property *(Rahl* vs. *De Jager,* 1 S. C. 88). Similarly, in *Nortje* vs. *Nortje* (6 S. C. 9), where a mutual will declared "that upon the decease of one of us the movables shall be publicly sold," that the proceeds of the sale should be divided between the survivor and the children, and "that the survivor shall remain in possession of the immovable property till his or her death, when the same shall be publicly sold, and the proceeds be divided amongst the children or their lawful heirs," the husband died first, and his wife adiated the inheritance, and accepted benefits under the will. It was decided that on the husband's death the children acquired a vested interest in the immovable property (7, 1 § 18).

Previously, in *Quin* vs. *Board of Executors* (Buch. 1870, p. 78), it had beeu decided that an insolvent's interest in a fideicommissary inheritance before the death of the fiduciary heir was such a f uture estate as vested in the trustee of his insolvent estate before the confirmation of the insolvency account and plan of distribution of the assets. De Villiers, C.J., with reference to this case, said: "I am not sure that the decision can be reconciled with Voefs view as expressed in his *Commentaries* (7, 1 § 18) unless—as I am inclined to think was the case— the Court felt itself justified in concluding from a consideration of the whole will that the testators, although using the term *fideicommissum,* intended to give the remaindermen a vested interest before the death of the fiduciary heir" (6 S. C. 13). This simply bears out what has been said above: if there is a usufruct, the remainderman's interest in the property subject to the usufruct vests immediately on the testator's death, but if there is a *fideicommissum,* the remainderman's interest in the fideicommissary property is postponed, and only vests or becomes absolute on the death of the fiduciary heir (assuming that the fideicommissary property is to pass over on death, and not on the happening of any other event or fulfilment of any other condition).

667. Where a usufruct is bequeathed for a certain fixed time, unconditionally, and the usufructuary dies before the expiry of such period, the usufruct for the unexpired term reverts to the owner of the usufructuary property, and the usufruct is regarded as extinguished by death. But where a usufruct is bequeathed for a certain time, with the condition that the usufruct shall at the end of that period be restored to another person, and the usufructuary dies before the expiry of such period, the usufruct for the remaining unexpired portion of such period goes to the usufructuary's heirs (7, 1 § 13).

Illustrations: A.leaves the farm X. to B., and the usufruct of the same farm to C. for five years. C. dies after one year. The usufruct reverts to B,, and C.'s heirs are not entitled to it. A. leaves the farm X. to B., and gives the usufruct thereof for five years to C, with the condition that on the expiry of the five years the usufruct shall go to D. C. dies one year after he begins to enjoy the usufruct. The usufruct for the next four years goes to C.'s heirs, and D. only takes the usufruct on expiry of the five years.

668. A usufruct may be constituted over any property which is capable of private ownership *(res in commercio),* and which cannot be consumed by use (perishables, for instance, are consumed by use). The property need not be such as will benefit the usufructuary. Thus, a usufruct of statuary and painting may be given (the benefit here being purely intellectual); or a usufruct of land may be given, coupled with the condition that more shall be spent on the land than the usufructuary derives therefrom. A usufruct may be constituted not only over particular things, but over universal property. Where a usufruct is constituted over a universal inheritance, nothing must be done in fraud of the rights of those entitled to legitimate portions (where legitimate portions are claimable as of right; which is not thecase in Cape Colony, Natal, the Transvaal, and Rhodesia). Where the *lex hoc edietali* is in force, no usufruct should be given so as to confer on a second spouse a greater portion than the lowest child's portion arising from the first marriage (7, 1 § 14). 669. A usufruct of a person's universal property includes the right of enjoying the fruits of movable and immovable property, and all fungibles (such things as waste in the using, and are therefore not specifically recovered, but are capable of substitution by other articles of the same quantity, weight, or value). In the case of a bequest of a universal usufruct, it does not matter when the property came into the possession of the testator, even acquisitions after the date of the will being included in the usufruct, provided they belonged to the testator at his death. If a testator leaves the usufruct of certain property of which he has only the bare ownership, he is considered to have left the hope of the usufruct *(spes ususfructus),* which he supposes will come to him (the testator) at some time or another, in such a manner that the usufruct of the property in question will come to the usufructuary after the merger of the usufruct in the ownership, whether such merger takes place in the lifetime of the testator, or only at the death of the testator (but in such a manner that the usufruct may be lawfully bequeathed by the testator). 'Where a testator bequeaths the usufruct of all his property to one person, and a particular legacy (such as a house) to nnother, the universal usufruct will not include the usufruct of the particular legacy, and the latter is acquired by the particular legatee in full ownership. A universal usufruct will not include the usufruct of fideicommissary property due to another, which the testator who bequeaths the universal usufruct possessed in a fiduciary capacity: for fideicommissary property is re-garded in the light of a debt due to another, and the fideicommissary property possessed by the deceased as fiduciary heir passes into the possession of another at the time when it was to be restored according to the terms of the *fideicommissum,* such time being the moment when the fiduciary heir dies, which is also the time when his will takes effect, and the universal usufruct bequeathed by the fiduciary heir comes into operation (7, 1 §§ 15—19).

Thus, A. is, during his life, fiduciary heir of the farm X., which is to pass on A.'s decease to B., as fideicommissary heir. A. makes a will, bequeathing the universal usufruct of the property of which he shall die possessed to D. A. dies. D. cannot claim the usufruct of X., which must be handed over, immediately on A.'s death, to B., who acquires X. in full ownership.

670. As a general rule, during the existence of a usufruct over property in favour of a person, the proprietor of such property can do nothing to the prejudice of the usufructuary, nor can he alter the form or condition of the usufructuary property so as to obstruct or diminish the exercise of the usufruct. Thus, the owner can acquire a servitude for the usufructuary property, because the value of the property is increased by such servitude; but he cannot relinquish such servitude, once it has been obtained. Where the usufructuary consents, the proprietor may, in Dutch Law (differing in this respect from Roman Law), impose a usufruct on the property. These rules were recognised in *De Villiers* vs. *Cape Divisional Council* (Buch. 1875, p. 59), where a question arose as to the usufructuary rights of a holder on quit-rent tenure. It was laid down that the proprietor of land is entitled, notwithstanding the usufruct, to exercise his rights of ownership, so far as the rights of the usufructuary are not disturbed. De Villiers, C.J., said: "Besides the restrictions upon the free use and enjoyment of the land by the grantees (on quit-rent tenure) and their assigns, there were others which considerably interfered with their powers of alienation. If they disposed of the land,

a fine immediately accrued under the old Dutch Law to the grantor, who, moreover, became entitled, within a year after he became aware of the sale, to re-purchase the land for the same price for which it had been sold. Upon non-payment of the rent, or any part of it, for three years, the land was forfeited to the *dominm*. In other respects the rights of the emphyteuta to the use and enjoyment of the land were complete. ... The title of the holder on loan was still more precarious. He had no right to alienate at all without the consent of the owner; and whether he alienated or not, the occupation might be determined at any time after the expiration of a year, without previous notice. The tenure differed little, if at all, from the *precarium* of the Roman Law." After giving this review of the old Dutch Law, the Court stated the general rule (as given above) at present prevailing (7, 1 § 20). 671. A person who has the usufruct of a house may use all the implements and appliances thereof, and may avail himself of servitudes constituted in favour of the house. In short, he may avail himself of everything which may enable him to have the full benefit and enjoyment of his occupation. In the same way, he may use gardens and out-houses which are accessory to the dwellinghouse. He cannot, however, injure the owner in any way by exercising his usufruct. He cannot alter the house or the rooms thereof in any way, and must look after the maintenance of the house. He cannot use various portions of the property for other purposes than those to which they were destined by the owner. A person who has the usufruct of a farm may avail himself of rural servitudes constituted in favour of such farm. He may use all the farming implements found on the farm, and may even use the seed found on or in the soil, provided he keeps up a fresh supply of seed continually, to replace the seed which has been used, so that it may be restored to the full owner on the termination of the usufruct. If a wood or forest grows on land subject to a usufruct, the usufructuary may not only cut down a reasonable quantity of timber, but may even sell the

same as fruits or produce. If there is not a wood or forest on the farm, and only a small patch of timber grows there, the usufructuary may take the same, if he requires it for the use of his vines (such as trellises, or supportingsticks), or for the necessary repair of the house. He may remove trees uprooted by tempest, and employ the wood for household purposes; and if such trees are injurious to his right of usufruct, he may call upon the proprietor of the land to remove them (7,1 §§ 21, 22).

Van Leeuwen (*Qent. For.* 1, 2, 15, 9) says: "If trees not fit for cutting have been uprooted or blown down by a storm, or have perished in any other way, they belong to the usufructuary, provided he put new ones in their place. " With this view Voet does not agree, holding that it is opposed to natural reason, and it is contrary to the opinion of Paulus if it is taken as law that a usufructuary may be compelled to plant fresh trees in place of those torn up by a storm.

672. The usufructuary cannot cut down fruit trees so as to cause loss to the proprietor; and, in the same way, he cannot alter pleasure grounds, containing walks or promenades, so as to make kitchen gardens of them (7, 1 § 22). 673. Where an estate is increased by alluvion, the usufruct of the additional portion of the estate belongs to the usufructuary. Where metals, limestone or chalk, sand and stones have been dug out of the soil before the usufruct begins, they belong in full ownership to the proprietor of the soil, and the usufructuary cannot make use of them. Voet draws a distinction with reference to metals, chalk, sand or stones dug out of the soil after the usufruct begins. If they are unfailing (i.e., such that the use of a moderate quantity by the usufructuary will not make any appreciable difference to the rights of the proprietor—*renascentia),* they are acquired by the usufructuary in full ownership as soon as they are dug out of the soil by him, or by some one on his behalf. If the supply on the property is limited (*si non renascantur),* the ownership in metals or stones dug out of the soil goes to the proprietor; and

in this case the usufructuary may use such metals or stones, but must repay their value to the proprietor when the usufruct terminates. A person who has the usufruct of a ship may navigate the same, provided he employs competent seamen, and guards against all risks. Where a person receives the usufruct of a flock of sheep or a herd of cattle he has the right to the young of such sheep or cattle, in so far as they exceed the original number of sheep or cattle. Where he has the usufruct of a special animal, such as a stallion, he may use the animal for other purposes than those for which it was used by its owner, but he must not diminish its value by ill-treatment (7, 1 §§ 23-27). 674. Where a usufructuary, or some one on his behalf, gathers fruits (whether natural fruits or such as are acquired by industry), they become his property by a right which is irrevocable; but if the fruits have not been gathered by the usufructuary, and he dies, his right to gather such fruits is not transmitted to his heir. Consequently, if ungathered fruits have been taken away by a robber or trespasser, the action to recover such fruits will lie in favour of the proprietor of the soil, and not of the usufructuary. A *bond fidt* possessor, on the other hand, will have a right to the fruits, and he ma sue for their recovery under such circumstances. The fruits or produce of a property may be gathered by the usufructuary at any time during the term of his usufruct, and it does not matter whether the fruits so gathered are ripe or not, provided it is not unusual to gather them before they ripen. Where a usufruct includes rents, the rents will go to the usufructuary for occupation by tenants during the period of the usufruct, even if the payment of such rent is made after the usufruct has terminated. Where a property subject to a usufruct (the rent derived from which is to go to the usufructuary) cannot be let, the usufructuary may himself occupy the property which is not let (7, 1 §§ 28—30).

Illustration: A. has the usufruct, including a right to the rents, of the farm X. , for five years from January 1st, 1875. Portion of the farm is let to B. for three years from January 1st, 1874. Another portion is let to C. for three years from January 1st, 1876. The remaining portion of the farm is unlet, and A. can occupy this remaining portion. C. vacates his portion of the farm on January 1st, 1879, and fails to pay his rent for 1878. In March, 1880, C. becomes insolvent, and surrenders his estate. A. can claim rent from B. for two years from January 1st, 1875, and B. must pay the first year's rent to the proprietor of the farm. A. can claim on C.'s insolvent estate for the rent for 1878.

675. A usufructuary can sell, let, or grant the enjoyment of his usufruct to another, provided that such ceded enjoyment does not last longer than it would have lasted had the usufructuary himself enjoyed the usufruct. The lessee of a usufruct, however, cannot be compelled to relinquish the usufruct at an unsuitable time, but he must receive reasonable previous notice. A usufructuary can likewise pledge his usufruct. Where a judgment has been given against a usufructuary, the fruits of the usufructuary property to which he is entitled during his usufruct may be taken in execution to satisfy the usufruct. But there can be no taking in execution where a testator, who bequeaths a usufruct, by his will directs that the usufruct shall not be liable for a debt incurred in favour of another person before the taking effect of the usufruct. A usufructuary may proceed against those who do anything, such as building or obstructing, which interferes with the usufruct, and the Court may bind the obstructor to give security providing against resultant damage. Where a general usufruct (and even the usufruct of special property) has been bequeathed to a person, and he cannot obtain the enjoyment thereof, he may sue to obtain the usufruct by an action of inheritance, in the same way as an heir can sue. In order to support the actions which a usufructuary can bring, he can demand from the proprietor of the usufructuary property such titledeeds or other documents as may be necessary to substantiate his claim (7, 1 §§ 31—34). 676. The expense of claiming, collecting, and preserving the fruits or produce falls on the usufructuary. Where a usufructuary, in order to vindicate the right to fruits and produce, is compelled to establish title to the property in question (as where a third party claims the usufructuary property, and the true owner is absent), he must bear the expense of making such claim, but has the right to claim restitution from the true owner on the expiry of the usufruct. He has a similar right to restitution for all expenses incurred by him in connection with the preservation of ownership. The usufructuary, as we have seen, must bear expenses incurred in connection with such reasonable repairs as are necessary to keep the usufructuary property in order. He must preserve such things as vines or fruit trees, and if they die he must replace them. He must properly feed and depasture usufructuary animals. Buildings which are ruined by age need not be repaired by the usufructuary. Where such ruined buildings are rebuilt, the usufructuary may claim compensation from the owner of the buildings. The usufructuary must pay ground-rent, quit-rent, drainage rates, and similar taxes, chiefly those of a temporary nature. Such expenses as are absolutely necessary for the preservation of the property need not be borne by the usufructuary. Where a person has hired the use of a house or land for a term of years, and bequeaths the usufruct thereof, the usufructuary need not pay the rent due on such house or land after the testator's death, but such rent must be paid by the testator's heir. A usufructuary need not pay the debts of the person who bequeathed a usufruct to him, out of the fruits or produce whereof he has the enjoyment; such debts must be subtracted from the whole of the property left by the testator, and the usufructuary will have the usufruct of the property remaining after payment of such debts. Where a usufructuary has been compelled to pay taxes and other charges (for which, if they had accrued during his tenure, he would have been personally liable) which became due in the testator's lifetime, he may, on the termination of his tenure as usufructu-

ary, claim a refund of such expenses from the proprietor of the usufructuary estate. A usufructuary must exercise the greatest care in the preservation of usufructuary property. When he gives up the usufruct he is absolved from paying for such repairs as are necessary to the property, which has deteriorated of itself; but he is liable for the expense of restoring such deterioration in value as has been caused by his act, or the act of his servants or agents (7, 1 §§ 35-41). 677. Where a person has the usufruct of fungibles *res fungibiles,* perishables, which can be replaced by others of the same species), which are consumed by use, and cannot be returned intact, he may, when his usufruct ends, return things of the same quantity, quality, and number, or may repay what they were worth at the time when the usufruct was acquired. Where a person leaves to another the usufruct of all his property, this will include fungibles, and they must be restored in the manner above stated. The fungible property may be used by the usufructuary in any way he pleases, and he may retain for himself the profits derived from such use, provided he returns the quantity, quality, number or value of the fungibles actually obtained at the time he acquires the usufruct. Thus, if a person obtains the usufruct (which may happen by the bequest of a universal usufruct, or by a special contract) of ten bushels of wheat, he may sow the same, and, if he reaps thirty bushels of wheat, he will retain twenty, and must hand back ten bushels to the original proprietor of the wheat, provided such bushels are equivalent in quantity, quality, and value to the original ten bushels (7, 5 §§ 1—4). 678. A right is said to vest *(dies cedit)* when anything becomes due in favour of a person; a right is said to be exercisable *(dies venit)* when anything which is due is claimable, that is to say, when the time for performance of the obligation which corresponds to the right arrives. In other words, in the case of property that has been bequeathed, *dies cedit* signifies that a legatee has acquired a right so perfect as to be transmissible to his heirs, while *dies venit* denotes that he can exercise such right. But there is an exception to the general rule relating to legacies in the case of the legacy of a usufruct. Where a usufruct has been bequeathed unconditionally, the right thereto vests in the usufructuary only from the time of adiation of the inheritance; and, where a usufruct has been bequeathed on condition that its enjoyment shall only commence from a certain date, the right vests *(dies cedit)* only when such day arrives. The same exception applies in the case of the personal servitudes *usus* (use) and *habitatio* (right of habitation). This is due to the fact that such personal servitudes attach to the person, and die with the person, so that no benefit accrues to a usufructuary dying before adiation, or to his heir. If, however, the heir does not adiate through negligence, the usufruct will be regarded as commencing from the date of delay on the heir's part, and he must pay the value thereof to the usufructuary or his heirs. If a usufruct has been left for particular terms, whether years or months (such as a bequest of the usufruct of a property from 1880 to 1885, and 1890 to 1895), different usufructs are considered to have been left, and there will be a separate vesting in regard to each period of usufruct. Where a person leaves a usufruct to two persons, who are named, who are to

C.L.—VOL. I. F F have the usufruct respectively in alternate years, the usufruct for the first year will go to the person first-named (7, 3, §§ 1—4).

See Grotius *(Introduction,* 2, 39, 10; *Maasdorp,* p. 157).

679. The *jus accrescendi* (right of accrual) in Roman Law was the right of survivorship, which became exercisable when there were co-heirs, one of whom would not take, or became (by death or otherwise) incapable of taking his share; and by virtue of this right such share accrued to the other co-heirs. This right was equally applicable to legacies or particular successions as to wills or universal successions. The surviving legatee took the share of the co-legatee who was conjoined with him, which such co-legatee had not by that time ac-

quired. In the case of inheritances, the testator had no power of direction with regard to the *jus accrescendi;* but he had such power in the case of legacies. In order that the *jus accrescendi* might apply in the case of legacies, there must be co-legatees in respect of the same thing, which must not be divided in respect of each legatee. A usufruct, being an incorporeal right, is not physically divisible, but it is legally divisible, and can therefore be divided into shares, which may be held separately or indivisibly; in the same way it may be bequeathed to several joint-usufructuaries, and such joint-usufructuaries may bring the action *communi dividundo* (for division of joint property) against each other. If a usufruct is left to two persons by testament, the share of one of them, on his failure to take, goes to the other by the *jus accrescendi*—a rule which does not apply in the case of other servitudes. This right of accrual in cases of usufruct is purely personal, and not real, as in the case of other legacies or inheritances, where one share accedes to another. A joint-legatee of a usufruct, who has ceased to possess or enjoy his own share, does not thereby lose his right of accrual to the share of the other legatee, provided he has not previously obtained the whole usufruct. Where A. and B. have a joint usufruct, and B., not being certain of his right to the usufruct, brings an action against C. (whom B. imagines to be the possessor of the usufructuary property, but who has, in reality, no right to it), and B. does not succeed in his claim, the portion of B. accrues to A., not to C. (who is not the actual possessor), nor to the true owner (for he is not entitled to the usufruct until the term of the usufruct expires); and if A., by nonuser, loses the usufruct, nothing reverts to B. by the law of accrual (for B. has not established his right to usufruct), and the whole usufruct reverts to the owner of the usufructuary property. Where there are two joint-legatees of a usufruct, and one of them acquires a share of the ownership, so that his usufruct is consolidated with or merged in his right of ownership, he does not lose his right of

accrual with reference to the share of his co-legatee. *The jus accrescendi* only takes place between persons whom the will conjoins in respect of a particular thing *(re),* or in respect of a particular thing and by special form of words at the same time *(re et verbis),* but not where persons are conjoined by words alone, without reference to a particular thing. It is a clear rule of modern Dutch Law that the construction in cases of inheritance and legacies will be against the *jus accrescendi,* unless it is quite clear that it was the testator's intention that *the jus accrescendi* should apply (see *Schorer,* §§ 152,163,182; Maasdorp's *Grotius,* pp. 470, 475,487). So, if a usufruct is left to two persons respectively in alternate years, and one dies or fails to enjoy the usufruct, the other cannot claim the forfeited usufruct by right of accrual, since he has had only the usufruct of particular years bequeathed to him (the conjunction of the legatees being not *re,* in respect of the usufruct, but only by words—*verbis tantum*—for the usufructs are regarded as separate, and as existing in respect of two independent persons, their conjunction in the will being a mere accident). In *Myiet's Executors* vs. *Ava* (14 S. C. 516) it was said by De Villiers, C.J.: "According to Julian *(Dig.* 7, 2, 1, 4), if a testator, having instituted two heirs, bequeaths the ownership after deduction of the usufruct to another, the heirs do not enjoy the *jus accrescendi.* Voet (7, 2 § 5), commenting upon this passage, states the reason of the rule to be that the usufruct was regarded as having been originally constituted in favour of each heir in proportion to his share of the inheritance. When once, therefore, the fiduciary heirs have entered upon their respective shares of inheritance, the separation of interests has taken place which, differing in this respect from the effect of a mere usufruct, prevents the operation of the *jus accrescendi* in favour of the survivor." Where husband and wife, by donation *inter vivos,* give each other all their property, reserving the usufruct of such property to the donor in each case, and one spouse dies, the other cannot by virtue of *the jus accrescendi* claim the usufruct of all the property, but only of that part of the property contributed by him or her, since they were not joined in the usufruct (7, 2 §§ 1-9).

See *De Pass* vs. *Colonial Government and Others* (4 S. C. 392); Grotius (2, 23, 5; *Maasdorp,* p. 113); Van der Keessel (§ 326); and Van Leeuwen *(Cens. For.* 1, 2, 15, 21).

680. A person who enters upon the enjoyment of a usufruct must give security for his occupation of the usufructuary property, to the effect that he will use it with care, that he will return the property at the termination of the usufruct in the same condition as it was in when he received it, and that his custody of the property will be free from fraud. The person who has the ultimate right to the property may claim payment of the security at any time after it shall appear that the property has been enjoyed in an improper or careless manner; but the security for return of the property can only be demanded when the usufruct expires, and the usufructuary does not return the property in the same condition as it was in when he received it. The degree of care which the usufructuary must exercise during his occupation is ordinary care, such as is expected from a reasonable man who is business-like in his methods. In modern Dutch Law, a usufructuary can be compelled to make an inventory of the property received by him, whereof he is to have the usufruct. Even if a universal usufructuary, when his usufruct was granted or bequeathed, obtained full power to alienate his interest, he must prepare and furnish an inventory. A usufructuary, in order to satisfy the requirement of security, must give sureties. If he cannot find suitable sureties he must apply to the Court for directions in the matter, and the Court may allow him to take the usufruct subject to such conditions for safe-guarding the property as the Court may deem fit to impose. Where a usufructuary contumaciously refuses to give security, when called upon to do so by the proprietor, he is deprived of the right of usufruct until such time as he furnishes security; and the fruits arising from the

property before the furnishing of such security will go, not to the usufructuary, but to the proprietor. Any person who is to derive benefit from the usufruct must give security. If there are several joint usufructuaries, each of them must give security. Where a usufruct is left to one person, with the direction that it shall presently be handed over to another, and the former person (the fiduciary) has no chance of ever regaining the usufruct, security need only be given by the person to whom the usufruct must pass (the fideicommissary). Where, on the death of the fideicommissary, or failure of some other condition, the usufruct may revert to, or remain in possession of the fiduciary, he must also give security. The security must be furnished to the person to whom the usufruct reverts, or is intended to revert, at its termination, or who owns the usufructuary property. Where there are several to whom the usufruct, at its termination, will revert, or who own the usufructuary property, security must be given to each. If the usufruct of a farm has been left unconditionally to one person, and the ownership conditionally to another, since the legatee of the ownership may not fulfil the condition and the farm may consequently revert to the heir, there is an uncertainty as to who will be ultimately entitled to the usufruct, and the usufructuary must give security to both the legatee of the farm and the testator's heir (or executor, as the case may be). So whenever it is uncertain which of two persons will ultimately be entitled to a usufruct, security must be given to both. A person to whom the usufruct will never revert is not entitled to security; and so, if a person to whom security was given afterwards loses his ownership in the usufructuary property—by virtue of which ownership he became entitled to the usufruct—he can no longer demand security. Where a person obtains a usufruct, and is ultimately to obtain the ownership of the usufructuary property, he need not give security. Voet states that this applies where a person is to obtain the ownership from a certain day; it is then certain that the property is to

come to the usufructuary or his heirs, and he is absolved from giving security. But it is submitted that this only applies where the right to the ownership vests in the usufructuary's lifetime; and that if a testator bequeaths the usufruct of a property to A., and the full ownership after A.'s death to A.'s heir, A. must give security in favour of his heir; for although A. has perfect freedom of testating with regard to his own property, the property of which he has the usufruct must inevitably pass to his heir, whether testamentary or *ab intestato,* and A. cannot deprive his heir thereof. Where a usufruct has been left to the Treasury or the Crown, security need not be given to the Treasury. A father who has the usufruct of his minor child's adventitious property need not give security; and Dutch Law (differing from Roman Law) extends this right to a mother, where the necessity for giving security is remitted by will. The inventory must, however, always be made. A person who gives another a usufruct by act or deed *inter vivos,* can expressly remit the obligation of the usufructuary to give security; and the heir of a testator who bequeaths a usufruct (to which heir the usufruct must ultimately come) can also remit the usufructuary's obligation to give security. Voet states clearly that a testator cannot, by will, remit the obligation of the usufructuary to give security; and he cites a case from the *Code* where a wife had left her husband the usufruct of all her property, and had expressed her desire that no security should be demanded of him, and it was decreed by the Emperors that the husband was bound to give security. Van Leeuwen *(Cens. For.* 1, 2, 15, 6) also states that a usufructuary " cannot be released from the necessity of giving this security, even though the testator desires that he should be. In spite of this desire the usufructuary is bound to give security for the protection of the owner's interest, and to make an inventory... of the property, included in the usufruct. " Grotius *(Introduction,* 2, 89, 2, 20; *Maasdorp,* pp. 156,159) says: "A life-usufructuary is bound to give security to the owner that he will not use the property in an improper manner, and that at the expiration of the usufruct it shall be returned to the owner in full ownership. Such security cannot be dispensed with even by last will.... Custom has decided that, if a man bequeaths to his wife or any other person the lifeusufruct of all his property, such legatee acquires the right to use and consume even things which perish with use, under such security and valuation as aforesaid, and this necessitates the making of au inventory of the property by the usufructuary, which, as already stated with respect to security, cannot be dispensed with." Schorer (§ 224) gives the reason for this limitation of the testator's right as being that "no one can validly renounce what is for the benefit of another," and quotes two decisions of the Court of Holland to that effect. He cites Groenewegen (Commentaries on the Code, 3, 83, 4) on the other side, who holds that " it is quite lawful for the testator to dispense with the usufructuary security." But Schorer dissents from Groenewegen (who is supported by Argentraeus and Sande), and agrees with the authorities on general Dutch Law, Voet and Grotius. Schorer also states: "The doctrine laid down by Grotius is so binding that if a penalty be provided by the testament in case security is demanded in spite of its having been dispensed with by the testator, such penalty is regarded as not written and null and void; and this is true in any case, whether the usufruct was given simply or with full power to alienate" (Maasdorp, p. 512). Van der Keessel (§ 371) says: " The security which it appears a usufructuary is amongst us bound to give, together with sureties, cannot be dispensed with by testament, unless the power of alienation has been conceded, in which case not the mere usufruct, but the property, subject to the burden of restoring it, is considered to have been left." For the latter part of his statement Van der Keessel cites Voet (7, 1 § 11; above, § 665), on reference to whom it will be seen that where a usufruct is left to a person with full power of alienation no usufruct has in reality been left, but full ownership limited by the oblig-

ation to restore the property. That is not a case of usufruct at all; and the nominal usufructuary has, for a limited period, the rights of a full owner. Van der Keessel, therefore, begs the question: the moment the power of alienation is conceded, there is no usufruct in the true sense of the word. Van der Keessel is, therefore, really in agreement with Voet and Grotius in every respect. From a review of the authorities, then, it would seem that a testator, in Dutch Law, has not the power to relieve a person from the obligation to give security. Voet, however, states that there is one way in which this may be evaded: it is lawful for a testator to bequeath a usufruct to one person, and to direct that one of the testator's heirs shall provide security for the restoration of the usufruct; in which case the usufructuary receives an additional legacy—that of security. Security which is due by a usufructuary, if not provided, can be claimed at any time during the period of the usufruct by a condictio incerti (claim for a thing not fixed in amount or value); and this claim is never prescribed. An action also lies against the usufructuary for damage to the usufructuary property (lex Aquilia); and, as we have seen, the property itself can be vindicated at the termination of the usufruct, unless the usufruct consists of money, fungibles, or perishables, in which case the same value or amount is claimable (7, 9 §§ 1—11).

As authorities for the statement of law that a testator cannot prevent the giving of security by a usufructuary, Voet cites Neostadius (Decisions of Court of Holland, No. 20; Decisions of the Supreme Court, No. 33, No. 91); Gayl (book 2, § 145), Peckius (On Willt of Spouses, 5, 24, 4); Sotomayor (Usufructs, c. 15); Carpzovius (Legal Definitions, 3, 13, 12, 14); Christinaeus (On the Laws of Mechlin, 9, 13, 3, 4); De Cabedo (1, § 136); Someren (The Law of Stepparmts, 7 5 1; 11, 3 § 2); Paul Voet (Institutes, Usufruct, 1 § 5); Dutch Consultations (part 1, 5,15, 20; part 2, 108, 178, 325; part 4, 231). As to cases where executors or surviving spouses need not make inventories, see Cape

Ord. 104, 1833, § 28, and Ord. 105, 1833, § 18; O. R. C. Statutes, chap. 54, § 33; and Heyne vs. Tomkin (3 C. L. J. 38).

681. Usufruct is terminated by death of the usufructuary. As it is a personal right, it is not transmissible to the usufructuary's heirs. If a testator bequeaths a usufruct to a man and his heirs, there are several usufructs, one in favour of the first legatee, and one in favour of each of his heirs. In such a case, fresh security must be given by each usufructuary, when he succeeds to the usufruct. Where a usufruct is left to a man and his heirs, only the first generation of heirs is considered as included, and not the heirs ad infinitum (to infinity), as is usually the case with other testamentary dispositions. If a usufruct is left to a corporation or to the State, or to a municipality, it will hold good for one hundred years, which is taken, in Dutch Law, to be the term of life of a long-lived man. (See In re Hoffmeester, 10 C. T. R. 758.) If a usufruct is left to several persons in undivided shares, the death of one of them does not terminate the usufruct; and it is only terminated by the death of all the usufructuaries. Where a person, as fiduciary, has to hand over a usufruct to a fideicommissary heir, the usufruct is terminated in the person of the fideicommissary, unless there is a right of reversion to the fiduciary, in wluch case the usufruct terminates with the death of the fiduciary heir. Where a usufructuary lets, sells, or makes over his right to another, the usufruct ends with the death of the usufructuary, and not with that of the lessee, purchaser, assignee, or grantee. Usufruct is also terminated when it is consolidated with or merged in the right of ownership of the usufructuary property. This happens where the usufructuary becomes owner of the property, or the usufruct reverts to one who is already owner of the property. Usufruct also terminates when the usufructuary abandons his right to the usufruct. It is not terminated where the usufructuary cedes his right, but lasts until the death of the original usufructuary. Where such cession cannot be made by the

usufructuary, the cession is treated as null and void. Where a usufructuary illegally transfers not only the usufruct but also the ownership of the usufructuary property, he loses the usufruct of the property, and the transferee has no right thereto. A usufructuary cannot be deprived of his usufruct solely on account of his misuse of the usufructuary property, since he has given security which may be called up at any time during the period of the usufruct. A usufruct is lost by non-user (according to Voet and Grotius, for a third of a century; according to other Dutch authorities, for thirty years; according to Roman Law, for three years in the case of movables, ten years in case of real property where the parties are present, and twenty years in the case of real property where the parties are absent from the country, or one of them is absent). This is the case even if the usufructuary was forcibly ejected from the property. A usufructuary does not make use of a property where neither he personally, nor another in his name, uses it. A person is said to use the property where he buys or hires a usufruct, or who receives it by way of gift, or who carries on the business of the usufructuary, such as a husband on behalf of his wife, or a wife on behalf of her absent husband. A usufruct is extinguished by total destruction of the property over which the usufruct is enjoyed. If part of a property be destroyed the usufruct continues as to the remaining part. Where the usufruct of a flock or herd of sheep or cattle is given generally, and not with reference to special sheep or cattle, the usufruct terminates when the number of sheep or cattle is so reduced that a flock or herd can no longer be said to exist. If the usufructary property does not perish, but undergoes an entire change in substance or form, the usufruct is lost: this happens where, by inundation, a field becomes a lake or pool; or where, by drainage, a lake becomes a field. Where a property has been completely destroyed, and a new property takes its place, a usufruct does not revive in respect of the new property. So, if a house is destroyed, and a new one is erected, or a ship is broken up,

and a new ship built out of the old materials, the usufruct does not revive. But if a house which is partly destroyed is restored, the usufruct revives; and, in like manner, if a person has the usufruct of a site, on which a house is built, and the house is destroyed, the usufruct of the site continues. If a usufruct is granted for a certain time, or until a certain condition is fulfilled, it is terminated on the expiration of the time or the fulfilment of the condition. If a usufruct is granted for a certain time, and the usufructuary dies before the expiration of that period, his right does not pass to his heirs for the remaining period, and the usufruct terminates (7, 4 §§ 1—14). 682. Where a person seeks to establish his right to a servitude, he must institute an action to secure an acknowledgment of his right *(actio confessoria)*. On the other hand, a person who asserts his full right of ownership, and seeks to prevent another from exercising a usufruct over his property, must institute an action for a declaration that such other person is not entitled to a usufruct. The action claiming a usufruct *(actio confessoria)* is in the nature of a real action, and lies in favour of the person for whose benefit a usufruct has been imposed on the property. It does not lie in favour of one who has been promised a usufruct by contract, and has not acquired it by quasi-delivery, for he has only a personal action on the contract. Nor does it lie in favour of the true owner of the property; for his property cannot be subject to a servitude in his own favour. The *actio confessoria* lies against any other person who is in possession of the usufructuary property; or against any person who disturbs the owner of the usufruct in his possession of the usufruct; or against a person who, in an action, holds himself out as being the possessor; and, in especial, the action lies against the owner of the servient tenement. The object of the action is to secure a declaration that the property is liable to the usufruct in question, and an order on the defendant compelling him to give possession to the plaintiff, together with the fruits arising from the property, or to suffer t he plaintiff to have the peace-

able use and enjoyment of the property. If, while the action is pending, or even before joinder in issue *(litis contestatio),* or before commencement of the suit, the usufruct is terminated by the death of the usufructuary, or in any other way, the usufructuary (if alive) or his heirs will have an equitable action to recover the fruits for the time during which the usufructuary was entitled to them, and any damages sustained by the usufructuary by reason of his not having had the usufruct. If, then, the usufruct is merely promised, the claim for it is made by personal action; if it is already established in the usufructuary's favour, it is sought by a real action *(actio in rem confessoria)*. The action by a person asserting full rights of ownership *(actio negatoria)* lies only in favour of the owner, and not a mere possessor. It is available against the person who wrongfully usurps a usufruct, or who, although a usufructuary, disturbs the true owner in the free possession and disposal over his property. The action, as we have seen, is for a declaration that the property is free from the usufruct, and for an order on the defendant to restore the property and the produce he has gathered, with payment of damages, or an order compelling him to desist from future disturbance. Both an owner deprived of possession, and one who is still in possession but is disturbed, may sue in this action (7, 6 §§ 1—4). 683. As we have seen (above, § 676) a usufructuary must bear the burden of certain taxes on the property whereof he has the usufruct. The principle and incidence of taxation differ greatly at the present time from the condition of things prevailing in Voet's day. But to a great extent the Courts still hold the usufructuary liable for taxes, especially if a person has a usufruct for life—since it is only just that a person who has such a full enjoyment, terminating only with his own existence, should bear the necessary burdens which the Legislature or the administration imposes on the land of which he has the full enjoyment. So a municipality is entitled to assessment rates on the value of fixed property, which rates are claimable from a person who has the life usufruct of the property (*Breda* vs. *Toivn Council of Cape Toicn*, 6 S. C. 71).

On the liability of usufructuaries, see *Burger* vs. *Jouberi's Truttees* (3 S. C. 410). In that case a testator sold to his son's children a farm, for a certain price, to be paid into the estate within six months. The inheritance coming to the son was not to be paid out to him, but was to be taken in part payment of the purchase-price fixed for the farm. The balance was to be raised by mortgaging the farm. The executors of the testator were to raise the loan. The son and his wife were to have the usufruct of the farm during their lives. In other words, the son's children received a free legacy of the farm, the purchase-price (which went into the estate) coming from their father's portion of inheritance and a loan on security of the farm. The son surrendered his estate in January, 1884, and the father died in April, 1884. It was decided that the usufructuary was bound to pay the interest which would become due on the mortgage to be raised, and that the trustees in insolvency could not, therefore, sell the usufruct of the insolvent without any encumbrance. De Villiers, C.J., said: "It is only right that the beneficiary should bear the encumbrances." As to rights of usufruct in cases of mutual wills, see *Haupt* vs. *Van den Heever's Executor* (6 S. C. 49); *De Montmort* vs. *Board of Executors* (2 S. C. 69); *Lucas* vs. *Hod«* (Buch. 1879, p. 132); *Smith* vs. *Sogers' Executors* (Foord, 66); *Naudi ys. Naudt's Executors* (10 S. C. 145); *Van Biljoen* vs. *Botha and Becker* (5 S. 175); and *Van Breda* vs. *Muster of Supreme Court* (7 S. C. 360).

684. The next personal servitude is use *(usus).* Use is the right to utilise the property of another person for one's daily needs, leaving the substance of the property intact. Use is a more limited right than usufruct. Both, however, concur in the following respects: (1) the thing must be used without prejudice to the substance; (2) security must be given for proper usage and restoration; (3) they originate and are terminated in the same way. Usufruct is divisible, and can

be bequeathed in parts, and admits of the right of accrual *(jus accrescendi);* while none of these things take place in the case of use *(usus).* Thus, a testator may leave the use of a property to one person, the usufruct to another, and the bare ownership to a third. Here the person who has the use first takes what is necessary for his wants, and the remaining produce of the property goes to the usufructuary. Usufruct includes use; but use does not include usufruct. The use of money, however, is the same as a usufruct thereof. A person who has the use of property cannot transfer the same to another, whether by sale, lease, or donation, unless it is clear from the terms of the will or grant that the testator or grantor intended that the usuary might let the property of which he has the use. The usuary of a house may let such portion thereof as is not needed for the use of himself and his family. A usuary must bear necessary expenses in connection with the preservation of the property (7, 8 §§ 1—5). 685. Habitation *(habitatio)* is a real right to inhabit the house of another without injury to the substance. There is more in *habitatio* than in *urns,* for a person who has the right of *habitatio* may let out the house for purposes of habitation, but not for other purposes, which a usufructuary may do. The right is not extinguished by non-user, as in the case of *usus. Habitatio* is extinguished by the death of the grantee, being a personal servitude; but not by the grantor's death. Voet inclines to the view that the grantor's heirs may revoke the grant of habitation, as it is a species of precarious tenure. Where there is a doubt as to whether *habitatio* or full ownership of a house has been left to a person, the presumption is that only the right of *habitatio* has been bequeathed; and the burden of proof that the full ownership has been left is on the legatee (7, 8 § § 6—9).

See Grotiua *(Introduction,* 2, 44, 1—10).

(3) Real Servitudes In General. 686. Real servitudes cannot exist, or be understood to exist, apart from immovable property *(praedia),* since they are ac-

cidents and conditions attaching to immovable property. Real servitudes cannot be let, whereas personal servitudes, such as usufruct and *habitatio,* may under certain circumstances be let to hire. As we have seen, in the case of real servitudes, there must be a dominant tenement enjoying the servitude, and a servient tenement over which the right is exercised. The immovable property to which a praedial or real servitude attaches is either urban or rural. Urban tenements are all such buildings as are erected for the purpose of habitation, whether they are situate in a town or in the country. Rural tenements are such immovable properties as, being situate in a town or in the country, are adapted and used for agricultural or pastoral purposes. Thus *praedia rastica* are distinguished from *praedia urbana,* not by situation, but by the use which they serve. As was stated in *Swarte* vs. *Landmark* (2 S. C. 8), "it is not the *place* where the property is situated which shews whether a *praedium* is *tirbanum* or *rusticum,* but the *use* to which the parties Lave devoted it." In *Nieuwoudt* vs. *Slarin* (18 S. C. 62), it was said by De Villiers, C J.: "I adhere to the view, expressed in *Suarts* vs. *Landmark,* that the test whether a tenement is rural or urban is not the place where the property is situated, but the use to which it is devoted. In that case, a small plot of land had been leased for the purpose of erecting a building for a shop, and the fact that under the lease the lessee had rights of grazing on the remainder of the lessor's farm was held not to make the tenement a rural one. *Prima fucie,* land, to the extent to which it is not actually built upon, is *praedium rusticum;* but if such land is a mere messuage adjoining a house, and required for the proper use and full enjoyment of the house, it is regarded in law as *praedium urbanum.* It follows that where land has been leased which exceeds in extent what is required for the proper use and full enjoyment of any house on it, such land must for the purposes of the lease be regarded as a rural tenement. The buildings may of course be leased separately from the remainder of the land, and in that case the buildings would be urban, and the lands rural tenements; but where the land and buildings are included in one and the same lease, the only test as to the nature of the tenancy is whether or not the remainder of the land was required for the proper use and full enjoyment of the buildings." That is to say, if the remainder of the land was not required for the proper use and full enjoyment of the buildings, such remainder would constitute a rural tenement. Where a garden is used for the purpose of deriving profit from the sale or use of agricultural products, and not as an appurtenant to a dwelling-house, it will be looked upon as a rural tenement; but an ornamental flower garden attached to a dwelling-house is an urban tenement (8, 1 §§ 1—3).

As to the impossibility of real servitudes existing without a *praedium,* see *Fain* vs. *Macdonald* (Buch. 1876, p. 166).

687. From the distinction between urban and rural tenements are derived urban and rural servitudes. Urban servitudes are those which exist in respect of urban tenements. Rural servitudes are those which exist in respect of rural tenements. The servitude, as to its classification, follows the nature of the dominant tenement, even if the servient tenement is not of the same nature as the dominant tenement. Thus, if the dominant tenement be rural, and the servient tenement urban, the servitude will be rural. If there are several servitudes, they must be reckoned according to the number, not of the dominant, but of the servient tenements. Thus, if there exists in favour of a farm a right of way over four other fanns, there are four separate servitudes. There is, however, an exception to this rule where there are several dominant tenements, and only one servient tenement. Here the number of servitudes will be reckoned according to the number of the dominant tenements. Thus, if four tenements have a right of way over one farm, there are four servitudes, for there is a right of way in favour of each dominant tenement (8, 1 §§ 4, 5).

See *Dreyer* vs. *Ireland* (Buch. 1874, p. 201).

688. The bare promise of a real servitude does not attach to the property over which it is proposed to constitute the servitude, unless there is a quasi-delivery, and in such a case only the promisor is personally bound; and in the case of such a bare personal promise & particular successor to the servient tenement, such as a purchaser or donee, is not liable to perform the promise, unless an express stipulation to that effect has been embodied in the contract of sale or deed of gift. It has been laid down *(Ebden* vs. *Anderson,* 2 S. 64) that there is no distinction between general and particular successors as purchasers of servient tenements. Voet, however, lays down that universal successors by inheritance may be sued by the person to whom the promise was made, and compelled to grant a right of servitude over the property in question to the plaintiff; and if there are several such successors, the action will lie against each of them *in solidum* (for the whole), a servitude being in its nature indivisible (8, 1 § 6). The rule affirmed in *Ebden* vs. *Anderson* (2 S. 64) relates to dominant tenements as well as to servient tenements. Where the owner of a farm granted to the owner of another farm, and "his heirs and successors," a right of way over the first farm, and the farms were divided into lots, the purchaser of one of the lots of the dominant tenement was held entitled to claim such right of way from the purchaser of a lot on the servient tenement, over which lot such right of way could be exercised in terms of the original agreement between the predecessors in title, although the defendant was not the owner of the whole of the servient farm, or even of the homestead situated thereon.

689. Before proceeding to treat separately of urban servitudes and rural servitudes, it is desirable to indicate certain rules of law which have reference in common to both urban and rural servitudes. They may be created and terminated in the same way. This may happen, according to Voet, by agreements and covenants accompanied by quasi-delivery *quasi traditione).* In *Ji-idd* vs. *Fourie* (2 E. D. C. 41) it was said

by Buchanan, J.: "The weighty authority of Voet is to the same effect as that of Groenewegen *(ad Grot.,* 2, 26, 1, 2). He notices the opinion of Grotius, only to controvert it. Speaking of the characteristics of servitudes (8, *i* § 1), he says, they may be created 'for instance, by agreements and covenants accompanied by a quasi-delivery, which consists in the mere exercise of the right and permission to do so, or by the pointing out of the place for the exercise of the servitude; and by our customs the delivery must be made with solemn forms according to the law of the place, iu order that the servient tenement may be affected by the real right of a servitude, and that creditors may be prevented from selling it by auction as if unaffected by such servitude; for the alienation of immovable property is, according to the common practice and by certain fixed laws, invalid if not made according to the laws of the place where it is situated; and under the term alienation, the creation of a servitude also falls.' And, again, Voet says (1, 8 § 20; above, § 532): 'As regards praedial servitudes, it is without doubt that they come within the number of immovable things, for they are nothing else than the rights and qualities of immovable things or estates.'"..." If the object of registration is to prevent fraud by giving notice to the world, I cannot, on principle, understand why express notice, given directly to the person sought to be affected by it, differs in its effect from notice which, by the operation of law, is held to be given to him by registration. Registration no doubt is the easiest and most certain means of proving notice, but in this case express and direct notice before purchase has been brought home to the purchaser *aliunde.* ... There is nothing so sacred in a deed of transfer as of itself to prevent this Court, as a Court of Law and Equity, from going behind it. A transfer deed is but the symbol of delivery. Actions to set aside or amend transfers are by no means uncommon in our Courts." *Saayman* vs. *La Grange* (Buch. 1879, p. 10) was cited, and Buchanan, J., proceeded: "The law of Holland, according to

Van Leeuwen *(R. D. L.* 2, 7, 4), adopted the rule requiring the tradition of immovables to be made *coram lege loci,* in order to prevent the commission of frauds. Further on in the same section, speaking of the Placaats regulating the mode of transfer of such property, he says: 'but, inasmuch as the *causa impulsiva* and object of the said Placaaten were only to prevent honest people, in buying, dealing with, or mortgaging immovable property (which wasfrequently not possessed in such full, free, and lawful ownership as might have been), from being defrauded and misled, and as through that means we could always ascertain the value, circumstances, and nature of the property possessed by the inhabitants in each place, the High Court has oftentimes held that the said Placaats by which the transfer, sale, alienation, and mortgage, if not made accordingly, are declared null and void, only apply to a third person, and not to the dealers themselves. Every alienation, however, which is acquired *titulo universali,* by inheritance, dowry, last will, community of property, *boedelscheyding,* is also excepted therefrom' *(R. D. L.,* 1 *Kotzi,* p. 191)....

Again, looking at the question in another way, a servitude may exist and yet not be registered, as, for example, a servitude imposed and acquired by last will, in which case Voet (8, 4 § 2) says there is no necessity for quasi-delivery, the disposition of the testator being sufficient for transferring to the legatees the real right. Or, a servitude may be acquired by prescription even without the knowledge of the owner of the servient tenement (8, 4 § 4).... The foundation for this, in all these cases, I take it, is the doctrine of notice. If I deal with a person who holds property under a will, I am bound to take notice of what rights or restrictions the will has conferred or imposed upon him. Or if one purchases c.L.—VOL. I. G G property over which some person other than the owner is exercising a right, this exercise of a right should put the purchaser on his guard, and compel him to inquire by what authority this right is exercised." Where a servitude has been bequeathed by last

will, as above stated, the legatee can claim it b action (8, §§ 1—*i).*

The owner of certain land sold a portion thereof to X., with a right of way over the remaining portion. This remaining portion was sold to another purchaser, Y., subject to the foregoing right of way in favour of X. The right of way was not registered as a servitude on T.'s transfer deed. X., before accepting his transfer deed, discovered that his servitude over Y.'s portion was not mentioned therein or registered on the deed, or in the Deeds Registry. He then brought an action against Y. to have the servitude registered as against Y.'s portion. It was decided that the transfer of the land to Y., without a reservation of the servitude over his portion, was a fraud on X.; that oral evidence of the sale to X. with the right of way was admissible; and that X. was entitled to have the servitude registered on X.'s title and on his own *(Richards* vs. *Nash and Another,* 1 S. C. 313). See the valuable judgment of Shippard, J., in *Jvdd* vs. *Fourie* (2 E. D. C. 41); *De Wet* vs. *ClotU* (1 M. 409); *Hiddinghvs. Topps* (4 S. 107); *Jansen* vs. *Fincham* (9 S. C. 289); *Parkin* vs. *Titterton* (2 M. 296); and, among English cases, *Steele* vs. *Thompson* (13 Moore, P. C. C. 280); *Doe* vs. *Alhop* (3 B. & A. 142); *Le Neve* vs. *Le Neve* (Amb. 436); *Bushell* vs. *Btishell* (1 S. & L. 103); and *Ford* vs. *White* (16 Beav. 120). Other South African cases are *Beningfield and Son* vs. *Durban Corporation* (18 N. L. R. 202), *Glass* vs. *Grahamstovm Brick Co.* (13 C. L. J. 277), and *Kama* vs. *Colonial Government* (8 C. T. R. 37; 15 S. C. 47).

690. So far is the rule, that in the acquisition of servitudes by prescription the knowledge of the owner of the servient tenement is not requisite, extended, that prescription will avail as against the true owner where a man has a grant of a servitude from one who is the mere possessor, and not the true owner, of the servient tenement; and it will also avail where the person exercising the servitude has received no grant from the possessor, but pretends that he has a grant, and openly exercises the right of servitude, without the knowledge of the true

owner. A strictly legal title is not necessary to acquire a servitude by prescription, so long as the person acquiring the servitude acts in good faith. So, if a man daily exercises a right of water-leading, and has obtained such right by long quasi-possession (sufficient to complete the term of prescription), he need not show by wbat title he has obtained the water-right, whether by bequest or otherwise; and it is enough, if he shows that for so many years he has had possession *non vi clam vel precario*—neither forcibly, secretly, nor on sufferance; lapse of years constituting the right to the servitude, although no title be proved (8, 4 § 4).

See *Frenchhoek Municipality* vs. *Hugo* (2 S. C. 242).

691. A negative servitude cannot be acquired by prescription, unless there has intervened some act by which the party claiming it has asserted it, and the opposing party has yielded to that assertion *(Jordaan* vs. *Winkelman and Others,* Buch. 1879, p. 86). Where the owner of a *praedium serviens* must refrain from doing some act, the servitude is termed negative—for instance, where he is prohibited from building in a certain position on his own land. The rule with regard to prescription applies, for example, where a man has for thirty years and more not exercised his right to raise in height the buildings on his own land. This gives the proprietor of the adjoining land, who has not acquired a servitude by grant, will, or contract, no right to forbid the subsequent increase in height of such buildings by their proprietor, on the ground that a servitude has been acquired by prescription. But if the adjoining party sent a letter of protest to the owner of the buildings, and the latter, on receipt of the letter, discontinued his building operations (entered into for the purpose of raising the buildings in height), resuming them after the lapse of some considerable period, the adjoining proprietor (following *Jordaan* vs. *Winkleman)* might then claim that such discontinuance was an admission of his right to a negative servitude (8, 4 § 5).

See *Vermaak* vs. *Palmer* (Buch. 1876, p.

34).

692. The prescriptive right to a servitude is gained after the lapse of a third of a century. It does not matter whether the user of such servitude has been continuous or intermittent (8, 4 § 6).

See *Jones* vs. *Capetown Town Council* (6 C. T. R. 73; 13S. C. 43;13 C. L. J. 140).

693. There cannot be a servitude of a servitude; in other words, a limited right to a servitude cannot be granted to another person by the holder of a servitude. Thus, if a person has a right of way, he cannot grant the usufruct of this right of way to another. Voet holds that the general rule does not apply to rights of way *(iter, actus* and *via)* already constituted, but to rights of way about to be constituted. The sense of the *Digest* is somewhat obscure, but, according to Voet's interpretation, it seems to be this—the test of the rule is the creation of the servitude. A testator cannot give a legatee the usufruct of a right of way, for a usufruct is a limited right, whereas real servitudes (such as rights of way) are unlimited. This means that a limited right in a right which is unlimited is a matter of impossibility. Where a right has already been constituted, however, such a servitude may be constituted, provided it is not a usufruct. Once the right of way is constituted, we know what it is; and a subtraction of that right of way in favour of a third party is allowable. But usufruct ends with the death of the usufructuary; if, then, a man lives ten years, and the right of way lasts in perpetuity, a temporary subtraction for ten years is made of a perpetual right—which is an impossibility in law. Once a subtraction in a right has been made, the subtraction must last as long as the right from which it is made; and usufruct or similar rights, being terminable at death, cannot be the basis of such a subtraction (8, 4 § 7). 694. Both urban and rural servitudes may not only be sold or bequeathed, but also be mortgaged, together with the properties (dominant tenements) to which they are attached. Neither urban nor rural servitudes can be pledged or mortgaged by themselves, independently of the dominant tenements to which they are attached. In the same way, they cannot be sold separately from the dominant tenement, since they are of advantage only to the owner of such dominant tenement. Urban or rural servitudes may be granted to the owner of an adjoining property who is a creditor of the owner of the servient tenement, on the understanding that the creditor may use the servitudes in question so long as the debt due by the owner of the servient tenement is unpaid, and may sell the same together with the dominant tenement if the debt is not paid within a certain time. Of course, the creditor cannot sell the servitudes apart from the dominant tenement which he owns, for such a sale would be valueless (unless he confers a right to use the dominant tenement for the purposes of the servitude). All praedial servitudes, whether urban or rural, are classed among indivisible things, whence they cannot be acquired, constituted, or taken away (discharged) in part. Consequently, one of two joint-owners cannot, against the will of the other, lawfully impose a servitude on a common estate held indivisibly. Where there are several jointowners of a property, and they successively grant the same servitude over it (such as a right of way), the grants of those first agreeing to the servitude are held in suspense, until the last of the jointowners has made his grant—all the grants being made by act *inter vivos*—and the grant by the last remaining joint-owner confirms the other grants, so that a servitude is validly constituted. Similarly, if one joint-owner grants the servitude by act *inter vivos,* and another confirms the grant by will, the first grant will be validated by the will. In like manner, if one joint-owner bequeaths a servitude, and his co-owners bequeath the same servitude by will, the servitude will be valid (8, 4 § § 8, 9). Illustrations: A., B., and C. jointly own the farm X., in undivided shares. A. gives K. a water-right on the said farm. The grant does not operate. Subsequently B. and C. sell the same water-right to K. The servitude in favour of K. then becomes operative. D. and E. own a house in undivided shares. D. sells to M. the right of building a shed against a wall of the house. The sale is inoperative. Subsequently, E. bequeaths to M. the right of building such a shed against the same wall. M., on proof of the sale, acquires the right to build the shed against the wall. Again, F. and G. own a farm P., and F. bequeaths to N. the right to depasture cattle on the farm. N. cannot exercise this right. Afterwards G. bequeaths to N. the right to depasture cattle on the farm. N. can then avail himself of the right 695. Roman-Dutch Law (differing in this respect from Roman Law) allows one person to acquire on behalf of another—whence it follows that one joint-owner of a common property held indivisibly can acquire a servitude in favour of such property for the benefit both of himself and his co-owner. In the same way, a usufructuary may acquire a servitude for the estate of which he has the usufruct. In like manner, the heir (or executor of the estate) of a testator may acquire a servitude in favour of a property, conditionally bequeathed as a legacy by such testator, in such manner that, if the condition is fulfilled, the legatee acquires both the property and the servitude, even where it was evident, when the servitude was acquired, that the ownership of the dominant tenement would pass away from the heir or executor to the legatee. Persons who have surface-rights over property *(superficies),* or who are holders by quitrent title *(emphyteusis),* may impose servitudes on the property which they hold to such an extent as to burden themselves, although such servitudes cannot burden the true owner *(dominus directus)* of the property. As soon as the surface rights or quit-rent tenure is ended, the servitude ceases to burden the property, which returns, without encumbrance, to the true owner (8, 4 § § 10, 11).

696. Both the owners of rural and urban servitudes can bring an action against a person who infringes or obstructs their rights of servitude. Thus, if the dominant tenement has a negative servitude that the building on the adjoining prop-

erty shall not be increased as to height, and the owner of such building increases the height thereof, the person entitled to the servitude may either institute an action or apply for an interdict to forbid such erection. The same remedies will apply where a person has a right of way over his neighbour's farm, and the neighbour erects a fence across the road. If the right of servitude is not wholly obstructed, no interdict can be claimed, and only a general action can be instituted (8, 4 § 12). 697. Servitudes cannot be constituted so as to benefit more than the dominant tenement. So, in the case of a servitude for digging sand, making lime, or quarrying stones, the owner of the dominant tenement cannot dig or quarry more than is necessary for the purposes of the dominant tenement. Where a person has a servitude of water-leading, he cannot give any of the water derived from this servitude to a neighbour, unless this was stipulated when the servitude was granted. In the same way, where he acquires another farm after obtaining a servitude of water-leading on his old property, he cannot lead this water to the newly-acquired property. Likewise, if he has a servitude of water-leading constituted so as to benefit one portion of his farm, he cannot thereafter divert the water so as to benefit another portion of the same farm. It is not the size of a property which determines the extent of a right of water-leading, but the extent of a servitude is limited by the express terms of the original agreement or grant. In the same way, unless there is an express agreement or reservation to that effect, a person who enjoys a servitude cannot in any mode allow the benefit thereof to a third party (8, 4 § 13). 698. With reference to water-rights, it may be here stated that every one may keep on his own property water brought there even by artificial means, and may prevent it from flowing down further, unless a servitude has been constituted, by virtue of which the water must be allowed to flow down. The water rising on a man's land may be acquired in various ways. Thus, a man may retain the rainwater which falls on his own property; and he may

dig a well on his own land, even if thereby he disturbs and taps the underground channels by which the water is conveyed to the land of a neighbouring proprietor. In other words, "a man may do whatever he pleases with water that rises upon his own property." This rule, however, is subject to an exception where there is a defined channel, known to the respective owners, which leads the water to a neighbour's land, and the neighbour has acquired a prescriptive right to such water. Thus, the Cape Supreme Court held (*Struben* vs. *Cape DistrictWaterworks Co.,* 9 S. C. 68) that the owner of land is entitled to the water which rises thereon, except in so far as such water has for thirty years or upwards been a source of a public stream, in which case his right in respect of the accustomed flow is limited by the rights of the public, so far as they are capable of being exercised, and by the riparian rights of the lower proprietors. With regard, however, to water other than that which flows in a defined channel as a public stream, it was decided that a person who, by digging a well in his own land for the *bond fide* purpose of improving the value of such land, abstracts underground water finding its way in undefined and to him unknown channels, is entitled to such water; and this is the case even when the abstraction causes a diminution in the supply of other wells, or even of a public stream. In the same way, by virtue of a right of servitude, a person may collect water on his own land, and keep it for his own purposes. This does not, however, refer to the ordinary rights of riparian proprietors acquired by prescription see *Hough* vs. *Van der Merwe,* Buch. 1874, p. 148; *Erasmuses. De Wet,* Buch. 1874, p. 204; *Kohler* vs. *Baartman and Others,* 12 S. C. 205 (8,4 § 14). 699. A real servitude, urban or rural, is valueless, which does not confer any benefit, either present or future, on the dominant tenement. A servitude may contain in itself both advantage to the dominant tenement (considered as real property), and pleasure to the owner of the dominant tenement (as an individual), but its nature will be determined according to its

relationship to the dominant tenement, not to the owner thereof. The mere fact, therefore, that a servitude gives pleasure and enjoyment to persons, does not deprive it of its characteristics as a real servitude (8, 4 § 15). 700. Different servitudes, in the case of real property, may be constituted in favour of several owners of different tenements (*praedia),* having reference to the same place (servient tenement), so long as the servitude which is later does not prejudice one which is prior in time. So, in *Ahlbom* vs. *Vickera* (9 S. C. 484), it was held that the owner of land on which there is an avenue, who has granted a right of way through the avenue to the owner of one tenement, is not on that account prevented from granting a right of way through the same avenue to the owner of another tenement, unless the second servitude interferes with the proper enjoTnent of the first. It was said by De Villiers, C.J., that "a servitude constitutes no greater limitation upon the rights of the owner of the servient tenement than is required for the due and proper enjoyment of the servitude by the owner of the dominant tenement. " Once a servitude has been granted, all things necessary for the exercise of the servitude are considered to have been granted at the same time, in favour of the dominant tenement. Thus, if a person has the right to draw water from a well on the servient tenement, he must be allowed access to the well, and consequently the grant of a right of way to the well is implied. So (*Hawkins* vs. *Munink,* 1 M. 465), where the dominant and servient tenements were on different sides of a river forming the boundary between them, and the proprietor of the dominant tenement had the right to take water from a fountain on the servient tenement, it was held that the servitude implied a right to a footbridge over the river; and that an unqualified right of servitude duly constituted by the transfer and title deeds of the land cannot be limited or impaired in the person of a particular successor by any merely personal agreements between the grantor of the servitude and the person in whose favour the servitude was granted, or any person subsequently acquiring the servient tenement from the grantor. From this it follows that any agreement impairing the right of servitude must be indorsed on the transfer or registered in the same manner as the right of servitude itself. In the same way, a person who has a servitude of water-leading may place a pipe in the watercourse, or take any other steps enabling him to draw oft" the water. Where a person has a right of way, and the way is obstructed by overhanging trees or in any other manner, he may demand the removal of the obstruction, so that he may freely enjoy his servitude. The owner of the dominant tenement can only take such steps as will secure his rights under the servitude; and he must not, in exercising his rights, do anything which may tend to interfere with or injure the owner of the servient tenement or any other neighbouring proprietor in the enjoyment of their rights. The owner of the servient tenement, again, is not bound to perform any personal duties. All that is required of him is that he shall allow something to be done by the owner of the dominant tenement—which will constitute an affirmative servitude—or that he will refrain from doing something himself—thereby constituting a negative servitude. The cause of a servitude should be perpetual— that is, the necessity for its exercise must not arise merely on one occasion, or on a few occasions, but the servitude must be such that it can be put into operation at any time; although, as we have seen, the exercise of the servitude need not be unintermittent. In other words, the nature of the servitude must be such that it may always be exercised, though it need not always be exercised. A servitude, though perpetual in its nature, may not be exercised if the time during which it has been specially agreed that it shall be exercised has gone *by.* Once a servitude has been granted, it cannot be arbitrarily withdrawn at the pleasure of the person who grants it. It is true that when a person has obtained leave to build on another's ground, and the building which has been erected can be removed without

any trouble, the permission can be withdrawn at any time. But when a building has been erected, and the removal thereof would cause great inconvenience and expense, the permission cannot be withdrawn arbitrarily *(Essack* vs. *Winter,* K. & B., Transv., p. 242). Voet says that where a man in reliance upon a grant (as of a servitude allowing a man to have a roof or verandah projecting over his neighbour's property), goes to expense in connection with building operations or otherwise, it is in the nature of a fraud on the part of the grantor arbitrarily to recall the grant. But a servitude is not lightly to be presumed, and so, according to Van Leeuwen *(R. D. L.* 2, 19, 5; 1 *Kotze,* p. 282), "if I, after a previous request from my neighbour, allow him to do something upon or over my property which I was not obliged to allow, I may at any time withdraw my permission and prohibit him, for this tacit condition is implied, namely, *until notice of prohibition."* Thus, where A. allowed B., at the request of the latter, to use a road over A.'s farm, leading to B.'s mill, but no servitude was granted to B. in express terms, B. instituted an action against A.'s successor in title for damages and for an interdict restraining the defendant from closing and impeding the road; and it was held that the plaintiff was not entitled to succeed *(Krige* vs. *Wilson,* K. & B., Transv., p. 58). Van Leeuwen *(Cent. For.* 2, 14, 5) also says: "When I, without express qualification, give leave for something to be done on my property, I am distinctly regarded as not having made this concession with the intention of making a present, or creating a servitude, but on sufferance; in common parlance, *tot wederseggens toe*—until recall" (8,4 § 16— 18). 701. As a general rule, the servient tenement must adjoin the dominant tenement. Sometimes, however, in the case of rural servitudes, the tenements need not adjoin, provided that the tenement between the dominant and the servient tenement is also subject to a servitude in favour of the dominant tenement. Thus a riparian proprietor may have a servitude as against a dozen estates situate higher up on the same stream than the

dominant tenement, and he may have his damages and an interdict for an interference by a proprietor, between whose estate and the plaintiff's there are several other estates, provided the stream in question flows over or through such estates. The same thing applies to urban tenements. The proprietor of one house in a town may have a right to let his rainwater run along a passage in a house several doors off (8, 4 § 19). 702. *Superficies* (surface right) is a servitude which, although praedial, may be exercised in respect of both urban and rural property. It confers rights to everything that is on or above the soil, whether the subject be a building, erected on the property of another with the consent of the proprietor of the soil, on condition that the person erecting the same shall continually possess it, or at any rate have the use of the building for a lengthy period, on payment of an annual charge; or whether the subject of the right consist of trees or other vegetation. This servitude may be imposed on property by agreement, or may be the subject of bequest, gift, or mortgage. In order to vindicate the same an equitable real action is available *(utilis actio in rem);* this action only lies to obtain the right of servitude—that is, the use or usufruct of the surface-rights —for the ownership of buildings erected above the surface belongs to the owner of the soil (43, 18 § 1). (4) Urban Servitudes In Particular. 703. The principal urban servitudes, affirmative and negative, known to the Roman Law, and to a considerable extent adopted in Roman-Dutch Law, are the following: *Servitus oneris ferendi* (bearing the weight of a building); *tigni immittendi* (inserting a beam in a neighbour's wall); *projiciendi et protegendi* (projecting a building or roof over a neighbour's property); *stillicidii et fluminis recipiendi vel avertendi* (conducting rain-water from one's roof into a neighbour's property, or receiving rain-water from a neighbour's roof into one's property); *non altius tollendi* (not exercising one's natural right to build higher); *altius tollendi* (allowing a neighbour to build higher than one is ordinarily entitled to build);*fenestrarum* making windows in one's own wall or the wall of another, practically in the same category as *servitus luminum* (that one's windows and supply of light shall not be interfered with) ; *ne luminibus officiatur* (that one's windows shall not be built up); *prospectus* (right to view); *ne prospectui officiatur* (that one's right to view shall not be obstructed); *non prospiciendi* (that one will not exercise a right to view); *cloacae* (driving a drain through another man's property); *fumi* (to pass one's smoke through a neighbour's chimney); *latrinae* (to construct a water-closet on a neighbour's property, or communicating with a cesspool on a neighbour's property). 704. By virtue of the servitude for sustaining a weight *(oneris ferendi)* the wall or pillar of the servient house or tenement is made liable to bear the weight, or part of the weight, of a neighbouring house or neighbouring houses. It corresponds to the English right of lateral support, although that right has been recognised to exist in South Africa within comparatively recent times. In *Murtha* vs. *Von Beek* (1 A. C. R. 121), where it was decided that the principle of lateral support is not applicable to claims in a diamond mine, no opinion was expressed as to the general application of the principle. The decision in that case was confined to mining claims. In *McFarlane* vs. *De Beer's Mining Board* (1 G. W. R. 898), the Griqualand High Court held that adjoining owners of land, who had issued licences for mining on their properties, were respectively entitled to lateral support from each other's land, as land-owners. The question was finally settled in *London and South African Exploration Co.* vs. *Rouliot* (8 S. C. 74), where it was laid down that the right of an owner of land to lateral support from adjacent land is recognised by Roman-Dutch Law. De Villiers, C.J., said that neither Groenewegen nor Voet (10,1 § 12) "refers specially to trenches or other excavations, but, the principle as to the right of support being once admitted, the removal of such support followed by damage must have been a wrong for which the action *in factum* lay. It is certainly an extraordinary circumstance "

that there is not much authority in Dutch text-books on the subject This was ascribed to the absence of mines, and, consequently, of the necessity for deep excavations, in Holland. The Court, therefore, resorted to other authorities not inconsistent with RomanDutch Law—the Roman Law (Gaius, in *Digest,* 10, 1, 18), *Code Civile* of France (§ 674, with the commentary of Pardessus), and the Scotch case of *Caledonian Railway Co.* vs. *Sprot* (2 McQ. 449). The principle of lateral support, according to Lord Cranworth, is "common to every system of jurisprudence." The same principle was adopted by the Transvaal High Court, in *Johannesburg Board of Executors* vs. *Victoria Buildings Co.* (Off. Rep. 1894, p. 49). The servitude of sustaining a weight imposes on the owner of the servient tenement not merely the passive duty of allowing the building to rest on his wall, but obliges him to keep his wall in repair, so as to be able fully to sustain the weight. During repairs to the supporting wall, the dominant owner cannot complain that sufficient support is not afforded to his building. Somewhat similar is the servitude conveying the right of inserting a beam in the wall of a neighbour's house *(tigni immittendi),* so that it rests on or in the wall of the dominant tenement, as well as on or in that of the servient tenement. Here no active duty is imposed on the owner of the servient tenement. He need not repair his wall so as to enable it to support the beams. The servitude may be agreed upon in general terms, without mention of the exact number of beams. The owner of the dominant tenement may insert such beams at various times, provided no damage is done to the servient tenement. New beams may be substituted for such as have decayed. It is different if the agreement stipulates for a specified number of beams, and directs in what manner they shall be inserted. The grant of a servitude must receive a strict interpretation, and where there is an express agreement it must not be departed from. In case of doubt, the presumption is in favour of freedom from the servitude. Even if there is no express agree-

ment, but a neighbour inserts into the wall of the servient tenement a certain number of beams, there being such knowledge and sufferance on the part of the owner of the servient tenement as amounts to consent, the law will construe the servitude strictly, and no right will be presumed in favour of the owner of the dominant tenement to insert other beams at will. In like manner, if the right to insert a beam is acquired neither by express nor tacit consent, but by prescription, the law will allow to the dominant tenement no other rights than those which were acquired by prescription. Where a right to insert a beam is obtained on the understanding that this shall be done for a certain purpose, and such purpose is not carried out, or the inserted beam is devoted to other uses than that originally agreed on, the owner of the beam forfeits his right, and may be called upon to remove the beam. Where a person gives to another the general right of inserting beams in his wall, and thereafter extends or widens such wall, the right to insert beams will not apply to that part of the wall which forms the extension or addition. Where a person has the right of replacing decayed beams by new beams, he will not, unless there is an express agreement to that effect, have the right of inserting beams additional to those which take the place of the decayed beams. The next right of a similar nature is the *servitus projiciendi,* or right of having a beam or portion of a building projecting over part of a neighbour's property. It is almost identical with the *servitus protegendi,* the right of building a protection or screen against the weather, which projects into a neighbour's ground. These servitudes differ from the foregoing, in that the owner of the dominant tenement is not entitled to support by or on the part of the owner of the servient tenement. There is no support derivable from the neighbour's wall. Where, then, a person makes part of his building project, and affixes it to, or inserts it in, his neighbour's wall, without having a servitude entitling him to do so, the neighbour may cut down or destroy the erection. But if only a projecting roof (without a servitude to that effect) has been made, and the same has not been inserted in the neighbour's wall, the neighbour cannot destroy the projecting erection, but must bring an action to restrain the defendant from having such a projection jutting over into his property (8, 2 §§ 1—4). 705. Every person is entitled to build his house to whatever height he pleases. In view of this, Voet holds that one cannot secure a servitude enabling one to raise one's own buildings to a greater height, and that the servitude *altiui tollendi* cannot apply to one's own property. It must, therefore, exist in respect of another property; and he defines it as the right to build on a neighbour's land, so as to improve the dominant tenement. It need not necessarily apply to the increase of the height of a house. Thus, it would be an exercise of the servitude *altius tollendi* to build a wall on a neighbour's land, where none formerly existed; or to increase the height of an existing wall on a neighbour's property. The definition of this servitude is discussed by Colquhoun (§ 945) in the following terms: "A *servitus altius tollendi* would arise in case of any one having agreed, or being obliged to permit another, to build an upper room or upper chamber on the top of his house; but here a difficulty arises—how could the Public Law, which restricted houses at Rome within a certain height, be infringed or altered by private compacts? This probably was rather the remission of a service existing, as where a house was already within the height allowed by law, and by virtue of an agreement between the parties was not to be raised higher, and was to overlook the neighbour's house; the abandonment of this contract would give a *servitus altius tollendi,* by rescinding the *servitus non altius tollendi,* by which it had been agreed that the house should not be raised to the full height allowed by law: *altius tollendi,* on the other hand, arises when a man promises to allow his neighbour to build his house higher than the laws passed simply for the reciprocal protection of neighbours permit." It should be borne in mind that no restrictions as to the

height of buildings exist in modern law, and that the maxim *cujus est solum, ejus est usque ad coelum,* applies universally. The servitude *altius tollendi* may then be taken to be a positive right, whereby one is enabled to build a wall on his neighbour's land, or to raise the height of an existing wall or house on such neighbour's land; the servitude *altius non tollendi* is a negative right, whereby a person agrees, in favour of the dominant tenement, that he shall not raise the height of an existing building on his land. The servitude *altius non tollendi,* according to Voet, frequently is implied in the servitude *ne luminibus officiatur* (that one's light shall not be obstructed or interfered with), for the right to have one's light unobstructed means that one's neighbour shall not build higher, for by such increase in height the light will be interfered with (8, 2 §§ 5—8). 706. Colquhoun, following the strict Roman Law, separates the servitudes relating to windows into *servitus fenestrarum,* where one stipulates for the right to make windows in one's own wall or in that of a neighbour, and *servitus luminum,* an agreement that a neighbour should not obstruct the windows which another had erected in such a position as to face the servient tenement (§§ 946, 947). Voet, on the other hand, treats of window servitudes under the general heading of *servitus luminum,* which he defines as a right to construct windows in another person's wall, with a corresponding duty on the part of the owner of the servient tenement to allow such windows to be made in his wall, and to continue to exist therein in such a manner that light is admitted to the dominant tenement. But the mere fact that one makes a window in another man's wall, without objection on his part, confers no right to receive light through such window (in the absence of grant or agreement), and the owner of the wall may obstruct the passage of light. Voet mentions a corresponding negative servitude, *servitus luminis non aperimdi,* whereby a person agrees not to place a window in his wall, overlooking his neighbour's property. This servitude passes, as against the servient

tenement, to a purchaser of, or particular successor to, the dominant tenement. The servitude *ne luminibus officiatur* is negative. It entitles the owner of the dominant tenement to have a full supply of light through his windows, and prevents the owner of the servient tenement from doing anything whereby the access of light through such windows is prevented, hindered, or obscured. If the owner of the servient tenement erects a building, which shuts out the view, but does not interfere with the light, he does not thereby infringe upon this servitude—though Voet says such an infringement would take place if the building were to shut out the sun from a part of the dominant tenement, such as a conservatory or hot-house, expressly designed to catch the direct rays of the sun. But the owner of the servient tenement cannot raise the height of his building, or form plantations of trees opposite the windows in question, so as to shut out the light from such windows. Where such a servitude is entered into in general terms, it includes not only windows then existing, but windows thereafter made, which face the servient tenement; for the servitude has regard, not so much to the windows in themselves, as to the access of light. Voet says that the servitudes *prospectus* (right of view), and *ne prospectui officiatur* (that one's view shall not he hindered or obstructed), are generally included in the servitudes relating to light. But the servitudes of view are more extended and comprehensive than those of light. Voet also mentions a special servitude, practically obsolete at the present time—*non prospiciendi in arcane alterius,* that the servient tenement shall not overlook and command a view of the yard, court, or garden of the dominant tenement (8, 2 §§ 9—12). In *Myburgh* vs. *Jamison* (4 S. 8), a person owned two adjacent properties, and sold one, with a condition in the transfer deed that no buildings should be erected thereon so as to obstruct the view from the other property. It was held that an obstruction of the view by trees was not within the meaning of the condition. In *Lewkowitch* vs. *Bellingham & Co.*

(Transv. Off. R. 1895, p. 50), where A. let to B. a certain wall for advertising purposes, and it was agreed that the lease might be cancelled if any building were erected so as to interfere with the view of the wall, it was held that the erection of a wooden hoarding, which interfered with the view of the wall, was such an obstruction as amounted to a building in terms of the contract. See also *St. Leger* vs. *Capetown Tovm Council* (5 C. T. R. 264; 12 S. C. 249) and *Laiorence* vs. *Roman* (17 C. L. J. 176).

707. The servitude *stillicidii vel fluminis recipiendi* consisted in the right to conduct the rain-water which fell upon one's roof into the property of a neighbour, whose tenement thus became servient. The servitude *stillicidii vel fluminis avertendi* consisted in the right to receive on one's own property, as the dominant tenement, the water which fell from a neighbour's property. To these corresponded the negative servitudes *non recipiendi* and *non avertendi,* that one should not conduct one's rain-water into a neighbour's property (the dominant tenement), and that one should not receive one's rain-water from a neighbour's property (the dominant tenement). A distinction was made in Roman Law between *stillicidium,* the ordinary fall of rain-water on a roof, and *ftumen,* the falling of water from a roof in one unbroken stream; but in modern usage these distinctions are of no importance. Ordinarily, every man has a right to the rain-water which falls on his own property. The right to this supply may be increased or diminished by the obtaining or granting of one of the above-mentioned servitudes. Once a servitude has been granted, the roof of a house must not be altered in such a manner that the water is caused to fall in a stronger stream than is permitted by the terms of the servitude; in other words, the owner of the dominant tenement, if he lets his water run into the servient tenement, must not exceed his rights so as to injure the servient tenement, and the owner of the servient

C.L.—VOL. I. H H tenement, who lets his water run into the dominant tenement, must act in a similar manner.

Where the owner of the servient tenement is liahle to receive the rain-water on his property, he cannot raise his buildings in such a manner that the rain-water is unable to reach his property, and if he does so raise his buildings, he must leave a clear space or passage between the servient and dominant tenements whereby the water can find its way from the dominant to the servient tenement (8, 2 § 18).

See Grotius *(Introduction,* 2, 34, 10—17); and Van Leeuwen *(R. D. L.* 2, 20, 8—10; 1 *Kotze,* pp. 289, 290; and *Cent. For.* 1, 2, 14, 20—21).

708. The Roman-Dutch authorities mention another servitude, known as *goot-recht,* which Grotius (2, 84, 24; *Maasdorp,* p. 149) briefly defines as the right to have a gutter or spout lying upon or discharging itself into the property of another. Van Leeuwen *(Cens. For.* 1, 2, 14, 22; *R. D. L.* 2, 20, 10; 1 *Kotze,* p. 290) treats of it more fully. He states that this servitude of *goot-recht,* or watercourse, is the right to let one's water run over the ground of another, who is bound to lead it off over his own land or in a gutter. This servitude refers only to clean water, produced by rainfall or some other natural cause. The owner of the dominant tenement must place at the outlet from his property a grating, to prevent stones or rubbish from passing into the servient tenement. This is a purely urban servitude, and must not be confused with the rural servitudes appertaining to what are known as "water-rights." It also dhTers from the servitude *cloacae,* which was the right of driving a drain through another man's property. Van Leeuwen *(Cens. For.* 1, 2, 14, 28; *R. D. L.* 2, 20, 11; 1 *Kotze,* p. 290) makes no distinction between this and the *servitus latrinae,* though Voet, while not going into detail, mentions them separately. It appears better, however, to retain the distinction, for *servitus latrinae* may consist in the right to discharge filth into a neighbour's cesspool, whereas the *servitus cloacae* does not confer a right to discharge dirty water into a neighbour's property, but to pass it through such property. The owner of the servient tenement need not

allow *faeces* to be passed through his property by virtue of the *servitus cloacae;* but in towns where modern drainage systems are in vogue, no objection can be raised to this, when done under municipal sanction and superintendence. The owner of the dominant tenement must clean and repair the sewer; and the sewerage must not constitute a nuisance as against the servient tenement. Where a sewer is used by two persons in common, both must contribute to the repair and cleansing thereof, unless the choking up or damage thereto has resulted from the act of one of the parties alone (8, 2 § 14). 709. With regard to urban tenements generally, it may be noted that where there is a doubt as to the ownership of a wall between two houses or gardens, it is presumed to be a common wall *(O'Reilly* vs. *Lucke,* 4 S. C. 104), and the burden of proof of ownership is on the person claiming the wall. The same rule applies to fences and empty spaces between two properties—unless, of course, such empty spaces are shown to belong to a third party. If a wall is built by one or two neighbours on a common boundary, it will be common property—following the maxim *quicquid inaedificatur solo, solo cedit* (see *Myburgh* vs. *Jamison,* 4 S. 8). A person who has two houses adjoining each other, and sells one of them, is considered to have sold half of the partition wall as part of the house, unless there is an agreement to a contrary effect. No one can do anything to a common or partition wall without his neighbour's consent, unless empowered to that effect under a servitude. Oveus or water-closets, as being calculated to do harm, should not be erected against a partywall; and if it is sought to remove the same, the presumption will be in favour of the person seeking the removal. Anything may be done which agrees with the original intention and object of those between whose properties a common wall stands. As to the question whether a neighbour can against the will of the owner of the adjoining tenement build upon the common wall, or against it, Voet lays it down that he may build up the central line of the common wall. Thus, if the wall be twelve inches in breadth, he may build upon it to the extent of six inches, at which point the middle line is reached. So, where defendant built upon the whole of a party-wall owned by him and plaintiff, and projected a roof over portion of plaintiff's property without his consent, he was ordered to remove the encroachment, as he was only entitled to cover one-half of the breadth of the wall. The weight of the erection must not be such that the wall is weakened, and caused to lean towards either house.

If an erection is made of such a nature and weight that there is a probability of its causing damage to the wall, the person who makes the erection may be called upon to provide security against damage.

Where a wall has been erected with the intention of marking the boundary between two estates, one party cannot build on it without the other's consent, for the original intention of the parties must be followed. Where a person builds on a wall beyond the middle or dividing line, without the consent of the other proprietor, but with his tacit acquiescence, the builder cannot be called on to remove the erection, and is only liable for compensation to the other owner.

As to common entrances *gemeene gang)* it may be stated that where the parties have agreed upon a hall, vestibule, lobby, door, gate, or portico as a common entrance, neither can (without the other's consent) in any way obstruct it, or render the passage more difficult (8, 2 §§ 15—18).

See Grotius *(Introduction, 2, 34, 4, 5, 25; Afaasdorp,* pp. 147—149); Pothier on *Partnership* (§ 140); Burge's *Commentaries* (vol. 3, p. 403); Van Leeuwon *(R. D. L.* 2, 20, 3; 1 *KotzS,* 287); and *Myburgh* vs. *Jamison* (4 § 8).

(5) Rural Servitudes In Particular. *A. Rights Common to Rural Servitudes.* 710. When a servitude conferring rights of way, water-rights, or any other rural servitude, has been unconditionally granted over land, or bequeathed by will, and no particular portion of the es-

tate has been indicated over which the servitude may be exercised, the owner of the dominant tenement has the right of election as to the portion on which he will exercise his servitude. If a servitude has been bequeathed so as to enure in favour of an estate of which there are several joint-owners, they should all of them agree as to the part over which the servitude is to be exercised. This right of election is grounded on the presumption that, where no particular portion of the estate is specified, the whole farm is subject to the servitude. In that case, whenever the owner of a dominant tenement exercises any right of way or water-right, he is considered to do so by virtue of a general, indefinite servitude. The owner of the dominant tenement, who has the right of election, must exercise that right like a good citizen *(civiliter).* He cannot, for instance, exercise his right of way over a farm by driving through the farmhouse, or through vineyards, when any other part of the farm is available for his purposes. In fact, where no particular portion of a farm is mentioned when the servitude is granted, that portion only is regarded as subject to the servitude which is not covered by buildings or cultivated ground. Once a particular part of an estate has been chosen for the exercise of a servitude, the person entitled to the servitude must abide by his election, and cannot arbitrarily use some other part of the estate for the purposes of the servitude; consequently, such portion of the farm as he has not chosen for the exercise of his servitude will be considered unburdened—unless the parties originally agreed that the servitude might be changed to another part of the farm. On the other hand, the owner of the servient tenement can change the venue or place for the exercise of the servitude from that previously determined upon by election or agreement, substituting another portion of his farm, so long as this does not prejudice the owner of the dominant tenement. As we have seen, a public stream between the dominant and servient tenements is no obstacle to a servitude, so long as it can be forded or crossed by a bridge (8, 8

§§ 8, 9). *B. Rights of Way.* 711. The term " rights of way" is here used in a general sense, not in the special meaning of the word *via.* The servitudes embracing rights of way, known to the Roman Law, were *iter, actus,* and *via.* Connected with them, but varying in their application and object, were the servitudes *pecoris ad aquam adpulsus* (driving cattle to water) and *jus pascendi* (right of pasturing cattle on another man's land, which comprised a sort of right of way, inasmuch as one was entitled to send one's cattle through the servient tenement in order to reach the pasture). The three first-mentioned servitudes were distinguished as follows: *iter,* or *senitus itineris,* is the right to use a footpath across another man's land, on which, however, a horse may even be ridden if the nature of the ground allows of it; *actus,* or *senitus actus,* is the right of driving cattle, beasts of burden, or vehicles, along a path or road over a neighbour's property; *via,* or *scrvitus viae,* comprehends *iter* and *actus,* and entitles one to drive laden carts or wagons, and to drag or draw stones or wood along a road over another man's property, provided no injury be done to the crops on the servient tenement. A person who has the servitude *iter* may exercise his rights under it for the benefit not of himself alone, but for that of his servants and visitors as well. Voet follows Grotius *(Introduction,* 2, 85, 1) in separating the right of walking along a path from the right of riding (bridleroad, *rij-pad),* whereas the Roman Law conjoins these rights. In any case, there is no difference in their mode of exercise; and Grotius even states "the right of bridle-road includes the right of foot-path, as the greater includes the less " *(Maasdorp,* p. 150). A person who enjoys the servitude *actus* is entitled to a reasonable width of road. If a place so narrow has been pointed out, that there is no room either for a beast or a vehicle, the servitude *iter* rather than the servitude *actus* is presumed to have been obtained; but if a beast may be driven along the path, even though a vehicle cannot be driven along it, the servitude *actus* is considered to have been granted. Voet quotes Modestinus as agreeing with Pomponius on this subject. As was stated by De Villiers, C.J. , in *Breda's Executors and Another-vs. MMs* (2 S.C. 189), "What it all amounts to is this—there may be *actus* without the right of driving vehicles; if the road in respect to which the *actus* was granted is wide enough to admit of vehicles passing over, in such cases the right to drive vehicles was also presumed to be granted. When Voet comes to consider *via* he shows that its meaning is more extensive than is generally supposed, and that *via* includes not only the right of driving vehicles, but of drawing stones and logs of wood." *Actus,* of course, includes *iter.* Where there is a doubt, the presumption is that *iter,* and not *actus,* has been granted; unless the grantor expresses a wish to the contrary. Where a person has the servitude *actus,* and daring the period of prescription avails himself only of the rights included under *iter,* he does not thereby lose the other rights appertaining to *actus.* Where a servitude *via* has been granted, the road used under the servitude must be wide enough to allow of the passage of both vehicles and cattle. So, where a person had the right of driving cattle to a certain stream to water, it was decided that, so long as the track remained unenclosed, it should be 150 feet wide, proof having been given that 400 head of cattle could be pastured on the dominant tenement *(Laubscfier* vs. *Rive and Others,* 5 S. 195). There is another right of way, arising of necessity, and known as *anood-weg* (way of necessity). According to Van Leeuwen *(R. D. L.* 2, 21, 7; 1 *Kotze,* 295), " every portion of land that has no special outlet must be accorded a right of approach over other intervening lands to the public roads (which may be used by every one in common), in the most direct line and with the least injury to such lands... and this is called a way of necessity, as well for a person on foot, as with a wagon, in order to gather and carry off the fruits of the land, or to drive cattle to and from it." Voet says that the owner who grants such a way of necessity may receive a reasonable compensation for the

same; or, at any rate, he need only grant it by way of sufferance *precario),* only to be used when necessity requires; and as little detraction to the rights of the owner of the servient tenement as possible must take place. The owner of the servient tenement may break up such a way of necessity or sufferance; but, where there is urgent necessity, he must restore the same. But roads used under the servitudes *iter, actus,* or *via,* cannot be broken up by cutting or digging; or even barred by means of a gate (see *Landman* vs. *Daverin,* 2 E. D. C. 8). A right of way by necessity can be claimed no further than the actual necessity of the case demands. The foregoing rights of way differ from those appertaining to a *via vicinalis.* A *via vicinalis, or* "neighbour's road," is a road, either in a village or leading to a town or village, which has been used by the people of the neighbourhood from time immemorial. Time immemorial in Cape Colony may be denned as the period required for prescription *(Peacock* vs. *Hodges,* Buch. 1876, p. 65). A *via vicinalis,* according to Grotius *Introduction,* 2, 85,10; *Maasdorp,* p. 151), cannot be closed, except by common consent of the neighbouring proprietors who use the road; and the profits derived from the sale of the road must be divided between such neighbours (8, 8 §§ 1—5). See *McKenzie* vs. *Shaw* (7 N. L. R. 84); *Gutridge* vs. *Holloway* (1N. L. R. 261); and *Vos* vs. *Colonial Government* (14 N. L. R. 201). As to right of way of necessity for the purpose of constructing fences between farms, see the Cape Fencing Act, No. 30,1883, § 24. As to *nood-weg,* see Grotius (2, 35,8), and *Schorer* (§ 216). *C. Water-Bights.* 712. Broadly speaking, a water-right is the right which a person has to a supply of water for the requirements of his estate, whether he be entitled to such water by virtue of the fact that it rises on his own property, or has the right to a supply by virtue of being a riparian proprietor (holding land on the banks of a public stream), or has acquired the right by virtue of a servitude, such servitude being either

that of *aquaeductus* or of *aquaehaustus.* A servitude, entitling one to a supply of water from a private stream, may also be acquired by prescription, where one is not entitled to the use of the water by virtue of one's ordinary rights as a riparian proprietor. 713. The first question, then, to consider is the right of an owner of property to water rising in his own land *(erumpens in suo).* Voet says that where water naturally, or through artificial means employed on the lower property, flows down from one property to another, there is no reason why the upper proprietor should not retain for his own uses water which rises on his own property, which consequently belongs to him; and, further, there is no reason why, in such a case, he should not grant to whomsoever he pleases the right of leading it in any direction that may be decided upon, and diverting it from the lower proprietors to whose estates it was accustomed to flow. This particularly refers to water rising on a man's property *(erumpens in suo).* In this case, says Voet, no servitude by prescription can be conceived as having been obtained by the lower proprietors in respect of the water, but the upper proprietor has retained for himself the fullest power of action; and if it is sought to establish a servitude in such a case, it would seem to consist in this rather than anything else, that the lower properties are burdened with a servitude, in favour of the upper one, by virtue of which they must receive the water flowing down from it. The upper proprietor, if he acts in good faith, is entitled, by digging wells or otherwise, to divert the flow of subterranean streams which otherwise find their way to the lower properties, and there appear on the surface; and, if this be the case, Voet argues that there is no reason why the upper proprietor should not divert water rising on his property, which flows openly over the surface of his property. This statement was thus explained by Bell, J., in *Retief* vs. *Lomv* (Buch. 1874, p. 165): "It applies to a case of a proprietor granting to a stranger the right of using water rising on the proprietor's own land, and therefore his own, and still reserving to himself full liberty. It applies to a case in which a servitude cannot be conceived, or if any can be conceived, it would only be that servitude which attaches to low-lying land of receiving the water which comes naturally from higher land. In other words, the author Voet is treating of the rights of persons to water which they could not have but for the liberality of the owner of the contiguous and higher grounds in which the water has its source."..." The obligation upon the lower ground to receive the water from the upper ground is not of the nature of a servitude generally, though for convenience' sake it may be classed under the title of servitude for want of a more appropriate title: for servitude is a service constituted by agreement or quasi-agreement, not *operatione naturae*" (by operation of nature). In *Silberbauer* vs. *Van Breda and Cape Town Municipality* (5 S. 281; quoted in *Vertnaak* vs. *Palmer,* Buch. 1876, p. 84) it was said by Watermeyer, J.: "It is impossible to dispute the law that a man might do whatever he pleased with water that rose upon his own property. It has been stated, and correctly, that so strong is the general rule that, whereas a servitude might be constituted by prescription on a lower proprietor to receive water which rises on lands of a higher proprietor, yet that prescription will not constitute a servitude upon the upper proprietor to enforce him to let the water run down." This statement of Watermeyer, J., is somewhat varied in the respective reports of the case; but a similar and unequivocal statement was made by Hodges, C.J.: "I believe the law of this Colony is quite clear—whatever may be the case as to water running over the land—that the rights of the freeholder to water rising from springs on his land is undisputed and indisputable. He may use it for any purposes relating to irrigation, or he may convey it away and use it as he pleases. Voet is very clear and distinct on this matter. " Similar views prevailed in *Erasmus* vs. *De Wet* (Buch. 1874, p. 204). But in *Mouton* vs. *Van der Merwe* (Buch. 1876, p. 18), De Villiers, C.J., referring

to the foregoing decisions, said: "There is no doubt that several eminent Judges of this Court in former times did lay down very strong views as to the rights of upper proprietors to all the water which rises upon their own land; and for that purpose they relied upon Voet. Voet goes to the extent of saying that the upper proprietor is entitled to all the water which rises upon his land, and for that *dictum* he quotes the *Code.* But on referring to the *Code* it will be found that it, at all events, does not fully bear out Voet. This Court would certainly be bound by a series of decisions to the same effect, but strong doubts have been thrown upon the general doctrine by the Privy Council in the appeal in the case of *Breda* vs. *sUberbauer* (5 S. at p. 248). I do not think that Voet's doctrine can be accepted to the full extent. In my opinion the upper proprietor cannot lay claim to all the water rising upon his land, if this water had been accustomed for a long series of years to flow down in a regular and defined course to the lower proprietor." This "long series of years" was more accurately defined in *Vermaak* vs. *Palmer,* where it was said by De Villiers, C.J., that "without here entering into the objections which may be raised to the notion of a servitude acquired by prescription in a case where there really has never been any adverse enjoment on the part of the person claiming the servitude as against the rights of the person from whom it is claimed, it is sufficient for the purpose of the present case to say that in our opinion the upper proprietor is not entitled to the exclusive and unlimited enjoyment of water rising on his own land, if for so long a period as thirty years, at all events, the water has flowed down beyond his land in a known and defined channel for the benefit of the lower proprietors. In such a case, the rules laid down in the case of *Hough* vs. *Van der Merwe* (Buch. 1874, p. 165) would apply, and the upper proprietor must be restricted to a reasonable use of the water." It will be seen, therefore, that no precise limit for the period of prescription has been fixed. To sum up, it may be gathered from the decisions in *Retief*

vs. *Louw* and *Breda* vs. *sUberbauer* that the law, following Voet, is as follows: (a) Over private waters the owner of the land on which such waters rise has full right of disposal. Water *erumpens in suo* is the property of the owner on whose land it rises, *(b)* The owner of water rising on his property cannot be deprived of his rights by prescription in favour of the lower proprietor. On the other hand, the views of De Villiers, C. J., which form the basis of decisions in the Cape Colony since 1876, may be summarised as follows: *(a)* The owner of land on which private waters rise has an absolute right to the exclusive use thereof, so long as no one else has acquired a right or servitude over such water *(Dreyer* vs. *Ireland.* (Buch. 1874, p. 193). *(b)* If such private stream has not been allowed to flow down in a definite and accustomed channel for any length of time to the land of a lower proprietor, the upper proprietor retains his right of exclusive usage, and the lower proprietor cannot restrain him from diverting the water of the stream *(Mouton* vs. *Van der Merwe,* Buch. 1876, p. 18).' (c) On the other hand, the upper proprietor is not entitled to the unlimited and exclusive use of water rising on his land, if this water has been allowed for the period of prescription—at least thirty years—to flow down in a definite and accustomed channel, so that lower proprietors have for that period enjoyed the common use of the water *(Vermaak* vs. *Palmer,* Buch. 1876, p. 25; the foregoing cases being all based on a discussion of *Voet,* 8, 8 § 6). *(d)* The general rule that a person may deal as he chooses with water rising on his own land, is subject to the limitation that the water thus rising is not the source, or the main source, of a public stream *(Van Heerden* vs. *Weise,* 1 A. C. R. 5).
See also *De Wet* vs. *Hiscock* (1 E. D. C. 249), and *Hiscock* vs. *De Wet* (1 A. C. R. 58).

714. It is necessary, in the next place, to distinguish between public streams and private streams. In *Van Heerden* vs. *Weise* (1 A. C. E. 5) it was said by De Villiers, C.J.: "Broadly stated, our law recognises two classes of natural

streams or water-courses— public and private. Under the designation of public streams are included all perennial rivers, whether navigable or not, and all streams which, although not large enough to be considered as rivers, are yet perennial, and are capable of being applied to the common use of the riparian proprietors. Under the designation of private streams are included rivers and streams which are not perennial, and streamlets which, although perennial, are so weak as to be incapable of being applied to common use." A perennial stream may be denned as one which is constant at its source, and which flows continuously in a bed having denned banks, for the greater part of the year. "The authorities no doubt say that a river may sometimes become dry in the heat of summer without forfeiting its character of a perennial and therefore a public river." This statement is exact so far as it goes; but the limitation must be added to the words "a perennial and therefore a public river," that it is capable of being applied to the common use of riparian proprietors. A stream does not become public if it is merely perennial, and incapable of being applied to the common use of riparian proprietors. It would seem from *Van Heerden* vs. *Weise* (1 A. C. R. p. 10) that a river which is generally dry except after rains is not perennial. The members of the Court in that case appear to have taken the view that where water flows for a period of at least six months in the year, even be it intermittently, the stream is perennial and public. But it is submitted that, in such territories as Cape Colony and Orange River Colony, a flow of even less than six months, provided there is a welldefined channel, having some spring or constant water-supply at the source (even though such supply disappears lower down in the bed), and not merely dependent on surface drainage (as to which see the learned remarks of Bigelow, J., in the United States of America: 9 Cush. 174), will constitute a perennial and public stream, so long as the stream, when containing water, is capable of being applied to the common use of the riparian proprietors.

A riparian proprietor is a person who owns land which abuts upon a public stream, or over any part of which there flows a public stream, or who—either expressly or presumptively from the terms of his grant—is owner, not only of the adjoining land, but of the stream up to the middle thereof. The terms of a grant must clearly indicate the title of the grantee to a portion of the stream. Thus, in *Beaufort West Municipality* vs. *Wernich* (2 S. C. 86), where defendant had purchased a lot of land " bounded on the west by the river Gamka," which was a portion of ground referred to in a previous grant as "being the reserved ground situate between the Gamka and Kuils River," it was held that the bank was the boundary, and that the defendant was not entitled to use any part of the river. But a riparian proprietor (see Sir H. Juta on *Water-rights*, p. 425) need not be the registered owner. Thus, in *Mouton* vs. *Van der Merwe* (Buch. 1876, p. 18), where the defendants had for forty to fifty years occupied and used as their own property certain land which the plaintiff contended was Government ground, and on which the source of the stream (the rights to which were in question) was found, the Court decided that as the defendants were *bond fide* occupiers, and no one, including plaintiffs, had shown a better title, they could to all intents and purposes be treated as owners of the land on which the water arose. 715. We now come to the rights of riparian proprietors, in regard to public streams. In *Retief* vs. *Louiv* (Buch. 1874, p. 165) it was said by Bell, C.J., that "a perennial stream, not in strict propriety capable of receiving the name of a river, flowing through but rising above private land, does not belong absolutely to the proprietor of the land through which it flows, but all the proprietors of land throughout its course have each a common right in the use of the water. This use, at every stage of its exercise by any one of the proprietors, is limited by a consideration of the rights of the other proprietors." This use was divided by De Villiers, C.J. (in *Hough* vs. *Van der Merwe*, Buch. 1874, p. 18), into ordinary or primary, and ex-

traordinary or secondary. Ordinary use, in the language of Bell, C.J., may be for the support of animal life; extraordinary use may be for the increase of mechanical life, and for the promotion of mechanical appliances. "The ordinary use is that which is required for the support of animal life and, in the case of riparian proprietors, for domestic purposes; the extraordinary use is that which is required for any other purpose than those just mentioned." In *Retief* vs. *Louw* it was laid down that if the upper proprietor requires all the water for the support of life, the lower proprietors must submit —that is, they receive nothing. If there be more than sufficient water for this purpose, sufficient must be allowed to pass for the supply of animal demands of all the lower proprietors before the upper proprietor can use the water for irrigation. The proprietors are in succession entitled to use the water for agricultural purposes. Agricultural uses being supplied throughout the course of the stream, the proprietors are then entitled to apply the water to mechanical purposes. No proprietor is entitled to use the water without regard to the wants of the other proprietors (except, of course, where he requires all of it for the support of animal life). The extent to which any one proprietor is entitled to use the water will depend on the circumstances of each case. In *Hough* vs. *Van der Merwe* these rules were somewhat differently stated by De Villiers, C.J.: "If the ordinary use is common to all the proprietors it would seem that the extraordinary use must be equally so. If, therefore, the upper proprietor in the enjoyment of his ordinary use deprives the lower proprietors of their ordinary use, he would not be liable to them in an action: but if an upper proprietor, in the enjoyment of his extraordinary use, deprives the lower proprietors of their extraordinary use, he would, according to the weight of authority, be liable to them in an action. " *A fortiori,* if the upper proprietor, in the enjoyment of his extraordinary use, deprives the lower proprietors of their ordinary use, he will likewise be liable. In other words, as to the ordinary use, the upper proprietor need only consider himself, but in the extraordinary use he must share equally with all the lower proprietors; and once he has had his ordinary use, he must, before having his extraordinary use, allow the lower proprietors to have their ordinary use. As to the rights of irrigation, it was laid down that " by our law the owner of land by or through which a public stream flows, is entitled to divert a portion of the water for the purposes of irrigation, provided, (1) that he does not thereby deprive the lower proprietors of sufficient water for their cattle and for domestic purposes; (2) that he uses no more than a just and reasonable proportion of the water, consistently with similar rights of irrigation in the lower proprietors; (8) that he returns it to the public stream with no other loss than that which irrigation has caused." This decision, so far as the question now under consideration is concerned, was recognised to be the law in the Transvaal, by Kotze, C.J., in *Meyer* vs. *Johannesburg Waterworks Co.* (Hertzog, p. 16; 10 C. L. J., p. 159). By irrigation is to be understood irrigation for the purposes of cultivation only. So, in *Struben* vs. *Collett* (17 C. L. J. 63; 9 C. T. R. p. 620), it was said that the fact that the defendant had water to spare for the purpose of irrigating the " veld" went to show that he used more water than he ought to have done. "The Court has laid down rules for the use of the water of perennial streams, and one of the first principles laid down as far back as the case of *Hough* vs. *Van der Merwe* is that the water, after being used for domestic purposes and the like, may be used for the purpose of irrigation, that is, irrigation for the purpose of cultivation, but certainly not for the purpose of watering ' veld,' while the owners below have not sufficient water to irrigate their cultivated land; and even where cultivated land is irrigated the Court has laid it down that the water should be turned into the channel without any more waste than was necessary for the purpose."

The general rules laid down by Voet on the subject of public streams may be here briefly summarised. In the first

place, an interdict (ne *quid in flumine publico ripave ejus fiat, quo pejus naviyetur*) is given against those who interfere with the navigation of a public stream, or divert the water so as to make it less navigable, or narrow the stream so that the water flows more rapidly. This interdict has no reference to private streams. As to its application, see *Port Elizabeth Divisional Council* vs. *Uitenhage Divisional Council* (Buch. 1868, p. 44). Another interdict *(ne quid in flumine publico fiat, quo aliter aqtm fluat, atque uti priori aestate fluxit)* lies against one who, without being entitled to do so, diverts the water of a public stream. Where the diversion has been made, the interdict is for restitution, and compensation may be claimed for loss caused by the diversion. It refers equally to streams which are and to those which are not navigable. The interdict *de aqua quotidiana et aestiva* refers to interference with or deprivation of one's ordinary supply of water, which one receives from a perennial stream, and which is derived from the ordinary source or sources of such stream, and does not originate elsewhere. This interdict is available to all the proprietors who suffer loss by the act of the upper proprietor. The distinction between public and private streams is based upon the *existimatio circumcolentium,* the opinion of those who live in the neighbourhood. This distinction, according to the judgment in *Van Ifeerden* vs. *Weise* (1 A. C. R. p. 8), although based upon Ulpian, is not wholly satisfactory. "The test becomes more intelligible when it is coupled, as has been done by Baldus *(ad Dig.* 1, 8, 3) and inferentially by Vinnius *(ad Inst.* 2, 1, 3), with the capability or otherwise of the stream itself to be used in common by the different riparian proprietors over whose land it flows." Such persons as have acquired, through long usage, a right to water from private streams of upper proprietors, may have an interdict for any interference with such right. A similar interdict applies to the case of a person who has acquired rights to take water from a fountain or spring belonging to another (43, 12 § 1; 43, 13 § 1; 43, 20

§ 1; 43 21 § 1; 43, 22 § 1). See, generally, *Jordaan* vs. *WinMeman* (Buch. 1879, p. 88;, *Southey* vs. *Schoombie* (1 E. D. C. 301), *Anderson* vs. *Pepworth* (1 N. L. R., N. S. 248), *Van Schalkwijk* vs. *Hauman* (14 S. C. 221), *Dreyer* vs. *Ireland* (Buch. 1874, p. 201), and *Dreyer* vs. *Letterstedi's Executors* (5 S. 88).

716. With regard to private streams, it may be stated generally that the rights of lower proprietors are either prescriptive, or depend upon grants of servitudes. The servitudes known to Dutch Law are *aquaediictus* (right of leading water), and *aquaeliaustus* (right to draw water). Under *aquaeductus,* water may be led from any part of the servient tenement, whether it be the source of a stream, or any part of its course, so long as the water does not come from a standing, as opposed to a running, body of water. A reach or pool in a river will be classed with the river to which it belongs as running water. The servitude is not extinguished when the stream dries up, but its user revives when the headspring or source begins to flow again; and the right is not lost if the water ceases to flow for a time which, in the case of an ordinary servitude, would be sufficient to discharge a servitude on account of disuse. The right to lead water from and through the servient tenement, even along the same channel, can be granted to more than one person; and this may be done in such a manner that they shall all exercise their right at the same time, or do so separately, on different days and at different hours, provided there is sufficient water for all. If the owner of the upper property uses artificial means to discharge the water upon the lower property, and the lower proprietor irrigates his land with this water, and does so for the period of prescription, the upper proprietor cannot grant to others the right of water-leading to the prejudice of such lower proprietor *(Vermaak* vs. *Palmer,* Buch. 1876, p. 25). Voet limits this prescriptive right to the case of water which flows to the lower proprietor by the operation of some artificial work situate upon the upper property; but De Villiers, C.J., extends the right to any case where the

lower proprietor has for the period of prescription (irrespective of any special grant) received water from the upper property. *Aquaehaustus* includes the right of drawing water from a fountain, well, private stream, or even from a tank or cistern, situate on the servient tenement (Grotius, *Introduction,* 2, 85, 18). This right, like other rural servitudes, implies a right of way to the fountain, well, or cistern, which cannot be impaired by merely personal agreement *(Hawkins* vs. *Munnik,* 1 M. 465). On the other hand, the granting of a right of way to a well or fountain implies the grant of a right to draw water. There is nothing to prevent the owner of the servient tenement from enclosing such tenement with a wall or hedge, so long as he leaves an entrance by which access may be had to the spring, well, or cistern. Where there is a public road between a servient and a dominant tenement, its existence is no obstacle to the grant of a right to draw water, since it is only necessary to pass over the road (a right open to every one) in order to fetch and carry the water. But a right of water-leading across a public road can only be granted by the authority of the Crown, or of a body in which jurisdiction over the public road is vested (such as a Divisional Council). Where there is no special grant of a servitude, but several neighbours use a common well, each of the neighbours will be liable for repairs, and a neighbour who renounces his right to draw water will at least be liable for repairs to or expenses connected with the well to the date of such renunciation (8, 3 §§ 6, 7). 717. It must be here noted that a servitude by prescription cannot be acquired by mere user during the period of prescription. In *Kohler and Others* vs. *Baartman and Others* (12 S. C. 205), two perennial streams took their rise upon a farm belonging to the defendants. After flowing over two other tenements belonging to defendants, on the lowest of which they joined, the amalgamated

O.L.—VOL. I. II stream flowed over the property of a third party, and thence on to a farm belonging to the plaintiffs. The plaintiffs had for one hundred years

used a furrow which conveyed water from a point on the tenement belonging to the third party. This water came from the amalgamated stream. There were several old judgments as between the plaintiffs and the third party, but none between plaintiffs and the predecessors of the defendants. The grant of title of the defendants' highest farm contained the condition that" all watercourses appearing on the diagram shall remain perfectly free and unencumbered." The claim was founded on the grant, and on an alleged prescriptive right, based on user for more than thirty years. The Court found that the plaintiffs had not, by acts adverse to any right in the owners of the farm on which the streams joined, asserted their right to the water, and that these owners had not continuously yielded to that assertion during a period of prescription. Consequently, it was held that no prescriptive right had been established. From this we may deduce that, in order to establish a prescriptive right to water from the land of an upper proprietor, certain conditions besides mere lapse of time are necessary: they are (a) an assertion of right to the water by an act or acts adverse to the right of the upper proprietors, and *(b)* a continual acquiescence in the assertion of the right of the lower proprietors, during the period of prescription, by the upper proprietors. Mere prescription only serves to indicate the sort of right to which claim is laid, and does not establish the right itself. In *Jordaan and Others* vs. *Winkleman and Others* (Buch. 1879, p. 79) it was said: "The object of inquiring into the length of time during which the water flowed down to the lower proprietors is not to ascertain whether they had acquired any prescriptive rights, but in order to ascertain the nature of the stream. One of the tests mentioned by the RomanDutch authorities *(Voet,* 48, 12 § 1) to distinguish a public from a private stream of water is the *existimatio circumcolenlium,* that is, the opinion of those who dwell on its banks. Where, as in the case of *Vermaak* vs. *Palmer,* the stream contains a large volume of water, the fact that the lower proprietors have from time immemorial,

or at all events for a long period, used the water for purposes of irrigation is almost conclusive proof that in the opinion of the riparian occupiers the stream is not a private one which the owner of the land on which it rises can dispose of at his pleasure." In *Struben* vs. *Cape District Waterworks Co.* (9 S. C. 77) it was said: "Where the public stream is limited in quantity, and that limited quantity is further reduced during several hours a day by a diversion to non-riparian proprietors, the strong presumption that injury may at certain seasons result to the lower proprietors must be rebutted by those who make the diversion. That presumption is not rebutted by proof that when the diversion has ceased they voluntarily discharge more water into the river than they had diverted. It is the wrongful diversion, while it lasts, which tends to the plaintiffs' injury and which the defendants must justify. That diversion, if repeated, may become the foundation of an adverse right on the part of the defendants, whilst their voluntary discharge of additional water at certain periods of the day would confer no right by prescription on the plaintiffs. Nor does the fact that no perceptible damage has yet been done rebut the presumption that damage may hereafter ensue." The foregoing principles were expressly made to apply to the case of public streams; but it is submitted that they apply with equal force to the case of private streams over which servitudes by grant or by prescription have been obtained. Similar rules would then apply in the case of an artificial watercourse, which, by long usage, and the common user of the riparian proprietors, has acquired the characteristics of a natural stream *(Myburgh* vs. *Van der Byl,* 1 S. C. 860). If the whole of a natural stream has "for upwards of thirty years been diverted by means of a furrow, and this artificial watercourse has during all that time been used by the riparian proprietors as a natural watercourse, it could not then have been successfully contended as between them that the upper proprietor was entitled to use all the water to the prejudice of the lower proprietor, because the watercourse was artificially constructed."

See *Mouton* vs. *Van der Merwe* (Buch. 1876, p. 18), *Silberbauer* vs. *Van Breda* 5 S. 231), *De Klerk* vs. *Niehaus* (7 C. T. R. p. 294), and *Oliver and Others* vs. *Fourie and Others* (9 C. T. E. 309). As to *aquaehaustus,* see *Meintjes* vs. *Oberholzer and Others* (3 S. 267).

718. There exists, in favour of an upper proprietor, a right similar to that obtained under the urban *servitus cloacae* (above, § 708). In *Ludolph and Others* vs. *Wegner and Others* (6 S. C. 197) it was said: "The action *aquae pluviae arcendae* is as old as the law of the twelve tables, and rests upon the broad principle that no one has a right to do any acts for the improvement or benefit of his own land to the prejudice of his neighbour, unless there is an obligation in the nature of a servitude to submit to such acts. There are three modes, according to Paulus *(Dig., 89, 8, 2),* in which such an obligation may be established—*lex, natura loci,* and *vetustas.* By *lex* he means a covenant between the neighbouring owners, giving the upper proprietor a right to discharge water upon the land of the lower proprietor, but of such a covenant there is no question in the present case. Under this term may also be included such an obligation as the law imposes upon one tenement to submit to the discharge of water from another tenement after thirty or more years' uninterrupted user by the upper proprietors upon the land of the lower proprietors without any resistance on the part of the latter. Such a servitude is not, however, acquired without proof of acts done in assertion of rights claimed on the part of the upper proprietors.... The second mode in which the obligation to receive water in a defined channel may be established is by proof that the situation of the locality, *natura loci,* is such that rain falling upon the tenement would naturally flow into the other through such channel.... If the locality is such that it is difficult to ascertain from the nature of the surface what is the natural channel, a third mode of proof comes in, and that is *vetustas,* or ancient custom." The Court then laid down the following rules as to the right of an up-

per proprietor to drain water into the property of a lower proprietor: "(1) A right to discharge water upon a neighbour's land may exist by virtue of a duly created servitude, or by virtue of the natural situation of the locality. (2) If it be difficult from the nature of the surface to ascertain what is the natural channel, then the course in which the water has immemorially flowed will be considered as having had a natural and legitimate origin. (8) Where water has flowed in an artificial channel for thirty years or more it may be presumed, in the absence of evidence to the contrary, to have flowed thus immemorially. (4) When once the right to discharge water into such a channel has been established, the person entitled to the right may increase the ordinary flow to the prejudice of the lower proprietor if such increase be occasioned in the ordinary course of draining, ploughing, or irrigating the upper land, and be not greater than is reasonable under the circumstances. If the channel becomes choked through neglect, he may compel the lower proprietor to clean it himself, or to allow him (the upper proprietor) to do so."

The subject of water rights is regulated, to some extent, by statute in the Transvaal (Law 11, 1894). § 1 defines "public stream" as "water flowing down in a defined channel, whether such channel shall contain water throughout the whole year or shall be dry during any period." § 2 declares that "Owners of farms on which private water takes its rise may deal therewith as they shall think fit. The expression 'private water' shall be applicable only to cases where the fountain or stream is not permanent, or not capable of sub-division, or does not run in any defined course on to the farms of other persons. The, owner of ground abutting on a public stream shall be entitled to use such water for household and agricultural purposes, provided he shall exercise his right in a reasonable manner." By § 3 " to enable him to exercise the right mentioned in art. 2 it shall be lawful for the owner of a piece of ground adjoining a public stream to lead or take out the water by

means of water furrows or otherwise." §§ 4, 5, 6, 7, 8, and 9 regulate the use of weirs. By § 10 "water led or taken out of a public stream by means of water furrows or otherwise shall not be Conducted beyond the limits of the farm on which it was taken out, and shall be returned to the public stream within the limits of such farm, unless the water so taken out shall have been used in a reasonable manner, or the lower proprietor wishes to use the water for domestic and agricultural purposes with the consent of the parties interested, in such wise that the water is not led in a wrong direction." As to Natal, see Law No. 26, 1887, "To enable Individuals and Companies to lead Water for purposes of Irrigation through Lands not their own." As to weirs, see *Goller* vs. *Van der Merwe* (1903 T. S. 18").

719. In connection with the right of drainage, it is necessary to bear in mind Voet's remarks on the subject of prohibiting access to rain-water, and prohibiting the use of the same *(aquae pluviaearcendae).* The foundation of the action *aquae pluviae arcendae* is the rule that no one can, without a servitude, let his water fall upon the property of another. The extent of this rule is greatly limited, as we have seen (§ 718) by the rules laid down in *Ludolph and Others* vs. *Wegner and Others* (6 S. C. 197). If no right to pass such water to the lower tenement has been established, a person who lets his water flow in such manner, whether by erecting mechanical works, or by plantations of willows or other trees, or who, when the water flows down naturally, increases the volume or speed of the flow, or alters it in any way so as to damage the lower proprietor, is liable in this action. This action, which is real (in respect of the tenement), and personal (in respect of the act complained of), is available to the owner of the tenement injured by the application of artificial means to aid, increase, or disturb the flow from the adjoining tenement—even if, at the time when the act complained of took place, the plaintiff was not the owner of the property: unless the person who sold the property to him had joined issue in this

action before the sale, in which case the purchaser could not bring the action for the same cause. A quit-rent tenant also has this action. It lies against the owner who, of himself, or through his tenant, has interfered with the water. The action is for a stoppage of the act complained of, and for payment of damages resulting from the injury to the lower proprietor. If there are several owners of the tenement from which the water flows, they will have to bear the damages jointly, not separately. The damage must have accrued before joinder in issue, and the plaintiff cannot recover damage before joinder in issue which has resulted through his own negligence. The action does not apply to the case of urban tenements. It does not apply, if the work which is alleged to cause the injurious flow of water to the lower tenement has only been made for the purpose of cultivation, or of reaping produce; or if a person has constructed a work on his own property for the purpose of keeping and retaining the rain-water which falls on his estate, or of retaining the surface drainage from another man's property, and thereby interferes with the flow to the lower proprietor's land. And if a person digs upon his own land, and thereby disturbs the supply of his neighbour's well or fountain, not with the intention of disturbing his neighbour, but in order to improve his own property, no action will lie. In the same way, if a person diverts a torrent, or stream of flood-water, so as to prevent it from reaching the plaintiff's land, he will not be liable for the injury caused to his neighbour by the loss of such water, which might otherwise have been useful to him—since every one may (in the absence of a servitude) turn off and hinder or impede the flow of water, so long as this is done with the intention to benefit himself, and not with the intention to injure the neighbour. This action only lies where the water does harm to the lower property, not where it is of no advantage to the lower property. But where a person turns off the water, which, after heavy rain-fall, is wont to overflow his pond or reservoir and injure his own property,

in such a manner as to divert it to the neighbour's property, and cause injury thereto, he will be liable in an action *(Meyer* vs. *Johannesburg Watenvorks Co.,* Hertzog, p. 17). This action will not lie against a private person, if he constructs the work by public authority (see *Eastern and South African Telegraph Co.* vs. *Cape Town Trainways Co.,* 10 C. T. R. 72). Nor will it lie against a private person, who constructs the work of his own private authority, if such work has existed from time immemorial; and such time immemorial will be reckoned to be, not a period longer than the life of the oldest of those who saw the work done, but a period longer than the life of the oldest of those who heard others say that they had seen the work done. Nor will the action lie if the work has been erected in accordance with a local statute on the subject, or if there has been leave and licence (literally, sufferance and permission) on the part of the neighbour who complains of the injury; or if the defendant's right to use the water in the manner complained of is based on a grant or prescriptive servitude; or, lastly, if it is not so much the water as the nature of the locality that causes the injury—for instance, where the water naturally flows from the upper to the lower tenements (89, 8 §§ 2—5).

The rights known as *heere waterinyen* and *ban waterinyen (Voet,* 39, 3 § 1) are peculiar to Holland, and have no general application in Roman-Dutch Law. See Grotius *(Introduction,* 2, 35, 15; and the learned note of Mr. Maasdorp, in his edition of *Grotiiu,* p. 151).

720. The servitude *pecoris ad aquam appulsus* (right of driving a herd of cattle or flock of sheep to water) partakes of the nature of rights of way and of water-rights. The cattle or sheep must be collected into a compact herd when driven over another person's farm, and must do no injury to trees, fruit, or crops. Where no particular spot has been definitely constituted a watering-place for the purpose of this servitude, the owner of the servient property may point out a convenient and easily accessible place for that purpose. He must not

be unreasonable; and if he is, the Court will interfere to restrain him. The cattle must use a defined track, of such width as circumstances permit. If the watering-place is at a great distance, the cattle must be allowed a reasonable rest on the servient tenement along the way. Any cattle pastured on the dominant tenement, whether belonging to the dominant owner or not, may have the advantage of the servitude *(Laubscher* vs. *Rive and Others* (5 S. 195; 1 Ros. 408). In case of doubt, the cattle to be driven to the watering-place must be regulated, as to their right to water, by the terms of the grant. *D. Other Rural Servitudes.* 721. The other rural servitudes known to Roman Law, and to some extent known to Roman-Dutch Law, are *glandis legendae,* a servitude conferring the right to gather fruits falling on another man's land (above, § 661); *jus pascendi,* the right to pasture cattle on another man's land. Under the *jus pascendi,* only cattle used for the purposes of the dominant tenement are included. Once this servitude has been imposed, the owner of the servient tenement cannot plough up the grazing ground. But "the owner of the servient tenement has the right to depasture his own cattle on the land." This right, however, only goes "to the extent to which the pasturage is sufficient for the cattle of the owner of the dominant tenement and himself. If the pasturage is just sufficient for the reasonable wants of the dominant tenement, the owner of the servient tenement cannot, in derogation of his own (? the dominant owner's) part, do anything whereby such pasturage would be rendered insufficient" (per De Villiers, C. J., in *Heidelberg Municipality* vs. *Uys,* 15 S. C. 161). The next servitude is *calcis coquendi* (the right to make lime), which may be exercised if it is for the benefit of the dominant tenement. No more lime can be made or burned than is needed for the dominant tenement alone. The same rule applies to the servitudes *arenae fodiendi* (right of digging sand on another man's land), *cretae eximendae* (right to quarry chalk or limestone), and *lapidis cedendi* (right to quarry or cut stones). Voet mentions other forms of servitude, which do not require special mention here. It is sufficient to state that a man can give another any rights over the grantor's property by servitude, so long as the grant is not against public morality (8, 3 §§ 10—12). (6) Loss Of Servitudes *(Praediales Servitutes)*. 722. Servitudes which have been promised, but not constituted, perish if no act is done to constitute the servitude. Servitudes which have once been constituted perish or become extinct by merger, where the same person becomes owner of the dominant and of the servient tenement. This applies to a shareholder in an undivided portion of the dominant tenement, who buys the servient tenement. A person purchasing part of a servient tenement does not lose his servitude over the remainder, if a servitude has been constituted over such remainder. Where one person becomes owner of both tenements, on the understanding that the newlyacquired ownership is revocable and temporary, the servitude which has been extinguished by the merger will be revived. Such is the case where the servient tenement is given by way of dowry (with a condition for restoration) to the husband, who owns the dominant tenement. But if the tenements have been merged, without any intention of subsequent separation, the servitude cannot be revived. A servitude is also destroyed by the destruction of the servient or dominant tenement. An inundation does not terminate the existence of a tenement. If the tenement which has been destroyed is restored, the servitude will revive. If a house, for instance, falls in, or is burnt, the rebuilding thereof will restore the servitude— unlike the case of a usufruct. Praedial servitudes, unlike personal ones, are in their nature perpetual, and therefore they may be revived. A praedial servitude is also lost by abandonment, express or implied. An abandonment is implied when two servitudes, one principal and the other accessory, are due at the same time, and the principal servitude is remitted; for, by remission of the principal, the accessory servitude is regarded as remitted. An abandonment is also implied,

when something is allowed to be done by the owner of the servient tenement which is necessarily and naturally repugnant to the servitude: for instance, if the servient owner is permitted to erect a building in a place assigned for use under a right of way, or to build higher, where there is a servitude in favour of the dominant tenement allowing rainwater to fall upon the servient tenement. So, where the plaintiff purchased lots of ground from a municipality, and the defendant had bought similar lots, against the transfer deed whereof was registered a servitude of grazing rights in favour of the land-owners in the municipality, the defendant reserving to himself only the right of building, and the defendant cultivated the land, and continued doing so for sixteen to eighteen years, it was held that the plaintiff was entitled neither to damages for obstruction of his grazing rights, nor to an interdict, as the cultivation of the land was necessarily repugnant to the grazing right, and the plaintiff had lost his right of servitude, seeing that he lay by for so many years, and made no objection *(Edmeades* vs. *Scheepers,* 1 S. C. 884). The dominant owner cannot plead that he was silent, and never openly acquiesced in the repugnant act. In such a case, the servient owner cannot be compelled to restore the property to its former condition; although Voet holds that the dominant owner is compellable to make good actual damage caused to the servient owner (Grotius, *Introd.,* 2, 87, 4). If two distinct principal servitudes are due by the same tenement, the abandonment of one of them does not destroy the other, whether they are owing in respect of the same dominant tenement, or of different dominant tenements. If the abandonment of one servitude would render the exercise of another servitude useless, where such other servitude has not been abandoned, the first servitude is considered to be abandoned only so far that the free exercise of the second servitude is not prejudiced by such abandonment (8,6 §§1-5). As to loss of servitudes, see *Van Niekerk* vs. *Wimble* (Buch. 1878, p. 191); and Van Leeuwen *(Cent. For.* 1, 2, 14, 43—

48).

723. As a servitude is indivisible, the abandonment thereof applies, as a general rule, to the whole servitude. But a servitude may be abandoned as to one portion of a farm, and retained as to the remainder. Where a dominant tenement is divided among several owners, one of them may abandon his right so far as his share is concerned, and the servitude will still continue for the benefit of the remaining divided shares in the property held by the other jointowners (see *Myburgh* vs. *Van der Byl,* 1 S. C. 860): for as many servitudes are regarded as existing as there are divided portions of the dominant tenement. In the same way, if a servient tenement is divided, servitudes are still regarded as existing in favour of the dominant tenement; and a servitude over one part may be abandoned without affecting the other divided parts. Where a dominant tenement is held in undivided shares, one joint-owner cannot abandon a servitude without the consent of the other jointowner. A bare possessor or usufructuary cannot abandon a servitude due to the usufructuary tenement. A guardian cannot abandon a servitude constituted in favour of his ward's property; nor can a husband abandon a servitude due to his wife's dotal estate, of which he has the administration and usufruct. The husband can, however, do this indirectly, by purchasing the estate which is servient to his wife's dotal property, and alienating the same afterwards, during the marriage, without reviving the servitude, which had become extinguished by merger. On dissolution of the marriage, however, the husband is liable for the value of the servitude. Servitudes are also lost by non-user during a third of a century (a period interpreted in the Cape Courts to mean thirty years). Mere interruption of the user, during the time before this period of prescription has elapsed, will not cause a loss of the servitude—for instance, the use of a right of water-leading on alternate days. Thus, the non-user, in the case of an intermittent servitude, must have lasted for the full period of prescription. The period of prescription need not be ful-

filled during the occupation of one possessor, but the possession of predecessors and successors will be reckoned together to make up the period of prescription. Servitudes are not lost where they are exercised, not by the grantee, but by a trustee, agent, usufructuary, or any other person having a similar relationship to the grantee, provided all the user is in the name, and by virtue of, the dominant tenement. A person is not regarded as having used a servitude, who exercises it indeed, but not as a servitude—for instance, where one has a servitude of water-leading by day, and only leads the water which is subject to the servitude by night (in which case he will lose his servitude by day, if he has abandoned it, or ceased to use it during the period of prescription). If a dominant tenement is divided into shares, non-user by one shareholder will not avail as against the other shareholders. But if a servient tenement is divided, a distinction is made according as the servitude is to be exercised over a distinct portion of the tenement, or over any portion of the tenement indiscriminately. In the former case, non-user will only affect the particular portion under servitude; in the latter, it affects the whole farm. Thus, if a person has a right of way over one part of a farm, and the farm is divided parallel to the road, or so as not to cut the road, only that portion over which the road runs will be subject to the right of way; and an abandonment by non-user will be entire, so as to discharge the servitude altogether. If, however, the farm is divided in portions which cross the road, the whole farm, and each of the divided portions, will be subject to the right of way; and the servitude will not be lost by non-user as to one portion, but there must be non-user as to all the portions. If a right of way has been granted over any portion of the servient tenement, such right of way to be changeable at the will of the dominant owner, and the servient tenement is thereafter divided, loss of the right by non-user as to one portion does not mean a loss of the right as to the other portions, provided they have been in use during the period of prescription.

Servitudes are not lost by non-user where they have not yet been established: where, for instance, the right of waterleading is granted, and the water has not yet been found. Voet, following Gaius, distinguishes between urban and rural servitudes in respect of loss by non-user. In the case of urban servitudes, since they are acquired by some act additional to user (such as building), they are lost not by non-user alone, but by non-user coupled with an act repugnant to the servitude (where, for instance, a person has a right to windows facing another man's property and a servitude of light—in which case the mere closing up of the windows by the dominant owner will not suffice, but the servient owner must be suffered to build higher, so that no light can be admitted to the windows). Rural servitudes, on the contrary, as they are acquired by simple user during the period of prescription, may be lost by non-user alone. Where a person exercises his servitude to a greater extent than be is entitled to, he does not thereby lose the servitude. Where the right of a person granting a servitude comes to an end, the servitude likewise ceases: for instance, where an heir has imposed a servitude on property bequeathed as a conditional legacy, while the condition is unfulfilled—in which case the property, when the legatee fulfils the condition, will be acquired by him free from the burden of servitude. Voet mentions a custom, which appears to be local, and not of general applicability in RomanDutch Law, whereby a servitude disappeared on transfer of the servient tenement, if the owner of the servitude and all interested parties were summoned by public proclamation to appear and prove the right to servitude, and failed to do so within the appointed time (8, 6 §§ 6-14).

As to loss of servitude by transfer to another property, see *Louw* vs. *De Villiers,* where it was held (10 S. C. 324) that the owner of a tenement, in favour of which a duly registered praedial servitude exists, cannot transfer the benefit of the servitude to another tenement belonging to him without the consent of the owner

of the servient tenement. See *Stewart's Trustee and Mamitz* vs. *Uniondal e Municipality* (7 8. C. 111).

(7) Actions Concerning Real Servitudes. 724. The actions relating to real servitudes are similar to those which concern personal servitudes. The *actio confessoria directa* (direct affirmative action) lies in favour of the owner of the dominant tenement, even if he is a part-owner of the servient tenement, though holding the dominant tenement privately. An equitable action also lies in favour of an hypothecary creditor, a quit-rent holder, or a person having surface rights. It does not lie in favour of a usufructuary, unless his usufruct entitles him to the benefit of a real servitude, when he may claim the usufruct itself, alleging in his claim that he has been obstructed in the enjoyment of the usufruct by deprivation of the real servitude. An upper proprietor has an equitable action, not to secure a servitude, but to have it declared that he is entitled to let his water flow down to the tenement of the lower proprietor. If there is more than one owner of the dominant tenement, each may bring an action claiming the full servitude *(in solidum).* If the Court declares that no servitude exists, this declaration, in an action by one owner, will affect all the other owners. But an owner can only be declared entitled to the payment of damages for loss which he has himself sustained, and his claim for damages will not estop the other proprietors from thereafter claiming damages. A question as to a disputed right of servitude may indirectly be tried by a personal action for damages, but the proper remedy is by a real action against all claiming right on the alleged servient tenement, to have the servitude declared to exist in favour of the dominant tenement, and to have the possessors and occupiers of the servient tenement interdicted from interrupting the enjoyment of the servitude *(Saunders* vs. *Hart,* 2 M. 295). The *actio confessoria* lies against any person who obstructs the servitude or its exercise, except that the action for the servitude to support a weight can only be brought against the owner of the building. The

hindrance to the servitude may be direct or consequential. An instance of consequential hindrance occurs where the owner of the servient tenement refuses to allow the owner of the dominant tenement to repair a road which he has the right to use. Generally, the action lies against the owner of the servient tenement; and, if there are two or more owners, against each of them for the whole servitude *(in solidum)*. The action claims the free and undisturbed exercise of the plaintiff s rights under the servitude, and security against future disturbance; and, furthermore, damages may be claimed resulting from loss of enjoyment during the period of disturbance. Where any duty of repair is cast on the owner of the servient tenement, he may be ordered to repair. Where he has broken down an erection whose existence is essential to the enjoyment of the servitude, he may be compelled to rebuild the same The action will not lie if the owner of the dominant tenement has agreed to the erection by the owner of the servient tenement which constitutes the obstruction. Where another tenement intervenes between the dominant and the servient tenement, and there is a servitude that the walls of the servient tenement shall not be raised, the action will not lie if the walls of the servient tenement are raised after the walls of the intervening tenement have been raised to the same or a greater height; although the action will revive if, during the period of prescription, the walls of the intervening tenement have again been lowered to their former height (8, 5 §§ 1—4). 725. The *actio negatoria contraria* (contrary negative action) lies in favour of an owner who claims that his tenement is free from a servitude, and is brought against one who desires or claims a right to exercise a servitude over such tenement. The action seeks a declaration that a tenement is free from the burden of a servitude which is claimed by the defendant. It will not matter if a servitude already exists over the tenement in question, so long as the servitude is not the one complained of, or is not due to the tenement in right whereof it is exercised. The ac-

tion may be brought if the servitude is not due at all, or if the owner of the dominant tenement exercises larger rights than he is entitled to under the servitude, or where the exercise of a servitude belonging to one tenement injures another tenement not subject to the servitude. Where parties have a common wall, an action for repairing the same may be instituted against each owner for the whole amount *(in soUdum)*, such owner having his recourse for a proportionate share of the outlay against the other owners. The *actio negatoria* also claims damages, and security against future disturbance of the plaintiffs property. The plaintiff can likewise claim the destruction of buildings erected in aid of the alleged right of servitude, which constitute a hindrance to or obstruction of his free rights of property (8, 5 §§ 5, 6). CHAPTER II. QUIT-RENT TENURE. 726. The subject of quit-rent tenure is one generally regulated by local enactments. Accordingly, the general principles of lawrelating to the subject will be very briefly treated of. Quit-rent tenure is that known in Roman Law as *emphyteusis*. It is not an absolute full ownership, though the quit-rent holder has an equitable ownership, conferring a right to an equitable vindicatory action *in rem*. He cannot demand a remission of rent on account of great drought or similar damage, as other tenants can. It is, in a certain sense, acquired by contract, but, being a real right, it is also acquired by transfer *coram lege loci*, or in the same way as servitudes are acquired, or by last will, or by long-continued prescription—in which case the possession may have been that of another's property in the capacity of quit-rent tenant, *nec vi, clam, nec precario*, or of one's own property during such period, rent being paid to another as direct owner *(dominus directus)*. The quit-rent tenure may also be acquired by way of donation, purchase, or other valid title. As against the State, forty years' possession is necessary to acquire quit-rent ownership of State property. As against others, the period of prescription (according to *Grotius*, 2, 40, 19), is thirty years.

Where a person has during a long period paid an uniform annual rent, it is presumed that this has been paid by way of quitrent, and not under an ordinary lease. The burden of proof that there is an ordinary lease is on the direct owner. Quit-rent tenure is usually granted by the Crown, as direct owner of all the land in a country. It may also be granted by churches, municipalities, and private persons who have absolutely free administration and disposition over their property. All persons who have capacity to contract may acquire quit-rent tenure; so minors, without the sanction of a Court, may acquire land by this mode of tenure on the authority of their guardians. Only immovable property is acquired by quit-rent tenure. The quit-rent must be paid to the direct owner. Quit-rent tenure may be acquired unconditionally, in favour of a person and his heirs, or specially, in favour of a special family or class of persons. The former may go to any heirs or successors; the latter only to the persons specially stipulated for as quit-rent holders.

The quit-rent holder has the fullest right to the fruits and produce of the property, and may take treasure found on the land of which he has the quit-rent tenure. He cannot take minerals and precious stones by mining the same in ground held on quit-rent tenure. The quit-rent tenant is subject to the same burdens as a usufructuary (see *De Villiers* vs. *Cape Divisional Council*, Buch. 1875, p. 50).

Quit-rent tenure ends with the expiry of time fixed for the quit-rent tenancy, or on failure of the special family or class of persons for whose benefit the grant was made (6, 3 §§ 1—14).

In the Cape Colony, quit-rent tenure is regulated by Acts No. 7 of 1856, No. 10 of 1875, No. 27 of 1887, No. 36 of 1888, No. 19 of 1889, and No. 37 of 1889; and see the case cited above (§ 726). As to Natal, see Law No. 17, 1861, Law No. 21, 1863, Law No. 17, 1865, Law No. 23, 1868, Law No. 16, 1876, and Law No. 33, 1887.

727. Where the quit-rent period has expired, and the direct owner accepts rent for the following year, the quit-rent

tenure, in case of doubt, is not presumed to have been prolonged. This mode of tenure expires with the total, not partial, destruction of the property subject to it. If the rent is paid by the acre, or similar unit of measurement, it will be diminished in proportion to the extent of the partial destruction of the property under quit-rent tenure. Where the destruction is not total, but so great that one cannot earn the amount of quit-rent from the remainder of the property, one may claim a reduction of the sum payable for quit-rent, in accordance with equity, or may abandon the quit-rent tenure. This, however, does not apply to quit-rent tenure from the Treasury or the Crown, which cannot be abandoned at will. Where the destruction of the property is due to the quit-rent tenant, he cannot claim reduction of quit-rent, or a right to abandon the property; whether the destruction be due to fraud or clear negligence.

C.L.—VOL. I. K K

And the liability for quit-rent will continue where the tenant has been forcibly deprived of possession without the act or connivance of the true owner, for the tenant might have recovered possession (6, 8 §§ 15—18).

728. Where war causes a loss of beneficial occupation, in that the tenant is compelled to abandon his property, he will not be liable for the rent during the period in which he has been deprived of beneficial occupation. Voet says a similar reduction must be made in case of an inundation which lasts for a full year and upwards, since there the tenant loses not merely the standing crops) but the sowing of a future crop as well. Quit-rent tenure is not lost where the tenant alienates his right of tenure without notice to the direct owner; but, according to Voet, the true owner has the right of retraction of the quit-rent property within the customary period; but Van Leeuwen *(R. D. L.* 4,19, 11; 2 *Kotze,* 156) is doubtful on the point, although he thinks that the *dominui directus* has the preference (see *Green* vs. *Griffitlis,* 4 S. C. 846). Van Leeuwen *(R. D. L.* 4, 19, 6; 2 *Kotze,* 158) says: "The possessor of property, on which there is any rent, redeemable or irredeemable, spe-

cially attached, has the retraction thereof within a year, whenever the said rent is sold to a third person" (6, 8 §§ 19—22).

This *jus retradus* must not be confused with the *jus retraetus* as applied to the sale of debts *(Seavilk* vs. *Colley,* 9 8. C. p. 45).

729. On the making over of a quit-rent tenure by sale, donation or otherwise, the new tenant or assignee must, according to Dutch Law, pay the *dominus directus* a sum equal to double the quit-rent as a recognition of his direct ownership *(recognitie).* Van der Keessel (§ 880) says that double rent should be paid upon every alienation. Voet holds that where a purchaser pays transfer duty, and a third party claims the emphyteutic property, and the dispute is thereafter settled by compromise, the duty (equal to twice the quit-rent) need not be paid to the owner a second time. The same rule, says Voet (who, according to Van der Keessel, must be read in this connection with caution, for the latter authority holds that the obligation to pay double quit-rent is general), applies in the case where the purchaser or assignee cedes his right to the claimant, as in that case there is no real alienation of the dominion or of the quit-rent tenure. The obligation to pay such duty, says Voet, does not arise where a person buys a right of quit-rent tenure for and in the name of another, since the purchase is really for the principal. The obligation to pay does not apply where the tenure is made over to one of several heirs (after the institution of an action to divide the joint inheritance), or to one of several owners (after the institution of an action to divide common property), and the other parties to the action receive a payment proportionate to their respective shares or holdings (6, 8 §§ 28—85). 730. Quit-rent tenure may, in strict law, be put an end to if the quit-rent holder has for three full years failed to pay quit-rent; although this penalty is very seldom enforced, in accordance with Koman-Dutch custom, and it is usual, in modern times, to exact either some penalty previously agreed upon, or payment of double quit-rent. In this

respect the local statutes or usages are followed (see *Colonial Government* vs. *Fryer and Huysamen,* 4 S. C. 86). No demand need be made by the direct owner for payment of quitrent; and arrival of the due date for payment will constitute a sufficient demand for quitrent. Payment must be made by the tenant or his authorised agent; for payment by an unauthorised agent is no recognition by the tenant of the ownership vested in the direct owner. A husband's neglect to pay quit-rent on property held by the wife, of which he has the control, will avail as against the wife. Remission of forfeiture by the *dominus directus* may be express or implied, and will avail as against the true owner. It is implied where, after the lapse of three years, the owner knowingly accepts rent for the fourth year, the quit-rent for the three years being unpaid. There must be an express declaration by the direct owner of his intention to exact forfeiture. If he does not make a demand for restoration of the property by the quit-rent tenant, his heir is precluded from doing so. The causes of forfeiture include unreasonable neglect and misuse of the property. Quitrent tenure may be lost by prescription, where the direct owner occupies the property for the period of prescription; or, where the quit-rent tenant denies the right of the direct owner to occupy and allows the period of prescription to elapse after such denial; or, where the tenant has transferred the property, as if it were his unencumbered, to another, and a period sufficient for prescription has elapsed after such transfer (6, 3 §§ 36—49). 731. Quit-rent tenure, on expiry, reverts to the direct owner, and becomes merged in the full ownership. The direct owner cannot of his own motion and authority evict the quit-rent holder, but must obtain an order of Court. For this he must resort to the vindicatory action. Improvements agreed upon at the beginning of the tenure belong to the direct owner, who need not pay compensation to the tenant for them; those not agreed upon, but afterwards made, which are beneficial, should be compensated for to the tenant (see *De Beers Co.* vs. *London and South*

African Exploration Co., 10 S. C. 859). In this respect the law makes no difference between the quit-rent holder and a *bond fide* possessor (as to whose rights see above, §§ 550, 608). Grotius says that similar rules apply *(Introd.* 2, 40, 24) to the right granted by a quit-rent tenant to another to enjoy the fruits of the property (6, 8 §§ 50—54).

The Natal Courts have followed the Cape Supreme Court in holding (*Vos* vs. *Colonial Government,* 14 N. L. R. 201) that quit-rent tenure is in the nature of *emphyteusis,* the *dominium plenum* (full or absolute ownership) remaining in the grantor or *dominus directus,* and the grantee having merely the right of possession. The usual conditions in such grants, relating to "outspan," roads, and watercourses, are common to emphyteutic tenure, but a further condition contained in a deed that the grant is subject to all such future duties and regulations as may be established, indicates a special grant far beyond that of simple *emphyteusis.* See also *Colonial Treasurer* vs. *Barff* (Morcom's Rep. 1871, p. 96), *Colonial Treasurer* vs. *Coetzee* (Morcom's Rep. 1872, pp. 28, 40), and *Orpen N. O.* vs. *Shaw* (3 C. L. J. 213). The Cape and Natal statutes make provision for the conversion of quit-rent tenure into freehold tenure. Sir John Cradock's Proclamation of August 6th, 1813, regulates the general law as to quit-rent tenure in Cape Colony. A grant of perpetual quit-rent confers the right to hold hereditarily and to alienate (§ 3). The Government reserves the rights to precious stones, gold and silver, and of making and repairing roads (§ 4). The rights of the Crown in places adjoining the sea are reserved (§ 5). The laws respecting freehold lands are to govern decisions on perpetual quit-rent (§ 6)— i.e., custom and the Common Law. Transfer of quit-rent land must take place *coram lege loci* (§ 10). Quit-rent lands are liable to the same burdens only as freehold land (§ 11).

INDEX TO VOL. I.

The numbers within brackets refer to the sections of the work.'

A.

ABANDONMENT. Page

EQUITY.
its application (4) 28
EVIDENCE.
cohabitation and marriage (369) 207
   See Burden Of Proof; Presumption;
Proof.
EXCEPTION.
against action by protutor (316) 180
vindication of ward's property (334)
191
rex venditae et traditae (561) 339
See Action.
(31) M M 2
EXCHANGE. Page
in form of donation (478). 276
See Donation.
EXCUSSION.
where several guardians are liable (324)
185
EXEMPTION.
from public duties (76) 68
See Immunity.
EXTERRITORIALITY.
its application (17) 37
of personal status (58) 56
See International Law; Private International Law;
Statutes.
   P.
FALCIDIAN LAW.
place in Roman Law (9) 32
abolished by Cape and Transvaal Law
(398) 231
claim under interdict *quod legatorum*
(646)..... 401
See Quod Leoatorum.
FATHER
is legitimate guardian of children (222)
139
when he may prohibit mother's
guardianship (240)...146
failure to appoint guardians (246) 148
security for loan from ward (254) 152
business continued by guardian (261)
156
liability to pay costs of child's action
(262) 157
co-tutor with son (273) 162
religion of child, rights as to (286) 168
marriage of minor child, consent to
(374) 208
difference with mother as to consent
(374) 209
security for usufruct (680) 438
See Child; Marriage; Parents; Wife.

FICTION OF LAW.
interpretation (24) 40
unborn persons (126) 93
FIDEICOMMISS UM.
ratification of acceptance by ward (268)
153
exclusion from community (398) 230
succession of children under marriage
contract (461).. 267
express terms in marriage contract
(461) 267
change under marriage contract (463)
268
repudiation by spouse (480) 276
acquired by usucapion (578) 352
vindication on sale (594) 362
FIDEICOMMISSUM—continued. Page
heir's right to vindicate (601) 371
bequest of usufruct to be restored (665)
423
fideicommissary's death in fiduciary's
lifetime (666)... 424
full ownership of fiduciary heir (666)
424
   See Antenuptial Contract; Usufruct.
FISCUS.
in Roman Law (91) 74
See Treasury.
FISHING.
trespass in (538) 316
in stagnant waters (538) 316
when fish *res nulliut* (538) 316
in public streams (538) 316
   Roman Law (538) 316
interruption of (538) 316
views of Grotius (538) 316
off sea-coast (538) 317
with the net (538) 317
with hook and line (538) 317
in private waters (538) 317
under Cape Statutes (538) 317
under Transvaal Statutes (538) 317
FORFEITURE OF BENEFITS.
divorce for desertion (491) 280
See Divorce; Judicial Separation.
FRAUD.
avoids promise of marriage (353) 201
consent of parents to marriage, obtaining (374).... 209
gift between spouses (477) 274
dowry, sale of (502) 287
See Dolus.
FBUCTUS INDUSTRIALES.
property given to spouse (471) 271
liability to refund (472) 272

   See Fruits.
FRUCTUS NATURALES.
(1) ungathered (550) 328
(2) gathered (550) 328
must have a just title (552) 330
absence of special usufruct (552) 330
variation in nature of title (552) 330
restoration by heir of deceased possessor (552).... 331
   See Fruits.
FRUITS, Page
fmet us industrialis (471) 271
fructus percepti (472) 272
fructus civiles (550) 328
fructus pendentes (550) 328
fructus exstantes (550) 328
rights of accession (550) 328
rights of owner (550) 328
rights of *maid fide* possessor (550) 328
restoration in inheritance action (551)
329
claimed in possessory interdict (643)
397
right of enjoyment (669) 427
irrevocable right of usufructuary (674)
430
not gathered under usufruct (674) 430
rights of *bond fide* possessor (674) 430
expenses of gathering (676) 431
See Fructus Industriales; Fructus
Natubales; Interest;
Ownership; Title; Usufruct.
   G.
GRANT.
to corporations (82) 70
revocation of servitude (700) 457
See Privilegium.
GROTTUS.
booty, when claimable (115) 84
judicial emancipation (141). 104
minor, liability on contract (179) 119
sureties to minors, restitution (195) 125
parent's acquisition of child's earnings
(211)....132
guardians, their security (249) 149
guardians, inventory by (251) 150
inventory, penalty for fraudulent (253)
151
insolvent guardian, action by (262) 157
delegation defined (272) 162
co-tutor, his authority (272) 162
guardian's fraud, liability of ward (279)
165
guardians, discharge of (285) 167
   Orphan Master, his liability (323)

CPSIA information can be obtained
at www.ICGtesting.com
Printed in the USA
BVOW04s0807041217
501906BV00013B/626/P